Documents of the English Reformation

Edited by
Gerald Bray

D1388634

James Clarke & Co Ltd
P.O. Box 60
Cambridge
CB1 2NT

Copyright © Gerald Bray 1994

First published by James Clarke & Co Ltd 1994

British Library Cataloguing-in-Publication Data
A record is available for this book from the British Library

ISBN 0 2276 7930 X

The Guernsey Press Co. Ltd., Guernsey,
Channel Islands.

CONTENTS

Reaction and Recovery (1553-1559)

The Progress of Protestantism (1560-1625)

The Protestant Schism and the Final Settlement (1625-1700)

Supplementary Texts

Appendixes

INTRODUCTION

There have been a number of important collections of Reformation documents in recent years, which have greatly enhanced scholarly knowledge of the period, and given historians much broader access to the source materials. Among the more important of these, the following may be mentioned immediately:

G. R. Elton ed., *The Tudor Constitution*, Second Edition, Cambridge, 1982.
A. G. Dickens and D. Carr, *The Reformation in England*, London, 1967.
J. P. Kenyon, *The Stuart Constitution*, Second Edition, Cambridge, 1986.

But useful though these collections are to those interested in political or economic developments, they are of but limited value to the theologian or to the student of Church history. Documents relating especially to the worship and doctrine of the Church are only partially represented, and are almost always abridged. Articles of Religion and Confessions of Faith are either omitted altogether or given fairly cursory treatment. The result is that it is very difficult to follow the development of the Church's theology, even though this was one of the main factors in political and social developments. Finally, there is no collection of documents currently in print which covers both the early Reformation and the Civil War period, though it is increasingly coming to be recognized that the one cannot be understood without the other.

With these needs in mind, the present collection has been compiled. It endeavours to provide a reasonably complete selection of source materials covering the period from 1526, the date of the first printed edition of the New Testament in English, to 1700, when the Act of Settlement established the principle of a Protestant monarchy and state. In selecting documents for inclusion, the emphasis has been on texts of a constitutional nature, i.e. those which represent the development of the Church's doctrine and government during the period under consideration. For the very early period, special consideration has been given to legal statutes which are still (at least partially) in force.

Little attempt has been made to be partisan in the selection, and documents of a Catholic or Puritan persuasion have been included to illustrate the mind of the Church as a whole. (Readers interested in pursuing the course of Dissent in greater detail are referred to the excellent collection of theological documents edited by Iain Murray, *The Reformation of the Church: A*

Collection of Reformed and Puritan Documents on Church Issues, Banner of Truth Trust, Edinburgh, 1965.

In addition to these documents, a few texts have been included which are seldom published nowadays and which are little known, though they are of considerable importance for understanding the doctrinal debates of the period. Examples of these are the Thirteen Articles of 1538, in which Archbishop Cranmer set out his response to the Lutheran Augsburg Confession of 1530, and the Canons of the Synod of Dort (1619), which established the basis on which "Calvinists" and "Arminians" (or more correctly, in the English context, "anti-Calvinists") separated from one another in the period leading up to the Civil War. There are also some documents, like the King's Declaration of 1628 and the Epistle Dedicatory to the Authorized Version of 1611, which have been included for the benefit of readers who may not have the Book of Common Prayer or the Authorized Version of the Bible (British Edition) ready to hand.

For this edition, spellings have generally been normalized according to current British standards, but the grammar and vocabulary of the original texts have been left intact, with only marginal exceptions, where it was felt that nothing of substance would be lost by updating the form of a word. Where non-technical words appear which have now fallen into disuse, an explanation of their meaning is given in parentheses. Proper names are normally rendered according to the modern style, e.g. Jerome (referring to the fourth-century Latin Father of the Church), and not Hierome or Hieronymus.

An important principle of this collection has been to publish all documents in full, which has inevitably led to the exclusion of material which is simply too long. In particular, the following documents have had to be omitted:

01. *The Institution of a Christian Man*, usually known as the *Bishops' Book*, which was published in 1537 as a commentary on the Ten Articles. It was reprinted by Bishop Charles Lloyd, *Formularies of Faith*, Oxford, 1825, and extracts may be found in Dickens and Carr, op. cit., pp. 85-89. A facsimile edition was published in 1976 by Walter J. Johnson Inc., 335, Chesnut Street, Norwood, NJ 07648, USA.

02. *A Necessary Doctrine and Erudition for any Christian Man*, usually known as the *King's Book*, which was published in 1543 as an answer to the Bishops' Book of 1537. It was reprinted by Bishop Charles Lloyd in the same edition as the above, and extracts may be found in Dickens and Carr, op. cit., pp. 114-118.

03. The *Books of Common Prayer* issued in 1549, 1552, 1559, 1637 and 1662. The first two of these are published in the Everyman's Library, no. 448, as *The First and Second Prayer Books of King Edward VI*, London, 1968. The third has been published in an edition by J. Booty, *The Book of Common Prayer 1559: The Elizabethan Prayer Book*,

50. *The Book of Common Prayer*, 1662.
51. *Statutes of the Realm*, 5, pp. 782-785.
52. Ibid., 6, pp. 74-76.
53. P. Schaff, op. cit., 3, pp. 738-741 and W. Cathcart ed., *The Baptist Encyclopaedia*, Philadelphia, 1881, pp. 1311-1321.
54. *Statutes of the Realm*, 7, pp. 636-638.

The Supplementary Texts may be found in the following sources:

01. *Statutes of the Realm*, 1, 316-318 and 2, 69-72.
02. Ibid., 1, p. 329.
03. Ibid., 2, pp. 84-86.
04. P. Schaff, op. cit., 3, pp. 3-73.

Special thanks are due to the Rev. Dr Roger Beckwith of Latimer House, Oxford, for his assistance with points of translation and to the Rev. Dr John Ashley Null, who pointed out to me both the importance and the relative inaccessibility of the Wittenberg Articles and the Edwardian Injunctions. Thanks are also due to Miss Wendy Bell, Librarian of Oak Hill College, London, who provided copies of important texts and essential bibliographical information. Much of the work on these texts was done at different times in the Library of the General Theological Seminary, New York, the University Library, Cambridge and in the Library of Samford University, Birmingham, Alabama, where the staff have been unfailingly kind and helpful. The collection was initially prepared as a resource for teaching Anglican Studies to my students at Oak Hill College in London. Circumstances have prevented me from using it in that capacity, but it is to those students, from whom I was so suddenly and so cruelly separated, that this work is humbly dedicated.

Note on Translations

Apart from the Canons of the Synod of Dort, original Latin or German texts are included in this edition. Where an official, or generally recognized translation exists, that has been included as well. In other cases, the documents have been specially translated for this edition. Every effort has been made to stay as close as possible to the original text, and to translate technical terms consistently, without sacrificing English style too much. Complete accuracy in this matter is unattainable, but the reader is asked to bear in mind the following points:

1. *Pietas* is normally rendered as *godliness*, not as *piety*.
2. *Iustitia* is normally rendered as *righteousness*, not as *justice*.
3. *Paenitentia* is normally rendered as *penitence*, not as *penance*

("Catholic") or *repentance* ("Protestant"). This is to preserve the ambiguity of the Latin, and to avoid taking sides in the controversy about the correct meaning of this word in some of the documents printed here. The reader is asked to bear in mind that either a "Catholic" or a "Protestant" translation may be possible, and that scholars often disagree as to which of the two was originally intended. This consideration also applies to the phrase *agite paenitentiam*, which is here translated as *do penitence* rather than as *repent*, even though the latter would be regarded today as better English.

Note on Dates

Dates in the text of the various documents are accompanied by a modern explanation or abbreviation in parentheses, e.g.:

The fourth day of May in the year of our Lord, one thousand five hundred and forty-seven (04 May 1547)
Easter 1539 (06 April 1539).

The Gregorian Calendar was introduced in Catholic Europe on 15 October 1582, but as it was not accepted in England until 1752, dates here are usually given in the Old (Julian) Style, which in the sixteenth and seventeenth centuries was ten days behind the New (Gregorian) Style. On the other hand, years are reckoned to have begun on 01 January, not on 25 March, as was the custom in England until 1752, and in Scotland until 1599. For example, 16 January 1593 (OS) would be 26 January 1594 (NS) but would appear here as 16 January 1594. In one or two cases, this difference affects the date of publication given for a particular document; e.g. Tyndale's first edition of the New Testament was published in February 1526 (NS), but is usually listed as 1525 in catalogues, which take the date on the title page as their point of reference. Likewise, the Thirty-eight Articles of Religion were published in 1563 by our reckoning, but in 1562 according to the Style in use at the time.

Note on Units of Account

Non-British readers may need to be reminded that until 15 February 1971, the pound sterling consisted of 20 shillings (20s.), each of which was in turn subdivided into 12 pence (12d.). It was also common for sums between one and five pounds to be denominated only in shillings and pence. Another unit of account used in sixteenth-century England was the mark, which was equivalent to thirteen shillings fourpence (13s. 4d.), or two-thirds of a pound sterling.

Before the Break with Rome

(1526-1534)

01. TYNDALE'S PREFACE TO THE NEW TESTAMENT (1526), 1534

History

It is universally acknowledged that the study and dissemination of the Bible was one of the most central aspects of the European Reformation. The process of rendering the sacred texts in the language of the people began with the work of John Wycliffe (c.1330-1384) and his Lollard associates, who produced two versions of the Bible in English, both of them translated from the Latin Vulgate. The first of these appeared about 1380 and the second sometime about 1388, after Wycliffe's death. The first Lollard Bible was condemned as heretical, but the second, by a strange irony, was accepted as "catholic" and even recommended for reading by people as indisputably orthodox as Sir Thomas More. However, this version remained in manuscript, and was never widely available. Moreover, by a decree of a synod held at Oxford in 1408, it was forbidden to translate or even to read the Bible in English without special permission. The New Testament (of the second version) was not published until 1731, and both versions were published together – in full – only in 1850!

Historians now agree that Lollardy still existed in England at the time of the Reformation, but it is uncertain how strong it was. On balance it seems that the surviving Lollards were attracted into the Reformers' camp, rather than that the first Reformers were affected by contemporary Lollardy. Whatever the truth of the matter, there is little or no sign of direct Lollard influence on the first printed version of the English New Testament, which was prepared by William Tyndale (c.1494-1526), an early convert to Lutheranism. Tyndale followed Luther in many respects, but his translation of the New Testament was an independent rendering from the Greek, not a calque from Luther's German, and it is a superior translation. Tyndale's English is noted for its freshness, which has stood the test of time. He himself revised his work in 1534, and again in 1535, but it is the 1534 version which is now accepted as standard. The Preface printed here is from that edition, and includes a separate section at the end, condemning the efforts of one George Joye to "improve" Tyndale's work.

Tyndale tried to gain support for his translation in England, but the Bishop of London was hostile, and in 1524 he felt that it would be wise to flee the country. He went to Wittenberg, Hamburg, Cologne and finally Antwerp. He was arrested there in 1535, and taken to Vilvoorde (near Brussels), where he was imprisoned and subsequently executed. There is some evidence that Henry VIII tried to save him, but he was never pardoned by the English king (for breaking the law of 1408 against translation) and his name remained virtually unmentionable until well into the reign of Elizabeth I. This did not deprive him of influence however, because his translation formed the basis of all subsequent Protestant versions, and it is estimated that up to 90% of the Authorized Version of 1611 can be traced back to him.

Theology

Tyndale's New Testament is a substantially Lutheran document, as the Preface and the Prologues to the various books clearly indicate. In particular, the Prologue to the Epistle to the Romans is no more than a translation of Luther's, with five additional paragraphs appended at the end. Tyndale also followed Luther's order of the New Testament books, relegating Hebrews, James, Jude and Revelation to the status of an appendix. It is known that Luther did this because he doubted the canonicity of these books, but Tyndale's position on this is unclear. Certainly there is nothing in his extant writings which would suggest that he doubted the full authority of these books, and it seems that his imitation of Luther at this point had no particular theological significance.

Tyndale goes beyond Luther, however, in his understanding of the Bible as covenant – a view which would later give rise to the most characteristic type of Puritan theology. In the Preface he gives us a very clear explanation of what this means. Later, in his response to George Joye, he develops his belief in *sola Scriptura*, a Lutheran formula which he nevertheless understands in his own way. Tyndale not only wished to affirm what Scripture affirms; he also wished to deny what Scripture does not clearly affirm. It was this second aspect of his thinking which was to become a major bone of contention between Conformists and Non-Conformists after the Elizabethan Settlement of 1559.

N.B. The paragraph numbering is included in this edition for ease of reference, and was not in the original text.

01. Here thou hast (most dear reader) the new testament or covenant made with us of God in Christ's blood. Which I have looked over again (now at the last) with all diligence, and compared it unto the Greek, and have weeded out of it many faults, which lack of help at the beginning, and oversight, did sow therein. If ought seem changed, or not altogether agreeing with the Greek, let the finder of the fault consider the Hebrew phrase or manner of speech left in the Greek words. Whose preterperfect tense and present tense is oft both one, and the future tense is the optative mode also, and the future tense is oft the imperative mode in the active voice, and in the passive ever. Likewise person for person, number for number, and an interrogation for a conditional, and such like as with the Hebrews is a common usage.

02. I have also in many places set light in the margin to understand the text by. If any man find faults either with the translation or with aught beside (which is easier for many to do, than so well to have translated it themselves of their own pregnant wits, at the beginning without fore-example) to the same it shall be lawful to translate it themselves and to put what they lust thereto. If I shall perceive either by myself or by the information of other, that aught be escaped me, or might be more plainly translated, I will shortly after cause it to be mended. Howbeit in many places, me thinketh it better to put a declaration in the margin, than to run too far from the text. And in many places, where the text seemeth at the first chop hard to be understood, yet the circumstances before and after, and often reading together, maketh it plain enough etc.

03. Moreover, because the kingdom of heaven, which is the Scripture and Word of God, may be so locked up, that he which readeth or heareth it cannot understand it; as Christ testifieth how that the scribes and Pharisees had so shut it up (Mt 23:13) and had taken away the key of knowledge (Lk 11:52) that their Jews which thought themselves within, were yet so locked out, and are to this day that they can understand no sentence of the Scripture unto their salvation, though they can rehearse the texts everywhere and dispute thereof as subtly as the popish doctors of dunces' dark learning, which with their sophistry, served us, as the Pharisees did the Jews. Therefore (that I might be found faithful to my Father and Lord in distributing unto my brethren and fellows of one faith, their due and necessary food: so dressing it and seasoning it, that the weak stomachs may receive it also, and be the better for it) I thought it my duty (most dear reader) to warn thee before, and to show thee the right way in, and to give thee the true key to open it withal, and to arm thee against false prophets and malicious hypocrites, whose perpetual study is to leaven the Scripture with glosses, and there to lock it up where it should save thy soul, and to make us shoot at a wrong mark, to put our trust in those things that profit their bellies only and slay our souls.

04. The right way; yea, and the only way to understand the Scripture unto our salvation, is that we earnestly, and above all thing, search for the profession of our baptism, or covenants made between God and us. As for an example: Christ saith (Mt 5:7): *Happy are the merciful, for they shall obtain mercy*. Lo, here God hath made a covenant with us, to be merciful unto us, if we will be merciful one to another, so that the man which sheweth mercy unto his neighbour may be bold to trust in God for mercy at all needs. And contrariwise, judgement without mercy shall be to him that showeth not mercy (Ja 2:13). So now, if he that showeth no mercy trust in God for mercy, his faith is carnal and worldly, and but vain presumption. For God hath promised mercy only to the merciful. And therefore the merciless have no God's word that they shall have mercy; but contrariwise, that they shall have judgement without mercy. And (Mt 6:14-15): *If ye shall forgive men their faults, your heavenly Father shall forgive you, but and if ye shall not forgive men their faults, no more shall your Father forgive you your faults*. Here also, by the virtue and strength of this covenant wherewith God of his mercy hath bound himself to us unworthy, may he that forgiveth his neighbour be bold when he returneth and amendeth to believe and trust in

God for remission of whatsoever he hath done amiss. And contrariwise, he that will not forgive cannot but despair of forgiveness in the end, and fear judgement without mercy.

05. The general covenant wherein all other are comprehended and included is this. If we meek ourselves to God, to keep all his laws after the example of Christ: then God hath bound himself to us to keep and make good all the mercies promised in Christ throughout all the Scripture.

06. All the whole law which was given to utter our corrupt nature, is comprehended in the ten commandments. And the ten commandments are comprehended in these two: love God and thy neighbour. And he that loveth his neighbour in God and Christ fulfilleth these two, and consequently the ten, and finally all the other. Now if we love our neighbours in God and Christ: that is to wit, if we be loving, kind and merciful to them, because God hath created them unto his likeness, and Christ hath redeemed them and bought them with his blood, then may we be bold to trust in God through Christ and his deserving, for all mercy. For God hath promised and bound himself to us, to show us all mercy and to be a Father Almighty to us, so that we shall not need to fear the power of all our adversaries.

07. Now if any man that submitteth not himself to keep the commandments do think that he hath any faith in God, the same man's faith is vain, worldly, damnable, devilish and plain presumption, as it is above said, and is no faith that can justify or be accepted before God. And that is it that James meaneth in his Epistle. *For how can a man believe*, saith Paul, *without a preacher?* (Ro 10:14). Now read all the Scripture and see where God sent any to preach mercy to any, save unto them only that repent and turn to God with all their hearts, to keep his commandments. Unto the disobedient that will not turn is threatened wrath, vengeance and damnation, according to all the terrible curses and fearful examples of the Bible.

08. Faith now in God the Father through our Lord Jesus Christ, according to the covenants and appointment made between God and us, is our salvation. Wherefore I have ever noted the covenants in the margins, and also the promises. Moreover, where thou findest a promise and no covenant expressed therewith, there must thou understand a covenant. For all the promises of the mercy and grace that Christ hath purchased for us are made upon the condition that we keep the law. As for an example, when the Scripture saith (Mt 7:7): *Ask and it shall be given you, seek and ye shall find, knock and it shall be opened unto you.* It is to be understood, if that when thy neighbour asketh, seeketh or knocketh to thee, thou then show him the same mercy which thou desirest of God, then hath God bound himself to help thee again, and else not.

09. Also ye see that two things are required to begin a Christian man. The first is a steadfast faith and trust in Almighty God, to obtain all the mercy that he hath promised us, through the deserving and merits of Christ's blood only, without all respect to our own works. And the other is that we

forsake evil and turn to God, to keep his laws and to fight against ourselves and our corrupt nature perpetually, that we may do the will of God every day better and better.

10. This have I said (most dear reader) to warn thee, lest thou shouldest be deceived and shouldest not only read the Scriptures in vain and to no profit, but also unto thy greater damnation. For the nature of God's Word is that whosoever read it or hear it reasoned and disputed before him, it will begin immediately to make him every day better and better, till he be grown into a perfect man in the knowledge of Christ and love of the law of God; or else make him worse and worse, till he be hardened that he openly resist the Spirit of God, and then blaspheme after the example of Pharaoh, Korah, Abiram, Balaam, Judas, Simon Magus and such other.

11. This to be even so, the words of Christ (Jn 3:19) do well confirm. *This is condemnation,* saith he, *the light is come into the world but the men loved darkness more than light, for their deeds were evil.* Behold, when the light of God's word cometh to a man, whether he read it or hear it preached and testified, and he yet have no love thereto, to fashion his life thereafter, but consenteth still unto his old deeds of ignorance; then beginneth his just damnation immediately, and he is henceforth without excuse, in that he refused mercy offered him. For God offereth him mercy upon the condition that he will mend his living, but he will not come under the covenant. And from that hour forward he waxeth worse and worse, God taking his Spirit of mercy and grace from him for his unthankfulness' sake.

12. And Paul writeth (Ro 1:21,26) that *the heathen, because when they knew God they had no lust to honour him with Godly living, therefore God poured his wrath upon them and took his Spirit from them, and gave them up unto their hearts' lusts to serve sin from iniquity to iniquity, till they were thoroughly hardened and past repentance.*

13. And Pharaoh, because when the word of God was in his country and God's people scattered throughout all his land, and yet neither loved them or it; therefore God gave him up, and in taking his Spirit of grace from him, so hardened his heart with covetousness that afterward no miracle could convert him.

14. Hereto pertaineth the parable of the talents (Mt 25:29). The Lord commandeth the talent to be taken away from the evil and slothful servant, and to bind him hand and foot and to cast him into utter darkness, and to give the talent unto him that had ten, saying: *to all that have, more shall be given. But from him that hath not, that he hath shall be taken from him.* That is to say, he that hath a good heart toward the Word of God and a set purpose to fashion his deeds thereafter and to garnish it with godly living and to testify it to other, the same shall increase more and more daily in the grace of Christ. But he that loveth it not, to live thereafter and to edify other, the same shall lose the grace of true knowledge and be blinded again and every day wax worse and worse and blinder and blinder, till he be an utter enemy of the Word of God, and his heart so hardened, that it shall be impossible to convert him.

15. And (Lk 12:47): *The servant that knoweth his master's will and prepareth not himself shall be beaten with many stripes; that is, shall have greater damnation.* And (Mt 7:26): *all that hear the Word of God and do not, thereafter build on sand*; that is, as the foundation laid on sand cannot resist violence of water, but is undermined and overthrown, even so the faith of them that have no lust nor love to the law of God built upon the sand of their own imaginations, and not on the rock of God's Word according to his covenants, turneth to desperation in time of tribulation and when God cometh to judge.

16. And the vineyard (Mt 21:33-41) planted and hired out to the husbandmen that would not render to the Lord of the fruit in due time, and therefore was taken from them and hired out to other, doth confirm the same. For Christ saith to the Jews, the Kingdom of Heaven shall be taken from you and given to a nation that will bring forth the fruits thereof, as it is come to pass. For the Jews have lost the spiritual knowledge of God and of his commandments and also of all the Scripture, so that they can understand nothing godly. And the door is so locked up that all their knocking is in vain, though many of them take great pain for God's sake. And (Lk 13:6-9) the fig tree that beareth no fruit is commanded to be plucked up.

17. And finally, hereto pertaineth with infinite other, the terrible parable of the unclean spirit (Lk 11:24-26) which, after he is cast out, when he cometh and findeth his house swept and garnished, taketh to him seven worse than himself, and cometh and entereth in and dwelleth there, and so is the end of the man worse than the beginning. The Jews, they had cleansed themselves with God's Word, from all outward idolatry and worshipping of idols. But their hearts remained still faithless to Godward and toward his mercy and truth, and therefore without love also and lust to his law, and to their neighbours for his sake, and through false trust in their own works (to which heresy, the child of perdition, the wicked Bishop of Rome with his lawyers hath brought us Christians), were more abominable idolaters than before, and become ten times worse in the end than at the beginning. For the first idolatry was soon spied and easy to be rebuked of the prophets by the Scripture. But the later is more subtle to beguile withal, and an hundred times of more difficulty to be weeded out of men's hearts.

18. This also is a conclusion, nothing more certain, or more proved by the testimony and examples of the Scripture, that if any that favoureth the Word of God be so weak that he cannot chasten his flesh, him will the Lord chastise and scourge every day sharper and sharper, with tribulation and misfortune, that nothing shall prosper with him but that all shall go against him, whatsoever he taketh in hand, and shall visit him with poverty, with sickness and diseases, and shall plague him with plague upon plague, each more loathsome, terrible and fearful than other, till he be at utter defiance with his flesh.

19. Let us therefore that have now at this time our eyes opened again through the tender mercy of God, keep a mean. Let us so put our trust in the mercy of God through Christ, that we know it our duty to keep the law of God and to love our neighbours for their Father's sake which created them, and for their Lord's sake, which redeemed them, and bought them so dearly with his blood. Let us walk in the fear of God and have our eyes open unto both parts of God's covenants, certified that none shall be partaker of the mercy save he that will fight against the flesh, to keep the law. And let us arm ourselves with this remembrance, that as Christ's works justify from sin and set us in the favour of God, so our own deeds through working of the Spirit of God help us to continue in the favour and the grace into which Christ hath brought us; and that we can no longer continue in favour and grace than our hearts are to keep the law.

20. Furthermore, concerning the law of God, this is a general conclusion, that the whole law, whether they be ceremonies, sacrifices, yea or sacraments either, or precepts of equity between man and man throughout all degrees of the world, all were given for our profit and necessity only, and not for any need that God hath of our keeping them, or that his joy is increased thereby or that the deed, for the deed itself, doth please him. That is, all that God requireth of us when we be at one with him and do put our trust in him and love him, is that we love every man his neighbour to pity him and to have compassion on him in all his needs and to be merciful unto him. This to be even so, Christ testifieth (Mt 7:12) saying: *This is the law and the prophets.* That is, to do as thou wouldst be done to (according, I mean, to the doctrine of the Scripture) and not to do that which thou wouldest not have done to thee, is all that the law requireth and the prophets. And Paul (Rm 13:8) affirmeth also that *love is the fulfilling of the law, and that he which loveth doth of his own accord all that the law requireth.* And (I Ti 1:5) Paul saith that *the love of a pure heart and good conscience and faith unfeigned is the end and fulfilling of the law.* For faith unfeigned in Christ's blood causeth to love for Christ's sake. Which love is the pure love only and the only cause of a good conscience. For then is the conscience pure, when the eye looketh to Christ in all her deeds, to do them for his sake and not for her own singular advantage, or any other wicked purpose. And John both in his gospel and also epistles, speaketh never of any other law than to love one another purely, affirming that we have God himself dwelling in us and all that God desireth, if we love one the other.

21. Seeing then that faith to God and love and mercifulness to our neighbours, is all that the law requireth, therefore of necessity the law must be understood and interpreted by them. So that all inferior laws are to be kept and observed as long as they be servants to faith and love, and then to be broken immediately, if through any occasion they hurt, either the faith which we should have to Godward in the confidence of Christ's blood, or the love which we owe to our neighbours for Christ's sake.

22. And therefore, when the blind Pharisees murmured and grudged at him and his disciples, that they brake the sabbath day and traditions of the elders, and that he himself did eat with publicans and sinners, he answereth (Mt 9:13) alleging Isaiah the prophet: *go rather, and learn what this meaneth – I require mercy and not sacrifice.* And (Mt 12:7): *Oh that ye wist what this meaneth, I require mercy and not sacrifice.* For only love and mercifulness understandeth the law, and else nothing. And he that hath not that written in his heart, shall never understand the law, no: though all the angels of heaven went about to teach him. And he that hath that graven in his heart shall not only understand the law, but shall also do of his own inclination all that is required of the law, though never law had been given: as all mothers do of themselves without law unto their children, all that can be required by any law, love overcoming all pain, grief, tediousness or loathsomeness; and even so, no doubt, if we had continued in our first state of innocency, we should ever have fulfilled the law, without compulsion of the law.

23. And because the law (which is a doctrine through teaching every man his duty, doth utter our corrupt nature) is sufficiently described by Moses, therefore is little mention made thereof in the new testament, save of love only, wherein all the law is included, as seldom mention is made of the new testament in the old law, save here and there are promises made unto them, that Christ should come and bless them and deliver them, and that the gospel and new testament should be preached and published unto all nations.

24. The gospel is glad tidings of mercy and grace and that our corrupt nature shall be healed again for Christ's sake and for the merits of his deservings only; yet on condition that we will turn to God, to learn to keep his laws spiritually, that is to say, of love for his sake, and will also suffer the curing of our infirmities.

25. The new testament is as much to say as a new covenant. The old testament is an old temporal covenant made between God and the carnal children of Abraham, Isaac and Jacob, otherwise called Israel, upon the deeds and observing of a temporal law. When the reward of the keeping is temporal life and prosperity in the land of Canaan, and the breaking is rewarded with temporal death and punishment. But the new testament is an everlasting covenant made unto the children of God through faith in Christ, upon the deservings of Christ. Where eternal life is promised to all that believe, and death to all that are unbelieving. My deeds, if I keep the law, are rewarded with the temporal promises of this life. But if I believe in Christ, Christ's deeds have purchased for me the eternal promise of the everlasting life. If I commit nothing worthy of death, I deserve to my reward that no man kill me; if I hurt no man, I am worthy that no man hurt me. If I help my neighbour, I am worthy that he help me again, etc. So that with outward deeds with which I serve other men, I deserve that other men do like to me in this world, and they extend no further. But Christ's deeds extend to life everlasting unto all that believe, etc. This be sufficient in this place concerning the law and the gospel, new testament and old; so that as there is but one God, one Christ, one faith and one baptism, even so thou understand that there is but one gospel, though many write it and many preach it. For all preach the same Christ and bring the same glad tidings. And thereto Paul's epistles, with the gospel of John and his first epistle, and the first epistle of Saint Peter, are most pure gospel and most plainly and richly described the glory of the grace of Christ. If ye require more of the law, seek in the prologue to the Romans and in other places where it is sufficiently intreated of.

26. Repentance. Concerning this word repentance, or (as they used) penance, the Hebrew hath in the Old Testament generally *sob (shub)* – turn, or be converted. For which the translation that we take for Saint Jerome's hath most part *converti* – to turn, or be converted, and sometime yet, *agere paenitentiam*. And the Greek in the New Testament hath perpetually *metanoeo* – to turn in the heart and mind, and to come to the right knowledge, and to a man's right wit again. For which *metanoeo* St Jerome's translation hath sometime *ago paenitentiam* – I do repent, sometime *paeniteo* – I repent, sometime *paeniteor* – I am repentant, sometime *habeo paenitentiam* – I have repentance, sometime *paenitet me* – it repenteth me. And Erasmus useth much this word *resipisco* – I come to myself, or to my right mind again. And the very sense and signification both of the Hebrew and also of the Greek word is – to be converted and to turn to God with all the heart, to know his will and to live according to his laws, and to be cured of our corrupt nature with the oil of his Spirit and wine of obedience to his doctrine. Which conversion or turning, if it be unfeigned, these four do accompany it and are included therein: Confession, not in the priest's ear, for that is but man's invention, but to God in the heart and before all the congregation of God, how that we be sinners and sinful, and that our whole nature is corrupt and inclined to sin and all unrighteousness, and therefore evil, wicked and damnable, and his law holy and just, by which our sinful nature is rebuked; and also to our neighbours, if we have offended any person particularly. Then, Contrition – sorrowfulness that we be such damnable sinners, and not only have sinned but are wholly inclined to sin still. Thirdly: Faith (of which our old doctors have made no mention at all in the description of their penance), yet God for Christ's sake doth forgive and receive us to mercy, and is at one with us and will heal our corrupt nature. And fourthly: Satisfaction, or amends-making, not to God with holy works, but to my neighbour whom I have hurt, and the congregation of God whom I have offended, (if any open crime be found in me), and submitting of a man's self unto the congregation or church of Christ, and to the officers of the same, to have his life corrected and governed henceforth of them, according to the true doctrine of the church of Christ. And note this: that as satisfaction or amends-making is counted righteousness before the world and a purging of the sin, so that the world when I have made a full amends, hath no further to complain. Even so, faith in Christ's blood is counted righteousness, and a purging of all sin before God.

27. Moreover, he that sinneth against his brother sinneth also against his Father, Almighty God. And as the sin committed against his brother is purged before the world with making amends and asking forgiveness, even so is the sin committed against God purged through faith in Christ's blood only. For Christ saith (Jn 8:24): *Except ye believe that I am he, ye shall die in your sins.* That is to say, if ye think that there is any other sacrifice or satisfaction to Godward than me, ye remain ever in sin before God, howsoever righteous ye appear before the world. Wherefore now, whether ye call this *metanoia*, repentance, conversion or turning again to God, either amending and etc. or whether ye say repent, be converted, turn to God, amend your living or what ye lust, I am content so ye understand what is meant thereby, as I have now declared.

28. Elders. In the Old Testament the temporal heads and rulers of the Jews which had the governance over the lay or common people are called elders, as ye may see in the four Evangelists. Out of which custom, Paul in his epistles and also Peter, call the prelates and spiritual governors which are bishops and priests, elders. Now whether ye call them elders or priests, it is to me all one: so that ye understand that they be officers and servants of the Word of God, unto the which all men both high and low that will not rebel against Christ, must obey as long as they preach and rule truly and no longer.

29. A prologue into the four Evangelists, showing what they were and their authority. And first of St Matthew. As touching the Evangelists, ye see in the New Testament clearly what they were. First Matthew (as ye read Mt 9:9, Mk 2:14, Lk 5:27) was one of Christ's apostles, and was with Christ all the time of his preaching, and saw and heard his own self almost all that he wrote.

30. Of Mark read (Ac 12:12-17) how Peter (after he was loosed out of prison by the angel) came to Mark's mother's house, where many of the disciples were praying for his deliverance. And Paul and Barnabas took him with them from Jerusalem and brought him to Antioch (Ac 12:25). And (Ac 13:5) Paul and Barnabas took Mark with them when they were sent out to preach; from whom he also departed, as it appeareth in the said chapter, and returned to Jerusalem again. And (Ac 15:37-40) Paul and Barnabas were at variance about him, Paul not willing to take him with them, because he forsook them in their first journey. Notwithstanding yet, when Paul wrote the epistle to the Colossians, Mark was with him, as he saith in the fourth chapter; of whom Paul also testifieth, both that he was Barnabas' sister's son and also his fellow worker in the Kingdom of God.

31. And (II Ti 4:11) Paul commandeth Timothy to bring Mark with him, affirming that he was needful to him, to minister to him. Finally, he was also with Peter when he wrote his first epistle, and so familiar that Peter

calleth him his son. Whereof ye see, of whom he learned his gospel, even of the very apostles, with whom he had his continual conversation, and also of what authority his writing is, and how worthy of credence.

32. Luke was Paul's companion, at the least way from the sixteenth chapter of Acts forth and with him in all his tribulation. And he went with Paul at his last going up to Jerusalem. And from thence he followed Paul to Caesarea, where he lay two years in prison. And from Caesarea he went with Paul to Rome, where he lay two other years in prison. And he was with Paul when he wrote to the Colossians, as he testifieth in the fourth chapter, saying: *The beloved Luke the physician saluteth you.*[1] And he was with Paul when he wrote the second epistle to Timothy, as he saith in the fourth chapter, saying: *Only Luke is with me.*[2] Whereby ye see the authority of the man, and of what credence and reverence his writing is worthy of, and thereto of whom he learned the story of his gospel, as he himself saith, how that he learned it and searched it out with all diligence of them that saw it and were also partakers at the doing. And as for the Acts of the Apostles, he himself was at the doing of them (at the least) of the most part, and had his part therein, and therefore wrote of his own experience.

33. John, what he was, is manifest by the first three Evangelists. First, Christ's apostle, and that one of the chief. Then Christ's nigh kinsman, and for his singular innocency and softness, singularly beloved and of singular familiarity with Christ, and ever one of the three witnesses of most secret things. The cause of his writing was certain heresies that arose in his time, and namely two, of which one denied Christ to be very man and to be come in the very flesh and nature of man. Against which two heresies he wrote both his gospel and also his first epistle, and in the beginning of his gospel saith that the word or thing was at the beginning, and was with God, and was also very God, and that all things was created and made by it, and that it was also made flesh; that is to say, became very man. *And he dwelt among us* (saith he) *and we saw his glory.*[3]

34. And in the beginning of his epistle he saith: *We show you of the thing that was from the beginning, which also we heard, saw with our eyes and our hands handled.*[4] And again: *We show you everlasting life, that was with the Father and appeared to us, and we heard and saw,*[5] and etc.

35. In that he saith that it was from the beginning, and that it was eternal life, and that it was with God, he affirmeth him to be very God. And that he saith, *we heard, saw and felt*, he witnesseth that he was very man also. John also wrote last, and therefore touched not the story that the other had compiled. But writeth most of faith and promises, and of the sermons of Christ.

36. This be sufficient concerning the four Evangelists and their authority and worthiness to be believed.

37. A warning to the reader if aught be escaped through negligence of the printer, as this text is that followeth, which if thou find any more such:

compare the English to the other books that are already printed, and so shalt thou perceive the truth of the English.

38. In the 23rd chapter of Matthew and in the 33rd leaf on the second side and last line, read the sentence thus: *Thou blind Pharisee, cleanse first the inside of the cup and platter, that the outside of them may be clean also.* (Mt 23:26).

William Tyndale, yet once more to the Christian Reader:

39. Thou shalt understand most, dear reader, when I had taken in hand to look over the New Testament again, and to compare it with the Greek, and to mend whatsoever I could find amiss, and had almost finished the labour; George Joye secretly took in hand to correct it also, by what occasion his conscience knoweth; and prevented me, insomuch that his correction was printed in great number, ere mine began. When it was spied and word brought me, though it seemed to divers other that George Joye had not used the office of an honest man, seeing that he knew that I was in correcting it myself; neither did walk after the rules of the love and softness which Christ and his disciples teach us, how that we should do nothing of strife to move debate, or of vainglory, or of covetousness; yet I took the thing in worth as I have done divers other in time past, as one that have more experience of the nature and disposition of the man's complexion, and supposed that a little spice of covetousness and vainglory (two blind guides) had been the only cause that moved him so to do, about which things I strive with no man: and so followed after and corrected forth and caused this to be printed, without surmise or looking on his correction.

40. But when the printing of mine was almost finished, one brought me a copy and showed me so many places, in such wise altered that I was astonied and wondered not a little what fury had driven him to make such change, and to call it a diligent correction. For throughout Matthew, Mark and Luke perpetually: and oft in the Acts, and sometime in John and also in the Hebrews, where he findeth this word *resurrection*, he changeth it into "the life after this life", or "very life" and such like, as one that abhorred the name of the resurrection.

41. If that change, to turn resurrection into life after this life, be a diligent correction, then must my translation be faulty in those places, and St Jerome's, and all the translators that ever I heard of, in what tongue soever it be, from the apostles unto this; his diligent correction (as he calleth it) which whether it be so or no, I permit it to other men's judgements.

42. But of this I challenged George Joye, that he did not put his own name thereto and call it rather his own translation; and that he played boo peep, and in some of his books putteth in his name and title, and in some keepeth it out. It is lawful for who will to translate and show his mind, though a thousand had translated before him. But it is not lawful (thinketh me) nor yet expedient for the edifying of the unity of the faith of Christ, that whosoever will, shall by his own authority, take another man's translation and put out and in and change at pleasure, and call it a correction.

43. Moreover, ye shall understand that George Joye hath had of a long time marvellous imaginations about this word resurrection, that it should be taken for the state of the souls after their departing from their bodies, and hath also (though he hath been reasoned with thereof and desired to cease) yet sown his doctrine by secret letters on that side of the sea, and caused great division among the brethren. Insomuch that John Fryth, being in prison in the Tower of London, a little before his death, wrote that we should warn him and desire him to cease, and would have then written against him, had I not withstood him. Thereto I have been since informed that no small number, through his curiosity, utterly deny the resurrection of the flesh and body, affirming that the soul, when she is departed, is the spiritual body of the resurrection, and other resurrection shall there none be. And I have talked with some of them myself, so doted in that folly, that it were as good persuade a post, as to pluck that madness out of their brains. And of this all is George Joye's unquiet curiosity the whole occasion, whether he be of the said faction also or not – to that, let him answer himself.

44. If George Joye will say (as I wot well he will) that his change is the sense and meaning of those Scriptures, I answer that it is sooner said than proved; howbeit let other men judge. But though it were the very meaning of the Scripture, yet if it were lawful after his example to every man to play boo peep with the translations that are before him, and to put out the words of the text at his pleasure, and to put in everywhere his meaning or what he thought the meaning were; that were the next way to stablish all heresies and to destroy the ground wherewith we should improve them. As for an example, when Christ saith (Jn 5:28-29): *The time shall come in the which all that are in the graves shall hear his voice and shall come forth; they that have done good unto resurrection of life (or with the resurrection of life), and they that have done evil, unto the resurrection (or with the resurrection) of damnation.* George Joye's correction is: *They that have done good shall come forth into the very life, and they that have done evil into the life of damnation*, thrusting clean out this word resurrection. Now by the same authority, and with as good reason, shall another come and say of the rest of the text: They that are in the sepulchres shall hear his voice, and so put in his diligent correction and mock out the text, that it shall not make for the resurrection of the flesh, which thing also George Joye's correction doth manifestly affirm. If the text be left uncorrupt it will purge herself of all manner false glosses, how subtle soever they be feigned, as a seething pot casteth up her scum. But if the false gloss be made the text, diligently overseen and correct, wherewith then shall we correct false doctrine and defend Christ's flock from false opinions and from the wicked heresies of ravening of wolves? In my mind therefore, a little unfeigned love after the rules of Christ, is worth much high learning, and single and slight understanding that edifieth in unity, is much better than subtle curiosity, and meekness better than bold arrogance and standing overmuch in a man's own conceit.

45. Wherefore, concerning the resurrection, I protest before God and our Saviour Jesus Christ, and before the universal congregation that believeth in him, that I believe according to the open and manifest Scriptures and Catholic Faith, that Christ is risen again in the flesh which he received of his mother, the Blessed Virgin Mary, and body wherein he died. And that we shall all, both good and bad, rise both flesh and body, and appear together before the judgement seat of Christ, to receive every man according to his deeds. And that the bodies of all that believe and continue in the true faith of Christ shall be endued with like immortality and glory as is the body of Christ.

46. And I protest before God that our Saviour Christ, and all that believe in him, that I hold of the souls that are departed as much as may be proved by manifest and open Scripture, and think the souls departed in the faith of Christ and love of the law of God, to be in no worse case than the soul of Christ was from the time that he delivered his spirit into the hands of his Father, until the resurrection of his body in glory and immortality. Nevertheless, I confess openly, that I am not persuaded that they be already in the full glory that Christ is in, or the elect angels of God are in. Neither is it any article of my faith, for if it so were, I see not but then the preaching of the resurrection of the flesh were a thing in vain. Notwithstanding, yet I am ready to believe it, if it may be proved with open Scripture. And I have desired George Joye to take open texts that seem to make for that purpose, as this is: *Today thou shalt be with me in Paradise*,[6] to make thereof what he could, and to make his dreams about this word resurrection go. For I receive not in the Scripture the private interpretation of any man's brain, without open testimony of any Scriptures agreeing thereto.

47. Moreover, I take God (which alone seeth the heart) to record to my conscience, beseeching him that my part be not in the blood of Christ, if I wrote of all that I have written throughout all my book, aught of an evil purpose, of envy or malice to any man, or to stir up any false doctrine or opinion in the church of Christ, or to be author of any sect, or to draw disciples after me, or that I would be esteemed or had in price above the least child that is born, save only of pity and compassion I had and yet have on the blindness of my brethren, and to bring them unto the knowledge of Christ, and to make every one of them if it were possible, as perfect as an angel of heaven, and to weed out all that is not planted of our Heavenly Father, and to bring down all that lifteth up itself against the knowledge of the salvation that is in the blood of Christ. Also, my part be not in Christ, if my heart be not to follow and live according as I teach, and also if mine heart weep not night and day for mine own sin and other men's indifferently, beseeching God to convert us all and to take his wrath from us, and to be merciful as well to all other men, as to mine own soul, caring for the wealth of the realm I was born in, for the king and all that are thereof, as a tender-hearted mother would do for her only son.

48. As concerning all I have translated or otherwise written, I beseech all men to read it for that purpose I wrote it – even to bring them to the knowledge of the Scripture. And as far as the Scripture approveth it, so far to allow it, and if in any place the Word of God disallow it, there to refuse it, as I do before our Saviour Christ and his congregation. And where they find faults, let them show it me if they be nigh, or write to me if they be far off; or write openly against it and improve it, and I promise them, if I shall perceive that their reasons conclude, I will confess mine ignorance openly.

49. Wherefore I beseech George Joye, yea and all other too, for to translate the Scripture for themselves, whether out of Greek, Latin or Hebrew. Or (if they will needs) as the fox when he hath pissed in the gray's hole challengeth it for his own, so let them take my translations and labours, and change and alter, and correct and corrupt at their pleasures, and call it their own translations, and put to their own names, and not to play boo peep after George Joye's manner. Which whether he have done faithfully and truly, with such reverence and fear as becometh the Word of God, and with such love and meekness and affection to unite, and circumspection that the ungodly have none occasion to rail on the verity, as becometh the servants of Christ, I refer it to the judgements of them that know and love the truth. For this I protest, that I provoke not Joye, nor any other man (but am provoked, and that after the spitefullest manner of provoking), to do sore against my will and with sorrow of heart that I now do. But I neither can nor will suffer of any man that he shall go, take my translation, and correct it without name, and make such changing as I myself durst not do, as I hope to have my part in Christ, though the whole world should be given me for my labour.

50. Finally, that New Testament thus diligently corrected, beside this so oft putting out this word resurrection, and I wot not what other change, for I have not yet read it over, hath in the end, before the Table of the Epistles and Gospels, this title: **Here endeth the New Testament diligently overseen and correct and printed now again at Antwerp, by me widow of Christopher of Eindhoven. In the year of our Lord 1534 in August.** Which title (reader), I have here put in, because by this thou shalt know the book the better. *Vale.*

[1] Cl 4:14   [3] Jn 1:14   [5] I Jn 1:2   [6] Lk 23:43
[2] II Ti 4:11   [4] I Jn 1:1

02. TYNDALE'S PREFACE TO THE PENTATEUCH, 1530

History

Having completed the translation of the New Testament, Tyndale turned his attention to the Old. Before his arrest, he had produced the Pentateuch, which was published in 1530. Soon afterwards, he also translated the prophet Jonah. Further work on the Old Testament was delayed because of revisions which he felt he had to make to the New. He eventually managed to complete Joshua to 2 Chronicles, but these were not published before his death, when they were incorporated into a complete edition of the bible by "Thomas Matthew", the pseudonym of John Rogers (1537).

The preface contains an account of Tyndale's attempts to secure the Bishop of London's support for his translation work, and also hints at the reasons why he felt obliged to leave England. It was reprinted in the 1534 edition, though the Prologue received a substantial addition, which deals specifically with "covenant theology".

Theology

Tyndale's overriding concern is to point out that the Bible was given for the "learning and comfort" of believers, and that this is the main reason why everyone needs a translation in his or her own language. He demonstrates his point by several quotations from the New Testament (which refer to the use of the Old), and also by rehearsing the main events of Patriarchal history. Particularly noteworthy are his assertions that even the most obnoxious stories from the Old Testament are full of consolation for the Christian, and also that believers today are subjected to exactly the same kinds of suffering and persecution as the characters of the Old Testament. The unity of the covenants was therefore not merely theoretical or historical, but had practical significance and application in the lives of individual Christians.

N.B. The paragraph numbering has been supplied for this edition, for ease of reference. Paragraphs added in 1534 are in parentheses, but to avoid confusion, the numbering sequence is not interrupted.

01. When I had translated the New Testament I added an epistle unto the latter end, in which I desired them that were learned to amend if aught were found amiss. But our malicious and wily hypocrites, which are so stubborn and hard-hearted in their wicked abominations that it is not possible for them to amend anything at all (as we see by daily experience, when both their livings and doings are rebuked with the truth) say, some of them that it is impossible to translate the Scripture into English, some that it is not lawful for the laypeople to have it in their mother tongue, some, that it would make them all heretics, as it would no doubt from many things which they of long time have falsely taught, and that is the whole cause wherefore they forbid it, though they other cloaks pretend. And some or rather every one, say that it would make them rise against the king, whom they themselves (unto their damnation) never yet obeyed. And lest the temporal rulers should see their falsehood, if the Scripture came to light, causeth them so to lie. And as for my translation, in which they affirm unto the laypeople (as I have heard say) to be I wot not how many thousand heresies, so that it cannot be mended or correct, they have yet taken so great pain to examine it, and to compare it unto that they would fain have it and to their own imaginations and juggling terms, and to have somewhat to rail at, and under that cloak to blaspheme the truth, that they might with as little labour (as I suppose) have translated the most part of the Bible. For they which in times past were wont to look on no more Scripture than they found in their Duns, or such like devilish doctrine, have yet now so narrowly looked on my translation that there is not so much as one i therein, if it lack a tittle over his head, but they have noted it, and number it unto the ignorant people for a heresy. Finally, in this they be all agreed, to drive you from the knowledge of the Scripture, and that ye shall not have the text thereof in the mother tongue, and to keep the world still in darkness, to the intent they might sit in the consciences of the people, through vain superstition and false doctrine, to satisfy their filthy lusts, their proud ambition, and unsatiable covetousness, and to exalt their own honour above king and emperor, yea and above God himself.

02. A thousand books had they lever to be put forth against their abominable doings and doctrine, than that the Scripture should come to light. For as long as they may keep that down, they will so darken the right way with the mist of their sophistry, and so tangle them that either rebuke or despise their abominations with arguments of philosophy and with worldly similitudes and apparent reasons of natural wisdom. And with wresting the Scripture unto their own purpose clean contrary unto the process, order and meaning of the text, and so delude them in descanting upon it with allegories, and amaze them expounding it in many senses before the unlearned laypeople (when it hath but one simple literal sense whose light the owls cannot abide) that though thou feel in thine heart and art sure how that all is false that they say, yet couldst thou not solve their subtle riddles.

03. Which thing only moved me to translate the New Testament. Because I had perceived by experience how that it was impossible to establish the laypeople in any truth, except the Scripture were plainly laid before their eyes in their mother tongue, that they might see the process, order and meaning of the text; for else, whatsoever truth is taught them, these enemies of all truth quench it again, partly with the smoke of their bottomless pit whereof thou readest (Re 9:2); that is, with apparent reasons of sophistry and traditions of their own making, founded without ground of Scripture, and partly in juggling with the text, expounding it in such a sense as is impossible to gather of the text, if thou see the process, order and meaning thereof.

04. And even in the Bishop of London's house I intended to have done it. For when I was so turmoiled in the country where I was that I could no longer there dwell (the process thereof were too long here to rehearse) I this wise thought in myself – this I suffer because the priests of the country be unlearned, as God it knoweth, there are a full ignorant sort which have seen no more Latin than that they read in their portesses and missals, which yet many of them can scarcely read, (except it be Albertus *De secretis mulierum*, in which yet, though they be never so sorrily learned, they pore day and night, and make notes therein, and all to teach the midwives, as they say, and Linwood, *A Book of Constitutions*, to gather tithes, mortuaries, offerings, customs and other pillage, which they call not theirs, but God's part and the duty of Holy Church, to discharge their consciences withal; for they are bound that they shall not diminish, but increase all things to the uttermost of their powers) and therefore (because they are thus unlearned, thought I) when they come together to the alehouse, which is their preaching place, they affirm that my sayings are heresy. And besides that, they add to of their own heads which I never spake, as the manner is to prolong the tale to short the time withal, and accused me secretly to the Chancellor and other the Bishop's officers. And indeed, when I came before the Chancellor, he threatened me grievously and reviled me, and rated me as though I had been a dog, and laid to my charge whereof there could be none accuser brought forth, (as their manner is not to bring forth the accuser) and yet all the priests of the country were the same day there. As I this thought, the Bishop of London came to my remembrance, whom Erasmus (whose tongue maketh of little gnats great elephants, and lifteth up above the stars whosoever giveth him a little exhibition), praiseth exceedingly among other in his annotations on the New Testament, for his great learning. Then thought I, if I might come to this man's service, I were happy. And so I gat me to London, and through the acquaintance of my master came to Sir Harry Gilford, the King's Grace's Controller, and brought him an oration of Isocrates which I had translated out of Greek into English, and desired him to speak unto my Lord of London for me, which he also did as he showed me, and willed me to write an epistle to my Lord, and to go to him myself, which I also did, and delivered my epistle to a servant of his own, one William Hebblethwaite, a man of mine old acquaintance. But God, which knoweth what is within hypocrites, saw that I was beguiled, and that that counsel was not the next way unto my purpose. And therefore he gat me no favour in my Lord's sight.

05. Whereupon my Lord answered me, his house was full, he had more than he could well find, and advised me to seek in London, where he said I could not lack a service. And so in London I abode almost a year, and marked the course of the world, and heard our praters, I would say our preachers, how they boasted themselves and their high authority, and beheld the pomp of our prelates, and how busied they were as they yet are, to set peace and unity in the world (though it be not possible for them that walk in darkness to continue long in peace, for they cannot but either stumble or dash themselves at one thing or another that shall clean unquiet altogether) and saw things whereof I defer to speak at this time, and understood at the last, not only that there was no room in my Lord of London's palace to translate the New Testament, but also that there was no place to do it in all England, as experience doth now openly declare.

06. Under what manner therefore should I now submit this book to be corrected and amended of them which can suffer nothing to be well? Or what protestation should I make in such a manner unto our prelates, those stubborn Nimrods which so mightily fight against God, and resist his Holy Spirit, enforcing with all craft and subtlety to quench the light of the everlasting testament, promises and appointment made between God and us; and heaping the fierce wrath of God upon all princes and rulers, mocking them with false feigned names of hypocrisy, and serving their lusts at all points, and dispensing with them even of the very laws of God, of which Christ himself testifieth (Mt 5:18), that not so much as one tittle thereof may perish, or be broken. And of which the prophet saith (Ps 119:4): *Thou hast commanded thy laws to be kept* me'od, that is in Hebrew *exceedingly*, with all diligence, might and power, and have made them so mad with their juggling charms and crafty persuasions that they think it a full satisfaction for all their wicked lying, to torment such as tell them truth, and to burn the word of their souls' health, and slay whoever believe thereon.

07. Notwithstanding, yet I submit this book and all other that I have either made or translated, or shall in time to come, (if it be God's will that I shall further labour in his harvest) unto all them that submit themselves unto the Word of God, to be corrected of them, yea and moreover to be disallowed and also burnt, if it seem worthy when they have examined it with the Hebrew, so that they first put forth of their own translating another that is more correct.

A Prologue showing the use of the Scripture

08. Though a man had a precious jewel and a rich, yet if he wist not the value thereof nor wherefore it served, he were neither the better nor richer by a straw. Even so, though we read the Scripture and babble of it never so much, yet if we know not the use of it and wherefore it was given, and what is therein to be sought, it profiteth us nothing at all. It is not enough therefore to read and talk of it only, but we must also desire God day and night instantly to open our eyes, and to make us understand and feel wherefore the Scripture was given, that we may apply the medicine of the Scripture, every man to his own sores, unless that we pretend to be idle disputers and brawlers about

vain words, ever gnawing upon the bitter bark without and never attaining unto the sweet pith within, and persecuting one another for defending of lewd imaginatiois and fantasies of our own invention.

09. Paul, in the third of the second epistle to Timothy (2 Ti 3:16) saith, that the Scripture is good to teach (for that ought men to teach, and not dreams of their own making, as the Pope doth) and also to improve, for the Scripture is the touchstone that trieth all doctrines, and by that we know the false from the true. And in the sixth to the Ephesians (Ep 6:17) he calleth it the sword of the Spirit, because it killeth hypocrites and uttereth and improveth their false inventions. And in the fifteenth to the Romans (Ro 15:4) he saith all that are written are written for our learning, that we through patience and comfort of the Scripture might have hope. That is, the examples that are in the Scripture comfort us in all our tribulations, and make us to put our trust in God, and patiently to abide his leisure. And in the tenth of the first to the Corinthians (I Co 10:1-13), he bringeth in examples of the Scripture to fear us and to bridle the flesh, that we cast not the yoke of the law of God from off our necks, and fall to lusting and doing of evil.

10. So now the Scripture is a light and showeth us the true way, both what to do and what to hope. And a defence from all error, and a comfort in adversity that we despair not, and feareth us in prosperity that we sin not. Seek therefore in the Scripture as thou readest it

1530 edition:

first the law, what God commandeth us to do. And secondarily the promises, which God promiseth us again, namely in Christ Jesu our Lord. Then seek examples, first of comfort, how God purgeth all them that submit themselves to walk in his ways, in the purgatory of tribulation, delivering them yet at the latter end, and never suffering any of them to perish that cleave fast to his promises. And finally, note the examples which are written to fear the flesh that we sin not. That is, how God suffereth the ungodly and wicked sinners that resist God and refuse to follow him, to continue in their wickedness, ever waxing worse and worse until their sin be so sore increased and so abominable, that if they should longer endure they would corrupt the very elect. But for the elect's sake God sendeth them preachers. Nevertheless, they harden their hearts against the truth and God destroyeth them utterly, and beginneth the world anew.

1534 edition:

chiefly and above all, the covenants made between God and us. That is to say, the law and commandments which God commandeth us to do. And then the mercy promised unto all them that submit themselves unto the law. For all the promises throughout the whole Scripture do include a covenant. That is, God bindeth himself to fulfil that mercy unto thee only, if thou wilt endeavour thyself to keep his laws, so that no man hath his part in the mercy of God, save he only that loveth his law and consenteth that it is righteous and good, and fain would do it, and ever mourneth because he now and then breaketh it through infirmity, or doth it not so perfectly as his heart would.

(11.) And let love interpret the law; that thou understand this to be the final end of the law, and the whole cause why the law was given – even to bring thee to the knowledge of God, how that he hath done all things for thee, that thou mightest love him again with all thine heart and thy neighbour for his sake as thyself, and as Christ loved thee. Because thy neighbour is the son of God also, and created unto his likeness as thou art, and bought with as dear blood as art thou. Whosoever feeleth in his heart that every man ought to love his neighbour as Christ loved him, and consenteth thereto, and enforceth to come thereto; the same only understandeth the law aright and can interpret it. And he that submitteth not himself in the degree he is in, to seek his neighbour's profit as Christ did his, can never understand the law, though it be interpreted to him. For that love is the light of the law, to understand it by.

(12.) And behold how righteous, how honest and how due a thing it is by nature, that every man love his neighbour unfeignedly even as himself, for his Father's sake. For it is the Father's great shame and his high displeasure, if one brother hurt another. If one brother be hurt of another, he may not avenge himself, but must complain to his Father or to them that have authority of his Father to rule in his absence. Even so, if any of God's children be hurt by any of his brethren, he may not avenge himself with hand or heart. God must avenge. And the governors and ministers of the law that God hath ordained to rule us by, concerning our outward conversation of one with another – they must avenge. If they will not avenge, but rather maintain wrong and be oppressors themselves, then we must tarry patiently till God come, which is ever ready to reap tyrants off the face of the earth as soon as their sins are ripe.

(13.) Consider also what wrath, vengeance and plagues God threateneth to them that are rebellious and disobedient.

(14.) Then go to and read the stories of the Bible for thy learning and comfort, and see everything practised before thine eyes, for according to those examples shall it go with thee and all men until the world's end. So that into whatsoever case or state a man may be brought, according to whatsoever example of the Bible it be, his end shall be according as he there seeth and readeth. As God there warneth ere he smite, and suffereth long ere he take extreme vengeance, so shall he do with us. As they that turn are there received to mercy, and they that maliciously resist perish utterly, so shall it be with us. As they that resist the counsel of God perish through their own counsel, so shall it be with us until the world's end. As it went with their kings and rulers, so shall it go with ours. As it was with their common people, so shall it be with ours. As it was with their spiritual officers, so shall it be with ours. As it was with their true prophets, so shall it be with ours until the world's end. As they had ever among them false prophets and true, and as their false persecuted the true and moved the princes to slay them, so shall it be with us until the end of the world. As there was among them but a few true-hearted to God, so shall it be among us; and as their idolatry was, so shall ours be until the end of the world. All mercy that is showed there is a promise unto thee if thou turn to God. And all vengeance and wrath showed there is threatened to thee, if thou be stubborn and resist.

(15.) And this learning and...

16. (This) comfort shalt thou evermore find in the plain text and literal sense. Neither is there any story so homely, so rude, yea or so vile (as it seemeth outward) wherein is not exceeding great comfort. And when some which seem to themselves great clerks say they wot not what more profit is in many gests of the Scripture if they be read without an allegory than in a tale of Robin Hood, say thou: that they be written for our consolation and comfort, that we despair not if suchlike happen to us. We be not holier than Noah, though he were once drunk. Neither better beloved than Jacob, though his own son defiled his bed. We be not holier than Lot, though his daughters through ignorance deceived him, nor peradventure holier than those daughters. Neither are we holier than David, though he brake wedlock, and upon the same committed abominable murder. All those men have witness of the Scripture that they pleased God and were good men, both before that those things chanced them, and also after. Nevertheless, such things happened them for our example – not that we should counterfeit their evil, but if while we fight with ourselves enforcing to walk in the law of God (as they did) we yet fail likewise, that we despair not, but come again to the laws of God and take better hold.

17. We read, since the time of Christ's death, of virgins that have been brought unto the common stews and there defiled, and of martyrs that have been bound and whores have abused their bodies. Why? The judgements of God are bottomless. Such things chanced partly for examples, partly God through sin healeth sin. Pride can neither be healed nor yet appear but through such horrible deeds. Peradventure they were of the Pope's sect and rejoiced fleshly, thinking that heaven came by deeds and not by Christ, and that the outward deed justified them and made them holy and not the inward spirit received by faith and the consent of the heart unto the law of God.

18. As thou readest therefore, think that every syllable pertaineth to thine own self, and suck out the pith of the Scripture, and arm thyself against all assaults. First, not with strong faith the power of God in creating all of naught. Then mark the grievous fall of Adam and of us all in him, through the light regarding the commandment of God. In the fourth chapter God turneth him unto Abel and then to his offering, but not to Cain and his

offering. Where thou seest that the deeds of the evil appear outwardly as glorious as the deeds of the good, yet in the sight of God, which looketh on the heart, the deed is good because of the man and not the man good because of his deed. In the sixth, God sendeth Noah to preach to the wicked and giveth them space to repent; they wax hard-hearted, God bringeth them to naught, and yet saveth Noah, even by the same water by which he destroyed them. Mark also what followed the pride of the building of the tower of Babel. Consider how God sendeth forth Abraham out of his own country into a strange land full of wicked people, and gave him but a bare promise with him that he would bless him and defend him. Abraham believed and that word saved and delivered him in all perils, so that we see how that man's life is not maintained by bread only (as Christ saith) but much rather by believing the promises of God. Behold how soberly and how circumspectly both Abraham and also Isaac behave themselves among the infidels. Abraham buyeth that which might have been given him for naught, to cut off occasions. Isaac, when his wells which he had digged were taken from him, giveth room and resisteth not. Moreover, they ear and sow and feed their cattle, and make confederations, and take perpetual truce, and do all outward things, even as they do which have no faith, for God hath not made us to be idle in this world. Every man must work godly and truly to the uttermost of the power that God hath given him, and yet not trust therein, but in God's word or promise, and God will work with us and bring that we do to good effect. And then when our power will extend no further, God's promises will work all alone.

19. How many things also resisted the promises of God to Jacob? And yet Jacob conjureth God with his own promises, saying: *O God of my father Abraham, and God of my father Isaac, O Lord, which saidst unto me: return unto thine own country, and unto the place where thou wast born and I will do thee good. I am not worthy of the least of those mercies, nor of that truth which thou hast done to thy servant. I went out but with a staff, and come home with two droves, deliver me out of the hands of my brother Esau, for I fear him greatly,*[1] etc. And God delivered him, and will likewise all that call unto his promises with a repenting heart, were they never so great sinners. Mark also the weak infirmities of the man. He loveth one wife more than another, one son more than another. And see how God purgeth him. Esau threatened him; Laban beguileth him. The beloved wife is long barren; his daughter is ravished, his wife is defiled, and that of his own son. Rachel dieth, Joseph is taken away, yea and as he supposed, rent of wild beasts. And yet how glorious was his end? Note the weakness of his children, yea and the sin of them, and how God through their own wickedness saved them. These examples teach us that a man is not at once perfect the first day he beginneth to live well. They that be strong therefore must suffer with the weak, and help to keep them in unity and peace one with another, until they be stronger.

20. Note what the brethren said when they were tached [i.e. detained, *ed.*] in Egypt, we have verily sinned (said they) against our brother in that we saw the anguish of his soul when he besought us, and would not hear him, and therefore is this tribulation come upon us. By which example thou seest, how that conscience of evil doings findeth men out at the last. But namely in tribulation and adversity; there temptation and also desperation, yea and the very pains of hell find us out. There the soul feeleth the fierce wrath of God, and wisheth mountains to fall on her, and to hide her (if it were possible) from the angry face of God.

21. Mark also, how great evils follow of how little an occasion. Dinah goeth but forth alone to see the daughters of the country, and how great mischief and trouble followed? Jacob loved but one son more than another, and how grievous murder followed in their hearts? These are examples for our learning, to teach us to walk warily and circumspectly in the world of weak people, that we give no man occasions of evil.

22. Finally, see what God promised Joseph in his dreams. Those promises accompanied him always, and went down with him even into the deep dungeon, and brought him up again, and never forsook him, till all that was promised was fulfilled. These are examples written for our learning (as Paul saith), to teach us to trust in God in the strong fire of tribulation and purgatory of our flesh. And that they which submit themselves to follow God, should note and mark such things; for their learning and comfort is the fruit of the Scripture and the cause why it was written. And with such a purpose to read it is the way to everlasting life, and to those joyful blessings that are promised unto all nations in the seed of Abraham; which seed is Jesus Christ our Lord, to whom be honour and praise for ever and unto God our Father through him. Amen.

---

[1] Gn 32:9-11

03. ACT FOR THE PARDON OF THE CLERGY, 1531 (22 Henry VIII, c.15)

History

At the same time that Tyndale was undermining traditional Church authority by preparing his translations of the Bible, a very different type of attack on the Church was being prepared in the highest circles in the land. By 1526 King Henry VIII realized that there was little chance of his producing a male heir. This was a serious matter, since he knew as well as anyone how easily the "Tudor peace", established by Henry VII in 1485 after a generation of civil war, could be broken by an uncertain succession. Henry had a daughter Mary, but although English law allowed succession to the throne through the female line, it was uncertain whether this extended to accepting a queen regnant. The only previous attempt by a woman to rule the country had been made by Matilda (1135-1154), and her claim had led to two decades of warfare. Henry needed a son in order to feel secure, and came to believe that remarriage was the only way he would get what he wanted.

At first it seemed as if the proceedings for an annulment of his marriage would go fairly smoothly, but Henry had reckoned without his wife, and her powerful Spanish connections. The case dragged on for several years before it became apparent that the Pope was not going to give the King his divorce. In response to this, Henry stirred up nationalist resentment against "foreign" domination, represented especially by the taxes which England paid to the Papacy. The Parliament which assembled in 1529 was anti-clerical in complexion – more so than the King – and was a ready instrument of the royal will.

Henry decided to put the squeeze on the higher clergy, including Cardinal Wolsey, in the hope that this would bend the Pope's will. His chosen device was the concept of *Praemunire*, which had been written into a number of statutes in the latter part of the fourteenth century. This stated that the Pope could not interfere with the Crown's rights when it came to presenting clergymen to benefices. It had gradually become a dead letter, and by 1526 papal "interference" in such matters was commonplace. Henry therefore had little difficulty in finding cause for complaint when he dusted off the old and half-forgotten statutes. Wolsey was disgraced in 1530, but the Pope did not budge. The King therefore extended the accusation to the clergy as a whole – an unprecedented, and quite obviously unjust act.

The "pardon" consisted of a subsidy (in reality a fine) of 100,000 pounds from the Province of Canterbury and later of another 18,840 pounds from the Province of York. The whole episode was intended to demonstrate that royal supremacy in and over the Church was not an empty formula, but a reality with which the Pope would have to reckon. It did not get Henry his annulment, but it began the process of divorce between Rome and England, which culminated with the Act of Supremacy in 1534.

Theology

In so far as the Act can be said to have a theology, it is that the laity have supreme jurisdiction over the clergy, and not the other way round. Lay control of the Church was to be an important Reformation principle, and this statute was its first concrete manifestation.

N.B. Paragraph numbers are those of the original Act. "Persons" should normally be taken to mean "parsons", i.e. ordained clergymen.

01. The King, our Sovereign Lord, calling to his blessed and most gracious remembrance that his good and loving subjects, the most reverend father in God the Archbishop of Canterbury and other bishops, suffragans, prelates and other spiritual persons of the province of the archbishopric of Canterbury, of this his realm of England, and the ministers under written, which have exercised, practised or executed in spiritual courts and other spiritual jurisdictions within the said province, have fallen and incurred into divers dangers of his laws by things done, perpetrated and committed contrary to the order of his laws, and specially contrary to the form of the Statutes of Provisors, Provisions and *Praemunire*; and His Highness, having alway tender eye with mercy and pity and compassion towards his said spiritual subjects, minding of his high goodness and great benignity so always to impart the same unto them as justice being daily administered, all rigour be excluded, and the great and benevolent minds of his said subjects largely and many times approved towards his Highness, and specially in their Convocation and Synod now presently being in the chapter house of the monastery of Westminster, by correspondence of gratitude to them to be requited: of his mere motion, benignity and liberality, by authority of this his Parliament, hath given and granted his liberal and free pardon to his said good and loving spiritual subjects and the said ministers and to every of them to be had, taken and enjoyed to and by them and every of them by virtue of this present Act in manner and form ensuing, that is to wit: The King's Highness of his said benignity and high liberality, in consideration that the said Archbishop, Bishops and Clergy of the said Province of Canterbury in their said Convocation now being, have given and granted to him a subsidy of one hundred thousand pounds of lawful money current in this realm, to be levied and collected by the said clergy at their proper costs and charges, and to be paid in certain form specified in their said grant thereof, is fully and resolutely contented and pleased that it be ordained, established and enacted by authority of this his said Parliament, that the most reverend father in God, William Archbishop of Canterbury, Metropolitan and Primate of All England, and all other bishops and suffragans, prelates, abbots, priors and their convents, and every person of the same convents and convents corporate, and every person of the same convents corporate, abbesses, prioresses and religious nuns and all other religious and spiritual persons, deans and chapters and other dignities of cathedral and collegial churches, prebendaries, canons and petty canons, vicars and clerks of the same, and every person of the same, all archdeacons, masters, provosts, presidents, wardens of colleges and of collegiate churches, masters and wardens of hospitals, all fellows, brethren, scholars, priests and spiritual conducts and every of the same, and all vicars general of dioceses, chancellors, commissaries, officials and deans rural, and all ministers hereafter generally rehearsed, of any spiritual court of courts within the said Province of Canterbury, that is to say – all judges, advocates, registers and scribes proctors constituted to judgements, and apparitors and all other which within the said province of the Archbishopric of Canterbury at any time heretofore have administered, exercised, practised or executed in any jurisdictions within the said province as officers or ministers of the said courts, or have been ministers or executors to the exercise or administration of the same, and all and singular politic bodies spiritual, in any manner wise corporated, and all persons, vicars, curates, chantry priests, stipendiaries and all and every person and persons spiritual of all the clergy of the said Province of Canterbury in this present Act of pardon hereafter not excepted, or to the contrary not provided for, by whatsoever name or surname, name of dignity, pre-eminence or office they or any of them be or is named or called the successors, heirs, executors and administrators of them and every of them, shall be by authority of this present pardon, acquitted, pardoned, released and discharged against his Highness, his heirs, successors and executors, and every of them of all and all manner offences, contempts and trespasses committed or done against all and singular Statute and Statutes of Provisors, Provisions and *Praemunire* and every of them, and of all forfeitures and titles that may grow to the King's Highness by reason of any of the same statutes, and of all and singular trespasses, wrongs, deceits, misdemeanours, forfeitures, penalties and profits, sums of money, pains of death, pains corporal and pecuniary, as generally of all other things, causes, quarrels, suits, judgements and executions in this present Act hereafter not excepted nor forprised, which may be or can be by his Highness in any wise or by any means pardoned, before and to the tenth day of the month of March in the twenty-second year of his most noble reign (10 March 1531), to every of his said loving subjects, that is to say: to the said Archbishop and other the said Bishops, suffragans, prelates, abbots, priors and convents, and every person of the same convent and convents corporate, and every person of the same convents corporate, abbesses, prioresses, nuns and spiritual persons in dignity and all other religious and spiritual persons, deans, chapters, prebendaries, canons, petty canons, vicars choral, and clerks, archdeacons, masters, provosts, presidents, wardens, fellows, brethren, scholars, priests and spiritual conducts, chancellors, vicars general of dioceses, commissaries official, deans rural, all judges, advocates, registers and scribes, proctors and apparitors, which have administered, practised or executed any jurisdiction in any spiritual court within the said province, and to the said politic bodies, spiritual persons, vicars, curates, chantry priests, stipendiaries and to all and every person and persons spiritual of the clergy of the said Province, and to all and every other person or persons before named.

02. Also the King's Highness is contented that it be enacted by authority of this present Parliament that this said free pardon shall be as good and effectual in the law to every of his said spiritual subjects of the said Province, and to every of them and to the said ministers and to every of them, and to all and every of the said bodies corporate and other persons before named, and to every of them by these general words before rehearsed in all things which be not hereafter in this present Act excepted, as the said pardon should have been if all offences, contempts, forfeitures, causes, matters, suits, quarrels, judgements, executions, penalties and all other things not hereafter excepted had been particularly, singularly and plainly pardoned, named, rehearsed and specified by proper or express words and names in their kinds, natures and qualities in words and terms thereunto requisite in the same pardon; and that his said subjects hereafter not excepted, nor any of them nor their said ministers, successors, heirs, executors nor administrators of any of them, nor any of them nor any of the said bodies corporate, be nor shall be sued, vexed nor inquieted in their bodies, goods, goods, lands nor chattels, for any manner, matter, cause, contempt, misdemeanour, forfeiture, trespass, offence or any other thing suffered, done or committed before the said tenth day of March (10 March 1531) against the King's Highness, his crown, prerogative, laws, statues or dignity, but only for such causes, matters and offences as be specially and plainly rehearsed in the exceptions, forprises and provisions in this present pardon hereafter mentioned and for none other; any statute or statutes, laws, customs, use or precedent heretofore made or used to the contrary in any wise notwithstanding.

03. Also the King's Highness of his bounteous liberality, by authority of this present Parliament, granteth and freely giveth unto his said spiritual subjects and their said ministers, that is to say: to the said Archbishop and all other the said bishops, suffragans, prelates, abbots, priors, convents, abbesses, prioresses, nuns and spiritual persons in dignity, and all other religious and spiritual persons, deans, chapters, prebendaries, canons, petty canons, vicars choral and clerks, archdeacons, masters, provosts, presidents, wardens, fellows, brethren, scholars, priests, spiritual conducts, chancellors, vicars general of dioceses, commissaries official, deans rural, judges, advocates, registers, scribes, proctors and apparitors, bodies corporate and politic, bodies spiritual, persons, vicars, curates, chantry priests, stipendiaries and to all other persons spiritual, men and women of the clergy or spiritualty of the said Province, and to every of them, all such goods, chattels, fines, issues, profits, amercements, forfeitures and sums of money by any of them forfeited, which to his Highness do or should belong or appertain by reason of any offence, contempt, misdemeanour, trespass, matter, cause or quarrel, suffered, done or committed by them or any of them before the said tenth day of March (10 March 1531), which be not hereafter specially and plainly forprised and excepted in this present Act of pardon: and that all and every of the said spiritual subjects and their said ministers and all and every of the said bodies corporate and other persons before named, may by himself and his or their attorney or attorneys according to the laws of this realm, plead and minister this present Act, and free pardon for his or their discharge of and for everything, that is thereby pardoned without any fee or other thing therefore in any wise paying to any person or persons for pleading, writing or entry of judgement, or for any other cause concerning the same, but only twelvepence to the clerk that shall enter the plea, matter or judgement for his or their discharge in that behalf; any statute or use to the contrary notwithstanding.

04. And furthermore the King's Highness is contented that it be enacted by authority of this present Parliament that his said free pardon in all manner courts of his laws and ells, where shall be reputed, deemed, judged, allowed and taken, as well in the words and clauses of the exceptions and forprises specified in this present pardon and Act, as in all and singular the other clauses, words and sentences mentioned and rehearsed in the said free pardon, most beneficially and availably to all and singular his said subjects, and to every of the said bodies corporate and politic, bodies spiritual, and to every person spiritual of the said clergy and spiritualty, and to their said ministers and officers, and to all other persons aforenamed, and to every of them, and to the successors, heirs, executors and ministrators of every of them, and most strongly in bar and discharge against his Highness, his heirs, successors and executors in everything, without obstacle, challenge or other delay, whatsoever it be, to be made, pleaded, objected or alleged by the King our Sovereign Lord, his heirs, successors or executors or by his or any of their general attorney or attorneys, or by any other person or persons for his Highness or any of his heirs, successors or executors.

05. And furthermore it is enacted by the King our Sovereign Lord, and by authority of this present Parliament, that if any officer or clerk, or any of his high courts, commonly called the King's Bench, chancery and common place, or of his exchequer, or any other officer or clerk of any other of his courts within this realm, after the feast of Easter next coming (09 April 1531) make out or write out any manner of writs or other process, or any extract or other precepts whereby any person or persons of his said subjects or any of the said bodies corporate or politic, bodies spiritual or any of them, shall be in any wise arrested, attached, distrained, summoned or otherwise vexed, troubled or grieved in his or their bodies, lands, tenements, goods or chattels,

or in any of them, for or because of any manner of thing acquitted, pardoned, released or discharged by this present Act of free pardon, he so offending and thereof lawfully condemned, shall yield and pay for recompense thereof to the party so grieved or offended, treble damages accounted as parcel of those damages all costs of the suit: and nevertheless all and singular such writs, process, extracts and precepts after the said feast of Easter to be made for or upon any manner thing acquitted, pardoned, released or discharged by this present Act of free pardon, shall be utterly void and of none effect.

06. Excepted always and forprised out of this pardon all manner of high treasons, all prepensed and voluntary murders, all robberies of churches and robberies done upon or to men's persons, all other felonies and robberies by the common law of felonous taking of money, goods and chattels above the value of twenty shillings, all felonous burning of houses, all carnal ravishment of women, all erasings of records, all outlawries of high treasons and all manner of felonies other than felonies to the said value of twenty shillings or under that sum; and that all other outlawries had or promulged upon or against any of the King's said subjects, for any cause not being treason, murder or felony above the said sum of twenty shillings, to be pardoned by the general words of this pardon aforesaid, so alway that the same said subjects and every of them so being outlawed, stand to right to answer or satisfy the party at whose suit he is outlawed according to the laws of this realm.

07. Also excepted and forprised out of this pardon all titles and actions of *Quare impedit*, and titles of presentations, donations and collations to benefices and other promotions spiritual, which the King our Sovereign Lord by force or means of any statute or statutes of Provisors, Previsions or *Praemunire*. And also excepted and forprised out of this pardon all ravishments of the King's wards, all wastes of the King's woods in his forests, parks and chases, all concealments of customs and subsidies, all riots, routs and unlawful assemblies, committed and done above the number of twenty persons. And also except all manner of alienations and gifts unto mortmain, and all alienations, gifts, assignments, wills and limitations of uses of any manors, lands, tenements, rents, annuities and other hereditaments, to the use of any manner of mortmain and all intrusions, had, made or done, in or into any manors, lands, tenements or other hereditaments since the feast of the nativity of our Lord God in the twenty-second year of the reign of our said Sovereign Lord (25 December 1530), and also all offences committed and done by digging down or casting down of any cross or crosses which stood or were set in any common or highway or ways, and all and singular debts other than debts growing upon recognizance, being already forfeited for surety of the peace, or for appearance at any day or place. And excepted or forprised out of this pardon all accounts and all actions, suits and impetitions for the same accounts and arrearages of accounts and for the said debt, or any of them hereby excepted and forprised, all homages and reliefs, all wilful escapes as well of convicts as of other persons; debts which were due to the most noble King Henry the VII, or to any person or persons to his use by any condemnation, recognizance, obligation or otherwise, all and singular those forfeitures due to our Sovereign Lord King Henry the VIII by any penal statute or statutes which be converted into the nature of debt by judgement or by agreement of the offenders before the said tenth day of March (10 March 1531), and all forfeitures and other penalties and profits grown or due by reason of any offence or act committed or done contrary to any statute or statutes, or contrary to the common law, whereof any seizure is made or any information given in the King's exchequer, or any suit commenced before the said tenth day of March (10 March 1531), or whereof the King's Highness by this bill signed, or otherwise, hath made any gift or assignment to any of his servants, other than such actions, suits, forfeitures, penalties and profits, grown or due, or which might grow or be due to the King's Highness by reason of any offence, contempt or act committed or done contrary to the said statute of Provisors, Provisions and *Praemunire*, or any of them. And also excepted, all issues, forfeited fines, amercements afferred, taxed, set, extreated or judged severally, or particularly extending above the sum of one hundred and twenty shillings, and that all and singular other fines, as well fines *per licentia concordandi* as other, and all other issues and amercements, as well real as other, which severally or particularly extend not above the said sum of one hundred and twenty shillings, whether they be totted or not totted, taken to the sheriff or not taken to his charge, extreated or not extreated, whether they be turned into debt or not debt, and not being levied or received by any sheriff or sheriffs, bailiff, ministers or other officers, shall be fully, clearly and plainly pardoned and discharged to every of the King's subjects before rehearsed, against the King our Sovereign Lord, his heirs and successors for ever.

08. And it is further enacted by the authority aforesaid, that in case it be objected to any sheriff or sheriffs, or other accountants in the King's court of his exchequer, or in any other his courts, that any sheriff or sheriffs, or other officers accountant, hath or have received or taken any such fines, issues, or amercements before pardoned, released or acquitted, that then every such sheriff and sheriffs and other accountants shall be discharged, released, pardoned and acquitted thereof by his or their oath, without any further trial in that behalf.

09. Provided alway that this Act of free pardon shall not in any wise extend or be prejudicial or available in anything to the reverend father in God, John Archbishop of Dublin, now being in the King's land and dominion of Ireland, nor shall in any wise extend to pardon, discharge, release or acquit the Bishop of Hereford, nor shall extend or be beneficial to Peter Ligham, Clerk; John Baker, Clerk; Adam Travers, Clerk; Robert Cliff, Clerk; Rowland Phillips, Clerk and Thomas Pelles, Clerk.

10. Provided also that this Act of pardon shall not extend or be prejudicial to the King our Sovereign Lord, his heirs or successors, in anything concerning or touching his right and title of dissolution of the college being in the University of Oxford, commonly called the Cardinal's College, which was lately founded by the late reverend father in God Thomas, late Cardinal and Archbishop of York; nor concerning the King's right and title to the site of the same college, nor shall extend or be in any wise beneficial or available to the dean and canons of the same college or any of them in anything concerning the King's rights and titles in all manors, lordships, lands and tenements, advowsons, churches, parsonages and other hereditaments of the said college or any of them.

11. Provided also that allowance shall be had to the clergy of the said Province of Canterbury out of the said sum of one hundred thousand pounds, of all and singular such sums of money as shall be reasonably taxed and assessed, to be paid by the persons before named, being fully excepted and forprised out and from the benefit of this free pardon, that is to say, the said Archbishop of Dublin and the said Bishop of Hereford and the said Peter Ligham, John Baker, Adam Travers, Robert Cliff, Rowland Phillips and Thomas Pelles, because that they and every of them shall not be contributors, nor charged to the payment of the said sum of one hundred thousand pounds.

12. Provided also that this Act of free pardon shall not extend or in any wise be beneficial to any clerk or other person of the said clergy or spiritualty, being in the said tenth day of March (10 March 1531) in the custody of the said Archbishop, or of any other Ordinary of the said Province, as a person attainted or convicted by the laws of this realm of any murder, felony, or other crime or offence for or concerning deliverance out of the said convict prison, till that he shall have made his purgation according to the laws or customs used in that behalf, or that he be thereof discharged by the King's pardon, or other lawful means.

13. Provided always that this Act shall not extend, nor in any wise be beneficial or available to any spiritual person, spiritual body corporated or politic, or other spiritual person having any dignity, benefice, promotion or other spiritual livelihood within the Province of York, other than to every of them which by his or their particular obligation, to be made in due and perfect form of the law according to the effect of a note or minute under written, do bind him or themself before the last day of May next coming (31 May 1531), in certain reasonable sum of money, not exceeding the sum of two years' value of his or their dignities, benefices, promotions, or other spiritual livelihood, being or lying within the said Province of York, to Sir Brian Tuke, Knight, Treasurer of the King's most honourable chamber, Christopher Hales, the King's general attorney, and Baldwin Malet, the King's solicitor, or to the over livers or over liver of them, or to any other like treasurer, attorney or solicitor, for the time being, or to any two of them to be paid to the King's use, upon certain conditions specified in the said note or minute, the which note or minute hereafter ensueth:

Noverint universi per praesentes me Johannem A. de T. in comitate Middlesex certicum teneri et firmiter obligari Briano Tuke milite, thesaurario camerae Domini Regis, Christophoro Hales, generali attornato eiusdem Domini Regis et Balduino Malet, solicitatori ipsius Domini Regis in — libris legalis monetae Angliae solvendis eisdem Briano, Christophoro et Balduino aut eorum uni executoribus vel assignatis suis ad usum Domini Regis in festo Sancti Bartholomaei apostoli proximo futuro post datum praesentium (24 August 1531) ad quam quidem solutionem etc. In cuius rei testimonium etc. Datum — die — anno regni Domini Henrici octavi Dei gratia Angliae et Franciae Regis, Fidei Defensoris et Domini Hiberniae.

(Let all men know by the presents that I, John, A(rchdeacon) of T(wickenham), in the County of Middlesex, am surely held and firmly obliged by Sir Brian Tuke, Knight, Treasurer of the Chamber of our Lord the King, Christopher Hales, General Attorney of the same Lord the King, and Baldwin Malet, Solicitor of the same Lord the King, to pay in — pounds of legal money of England to the same Sir Brian, Christopher and Baldwin, or to their all and singular executors or deputies, for the use of our Lord the King, on the feast of St Bartholomew the Apostle next following after the date of the presents (24 August 1531), in settlement, etc. In witness of which, Given the — day of the — year of the reign of our Lord Henry VIII, by the grace of God, King of England and France, Defender of the Faith and Lord of Ireland.)

The condition of this obligation is such that where the most reverend father in God, William Archbishop of Canterbury, Metropolitan and Primate of all England, and other prelates and the clergy of the Province of Canterbury, in their synodal convocation begun in the Cathedral Church of Saint Paul of London, in the fifth day of November in the year of our Lord God 1529 (05 November 1529), and lately for certain urgent causes prorogued unto the chapter house set within the monastery of Saint Peter of Westminster, have granted to our said Sovereign Lord the King a subsidy of one hundred thousand pounds of current money within this realm, to be levied and collected of the goods and possessions ecclesiastical of the same Province, and to be paid to our said Sovereign Lord in five years from and after the Annunciation of our Lady Saint Mary last past (25 March 1530) in certain form specified in the grant of the same subsidy. If the before bounden John A., his executors or assigns do pay or cause to be paid to the collector or collectors of such subsidy as hereafter shall be granted to the King's Highness by the bishops and other prelates and the clergy of the Province of York, in the synodal convocation of the same bishops, prelates and clergy to be holden or kept in the same province, as much and as many of all and singular those sums of money which shall be assized, taxed and set for and upon the said John A., now hath in the same province of York as by the same John A., or his executors, shall be due to be paid according to the form and effect of the same grant hereafter to be made; and in case that no such subsidy shall be granted to the King our Sovereign Lord by the said bishops, prelates and clergy of the said Province of York before the feast of Saint Michael the Archangel next coming (29 September 1531), or that a subsidy shall be granted to the King by the same bishops, prelates and clergy before the same feast, which subsidy shall not extend or amount to such like rate and portion for the Province of York in comparison of the said sum of one hundred thousand pounds current money of England, now granted unto the King's Highness by the said clergy of the Province of Canterbury, as the subsidy last granted to his Highness by the prelates and clergy of the Province of York in their convocation begun the twenty-second day of March in the year of Our Lord 1522 (22 March 1522) and afterward prorogued to Westminster, was in comparison to the rate and portion of the subsidy granted to his Highness by the prelates and clergy of the Province of Canterbury, in their convocation begun at Paul's Church in London, the fifth day of November in the year of Our Lord 1529 (05 November 1529); then if the said John A. or his executors do pay or cause to be paid to the treasurer of the King's chamber, for the time being, for all his said spiritual dignities, benefices, livelihood and other spiritual possessions and promotions being or lying in the said Province of York, such and like sums of money after the rates of the yearly values of the same his spiritual dignities, benefices, livelihood, possessions and promotions as the same John A. or any other spiritual person or spiritual body corporate or politic, shall pay, for and in contribution to the payment of the said subsidy of one hundred thousand pounds, granted by the said clergy of the said Province of Canterbury, for other spiritual dignities, benefices, livelihood and other spiritual possessions and promotions, being of like yearly values and being or lying within the same Province of Canterbury, and in the same feasts within the same five years to be paid, in which the said subsidy of one hundred thousand pounds is granted to be paid, then this present obligation shall be void and of none effect, or else it shall stand in full strength and virtue.

04. THE SUPPLICATION OF THE COMMONS, 1532

History

This document was prepared by Thomas Cromwell as early as 1529, and submitted to the House of Commons in 1532. It is perhaps the best example of how the King was able to use lay resentment of the clergy to further his own ends. The supplication could not go unanswered, and the Bishops drafted a lengthy reply to it, though with little success. By 1532 Henry was determined to have his way, and there was little the clergy could do but submit to his will.

Theology

What is most noticeable about the theology of this document is its insistence that the truth of the Catholic faith has been preserved in the Church of England, in spite of the clerical abuses which the Commons are censuring. There is no hint of anything Protestant in the doctrinal sense, and indeed the opening paragraphs suggest that reform of the clergy is needed if Protestant opinions are to be effectively dealt with.

N.B. The paragraph numbering is that of the original document.

To the King our Sovereign Lord:

In most humble wise show unto your excellent Highness and your most prudent wisdom, your faithful, loving and most humble obedient subjects the Commons in this your present Parliament assembled. Where of late, as well through new fantastical and erroneous opinions, grown by occasion of frantic, seditious, and overthwartly framed books compiled, imprinted, published and made into the English tongue, contrary and against the very true Catholic and Christian faith, as also by the extreme and uncharitable behaviour and dealing of divers ordinaries, their commissaries and substitutes, which have heretofore had and yet have the examination in and upon the said errors and heretical opinions; much discord, variance and debate has risen, and more and more daily is like to increase and ensue amongst the universal sort of your said subjects, as well spiritual and temporal, each against the other, in most uncharitable manner, to the great inquietation, vexation, and breach of your peace within this your most Catholic realm:

The special particular griefs whereof, which most principally concern your said Commons and lay subjects, and which are, as they undoubtedly suppose, the very chief fountains, occasions and causes that daily breed, foster and nourish and maintain the said seditious factions and deadly hatred, and most uncharitable part-taking, either part and sort of said subjects spiritual and temporal against the other, hereafter following do ensue:

01. First, where the prelates and spiritual ordinaries of this your most excellent realm of England, and the clergy of the same, have in their convocations heretofore made and caused to be made, and also daily do make, many divers fashions of laws, constitutions and ordinances, without your knowledge or most royal assent, and without the assent and consent of any of your lay subjects; unto the which laws your said lay subjects have not only heretofore and daily been constrained to obey as well in their bodies, goods and possessions, but also be compelled to incur daily into the censures of the same, and be continually put to importable charges and expenses against all equity, right and good conscience. And yet (neither) your said humble subjects nor their predecessors could ever be privy to the said laws; nor any of the said laws have been declared unto them in the English tongue, or otherwise published, by knowledge whereof they might have eschewed the penalties, dangers or censures of the same; which laws so made your said most humble and obedient subjects, under the supportation of your majesty, suppose to be not only to the diminution and derogation of your imperial jurisdiction and prerogative royal, but also to the great prejudice, inquietation and damage of your said subjects.

02. Also now where of late there has been devised by the most reverend father in God, William, Archbishop of Canterbury, that in the courts which he calls his courts of the Arches and Audience shall be but only ten proctors at his deputation, which be sworn to preserve and promote the only jurisdiction of the said courts; by reason whereof, if any of your lay subjects should have any lawful cause against the judges of the said courts, or any doctors or proctors of the same, or any of their friends or adherents, they can nor may in any wise have indifferent counsel; and also all causes depending in any of the said courts may, by the confederacy of the said few proctors, be in such wise tracted and delayed, as your subjects suing in the same shall be put to importable charges, costs and expense. And in case that any matter there being preferred should touch your crown, regal jurisdiction and prerogative royal, yet the same shall not be disclosed by any of the said proctors for fear of loss of their offices. Wherefore your said most obedient subjects, under the protection of your majesty, suppose that your Highness should have the nomination of some convenient number of proctors to be always attendant in the said courts of the Arches and Audience, there to be sworn as well to the preferment of your jurisdiction and prerogative royal as to the expedition of all the causes of your lay subjects repairing and suing to the same.

03. And where also many of your said most humble and obedient subjects, and specially those that be of the poorest sort within this your realm, be daily convented and called before the said spiritual ordinaries, their commissaries and substitutes, *ex officio*; sometimes, at the pleasure of the said ordinaries and substitutes, for malice without any cause; and sometimes – at the only promotion and accusement of their summoners and apparitors, being very light and indiscreet persons, without any lawful cause of accusation or credible frame proved against them, and without any presentment in the visitation – be inquieted, disturbed, vexed, troubled and put to excessive and importable charges for them to bear, and many times be suspended and excommunicate for small light causes upon the only certificate of the proctors of the adversaries made under the feigned seal which every proctor has in his keeping; whereas the party suspended and excommunicated many times never had any warning; and yet when he shall be absolved, if it be out of court, he shall be compelled to pay his own proctor twenty pence, to the proctor which is against him another twenty pence, and twenty pence to the scribe, besides a privy reward that the judge shall have, to the great impoverishing of your said poor lay subjects.

04. Also your said most humble and obedient subjects find themselves grieved with the great and excessive fees taken in the said spiritual courts, and specially in the said courts of the Arches and Audience, where they take for every citation two shillings and sixpence; for every inhibition six shillings and eightpence; for every proxy sixteen pence; for every certificate sixteen pence; for every libel three shillings and fourpence; for every answer to any libel three shillings and fourpence; for every act, if it be but two words, to the registrar, fourpence; for every personal citation or decree three shillings and fourpence; for every sentence or judgement to the judge twenty-six shillings and eightpence; for every *significavit* twelve shillings; for every commission to examine witnesses twelve shillings; which is thought to be importable to be borne by your said subjects, and very necessary to be reformed.

05. And where also the said prelates and ordinaries daily do permit and suffer the parsons, vicars, curates, parish priests and other spiritual persons having cure of souls, within this your realm ministering, to exact and take of your humble and obedient subjects divers sums of money for the sacraments and sacramentals of Holy Church, sometimes denying the same without they be first paid the said sums of money, which sacraments and sacramentals your said most humble and obedient subjects, under the protection of your Highness, do suppose and think ought to be in most reverend, charitable and godly wise freely ministered unto them at all times requisite, without denial or exaction of any manner sums of money to be demanded or asked for the same.

06. And also where, in the spiritual court of the said prelates and ordinaries, be limited and appointed so many judges, scribes, apparitors, summoners, appraisers, and other ministers for the approbation of

testaments, which coveting so much their own private lucres, and satisfaction of the appetites of the said prelates and ordinaries, that when any of your said loving subjects do repair to any of the said courts for the probate of any testaments, they do in such wise make long delays, or excessively take of them so large fees and rewards for the same, as is importable for them to bear, directly against all justice, law, equity and good conscience. Wherefore your said most humble and obedient subjects do therefore, under your gracious correction and supportation, suppose it were very necessary that the said ordinaries, in the deputation of such judges, should be bound to appoint and assign such discreet, gravous and honest persons, having sufficient learning, wit, discretion and understanding, and also being endued with such spiritual promotion, stipend and salary as they, being judges in their said courts, might and may minister, to every person repairing to the same, justice, without taking any manner fee or reward for any manner sentence or judgement to be given before them.

07. And also whereas divers spiritual persons being presented as well by your Highness and by other patrons within this your realm to divers benefices or other spiritual promotions, the said ordinaries and their ministers do not only take of them, for their letters of institution and induction, many great and large sums of money and rewards; but also do pact and covenant with same, taking sure bonds for their indemnity to answer to the said ordinaries, the firstfruits of the said benefices after their institution, so as they, being once presented or promoted as is aforesaid, be by the said ordinaries very uncharitably handled, to their no little hindrance and impoverishment, which your said subjects suppose not only to be against all laws, right and good conscience, but also to be simony, and contrary to the laws of God.

08. And also whereas the said spiritual ordinaries do daily confer and give sundry benefices unto certain young folks, calling them their nephews or kinsfolk, being in their minority and within age, not apt nor able to serve the cure of any such benefice; whereby the said ordinaries do keep and detain the fruits and profits of the same benefices in their own hands, and thereby accumulate to themselves right great and large sums of money and yearly profits, to the most pernicious example of all your said lay subjects; and so the cures and other promotions given unto such infants be only employed to the enriching of the said ordinaries, and the poor silly souls of your people and subjects, which should be taught in the parishes given as aforesaid, for lack of good curates, do perish without doctrine or any good teaching.

09. And also where a great number of holy days which now at this present time, with very small devotion, be solemnized and kept throughout this your realm – upon the which many great, abominable and execrable vices, idle and wanton sports, be used and exercised – which holy days, if it may stand with your gracious pleasure, and specially such as fall in the harvest, might, by your majesty, by the advice of your most honourable council, prelates and ordinaries, be made fewer in number; and those that shall hereafter be

ordained to stand and continue might and may be the more devoutly, religiously, and reverently observed, to the laud of Almighty God, and to the increase of your high honour and fame.

10. And furthermore, where the said spiritual ordinaries, their commissaries and substitutes, sometimes for their own pleasures, sometimes by the sinister procurement of other spiritual persons, use to make out process against divers of your said subjects, and thereby compel them to appear before themselves, to answer at certain day and place to such articles as by them shall be, or office afore themselves, then proposed, and that secretly and not in open places; and forthwith upon their appearance, without cause or any declaration them made or showed, commit or send them to ward, where they remain without bail or mainprize, sometimes for half a year, sometime a whole year and more, before they may in any wise know either the cause of their imprisonment or the name of their accuser; and finally, after their great costs and charges therein, when all is examined and nothing can be proved against them, but they clearly innocent for any fault or crime that can be laid unto them in that part, be set again at large without any recompence or amends in that behalf to be towards them adjudged.

11. And also, if percase upon the said process and appearance any party be, upon the said matter, cause, or examination brought forward and named, either as party or witness, and then upon the proof and trial thereof, not able to prove and verify his said accusation or testimony, against the party so accused, to be true, then the person so causelessly accused is for the most part without any remedy for his charges and wrongful vexation, to be towards him adjudged and recovered.

12. Also upon the examination of the said accusation, if heresy be ordinarily laid unto the charge of the party so accused, then the said ordinaries or their ministers use to put to them such subtle interrogatories, concerning the high mysteries of our faith, as are able quickly to trap a simple, unlearned, or yet a well-witted layman without learning, and bring them by such sinister introduction soon to his own confusion. And forthwith, if there chance any heresy to be, by such subtle policy, by him confessed in words and yet never committed nor thought in deed, then put they, without further favour, the said person either to make his purgation, and so thereby to lose his honesty and credence for ever, or else, as some simple silly soul precisely standing to the clear testimony of his own well-known conscience, rather than to confess his innocent truth, to abide the extremity in that behalf, and so is utterly destroyed. And if it fortune the said party so accused to deny the said accusation, and so put his adversaries to prove the same untruly, forged, and imagined against him, then for the most part, such witnesses as be brought forth for the same, be they but two in number, never so sore defamed, of little truth or credence, adversaries or enemies to the party, yet they shall be allowed and enabled only by discretion of the said ordinaries, their commissaries and substitutes; and there, upon sufficient cause to proceed to judgement, to deliver the party so accused either to the secular hands after abjuration, without remedy, and afore, if he submit himself, to compel him, when best happeneth, to make his purgation and bear a faggot, to his extreme shame and undoing.

In consideration whereof, most gracious Sovereign Lord – and forasmuch as there is at this present time, and by a few years past has been, outrageous violence on the one part, and much default and lack of patient sufferance, charity and good will on the other part – a marvellous disorder of the godly quiet, peace and tranquillity that this your realm heretofore ever hitherto has been in, through your politic wisdom, in most honourable fame and Catholic faith preserved; it may therefore, most benign Sovereign Lord, like your excellent goodness for the tender and universally indifferent zeal, benign love, and favour that your Highness beareth towards both the said parties, the said articles (if they shall be by your most clear and perfect judgement thought any instruments or causes of the said variance and disorder, or those and all other occasions whatsoever accounted by your Highness to make towards the said factions) deeply and weightily, after your accustomed ways and manner, searched, weighed and considered, graciously to provide (all violence on both sides utterly and clearly set apart) some such necessary and behoveful remedies as may effectually reconcile and bring in perpetual unity your said subjects, spiritual and temporal; and for the establishing thereof, to make and ordain, on both sides, such strait laws against the breakers, transgressors and offenders as shall be too heavy, dangerous and weighty for them or any of them to bear, suffer and sustain.

Whereunto your said Commons most humbly, heartily and entirely beseech your grace, as the only head, sovereign lord, protector and defender of both the said parties, in whom and by whom the only sole redress, reformation and remedy herein absolutely rests and remains. By occasion whereof all your said Commons in their conscience surely account that, beside the marvellous fervent love that your Highness shall thereby and (*sic*) engender in their hearts towards your grace, you shall do the most princely feat, and show the most honourable and charitable precedent and mirror that ever did sovereign lord upon his subjects; and therewithal merit and deserve of our merciful Lord eternal bliss, whose goodness grant your grace in most godly, princely and honourable estate long to reign, prosper and continue as the sovereign lord over all your said most humble and obedient subjects.

05. THE REPLY OF THE ORDINARIES, 1532

History

The bishops could not ignore the challenge presented by the supplication from the House of Commons, particularly as it came hard on the heels of a number of other humiliations. They mounted a spirited defence of their position, pointing out that some laymen had used brute force against the clergy, who by and large were innocent of the charges laid against them. Unfortunately, in spite of the large measure of truth which their reply contained, the bishops lacked the sympathy of Parliament and the nation. In the ensuing contest they found that they had little choice but to submit to the King and accept whatever fate he might have in store for them.

Theology

As one might expect, the theology which underlies this document is one which refuses to allow that the state has any business interfering in Church affairs. The Church is a spiritual corporation, answerable to God and not to the King. This view was not to be acceptable to the Protestant Establishment in England, though it was to become a major plank in the platform of later Dissenters, both Catholic and Puritan.

N.B. The paragraph numbers have been supplied for ease of reference.

01. After our most humble wise, with our most bounden duty of honour and reverence to your excellent majesty, endued by God with incomparable wisdom and goodness. Please it the same to understand that we, your orators and daily bounden bedesmen the ordinaries, have read and perused a certain supplication which the Commons of your grace's most honourable Parliament now assembled have offered up unto your Highness, and by your grace's commandment delivered to us, to make answer thereto. And as the time has served and permitted, we have, according to your Highness's commandment, made thereunto this answer following, beseeching your grace's indifferent benignity graciously to hear the same. First, where in the said supplication it is induced, as for a preface, that much discord, variance and debate has arisen amongst your grace's subjects, spiritual and temporal, and more and more daily is like to increase and ensue, to the great unquietness and breach of your peace within your grace's most Catholic realm, as well through new fantastical and erroneous opinions grown by occasion of seditions and overthwart framed books compiled, imprinted, and made in English tongue in the parts beyond the sea, contrary and against the very true Catholic and Christian faith, as also by the uncharitable behaviour and dealing of divers ordinaries, their commissaries and substitutes, in the common and often vexation of your grace's said subjects in the spiritual courts, and also by other evil examples and misuses of spiritual persons.

02. To this we, your said orators and daily bounden bedesmen the ordinaries, answer, assuring your majesty that in our hearts and conscience there is no such discord, debate, variance or breach of peace on our part against our brethren in God and ghostly children, your subjects, as is induced in this preface; but our daily prayer is and shall be that all unity, concord and peace may increase among your grace's true and faithful subjects, our said ghostly children, whom, God be our witness, we love, have loved, and shall love ever with hearty affection; never intending any hurt or harm towards any of them in soul or body; and never enterprised anything against them of trouble, vexation, or displeasure; but only have, as we dare surely affirm, with all charity, exercised the spiritual jurisdiction of the Church, as we are bound of duty, upon certain evil-disposed persons infected and utterly corrupt with the pestilent poison of heresy; and to have had peace with such, had been against the Gospel of our Saviour Christ, wherein he saith: *Non veni mittere pacem sed gladium.* (I have not come to put peace, but a sword).[1] Wherefore, forasmuch as we perceive and know right well that there be as well-disposed and as well-conscienced men of your grace's Commons, in no small number assembled, as ever we know at any time in Parliament; and with that consider how on our part there is given no such occasion why the whole number of the spiritualty and clergy should be thus noted unto your Highness, omitting and leaving the conjectures of men, which though they be probable and in many's knowledge evident, yet they may and do sometime err; we humbling our hearts to God and remitting the judgement of this our inquietation to him, and trusting as his Scripture teacheth us, that if we love him above all, *omnia co-operabuntur in bonum* (everything will work together for good),[2] we shall endeavour ourselves to declare unto your Highness the innocency of us your poor orators, as far as the truth of God's Word and learning of the Church with the sincerity of our acts and deeds will maintain the same, with this determination and purpose not to colour, by wordy reasons of man's wit, any our doings or proceedings, but to refer the truth to be defended by God and your Highness, in whose virtue, learning and Christian religion we can never doubt.

03. And where, after the general preface of the said supplication, your grace's Commons descend to special particular griefs, and first report that the clergy of this your realm, being your Highness's subjects, in their convocations by them holden within this your realm, have made and daily make divers factions of laws concerning temporal things, and some of them

be repugnant to the laws and statutes of your realm, not having nor requiring your most royal assent to the same laws so by them made, neither any assent or knowledge of your lay subjects is had to the same, neither to them published and known in their mother tongue, albeit divers and sundry of the said laws extend, in certain causes, to your excellent person, your liberty and prerogative royal, and to the interdiction of your lands and possessions, and so likewise to the goods and possessions of your lay subjects, declaring the infringers of them, so by them made, not only to incur into the terrible censures of excommunication, but also the detestable crime and sin of heresy, by the which divers of your most humble and obedient lay subjects be brought into this ambiguity, whether they may do and execute your laws according to your jurisdiction royal of this realm, for dread of the same censures and pains comprised in the said laws, so by them made in their convocations, to the great trouble and inquietation of your said humble and obedient lay subjects, to the impeachment of your jurisdiction and prerogative royal. To this article we say that forasmuch as we repute and take our authority of making of laws to be grounded upon the Scripture of God and the determination of Holy Church, which must also be a rule and squire to try the justice and righteousness of all laws, as well spiritual as temporal, we verily trust that in such laws as have been made by us or by our predecessors, the same being sincerely interpreted, and after the good meaning of the makers, there shall be found nothing contained in them but such as may be well justified by the said rule and squire. And if it shall otherwise appear, as it is our duty, whereunto we shall always most diligently apply ourselves, to reform our ordinances to God's commission and to conform our statutes and laws, and those of our predecessors, to the determination of Scripture and Holy Church, so we hope in God, and shall daily pray for the same, that your Highness will, if there appear cause why, with the assent of your people, temper your grace's laws accordingly; whereby shall ensue a most sure and perfect conjunction and agreement, as God being *lapis angularis* (the cornerstone) to agree and conjoin the same.

04. And as concerning the requiring of your Highness's royal assent to the authorizing of such laws as have been by our predecessors, or shall be made by us, in such points and articles as we have by good authority to rule and order by provisions and laws; we, knowing your Highness's wisdom, virtue and learning, nothing doubt but that the same perceiveth how the granting thereunto dependeth not upon our will and liberty, and that we, your most humble subjects, may not submit the execution of our charges and duty, certainly prescribed by God, to your Highness's assent; although, of very deed, the same is most worthy for your most princely and excellent virtues, not only to give your royal assent, but also to devise and command what we should, for good order and manners, by statutes and laws, provide in the Church. Nevertheless, considering we may not so, nor in such sort, restrain the doing of our office in the feeding and ruling of Christ's people,

your grace's subjects, we – most humbly desiring your grace, as the same has done heretofore, so from henceforth to show your grace's mind and opinion unto us, what your Highness's wisdom shall think convenient, which we shall most gladly hear and follow, if it shall please God to inspire us so to do – with all submission and humility, beseech the same, following the steps of your most noble progenitors, and conformably to your own acts, to maintain and defend such laws and ordinances as we, according to our calling and by the authority of God shall, for his honour, make to the edification of virtue and the maintaining of Christ's faith, whereof your Highness is defender in name, and has been hitherto in deed, a special protector.

05. Furthermore, in the same first article, where your lay subjects say that sundry of the said laws extend, in certain causes, to your excellent person, your liberty and prerogative royal, and to the interdiction of your lands and possessions: To this your said orators say, in answer to the former article as submitted, that having the trying and examining of the laws made in the Church, by us or our predecessors, to the just and straight rule of God's law – which giveth measure of power, prerogative and authority to all emperors, kings, princes and potentates and all other – we have such estimation and have conceived such opinion of your Highness's goodness and virtue, that whatsoever any persons, not so well learned as your grace is, will pretend unto the same, whereby we, your most humble subjects, might be brought into your grace's displeasure and indignation, submitting that we should by usurpation and presumption extend our laws to your most noble person, prerogative and realm, yet the same your Highness being so highly learned will, of your own most bounteous goodness, facilely discharge and deliver us from that contention – the matter whereof not well understood is hateful – when it shall appear that no such laws be made by us, nor, as far as we perceive and remember, by our predecessors neither, nor finally no laws, as we verily trust, but such as be good, wholesome and convenient, and maintainable by the Word of God and the determination of Christ's Catholic Church.

06. Furthermore, there be joined, with mention of your grace's person, other griefs that likewise some of the said laws extend to the goods and possessions of your said lay subjects, declaring the transgressors not only to fall into the terrible censures of excommunication, but also to the detestable crime of heresy. To this we, your grace's said orators, answer that we remember no such; and yet if there be any such, it is but according to the common law of the Church, and also to your grace's laws, which determine and decree that every person, spiritual or temporal, condemned of heresy shall forfeit his moveables or immoveables to your Highness, or to the lord spiritual or temporal that by law hath right to them. Other statutes we remember none that toucheth the loss of their lands or goods. If there be, good it were that they were brought forth to be weighed and pondered accordingly as above.

07. Item, where they say that for fear of the said pains and censures comprised in the said laws, divers of your lay subjects be brought into this ambiguity, whether they may do and execute your grace's laws, according to your jurisdiction royal of this your realm: To this your said orators answer and say, that they be sorry that they, being your most humble subjects in heart, should be noted to be let or impediment to the execution of your grace's laws. For we your said orators are, have been, and ever intend to be of that humble, reverent mind toward your grace's Highness, and of that charitable affection toward our ghostly children, your laypeople and subjects, that in our conscience, we neither yet have given to your worshipful Commons any just cause so to note us, neither during our lives intend to make any impeachment otherwise than by our most humble suit unto your Highness, and giving advice and counsel or doctrine to your lay subjects, to consider the right and justice of such matters as, in the making or executing, might appear to be to the great prejudice of the liberties of Christ's Church; but rather to endure and sustain patiently, as we do, the same. And if we be otherwise a let than thus, or as ministers of God's Word in the feeding and ruling of your grace's people in spiritual food, doctrine and correction, according to the determination of Christ's Catholic Church, your Highness shall find no difficulty of our reformation.

08. Item, as touching the second principal article of the said supplication, where they say that divers and many your grace's obedient subjects, and especially they that be of the poorest sort, be daily called before us, the special ordinaries and commissaries and substitutes *ex officio* – sometime at the pleasure of us, the said ordinaries or commissaries and substitutes, for displeasure, without any probable cause, and sometime at the only promotion of our summoners, being light and indiscreet persons, without any credible fame first proved against them, and without any presentment in the visitation or lawful accusation: To this we, your grace's said orators, do answer and say, and first we most humbly desire your Highness by your high wisdom and learning to consider, that albeit, in the ordering of Christ's people, your grace's subjects, God, of his special goodness assisteth His Church and inspireth, by the Holy Ghost as we verily trust, such wholesome rules and laws as tend to the wealth of his elect folk, the increase and augmentation of his faith, honour and glory – yet upon consideration to man unknown, his infinite wisdom leaveth and permitteth men to walk in their infirmity and frailty. So that we cannot, nor will arrogantly presume of ourselves, as though being in name spiritual men, we were also all, in all our acts and doings, clean and void from all temporal affections and carnality of this world, in that the laws of the Church made for spiritual and ghostly purpose be not sometimes applied to worldly intent; which we ought and do lament (as becometh us) very sore. Nevertheless, inasmuch as the evil acts and deeds of men be the more defaults of those particular men, and not of the whole order of the clergy, nor of the laws wholesomely by them made, our request and petition shall be, with all humility and reverence, that all laws well made be not therefore called evil, because at all times and by all men they be not well executed, and that in such defaults as shall appear, such distribution may be used as St Paul speaketh of: *ut unusquisque onus suum portet* (that each one bear his own burden),[3] and remedy to exhibit to reform the offenders; unto the which your Highness shall perceive as great towardness in your said orators as can be required upon declaration of the particulars and special articles in that behalf. And other answer than this cannot be made in the name of your whole clergy, considering that in many of the particularities which be alleged as defaults, if the whole clergy should confess or deny them, they be not all true or all false generally in the whole; for though *in multis offendimus omnes* (in many things we all offend),[4] as St James saith, yet not *in omnibus offendimus omnes* (in everything we all offend); and the whole number can neither justify nor condemn particular acts to them unknown but thus. He that calleth a man *ex officio* for correction of sin doeth well. He that calleth men for pleasure and vexation doeth evil. Summoners should be honest men. If they offend in their office, they should be punished. To prove first the same, before men be called, it is not necessary. He that is called according to the laws *ex officio* or otherwise cannot complain. He that is otherwise ordered should have, by reason, convenient recompense and so forth; that that is well to be allowed, and misdemeanour, when it appeareth, reproved.

09. Item, where they say in the same article that upon their appearance *ex officio* at the only pleasure of us the said ordinaries or commissaries and their substitutes, they be committed to prison without bail or mainprize, and there they lie, some half a year or more before they come to their deliverance: To this your said orators answer, we use no person before conviction but for sure custody, only of such as be suspected of heresy, in which crime, thanked be God, there has fallen no such notable personage in our time, or of such qualities as hath given occasion of any sinister suspicion to be conceived of malice or hatred to his person other than the heinousness of that crime deserveth. Truth it is that certain apostates, friars, monks, lewd priests, bankrupt merchants, vagabonds and lewd idle fellows of corrupt intent, have embraced the abominable and erroneous opinions lately sprung up in Germany, and by them some seduced in simplicity and ignorance. Against these, if justice has been exercised according to the laws of the Church, and conformably to the laws of this realm, we be without blame. If we have been too slack and remiss, we shall gladly do our duty from henceforth. If any man hath been under pretence of this crime particularly offended, it were pity to suffer any man wronged; and thus it ought to be, and otherwise we cannot answer, no man's special case being declared in the said petition.

10. Item, where they say further that they so appearing *ex officio* be constrained to answer to many subtle questions and interrogatories, by the which a simple, unlearned, or else a well-witted layman without learning, sometime is, and commonly may be, trapped and induced to the peril of open penance, to their shame, or else to redeem the same penance for money, as is commonly used: To this your said orators answer, we should not use subtlety, for we should do all things plainly and openly; and if we do otherwise, we do amiss. We ought not to ask questions, but after the capacities of the man. Christ has defended his true doctrine and faith in his Catholic Church from all subtlety, and so preserved good men in the same, as they have not (blessed be God) been vexed, inquieted or troubled in Christ's Church therefor, and evil men fall in danger by their own subtlety; for among all other matters protested before God, we neither have known, read or heard of any one man damaged, hurt or prejudiced by spiritual jurisdiction in this behalf, neither in this realm nor any other, but only by his own deserts. Such is the goodness of God in maintaining the cause of his Catholic faith.

11. Item, where they say that they be compelled to do open penance, or else to redeem the same for money: To this your said orators answer, as for penance, it consisteth in the arbiter of a judge who ought, without affection, enjoin such penance as might profit for correction of the fault. Wherefore we disallow that judge's doing, who taketh money for penance, for lucre or advantage, not regarding the reformation of sin as he ought to do; but when open penance may sometime work in certain persons more hurt than good, it is commendable and allowable in that case to punish by the purse and preserve the fame of the party; foreseeing alway the money be converted *in usus pios et eleemosynam* (to godly uses and works of mercy); and thus we think of the thing, and that the offenders herein should be punished.

12. Item, where they complain that two witnesses be admitted, be they never so defamed, of little truth and credence, adversaries or enemies to the parties, yet in many causes they may be allowed by the discretions of the said ordinaries, their commissaries or substitutes, to put the party accused or defamed, of office, to open penance, and then to redemption for money, so that every of your subjects, upon the only will and pleasure of the ordinaries, their commissaries and substitutes, without any accuser, proved fame or presentment, is or may be infamed, vexed and troubled, to the peril of their lives, their shames, costs and expenses: To this your said orators answer, the Gospel of Christ teacheth us to believe two witnesses; and as the cause is, so the judge must esteem the qualities of the witness, and in heresy no exception is necessary to be considered if their tale be likely; which hath been highly provided, lest heretics without jeopardy might else plant their heresies in lewd and light persons, and taking exception to their witness, take boldness to continue their folly. This is the universal law of Christendom and hath universally done good. Of any injury done to any man thereby, we know not.

13. Item, where they say that it is not intended by them to take away from us our authority to correct and punish sin, and especially the detestable crime of heresy: To this your said orators answer, in the persecution of heretics we regard our duty and office whereunto we be called, and if God would discharge us thereof, or cease that plague universal – as by your mighty hand, and directing the hearts of princes, and specially of your Highness (laud and thanks be unto him), his goodness doth commence and begin to do – we should and shall have great cause to rejoice, as being our authority therein costly, dangerous, full of trouble and business, without any fruit, pleasure or commodity worldly, but a continual conflict and vexation, with pertinacity, wilfulness, folly and ignorance, whereupon followeth their bodily and ghostly destruction, to our great sorrow and lamentation.

14. Item, where they desire that by the assent of your Highness, if the laws heretofore made be not sufficient for the repressing of heresy, that more dreadful and terrible be made. To this your said orators answer, this is undoubtedly a more charitable request than (as we trust) necessary, considering that by the aid of your Highness, the pains of your grace's statutes already made, freely executed, your realm may be in short time clean purged from the few small dregs that do remain, if any do remain.

15. Item, whereas they desire some reasonable declaration may be known to your people how they may (if they will) avoid the peril of heresy: To this your said orators and bedesmen say and answer, that there can be no better declaration known than is already by our Saviour Christ, the apostles and the determination of the Church, which if they keep they shall not fail clearly to eschew heresy.

16. Item, where they desire that some charitable fashion may be devised by your most excellent wisdom for the calling of any of your subjects before them, that it shall not stand in the only will and pleasure of the ordinaries, at their own imagination, without lawful accusation, proved fame by honest witness, presentment in the visitation, or other lawful presentment according to your laws, or by such other charitable means as shall be thought by your most excellent wisdom measurable in that behalf for the quietness of your subjects: To this your said orators answer, that a better provision cannot be devised than is already devised by the clergy, in our opinion; and if any default appear in the execution, it shall be amended upon the declaration of the particulars and the same proved.

17. Item, where they say that your grace's subjects be originally accited to appear out of the diocese that they dwell in, and many times be suspended and excommunicated for small and light causes upon the only certificate devised by the proctors, etc., and that also your said most humble and obedient subjects find themselves grieved with the great and excessive fees taken in the spiritual courts, etc.: To this article – for because it concerneth most specially the spiritual courts of me, the Archbishop of Canterbury – please it your grace to understand that about twelve months past I reformed certain things objected here; and now, within these ten weeks, I reformed many other things in my said courts, as it is I suppose not unknown unto your grace's Commons; and some of the fees of the officers in my courts I have brought down to halves, some to the third part and some wholly taken away and extincted; and yet it is objected as though I had taken no manner of reformation therein. Nevertheless I will not cease yet; but in such things as I shall see your grace's Commons most offended, I will set up some redress accordingly, so as I trust your grace's worshipful Commons will be contented in that behalf. And I, your grace's most humble chaplain, the said Archbishop of Canterbury, entirely beseech your grace to consider what high services the doctors of civil law, which have been brought up and had their experience and practice in my said poor courts, have done to your grace and your grace's most noble progenitors concerning treaties, truces, confederations and leagues, drawn, devised and concluded with outward princes; and how that without such learned men in civil law, your most noble grace and your progenitors could not have been so honourably and so conveniently served in that behalf, as at all times you and they have been, which thing percase, when such learned men in civil law shall fail within this your realm, will appear more evident than it doth now. The decay whereof grieveth me to foresee and remember, not so greatly for any cause concerning specially the pleasure or profit of myself, being a man spent, and at the point to depart this world, and having no penny of any advantage by my said courts, but principally for the good love and zeal that I bear to the honour of your most noble grace and of this your realm, that it may continue in as high estimation in outward realms, by the honourable service of learned men in civil law, being ambassadors, after my death, as it hath at all times hitherto; of which learned men having good experience, your grace shall not fail to have good choice, when time shall require, if the doctors of my court, the Arches, may be entertained there, as they have been in times past, being there for a season practising and preparing themselves to be able to do your grace acceptable service when your grace shall call them and command them. And albeit there is, by the assent of the Lords temporal and the Commons of your Parliament, an Act passed thereupon already, the matter depending afore your majesty by way of supplication offered up unto your Highness by your said Commons; yet forasmuch as we, your grace's most humble chaplains, the archbishops of Canterbury and York, be straitly bounden by oath to be intercessors for the right of our churches, and forasmuch as the spiritual prelates of the clergy, being of your grace's Parliament, consented not to the said Act, for divers great causes moving their consciences, we, your grace's said chaplains, in our most humble manner show unto your Highness that it appertaineth to the archbishops of Canterbury and York, the right of their churches for the space of four hundred years or thereabouts, to have spiritual jurisdiction over all them your grace's subjects dwelling within their provinces, and to have authority to call them before them by citation, not only in spiritual causes devolved to them by way of appeal, but also by way of querimony and complaint; which right and privilege pertaineth not only to the persons of the said archbishops, but also to the dignities and pre-eminences of their churches. Insomuch as when the archbishop of either of the sees dieth, the said privileges do not only remain to his successor (by which he is named *Legatus natus*), but also, in the mean time of vacation, the same privilege resteth in the churches of Canterbury and York, and is executed by the prior, dean and chapters of the said churches; and so the said Act is directly against the liberty and privileges of the churches of Canterbury and York, lawfully prescribed by so long time as is aforesaid; and what dangers be to them which study and labour to move and induce any persons to break or take away the liberties and privileges of the Church, whoso will read the general Councils of Christendom and holy canons of the Fathers of the Catholic Church ordained in that behalf, shall soon perceive, as well as though they were here expressed. And further, we think verily that our churches to whom the said privileges were granted, can give no cause why the Pope himself (whose predecessors granted that privilege) or any other (the honour of your grace ever except) may justly take away the same privilege, so lawfully prescribed, from our churches, though we had greatly offended, abusing the said privileges; but where in our persons we trust we have given no cause why to lose that privilege, we most entirely and most humbly beseech your grace that, of your superabundant goodness and absolute power, it may please the same to set such an order and direction in this behalf as we may enjoy the privileges of our churches, lawfully prescribed and admitted so long as before, by the consent of your most noble grace, your progenitors, the temporal lords and spiritual prelates, and all the Commons, both spiritual and temporal, of this your grace's realm.

18. Item, where they say that the executors be put to travel to far places out of the shire they dwell in: To this we, your grace's said orators, answer that there be none so far called, unless it be by my lord of Canterbury by virtue of his prerogative, approved by a statute lately by them (as much as in them is) passed. And as touching inferior ordinaries, having ample and large jurisdictions and dioceses, there be in every shire for the most part appointed and remaining, certain commissaries, officials or substitutes for the expedition of testaments and other causes, except it be so that the parties themselves will come further for the same cause, or that the bishop or his officer does sometime upon consideration – for that the testament containeth many and great legacies or such other – does call the executors before them where they be; which they may do, by the common rule of the laws of the Church, within any part of their dioceses.

19. Item, where they complain that there is exacted and demanded in divers parishes of this your realm, other manner of tithes than hath been accustomed to be paid this hundred years past, and in some parts of this your realm there is exacted double tithes, that is to say, threepence or twopence half-penny, for one acre, over and beside the tithe for the increase of the cattle that pastureth the same: To this we, your grace's said orators, answer that tithes being due by God's law, be so duly paid (thanked be God) by all good men, as there needeth not any exaction or demand in the most parts of this your grace's realm. As for double tithes, they cannot be maintained due for one

increase; whether it be in any place unduly exacted or no, in fact we know not. This we know in learning, that a hundred years, not seven hundred, of non-payment, may not debar the right of God's law. The manner of payment and person unto whom to pay may be, in time, altered, but the duty cannot by any means be taken away.

20. Item, where they say that any mortuary is due, sometime curates, before they will demand it, will bring citation for it, and then will not receive the mortuaries till he may have such costs as he says he has laid out for the suit of the same, where indeed, if he would charitably first have demanded it, he needed not to have sued for the same, for it should have been paid with good will: To this we, your said orators, answer that these curates thus offending, if they were known, ought to be punished; but who thus doeth, we know not.

21. Item, where they say that if any spiritual person has obtained the possession of any profit for the time of thirty or forty years, albeit such profit began sometime by sufferment, sometime by devotion, yet it is said that the said prescription maketh a good title in the law against any layperson, which things be used to the importable charges of your subjects: To this we, your said orators, answer that true it is that the time of thirty or forty years maketh a lawful prescription by the law used and approved throughout all Christendom; but whether, by the reason of the same, any importable charges be put upon your subjects we know not, but surely trust the contrary; otherwise we cannot determinately answer, except the specialty were disclosed.

22. Item, where they say that divers spiritual persons – being presented, as well by your Highness as by other patrons within this your realm, to divers benefices and other spiritual promotions – we the said ordinaries and our ministers do not only take of them, for their letters of institutions and inductions, many great and large sums of money and reward, etc.: To this we, your said orators, answer that this is a particular abuse, and that he that taketh rewards doeth not well; and if any penny be exacted above the accustomed rate usually received, and after a convenient proportion, it is not well done; but in taking the accustomed fees for the sealing, writing and registering of the letters, which is very moderate, we cannot think it reputed as any offence; neither have not heard any priests, by our days, complain of any excess therein.

23. Item, where they say in the same article that such as be presented to benefices as aforesaid, be long delayed, without reasonable cause, to the intent that we, the ordinaries, may have the profit of the benefice during the vacation, unless they will pact and convent with us by temporal bonds, after such fashion and condition as we will, whereof some bonds contain that we the ordinaries should have part of the profit of the said benefices after their institution so that they, being once presented or promoted as is aforesaid, be by us the said ordinaries, sometime uncharitably handled, not only to the hurt of the lay patrons but also to the hindrance and impoverishment of their clerks by them presented, which your said subjects suppose not only

to be against right and good conscience, but also seemeth to be simony and contrary to the laws of God: To this we, your grace's humble orators, do say that a delay without reasonable cause, and for a lucrative intent, is detestable in spiritual men, and the doers cannot eschew punishment, the same being proved; but otherwise a delay is sometimes expedient to examine the clerk, and sometimes necessary where the title is in variance. All other bargains and covenants, being contrary to the law, ought to be punished, as the quality is of the offence, more or less, as simony or inordinate covetousness, with condign pains accordingly; but in facts particular and special defaults the whole clergy cannot give no more special answer than this.

24. Item, where they say that we give benefices to our nephews and kinsfolk, being in young age or infants, whereby the cure is not substantially looked unto, nor the parishoners taught as they should be: To this we, your humble orators, say that that thing which is not lawful in others is in spiritual men more detestable. Benefices should be disposed not *secundum carnem et sanguinem sed secundum merita* (according to flesh and blood but according to merit). And where this is a default it is not authorized by the clergy as good, but reproved; wherefore in this the clergy is not to be blamed, but the default (as it may appear) laid to particular men, and not to be answered unto otherwise by the whole clergy.

25. Item, where they say that we, your said orators, take the profit of such benefices for the time of minority of our said kinsfolk: To this your said orators answer that if it be done to our own use and profit it is not well, but to be reformed in such as do use the same; otherwise, if it be bestowed to the bringing up and use of the same parties, or applied to the maintenance of the Church and God's service, or distributed among poor people of the parish or elsewhere, we do not see but that it may be allowed.

26. Item, where they say that they think a great number of holy days which now at this present time, with very small devotion, be solemnized and kept throughout this your realm, upon the which many great, abominable and execrable vices, idle and wanton sports be exercised and used, which holy days (if it might stand with your grace's pleasure), and especially such as fall in the harvest, might by your majesty, by the advice of your most honourable council, prelates and ordinaries, be made fewer in number, and these that shall hereafter be ordained may be the more devoutly, religiously and reverently observed in the law of Almighty God and to the increase of your Highness's honour and fame: To this we, your said orators and bedesmen, answer that we be right heavy in our hearts to hear that any such abominable or execrable vice should be used at any time, and especially on the holy day; whereunto we intend hereafter to have a special regard for the reformation of the same with all diligence. Moreover we, your said bedesmen, say that we think (your grace's Highness not offended) it is neither reasonable nor convenient that a thing that is instituted by our holy fathers and predecessors, to the honour of God and his blessed saints, should be taken away for the abuse of the same, seeing that there is nothing so good but it may be abused, as the blessed sacrament of the altar and all other holy sacraments; which no good Christian man will think that, for such abuse, they should be taken away, but rather the abuse to be amended and reformed. And as touching the holy days in harvest, there be in August but St Lawrence (10 August), the Assumption of our Blessed Lady (15 August), Saint Bartholomew (24 August) and in September the Nativity of our Lady (08 September), the Exaltation of the Cross (14 September) and Saint Matthew the Apostle (21 September), before which days harvest is commonly ended. And to take away any of these, we suppose, no man will be contented, seeing that they be of so great antiquity and incorporated in the law, and of them that be so high in the favour of God, by whose intercession and means we may better obtain his favour towards us in his benefits, which is specially to be regarded in the harvest time.

27. Item, where they say that divers and many spiritual persons, not contented with the convenient livings and promotions of the Church, daily intromit and exercise themselves in secular offices and rooms, as stewards, receivers, auditors, bailiffs and other temporal offices, withdrawing themselves from the good contemplative life that they have professed into the service of God, not only to the damage but also to the perilous example of your loving and obedient subjects: To this we, your said bedesmen and orators, answer that beneficed men may lawfully be stewards and receivers to their own bishops, as it evidently appeareth in the laws of the Church; and we, by the said laws, ought to have no other. And as for priests to be auditors and bailiffs, we know none such.

28. And where finally, they, in conclusion of their supplication, do repeat and say that forasmuch as there is at this present time, and by a few years past hath been, much misdemeanour and violence upon the one part, and much default and lack of patience, suffrance, charity and good will on the other part, and a marvellous discord of the quiet and godly peace and tranquillity, that this your realm hath heretofore been in, ever hitherto, through your politic wisdom, in most honourable fame and Catholic faith, inviolably preserved: To the first part thereof, as touching such discord as is reported, and also the misdemeanour which is imputed to us and our doings, we trust we have sufficiently answered to the same as above, humbly beseeching your grace, of your most excellent goodness, so to esteem and weigh the premises, as well our such answer as the contents of their supplication, as shall be thought good and expedient by your Highness's wisdom. Furthermore, we ascertain your grace as touching the violence which they seem to lay to our charges, albeit divers of the clergy of this your realm have sundry times been rigorously handled, and with much violence entreated by certain ill-disposed and seditious persons of the lay fee, so injured in their own persons, thrown down in the kennel in the open street at midday, even here, within your city and elsewhere, to the great reproach, rebuke and disquietness of the clergy and ministers of God's Church within this your realm, the great danger of souls of the said misdoers, and perilous example of your said subjects. Yet we think verily, and do affirm the same, that no violence hath been so used on our behalf towards your said lay subjects in any case; unless they do esteem this to be violence that we do commonly use, as well for the health of their souls as for the discharge of our duties, in taking, examining and punishing of heretics according to the law; wherein we doubt not but that your grace and divers of your grace's subjects do right well perceive and understand what charitable demeanour and entreaty we have used with such as have been before us for the same cause of heresy, and what means we have devised and studied for favour and safeguard specially of their souls; and that so charitably (as God be our judge) and without all violence as we could possibly devise. In execution whereof, and also of other laws of the Church for repression of sin and reformation of mislivers, it hath been to our great comfort that your grace and most excellent Highness hath herein, of your benign goodness, assisted and aided us, to the said ordinaries and ministers of God's Church, in this behalf for the great zeal and entire love which your grace beareth to God, his Church, and his ministers; specially in the defence of his faith, whereof your grace only and most worthily amongst all Christian princes beareth the title and name.

29. And as to their final petition and conclusion we, your grace's said most humble bedesmen, in our most lowly wise beseech your grace's majesty – in case there be any such marvellous discord and grudge amongst your subjects as is reported in the said supplication – all the premises considered and tendered by your great politic wisdom, to repress the misdoers and such as be the occasion of the said marvellous discord, and to reconcile and bring to perpetual unity your said subjects. For in this behalf we, your grace's said orators and humble bedesmen, protest in our consciences that we find, in our behalf, no such grudge nor displeasure towards your lay subjects, our ghostly children, as above. We therefore, your most humble bedesmen and orators, beseech your grace's Highness – upon the tender zeal and entire love which your grace doth bear to Christ's faith and to the laws of his Church, specially in this your grace's own realm – of your accustomed and incomparable goodness unto us your said bedesmen, to continue our chief protector, defender and aider in and for the execution of our office and duty, specially touching repression of heresy, reformation of sin, and due behaviour and order in the premises of all your grace's subjects, spiritual and temporal, which (no doubt thereof) shall be much to the pleasure of God, great comfort to many's souls, quietness and unity of all your whole realm, and as we think verily, most principally to the great comfort of your grace's majesty, which we beseech lowly upon our knees, so entirely as we can, to be the author of unity, charity and concord as above, for whose preservation we do and shall continually pray to Almighty God long to reign and prosper in most honourable estate to his pleasure.

1 Mt 10:34   2 Ro 8:28   3 Ga 6:5   4 Ja 3:2

06. THE SUBMISSION OF THE CLERGY, 1532

History

The battle of wits between the clergy and the King was quickly over. On 15 May 1532, the clergy surrendered in the following terms. Two years later this submission was given statutory confirmation.

We your most humble subjects, daily orators and bedesmen of your clergy in England, having our special trust and confidence in your most excellent wisdom, your princely goodness and fervent zeal to the promotion of God's honour and Christian religion, and also in your learning, far exceeding, in our judgement, the learning of all other kings and princes that we have read of, and doubting nothing but that the same shall still continue and daily increase in your majesty:

First, do offer and promise, *in verbo sacerdotii* (on the word of the priesthood), here unto your Highness, submitting ourselves most humbly to the same, that we will never from henceforth enact, put in ure, promulge, or execute any new canons or constitutions provincial, or any other new ordinance, provincial or synodal, in our Convocation or Synod in time coming, which Convocation is, always has been, and must be assembled only by your Highness's commandment or writ, unless your Highness by your royal assent shall license us to assemble our Convocation and to make, promulge and execute such constitutions and ordinances as shall be made in the same; and thereto give your royal assent and authority.

Secondly, that whereas divers of the constitutions, ordinances and canons provincial or synodal, which have been heretofore enacted, be thought to be not only much prejudicial to your prerogative royal, but also overmuch onerous to your Highness's subjects, your clergy aforesaid is contented, if it may stand so with your Highness's pleasure, that it be committed to the examination and judgement of your grace, and of thirty-two persons, whereof sixteen to be of the upper and nether house of the temporalty, and other sixteen of the clergy, all to be chosen and appointed by your most noble grace. So that finally, whichsoever of the said constitutions, ordinances or canons, provincial or synodal, shall be thought and determined by your grace and by the most part of the said thirty-two persons not to stand with God's laws and the laws of your realm, the same to be abrogated and taken away by your grace and the clergy; and such of them as shall be seen by your grace, and by the most part of the said thirty-two persons, to stand with God's laws and the laws of your realm, to stand in full strength and power, your grace's most royal assent and authority once impetrate and fully given to the same.

07. ACT FOR THE CONDITIONAL RESTRAINT OF ANNATES, 1532 (23 Henry VIII, c. 20)

History

As a last attempt to get his way with the Pope, Henry decreed in 1532 that annates would temporarily be withheld. These were the so-called "first-fruits", or first year's revenues from a bishopric or archbishopric, which the new incumbent of a see paid to Rome. The sums involved were considerable, though the Act characteristically exaggerates their importance. Nevertheless, there is some evidence that the Pope was concerned by the move, because he was quick to despatch the bulls necessary for the consecration of Thomas Cranmer as Archbishop of Canterbury.

The Act was confirmed by letters patent dated 09 July 1533, and made obsolete in the following year, when all payments to Rome were stopped.

N.B. The paragraph numbering is that of the original statute.

01. Forasmuch as it is well perceived, by long-approved experience, that great and inestimable sums of money have been daily conveyed out of this realm, to the impoverishment of the same; and specially such sums of money as the Pope's Holiness, his predecessors and the court of Rome by long time have heretofore taken of all and singular those spiritual persons which have been named, elected, presented, or postulated to be archbishops or bishops within this realm of England, under the title of annates, otherwise called first-fruits; which annates, or first-fruits, heretofore have been taken of every archbishopric or bishopric within this realm, by restraint of the Pope's bulls, for confirmations, elections, admissions, postulations, provisions, collations, dispositions, institutions, installations, investitures, orders, holy benedictions, palls or other things requisite and necessary to the attaining of those their promotions; and have been compelled to pay, before they could attain the same, great sums of money, before they might receive any part of the fruits of the said archbishopric, whereunto they were named, elected, presented or postulated; by occasion whereof, not only the treasure of this realm has been greatly conveyed out of the same, but also it has happened many times, by occasion of death, unto such archbishops and bishops, so newly promoted, within two or three years after his or their consecration, that his or their friends, by whom he or they have been holpen to advance and make payment of the said annates, or first-fruits, have been thereby utterly undone and impoverished:

And for because the said annates have risen, grown and increased by an uncharitable custom, grounded upon no just or good title, and the payments thereof obtained by restraint of bulls, until the same annates or first-fruits have been paid, or surety made for the same; which declares the said payments to be exacted and taken by constraint, against all equity and justice:

The noblemen therefore of this realm, and the wise, sage, politic Commons of the same, assembled in this present Parliament, considering that the court of Rome ceases not to tax, take and exact the said great sums of money, under the title of annates, or first-fruits, as is aforesaid, to the great damage of the said prelates and this realm; which annates or first-fruits were first suffered to be taken within the same realm for the only defence of Christian people against the infidels, and now they be claimed and demanded as mere duty, only for lucre, against all right and conscience; insomuch that is evidently known that there has passed out of this realm unto the court of Rome, since the second year of the reign of the most noble prince of famous memory, King Henry VII, unto this present time, under the name of annates or first-fruits, paid for the expedition of bulls of archbishoprics and bishoprics, the sum of eight hundred thousand ducats, amounting in sterling money at the least to eight score thousand pounds, besides other great and intolerable sums which have yearly been conveyed to the said court of Rome by many other ways and means, to the great impoverishment of this realm :

And albeit that our said sovereign the King and all his natural subjects, as well spiritual as temporal, be as obedient, devout, Catholic and humble children of God and Holy Church as any people be within any realm christened; yet the said exaction of annates or first-fruits be so intolerable and importable to this realm that it is considered and declared by the whole body of this realm now represented by all the estates of the same, assembled in this present Parliament, that the King's Highness before Almighty God is bound, as by the duty of a good Christian prince, for the conservation and preservation of the good estate and commonwealth of this his realm, to do all that in him is to obviate, repress and redress the said abuses and exactions of annates or first-fruits; and because that divers prelates of this realm be now in extreme age and in other debilities of their bodies, so that of likelihood bodily death in short time shall or may succeed unto them; by reason whereof great sums of money shall shortly after their deaths be conveyed unto the court of Rome for the unreasonable and uncharitable causes abovesaid, to the universal damage, prejudice and impoverishment of this realm, if speedy remedy be not in due time provided:

It is therefore ordained, established and enacted by authority of this present Parliament, that the unlawful payments of annates or first-fruits and all manner contributions for the same for any archbishopric or bishopric, or for any bulls hereafter to be obtained from the court of Rome, to or for the aforesaid purpose and intent, shall from henceforth utterly cease, and no such hereafter to be paid for any archbishopric or bishopric within this realm, other or otherwise than hereafter in this present Act is declared; and that no manner person nor persons hereafter to be named, elected, presented or postulated to any archbishopric or bishopric within this realm shall pay the said annates or first-fruits for the said archbishopric or bishopric, nor any other manner of sum or sums of money, pensions or annuities for the same, or for any other like exaction or cause, upon pain to forfeit to our said Sovereign Lord the King, his heirs and successors, all manner his goods and chattels for ever, and all the temporal lands and possessions of the same archbishopric or bishopric during the time that he or they which shall offend, contrary to this present Act, shall have, possess or enjoy the archbishopric or bishopric, wherefor he shall so offend contrary to the form aforesaid.

02. And furthermore it is enacted by authority of this present Parliament that every person hereafter named and presented to the court of Rome by the King, or any of his heirs and successors, to be bishop of any see or diocese within this realm hereafter, shall be letted, deferred or delayed at the court of Rome from any such bishopric whereunto he shall be so presented, by means of restraint of bulls apostolic, and other things requisite to the same; or shall be denied at the court of Rome, upon convenient suit made, any manner bulls requisite for any of the causes aforesaid, every such person or persons so presented may be, and shall be, consecrated here in England by the archbishop in whose province the said bishopric shall be, so alway that the same person shall be named and presented by the King for the time being to the same archbishop:

And if any persons being named and presented as is aforesaid, to any archbishopric of this realm, making convenient suit as is aforesaid, shall happen to be letted, deferred, delayed or otherwise disturbed from the same archbishopric for lack of pall, bulls or other things to him requisite, to be obtained in the court of Rome in that behalf, that then every such person named and presented to be archbishop may be, and shall be consecrated and invested, after presentation made as is aforesaid, by any other two bishops within this realm whom the King's Highness or any of his heirs or successors, kings of England, for the time being will assign and appoint for the same, according and in like manner as divers other archbishops and bishops have been heretofore, in ancient time, by sundry the King's most noble progenitors, made, consecrated and invested within this realm:

And that every archbishop and bishop hereafter, being named and presented by the King's Highness, his heirs or successors, kings of England, and being consecrated and invested as is aforesaid, shall be installed accordingly and shall be accepted, taken, reputed, used and obeyed, as an archbishop or bishop of the dignity, see or place whereunto he shall be so named, presented and consecrated, requires; and as other like prelates of that province, see or diocese have been used, accepted, taken and obeyed, which have had and obtained completely their bulls and other things requisite in that behalf from the court of Rome. And also shall fully and entirely have and enjoy all the spiritualities and temporalities of the said archbishopric or bishopric, in as large, ample and beneficial manner as any of his or their predecessors had and enjoyed in the said archbishopric or bishopric, satisfying and yielding unto the King our Sovereign Lord, and to his heirs and successors, kings of England, all such duties, rights and interests as before this time had been accustomed to be paid for any such archbishopric or bishopric, according to the ancient laws and customs of this realm and the King's prerogative royal.

03. And to the intent our said holy father the Pope and the court of Rome shall not think that the pains and labours taken and hereafter to be taken about the writing, sealing, obtaining and other businesses sustained, and hereafter to be sustained by the offices of the said court of Rome, for and about the expedition of any bulls hereafter to be obtained or had for any such archbishopric or bishopric shall be irremunerated, or shall not be sufficiently and condignly recompensed in that behalf; and for their more ready expedition to be had therein: it is therefore enacted by the authority aforesaid that every spiritual person of this realm hereafter to be named, presented or postulated to any archbishopric or bishopric of this realm, shall and may lawfully pay for the writing and obtaining of his or their said bulls at the court of Rome, and besealing the same with lead, to be had without payment of any annates or first-fruits, or other charge or exaction by him or them to be made, yielded or paid for the same, five pounds sterling, for and after the rate of the clear and whole yearly value of every hundred pounds sterling, above all charges of any such archbishopric or bishopric, or other money, to the value of the said five pounds, for the clear yearly value of every hundred pounds of every such archbishopric or bishopric, and not above, nor in any other wise, anything in this present Act before written notwithstanding.

And forasmuch as the King's Highness and this his high court of Parliament neither have, nor do intend to use in this or any other like cause, any manner of extremity or violence, before gentle courtesy and friendly ways and means first approved and attempted, and without a very great urgent cause and occasion given to the contrary, but principally coveting to disburthen this realm of the said great exactions and intolerable charges of annates and first-fruits, have therefore thought convenient to commit the final order and determination of the premises in all things, unto the King's Highness. So that if it may seem to his high wisdom and most prudent discretion meet to move the Pope's Holiness and the court of Rome amicably, charitably and reasonably to compound, either to extinct and make frustrate the payment of the said annates or first-fruits, or else by some friendly, loving and tolerable composition, to moderate the same in such wise as may be by this his realm easily borne and sustained; that then those ways and compositions once taken, concluded and agreed between the Pope's Holiness and the King's Highness shall stand in strength, force and effect of law, inviolably to be observed.

04. And it is also further ordained and enacted by the authority of this present Parliament that the King's Highness at any time or times on this side of the feast of Easter, which shall be in the year of our Lord God one thousand five hundred and three and thirty (13 April 1533), or at any time on this side the beginning of the next Parliament, by his letters patent under his great seal, to be made and to be entered of record in the roll of this present Parliament, may and shall have full power and liberty to declare, by the said letters patent, whether that the premises, or any part, clause or matter thereof, shall be observed, obeyed, executed, performed and take place and effect, as an act and statute of this present Parliament, or not; so that if his Highness, by his said letters patent, before the expiration of the terms above limited, thereby do declare his pleasure to be that the premises, or any part, clause or matter thereof shall not be put in execution, observed, continued nor obeyed – in that case all the said premises, or such part, clause or matter thereof, as the King's Highness so shall refuse, disaffirm or not ratify, shall stand and be from henceforth utterly void and of none effect. And in case that the King's Highness, before the expiration of the terms afore prefixed, do declare by his said letters patent, his pleasure and determination to be that the said premises, or every clause, sentence and part thereof, that is to say the whole, or such part thereof as the King's Highness so shall affirm, accept and ratify, shall in all points stand, remain, abide and be put in due and effectual execution, according to the purport, tenor, effect and true meaning of the same; and to stand and be from henceforth for ever after, as firm, steadfast and available in the law, as though the same had been fully and perfectly established, enacted and confirmed, to be in every part thereof, immediately, wholly and entirely executed in like manner, form and effect, as other Acts and laws; the which be fully and determinately made, ordained and enacted in this present Parliament.

05. And if that on the aforesaid reasonable, amicable and charitable ways and means, by the King's Highness to be experimented, moved or compounded, or otherwise approved, it shall and may appear, or be seen unto his grace, that this realm shall be continually burdened and charged with this, and such other intolerable exactions and demands as heretofore it hath been; and that thereupon, for continuance of the same, our said holy father the Pope, or any of his successors, or the court of Rome, will or do, or cause to be done at any time hereafter, so as is above rehearsed, unjustly, uncharitably and unreasonably vex, inquiet, molest, trouble or grieve our said Sovereign Lord, his heirs of successors, kings of England, or any of his or their spiritual or lay subjects, or this his realm, by excommunication, excommengement, interdiction, or by any other process, censures, compulsories, ways or means:

Be it enacted by the authority aforesaid, that the King's Highness, his heirs and successors, kings of England, and all his spiritual and lay subjects of the same, without any scruples of conscience, shall and may lawfully, to the honour of Almighty God, the increase and continuance of virtue and good example within this realm, the said censures, excommunications, interdictions, compulsories, or any of them notwithstanding, minister or cause to be ministered, throughout this said realm, and all other the dominions or territories belonging or appertaining thereunto, all and all manner of sacraments, sacramentals, ceremonies or other divine service of Holy Church, or any other thing or things necessary for the health of the soul of mankind, as they heretofore at any time or times have been virtuously used or accustomed to do within the same; and that no manner such censures, excommunications, interdictions, or any other process or compulsories, shall be by any of the prelates or other spiritual fathers of this region, nor by any of their ministers or substitutes, be at any time or times hereafter published, executed or divulged in any manner of wise.

Be it remembered that on the ninth day of July, in the twenty-fifth year of the reign of King Henry (09 July 1533), the same Lord the King, by his letters patent, sealed under his great seal, ratified and confirmed the aforesaid Act, and gave to the Act his royal assent.

08. ACT IN RESTRAINT OF APPEALS, 1533 (24 Henry VIII, c. 12)

History

This Act was passed with great urgency in February 1533, in order to expedite the King's divorce. Henry had already secretly married Anne Boleyn (in January 1533) and she was known to be pregnant. The immediate circumstances however do not tell the whole story, since this Act was to become the legal basis for the final separation from Rome in the following year.

The Act was repealed by Mary I in 1554 but revived by Elizabeth I in 1559.

N.B. The paragraphs are numbered in accordance with the original document.

01. Where by divers sundry old authentic histories and chronicles it is manifestly declared and expressed that this realm of England is an empire, and so hath been accepted in the world, governed by one supreme head and king, having the dignity and royal estate of the imperial crown of the same, unto whom a body politic, compact of all sorts and degrees of people divided in terms and by names of spiritualty and temporalty, be bounden and ought to bear, next to God, a natural and humble obedience; he being also institute and furnished by the goodness and sufferance of Almighty God with plenary, whole and entire power, pre-eminence, authority, prerogative and jurisdiction, to render and yield justice, and final determination to all manner of folk, residents or subjects within this his realm, in all causes, matters, debates and contentions happening to occur, insurge or begin within the limits thereof, without restraint or provocation to any foreign princes or potentates of the world; the body spiritual whereof having power, when any cause of the law divine happened to come in question, or of spiritual learning, then it was declared, interpreted and showed by that part of the said body politic, called the spiritualty, now being usually called the English Church, which always hath been reputed and also found of that sort, that both for knowledge, integrity and sufficiency of number, it hath been always thought, and is also at this hour, sufficient and meet of itself, without the inter-meddling of any exterior person or persons, to declare and determine all such doubts, and to administer all such offices and duties as to their rooms spiritual doth appertain; for the due administration whereof and to keep them from corruption and sinister affection, the King's most noble progenitors, and the antecessors of the nobles of this realm, have sufficiently endowed the said Church both with honour and possessions; and the laws temporal, for trial of property of lands and goods, and for the conservation of the people of this realm in unity and peace, without ravin or spoil, was and yet is administered, adjudged and executed by sundry judges and ministers of the other part of the said body politic, called the temporalty; and both their authorities and jurisdictions do conjoin together in the due administration of justice, the one to help the other:

And whereas the King, his most noble progenitors, and the nobility and Commons of this said realm, at divers and sundry Parliaments, as well in the time of King Edward I (1272-1307), Edward III (1327-1377), Richard II (1377-1399), Henry IV (1399-1413) and other noble kings of this realm made sundry ordinances, laws, statutes and provisions for the entire and sure conservation of the prerogatives, liberties and pre-eminences of the said imperial crown of this realm, and of the jurisdiction spiritual and temporal of the same, to keep it from the annoyance as well of the see of Rome as from the authority of other foreign potentates, attempting the diminution or violation thereof, as often, and from time to time, as any such annoyance or attempt might be known or espied:

And notwithstanding the said good statutes and ordinances made in the time of the King's most noble progenitors, in preservation of the authority and prerogative of the said imperial crown, as is aforesaid; yet nevertheless since the making of the said good statutes and ordinances, divers and sundry inconveniences and dangers, not provided for plainly by the said former acts, statutes and ordinances, have arisen and sprung by reason of appeals sued out of this realm to the see of Rome, in causes testamentary, causes of matrimony and divorces, right of tithes, oblations and obventions, not only to the great inquietation, vexation, trouble, cost and charges of the King's Highness, and many of his subjects and residents in this his realm, but also to the great delay and let to the true and speedy determination of the said causes, for so much as the parties appealing to the said court of Rome most commonly do the same for the delay of justice.

And forasmuch as the great distance of way is so far out of this realm, so that the necessary proofs, nor the true knowledge of the cause, can neither there be so well known, nor the witnesses there so well examined, as within this realm, so that the parties grieved by means of the said appeals be most times without remedy:

In consideration whereof the King's Highness, his nobles and Commons, considering the great enormities, dangers, long delays and hurts, that as well to his Highness as to his said nobles, subjects, commons and residents of this his realm, in the said causes testamentary, causes of matrimony and divorces, tithes, oblations and obventions, do daily ensue, does therefore by his royal assent, and by the assent of the Lords spiritual and temporal, and the Commons, in this present Parliament assembled, and by authority of the same, enact, establish and ordain that all causes testamentary, causes of matrimony and divorces, rights of tithes, oblations and obventions (the knowledge whereof by the goodness of princes of this realm, and by the laws and customs of the same, appertaineth to the spiritual jurisdiction of this realm) already commenced, moved, depending, being, happening, or hereafter coming in contention, debate or question within this realm, or within any of the King's dominions or marches of the same, or elsewhere, whether they concern the King our Sovereign Lord, his heirs and successors, or any other subjects or residents within the same, of what degree soever they be, shall be from henceforth heard, examined, discussed, clearly, finally and definitively adjudged and determined within the King's jurisdiction and authority, and not elsewhere, in such courts spiritual and temporal of the same, as the natures, conditions and qualities of the causes and matters aforesaid in contention, or hereafter happening in contention, shall require, without having any respect to any custom, use or suffrance, in hindrance, let or prejudice of the same, or to any other thing used or suffered to the contrary thereof by any other manner of person or persons in any manner of wise; any foreign inhibitions, appeals, sentences, summons, citations, suspensions, interdictions, excommunications, restraints, judgements or any other process or impediments, of what natures, names, qualities or conditions soever they be, from the see of Rome or any other foreign courts or potentates of the world, or from and out of this realm, or any other the King's dominions, or marches of the same, to the see of Rome, or to any other foreign courts or potentates, to the let or impediment thereof in any wise notwithstanding.

And that it shall be lawful to the King our Sovereign Lord, and to his heirs and successors, and to all other subjects or residents within this realm, or within any the King's dominions or marches of the same – notwithstanding that hereafter it should happen any excommengement, excommunications, interdictions, citations or any other censures, or foreign process out of any outward parts, to be fulminated, provulged, declared or put in execution within this said realm, or in any other place or places, for any of the causes before rehearsed, in prejudice, derogation, or contempt of this said Act, and the very true meaning and execution thereof – may and shall nevertheless as well pursue, execute, have and enjoy the effects, profits, benefits and commodities of all such processes, sentences, judgements and determinations done, or hereafter to be done, in any of the said courts spiritual or temporal, as the cases shall require, within the limits, power and authority of this the King's said realm, and dominions and marches of the same, and those only, and none other to take place, and to be firmly observed and obeyed within the same.

As also that all the spiritual prelates, pastors, ministers and curates within this realm, and the dominions of the same, shall and may use, minister, execute and do, or cause to be used, ministered, executed and done, all sacraments, sacramentals, divine services, and all other things within the said realm and dominions, unto all the subjects of the same, as Catholic and Christian men ought to do; any former citations, processes, inhibitions, suspensions, interdictions, excommunications or appeals, for or touching the causes aforesaid, from or to the see of Rome, or any other foreign prince or foreign courts, to the let or contrary thereof in any wise notwithstanding.

And if any of the said spiritual persons, by the occasion of the said fulminations of any of the same interdictions, censures, inhibitions, excommunications, appeals, suspensions, summons or other foreign citations for the causes beforesaid, or for any of them, do at any time hereafter refuse to minister, or cause to be ministered, the said sacraments and sacramentals, and other divine services, in form as is aforesaid, shall for every such time or times that they or any of them do refuse so to do, or cause to be done, have one year's imprisonment, and to make fine and ransom at the King's pleasure.

02. And it is further enacted by the authority aforesaid, that if any person or persons inhabiting or resident within this realm or within any of the King's said dominions, or marches of the same, or any other person or persons, of what estate, condition or degree soever he or they be, at any time hereafter, for or in any the causes aforesaid, do attempt, move, purchase or procure, from or to the see of Rome, or from or to any other foreign court or courts out of this realm, any manner foreign process, inhibitions, appeals, sentences, summons, citations, suspensions, interdictions, excommunications, restraints or judgements, of what nature, kind or quality soever they be, or execute any of the same process, or do any act or acts to the let, impediment, hindrance, or derogation of any process, sentence, judgement or determination, had, made, done or hereafter to be had, done or made in any courts of this realm or the King's said dominions, or marches of the same, for any of the causes aforesaid, contrary to the true meaning of this present Act and the execution of the same, that then every such person or persons so doing, and their fautors, comforters, abettors, procurers, executors and counsellors, and every of them, being convict of the same, for every such default shall incur and run in the same pains, penalties and forfeitures, ordained and provided by the statute of provision and *praemunire*, made in the sixteenth year of the reign of the right noble prince King Richard II (1393), against such as attempt, procure, or make provision to the see of Rome, or elsewhere, for anything or things, to the derogation or contrary to the prerogative or jurisdiction of the crown and dignity of this realm.

03. And furthermore, in eschewing the said great enormities, inquietations, delays, charges and expenses hereafter to be sustained in pursuing of such appeals, and foreign process, for and concerning the causes aforesaid, or any of them, do therefore by authority aforesaid, ordain and enact that in such cases where heretofore any of the King's subjects or residents have used to pursue, provoke or procure any appeal to the see of Rome, and in all other cases of appeals, in or for any of the causes aforesaid, they may and shall from henceforth take, have and use their appeals within this realm

and not elsewhere, in manner and form as hereafter ensueth and not otherwise; that is to say, first from the archdeacon or his official, if the matter or cause be there begun, to the bishop diocesan of the said see if in case any of the parties be grieved. And in like wise if it be commenced before the bishop diocesan or his commissary, from the bishop diocesan or his commissary, within fifteen days next ensuing the judgement or sentence thereof there given, to the Archbishop of the Province of Canterbury, if it be within his province, and if it be within the Province of York then to the Archbishop of York; and so likewise to all other archbishops in other the King's dominions, as the case by order of justice shall require; and there to be definitively and finally ordered, decreed and adjudged according to justice, without any other appellation or provocation to any other person or persons, court or courts.

And if the matter or contention for any of the causes aforesaid be or shall be commences by any of the King's subjects or residents, before the archdeacon of any archbishop or his commissary, then the party grieved shall or may take his appeal within fifteen days next after judgement or sentence there given, to the court of the Arches or Audience of the same archbishop or archbishops; and from the said court of the Arches or Audience, within fifteen days then next ensuing after judgement or sentence there given, to the archbishop of the same province, there to be definitively and finally determined, without any other or further process or appeal thereupon to be had or sued.

04. And it is further enacted by the authority aforesaid that all and every matter, cause and contention now depending, or that hereafter shall be commenced by any of the King's subjects or residents for any of the causes aforesaid, before any of the said archbishops, that then the same matter or matters, contention or contentions, shall be before the same archbishop where the said matter, cause or process shall be so commenced, definitively determined, decreed or adjudged without any other appeal, provocation or any other foreign process out of this realm, to be sued to the let or derogation of the said judgement, sentence or decree, otherwise than is by this Act limited and appointed; saving always the prerogative of the Archbishop and Church of Canterbury, in all the foresaid cases of appeals, to him and to his successors, to be sued within this realm, in such and like wise as they have been accustomed and used to have heretofore.

And in case any cause, matter or contention, now depending for the causes before rehearsed, or any of them, or that hereafter shall come in contention for any of the same causes, in any of the foresaid courts, which has, does, shall or may touch the King, his heirs or successors, kings of this realm; that in all and every such case or cases the party grieved, as before is said, shall or may appeal from any of the said courts of this said realm, where the said matter, now being in contention, or hereafter shall come in contention, touching the King, his heirs or successors (as is aforesaid) shall happen to be ventilated, commenced or begun, to the spiritual prelates and other abbots and priors of the Upper House, assembled and convocate by the King's writ in the Convocation being, or next ensuing, within the province or provinces where the same matter of contention is or shall be begun; so that every such appeal be taken by the party grieved within fifteen days next after the judgement or sentence thereupon given or to be given; and that whatsoever be done, or shall be done and affirmed, determined, decreed and adjudged by the foresaid prelates, abbots and priors of the Upper House of the said Convocation, as is aforesaid, appertaining, concerning or belonging to the King, his heirs and successors, in any of these foresaid causes of appeals, shall stand and be taken for a final decree, sentence, judgement, definition and determination, and the same matter, so determined, never after to come in question and debate, to be examined in any other court or courts.

And if it shall happen any person or persons hereafter to pursue or provoke any appeal contrary to the effect of this Act, or refuse to obey, execute and observe all things comprised within the same, concerning the said appeals, provocations and other foreign processes to be sued out of this realm, for the causes aforesaid, that then every such person or persons so doing, refusing, or offending contrary to the true meaning of this Act, their procurers, fautors, advocates, counsellors and abettors, and every of them, shall incur into the pains, forfeitures and penalties ordained and provided in the said statute made in the said sixteenth year of King Richard II (1393), and with like process to be made against the said offenders, as in the same statute made in the said sixteenth year more plainly appears.

09. ACT FOR THE SUBMISSION OF THE CLERGY AND RESTRAINT OF APPEALS, 1534 (25 Henry VIII, c. 19)

History

It now remained only to put the moves made against the Papacy between 1531 and 1533 on a more solid legal foundation. There was no hope of any divorce appeal being granted in Rome, and the King's remarriage made further delay impossible. The following Act merely turned into statute law things which had already occurred. As with other legislation of its type, it was repealed by Mary I in 1554 and reinstated by Elizabeth I in 1559; parts of it, indeed, are still in force today.

N.B. For this edition, paragraph numbers follow the original document, and the portions of the Act which are still in force are indicated in **bold type**.

01. Where the king's humble and obedient subjects, the clergy of this realm of England, have not only acknowledged according to the truth, that the convocations of the same clergy is, always has been, and ought to be assembled only by the King's writ, but also submitting themselves to the King's Majesty, have promised *in verbo sacerdotii* **(by the word of their priesthood) that they will never from henceforth presume to attempt, allege, claim or put in ure, or enact, promulge or execute any new canons, constitutions, ordinance provincial or other, or by whatsoever other name they shall be called in the Convocation, unless the King's most royal assent and licence may to them be had, to make, promulge and execute the same; and that his Majesty do give his most royal assent and authority in that behalf:**

And where divers constitutions, ordinances and canons, provincial or synodal, which heretofore have been enacted, and be thought not only to be much prejudicial to the King's prerogative royal, and repugnant to the laws and statutes of this realm, but also overmuch onerous to his Highness and his subjects; the said clergy have most humbly besought the King's Highness that the said constitutions and canons may be committed to the examination and judgement of his Highness, and of two-and thirty persons of the King's subjects, whereof sixteen to be of the upper and nether house of the Parliament of the temporalty, and the other sixteen to be of the clergy of this realm; and all the said two-and-thirty persons to be chosen and appointed by the

King's Majesty, and that such of the said constitutions and canons as shall be thought and determined by the said two-and-thirty persons, or the more part of them, worthy to be abrogated and annulled, shall be abolished and made of no value accordingly; and such other of the same constitutions and canons as by the said two-and-thirty or the more part of them, shall be approved to stand with the laws of God and consonant to the laws of this realm, shall stand in their full strength and power, the King's most royal assent first had and obtained to the same:

Be it therefore now enacted by authority of this present Parliament, according to the said submission and petition of the said clergy, that they, nor any of them, from henceforth shall presume to attempt, allege, claim or put in ure any constitutions or ordinances, provincial or synodal, or any other canons, nor shall enact, promulge or execute any such canons, constitutions or ordinance provincial, by whatsoever name or names they may be called, in their convocations in time coming (which alway shall be assembled by authority of the King's writ), unless the same clergy may have the King's most royal assent and licence to make, promulge and execute such canons, constitutions and ordinances, provincial or synodal, upon pain of every one of the said clergy doing contrary to this Act, and being therefore convict, to suffer imprisonment and make fine at the King's will.

02. And forasmuch as such canons, constitutions and ordinance as heretofore have been made by the clergy of this realm cannot now at the session of the present Parliament, by reason of shortness of time, be viewed, examined and determined by the King's Highness, and thirty-two persons to be chosen and appointed according to the petition of the said clergy in form above rehearsed: be it therefore enacted by authority aforesaid that the King's Highness shall have power and authority to nominate and assign at his pleasure the said two-and-thirty persons of his subjects, whereof sixteen to be of the clergy, and sixteen to be of the temporalty of the upper and nether house of the Paliament, and if any of the said two-and-thirty persons so chosen shall happen to die before their full determination, then his Highness to nominate other from time to time of the said two houses of Parliament, to supply the number of the said two-and-thirty; and that the same two-and-thirty, by his Highness so to be named, shall have power and authority to view, search and examine the said canons, constitutions and ordinance, provincial and synodal, heretofore made, and such of them as the King's Highness and the said two-and-thirty, or the more part of them, shall deem and adjudge worthy to be continued, kept and obeyed, shall be from thenceforth kept, obeyed and executed within this realm, so that the King's most royal assent under his great seal be first had to the same; and the residue of the said canons, constitutions, or ordinance provincial, which the King's Highness and the said two-and-thirty persons or the more part of them shall not approve, or deem and judge worthy to be abolished,

abrogate and made frustrate, shall from thenceforth be void and of none effect, and never be put in execution within this realm.

03. Provided alway that no canons, constitutions or ordinances shall be made or put in execution within this realm by authority of the convocation of the clergy, which shall be contrariant or repugnant to the King's prerogative royal, or the customs, laws or statutes of this realm; anything contained in this Act to the contrary hereof notwithstanding.

04. And be it further enacted by authority aforesaid that from the feast of Easter which shall be in the year of our Lord God 1534 (05 April 1534), no manner of appeals shall be had, provoked or made out of this realm, or out of any of the King's dominions to the Bishop of Rome, nor to the see of Rome, in any causes or matters happening to be in contention, and having their commencement or beginning in any of the courts within this realm, or within any the King's dominions, of what nature, condition or quality soever they be of, but that all manner of appeals, of what nature or condition soever they be of, or what cause or matter soever they concern, shall be made and had by the parties grieved, or having cause of appeal, after such manner, form and condition as is limited for appeals to be had and prosecuted within this realm in causes of matrimony, tithes, oblations and obventions, by a statute thereof made and established since the beginning of this present Parliament, and according to the form and effect of the said statute; any usage, custom, prescription or anything or things to the contrary hereof notwithstanding.

And for lack of justice at or in any of the courts of the archbishops of this realm, or in any the King's dominions, it shall be lawful to the parties grieved to appeal to the King's Majesty in the King's court of chancery, and that upon every such appeal a commission shall be directed under the great seal to such persons as shall be named by the King's Highness, his heirs or successors, like as in case of appeal from the admiral's court, to hear and definitively determine such appeals and the causes concerning the same. Which commissioners, so by the King's Highness, his heirs or successors, to be named or appointed, shall have full power and authority to hear and definitively determine every such appeal, with the causes and all circumstances concerning the same; and that such judgement and sentence, as the said commissioners shall make and decree, in and upon any such appeal, shall be good and effectual, and also definitive; and no further appeals to be had or made from the said commissioners for the same.

05. And if any person or persons, at any time after the said feast of Easter, provoke or sue any manner of appeals, of what nature or condition soever they be of, to the said Bishop of Rome, or to the see of Rome, or do procure or execute any manner of process from the see of Rome, or by authority thereof, to the derogation or let of the due execution of this Act, or contrary to the same, that then every such person or persons so doing, their aiders, counsellors and abettors, shall incur and run into the dangers, pains and penalties contained and limited in the Act of Provision and *Praemunire* made in the sixteenth year of the King's most noble progenitor, King Richard II (1393), against such as sue to the court of Rome against the King's crown and prerogative royal.

06. Provided always, that all manner of provocations and appeals hereafter to be had, made or taken from the jurisdiction of any abbots, prior, and other heads and governors of monasteries, abbeys, priories and other houses and places exempt, in such cases as they were wont or might afore the making of this Act, by reason of grants or liberties of such places exempt, to have or make immediately any appeal or provocation to the Bishop of Rome, otherwise called Pope, or to the see of Rome, that in all these cases every person and persons, having cause of appeal and provocation, shall and may take and make their appeals and provocations immediately to the King's Majesty of this realm, into the court of chancery, in like manner and form as they used afore to do to the see of Rome; which appeals and provocations so made shall be definitively determined by authority of the King's commission in such manner and form as in this Act is above mentioned; so that no archbishop or bishop of this realm shall intermit or meddle with any such appeals, otherwise or in any other manner than they might have done afore the making of this Act; anything in this Act to the contrary thereof notwithstanding.

07. Provided also that such canons, constitutions, ordinances and synodals provincial being already made, which be not contrariant or repugnant to the laws, statutes and customs of this realm, nor to the damage or hurt of the King's prerogative royal, shall more still be used and executed as they were afore the making of this Act, till such time as they be viewed, searched or otherwise ordered and determined by the said two-and-thirty persons, or the more part of them, according to the tenor, form and effect of this present Act.

10. ACT RESTRAINING THE PAYMENT OF ANNATES AND CONCERNING THE ELECTION OF BISHOPS, 1534
(25 Henry VIII, c. 20)

History

Once again we are dealing with a piece of tidying-up legislation which, as it turned out, has become part of the permanent law of the land. It was superseded by another act for the election of bishops, passed in 1547, but it was subsequently restored in 1559 and has remained substantially unchanged ever since, apart from the sixth article, which was repealed in 1967.

Annates were annexed to the Crown by a further Act, also passed in 1534, and there the situation remained until 1703, when Queen Anne set aside what was to become known as her Bounty as a means to pay the clergy. That in turn was reorganized in 1947, to become the Church Commissioners, a body which remains responsible for ecclesiastical revenues and which continues to make a substantial contribution towards the payment of the clergy.

01. Where since the beginning of this present Parliament, for repression of the exaction of annates and first-fruits of archbishopric and bishoprics of this realm wrongfully taken by the Bishop of Rome, otherwise called the Pope, and the see of Rome, it is ordained and established by an Act, among other things, that the payments of the annates or first-fruits, and all manner contributions of the same, for any such archbishopric or bishopric, or for any bulls to be obtained from the see of Rome, to or for the said purpose or intent, should utterly cease, and no such be paid for any archbishopric or bishopric within this realm, otherwise than in the same Act is expressed; and that no manner of person or persons to be named, elected, presented or postulated to any archbishopric or bishopric within this realm should pay the said annates or first-fruits, nor any other manner of sum or sums of money, pensions or annuities for the same, or for any other like exaction or cause, upon pain to forfeit to our Sovereign Lord the King, his heirs and successors, all manner his goods and chattels for ever, and all the temporal lands and possessions of the said archbishopric or bishopric during the time that he or they should offend contrary to the said Act, should have, possess and enjoy the said archbishopric or bishopric. And it is further enacted that if any person named or presented to the see of Rome by the King's Highness, or his heirs and successors, to be bishop of any see or diocese within this realm, should happen to be let, delayed or deferred at the see of Rome from any such bishopric whereunto he should be so presented, by means of restraint of bulls of the said Bishop of Rome, otherwise called the Pope, and other things requisite to the same, or should be denied at the see of Rome, upon convenient suit made, for any bulls requisite for any such cause, that then every person so presented might or should be consecrated here in England by the archbishop in whose province the said bishopric shall be; so always that the same person should be named and presented by the King for the time being to the said archbishop. And if any person being named and presented as is before said, to any archbishopric of this realm, making convenient suit, as is aforesaid, should happen to be let, delayed, deferred or otherwise disturbed from the said archbishopric, for lack of pall, bulls or other things to him requisite to be obtained at the see of Rome, that then every such person so named and presented to the archbishop might and should be consecrated and invested, after presentation made as is aforesaid, by any other two bishops within this realm, whom the King's Highness, or any his heirs or successors, kings of England, would appoint and assign for the same, according and after like manner as divers archbishops and bishops have been heretofore in ancient time by sundry the King's most noble progenitors made, consecrated and invested within this realm. And it is further enacted by the said Act that every archbishop and bishop, being named and presented by the King's Highness, his heirs and successors, kings of England, and being consecrated and invested as is aforesaid, should be installed accordingly and should be accepted, taken and reputed, used and obeyed as an archbishop or bishop of the dignity, see or place whereunto he shall be so named, presented and consecrated, and as other like prelates of that province, see or diocese have been used, accepted, taken and obeyed, which have had and obtained completely their bulls and other things requisite in that behalf from the see of Rome, and also should fully and entirely have and enjoy all the spiritualities and temporalities of the said archbishopric or bishopric in as large, ample and beneficial manner as any of his or their predecessors had or enjoyed in the said archbishopric or bishopric, satisfying and yielding unto the King's Highness and to his heirs and successors, all such duties, rights, and interests as beforetime have been accustomed to be paid for any such archbishopric or bishopric, according to the ancient laws and customs of this realm and the King's prerogative royal, as in the said Act amongst other things is more at large mentioned.

And albeit the said Bishop of Rome, otherwise called the Pope, has been informed and certified of the effectual contents of the said Act, to the intent that by some gentle ways the said exactions might have been redressed and reformed, yet nevertheless the said Bishop of Rome hitherto has made no answer of his mind therein to the King's Highness, nor devised nor required any reasonable ways to and with our said Sovereign Lord for the same: wherefore his most royal Majesty of his most excellent goodness, for the wealth and profit of this his realm and subjects of the same, has not only put his most gracious and royal assent to the aforesaid Act, but also has ratified and confirmed the same, and every clause and article therein contained, as by his letters patent under his great seal enrolled in the Parliament roll of this present Parliament more at large is contained.

02. And forasmuch as in the said Act it is not plainly and certainly expressed in what manner and fashion archbishops and bishops shall be elected, presented, invested and consecrated within this realm, and in all other the King's dominions; be it now therefore enacted by the King our Sovereign Lord, by the assent of the Lords spiritual and temporal, and the Commons, in this present Parliament assembled, and by the authority of the same, that the said Act and everything therein contained shall be and stand in strength, virtue and effect; except only that no person or persons hereafter shall be presented, nominated or commended to the said Bishop of Rome, otherwise called the Pope, or to the see of Rome, to or for the dignity or office of any archbishop or bishop within this realm, or in any other the King's dominions, nor shall send nor procure there for any manner of bulls, briefs or palls; but that by the authority of this Act, such presenting, nominating or commending to the said Bishop of Rome or to the see of Rome, and such bulls, briefs, palls, annates, first-fruits and every other sums of money heretofore limited, accustomed or used to be paid at the said see of Rome, for procuration or expedition of any such bulls, briefs or palls, or other thing concerning the same, shall utterly cease and no longer be used within this realm or within any the King's dominions; anything contained in the said Act aforementioned to the contrary thereof notwithstanding.

03. And furthermore be it ordained and established by the authority aforesaid, that at every avoidance of every archbishopric or bishopric within this realm, or in any other the King's dominions, the King our Sovereign Lord, his heirs and successors, may grant to the prior and convent, or the dean and chapter of the cathedral churches or monasteries where the see of such archbishopric or bishopric shall happen to be void, a licence under the great seal, as of old time has been accustomed, to proceed to election of an archbishop or bishop of the see so being void, with a letter missive, containing the name of the person which they shall elect and choose; by virtue of which licence the said dean and chapter, or prior and convent, to whom any such licence and letters missive shall be directed, shall with all speed and celerity in due form elect and choose the said person named in the said letters missive, to the dignity and office of the archbishopric or bishopric so being void, and none other.

And if they do defer or delay their election above twelve days next after such licence and letters missive to them delivered, that then for every such default the King's Highness, his heirs and successors, at their liberty and pleasure shall nominate and present, by their letters patent under their great seal, such a person to the said office and dignity so being void, as they shall think able and convenient for the same.

And that every such nomination and presentment to be made by the King's Highness, his heirs and successors, if it be to the office and dignity of a bishop, shall be made to the archbishop and metropolitan of the province where the see of the same bishopric is void, if the see of the said archbishopric be then full, and not void; and if it be void, then to be made to such archbishop or metropolitan within this realm or in any the King's dominions as shall please the King's Highness, his heirs and successors; and if any such nomination or presentment shall happen to be made for default of such election to the dignity or office of any archbishop, then the King's Highness, his heirs and successors, by his letters patent under his great seal, shall nominate and present such person, as they will dispose to have the said office and dignity of archbishopric being void, to one such archbishop and two such bishops, or else to four such bishops within this realm, or in any of the King's dominions, as shall be assigned by our said Sovereign Lord, his heirs and successors.

04. And be it enacted by authority aforesaid that whensoever any such presentment or nomination shall be made by the King's Highness, his heirs or successors, by virtue and authority of this Act, and according to the tenor of the same; that then every archbishop and bishop, to whose hands any such presentment and nomination shall be directed, shall with all speed and celerity invest and consecrate the person nominate and presented by the King's Highness, his heirs and successors, to the office and dignity that such person shall be so presented unto, and give and use to him pall, and all other benedictions, ceremonies and things requisite for the same without suing, procuring or obtaining hereafter any bulls or other things at the see of Rome, for any such office or dignity in any behalf.

And if the said dean and chapter, or prior and convent, after such licence and letters missive to them directed, within the said twelve days do elect and choose the said person mentioned in the said letters missive, according to the request of the King's Highness, his heirs or successors, thereof to be made by the said letters missive in that behalf, then their election shall stand good and effectual to all intents.

And that the person so elected, after certification made of the same election under the common and convent seal of the electors, to the King's Highness, his heirs and successors, shall be reputed and taken by the name of lord elected of the said dignity and office that he shall be elected unto.

And then making such oath and fealty only to the King's Majesty, his heirs and successors, as shall be appointed for the same, the King's Highness, by his letters patent under his great seal, shall signify the said election, if it be to the dignity of a bishop, to the archbishop and metropolitan of the province where the see of the said bishopric was void, if the see of the said archbishop be full and not void; and if it be void, then to any other archbishop within this realm, or in any other the King's dominions; requiring and commanding such archbishop, to whom any such signification shall be made, to confirm the said election and to invest and consecrate the said person so elected to the office and dignity that he is elected unto, and to give and use to him all such benedictions, ceremonies and other things requisite for the same, without any suing, procuring or obtaining any bulls, letters or other things from the see of Rome for the same in any behalf. And if the person be elected to the office and dignity of an archbishop, according to the tenor of this Act, then after such election certified to the King's Highness in form aforesaid, the same person so elected to the office and dignity of an archbishop shall be reputed and taken lord elect to the said office and dignity of archbishop, whereunto he shall be so elected; and then after he has made such oath and fealty only to the King's Majesty, his heirs and successors, as shall be limited for the same, the King's Highness, by his letters patent under his great seal, shall signify the said election to one archbishop and two other bishops, or else to four bishops within this realm, or within any other the King's dominions, to be assigned by the King's Highness, his heirs or successors, requiring and commanding the said archbishop and bishops, with all speed and celerity, to confirm the said election and to invest and consecrate the said person so elected to the office and dignity that he is elected unto, and to give and use to him such pall, benedictions, ceremonies and all other things requisite for the same, without suing, procuring or obtaining any bulls, briefs or other things at the said see of Rome, or by the authority thereof in any behalf.

05. And be it further enacted by authority aforesaid that every person and persons being hereafter chosen, elected, nominated, presented, invested and consecrated to the dignity or office of any archbishop or bishop within this realm, or within any other the King's dominions according to the form, tenor and effect of the present Act, and suing their temporalties out of the King's hand, his heirs or successors, as has been accustomed, and making a corporal oath to the King's Highness and to none other, in form as is afore rehearsed, shall and may from henceforth be thronized or installed as the case shall require, and shall have and take their only restitution out of the King's hands, of all the possessions and profits spiritual and temporal, belonging to the said archbishopric or bishopric whereunto they shall be so elected or presented, and shall be obeyed in all manner of things, according to the name, title, degree and dignity that they shall be so chosen or presented unto, and do and execute in everything and things touching the same, as any archbishop or bishop of this realm, without offending the prerogative royal of the crown and the laws and customs of this realm, might at any time heretofore do.

06. And be it further enacted by the authority aforesaid, that if the prior and convent of any monastery, or dean and chapter of any cathedral church, where the see of any archbishop or bishop is within any of the King's dominions, after such licence as is afore rehearsed, shall be delivered to them, proceed not to election, and signify the same according to the tenor

of this Act, within the space of twenty days next after such licence shall come to their hands; or else if any archbishop or bishop, within any the King's dominions, after any such election, nomination or presentation shall be signified unto them by the King's letters patent, shall refuse, and do not confirm, invest and consecrate with all due circumstance as is aforesaid, every such person as shall be so elected, nominated or presented, and to them signified as is above mentioned, within twenty days next after the King's letters patent of such signification or presentation shall come to their hands; or else if any of them, or any other person or persons, admit, maintain, allow, obey, do or execute any censures, excommunications, interdictions, inhibitions or any other process or act, of what nature, name or quality soever it be, to the contrary, or let of due execution of this Act; that then every prior and particular person of his convent, and every dean and particular person of the chapter, and every archbishop and bishop, and all other persons, so offending and doing contrary to this Act, or any part thereof, and their aiders, counsellors, and abetters, shall run into the dangers, pains and penalties of the Statute of the Provision and *Praemunire*, made in the five-and-twentieth year of the reign of King Edward III (1351) and in the sixteenth year of King Richard II (1393).

11. THE ECCLESIASTICAL LICENCES ACT, 1534 (25 Henry VIII, c. 21)

History

This Act was the centrepiece of the legislation granting plenary powers in ecclesiastical matters to the King. It put an end to the papal power to grant dispensations, which were exceptions to Canon Law, and also stopped the payment of Peter's Pence, a tax of two hundred pounds which for centuries had been paid to Rome. Much of this statute is still in force, particularly the provisions allowing the archbishops to grant special licences for marriages.

N.B. For this edition, paragraph numbers are those of the original document. Sections which have been repealed are italicized. These are: 1, 2, 15, 21 and 23, repealed by the Statute Law Revision Act, 1969; 16, repealed by the Criminal Law Act, 1967; and 19, 20 and 22, repealed by the Statute Law Revision Act, 1948.

01. *Most humbly beseeching your most royal majesty, your obedient and faithful subjects, the Commons of this your present Parliament assembled, by your most dread commandment, that where your subjects of this your realm and of other countries and dominions, being under your obeisance, by many years past have been, and yet be greatly decayed and impoverished by such intolerable exactions of great sums of money as have been claimed and taken, and yet continually be claimed to be taken out of this your realm and your other said countries and dominions, by the Bishop of Rome, called the Pope, and the see of Rome, as well in pensions, censes, Peter's pence, procurations, fruits, suits for provisions, and expeditions of bulls for archbishoprics and bishoprics, and for delegacies and rescripts in causes of contentions and appeals, jurisdictions legatine, and also for dispensations, licences, faculties, grants, relaxations, writs called* perinde valere, *rehabilitations, abolitions and other infinite sorts of bulls, briefs and instruments of sundry natures, names and kinds, in great numbers heretofore practised and obtained otherwise than by the laws, laudable uses and customs of this realm should be permitted, the specialties whereof be overlong, large in number and tedious here particularly to be inserted; wherein the Bishop of Rome aforesaid has not been only to be blamed for his usurpation in the premises, but also for his abusing and beguiling your subjects, pretending and persuading to them that he has full power to dispense with all human laws, uses and customs of all realms, in all causes which be called spiritual, which matter has been usurped and practised by*

*him and his predecessors by many years, in great derogation of your
imperial crown and authority royal, contrary to right and conscience:*

*For where this your grace's realm recognizing no superior under God,
but only your grace, has been and is free from subjection to any man's laws,
but only to such as have been devised, made and ordained within this realm,
for the wealth of the same, or to such other as, by suffrance of your grace
and your progenitors, the people of this your realm have taken at their free
liberty, by their own consent to be used amongst them, and have bound
themselves by long use and custom to the observance of the same, not as to
the observance of the laws of any foreign prince, potentate or prelate, but
as to the accustomed and ancient laws of this realm, originally established
as laws of the same, by the said suffrance, consents and custom, and none
otherwise:*

*It stands therefore with natural equity and good reason, that in all and
every such laws human made within this realm, or induced into this realm
by the said suffrance, consents and custom, your royal majesty and your
lords spiritual and temporal, and Commons, representing the whole state
of your realm in this your most High Court of Parliament, have full power
and authority not only to dispense but also to authorize some elect person
or persons to dispense with those, and all other human laws of this your
realm, and with every one of them, as the quality of the persons and matter
shall require; and also the said laws, and every of them, to abrogate, annul,
amplify or diminish, as it shall be seen unto your majesty and the nobles
and Commons of your realm present in your Parliament, meet and
convenient for the wealth of your realm, as by divers good and wholesome
Acts of Parliaments made and established as well in your time, as in the
time of your most noble progenitors, it may plainly and evidently appear:*

*And because that it is now in these days present seen that the state, dignity,
superiority, reputation and authority of the said imperial crown of this
realm, by the long suffrance of the said unreasonable and uncharitable
usurpations and exactions practised in the times of your most noble
progenitors, is much and sore decayed and diminished, and the people of
this realm thereby impoverished, and so or worse be like to continue, if
remedy be not therefore shortly provided:*

*It may therefore please your most noble majesty, for the honour of
Almighty God and for the tender love, zeal and affection that ye bear, and
always have borne to the wealth of this your realm and subjects of the same,
for as much as your majesty is supreme head of the Church of England, as
the prelates and clergy of your realm, representing the said Church, in their
synods and convocations have recognized, in whom consisteth full power
and authority, upon all such laws as have been made and used within this
realm, to ordain and enact by the assent of your lords spiritual and
temporal, and the Commons in this your present Parliament assembled,
and by authority of the same, that no person or persons of this your realm*

or of any other your dominions shall from henceforth pay any pensions, censes, portions, Peter's pence or any other impositions, to the use of the said bishop, or the see of Rome, like as heretofore they have used, by usurpation of the said Bishop of Rome and his predecessors, and suffrance of your highness and your most noble progenitors, to do; but that all such pensions, censes, portions and Peter's pence, which the said Bishop of Rome, otherwise called the Pope, has heretofore taken and perceived, or caused to be taken and perceived to his use, and his chambers which he calls apostolic, by usurpation and suffrance as is abovesaid, within this your realm, or any other your dominions, shall from henceforth clearly surcease and never more be levied, taken, perceived, nor paid to any person or persons in any manner of wise; any constitution, use, prescription or custom to the contrary thereof notwithstanding.

02. And be it further enacted by the authority aforesaid that neither your highness, your heirs nor successors, kings of this realm, nor any your subjects of this realm, nor of any other your dominions shall from henceforth sue to the said Bishop of Rome, called the Pope, or to the see of Rome, or to any person or persons having or pretending any authority by the same, for licences, dispensations, compositions, faculties, grants, rescripts, delegacies or any other instruments or writings, of what kind, name, nature, or quality soever they be of, for any cause or matter, for the which any licence, dispensation, composition, faculty, grant, rescript, delegacy, instrument or other writing heretofore has been used and accustomed to be had and obtained at the see of Rome, or by authority thereof, or of any prelate of this realm; nor for any manner of other licences, dispensations, compositions, faculties, grants, rescripts, delegacies or any other instruments or writings that in causes of necessity may lawfully be granted without offending of the Holy Scriptures and laws of God:

But that from henceforth every such licence, dispensation, composition, faculty, grant, rescript, delegacy, instrument and other writing aforenamed and mentioned, necessary for your highness, your heirs or successors, and your and their people and subjects, upon the due examinations of the causes and qualities of the persons procuring such dispensations, licences, compositions, faculties, grants, rescripts, delegacies, instruments, or other writings, shall be granted, had and obtained from time to time within this your realm, and other your dominions, and not elsewhere, in manner and form following, and none otherwise, that is to say:

The Archbishop of Canterbury for the time being, and his successors, shall have power and authority from time to time by their discretions to give, grant and dispose by an instrument under the seal of the said archbishop unto your majesty, and to your heirs and successors, kings of this realm, as well all manner such licences, dispensations, compositions, faculties, grants, rescripts, delegacies, instruments and all other writings, for causes not being contrary or repugnant to the Holy Scriptures and laws of God, as heretofore has been used and accustomed to be had and obtained by your highness, or any your most noble progenitors, or any of your or their subjects, at the see of Rome, or any person or persons by authority of the same; and all other licences, dispensations, faculties, compositions, grants, rescripts, delegacies, instruments and other writings, in, for and upon all such causes and matters as shall be convenient and necessary to be had for the honour and surety of your highness, your heirs and successors, and the wealth and profit of this your realm; so that the said archbishop or any of his successors, in no manner wise shall grant any dispensation, licence, rescript or any other writing afore rehearsed, for any cause or matter repugnant to the law of Almighty God.

03. Be it also enacted by authority aforesaid that the said archbishop and his successors, after good and due examination by them had, of the causes and qualities of the persons procuring for licences, dispensations, compositions, faculties, delegacies, rescripts, instruments or other writings, shall have full power and authority by themselves, or by their sufficient and substantial commissary or deputy, by their discretions, from time to time, to grant and dispose by an instrument under the name and seal of the said archbishop, as well to any of your subjects as to the subjects of your heirs and successors, all manner licences, dispensations, faculties, compositions, delegacies, rescripts, instruments or other writings, for any such cause or matter, whereof heretofore such licences, dispensations, compositions, faculties, delegacies, rescripts, instruments, or writings, have been accustomed to be had at the see of Rome, or by authority thereof, of any prelate of this realm.

And that the said archbishop and his commissary shall not grant any other licence, dispensation, composition, faculty, writing or instrument, in causes unwont and not accustomed to be had or obtained at the court of Rome, nor by any authority thereof, nor by any prelate of this realm, until your grace, your heirs or successors, or your or their council shall first be advertised thereof, and determine whether such licences, dispensations, compositions, faculties or other writings, in such causes unwont and not accustomed to be dispensed withal or obtained, shall commonly pass as other dispensations, faculties or other writings, shall or no, upon pain that the grantors of every such licence, dispensation or writing, in such causes unwont, contrary to this Act, shall make fine at the will and pleasure of your grace, your heirs and successors; and if it be thought and determined by your grace, your heirs and successors, or your or their council, that dispensations, faculties, licences or other writings, in any such cause unwont, shall pass, then the said archbishop or his commissary, having licence of your highness, your heirs or successors for the same, by your or their bill assigned, shall dispense with them accordingly.

04. Provided always that no manner of dispensations, licences, faculties or other rescripts or writings hereafter to be granted to any person or persons

by virtue or authority of this Act, by the said archbishop or his commissary being of such importance that the tax of the expedition thereof at Rome extended to the sum of four pounds or above, shall in any wise be put into execution, till the same licence, dispensation, faculty, rescript or other writing, of what name or nature soever it be of, be first confirmed by your highness, your heirs or successors, kings of this realm, under the great seal, and enrolled in your chancery in a roll, by a clerk to be appointed for the same; and that this Act shall be a sufficient warrant to the chancellor of England for the time being, or to him whom your grace, your heirs or successors, shall depute to be keeper of the great seal, to confirm in your name, your heirs or successors, the aforesaid writings, passed under the said archbishop's seal, by letters patent, in due form thereof to be made under your great seal, remitting as well the said writing under the archbishop's seal as the said confirmation under the great seal, to the parties from time to time procuring for the same:

And that all such licences, dispensations, faculties and other rescripts and writings, for the expedition of the which the said taxes to be paid at Rome were under four pounds, which be matters of no great importance, shall pass only by the archbishop's seal, and shall not of any necessity be confirmed by the great seal unless the procurers of such licence, faculty or dispensation desire to have them so confirmed; in which case they shall pay for the said great seal, to the use of your highness, your heirs and successors, five shillings sterling, and not above, over and besides such tax as shall be hereafter limited for the making, writing, registering, confirming and enrolling of such licences, confirmations and writings under the said tax of four pounds.

And that every such licence, dispensation, composition, faculty, rescript and writing, of whatever name or nature soever it be, for such causes as the tax was wont to be four pounds or above, so granted by the archbishop, and confirmed under the great seal, and all other licences, dispensations, faculties, rescripts and writings hereafter to be granted by the archbishop by virtue and authority of this Act, whereunto the great seal is not limited of necessity to be put to, by reason that the tax of them is under four pounds, shall be accepted, approved, allowed and admitted good and effectual in the law, in all places, courts and jurisdictions, as well spiritual as temporal, within this realm, and elsewhere within your dominions, and as beneficial to the persons obtaining the same, as they should have been if they had been obtained, with all things requisite, of the see of Rome, or of any other person by authority thereof, without any revocation or repeal hereafter to be had of such licences, dispensations, faculties, rescripts or writings, of what nature soever they be.

And that all children procreated after solemnization of any marriages to be had or done by virtue of such licences or dispensations shall be admitted, reputed and taken legitimate in all courts, as well spiritual as temporal, and in all other places, and inherit the inheritance of their parents and ancestors within this your realm, and all other your dominions, according to the laws and customs of the same; and all acts to be done, had or executed according to the tenor of such licences, dispensations, faculties, writings or other instruments to be made or granted by authority of this Act, shall be firm, permanent and remain in force; any foreign laws, constitutions, decrees, canons, decretals, inhibitions, use, custom, prescription or any other thing had, or hereafter to be made to the contrary notwithstanding.

05. And be it further enacted that the said archbishop and his successors shall have power and authority to ordain, make and constitute a clerk, which shall write and register every such licence, dispensation, faculty, writing or other instrument to be granted by the said archbishop, and shall find parchment, wax and silken laces convenient for the same, and shall take for his pains such sums of money as shall be hereafter in this present Act to him limited in that behalf for the same; and that likewise your grace, your heirs and successors, shall by your letters patent, under your great seal, ordain, depute and constitute one sufficient clerk, being learned in the course of the chancery, which shall always be attendant upon the lord chancellor or the lord keeper of the great seal for the time being, and shall make, write and enrol the confirmations of all such licences, dispensations, instruments and other writings as shall be thither brought under the archbishop's seal, there to be confirmed and enrolled; and shall also entitle in his books, and enrol of record, such other writings as shall thither be brought under the archbishop's seal, not to be confirmed, taking for his pains such reasonable sums of money as hereafter by this Act to him shall be limited for the same; and that as well the said clerk appointed by the said archbishop, as the said clerk to be appointed by your highness, your heirs or successors, shall subscribe their names to every such licence, dispensation, faculty or other writing that shall come to their hands to be written, made, granted, sealed, confirmed, registered and enrolled by authority of this Act, in form as before rehearsed.

06. And forasmuch as the charges of obtaining the said licences, dispensations, faculties and other rescripts or writings aforenamed at the court of Rome, by the losses and exchanges and in conducting of couriers, and waging solicitors to sue for any such licences, dispensations, faculties, instruments and other rescripts or writings, have been grievous and excessive to your people, and many times greater sums have been demanded for the speedy expedition in the court of Rome, than be expressed in the old tax limited to be paid for the said expeditions, whereby your people have been brought to an uncertainty upon the payment for expeditions of such things, and by reason thereof have been constrained to pay more than they were wont to do, to the great impoverishing of this realm, as is aforesaid: and sometimes the speeding of such dispensations, faculties, licences and other writings at Rome has been so long deferred that the parties labouring for the same have suffered great incommodities and loss for lack of quick speed, which hereafter may be had within this your realm, to the great commodity of your people whereby the charges of making exchanges, conducting of couriers and solicitors for the said dispensations, shall be abated, and your people so much relieved and eased; to the intent that all ambiguity and uncertainty of payments for dispensations, faculties, licences and other rescripts and writings may be taken away, that no fraud or exaction shall be exercised upon your people by such officers as shall be appointed by this Act, to take pains speeding such dispensations, faculties and licences, but that your people may be sure and certain what they be appointed to pay for the same:

Be it enacted by the present Parliament and by the authority of the same that there shall be two books drawn and made of one tenor, in which shall be contained the taxes of all customable dispensations, faculties, licences and other writings wont to be sped at Rome, which books, and every leaf of those books, and both sides of every leaf, shall be subscribed by the Archbishop of Canterbury, the Lord Chancellor of England, the Lord Treasurer of England and the two chief justices of both benches for the time being; to the which books all suitors for dispensations, faculties, licences and other writings afore rehearsed, shall have recourse if they require it; and one of the said books shall remain in the hands of him which shall be appointed to be registrar and scribe of the said dispensations, faculties and licences under the said Archbishop of Canterbury, in form as is before said; and the other book shall remain with the clerk of the chancery, which by your grace, your heirs or successors, shall be appointed as is afore rehearsed; which clerk of the chancery shall also entitle, and note particularly and daily, in his book ordained for that purpose, the number and quality of the dispensations, faculties, licences and other rescripts and writings, which shall be sealed only with the seal of the said archbishop, and also which shall be sealed with the said seal, and confirmed with the great seal, in form as is before said, that all fraud and concealment in this behalf may be avoided.

07. And be it enacted by this present Parliament and by the authority of the same, that no man suing for dispensations, faculties, licences or other rescripts or writings which were wont to be sped at Rome, shall pay any more for their dispensations, licences or rescripts than shall be contained, taxed and limited in the said duplicate books of taxes, only compositions excepted, of which being arbitrary, no tax can be made, wherefore the tax thereof shall be set and limited by the discretion of the said Archbishop of Canterbury and the Lord Chancellor of England, or the lord keeper of the great seal for the time being; and that such as shall exact or receive of any suitor more for any dispensation, faculty or licence than shall be contained in the said book of taxes, shall forfeit ten times so much as he shall so extortionately exact and receive; the one half of the which forfeiture to be to the use of your grace, your heirs or successors, and the other half thereof

to be to such of your subjects as will sue for the same by action, bill, or plaint in any of your grace's courts, wherein the defendant shall have none essoin nor protection allowed, neither shall be admitted to wage his law.

08. Be it also enacted by this Parliament and authority of the same that the tax or sum appointed to be paid for every such dispensation, licence, faculty, instrument, rescript or other writing to be granted by authority of this Act, shall be employed and ordered as hereafter ensues; that is to say, if the tax extend to four pounds or above, by reason whereof the dispensation, licence, faculty, rescript or writing, which shall pass by the said archbishop's seal, musty be confirmed by the appension of the great seal, then the said tax so extending to four pounds or above shall be divided into three parts, whereof two shall be perceived by the said clerk of the chancery to be appointed as is aforesaid, to the use of your highness, your heirs and successors, and to the use of the lord chancellor, or the keeper of the great seal for the time being, and to the use of the said clerk, in such wise as hereafter shall be declared; and that the third part shall be taken by the said clerk of the archbishop, to the use of the same archbishop and his commissary, and his said clerk and registrar, in such wise as hereafter shall be ordained and limited by this Act; that is to say, the said two parts shall be divided in four parts, of which three parts shall be taken to the only use of your highness, your heirs and successors, and the fourth part shall be divided in three parts, whereof the Chancellor of England or lord keeper of the great seal for the time being, shall have two parts, and the said clerk of the chancery the third part for his pains, travel and labours that he is limited to write and do by virtue of this Act; and the said third part of the whole tax appointed to the said archbishop, and his officers, as is aforesaid, shall be divided into three parts, whereof the archbishop shall have to his use two parts, and his officers shall have the third part thereof; of which third part to be divided into two parts, the said clerk or registrar, which shall find parchment, wax and silk, and shall devise and write the said dispensations, licences, faculties, rescripts or other writings, and register the same, shall have for his said labour, and for receiving and repaying of the sums of money that shall come to his hands for dispensations, faculties, licences and other rescripts aforesaid, the one moiety thereof, and the commissary of the said archbishop appointed to seal the said dispensations, faculties, licences and other rescripts, shall have the other part.

And if the tax be under four pounds and not under forty shillings, then the said tax shall be divided into three parts, as is aforesaid, whereof the king's highness, his heirs and successors, shall have two parts thereof, abating three shillings fourpence, which shall be to the said clerk of the chancery for subscribing, entitling and enrolling the said dispensations, licences, faculties, rescripts and other writings aforesaid, and receiving of the king's money so taxed; and the archbishop and his officers shall have the third part, which third part shall be divided into two parts, whereof the archbishop shall have the one entirely to himself, his scribe and commissary shall have the other part thereof, equally to be divided amongst them for their costs and pains in that behalf.

And if the tax be under forty shillings and not under twenty-six shillings eightpence, the same tax shall be divided into two parts, whereof the one part shall be to your grace, your heirs and successors, deducting thereof two shillings for the clerk of the chancery for his pains, as is aforesaid; and the other part shall be to the said archbishop and his officers, which other part shall be divided into two parts, whereof the archbishop shall have the one and the commissary and scribe shall have the other, equally divided amongst them. And if the tax be under twenty-six shillings eightpence and not under twenty shillings, the same shall be divided into two parts, whereof your grace, your heirs and successors, shall have the one part entirely, abating two shillings thereof to the said clerk of the chancery; and the archbishop and his officers shall have the other part, and the same other part shall be divided into three parts, whereof the archbishop shall have one, his commissary the second, and his scribe or registrar the third; and in case the tax be under twenty shillings the same shall be perceived to the use of the said commissary, clerk of the said archbishop, and clerk of the chancery, to be equally divided amongst them for their pains and labours by them to be sustained, by authority of this Act, as aforesaid.

09. Provided always that this Act shall not be prejudicial to the Archbishop of York, or to any bishop or prelate of this realm; but that they may lawfully, notwithstanding this Act, dispense in all cases in which they were wont to dispense by the common law or custom of this realm afore the making of this Act.

10. Provided also and be it enacted by the authority aforesaid, that if it happen the see of the archbishopric of Canterbury to be void, that then all such manner of licences, dispensations, faculties, instruments, rescripts and other writings which may be granted by virtue and authority of this Act, shall during the vacation of the same see, be had, done and granted under the name and seal of the guardian of the spiritualties of the said archbishopric for the time being, according to the tenor and form of this Act, and shall be of like force, value and effect, as if they had been granted under the name and seal of the archbishop for the time being.

11. And be it further enacted that if the aforesaid Archbishop of Canterbury for the time being, or the said guardian of the spiritualties for the time being, hereafter refuse or deny to grant any licences, dispensations, faculties, instruments or other writings, which they be authorized to do by virtue and authority of this Act, in such manner and form as is afore remembered, to any person or persons that ought of a good, just and reasonable cause to have the same, by reason whereof this present Act, by their wilfulness, negligence or default, should take no effect; then the Chancellor of England, or the lord keeper of the great seal for the time being, upon nay complaint thereof made, shall direct the king's writ to the said archbishop or guardian denying or refusing to grant such licences, dispensations, faculties or other writings, enjoining him by the said writ, upon a certain pain therein to be limited by the discretion of the said chancellor or keeper of the great seal, that he shall in due form grant such licence, dispensation, faculty or other writing, according to the request of the procurers of the same, or else signify unto your highness, your heirs or successors, in the court of chancery, at a certain day, for what occasion or cause he refused and denied to grant such licences, faculties or dispensations.

And if it shall appear to the said chancellor or lord keeper of the great seal, upon such certificate, that the cause of refusal or denial of granting such licences, faculty, or dispensation was reasonable, just and good, that then it so being proved by due search and examination of the said chancellor or lord keeper of the great seal, to be admitted and allowed.

And if it shall appear upon the said certificate that the said archbishop or guardian of the spiritualties for the time being, of wilfulness in contemning the due execution of this Act without a just and reasonable cause, refused or denied to grant such licence, faculty or dispensation, that then your highness, your heirs or successors, being thereof informed, after due examination had, that such licences, faculties or dispensations may be granted without offending the Holy Scriptures and laws of God, shall have power and authority in every such case, for the default, negligence and wilfulness of the said archbishop or guardian, to send your writ of injunction under your great seal, out of your said court of chancery, commanding the archbishop or guardian that so shall deny or refuse to grant such licence, faculty or dispensation, to make sufficient grant thereof, according to the tenor and effect of this Act, by a certain day and under a certain pain in the said writ to be contained, and to be limited by your highness, your heirs or successors, kings of this realm.

And if the said archbishop or guardian, after the receipt of the said writ, refuse or deny to grant such licences, faculties or dispensations, as shall be enjoined by him by virtue of the said writ, and show and prove before your majesty, your heirs or successors, no just or reasonable cause why he should do so; then the said archbishop or guardian that so shall refuse to put this Act in execution according to the said writ of injunction, shall suffer, lose and forfeit to your highness, your heirs and successors, such pain and penalty as shall be limited and expressed in the said writ of injunction. And over that, it shall be lawful to your highness, your heirs and successors, for every such default and wilfulness of the said archbishop or guardian for the time being, to give power and authority, by commission under your great seal, to such two spiritual prelates or persons to be named by your highness, your heirs or successors, as will do and grant such licences, faculties and dispensations, refused or denied to be granted by the said archbishop or guardian in contempt of this Act.

12. And be it further enacted by the authority aforesaid that the said two spiritual prelates or persons, to whom in such cases any such commission shall be directed, shall have power and authority to grant every such licence, faculty, dispensation, instrument and other writings, so refused to be granted by the said archbishop or guardian for the time being, by an instrument under their seals, taking like fees and charges for the same as is before rehearsed, and not above, under the pains afore remembered. And that every such licence, faculty and dispensation so granted for any cases or matters, whereunto any confirmation under the king's great seal is appointed by this Act, to be had in manner and form above declared, shall be had and obtained accordingly. And such licences and confirmations shall be had for like fees and charges as they are above specified, and not above, under the pains above mentioned. And that every such licence, faculty, dispensation and other writing to be granted by the said prelates or persons to be assigned by the king's highness, his heirs and successors, as is aforesaid, shall be of as good value, strength and effect, and as beneficial and profitable to the persons procuring the same, as if they had been made, granted and obtained under the name and seal of the said archbishop.

13. Provided always that this Act, nor anything or things therein contained, shall be hereafter interpreted or expounded, that your grace, your nobles and subjects, intend, by the same, to decline or vary from the congregation of Christ's Church in any things concerning the very articles of the Catholic faith of Christendom, or in any other things declared by Holy Scripture and the Word of God, necessary for your and their salvations, but only to make an ordinance by policies necessary and convenient to repress vice, and for good conservation of this realm in peace, unity and tranquillity, from ravin and spoil, ensuing much the old ancient customs of this realm in that behalf; not minding to seek for any relief, succours or remedies for any worldly things and human laws, in any cause of necessity, but within this realm, at the hand of your highness, your heirs and successors, kings of this realm, which have and ought to have an imperial power and authority in the same, and not obliged, in any worldly causes, to any other superior.

14. Provided alway that the said Archbishop of Canterbury, or any other person or persons, shall have no power or authority by reason of this Act to visit or vex any monasteries, abbeys, priories, colleges, hospitals, houses or other places religious, which be or were exempt before the making of this Act, anything in this Act to the contrary thereof notwithstanding; but that redress, visitation and confirmation shall be had by the king's highness, his heirs and successors, by commission under the great seal, to be directed to such persons as shall be appointed requisite for the same, in such monasteries, colleges, hospitals, priories, houses and places religious exempt; so that no visitation nor confirmation shall from thenceforth be had nor made, in or at any such monasteries, colleges, hospitals, priories, houses and places religious exempt, by the said Bishop of Rome, nor by any of his authority, nor by any out of the king's dominions; nor that any person, religious or other, resident in any of the king's dominions, shall from henceforth depart out of the king's dominions to or for any visitation, congregation or assembly for religion, but that all such visitations, congregations and assemblies shall be within the king's dominions.

15. *Provided also that this present Act or anything therein contained, or any licence or dispensation hereafter to be made by virtue and authority thereof, shall not extend to the repeal or derogation of the late Act, made since the beginning of the present Parliament, for reformation of pluralities of benefices, and for non-residences of spiritual persons upon their dignities or benefices, nor to anything contained or mentioned in the said Act; nor that this Act, nor anything to be done by authority thereof, shall not be taken, expounded or interpreted to give licence to any person or persons to have any more number of benefices than is limited in the said Act; and that the same Act for pluralities and non-residences of benefices, and everything therein contained, shall stand good and effectual in all intents, according to the true meaning thereof; anything in this present Act, or any licence or dispensation to be had by authority thereof, in any wise notwithstanding.*

16. *And be it further enacted by authority aforesaid that if any person or persons, subject or resident within this realm, or within any of the king's dominions, at any time hereafter sue to the court of Rome, or the see of Rome, or to any person claiming to have his authority by the same, for any licence, faculty, dispensation or other thing or things contrary to this Act, or put in execution any licence, faculty or dispensation, or any other thing or things hereafter to be obtained from Rome, or the see of Rome, or from any claiming authority by the same, for any of the causes above-mentioned in this Act, or for any other causes that may be granted by authority of this Act, or attempt to do anything or things contrary to this Act, or maintain, allow, admit or obey any manner of censures, excommunications, interdictions or any other process from Rome, of what name or nature soever it be, to the derogation or let of the execution of this Act, or of any thing or things to be done by reason of the said Act; that then every such person or persons so doing, offending and being thereof convicted, their aiders, counsellors and abettors, shall incur and run into the pain, loss and penalty comprised and specified in the said Act of Provision and Praemunire, made in the sixteenth year of your most noble progenitor, King Richard II (1393), against such as sue to the court of Rome against your crown and dignity royal.*

17. Provided alway that this Act, or anything therein contained, shall not hereafter be taken nor expounded to the derogation or taking away of any grants, or confirmations of any liberties, privileges or jurisdiction of any monasteries, abbeys, priories or other houses or places exempt, which heretofore the making of this Act have been obtained at the see of Rome, or by authority thereof; but that every such grant and confirmation shall be of the same value, force and effect as they were before the making of this Act, and as if this Act had never been made. Provided always that the abbots, priors and other chief rulers and governors of such monasteries, abbeys, priories and other houses and places exempt, shall not hereafter pay any pension, portion or other cense to the see of Rome; nor admit or accept any visitation, nor any confirmation from or by the said see of Rome, or by authority thereof, of or for any person to be elected, named or presented to be heads of any such monasteries, abbeys, priories, places or houses exempt, nor shall make any corporal oath to the Bishop of Rome, otherwise called the Pope, upon the pains limited in this Act; but that every such visitation and confirmation of such heads elect – in any such monasteries, abbeys, priories, houses or places exempt, where after their election they were bounden to have and obtain any confirmation of their election, or of the person named, presented or elected – shall be from henceforth had, made and done within this realm, at and within every such abbeys, monasteries, priories and other houses and places exempt, by such person and persons as shall be appointed, by authority of the king's commission, from time to time, as the case shall require, and not by the see of Rome, nor by the authority thereof; anything in this next proviso above specified to the contrary thereof notwithstanding.

18. Provided always that in such monasteries, abbeys, priories and houses exempt, where after election, presentation or nomination of their heads, no such confirmation is requisite to be had, nor has been used to be taken by reason of such privileges as they have concerning the same, that in every such monasteries, abbeys, priories and places exempt, they shall not be bounden to obtain, have or take any confirmation for the same within this realm, by authority of this Act, but use their privileges therein as they have done before the making of this Act; anything in this Act, or any the provisions next above rehearsed, to the contrary thereof notwithstanding.

19. *Provided also and be it enacted, that this Act, or anything or things, word or words therein, or in the preamble thereof mentioned or contained, is not intended or meant, nor shall be expounded nor interpreted, that any dispensations, licences or confirmations for marriages, granted to any the king's subjects born under his obeisance, at any time before the twelfth day of March in the year of our Lord God 1533* (12 March 1533), *shall be appaired, or of any less value, strength, force or effect than they were at the said twelfth day of March; nor that this Act, or anything therein contained, shall not extend to the derogation, appairing or annulling of any licences, dispensations, confirmations, faculties or indulgences at any time before the said twelfth day of March in the year of our Lord God 1533* (12 March 1533), *had or obtained at the see of Rome, or by authority thereof, to or for any subjects born in this realm, or in any the king's dominions, or to or for the hospital of the Prior of St John of Jerusalem in England, or any commandries or members thereof, or to or for any other* *cathedral churches, hospitals, monasteries, abbeys, priories, colleges, conventual churches, parochial churches, chapels, fraternities, brotherhoods, or bodies politic within this realm, or in any other the king's dominions; but that every such licence, dispensation, confirmation, faculty and indulgence granted before the said twelfth day of March to any such subject, or to the said hospital of the Prior of St John of Jerusalem in England, commandries or members thereof, or to any other cathedral church, hospital, monastery, abbey, priory, college, church conventual, parochial church, chapel, fraternity, brotherhood or body politic, or to their predecessors or ancestors within this realm, or in any other the king's dominions, shall be of the same force, strength, value and effect, and may be from time to time put in execution at all times hereafter, by and to them that will use and have the same, as they might have been before the making of this Act, and as if this Act had never been had nor made; anything in the said Act to the contrary hereof notwithstanding.*

20. *Provided always that such licences, dispensations, confirmations or faculties heretofore obtained at the see of Rome or by authority thereof, contrary to the express provisions of the laws and statutes of this realm heretofore made, shall not at anytime hereafter be used or put in execution in any case, to the derogation, or contrary to the said laws and statutes of this realm, and the provisions of the same; anything in this proviso to the contrary thereof notwithstanding.*

21. *And be it enacted by authority of this present Parliament, that the king our sovereign lord, by the advice of his honourable council, shall have power and authority from time to time, for the ordering, redress and reformation of all manner of indulgences and privileges thereof within this realm, or within any of the king's dominions, heretofore obtained at the see of Rome or by authority thereof, and of the abuses of such indulgences and privileges thereof as shall seem good, wholesome and reasonable for the honour of God and weal of his people; and that such order and redress as shall be taken by his highness in that behalf shall be observed and firmly kept upon the pains limited in this Act for the offending of the contents of the same.*

22. *Provided alway, and be it enacted by the authority of this present Parliament, that this present Act, or anything or things therein contained, shall not begin to take effect nor be put in execution till the feast of the Nativity of St John Baptist next coming (24 June 1534), except the king's majesty, on this side the said feat, by his letters patent under his great seal, to be enrolled in the Parliament roll of this present Parliament, do declare and express, that it is his pleasure that it shall begin and take effect at any time afore the said feast; and if his highness happen so to do, that then, immediately after such declaration of his pleasure by his said letters patent in form aforesaid, this said Act shall begin and be put in execution afore the said feast, according to his said letters patent; anything in this proviso to the contrary hereof notwithstanding.*

23. *And be it further enacted by authority aforesaid that the king's majesty at all times on this side the said feast shall have full power and authority, by his letters patent under his great seal, to be enrolled in the Parliament roll of this present Parliament, to abrogate, annul and utterly repeal and make void this Act and everything and things therein contained, or else as much and such part thereof as shall be declared and limited on this side the said feast by his said letters patent to be void and repealed; and that all such repeal and annulling so to be made in form aforesaid by his highness on this side the said feast, shall be as good and effectual as though it had been done and had by authority of Parliament; anything or things contained in this present Act to the contrary notwithstanding; and if no such repeal be had or made by the king's majesty on this side the said feast, in form as is afore rehearsed, that then the said Act, or as much and such thereof as shall not be repealed on this side the said feast, shall immediately after the said feast stand firm, good and effectual, and from thenceforth be put in due execution according to the tenor thereof; anything in this Act or in any the provisions aforesaid to the contrary hereof notwithstanding.*

12. THE ABJURATION OF PAPAL SUPREMACY BY THE CLERGY, 1534

History

Once the Act restraining the payment of annates had been passed and all legal and financial transactions between the English Church and Rome had been abrogated, it was but a short step to the repudiation of papal supremacy. Henry recognized that this was a spiritual matter more than a temporal one, and so it was left to the clergy in their Convocations to make the first move. Canterbury did so almost at once, on 31 March 1534. York followed some time later, the deliberations taking place on, and shortly after, 05 May and ratified by the Archbishop on 02 June. Meanwhile, the clergy of the University of Cambridge had taken a similar step (02 May).

The King thus felt able to proclaim the abolition of the papal supremacy on 09 June, though this was not agreed by the University of Oxford until 27 June. The entire proceeding was then approved by Parliament and passed into statute during the November 1534 session.

Convocation of Canterbury

On the last day of March (31 March 1534), in the presence of the most reverend Ralph Pexsall, the clerk of the crown in the chancery of the lord the King, in the name of the said King, presented a royal writ for summoning Convocation and proroguing it to the fourth day of November following (04 November 1534). And afterwards was exhibited a writing by William Saye, notary public, concerning the answer of the Lower House to the question, viz. "Whether the Roman pontiff has any greater jurisdiction bestowed on him by God in the Holy Scriptures in this realm of England, than any other foreign (*externus*) bishop? Noes 34, doubtful 1, ayes 4.

Convocation of York

By virtue of a royal writ this synod, convened on the fifteenth day of May (15 May 1534), sent to the lord the King, by the archbishop's certificate, the sentence of their decision against the Pope's supremacy: "To the most illustrious and excellent prince and lord, the lord Henry VIII, by the grace of God King of England and France, Defender of the Faith, and Lord of Ireland, Edward, by divine permission archbishop of York, primate of England, and metropolitan, greeting. We make known and declare to your royal highness, by the tenor of the presents, that when, according to the mandate of your royal majesty, the following conclusion was proposed in the presence of the prelates and clergy of the province of York, gathered together in the sacred synod of the province or Convocation of the prelates and clergy of the same province of York, held in the chapter house of the metropolitan church of York on the fifth day of May, in the present year of our Lord 1534 (05 May 1534), and continued from day to day: "That the Bishop of Rome has not, in Scripture, any greater jurisdiction in the kingdom of England than any other foreign bishop". And when further, on behalf of the presidents deputed by you in the same synod, the said prelates and clergy were asked and demanded to confirm and endorse that opinion by their consent, if they thought or judged it consonant to the truth and not repugnant to the Holy Scriptures; at length the said prelates and clergy of the province of York aforesaid, after careful discussion had in that behalf, and mature deliberation, unanimously and concordantly with no dissentient affirmed the conclusion above mentioned to have been and to be true, and concordantly consented to the same. Which all and singular we notify to your highness by the tenor of the presents. In testimony of which, all and singular, we have caused our seal to be affixed to the presents. Given in our castle of Cawood, the second day of June, in the year of our Lord 1534 (02 June 1534), and the third of our consecration.

The Henrician Reformation

(1534-1547)

13. THE ACT OF SUPREMACY, 1534
(26 Henry VIII c.1)

History

This act, passed by Parliament in November 1534, wrote into the statutes of the realm the decision of the Convocations of Canterbury and York taken earlier in 1534 and proclaimed by the King on 09 June. The title was dropped by Mary I (1553) and altered to that of Supreme Governor by Elizabeth I (1559), which it remains to this day.

Theology

The claim to supreme headship included the right to teach doctrine and reform the Church, but not the right to preach, ordain or administer the sacraments and rites of the Church. This right was known as the *potestas ordinis* and was reserved to the clergy. Henry VIII maintained that he was doing no more than assert the ancient rights of the secular power, which the Papacy had usurped in the course of the centuries. It was a view which was shared by the Lutheran princes in Germany and it could claim some support from the practice of the Eastern Orthodox Churches, where the Emperor (or Tsar) played a major part in Church affairs.

Opposition to Henry centred mainly on the claim to teach doctrine. In the Early Church, doctrine had been established by Ecumenical Councils which were called together by the Roman (later Byzantine) Emperor who presided over their deliberations and put their decisions into effect. But the decisions themselves were made by the assembled bishops, however much imperial pressure they may have been subjected to. Henry ignored this, possibly because he sensed that the majority of the bishops would not have supported him in his breach with Rome.

Another difficulty, which surfaced at the accession of Elizabeth, was the claim inherent in the title "Supreme Head". Many Protestants felt that this title belonged only to Christ, whom St Paul called the Head of the Church. To accommodate this objection, Elizabeth altered the title to that of "Supreme Governor" – a change of form, but not of substance.

Albeit the King's Majesty justly and rightfully is and oweth to be the Supreme Head of the Church of England, and so is recognized by the clergy of this realm in their Convocations, yet nevertheless for corroboration and confirmation thereof, and for increase of virtue in Christ's religion within this realm of England, and to repress and extirp all errors, heresies, and other enormities and abuses heretofore used in the same; be it enacted by authority of this present Parliament, that the King our Sovereign Lord, his heirs and successors, kings of this realm, shall be taken, accepted, and reputed the only Supreme Head on earth of the Church of England, called *Anglicana Ecclesia*, and shall have and enjoy, annexed and united to the imperial crown of this realm, as well the style and title thereof, as all honours, dignities, pre-eminences, jurisdictions, privileges, authorities, immunities, profits, and commodities, to the said dignity of Supreme Head of the same Church belonging and appertaining; and that our said Sovereign Lord, his heirs and successors, kings of this realm, shall have full power and authority from time to time to visit, repress, redress, reform, order, correct, restrain, and amend all such errors, heresies, abuses, offences, contempts, and enormities, whatsoever they be, which by any manner spiritual authority or jurisdiction ought or may lawfully be reformed, repressed, ordered, redressed, corrected, restrained, or amended, most to the pleasure of Almighty God, the increase of virtue in Christ's religion, and for the conservation of the peace, unity and tranquillity of this realm; any usage, custom, foreign laws, foreign authority, prescription, or any other thing or things to the contrary hereof notwithstanding.

14. THE SUFFRAGAN BISHOPS ACT, 1534
(26 Henry VIII, c. 14)

History

This Act made provision for the appointment of suffragan bishops, to assist the diocesans in their duties. Several of these bishops have since become diocesans, as new sees have been created. Most of the Act is still in force, though of course it has been supplemented by more recent legislation. Parts of article 2 were repealed by the Statute Law Revision Act of 1888, and of article 4 by the Criminal Law Act, 1967. Article 7 was repealed by the Statute Law Revision Act, 1977 and most of the rest of article 4 by the Dioceses Measure, 1978.

N.B. All parts of this Act which have been repealed are italicized in the text. Paragraph numbers are those of the original document.

01. Albeit that since the beginning of the present Parliament good and honourable ordinances and statutes have been made and established for elections, presentations, consecrations and investing of archbishops and bishops of this realm, and in all other the King's dominions, with all ceremonies appertaining unto the same, as by sundry statutes thereof made more at large is specified; yet nevertheless no provision hitherto has been made for suffragans, which have been accustomed to be had within this realm for the more speedy administration of the sacraments, and other good, wholesome and devout things and laudable ceremonies, to the increase of God's honour and for the commodity of good and devout people. Be it therefore enacted by authority of this present Parliament that the towns of Thetford, *Ipswich*, Colchester, Dover, *Guildford*, Southampton, Taunton, Shaftesbury, Molton, Marlborough, Bedford, *Leicester*, *Gloucester*, Shrewsbury, *Bristol*, Penrith, Bridgewater, Nottingham, Grantham, Hull, Huntingdon, Cambridge and the towns of Perth and Berwick, St German's in Cornwall, and the Isle of Wight shall be taken and accepted for sees of bishops suffragan to be made in this realm, *and in Wales*, and the bishops of such sees shall be called suffragans of this realm. And that every archbishop and bishop of this realm, *and of Wales*, and elsewhere within the King's dominions, being disposed to have any suffragan, shall and may at their liberties, name and elect, that is to say, every of them for their particular diocese, two honest and discreet spiritual persons, being learned and of good conversation, and those two persons, so by them to be named, shall present to the King's Highness, by their writing under their seals, making humble request to his Majesty to give to one such of the two said persons, as shall please his Majesty, such title, name, style and dignity of bishop of such of the sees above specified, as the King's Highness shall think most convenient for the same; and that the King's Majesty, upon every such presentation, shall have full power and authority to give to one of those two persons, so to his highness to be presented, the style, title and name of a bishop of such of the sees aforesaid, as to his Majesty shall be thought most convenient and expedient, so it be within the same province whereof the bishop that doth name him is. And that every such person to whom the King's Highness shall give any such style and title of any of the sees aforenamed shall be called bishop suffragan of the same see whereunto he shall be named.

And after such title, style and name so given as is aforesaid, the King's Majesty shall present every such person, by his letters patent under his great seal, to the Archbishop of Canterbury, if the town whereof he has his title be within the province of Canterbury, and likewise to the Archbishop of York, if the town whereof he has his title be within the province of York, signifying and declaring by the same letters patent the name of the person presented, and the style and title of dignity of the bishopric whereunto he shall be nominated, requiring the same archbishop, to whom such letters patent shall be directed, to consecrate the said person so nominated and presented to the same name, title, style and dignity of bishop, that he shall be nominated and presented unto, and to give him all such creations, benedictions and ceremonies, as to the degree and office of a bishop suffragan shall be requisite.

02. And be it also enacted by authority aforesaid, that all and every such person and persons as shall be nominated, elected, presented and consecrated, as is afore rehearsed, shall be taken, accepted and reputed in all degrees and places according to the style, title, name and dignity that he shall be so presented unto, *and have such capacity, power and authority, honour, pre-eminence and reputation, in as large and ample manner, in and concerning the execution of such commission, as by any of the said archbishops or bishops within their diocese shall be given to the said suffragans, as to suffragans of this realm heretofore has been used and accustomed.*

03. And be it further enacted by authority aforesaid, that every archbishop of this realm, to whom any the King's letters patent in the cases afore rehearsed, shall be directed, having no lawful impediment, shall perform and accomplish the effects and contents of this Act within the time of three months next after such letters patent shall come to their hands; any usages, customs, foreign laws, privileges, prescriptions, or other thing or things heretofore used, had, or done to the contrary hereof notwithstanding.

04. Provided always that no such suffragans, which shall be made and consecrate by virtue of the authority of this Act, shall take or perceive any manner of profits of the places and sees whereof they shall be named, *nor use, have or execute any jurisdiction or episcopal power or authority within their said sees, nor within any diocese or place of this realm, or elsewhere within the King's dominions, but only such profits, jurisdiction, power and authority as shall be licensed and limited to them to take, do and execute by any archbishop or bishop of this realm, within their diocese to whom they shall be suffragans, by their commission under their seals.*

And that every archbishop and bishop of this realm, for their own peculiar diocese, may and shall give such commission or commissions to every such bishop suffragan as shall be so consecrated by authority of this Act, as has been accustomed for suffragans heretofore to have, or else such commission as by them shall be thought requisite, reasonable and convenient; and that no such suffragan shall use any jurisdiction ordinary or episcopal power, otherwise, nor longer time, than shall be limited by such commission to him to be given as is aforesaid, upon pain to incur into the pains, losses, forfeitures and penalties mentioned in the Statute of Provisions, made in the sixteenth year of King Richard II (1393).

05. Provided always that the bishop that shall nominate the suffragan to the King's Highness, or the suffragan himself that shall be nominate, shall provide two bishops or suffragans to consecrate him, with the archbishop, and shall bear their reasonable costs.

06. Provided also that the residence of him that shall be suffragan over the diocese where he shall have commission shall serve him for his residence, as sufficiently as if he were resident upon any other his benefice; any Act heretofore made to the contrary notwithstanding.

07. *Be it further enacted that all such suffragans as shall hereafter exercise the offices aforesaid, by the commission of the bishop, for the better maintenance of his dignity, may have two benefices with cure; any former Act made to the contrary notwithstanding.*

15. THE WITTENBERG ARTICLES, 1536

History

Shortly after breaking with Rome, Henry VIII and Archbishop Cranmer started looking for allies among the Continental Protestants. An English delegation went to Germany in 1535 in an attempt to forge some kind of agreement with the Lutherans. This delegation brought a number of proposals with it, to which the Duke of Saxony and the Landgrave of Hesse replied in the so-called "Christmas Articles" of 1535. These called for a full acceptance of the Augsburg Confession in England, in return for which Henry VIII was nominated to be commander-in-chief of the Protestant cause in Europe. Henry accepted this, but soon negotiations broke down over the question of his divorce, which the Lutheran theologians were not prepared to recognize. Later in the year, when Anne Boleyn was executed, negotiations were broken off completely. Luther may have come to terms with an adulterer, but not with one who was a murderer as well! The main author of the text seems to have been Luther's assistant, Philipp Melanchthon. Luther himself took part in the negotiations, and the English Church was represented by Edward Fox, Nicholas Heath and Richard Barnes.

Before the final break came, the theologians at Wittenberg had managed to prepare a draft confession, which the English delegates could take home with them. Whether they did so or not is unknown, since all evidence of it has vanished in England, and the German copy was not rediscovered until 1904. Until then, the only ones which were known were 6 and 12-15, which V. L. von Seckendorf included in his *Historia Lutheranismi* (Leipzig, 1692). The original texts are in Latin and German, and were published by Georg Mentz (*Die Wittenberger Artikel von 1536*, Leipzig, 1905). For this edition, parallel Latin (or German, where the Latin in missing) and English texts have been printed. Numbers in parentheses after the heading of each article refer to the corresponding articles in the Lutherans' Augsburg Confession (1530), from which the material was ultimately derived.

Theology

The Wittenberg Articles were less categorical than the Christmas Articles in their insistence on conformity to the Augsburg Confession, but there is no doubt that their main thrust was similar. But compared with the Lutheran document, the Wittenberg Articles placed considerably more weight on the themes of repentance, justification and good works, which had become the mainstays of Lutheran theology by the mid-1530s. A good deal of attention was also paid to the question of priestly marriage and monastic celibacy, which were burning issues in both England and Germany, though little is said about civil government – in contrast to what was later to become a standard feature of English confessional statements. One of the more remarkable features is the provision made for theological training of both men and women in the ancient universities. That was soon implemented to a large extent for men, but it is a tragedy that women were excluded for over 300 years, and that by the time provision was made for them, education was becoming secularized. Not until the 1970s would women be accepted for theological training on the same basis as men, even though Luther and the English delegates to Wittenberg had been prepared for it so many centuries ago!

N.B. Phrases which were incorporated into the Ten Articles (1536) are italicized, and those which were used in the Thirteen Articles (1538) are in bold type.

01. De symbolis (01,03,07,17)

Quod ad primum, tertium, septimum et decimum septimum *articulos* confessionis nostrae *attinet*, confitemur simpliciter et plane sine ulla ambiguitate, nos *credere*, tenere, docere et defendere *omnia ea quae sunt in Canone Bibliae et in tribus symbolis Apostolico, Niceno et Athanasii*, ad illum ipsum sensum, quem et tradunt illa symbola et approbati sancti patres eadem tractant et defendunt. Et volumus ea teneri et haberi pro sacrosanctis et immotis et non labefactandis cuiusquam *auctoritate aut opinione contraria*. Ad haec sentimus eos *articulos fidei* in illis traditos *ita necessarios esse ad* animarum *salutem, ut qui contrarium* sentiunt, *non possint esse membra ecclesiae*, sed sint prorsus idololatrae.

Porro sentimus summa fide retinendam esse ipsam *verborum formam in illis articulis*, quae extat *in ipsis symbolis*, nec ab ea forma verborum unquam recedendum esse.

01. The Creeds (01,03,07,17)

Concerning the first, third, seventh and seventeenth *articles* of our Confession, we confess simply and clearly, without any ambiguity, that we *believe*, hold, teach and defend *everything which is in the Canon of the Bible and in the three Creeds, i.e. the Apostles', Nicene and Athanasian Creeds*, in the same meaning which the Creeds themselves intend and in which the approved holy Fathers use and defend them. And we desire that these creeds be held and considered very holy, unchangeable and not subject to alteration *by any man's authority or contrary opinion*. In addition, we hold that *the articles of faith* given in them *are so necessary for* the *salvation* of souls *that those who* believe *differently cannot be members of the Church*, but are complete idolaters.

Furthermore, we maintain that the very *form of words in those articles* should be retained most precisely, just as it is *in the creeds themselves*, and that there should never be any

Proinde magno consensu *damnamus* Valentinianorum, Manichaeorum, Samosatensorum, Arianorum, Pneumatomachorum et reliquorum similes haereses omnes, *quas hactenus ecclesia in sanctis synodis quattuor Nicena, Constantinopolitana, Ephesina et Chalcedonensi damnavit.*

drawing back from the form of words. Therefore *we* unanimously *condemn* the heresies of the Valentinians, Manichaeans, Adoptionists, Arians and Macedonians, and all other heresies like them, *which the Church* long ago *condemned in the four holy councils of Nicaea, Constantinople, Ephesus and Chalcedon.*

02. De peccato originali (02)

02. Original Sin (02)

Quod ad secundum articulum attinet de peccato originis, prorsus et sine ulla ambiguitate sentimus, docemus et defendimus id, quod docet S. Paulus, et ad eum sensum, quem interpretatur et defendit S. Augustinus adversus Pelagianos et caeteri, qui sequuntur Augustini sententiam, ut Anselmus et Bonaventura, et hanc Augustini sententiam de peccato originis veram esse sentimus et recte approbatam in synodis.

Deinde maxime probamus definitionem Anselmi, qui ait **peccatum originis esse carentiam iustitiae originalis debitae inesse**, sicut enim iustitia originis fuit non tantum acceptatio, sed etiam integritas virium, hoc est rectitudo voluntatis, seu aptitudo ad vere oboediendum legi Dei, seu perfecta habitualis oboedientia erga Deum, ita econtra peccatum originis est non tantum reatus seu imputatio, sed etiam corruptio secuta lapsum Adae in omnibus secundum naturam propagatis. Et haec corruptio non tantum defectus est rectitudinis, quae fuerat in natura hominis ante lapsum, videlicet non habere rectitudinem voluntatis seu aptitudinem ad

Concerning the second article about original sin, we clearly and without any ambiguity hold, teach and defend what St Paul teaches, as St Augustine interprets and defends it against the Pelagians, as well as others who follow Augustine's teaching, like Anselm and Bonaventure; and we hold that Augustine's is the true understanding of original sin and that it was rightly approved by the councils.

Furthermore, we particularly approve the definition of Anselm, who says that **original sin is a lack of that original righteousness which ought to be in (man)**, for just as original righteousness was not only Adam's acceptability to God, but also the integrity of his own faculties, i.e. an uprightness of will or a natural inclination towards true obedience to the law of God, or habitually perfect obedience to God; so, on the other hand, original sin is not just guilt or the imputation (of guilt), but also corruption, which after Adam's fall, is in all who are born according to nature. This corruption is not only a lack of the righteousness which had been in

perfectam oboedientiam, ad verum timorem Dei, ad veram fidem, ad veram dilectionem Dei et proximi, sed etiam est concupiscentia, hoc est rebellio contra legem Dei et inclinatio ad omnis generis peccata contra primam et secundam tabulam legis Dei.

Tenemus et hoc, quod omnes homines, secundum naturam propagati, nascuntur cum peccato originis, et hoc peccatum originis est vere peccatum afferens nunc quoque aeternam mortem eis, qui non renascuntur per baptismum et Spiritum Sanctum.

03. De baptismo (09)

Quod ad articulum nonum attinet, etiam plane et sine ulla ambiguitate confitemur, docemus et defendimus *universalis ecclesiae consensum de baptismo videlicet, quod baptismus a Christo institutus sit et sit necessarius ad salutem, et quod per baptismum offerantur remissio peccatorum et gratia Christi infantibus et adultis, et quod non debeat iterari baptismus, et quod infantes debeant baptizari, et quod infantes per baptismum consequantur remissionem peccatorum, gratiam et fiant filii Dei, quia promissio gratiae et vitae aeternae pertinet non solum ad adultos, sed etiam ad infantes*, et haec promissio per ministerium in ecclesia infantibus et adultis administrari

human nature before the Fall, viz. (the fact that since the Fall) we do not have any reliable knowledge of God, nor uprightness of will, nor a predisposition towards perfect obedience, towards true fear of God, towards true faith, towards true love of God and of one's neighbour. (This corruption) is also concupiscence, i.e. rebellion against God's Law and the inclination to sins of every kind, contrary to the first and second tables of God's Law.

We also hold that every human being engendered according to nature is born with original sin, which original sin is truly sin, bringing eternal death even now to those who are not born again by Baptism and the Holy Spirit.

03. Baptism (09)

Concerning the ninth article, we also openly and without any ambiguity confess, teach and defend *the universal consensus of the Church concerning baptism, viz. that baptism was instituted by Christ and is necessary for salvation, that through baptism remission of sins and the grace of Christ are offered to children as well as to adults, that baptism should not be repeated, that children should be baptized and that through baptism, children obtain remission of sins and grace, and become sons of God, because the promise of grace and of eternal life belongs not only to adults but also to children*, and this promise ought to be granted by the ministry in the Church to children as

debet.

Quia vero *infantes nascuntur cum peccato originis, habent opus remissione illius peccati*, et illud ita remittitur, ut reatus tollatur, sed materiale peccati, videlicet corruptio naturae seu concupiscentia, manet in hac vita, etsi incipit sanari, quia Spiritus Sanctus in ipsis etiam infantibus est efficax et eos mundat suo quodam modo. Nemo enim intrare potest in regnum caelorum, nisi renatus ex aqua et Spiritu Sancto. *Probamus* igitur sententiam ecclesiae, quae *damnavit Pelagianos*, qui negabant in infantibus esse peccatum originis, *damnamus et Anabaptistas*, qui negant infantes baptizandos esse.

De adultos vero docemus, quod ita *consequuntur per baptismum remissionem peccatorum* et gratiam, *si baptizandi attulerint paenitentiam veram, confessionem articulorum fidei*, et promissione, quae est addita baptismo, se confirment et credant, vere ipsis ibi donari remissionem peccatorum et iustificationem propter Christum, sicut Evangelium dicit (Mc 16:16): Qui crediderit et baptizatus fuerit, et *Petrus ait in Actis (2:38): Paenitentiam agite, et baptizetur unusquisque vestrum in nomine Iesu Christi in remissionem peccatorum et accipietis donum Spiritus Sancti*. Et cum eunuchus petivisset baptismum, inquit Philippus (Ac 8:37): Si credis ex toto corde, licet. Et respondet eunuchus: Credo Filium Dei esse Iesum. *Et ad Titum 3 (v.5): Non ex operibus*

well as to adults.

Because *children are born with original sin, they need remission of that sin*, and it is forgiven in such a way that guilt is removed, but the matter of sin, viz. corruption of nature or concupiscence, still remains in this life, although it begins to be healed, because the Holy Spirit is efficacious in children as well and cleanses them in his own way. Nobody can enter the kingdom of heaven unless he is born again of water and of the Holy Spirit. Therefore *we approve* the statement of the Church which *condemned the Pelagians* who denied that children possess original sin, and *we also condemn the Anabaptists* who deny that children are to be baptized.

Concerning adults, we teach that *by baptism they obtain remission of sins* and grace *if on coming to baptism they bring true penitence, confession of the articles of faith*, assure themselves of the promise which is attached to baptism, **and believe that by it they are truly granted remission of sins and justification on account of Christ**, as the Gospel (Mk 16:16) says: He who believes and is baptized... and as *Peter* says (Ac 2:38): *Do penitence and be baptized, every one of you, in the name of Jesus Christ for the remission of sins, and you will receive the gift of the Holy Spirit.* And when the eunuch asked for baptism, Philip said (Ac 8:37): "If you believe with all your heart, you may. And he answered and said, I believe that Jesus is the Son of God." *And in Ti 3 (v.5): Not by works*

iustitiae, quae fecimus nos, sed secundum suam misericordiam salvos nos fecit per lavacrum regenerationis et renovationis Spiritus Sancti etc. Et Petrus ait (I Pe 3:21): Bonae conscientiae pactum.

of righteousness which we have done, but according to his mercy he saved us by the washing of regeneration and renewing of the Holy Spirit", and Peter (I Pe 3:21) calls it the covenant of a good conscience.

04. De paenitentia et iustificatione (04,05,06,12,20)

04. Penitence and Justification (04,05,06,12,20)

Quod ad quartum, quintum, sextum, doudecimum et vicesimum articulos attinet de doctrina paenitentiae et iustificationis et bonorum operum, confitemur, docemus et defendimus eam doctrinam, quae de his rebus traditur in Canone Bibliae, quam in ecclesia sancti patres Ambrosius, Augustinus et quidam horum similes docuerunt, et iudicamus, magnopere prodesse, ut haec doctrina pure traditur in ecclesiis, ut gloria Christi illustretur et eius beneficia recte intelligantur et conscientiae habeant firmam consolationem et discant veros cultus Dei. Cum igitur Christus clare mandaverit, ut praedicentur paenitentia et remissio peccatorum in nomine ipsius, nos quoque docemus, quod ad consequentiam salutem et vitam aeternam necesse sit habere paenitentiam et remissionem peccatorum.

Concerning the fourth, fifth, sixth, twelfth and twentieth articles, covering the doctrines of penitence, justification and good works, we teach and defend the doctrine concerning these things which is handed down to us in the Canon of the Bible, which the holy fathers Ambrose, Augustine and others like them have taught in the Church, and we judge it very profitable that this doctrine be transmitted in the churches so that Christ's glory may be magnified and his benefits rightly understood, and that consciences may have steadfast consolation and learn (what) true worship of God (is). Therefore, since Christ has clearly commanded that penitence and remission of sins be preached in his name, we also teach that penitence and remission of sins are necessary in order to obtain salvation and eternal life.

Primum igitur de paenitentia confitemur et defendimus consensum Catholicae Ecclesiae, quae sentit iuxta Scripturas, *quod lapsis post baptismum necessaria sit paenitentia, et quod lapsi, qui in hac vita non agunt paenitentiam, certo damnetur*, contra autem, *quod lapsi*, quandocunque et quocunque

First then, concerning penitence, we confess and defend the consensus of the Catholic Church which holds, in accordance with the Scriptures, *that penitence is necessary for those who have lapsed after baptism, and that the lapsed who do not do penitence in this life will certainly be damned.* However, we also maintain

tempore *agunt paentientiam* et *convertuntur, vere consequuntur remissionem peccatorum*, et quod Ecclesia debet talibus impartire absolutionem. Damnamus igitur Novatianos, qui secus senserunt.

Ut autem sine ulla ambiguitate constet, quid sit paenitentia, clare et plane profitemur iuxta Scripturam canonicam et sanctos patres, *paenitentiam* veram et integram, *quam Christus praecipit, constare his tribus partibus, contritione, fide,* seu fiducia misericordiae Dei, quae propter Christum promissa est, *et novitate vitae seu nova oboedientia. Est autem contritio* cum *conscientia,* quae arguitur Verbo Dei, *agnoscit peccatum* et *vere sentit, Deum irasci peccato, et veros terrores concipit et dolet* se pecasse, *vere pudefit et sentit, se nulla nostra opera aut merita posse opponere irae Dei,* sicut multis exemplis et sententiis in Scriptura praecipitur et describitur contritio, ut in Ps. (38:4): Non est pax ossibus meis a facie peccatorum meorum. Et in Actis dicitur (2:37): His auditis compuncti sunt corde etc.

In his terroribus et doloribus necesse est proponi doctrinam de fide in Christum et remissione peccatorum. Cum igitur fides accedit, hi pavores et dolores fiunt timor filialis et bona opera, cultus Dei et sacrificia, de quibus dicit Ps (51:17): sacrificium Deo spiritus contribulati, cor contritum et humiliatum Deus

that the lapsed truly obtain remission of sins whenever and as often *as they do penitence and are converted*, and that the Church should grant absolution to such people. Therefore we condemn the Novatians, who thought otherwise.

But so that the nature of penitence might be understood without any ambiguity, we state clearly and openly, in accordance with canonical Scripture and the holy fathers, that the true and genuine *penitence which Christ commands consists of these three parts: contrition, faith,* i.e. trust in the mercy of God which is promised on account of Christ, *and newness of life, or the new obedience. Contrition is* when a *conscience* which is convicted by God's Word *recognizes its sin, truly realizes that God is angry with the sin, and is genuinely terror-stricken and grieves* that it has sinned, *i.e. is truly ashamed and realizes that it is unable to make any of our own works or merits stand up against God's wrath.* Contrition is commanded and described by many examples and statements in Scripture, as in Ps (38:4): Neither is there peace for my bones because of my sin. And in Acts (2:37), it is said: Now when they heard this, they were pricked in their heart, etc.

In these terrors and sorrows the doctrine concerning faith in Christ and the remission of sins must be presented. For when faith comes, these terrors and sorrows turn into filial fear, good works, worship of God and those sacrifices of which Ps (51:17) says: The sacrifice to God of a troubled spirit; a contrite and a

non despicies.

Ideo *secundum partem paenitentiae esse fidem necesse est, qua credimus, nobis ipsis a Deo remitti peccata et nos iustificari* ac iustos reputari et fieri *filios Dei non propter dignitatem* contritionis aut aliorum *operum, sed* gratis *propter Christum.* Hac fide eriguntur in terroribus conscientiae et redduntur pacata corda et liberantur a terroribus peccati et mortis, sicut Paulus inquit (Ro 5:1): Iustificati fide pacem habemus erga Deum. Quia si iudicio Dei adversus peccatum opponeremus dignitatem nostram et merita nostra pro peccato, promissio reconciliationis fieret nobis incerta et conscientiae nostrae adigerentur ad desperationem, sicut Paulus ait (Ro 4:15): Lex iram operatur, sed opponi debent pro peccato meritum Christi et gratuita promissio misericordiae, quae donatur propter Christum, sicut Paulus inquit (I Co 15: 56-57): Aculeus mortis peccatum est, potentia peccati lex, gratia autem Deo, qui dat nobis victoriam per Dominum nostrum Iesum Christum.

Haec autem *fides* quae, ut dictum est, consolatur perterrefactas mentes, concipitur et *confirmatur ex Evangelio et ex absolutione, quae singulis applicat promissionem gratiae.* Cumque hoc modo per verbum Evangelii et absolutionem, quae et ipsa est vox Evangelii, sustentant se conscientiae, simul concipiunt Spiritum Sanctum, sicut Paulus docet ad Galatas (3:14): Ut promissionem Spiritus accipiamus

humbled heart, O God, thou wilt not despise.

Therefore *the second element of penitence must be faith, by which we believe that our sins are forgiven us by God and that we are justified* and accounted righteous and become *sons of God, not because of the worthiness* of our contrition or of other *works, but* freely *for Christ's sake.* By this faith terrified consciences are lifted up and hearts are made peaceful and set free from the terrors of sin and death, as Paul says (Ro 5:1): Being justified by faith, we have peace with God. For if, to God's judgement against sin, we were to oppose our worthiness and our merits (as a satisfaction) for sin, the promise of reconciliation would become uncertain for us, and our consciences would be driven to despair, as Paul says (Ro 4:15): The law works wrath. What ought to be offered for sin is Christ's merit and the free promise of mercy which is given for his sake, as Paul says (I Co 15: 56-57): The sting of death is sin, and the strength of sin is the law. But thanks be to God, who gives us the victory through our Lord Jesus Christ.

This faith which, as was said, comforts terrified minds *is* engendered and *strengthened by the Gospel and by absolution, which applies the promises of grace to individuals.* When consciences raise themselves up in this way through the word of the Gospel and through absolution, which is itself a the voice of the Gospel, they also receive the Holy Spirit, as Paul teaches in Ga 3:14: That we might receive the

per fidem. Item (Ro 10:17): Fides ex auditu est.

Et cum Spiritus Sanctus sit efficax, parit iam novos motus in cordibus consentientes legi Dei, scilicet fidem, dilectionem Dei, timorem Dei, odium peccati, propositum non peccandi, et reliquos bonos fructus iuxta illud (Ie 31:33): Dabo legem meam in cordibus eorum. Igitur *iustificatio*, quae fit fide hoc modo, ut dictum est, *est renovatio* et regeneratio.

Haec est sententia et Scripturae et sanctorum patrum de remissione peccatorum et de fide. Sic enim et Bernardus inquit: Necesse est primo omnium credere, quod remissionem peccatorum habere non possis nisi per indulgentiam Dei, sed adde adhuc, ut credas et hoc, quod per ipsum peccata tibi donantur. Hoc est testimonium, quod perhibet Spiritus Sanctus in corde tuo, dicens: Dimissa sunt tibi peccata tua, sic enim arbitratur Apostolus gratis iustificari hominem per fidem. Haec sunt verba divi Bernardi in sermone de annuntiatione, et huiusmodi multa praeclara testimonia in hanc sententiam extant passim in praecipuis partibus.

Haec autem fides, de qua loquimur, non tantum est notitia in intellectu, **sed etiam est fiducia** in volutate, qua voluntas nostra vult et accipit beneficium Christi et acquiescit propter Christum et repugnat dubitationi et vincit terrores peccati et mortis et certo statuit, quod propter mediatorem Christum

promise of the Spirit through faith, and also (Ro 10:17): Faith is by hearing.

Since the Holy Spirit is effective, he also creates new promptings in our hearts, which assent to God's law, viz. faith, the love of God, the fear of God, hatred of sin, the determination not to sin, and other good fruits, in accordance with the passage (Je 31:33): I will put my law in their hearts. Therefore *justification*, which comes about through faith in the manner described, *is renewal* and regeneration.

This is the view both of Scripture and of the Church [*lit.* Holy] fathers concerning the remission of sins and faith. For Bernard also says: You must above all things believe that you cannot have remission of sins except by God's forgiveness, but you must add this: that you also believe that your own sins are forgiven through him. This is the testimony which the Holy Spirit implants in your heart, saying, "Your sins are forgiven you"; for so the Apostle concludes that man is freely justified through faith. These are the words of St Bernard in his Sermon on the Annunciation, and many clear statements of this kind are found here and there in the foremost Church fathers.

This faith of which we are speaking is not only a matter of knowledge in the intellect, **but also trust** in the will, through which our will desires and receives Christ's benefits and through Christ becomes full of peace, strives against doubt, conquers the terrors of sin and death,

habeamus Deum placatum et propitium et simus filii.

Complectitur ergo haec fides omnes articulos fidei et in eis hunc quoque, videlicet remissionem peccatorum, quia hic est finis, ad quem reliqui de Christo destinati sunt. Ideo enim Filius Dei incarnatus, passus, resuscitatus est etc., ut nos habeamus remissionem peccatorum et vitam aeternam propter ipsum. Quare non loquimur de fide, qualis est in impiis et diabolis. Nam hi non credunt omnes articulos fidei, non enim credunt remissionem peccatorum, sed loquimur de hac ipsa fide, quae et ceteros articulos credit et hunc, quod nobis donetur remissio peccatorum propter Christum.

Ad haec plane et clare docemus, quod oporteat in omni vita coniungi haec duo contritionem et fidem. Non enim potest existere haec fides in his, qui carnali securitate contemnunt iudicium Dei et indulgent vitiosis affectibus nec habent contritionem iuxta illud Esaiae 66 (v. 2): Ad quem respiciam, nisi ad contritum spiritu et trementem sermones meos. Rursus contritio sine hac fide fit desperatio. Ideo docenda est ecclesia, quod haec fides seu fiducia, quae credit, nobis remitti peccata propter Christum et nos iustos reputari, sit praecepta, quia praeceptum est credere promissioni Dei. Promissio enim requirit fidem, Ro 4 (v.13). Et Iohannes ait (I Io 5:10): Qui non credit, mendacem facit eum, et Christus inquit (Io 6:40): Haec est voluntas eius, qui

and decrees with certainty that because of our Mediator Christ we may now have a placated and gracious God, and that we may be his sons.

Therefore this faith embraces all articles of faith, and among them also this article concerning the remission of sins, since this is the end to which the other articles concerning Christ are pointed. It is for this reason that God's Son became man, suffered, rose again, etc., that we might have remission of sins and eternal life for his sake. Therefore we are not speaking of the "faith" of the wicked and the devils. For they do not believe all the articles of faith, because they do not believe in the remission of sins, but we are speaking of that faith which believes both the other articles of faith and this; that remission of sins is granted to us for Christ's sake.

In addition to these things we clearly and distinctly teach that in our entire life these two things ought to be conjoined: contrition and faith. For this faith cannot exist in those who in carnal security despise God's judgement, indulge in vile affections, and have not the contrition spoken of by Isaiah 66 (v.2): On whom shall I look if not on him who is contrite in spirit, and trembles at my word? Furthermore, contrition without this faith becomes despair. Therefore the Church must be taught that this faith or trust, which believes that our sins are forgiven and that we are accounted righteous for Christ's sake, is what God commands, since it has been commanded that we believe God's promise. For a promise

misit me, ut omnis qui videt Filium et credit in eum, habeat vitam aeternam.

requires faith Ro 4 (v.13). And John says (I Jn 5:10): He who does not believe has made him a liar, and Christ says (Jn 6:40): This is the will of him who sent me, that everyone who sees the Son and believes in him may have everlasting life.

05. De bonis operibus (06, 18, 20)

05. Good Works (06, 18, 20)

Tertia pars paenitentiae est novitas vitae seu nova oboedientia, sicut Iohannes ait (Lc 3:8): *Facite fructus dignos paenitentiae*, et Esaias (1:16): Desinite male facere, etc. Confitemur enim, quod sentit et confitetur ecclesia catholica Christi, quod reconciliationem necessario sequi debeat nostra oboedientia erga Deum, hoc est bona opera nobis mandata a Deo. *Etsi enim acceptatio ad vitam aeternam coniuncta est cum iustificatione*, hoc est, cum remissione peccatorum et reconciliatione, et **bona** *opera* **non sunt pretium** pro vita aeterna, *tamen sunt necessaria ad salutem*, quia sunt debitum, quod necessario reconciliationem sequi debet, sicut *Paulus ait (Ro 8:12): debitores sumus, et Christus inquit (Mt 19:17): Si vis ad vitam ingredi, serva mandata, et Paulus de malis operibus (Ga 5:21): Qui talia agunt, regnum Dei non possidebunt.* Sed necesse est ad doctrinam de bonis operibus illustrandam multa moneri ecclesiam. Primum, qualia opera requirantur, secundo, quomodo fieri possint, tertio, quomodo placeant Deo, quarto, de peccatis mortalibus, quae qui admittunt, excidunt gratia Dei. Quinto, quae sit necessitas et dignitas seu meritum bonorum operum.

The third part of penitence is newness of life, i.e. the new obedience, as John (the Baptist) says (Lk 3:8): Make fruits worthy of penitence, and Isaiah (1:16): Cease to do evil, etc. For we confess what the catholic Church of Christ holds and confesses, that obedience to God, that is, the good works commanded us by God, ought of necessity to follow reconciliation. *For although acceptance into eternal life is conjoined with justification* i.e. with the remission of sins and reconciliation, and (although) **good works are not a payment** for eternal life, *nevertheless they are necessary for salvation*, because they are a debt which ought of necessity to follow reconciliation, as *Paul says (Ro 8:12): We are debtors, and Christ says (Mt 19:17): If you want to enter into life, keep the commandments, and Paul (says) concerning evil deeds (Ga 5:21): Those who do such things will not possess the kingdom of God.* But it is necessary that the Church be often admonished about putting this doctrine concerning good works into practice. First, (it must teach) what kinds of works are demanded; secondly, how they might be done; thirdly, how they please God; fourthly, concerning mortal sins,

which those who commit them perish from the grace of God. Fifthly, what the necessity, worth or merit of good works is.

Primum igitur docemus, *requiri opera a Deo* mandata et quidem *non tantum externa civilia opera, sed etiam spirituales motus, timorem Dei, fiduciam,* invocationem, dilectionem, patientiam, odium peccati, propositum non peccandi et similes motus ac virtutes, oportet enim in cordibus nostris inchoari legem Dei iuxta illud (Ie 31:33): Dabo legem meam in corda eorum, et *Christus* inquit (Mt 5:20): *Nisi abundaverit iustitia vestra plus quam Pharisaeorum, non intrabitis in regnum caelorum,* hoc est, oportet nos non tantum externa civilia opera facere, sed etiam habere spirituales motus consentientes legi Dei, timorem Dei, fidem, invocationem, sicut ait Paulus (Ro 8:14): Qui Spiritu Dei aguntur, hi sunt filii Dei. Haec novitas in hac vita tantum inchoatur, sed crescere eam oportet et nos magis magisque sanctificari, sicut ait Paulus (II Co 5:2, 3): Desiderantes ergo superindui, si tamen induti, non nudi reperiemur. Oportet igitur in salvandis esse hanc inchoatam novitatem eamque confirmari et crescere.

De secundo docemus, quod non possunt existere in nobis invocatio, dilectio et reliquae virtutes, nisi prius fide corda erigantur per Evangelium, quia donec sentiunt iram Dei, negant se exaudiri, non diligunt Deum, sicut scriptum est (Ro 10:14): Quomodo invocabunt, si non credent? Adesse

First therefore, we teach that *the works* commanded *by God are required,* and *not only external, civil works but also spiritual promptings, viz. the fear of God, trust,* prayer, love, patience, hatred of sin, the determination not to sin, and similar promptings and virtues, for the law of God ought to begin in our hearts according to this (Je 31:33): I will put my law in their hearts, and *Christ says (Mt 5:20): Unless your righteousness exceeds the righteousness of the scribes and the Pharisees, you will not enter the kingdom of heaven.* This means not only that we ought to do external, civil good works, but that we ought also to have spiritual promptings which agree with God's law, the fear of God, faith and prayer, as Paul says (Ro 8:14): As many as are led by the Spirit of God are sons of God. This newness merely begins in this life but it ought to increase, and we ought to be more and more sanctified, as Paul says (II Co 5:2, 3): Desiring to be clothed, so that being clothed, we should not be found naked. Therefore there ought to be this incipient newness of life in those who are being saved, and it ought to be strengthened and grow.

Concerning the second point, we teach that prayer, love and other virtues cannot exist in us unless our hearts are first raised up by faith through the Gospel, since as long as they feel God's wrath, they do not believe that their prayers are heard, and they do not love God, as it is

igitur fidem oportet, qua cum erigimur et agnoscimus Deum placatum esse et, sicut ait Paulus (Ro 8:15): Clamamus Abba, Pater, tum demum vere invocamus et diligimus, estque fides ipsa praecipuum opus et praecipuus cultus Dei, quia agnoscit Christum mediatorem. Praeterea ut hae virtutes efficiantur, diximus dari Spiritum Sanctum, qui per verbum fide concipitur, ut dictum est; fiunt enim haec virtutes in nobis movente et adiuvante nos Spiritu Sancto.

Tertio quaeritur, quomodo haec oboedientia, hoc est et novitas et bona opera Deo placeant. Nam et de hoc loco valse refert et necesse est ecclesiam recte doceri, ut utrumque intelligat, videlicet quod nemo legi satisfaciat, item quare placeat oboedientia, quamquam procul absit a perfectione. De utroque diligenter disputaverunt sancti patres, sed recentiores multa absurda confinxerunt.

Confitemur igitur oboedientiam illam in sanctis inchoatam non satisfacere, item adhuc in sanctis in hac vita haerere concupiscentiam, quae etiamsi cepit mortificari, tamen non est penitus abolita. Est autem concupiscentia sua natura peccatum, etsi non imputatur credentibus et repugnantibus. Adhaec gignit concupis-

written (Ro 10:14): How then shall they pray if they do not believe? Therefore faith must be present – faith by means of which we are not only raised up and recognize that God has been placated, and (whereby), as Paul says (Ro 8:15): We cry, Abba, Father, but by which we finally really pray and love. This very faith is the foremost work and the foremost worship of God, because it recognizes Christ as our Mediator. Beyond that, we have said that it was in order that these virtues might be effected that the Holy Spirit was given, who through the Word is received by faith, as has been said; for these virtues are wrought in us by the activity and aid of the Holy Spirit.

Thirdly, it is asked how this obedience, that is, both newness (of life) and good works, might please God. For it is very important and necessary that the Church be correctly taught on this point, in order that it may understand both matters, namely, that nobody keeps the law satisfactorily, but also, why obedience pleases God, even though it is far from perfection. The holy fathers carefully considered both questions, but more recent (teachers) have invented many absurd (things about them).

Therefore we confess that the obedience which is begun in the saints is not sufficient, for in this life concupiscence still inheres in the saints, and even though it has begun to be mortified, yet it has not been entirely abolished. Concupiscence is by its very nature sin, even though it is not imputed to those who believe,

centia vitiosos affectus. Quoties enim dubitant sancti se Deo curae esse? Quoties labascit fides? Quis timet, quantum debet? Quis satis ardenter diligit Deum?

Quis satis patienter obtemperat in adversis? Quem non interdum incedunt odia et aliae cupiditates? Quis satisfacit suae vocationi? Quoties sancti fremunt, cum vident impios et tyrannos florere et omnibus vitae commodis frui, se vero duriter exerceri omni genere calamitatum? Haec vitia non sunt extenuanda, sed sunt sua natura vere peccata, sed non imputantur credentibus. Et in tanta potentia Diaboli quoties incidit haec infirma natura in Diaboli insidias? Ideo clare testaur Scriptura, sanctos non satisfacere legi et habere eos peccata. I Io 1 (v.8): Si dixerimus, quod peccatum non habemus, ipsi nos seducimus. Idem copiose docent Augustinus et Hieronymus.

Quare haec nostra oboedientia non satisfacit legi nec possunt conscientiae ea niti et eam opponere iudicio Dei tamquam legis impletionem, in qua non possit accusari imperfectio aut naturalis infirmitas, quae retardat in bonis operibus. Hanc doctrinam in ecclesia extare necesse est ad prohibendam falsam fiduciam operum et propriae dignitatis, quemadmodum quidam finxerunt se habere superflua merita eaque aliis largiti sunt, ut propter ea opera salvarentur, sed discant veram

and who strive against it. Also, concupiscence brings forth evil lusts. For how often do even the saints (not) doubt whether God takes any notice of them? How often does faith (not) begin to waver? Who fears (God) as much as he should? Who loves God strongly enough? Who submits patiently enough in adversities? Whom do not hatred and other evil desires occasionally invade? Who satisfies (the demands of) his calling? How often do the saints (not) murmur when they see the wicked and the tyrants flourishing and enjoying all the advantages of life, while they are sorely tried by all kinds of calamities? Such shortcomings are not to be minimized, but are by their nature actually sins, though they are not imputed to believers. And because the Devil is so powerful, how often does our weak nature (not) fall into his snares? Thus Scripture clearly bears witness that the saints do not satisfy the law, and that they have sin. I Jn 1 (v.8): If we say we have no sin, we deceive ourselves. Augustine and Jerome teach the same thing at great length.

Wherefore (it is clear that) our obedience does not satisfy the law, nor can consciences find rest and set this (obedience) up against the judgement of God as if it were the fulfilment of the law, in which there is no possible accusation of imperfection or of the natural weakness which hinders us from good works. It is necessary that this doctrine be taught in the Church in order to avoid false trust in works and in our own worthiness, to the point that some have imagined that they possess

humilitatem etiam sancti et confugiant ad misericordiam iuxta illud (Ga 3:22): Conclusit omnes sub peccatum, ut omnium misereatur. Item (Ps 143:2): Non intres in iudicium cum servo tuo, quia non iustificabitur in conspectu tuo omnis vivens. Cum igitur constet, sanctos non satisfacere legi et habere peccata, necesse est rursus sanctis proponi veram et firmam consolationem. Teneat igitur conscientia, quod persona sit iusta, id est, habeat remissionem peccatorum seu sit reconciliata et accepta ad vitam aeternam gratis per misericordiam propter mediatorem Christum, etiam si nos simus indigni. Deinde vero quod illa inchoata oboedientia sit necessaria ac, tametsi procul abest a perfectione legis, placeat tamen, quia sumus in Christo, propter quem condonantur nobis reliquiae peccati.

Et haec oboedientia in reconciliatis fide iam reputatur esse iustitia et quaedam legis impletio, non quidem possit opponi iudicio Dei iuxta illud (I Co 4:4): Nihil mihi conscius sum, sed in hoc non iustificatus sum, verum placet, quia sumus in Christo, sicut docet Paulus Ro 6 (v. 14): Iam non estis sub lege, sed sub gratia, id est, lex iam non accusat vos, tametsi non potestis satisfacere legi, sed iam filii estis, ideo non accusat vos. Et Ro 8 (v. 1): Nulla nunc condemnatio est his, qui

superfluous merits and have granted them to others sot hat they may be saved by them. But even saints must learn true humility and take refuge in God's mercy as it is written (Ga 3:22): God has concluded all in sin, in order to have mercy on all. Likewise (Ps 143:2): Enter not into judgement with thy servant, for in thy sight shall no man living be justified. Since therefore it is established that the saints do not satisfy (the demands of) the law but have sin, it is necessary that true and firm consolation be set before the saints again. Therefore let conscience firmly hold that a person is just, i.e., that he has the remission of sins, or has been reconciled and accepted into eternal life, freely through mercy for the sake of Christ the Mediator, even though we are unworthy. But let us also believe thereafter that this incipient obedience is necessary and that, even though it is far from perfectly fulfilling the law, nevertheless it may be pleasing to God because we are in Christ, for whose sake the remains of sin in us are forgiven.

And this obedience in those who have been reconciled by faith is now reckoned as righteousness and as a kind of fulfilment of the law, not indeed as if it could be made to stand against God's judgement, according to the passage (I Co 4:4): I know nothing against me, but I am not thereby justified, but it pleases God because we are in Christ, as Paul teaches in Romans 6 (v. 14): Now you are not under the law but under grace; that is, the law no longer accuses you, even though you are not

in Christo Iesu ambulant, etc. Non ait eos non habere peccatum, sed nunc non condemnari, quia propter Christum sunt facti filii.

Addit enim (Ro 8:3): Cum legi esset impossibile iustificare, missus est Filius etc. Itaque quod dicitur, legem fieri possibilem per gratiam, recte et utiliter dicitur. Duo autem complectitur haec sententia: et quod a Spiritu Sancto iuvemur et quod placeat inchoata oboedientia, non quia perfecta sit, sed propter gratiam. Quare hac fide in omni vita opus est, haec perpetuo lucere et consolari nos debet contra infirmitatem naturae et appraehendere mediatorem Christum et statuere, quod vere propter ipsum habeamus remissionem peccatorum et simus filii. Facile autem iudicari potest a peritis conscientiis, hanc doctrinam et consolationem maxime necessarium esse ecclesiae. Nam pii adigerentur ad desperationem, si sentiendum esset, tunc demum eos placere, cum legi satisfacerent. Ideo autem piis hae reliquiae peccati non imputantur, quia in paenitentia, hoc est, agnitione suae infirmitatis et vera contritione appraehendunt mediatorem Christum, sicut ait Paulus (Ro 8:33): Quis accusabit electos, cum habeamus interpellatorem Christum.

Sed hic addendum est de quarto loco, cum indulgent homines vitiosis affectibus et admittunt facta contra

able to satisfy the law, but now you are God's sons, and therefore it does not accuse you, and Ro 8 (v.1): There is therefore now no condemnation to those who walk in Christ Jesus. He does not say that they have no sin, but that now they are not condemned because through Christ they are made sons. For he adds (Ro 8:3): Since it was impossible for the law to justify, the Son was sent, etc. And so the statement that the law is made possible through grace is correct and beneficial. However, this statement implies two things: both that we be aided by the Holy Spirit and that the obedience begun in us please God, not because it is perfect but because of grace. Therefore we need to have this faith throughout our entire life; it ought to shine perpetually; it ought to comfort us against the weakness of our nature and lay hold of Christ the Mediator, and establish that we really have the remission of sins and are sons of God for his sake. It can easily be judged by experienced consciences that this doctrine and consolation is most necessary for the Church. For the godly would be driven to despair if they had to think that they please God only when they satisfy the law. Therefore what remains of sin is not imputed to the godly, because in penitence, i.e. in recognizing their own weakness and in true contrition, they lay hold of the Mediator Christ, as Paul says (Ro 8:33): Who will accuse the elect, when we have Christ as our intercessor?

But now we must add, concerning the fourth point, that when people indulge in sinful passions and do

legem Dei, tales non manent in gratia. Et hi lapsus sunt peccata mortalia, de quibus idem docemus, quod consensus catholicae ecclesiae docet et Paulus inquit (Ga 5:21): Qui talia agunt, non possidebunt vitam aeternam. Necesse est igitur renatos cum vera fide simul retinere iustitiam bonae conscientiae et resistere vitiosis affectibus et oboedire legi Dei, ideoque Paulus inquit (II Co 1:12): Haec est gloriatio nostra, testimonium conscientiae nostrae, et I Ti 1 (v. 5): Summa mandati est dilectio ex corde puro et conscientia bona et fide non ficta. Ro 8 (v. 13): Si actiones carnis mortificabitis, vivetis.

De quinto igitur docendae sunt ecclesiae de necessitate et de dignitate huius oboedientiae, videlicet quod, quamquam oboedientia nostra seu iustitia bonae conscientiae non sit pretium, propter quod datur vita aeterna, sicut nemo sanctorum statuere potest, ullum suum opus dignum esse, propter quod habeat remissionem peccatorum et sit acceptus ad vitam aeternam, et Ps (143:2) inquit: Non iustificabitur in conspectu tuo omnis vivens, tamen haec oboedientia seu iustitia bonae conscientiae sit necessaria, quia debitum est, quod necessario sequi reconciliationem debet, sicut Paulus inquit (Ro 8:12): Debitores sumus; item (II Co 5:3): Superindui desiderantes, si tamen induti, non nudi reperiemur. Quare necessaria est in salvandis haec inchoata novitas, et

things which are contrary to God's law, they do not remain in grace. And these lapses are mortal sins, concerning which we teach what the consensus of the catholic Church teaches, and (what) Paul says (Ga 5:21): Those who do such things will not possess eternal life. It is therefore necessary that those who have been born again retain, together with true faith, the righteousness of a good conscience; and that they resist sinful passions and obey God's law. Therefore Paul says (II Co 1:12): Our rejoicing is this, the testimony of our conscience, and I Ti 1 (v. 5): Now the sum of the commandment is love out of a pure heart and of a good conscience and of faith unfeigned; and Ro 8 (v. 13): If you mortify the deeds of the flesh you will live.

Concerning the fifth point, churches ought to be taught about the necessity and worthiness of this obedience, viz. that, although our obedience or the righteousness of a good conscience is not a payment for which eternal life is given, just as no one of the saints can assert that any good work of his is a worthy deed for which he may have remission of sins and be accepted into eternal life, and Ps (143:2) says: In thy sight shall no man living be justified; nevertheless, this obedience or righteousness of a good conscience is necessary because it is a debt which must follow reconciliation, as Paul says (Ro 8:12): We are debtors, and also (II Co 5:3): desiring to be clothed, so that being clothed, we shall not be found naked. Therefore this incipient newness of life is necessary in those

cum sine ulla dubitatione sit mandatum Christi: Agite poenitentiam, item: Diligite vos mutuo, certe debitum esse constat.

Praeterea cum in iustificatione fiat renovatio, haec ipsa nova vita est oboedientia erga Deum. Quare non potest retineri iustificatio, nisi retineatur haec inchoata oboedientia iuxta illud (I Io 3:10): Omnis qui non facit iustitiam, non est ex Deo. Item (I Io 3:8): Qui facit peccatum, ex Diabolo est.

Iam et dignitas magna est huius inchoatae oboedientiae. Quamquam enim est imperfecta, tamen quia personae sunt in Christo, reputatur haec oboedientia esse quaedam legis impletio et est iustitia, sicut saepe vocat Scriptura, ut (Ps 119:121): Feci iudicium et iustitiam, et Iohannes (I Io 3:7) ait: Qui facit iustitiam iustus est, et Iacobus (2:24): Iustificamur non ex fide solum, sed etiam ex operibus. Id non sic accipi debet, quod consequamur remissionem peccatorum et reconciliationem propter opera, sed sententia est, quod utraque iustitia necessaria sit, primum fides, qua coram Deo iustificamur, id est, consequimur remissionem peccatorum et reconciliationem seu regeneramur et efficimur filii; deinde et altera iustitia, videlicet iustitia operum seu iustitia bonae conscientiae debita et necessaria est.

Et cum Christus inquit (Mt 19:17): Si vis in vitam ingredi, serva mandata, docet hanc oboedientiam esse quandam legis impletionem. Sed

who are to be saved; also, since this is most certainly the commandment of Christ: Do penitence and love one another, it is certainly a bounden duty.

Moreover, since renewal occurs in justification, this new life is obedience to God. Therefore justification cannot be retained unless this incipient obedience is retained, according to the passage (I Jn 3:10): Whoever does not do righteousness is not of God; and (I Jn 3:8): He who commits sin is of the Devil.

Now the value of this incipient obedience is great, for although it is imperfect, nevertheless because the people concerned are in Christ, this obedience is reckoned to be a kind of fulfilment of the law and is righteousness, even as Scripture often calls it (Ps 119:121): I have done judgement and justice, and John says (I Jn 3:7): He who does righteousness is righteousness, and (Ja 2:24): We are justified not by faith only, but by works. This should not be understood as if we obtain remission of sins and reconciliation on account of our works, but the meaning is that both righteousnesses are necessary. First, faith is necessary, for by it we are justified before God, that is, by it we obtain remission of sins and reconciliation; i.e. we are born again and made sons; and then also that another righteousness is necessary and owed, namely, the righteousness of works, i.e. the righteousness of a good conscience.

And when Christ says (Mt 19:17): If you want to enter into life, keep the commandments, he is teaching that this obedience is a kind of fulfilment

huic loco addenda est interpretatio, constat enim ex aliis Scripturis locis, quod nemo legi satisfaciat. Quare necesse est doceri, quomodo intelligi haec sententia debeat: Serva mandata. Addendum est enim Evangelium de Christo, videlicet quod primum quaerenda sit iustificatio fide in Christum et quod placeat postea inchoata oboedientia et reputatur esse quaedam legis impletio, et Iohannes ait (I Io 3:9): Qui natus ex Deo non peccat, id est, Spiritus Sanctus parit bona opera. Et haec placent non quia nihil sit vitii in natura hominis, sed quia iam sumus in Christo. Ut igitur sciamus, hanc imperfectam oboedientiam in credentibus Deo placere, ornantur bona opera honestissimis praeconiis a Spiritu Sancto, vocantur sacrificia et cultus Dei.

Ad haec bona opera sunt meritoria iuxta illud (I Co 3:8): Unusquisque accipiet mercedem iuxta proprium laborem. Etsi enim conscientia non potest statuere, quod propter dignitatem operum detur vita aeterna, sed nascimur filii Dei et haeredes per misericordiam, tamen haec opera in filiis merentur praemia corporalia et spiritualia et gradus praemiorum. Si enim fides, quae accipit remissionem peccatorum et donationem vitae aeternae, niteretur dignitate operum, fieret incerta et adigerentur conscientiae ad desperationem, et debet fides niti mediatore Christo. Ideo Paulus dicit (Ro 6:23): Donum Dei

of the law. But a qualification must be added to this passage, for from other parts of Scripture it is evident that no-one can satisfy the law. Therefore it must also be taught how this phrase "keep the commandments" is to be understood. For the Gospel concerning Christ must be taken into account, namely, that justification must be sought first by faith in Christ and that thereafter this incipient obedience pleases God and is regarded as a fulfilment of the law, as John says (I Jn 3:9): Whoever is born of God does not commit sin; that is, that the Holy Spirit brings forth good works. And those good works please God, not because there is no trace of sin in man's nature, but because we are now in Christ. In order therefore that we may know that such obedience in believers, albeit imperfect, pleases God, good works are glorified by the Holy Spirit with the most noble recommendations and are called sacrifices and worship of God.

In addition to this, good works are meritorious according to that wellknown passage (I Co 3:8): Every man shall receive his own reward according to his labour. For although the conscience cannot claim that eternal life is given on account of the worthiness of the works, but knows that we are born again as sons and heirs of God by mercy, nevertheless these works in those who are sons deserve rewards, both bodily and spiritual, and also degrees of reward. For if faith, which receives the forgiveness of sins and the gift of eternal life, relies on the worthiness of the deeds, it becomes uncertain,

vita aeterna per Iesum Christum. Sed hac fide vivificantur et renovantur corda. Ideo coniuncta est inchoata oboedientia et quidem debita est. Cum autem et fides opus sit et cum ea debeat coniuncta esse inchoata oboedientia, Scriptura loquitur more legis: Reddet unicuique iuxta opera sua, id est, iuxta iustitiam et iniustitiam. Et tamen fides, quamquam ut (est ?) opus, accipit reconciliationem non propter dignitatem nostram, sed per misericordiam.

and consciences are driven to despair, but faith must rely on Christ the Mediator. Therefore Paul says (Ro 6:23): For the gift of God is eternal life through Jesus Christ. But it is by means of this faith that hearts are quickened and renewed. Therefore incipient obedience is added to it and is indeed required. But since faith also is a work and since incipient obedience must be added to it, Scripture says, in the manner of a law, that God will render to each one according to his works, i.e. according to righteousness and unrighteousness. Nevertheless faith, although it is a work, receives reconciliation, not on account of our worthiness, but on account of mercy.

06. De coena Domini (10)

Quod ad decimum articulum confessionis nostrae attinet, **constanter credimus et docemus, quod in sacramento corporis et sanguinis Domini** *vere substantialiter et realiter* adsint *corpus et sanguinis Christi sub speciebus panis et vini*, et quod sub eisdem speciebus vere et *corporaliter exhibeantur et distribuantur* omnibus *illis, qui sacramentum accipiunt.*

06. The Lord's Supper (10)

Concerning the tenth article of our confession, **we firmly believe and teach that in the sacrament of the Lord's body and blood, Christ's body and blood are** *truly, substantially and really* **present** *under the species of bread and wine,* **and that under the same species they are truly** and *bodily* **presented and distributed** *to all those who receive the sacrament.*

07. De confessione et satisfactione (11)

Quod ad undecimum articulum attinet, profitemur et docemus *absolutione* privata *singulis applicari promissionem gratiae.* Ideo docemus in ecclesiis *privatam absolutionem necessario retinen-*

07. Confession and Satisfaction (11)

Concerning the eleventh article, we profess and teach that *the promise of grace is applied to individuals in* private *absolution.* Therefore we teach that in the churches *private absolution must be retained* and that

dam esse et docendos homines, ut eam petant. Nam *vox illa absolutionis* est vox Evangelii, quod Christus per Ecclesiae ministerium iussit annuntiari multis et singulis, et *vult, ut voci Evangelii sonanti per ministrum credamus, tamquam voci Dei de coelo sonanti,* quemadmodum testatur inquiens (Io 20:23): **Quorum remiseritis peccata,** remittentur eis. *Item (Lc 10:16): Qui vos audit, me audit.*

Retinemus igitur confessionem arcanam, quae fit ministris ecclesiae, ut petatur absolutio propter consolationem uberrimam, et ut retineatur in ecclesia intellectus et beneficium potestatis clavium, quorum utrumque retineri maxime opus est, deinde et propter alias utilitates. **Nam in ea confessione explorari fides indoctorum potest, ut instituantur,** et saepe opus est **imperitis** consilio. Sed de hac confessione docemus, quod non sint onerandae conscientiae enumeratione delictorum, quia enumeratio illa non est praecepta in Evangelio, sicut praecipui scriptores fatentur eam non esse iuris divini. Ad haec ista enumeratio, de qua praecipiunt Romani pontifices, impossibilis est, qui iubent fieri enumerationem omnium peccatorum. Scriptum est enim (Ps 19:12): Delicta quis intelligit?

Porro de satisfactionibus cum constet canonicas satisfactiones olim in ecclesia fuisse ritum publicae

people should be taught to ask for it. For *the very voice of absolution* is the voice of the Gospel, which Christ has commanded should be proclaimed through the Church's ministry to everyone, both collectively and individually, and *he wants us to believe the voice of the Gospel which sounds forth through the minister as if we were hearing the voice of God sounding forth from heaven,* as he testifies (Jn 20:23): **Whosesoever sins you remit,** they are remitted to them, and also (Lk 10:16): He who hears you hears me.

Therefore we retain secret confession, which is made to the ministers of the Church, in order that absolution may be sought for the sake of its very rich consolation, and that the understanding and the benefit of the power of the keys be retained in the Church, for (these and) other reasons as well. **For in that confession the faith of the unlearned may be examined to see how well they are instructed, since the inexperienced** are often in need of counsel. However, we teach concerning this confession that consciences should not be burdened by enumerating sins because such enumeration is not commanded in the Gospel, and also leading writers state that it is not of divine right. In addition, that enumeration which the Roman bishops teach is impossible, because they demand an enumeration of all sins. For it is written (Ps 19:12): Who understands his errors?

Furthermore, as far as satisfactions are concerned, since it is clear that the canonical satisfactions were formerly part of the rite of public

ponitentiae, de quo ipsi sancti patres senserunt eos ritus tum disciplinae, tum exempli causa institutos esse, non ut mererentur remissionem culpae aut compensarunt mortem aeternam vel purgatorium, nos quoque sentimus, non esse plus tribuendum illis ritibus, quam tribuerunt ipsi sancti patres recte intellecti et quam sinit Evangelium, quod docet nos, solum Christi esse hostiam, solam Christi mortem esse oblationem, satisfactionem et compensationem, propter quam Deus et culpam et mortem aeternam nobis remittit.

Caeterum vera contritio mortificat carnem et nova oboedientia debet cohercere carnem variis exercitiis, sicut Paulus ait (I Co 9:27): Castigo corpus meum et in servitutem redigo. Et haec non sunt opera indebita, sed debita.

Est etiam retinenda distinctio remissionis culpae et remissionis poenae temporalis. Cum enim Deus saepe puniat peccata praesentibus et temporalibus poenis, valde prodest hoc quoque in ecclesia doceri, *quod non solum consequamur vitam aeternam*, cum agimus poenitentiam, *sed etiam* quod *remissionem aut mitigationem* praesentium *poenarum* et calamitatum *paenitentia et bona opera* nostra mereantur, *sicut Paulus inquit (I Co 11:31): Si nos ipsi iudicaremus, non iudicaremur a Domino, et Zacharias (1:3): Convertimini ad me et ego convertar ad vos; et Esaias 58 (vv. 7,11): Frange esurienti panem tuum, etc. tunc eris*

penance in the Church, about which the holy fathers themselves believed that those rites had been instituted for the sake of discipline and example, and did not believe that they merited remission of guilt, or compensated for eternal death or purgatory, we also think that more ought not to be attributed to these rites than the holy fathers, who rightly understood them, attributed to them. Nor ought more to be attributed to them than the Gospel allows. The Gospel teaches us that Christ alone is the sacrifice, and that Christ's death alone is the oblation, satisfaction and compensation, because of which God remits to us guilt and eternal death.

But genuine contrition mortifies the flesh, and the new obedience ought to coerce the flesh by various exercises, as Paul says (I Co 9:27): I keep under my body and bring it into subjection. These are not unrequired works, but required ones.

Also the distinction should be retained between the remission of guilt and the remission of temporal punishment. For since God often punishes sin by present and temporal punishments, it is very worthwhile that it be taught in the Church that *we not only receive eternal life* when we do pentience, *but also* that our *pentience and good works merit the remission or mitigation of* temporal *punishments* and calamities, *as Paul says (I Co 11:31) that if we would judge ourselves, we would not be judged by The Lord*, and Zechariah *(1:3): Turn to me and I will turn to you, and Isaiah 58 (vv. 7,11): Share your bread with the hungry... then*

velut hortus irrigans, et Deus remisit poenam Ninivitis propter ipsorum paenitentiam (Io 3:10). Et de hac remissione poenarum vere intelligi potest (Tb 4:11; 12:9): Eleemosina liberat a morte, hoc est, meretur remissionem praesentium poenarum. *Haec sunt inculcanda ecclesiis, et ut excitentur ad bene operandum, et in his ipsis operibus exerceant et confirment fidem petentes et expectantes a Deo mitigationem praesentium calamitatum.*

you will be a spring of water whose waters do not fail, and God remitted the punishment of the Ninevites because of their penitence (Jo 3:10). And it is concerning this remission of punishments that the passage can be rightly understood (Tb 4:11; 12:9): Alms deliver from death; that is, they merit the remission of present punishments. *These things ought to be taught to the churches, both so that they may be incited to do good works and to exercise and strengthen their faith in such good works, seeking and asking of God mitigation of present calamities.*

08. De usu sacramentorum (13)

08. The Right Use of the Sacraments (13)

Quod ad tertium decimum articulum confessionis nostrae attinet, docemus, quod sacramenta instituta sunt, non modo ut sint notae professionis inter Christianos, sed magis ut sint certa quaedam testimonia et efficacia signa gratiae et voluntatis Dei erga nos, hoc est, per quae Deus invisibiliter operetur in nobis et suam gratiam in nos invisibiliter diffundat...
wo wir anders recht gebrauchen, item dass sie sind gegeben den Glauben zu erwecken und zu sterken in denen, so ihr brauchen.

Concerning the thirteenth article of our confession, **we teach that the sacraments were instituted not only to be marks of Christian profession but, in addition, to be steadfast witnesses and efficacious signs of grace and of God's will towards us, that is, means through which God works invisibly in us and invisibly pours his grace into us...**

provided that we use them rightly, in that they were given in order to awaken and strengthen faith in those who thus use them.

Weiter lehren wir, dass man der Sakramente also gebrauchen soll, dass neben wahrhaftiger Reu und **Buss auch soll dasein der Glaube** und nämlich solcher Glaube, wie droben vom Glauben gesagt ist, durch welchen wir gerecht werden,

Moreover we teach that the sacraments are to be used in such a way that, besides true contrition and repentance, **faith also should be present**: and namely such faith as is said above about faith, by which we are justified, that is, the faith which

das ist, der do nicht allein glaubt in gemein, dass ein Gott sei etc., sondern der do auch **glaubt den gegenwärtigen Verheissungen, so durch die Sakramente dargeboten, gereicht und übergeben werden. Denn wir halten das nicht für** beständig und **recht, dass etliche sagen, dass die Sakramente Gnade bringen** *ex opere operato sine bono modo utentis* allein von wegen des getannen Werks, obgleich der es empfehet, keinen Glauben hat, **denn in denen, so zur Vernunft gekommen sind, ist von Noten dass, der die Sakramente empfeht, den Glauben mitbringe, welcher glaubt denselbigen Verheissungen und die verheissenen Güter (so in den Sakramenten angeboten werden) empfahe**, und dieser Brauch der Sakramente ist den frommen Herzen und blöden Gewissen sehr tröstlich.

does not only believe in general that God exists etc., but **the faith which also believes the present promises that are held forth, presented and distributed through the sacraments. For we hold that it is not** true and **correct to say, as some do, that the sacraments confer grace by virtue of the mere performance of the rite (***ex opere operato***) without the good intention of the recipient,** i.e. only on the basis of the work done, even though the recipient should have no faith, **for in those who have come to penitence it is necessary that he who would receive the sacraments rightly bring with him the faith which believes the same promises, and may receive the promised blessings which are offered in the sacraments**. This use of the sacraments is very comforting to believing hearts and tender consciences.

09. *Von dem Kirchenregiment (08, 14)*

09. *Church Order (08, 14)*

Den achten und vierzehnten Artikeln belangend **lehren wir** einträchtlich, **dass niemand soll** in der Christenheit **öffentlich lehren oder Sakrament reichen, er sei denn ordentlich dazu berufen von denen, die da recht** und Macht **haben**, Kirchendiener **zu berufen und anzunehmen**.

Item wir lehren auch, dieweil beide, die Sakramente in der Christenheit und auch das Wort Gottes, ihre Kraft haben nicht von wegen der Würdigkeit des Dieners, sondern **von wegen der Ordnung** oder Einsetzung und Befehls **Christi, so**

Concerning the eighth and fourteenth articles, **we** unanimously **teach that nobody should teach or administer the sacraments publicly** anywhere in Christendom **without having been regularly called by those who have the right** and power **to call and ordain** Church ministers.

Moreover, since in Christendom both the sacraments and the Word of God have their power, not because of the worthiness of the minister but **because of the order** or institution and command **of Christ**, we also teach that **they are** just as **effica-**

sind sie gleich **kräftig, wenn sie durch böse Diener gereicht** werden, als wo sie durch fromme gereicht werden, darum verdammen wir, die da sagen, dass man nicht möge das Wort und Sakrament annehmen von bösen Dienern, als sei es darum unkräftig und vergeblich.

cious **when** they are **administered by evil ministers** as when they are administered by godly ones. Therefore we condemn those who say that one may not receive the Word and the sacraments from evil ministers, as if the Word and the sacraments were for that reason inefficacious and void.

10. Von Kirchenordnungen (07, 15)

Den fünfzehnten Artikel unser Konfession und das letzte Stück des siebten Artikels belangend, lehren wir, dass die Bischöfe oder Pfarrer die Macht haben, Kirchenordnungen und Zeremonien zu machen und dergleichen Satzungen als von Feiertagen und Unterschied der Kirchendiener etc., darzu dass alles ordentlich und friedlich zugehe in den Kirchen, und dass solche Ordnung und Zeremonien, welche ohne Sünde mögen gehalten werden und darzu dienen, dass es friedlich und ordentlich zugehe, sollen von jedermann um Friedens und christlicher Liebe willen gehalten werden.

Zu dem lehren wir auch, dass man hierin die christliche Freiheit behalten solle, nämlich dass die Leute verstehen, dass solche Satzungen nicht der Meinung zu halten, als seien sie nötig zur Seligkeit, und dass die Gewissen nicht verletzt werden, ob sie unterweilen nicht gehalten werden, so doch dass, der sie nachlässt, solches tue aus rechtem Verstand des Geistes und nicht mit Verachtung der Ärgernis, denn wie das man mit dem Gebrauch der christlichen Freiheit mässig

10. Church Ordinances (07, 15)

Concerning the fifteenth article and the last part of the seventh article of our Confession we teach that bishops or pastors have the authority to establish ecclesiastical rites and ceremonies as well as such usages as feast days, ranks of clergymen, etc. Moreover, we teach that all things in the churches should be done with order and peace and that such rites and ceremonies as may be observed without sin and which serve the cause of peace and order ought to be observed by everyone for the sake of peace and Christian love.

Moreover we also teach that in this way Christian freedom should be maintained, that is, that people should understand that they are to observe such usages not as if they were necessary for salvation, and that consciences should not be violated if sometimes such usages are not observed, as long as he who omits them does this with the right understanding and not with the contempt that comes from dislike; for one must be moderate in the use of Christian freedom lest the

fahren soll, dass die unverständigen nicht dadurch geärgert, noch um das Missbrauchs willen unsrer Freiheit von der rechten Lehre des Evangelii abgeschreckt werden, und dass man nicht ohne sondere bewegende Ursachen die gewöhnlichen Kirchenordnungen ändern soll, sondern dass man um Friede und Einigkeit willen die alten Gewohnheiten halte, so man ohne Sünde halten kann.

Darüber sagen wir auch, dass wo die Bischöfe ihre Satzung machen, der Meinung als sollte man dadurch Gnade und Vergebung der Sünde erlangen oder genügen für die Sünde, oder dass die Gewissen damit verbunden und verstrickt werden und die Leute dafür halten, als seien es sondere Gottesdienste nötig zur Seligkeit und wähnen, sie tun Sünde, wo sie dieselben an Verachtung und Ärgernis nachlassen; solchen Wahn halten wir dem Evangelio und der Lehre vom Glauben ganz entgegen sein, und lehren, dass keine Bischöfe solche Satzungen Macht haben zu machen oder zu fordern.

Endlich lehren wir auch, dass gleich wie es **nicht Not ist, dass solche Kirchensatzungen oder Zeremonien von Menschen eingesetzt allenthaben gleich und einerlei sind, denn ein einzelnes Land** hat ihre Feste und ein einzelnes Kirchspiel hat **seine eigene Weise und Ordnung**, die den andern nicht allerdinge gleich sind, also auch wird durch solche Ungleichheit nicht verletzt noch zertrennt die recht geistliche Einigkeit der Kirchen, dann dass dieselbige bleibe und erhalten werde, ist genug, dass man einig sei der rechten Lehre

unlearned be thereby offended or frightened away from the correct doctrine of the Gospel because of the misuse of our freedom. Therefore the customary Church ordinances ought not to be altered without special, cogent reasons, but for the sake of peace and unity the old custom should be retained as far as it can be without sin.

Moreover, we also say that when bishops set up their rite with the intention that one should obtain grace and forgiveness of sins or satisfaction for sin through them, or when consciences are thereby bound and ensnared and people imagine that special worship is necessary for salvation and that they are sinning if they omit such observance, with no contempt for them or offence being involved, we consider such an error contrary to the Gospel and the doctrine of faith, and we teach that no bishops have the authority to establish or impose such rites.

Finally we also teach that just as **it is not necessary that such Church rites or ceremonies instituted by men should be observed uniformly in all places, since each country** has its feast days and each Church district **has its own custom and usage** which are not exactly like the others, even so the true spiritual unity of the churches is not harmed or dissolved by such diversity, for it is sufficient for the maintenance of true unity that there be unity in the preaching of the Gospel and in the correct use of the sacraments, and that people live in love with one

des Evangelii und des rechten Brauchs der Sakramente und demselbigen gemäss in der Liebe gegeneinander lebe, wie S. Paulus sagt (Ep 4:5): **Ein Glaube, eine Taufe, etc.**

another, as St Paul says (Ep 4:5): **One faith, one baptism, etc.**

11. Von weltlichen Ständen (16)

Den sechszehnten Artikel belangend lehren wir erstlich, dieweil das Reich Christi geistlich ist, das ist, dass do in der Menschen Herzen recht Erkenntnis Gottes, Furcht und Glauben, eine ewige Gerechtigkeit und ewiges Leben anrichtet, darum so zerreisst nicht das weltliche Reich oder Landregierung und Hausregiment, sondern bestätigt dieselben und befielt, dass man sie erhalte als göttliche Ordnung, gute Kreaturen Gottes.

Denn Gott will, dass wir gebrauchen und unterworfen sein sollen aller weltlichen geordneten Oberkeit, darunter wir leben, und gebäut, dass wir durch solchen Gehorsam die Liebe erzeigen.

Zum anderen lehren wir, weil solche geordnete weltliche Regimente und Oberkeit Gott gefallen, so mag ein Christ nach göttlichem Gesetz ohne Sünde Oberkeit und Richteramt führen und aus kaiserlichen und anderen gewöhnlichen Rechten recht sprechen, Übeltäter nach gemeinem Recht strafen, rechte Kriege führen, kaufen und verkaufen, eigene Güter haben, auf gelegten Eid tun, ehelich sein, etc.

Endlich lehren wir, dass alle Christen von Noten ihrer Oberkeit sollen gehorsam sein in allen Din-

11. Civil Affairs (16)

Concerning the sixteenth article we teach first, that Christ's kingdom is a spiritual kingdom, that is, a kingdom which establishes in the hearts of men correct knowledge of God, fear and faith, eternal righteousness and everlasting life, and that therefore it does not destroy either the civil empire, local government, or domestic authority, but rather it confirms all of them and commands us to maintain them as the ordinance of God, as good creations of God.

For God wants us to use and to be subject to all civil governments under which we live, and he commands us to show love by such obedience.

Secondly, since such government and civil authority are pleasing to God, we teach that according to divine law a Christian may without sin hold civil office, sit as a judge, decide matters by imperial or other existing laws, punish evildoers according to common law, engage in just wars, serve as a soldier, buy, sell and possess property, take required oaths, be married, etc.

Finally, we teach that all Christians are obliged to be subject to civil authority in all things, except that if

gen, ohne wo sie etwas gebieten, dass ohne Sünde nicht geschehen kann, dann in solchem Fall soll man Gott mehr gehorsam sein dann den Menschen. Ac 5:29.

rulers command what cannot be obeyed without sin, Christians must obey God rather than men. Ac 5:29.

12. De missa (24)

De lectionibus et precationibus in missa non est controversia. Cum enim Paulus (I Co 14:26) etiam in publicis caeremoniis velit **recitari** aliquas **sacras lectiones** utiles ad excitandas mentes ad timorem et fidem et addi **precationes** et gratiarum actionem, hic mos in ecclesia **non abolendus,** sed diligenter **conservandus est.** Primum enim maxime prodest in communi **coetu fieri precationem, quia Christus** nominatim ecclesiae **dedit promissiones, cum ait (Mt 18:19, 20): Si duo ex vobis consenserint super terram de omni re, quamcunque petierint, fiet illis a patre meo, qui in caelis est; ubi enim sunt duo vel tres congregati in nomine meo, ibi sum in medio eorum.** Invitat igitur nos Christus amplissima promissione, ut in precatione **nos ecclesiae adiungamus, vult Deus, ecclesiam sic inter se devinctam esse, ut alii aliorum necessitate afficiantur et pro aliis orent, et promittit, se has preces exauditurum esse;** ut hoc discamus et hanc fidem exerceamus, publica consuetudo ecclesiae in publicis precationibus, in missa et aliis ceremoniis monere nos debet. Iubet et Paulus (II Co 1:11) per multos fieri precationes, ut vicissim multi agant gratias Deo, quod Deus exaudiverit preces, quod respexerit afflictos.

12. The Mass (24)

Concerning lessons and prayers in the mass, there is no controversy. For since even Paul (I Col 14:26) wants some **lessons from Holy Scripture to be read** in the public service – lessons that are beneficial for stirring up minds to fear and faith – and also wants prayers and thanksgivings **to be added, this custom ought not to be abolished** in the Church, **but** carefully **preserved.** For first of all, it is very useful that **prayer be made in common worship, since Christ** expressly **gave promises** to the **Church when he said (Mt 18:19, 20): If two of you agree on earth concerning anything, whatever you ask for, it shall be done for them by my Father in heaven. For where two or three are gathered together in my name, there am I in the midst of them. Therefore Christ invites us** with this very full promise **to join the Church** in prayer, **for God wants the Church to be so closely bound together that we feel each other's needs and pray for them, and God promises that he will hear these prayers.** The public custom of the Church in public prayers, in the mass, and in other services ought to admonish us that we may learn this and exercise this faith. In II Co 1:11 Paul also urges that prayers be made by many in order that many might, in turn, thank God, that he would hear their prayers and take care of the afflicted.

Deinde exemplum Ecclesiae utilissimum est. Monet enim multos, ut ipsi quoque **excitentur ad credendum et invocandum**, praesertim si populus in concionibus admoneatur de promissionibus ecclesiae factis. Ita enim intelligent aliorum exempla, et mos ecclesiae proderit ipsis ad aedificationem, ut docet Paulus (I Co 14:19).

Next, the example of the Church is most useful. For it encourages many **to be stirred up** themselves **to believe and to pray**, especially if the people are instructed in sermons concerning the promises given to the Church. For thus they will learn of the example of others, and the custom of the Church will help their edification, as Paul teaches (I Co 14:19).

Tertio **prodest etiam exemplum** ecclesiae, ut moneat singulos, quarum rerum cura affici et quid petere debeant. Nam populus non admonitus non intelligit **publicas necessitates**. Ibi autem non solum audit privata dona petenda esse, sed etiam discit, **singulos debere affici publicis curis, orare pro universa ecclesia, ut liberetur ab erroribus, scandalis, disidiis, impiis cultibus, ut propagetur vera doctrina, ut veri cultus praestentur Deo**, et nos regamur et sanctificemur per Spiritum Sanctum. Discit item Deo placere precationes de rebus corporalibus, de pace, **de felici gubernatione, de proventu frugum, contra pestilentiam et similia** mala.

Thirdly, **the example** of the Church **is also helpful** in that it teaches individuals what they should be concerned about and what they should ask for. For uninstructed people do not know what **the public needs** are. **In public services** they not only hear that private gifts are to be prayed for but also to learn that **individuals ought to be concerned with matters of public interest and pray for the universal Church, that it be set free from errors, scandals, dissensions and wicked customs, that true doctrine might be propagated and true worship rendered to God**, and (that) we may be governed and sanctified by the Holy Spirit. Likewise they learn that prayers for secular matters, for peace, **for good government, for the growth of crops and for preservation from pestilence and similar** evils are pleasing to God.

Huiusmodi precationes in publicis caeremoniis, in missa et aliis sentimus pie et necessario **institutas esse.** Est enim mandatum Dei, et ut **invocemus eum in omnibus periculis**, et ut populus in publicis ritibus de hac invocatione

Prayers of this sort in public services, in the mass, and in other gatherings we believe to have been **instituted out of godliness and necessity.** For it is the command of God, both that **we call upon him in all dangers** and that people be

doceatur, ut discat Deo credere et a Deo petere et expectare auxilium.

Sed de usu sacramenti corporis et sanguinis Domini in missa, improbamus eos, qui sentiunt, usum sacramenti cultum esse applicandum pro aliis vivis et mortuis et mereri illis remissionem culpae et poenae, idque ex opere operato. Haec enim sunt ignota veteri Ecclesiae et dissentiunt a Scripturis Sacris et obscurant doctrinam de fide et alieni operis fiduciam pariunt.

Sed cum Christus dixerit (Lc 22:19): Hoc facite in mei commemorationem, instituit hoc sacramentum, ut ibi fiat vera fide recordatio mortis ipsius et beneficiorum, quae nobis morte sua meruit. Et haec beneficia per sacramentum applicantur sumenti, cum fidem hace recordatione exuscitat et credit, Christum vere nobis donare sua beneficia, cum tantum testimonium nobis exhibeat, quod nos sibi adiungat, quod nos velit tamquam sua membra servare, quod nos mundet suo sanguine.

Haec fides, qua accipiuntur beneficia Christi, est spiritualis cultus Dei, et quia cum ea fide debet esse coniuncta gratiarum actio, qua corda vere pro remissione peccatorum et redemptione gratias agant

taught in public services concerning such prayer, in order that they may learn to believe God and to seek and expect help from him.

But concerning the celebration of the sacrament of the body and blood of the Lord in the mass, we blame those who think that the celebration of the mass is a service to be held for other people living and dead, and that it merits for them the remission of guilt and punishment, and this by virtue of the mere performance of the rite (ex opere operato). For these ideas were unknown to the ancient Church, and they disagree with the Holy Scriptures, obscure the doctrine concerning faith and produce trust in the work of another.

But when Christ said (Lk 22:19): Do this in remembrance of me he instituted this sacrament in order that in it by true faith there might be a memorial of his death and of the benefits which he merited for us by his death. And these benefits are granted through the sacrament to the recipient when by means of this memorial he rouses up his faith and believes that Christ really grants us his benefits when he presents to us such great evidence that he unites us to himself, that he wants to preserve us as his members, and that he cleanses us by his blood.

This faith, by which Christ's benefits are received, is the spiritual worship of God; and since to this faith there must be joined the giving of thanks, whereby our hearts truly give thanks to God the Father and

Deo Patri et Domino nostro Iesu Christo, idea vetus ecclesia hunc usum sacramentorum vocavit Eucharistiam, sicut Cyprianus suavissime inquit de communicantibus: Pietas inter data et condonata se dividens gratias agit tam uberis beneficii largitori, id est: Pietas utrumque considerat, quanta sit magnitudo beneficii nobis donati, gratiae et vitae aeternae, et e regione, quanta sit magnitudo malorum nostrorum, hoc est, peccatorum et mortis aeternae. Existit igitur ardens gratiarum actio, cum videmus, nobis ineffabili clementia tanta peccata remitti et nos insuper donari Spiritu Sancto et gloria illa aeternae vitae.

Et in hanc sententiam sentimus hanc sacratissimam ceremoniam vocari sacrificium a sanctis patribus, qui certe non senserunt id opus applicatum pro aliis mereri eis remissionem culpae et poenae idque ex opere operato, sed senserunt in usu sacramenti exercendam esse fidem at gratiarum actionem faciendam esse.

Cum igitur Christus sic instituerit usum sacramenti, ut esset communio, in qua porrigeretur aliquibus sacramentum, et hunc morem diu servaverit vetus ecclesia nec habuerit privatas missas, sentimus nos, talem ritum, in quo fit communio aliquorum, pium et consentaneum esse Evangelio.

our Lord Jesus Christ for the remission of sins and redemption, therefore the ancient Church called this celebration of the sacrament the Eucharist, as Cyprian says most delightfully about those who receive the sacrament: Godliness, distinguishing between the things given and the things forgiven, gives thanks to the Giver of so rich a benefit; that is, godliness considers both things: 1. how great is the magnitude of the benefit given to us – grace and eternal life and 2. by contrast, how great is the magnitude of our evils, of our sins and eternal death. Therefore enthusiastic thanksgiving arises when we see that such great sins are remitted by ineffable clemency and that, besides, we are given the Holy Spirit and the glory of eternal life.

We hold that it was in this sense that this most holy ceremony was called a sacrifice by the holy fathers, who certainly did not think that this rite performed for others' merits remission of guilt and remission of punishment for them, and that *ex opere operato*, but they thought that in the celebration of the sacrament their faith should be exercised and thanksgiving should be made.

Since therefore, Christ so instituted the celebration of the sacrament as to be a Communion in which the sacrament might be distributed to others, and since the ancient Church preserved this custom for a long time and did not hold private masses, we hold that a rite in which the Communion of others (besides the celebrant) takes place is godly and in keeping with the Gospel.

Deinde privatae missae solitae sunt fieri cum illa opinione de usu sacramenti, quod necesse est, existere in ecclesia hunc cultum applicandum pro aliis, ut mereatur eis remissionem culpae et poenae, **tales igitur missae abrogandae sunt.** Et ut haec scandala tollantur et Christi institutio, videlicet communio, servetur, sentimus, neminem cogendum esse, ut celebret privatas missas. Cum enim Paulus dicat (I Co 11:27) reos esse corporis et sanguinis Domini illos, qui abutantur sacramento, **summa cura praestandum est, ut pius et sanctus usus ad gloriam Christi et salutem ecclesiae restituatur.**

It was at a later time that private masses were commonly celebrated with this idea of the sacrament, that it must be done for others in the Church, that it might earn the remission of guilt and punishment for them. Therefore **such masses ought to be abolished.** And in order that these offences might be removed and Christ's institution, Communion, be preserved, we hold that no-one ought to be compelled to celebrate private masses. For since Paul says (I Co 11:27) that those who misuse the sacrament are guilty of the body and blood of the lord, **great care must be taken that a godly and holy celebration be restored, to the glory of Christ and the well-being of the Church.**

13. De utraque specie (22)

Non dubium est, quin vetus ecclesia in oriente et occidente usa sit utraque specie sacramenti corporis et sanguinis Christi, videlicet specie panis et specie vini. Nam et Paulus hunc morem testatur fuisse in ecclesia Corinthiorum, et Christus eum instituit sacramentum, non solum pro parte ecclesiae, videlicet pro sacerdotibus, sed pro universa ecclesia hunc usum sacramenti ordinavit, et extant Hieronymi et aliorum sententiae, quae ostendunt, hunc morem diu mansisse in ecclesia, et in capitulo: Comperimus praecepit Gelasius, ut utraque species sumatur. Quare recens prohibitio tantum est humana traditio, quare non habet auctoritatem mutandi institutum Christi, nec sunt cogendi homines propter

13. Of Both Kinds (22)

There is no doubt that the ancient Church in east and west celebrated the sacrament of Christ's body and blood under both kinds, namely, under the species of bread and the species of wine. For Paul also bears witness that this was the custom in the church of the Corinthians, and Christ instituted the sacrament not only for a part of the Church, namely for the priests, but he ordained this form of celebrating the sacrament for the whole Church. There exist statements of Jerome and of others which prove that this custom continued for a long time in the Church. Also Gelasius, in the chapter headed *Comperimus*, ordered both kinds to be received. Hence the recent prohibition of such reception is a mere human tradition which does

humanam traditionem, ut contra conscientiam mutent morem traditum a Christo et usurpatum in veteri ecclesia, cum constet, hunc usum legitimum et pium esse.

not have the authority to change Christ's institution, nor should people be compelled for the sake of human tradition to alter, against their conscience, the custom handed down by Christ and followed in the ancient Church, when it is clear that this practice is legitimate and godly.

14. De coniugio sacerdotum (23)

De virginitate et de continentia et de coniugio manifestam Pauli sententiam I Corinth. 7 sequimur et defendimus. Et quemadmodum Christus (Mt 19:12) laudat eunuchos, qui se castraverunt propter regnum Christi, ita nos quoque docemus, virginitatis conservationem bonum opus esse et utlie ad assiduitatem praestandam in studiis et in meditatione, in precatione, in ministeriis ecclesiasticis, sicut Paulus inquit (I Co 7:32-33): Maritum ea curare, quae sunt mundi, coelibem vero, quae sunt Domini. Nam maritum impediunt occupationes domesticae, quominus possit praestare illam assiduitatem, utilem studiis et ministeriis publicis, sed coelebs est expeditior, quare et maiorem intentionem animi adhibere potest in discendo, docendo et ceteris functionibus et minus ab his curis abducitur. Itaque commodum est eligere et habere in ecclesiis ministros pure coelibes, et adhortandi sunt hi, qui videntur idonei, ut donum Dei propter utilitatem ecclesiae conservent sua diligentia et temperantia, et docendi, quod Deo placeat hoc officium et habeat magna praemia.

14. The Marriage of Priests (23)

Concerning virginity, continence and marriage, we follow and defend the clear teaching of Paul in I Corinthians 7. And even as Christ (Mt 19:12) praises eunuchs who castrated themselves for the sake of the kingdom of Christ, so we also teach that the retention of virginity is a good work, and useful for giving constant attention to studies and meditation, to prayer and to ecclesiastical offices, even as Paul says (I Co 7:32-33) that he that is married cares for the things that are of the world, whereas the celibate (cares for) the things that belong to the Lord. For domestic concerns hinder the married person from being able to show that constant attention which is beneficial to studies and public duties; but a celibate is freer and can give greater attention to learning, teaching and other functions, and is less often diverted from these pursuits. And so it is advantageous to choose and have in the churches ministers who are completely celibate. Those who seem to be suited to that ought to be encouraged to preserve the gift of God for the benefit of the Church with diligence and temperance, and they ought to be instructed that this estate pleases

Sed quia Christus est testator, non omnes idoneos esse ad perpetuum coelibatum, ideo sentimus his, qui non sunt idonei ad coelibatum, coniugium nec prohibendum esse nec prohiberi posse voto aut lege humana, quia votum et leges humanae non possunt nos liberare a lege divina et iure naturae. Est autem lex divina (1 Co 7:2, 9) ut unusquisque, qui non habet donum continentiae habeat uxorem vitandae fornicationis causa. Et ius naturae est appetitio coniunctionis conformis rectae rationi. Ad hanc naturalem, ut vocant "storgen" accessit iam concupiscentia, quae magis inflammat naturam, ut magis opus sit coniugio, tamquam remedio.

Illa autem lex, quae sacerdotibus prohibet coniugia, mere humana traditio est. Imo haec nova traditio, quae prohibet coniugia sacerdotibus et coniugia sacerdotibus et contracta distrahit, non est orta a conciliis, sed a solis Romanis episcopis.

Est autem mundicies coram Deo non polluere conscientiam, sed oboedire Deo. Quare impurus coelibatus non est mundicies, sed coniugium, cum sit sanctificatum Verbo Dei, est mundicies sicut Paphnutius dixit consuetudinem coniugalem esse continentiam. Certo enim scimus, hoc vitae genus Deo placere, et est plenum exercitiis pietatis, ideoque ecclesia longo tempore non solum in oriente, sed etiam in occidente habuit sacerdotes coniuges.

God and has great rewards.

But since Christ himself bears witness that not all are suited to perpetual celibacy, therefore we hold that marriage ought not to be forbidden those who are not suited to celibacy; neither can it be prohibited by human vows or laws, because human vows are not able to free us from the divine law and the right of nature. For this is a divine law (I Co 7:2, 9), that everyone who does not have the gift of continency should have a wife in order to avoid fornication. And the right of nature is a desire for union in keeping with right reason. To this natural drive, which (the Greeks) call "storge", there has been added concupiscence, which inflames nature all the more, so that there is all the more need of marriage as a kind of remedy.

The law however, which prohibits the marriage of priests, is a purely human tradition. Indeed, this new tradition, which forbids the marriage of priests and which dissolves marriages, did not arise from the councils, but only from the Roman bishops.

Purity before God, however, consists in not polluting one's conscience but in obeying God. Therefore impure celibacy is not purity, but marriage is purity, since it is sanctified by the Word of God. Thus Paphnutius said that conjugal custom is continency. For we well know that this state of life pleases God and gives full scope for the exercise of godliness, and for that reason the Church for a long time, not only in the east but also in the west, had priests who were married.

Et testantur historiae, hunc morem vi in Hispania et Germania mutatum esse, et Graecae ecclesiae habent adhuc sacerdotes maritos. Quare coniugium non est immundicies aut res indigna ministris ecclesiarum. Qualia autem exempla, quantam immundiciem, quam indignam ecclesiis pepererit lex Romani episcopi non est obscurum. Cumque lex divina praecipiat coniugium his, qui non praestant continentiam, iudicamus, prohibitionem pontificiam de coelibatu illicitam esse et coniugium sacerdotibus permittendum esse.

And history books bear witness to the fact that this custom was changed in Spain and Germany by force, and the Greek churches still have married priests. And so marriage is not impurity or a state unbecoming to ministers in the churches. But what sad examples and how much shameful impurity the law of the Bishop of Rome has imposed on the churches is no secret. And since a divine law prescribes marriage for those who cannot show continence, we judge that the papal prohibition concerning marriage is illegitimate, and that the marriage of priests ought to be permitted.

15. De votis monasticis (27)

15. Monastic Vows (27)

Multae sunt graves causae, quare opus sit de publico alere studiosos et pios destinatos sacris litteris, ut inde sumi possint ecclesiarum doctores. Cum enim tenuiores non possint suis facultatibus tolerare sumptus studiorum, et divites magis conferant se ad alias artes, quibus magni honores, magna praemia in republica proposita sunt, necesse est, ecclesiam curare, ut publicis reditibus foveantur aliqui, qui dent operam sacris litteris et ceteris artibus, quibus ecclesia opus habet. Hoc nisi fit, multis in locis defuturi sunt ecclesiis pastores, et pertinet haec cura ad reges et principes, prospicere, ne desint ecclesiis pastores, et suppeditare sumptus docentibus et discentibus. Ideo enim Esaias (49:23) vocat reges nutricios ecclesiae et reginas nutrices, ut doceat, quod reges et res publicae debeant defendere doctores et suppeditare

There are many weighty reasons why there is need of support from public funds for students and godly persons who prepare for the study of theology, so that from their midst the teachers of the Church may be taken. For since poor people are not able to afford the expense of study from their own resources, and rich people prefer other professions in which great honours and great rewards in the state are offered, it is necessary that the Church take care that some people be supported by its public revenues, who will devote themselves to sacred studies and the other arts which the Church has need of. Unless this happens, churches in many places will be lacking pastors, and it is the responsibility of kings and princes to see to it that there be no lack of pastors for the churches, and to provide expenses for teachers and students. That is why Isaiah

sumptus. Nec iniquum est, hos, quorum studia ad utilitatem ecclesiae destinata sunt, vicissim ab ecclesiis ali, sicut Paulus inquit (I Co 9:7): Quis militat suis stipendiis?

Hoc consilio apparet initio coetus in collegiis et monasteriis institutos esse, ut frequentia aliqua esset versantium in sacris litteris, ex quibus eligi possint doctores, idque leges in codice et historiae testantur.

Prodest igitur ad hunc usum, emendatis opinionibus et cultibus impiis, conservare collegia et monasteria.

Non enim satis est, iuventutem, quae admovenda est olim ecclesiae gubernaculis, litteras discere, sed etiam disciplina quadam et piis exercitiis assuefacienda est ad amorem ceremoniarum et pietatem, nam qui non sunt tali diligentia assuefacti, plerumque magis sunt prophani quam expedit.

Ad haec opus est ecclesiae doctis et peritis pastoribus. Plurimum autem ad doctrinam confirmandam et formanda iudicia conducit illa familiaris cum doctis et peritis rerum spiritualium conversatio. Nemo enim potest solidam doctrinam sine tali collatione consequi. Si autem omnino deerunt pastores ecclesiis

(49:23) calls kings nursing fathers of the church, and queens nursing mothers, (for he wishes) to teach that kings and states ought to protect teachers and provide for their expenses. Nor is it unjust that those whose studies are destined for the benefit of the Church should in turn be supported by the churches, as Paul says (I Co 9:7): Who goes to war at his own expense?

The foundations in colleges and monasteries appear to have been made with this purpose, that there might be a certain group of people who engaged in sacred studies, from whose midst teachers could be chosen. This fact is borne witness to by the laws in the Codex [Iustinianus, *ed.*] and by stories in history books.

Therefore it is for the benefit of this practice that colleges and monasteries should be preserved, after false opinions and ungodly practices have been reformed.

For it is not enough for the youth who must one day become the rulers of the Church, merely to learn their letters; they must also, by means of a certain discipline and of godly practices, get accustomed to loving ceremonies and godliness, because those who are not so accustomed are often more worldly than is proper.

In addition, the Church has need of learned and experienced pastors. For living close to men who are learned and experienced in spiritual matters contributes very much to confirming doctrine and to forming sound judgements. For no-one is able to acquire sound doctrine without such common life. And if

aut erunt pastores indocti et inexercitati et tyrones, qualem statum futurum ecclesiae putabimus? Vastitas et barbaries futura est, amissis litteris, extincta doctrina.

Paulus (I Ti 3:6) vetat eligi neophytos, quia sciebat opus esse peritis et exercitatis doctoribus. Nazianzenus deplorat ecclesiae calamitatem, quia hi, qui antea non didicissent, subito fierent doctores, non doctrina sed suffragiis erecti. Basilius ait, sibi doctrinam praesentium patrum, quos audierit, adhuc personare in auribus. Quare valde optandum est, ut talia sint monasteria, in quibus floreat et propagetur doctrina et recte assuefiat iuventus et praeparetur ad ministeria ecclesiae, ut haberi possint eruditi et exercitati doctores ecclesiarum. Talia fuerunt olim collegia episcoporum, ut ex Ambrosii et Augustini historiis et aliis apparet, in quibus diu propagata est doctrina.

Postea cum in talibus collegiis studia doctrinae negligerentur, magna mutatio doctrinae secuta est, quae non leviter nocuit ecclesiae. Itaque conservata politia collegiorum et monasteriorum emendentur opiniones, tollatur superstitio, abiiciantur impii cultus et renoventur studia doctrinae ad utilitatem ecclesiae. Nos enim iudicamus, opiniones illas impias esse, sentire,

pastors are entirely lacking in the churches, or if they are untrained and unlearned recruits, what shall we think of the future state of the Church? There will be desolation and barbarity once learning has been lost and doctrine has become extinct.

Paul (I Ti 3:6) forbids the choosing of novices because he knows there is always need of experienced and trained teachers. Gregory of Nazianzus deplores the calamity that befell the Church because those who had not taught before were suddenly made teachers – set up not because of their training, but by popular election. Basil says that he can still hear ringing in his ears the teaching of the outstanding fathers whose lectures he heard. Therefore it is very much to be desired that there be monasteries in which Christian doctrine may flourish and be propagated, in which the young may be rightly educated and prepared for the ministry of the Church, in order that they can be considered learned and trained teachers of the churches. Such were once in ancient times the bishops' schools, in which Christian doctrine was long preserved, as appears in the histories and other books of Ambrose and Augustine.

Thereafter, when the study of Christian doctrine was neglected in such communities, a great change in Christian doctrine ensued – a change which harmed the Church to no little degree. Therefore let us preserve the organization of the colleges and monasteries, but let the opinions held there be improved; let superstition be removed, let ungodly practices be abolished, and let the study of

quod monastica vota mereantur remissionem peccatorum et vitam aeternam aut sint iustitia vel perfectio christiana.

Et quamquam licita vota servanda sunt, tamen vota monastica sunt illicita, facta cum falsa persuasione, quod illa opera sine mandato Dei excogitata non sint res indifferentes, sed sint cultus et mereantur remissionem peccatorum et vitam aeternam. Quare sunt irrita vota.

Quod igitur ex Paulo (I Ti 5:12) obiicitur de viduis, quae primam fidem irritam fecerint, etiamsi tunc fuissent aliqua vota, tamen ille locus non potest accommodari ad vota monastica horum temporum quae, cum fiant cum impia opinione, non sunt vota. Transferunt enim gloria Christi in humanas observationes, et veros cultus in ecclesia obscurant, scilicet fidem in Christum et bona opera vocationis. Quis enim non anteferebat observationes monachorum functioni magistratus et patris familias? Haec enim tamquam prophana et immunda opera vix excusabilia videbantur, fides vero obscurabatur, quia non docebant, gratis donari remissionem peccatorum propter Christum, sed tribuebant hunc honorem suis observationibus.

Christian doctrine be renewed for the benefit of the Church. For we consider that those opinions are godless which hold that monastic vows merit the remission of sins and eternal life, or that they constitute righteousness or Christian perfection.

And although proper vows should be kept, nevertheless monastic vows are illicit if they are made under the false conviction that those works which have been invented without God's command are not matters of indifference, but worship of God, and that they merit remission of sins and eternal life. Therefore they are vows (that are) not binding.

As for what is cited from Paul to the contrary concerning the widows (I Ti 5:12), that they have made their first faith non-binding, even if at that time there had been vows, that passage can nevertheless not be applied to monastic vows of the present time. Since they are made with godless intention, they are not valid vows. For they transfer the glory of Christ to human observances and obscure true worship of in the Church, viz. faith in Christ and the good works of one's calling. For who did not place monks' observances ahead of the functions of a magistrate and of a housefather? For these works which were so profane and unclean seemed scarcely excusable. Faith was truly obscured because people were not teaching that the remission of sins was given freely for Christ's sake, but they attributed this honour to their own observances.

Et has opiniones et haec exempla imitabatur reliqua ecclesia et superstitiose sentiebat opera traditionum humanarum cultus esse, ac mereri remissionem peccatorum et vitam aeternam. Cum autem has opiniones damnet Evangelium, constat vota monastica cum hac persuasione facta non esse licita.

Ad haec non omnes idonei ad perpetuam continentiam. Debet autem votum esse de re possibili.

Et constat multos iuvenes et puellas intrudi in monasteria et cogi, ut faciant vota ante iustam aetatem, qua in re quantum sit periculi, non est obscurum.

Concedendum est igitur his, qui malunt in alio vitae genere pie vivere, ut discedant ex monasteriis.

Recte faciunt et illi, qui discedunt a monachis, ubi in monasteriis coguntur observare impios cultus, ut abusus missarum, indulgentias et pleraque alia. Si qui autem idonei ad vitam monasticam malunt in illis collegiis vivere, si sunt emendatae opiniones et cultus, et utuntur ordinationibus velut rebus indifferentibus, hos non repraehendimus, ac multos sanctos at praestantes viros hoc animo pie vixisse in monasteriis iudicamus; imo optandum est, ut sint talia collegia doctorum et piorum virorum, in quibus ad utilitatem communem ecclesiae colantur studia doctrinae christianae et adolescentes non solum doctrina erudiantur, sed etiam piis exercitiis et illa paedagogia rituum assuefiant ad pie-

And the rest of the Church imitated these examples and opinions, and superstitiously believed that the works of human tradition were a service to God, and that they merited remission of sins and life everlasting. But since the Gospel condemns these opinions, it is clear that monastic vows made with such a conviction are not binding.

Furthermore, not everyone is suited to perpetual continency. But a vow ought to be made in matters that are possible.

It is clear that many young boys and girls were pushed and shoved into the monasteries in order to make vows before the right age. How great a danger there is in that sort of affair is no secret.

Therefore permission to leave the monasteries must be granted to those who prefer to live godly in another state of life.

Those who leave the monasteries where they are forced to observe godless activities, such as abuses of the mass, indulgences, and many other things, also act rightly. But if those who are suited to monastic life prefer to live in those communities, if their opinions and activities are corrected, and if they treat the observances as matters of indifference, we do not have anything against this, for we judge that many saintly people lived godly lives in monasteries in this spirit. In fact, it is much to be desired that there be such communities of learned and godly men, in whose midst the study of Christian doctrine is cultivated for the general benefit of the Church, and in which young people are not

tatem, sed ita, ne votis irretiti cum periculo conscientiae retineantur. Et hoc vitae genus, quia destinatum esset ad utilitatem ecclesiae, ad docendos et exercendos eos coetus, ex quibus sumi possent ecclesiarum doctores, esset pium et placeret Deo; haberet enim cultus a deo mandatos. Est enim mandatum Dei, ut accessuri ad ministeria doceantur et exerceantur, et propter hunc finem probat Deus paedagogiam rituum.

Possunt et monialium collegia esse, ubi puellae discant litteras et doctrinam pietatis, sed non sunt retinendae in monasteriis iuvenculae, quae nubere cupiunt, nec deinceps ullae votis onerandae sunt. Est enim Pauli doctrina servanda, qui ita suadet virginitatem, ne velit laqueos iniici conscientiis.

only educated in Christian doctrine but also trained in godliness by godly practices and by the usual training in ritual, as long as those who have been ensnared by vows are not forced to remain in them, to the jeopardy of their consciences. This kind of common life, since it had been intended to benefit the Church, to teach and to train those groups from whose midst the teachers of the churches could be taken, would be godly and God-pleasing, for it would be service commanded by God. For the command of God is that those who will enter the ministry be taught and trained, and God approves a discipline of ordered life which is directed to this goal.

Communities in which girls may learn the arts and the Christian teaching of godliness may also exist, but girls who desire to marry ought not to be retained in cloisters, nor should they be burdened with vows. For Paul's instruction is to be followed, when he advised virginity in such a way as not to put snares on consciences.

16. Von den Heiligen (21)

Vom einundzwanzigsten Artikel in der Konfession.

Der Heiligen Gedächtnis und Feier verwerfen wir nicht, sondern **achten, dass um dieser Ursache willen, Nutz** und christlich **sei ihr Gedächtnis zu halten:**

Erstlich dass wir an ihnen sehen, dass **Gott der Christenheit hat**

16. The Saints (21)

Concerning the twenty-first article in the Confession.

We do not reject the remembrance of saints and the celebration of their days, but **for the following reasons consider that it is beneficial** and Christian **to keep their remembrance:**

First, we ought to learn from them that **God wanted to set before**

Exempel vorstellen wollen, darin er beweist, dass er wolle gnädig sein allen, so sich bekehren, und wolle, dass sie selig werden, dass wir auch für solche Exempel danksagen und unseren Glauben damit stärken als, **so wir hören, dass Petro** solche grosse Sünde **vergeben ist,** sollen wir dabei auch Trost empfangen und **glauben, Gott werde uns auch vergeben, so wir uns bekehren.** Auch soll man Gott danken, dass er der Kirche nicht allein solche Exempel, sondern auch nützliche Lehrer gegeben hat, Prophete, Apostel, Bischöfe.

Zum anderen so ist auch nützlich den Leuten **vorhalten Exempel des Glaubens und anderer Tugend, dass wir solchen nachfolgen,** jeder nach seinem Beruf, denn die Exempel dienen zu vermahnen und zu lehren, als so wir hören, dass Gott mit grossen Mirakeln die Könige erhalten und herrlich gemacht hat, **welche Abgotterei abgetan haben,** werden wir mit solchen **Exempeln** gestärkt, dass wir Gottes Ehre, auch desto ernstlicher fordern und von Gott Hilfe gewarten. So wir **der Martyrer Beständigkeit** hören, werden wir auch desto getröster, **dass wir** wie sie Gott gehorsam sein und Verfolgung **desto geduldiger leiden.**

Zum dritten soll man **auch Gott danken, dass er den Heiligen diese Gaben gegeben hat, und sollen sie auch gelobt werden, dass sie Gottes Gaben wohl gebraucht haben** und dem Fleisch gewährt, sie auszuschütten, auch dass sie solche Gaben haben **angewandt** andern Leuten und **der Kirchen zu Nutz.**

Christendom examples in whom he might show that he pleases to be gracious to all who repent, that he wants them to be saved, and that he wants us to give thanks for such examples and thereby strengthen our faith. When for instance, **we hear** what awful sins **were remitted to Peter, we should** take comfort and **believe that God will forgive us also if we repent.** Also we should thank God that he has given the Church not only such examples, but also profitable teachers, prophets, apostles and bishops.

Secondly, it is profitable **to hold before** the people **examples of faith and of other virtues, so that we may follow after them,** each one in his own calling; for these examples serve to encourage and teach, so that when we, for example, hear that God with great miracles protected and exalted kings **who put away idolatry,** we are strengthened by such **examples** to promote God's honour more earnestly and to expect help from him. When we hear of **the martyrs' steadfastness,** we are more content to obey God as they did and to **suffer** persecution **so much more patiently.**

Thirdly, we should **thank God that he gave these gifts to the saints, and they should be praised for having really used God's gifts and** resisted the desire of the flesh to squander them, and that they **used** such gifts **for the benefit** of other people and **of the churches.** Thus the praise and merit which belongs

Und soll man von der Tugenden und guten Werken Lobe und Verdienst reden.

Diese Ehre von den Heiligen zu rühmen, lassen wir zu, wie S. Basilius und S. Hieronymus allein von solchen Ehren reden, **denn Basilius** spricht also **in der predigt von Martyre Gordio: Die Heiligen bedürfen unsers Preisens nicht zu ihr Seligkeit, aber wir bedürfen ihr Gedächtnis, ihrem Exempel nachzufolgen, und in einer anderen Predigt: Das heisst die Martyrer preisen und loben, nämlich die Kirche vermahnen ihr Exempel und Tugend nach- zufolgen.**

Aber von der Anrufung der Heiligen ist in göttlicher Schrift kein Gebot und kein Exempel, auch wird solches nicht gelehrt von den alten heiligen Vätern, derhalben tun diejenige nicht wider die Heilige Schrift, auch nicht wider die alte Kirche, so die Heiligen nicht anrufen.

Dazu das Vertrauen auf ein Mittler oder Versöhner gehört allein Christo und nicht den Heiligen, dann allein Christi Verdienst gelten für unsere Sünde, und der himmlische Vater hat uns diesen allein zu einem Mittler und Priester vorgestellt und zugesagt, dass er uns um dieses Christi willen erhören wolle.

17. Von Bildern

Bilder Christi und der Heiligen, nämlich ihre Historien gemalt oder sonst nachgemacht in Kirchen und an anderen Orten, haben zu diesem Brauch, dass sie wie Gregorius

to virtues and good works should be spoken of.

This veneration of the saints we permit in the sense that only St Basil and St Jerome speak of it, for **Basil** speaks thus **in his sermon concerning the martyr Gordius: "The saints do not need our praise for their salvation, but we need to remember them in order to follow their example."** In another sermon he says: **"To praise and bless the martyrs is the same thing as to admonish the Church to follow their examples and their virtues."**

As for the invocation of the saints, there is no command and no example of this in Holy Scripture, nor was this taught by the ancient fathers. So those who do not invoke the saints are not contradicting Holy Scripture or the ancient Church.

In addition, trust in a mediator or reconciler belongs to Christ alone and not to the saints, for Christ's merit alone avails for our sins, and the heavenly Father has set him alone before us as the one Mediator and Priest, and has promised to hear us for the sake of this Christ.

17. Images

Images of Christ and of the saints, i.e. representations of their story by means of paintings and the like in churches and elsewhere, are the books of the illiterate, as Gregory

spricht, der Bücher sind, dass ist, dass sie Ungelehrten uns die Historie weisen, wie geschriebene Bücher, solches ist ein Mittelding an ihm selb, davon die Christen nicht zanken sollen.

Doch **dieweil solches Gemälde den Ungelehrten diesen Nutz bringt, dass sie darin gleich als in Büchern die Historien sehen und lernen**, verwerfen wir die Bilder an ihm selb nicht, tun sie auch nicht ab, sondern wir strafen den Missbrauch.

Denn wir lehren, man soll die Bilder nicht anbeten, man soll auch nicht halten, dass sie eine Kraft haben, auch soll man nicht halten, dass ein Gottesdienst sei, Gott oder der Heiligen Bilder aufstellen, oder **dass Gott gnädiger sei oder nicht wirke, so er angeruft wird bei diesem Bild, denn sonst.**

Denn Gott will, dass man ihn allein durch sein Wort und seine Sakramente mit Glauben fasse, darum ist es ein gottloser Irrtum Gott anbinden an gewisse Bilder ohne Gottes Wort, auch ist dieses ein gottloser Irrtum, dass ein Werk bei diesem Bild Gott mehr gefalle, denn an anderen Orten, sondern man soll glauben, dass Gott zugleich an allen Orten erhöre diejenige, so ihn ernstlich anrufen. Also straft auch Jesaja (66:1) diejenige, so nicht halten, dass Gott zugleich an allen Orten erhöre, welche ihn anrufen im rechten geistlichen Gottesdienst, denn also spricht er: Der Himmel ist des Herrn Stuhl, etc., wo wohnt Gott etc., in den erschrockenen Herzen. Und Christus spricht (Io 4:21, 23):

says; that is, they explain the story like written books. As such, they are a means if access to (Christ) himself, which Christians should not argue about.

Because such representation provides for the illiterate the advantage of seeing and learning the stories as if from books, we do not reject pictures in themselves, nor do we abolish them, but we do object to their misuse.

For we teach that images are not to be worshipped, nor is to be thought that they have power, nor should people think that setting up images of God or of the saints is serving God, or **that God is more gracious or does not act unless he is invoked before such an image.**

For God wants men to grasp him only in faith through his Word and his sacraments; therefore it is a godless error to bind God to certain images without God's word. It is also a Godless error to think that such a deed performed before such an image pleases God more than if done elsewhere, for we should believe that God in all places hears those who earnestly call upon him. Hence Isaiah (66:1) reproved those who do not believe that God everywhere hears those who call upon him in true spiritual worship, for he says that heaven is the Lord's throne, etc., where God dwells etc. in humble hearts. Christ says (Jn 4:21, 23): "You shall not worship the father on this mountain, nor in Jerusalem, but

Ihr werdet weder auf diesem Berg noch zu Jerusalem anrufen, sondern die wahrhaftigen Anrufer werden den Vater anrufen in Geist und in der Wahrheit, und Paulus spricht (I Ti 2:8): Ich will, dass die Menschen beten an allen Orten.

in spirit and in truth", and Paul says (1 Ti 2:8): I will that men pray everywhere.

16. THE TEN ARTICLES, 1536

History

These articles were promulgated soon after the return of the English delegates to Wittenberg. They were drawn up at the King's request, and reflect his basically traditionalist views. Each one, except the ninth, begins with the phrase: *"...and we will that all bishops and preachers shall instruct and teach our people committed by us unto their spiritual charge..."*, which underlines Henry's supreme headship of the Church. The articles remained part of the Church of England's official statements until 1553, when they were superseded by the Forty-two Articles of Edward VI, though they were not officially repealed. They were never widely used, and as early as 1537 the so-called Bishops' Book provided a protestantizing commentary which effectively limited their authority.

Theology

Lutheran influence is prominent in Article 05 on Justification, and following Luther's practice only three of the traditional seven sacraments are mentioned. On the other hand, traditional Catholic practices like the veneration of images, the cult of the saints and prayers for the dead are reaffirmed. Article 04 on the Lord's Supper allows for a breadth of interpretation which could permit either a Lutheran or a Catholic position on transubstantiation. The need to respond to Protestant attacks is particularly apparent in the defence of penance in Article 03. There is an extensive appeal to Scripture in that Article, which suggests that there was a conscious attempt being made to persuade Protestants that penance had biblical warrant. Another concession to Protestant sensibilities is apparent in the rejection of purgatory and the devotional practices connected with it. With one exception, biblical quotations are in Latin, a reminder that there was as yet no official English translation of the Scriptures. On balance, the Ten Articles reflect an early stage in the process of reformation, when traditionalist views were still strong. However, the fact that a number of Protestant ideas were admitted, and given at least qualified approval, shows which way the wind was blowing.

N.B. For ease of reference, the paragraphs of articles 01, 02, 03 and 05 have been numbered for this edition.

The Preface

Henry the VIII, by the grace of God, King of England and of France, Defensor of the Faith, Lord of Ireland, and in earth Supreme Head of the Church of

England, to all and singular, our most loving, faithful and obedient subjects, greeting.

Among other cures appertaining unto this our princely office, whereunto it hath pleased Almighty God of his infinite mercy and goodness to call us, we have always esteemed and thought, like as we also yet esteem and think, that it most chiefly belongeth unto our said charge diligently to foresee and cause, that not only the most holy Word and commandments of God should most sincerely be believed, and most reverently be observed and kept of our subjects, but also that unity and concord in opinion, namely in such things as doth concern our religion, may increase and go forthward, and all occasion of dissent and discord touching the same be repressed and utterly extinguished.

For the which cause, we being of late, to our great regret, credibly advertised of such diversity in opinions, as have grown and sprung in this our realm, as well concerning certain articles necessary to our salvation, as also touching certain other honest and commendable ceremonies, rites and usages now of long time used and accustomed in our churches, for conservation of an honest policy and decent and seemly order to be had therein, minding to have that unity and agreement established through our said Church concerning the premises, and being very desirous to eschew not only the dangers of souls, but also the outward unquietness which by occasion of the said diversity in opinions (if remedy were not provided) might perchance have ensued, have not only in our own person at many times taken great pains, study, labours and travails, but also have caused our bishops, and other the most discreet and best learned men of our clergy of this our realm, to be assembled in our Convocation, for the full debatement and quiet determination of the same. Where, after long and mature deliberation, and disputations had of and upon the premises, finally they have concluded and agreed upon the most special points and articles, as well such as be commanded of God, and are necessary to our salvation, as also divers other matters touching the honest ceremonies and good and politic orders, as is aforesaid; which their determination, debatement and agreement, for so much as we think to have proceeded of a good, right and true judgement, and to be agreeable to the laws and ordinances of God, and much profitable for the establishment of that charitable concord and unity in our Church of England, which we most desire, we have caused the same to be published, willing, requiring and commanding you to accept, repute and take them accordingly. And further, we most heartily desire and pray Almighty God, that it may please him so to illumine your hearts that you and every of you may have no less desire, zeal and love to the said unity and concord, in reading, divulging and following the same, than we have had, and have in causing them to be thus devised, set forth and published.

And because we would the said articles and every of them should be taken and understanden of you after such sort, order and degree as appertaineth accordingly, we have caused, by the like assent and agreement of our said bishops and other learned men, the said articles to be divided into two sorts; whereof the one part containeth such as be commanded expressly by God, and be necessary to our salvation; and the other containeth such things as have been of a long continuance for a decent order and honest policy, prudently instituted and used in the churches of our realm, and be for that same purpose and end to be observed and kept accordingly, although they be not expressly commanded of God, nor necessary to our salvation. Wherefore we will and require you to accept the same, after such sort, as we have here prescribed them unto you, and to conform yourselves obediently unto the same. Whereby you shall not only attain that most charitable unity and loving concord, whereof shall ensue your incomparable commodity, profit and lucre, as well spiritual as other, but also you shall not a little encourage us to take further travails, pains and labours for your commodities, in all such other matters as in time to come may happen to occur, and as it shall be most to the honour of God, the profit, tranquillity and quietness of all you our most loving subjects.

01. The principal articles concerning our faith

01. First, as touching the chief and principal articles of our faith, since it is thus agreed as hereafter followeth, by the whole clergy of this our realm, we will that all bishops and preachers shall instruct and teach our people, by us committed to their spiritual charge, that they ought and must most constantly believe and defend all those things to be true, which be comprehended in the whole body and canon of the Bible, and also in the three creeds, or symbols, whereof one was made by the apostles, and is the common creed which every man useth; the second was made by the holy council of Nicaea, and is said daily in the mass; and the third was made by Athanasius, and is comprehended in the Psalm *Quicunque vult*; and that they ought and must take and interpret all the same things according to the selfsame sentence and interpretation, which the words of the selfsame creeds or symbols do purport, and the holy approved doctors of the Church do entreat and defend the same.

02. That they ought and must repute, hold and take all the same things for the most holy, the most sure and the most certain and infallible words of God, and such as neither ought, nor can be altered or convelled, by any contrary opinion or authority.

03. That they ought and must believe, repute and take all the articles of our faith contained in the said creeds to be so necessary to be believed for man's salvation, that whosoever being taught will not believe them as is aforesaid, or will obstinately affirm the contrary of them, he or they cannot be the very members of Christ and his espouse the Church, but be very infidels or heretics, and members of the Devil, with whom they shall perpetually be damned.

04. That they ought and must most reverently and religiously observe and keep the selfsame words, according to the very same form and manner of speaking, as the articles of our faith be already contained and expressed in the said creeds, without altering in any wise, or varying from the same.

05. That they ought and must utterly refuse and condemn all those opinions contrary to the said articles, which were of long time past condemned in the four holy councils, that is to say, in the Council of Nicaea, Constantinople, Ephesus and Chalcedon, and all other since that time in any point consonant to the same.

02. The sacrament of baptism

01. Secondly, as touching the holy sacrament of baptism, we will that all bishops and preachers shall instruct and teach our people committed by us unto their spiritual charge, that they ought and must of necessity believe certainly all those things which hath been always by the whole consent of the Church approved, received and used in the sacrament of baptism; that is to say, that the sacrament of baptism was instituted and ordained in the New Testament by our Saviour Jesus Christ, as a thing necessary for the attaining of everlasting life, according to the saying of Christ, *Nisi quis renatus fuerit ex aqua et Spiritu Sancto, non potest intrare in regnum caelorum*, that is to say, No man can enter into the kingdom of heaven, except he be born again of water and the Holy Ghost.[1]

02. That it is offered unto all men, as well infants as such as have the use of reason, that by baptism they shall have remission of sins, and the grace and favour of God, according to the saying of Christ, *Qui crediderit et baptizatus fuerit, salvus erit*; that is to say, Whosoever believeth and is baptized shall be saved.[2]

03. That the promise of grace and everlasting life (which promise is adjoined unto this sacrament of baptism) pertaineth not only unto such as have the use of reason, but also to infants, innocents and children; and that they ought therefore and must needs be baptized; and that by the sacrament of baptism they do also obtain remission of their sins, the grace and favour of God, and be made thereby the very sons and children of God. Insomuch as infants and children dying in their infancy shall undoubtedly be saved thereby, and else not.

04. That infants must needs be christened because they be born in original sin, which sin must needs be remitted; which cannot be done but by the sacrament of baptism, whereby they receive the Holy Ghost, which exerciseth his grace and efficacy in them, and cleanseth and purifieth them from sin by his most secret virtue and operation.

05. That children or men once baptized can, nor ought ever to be baptized again.

06. That they ought to repute and take all the Anabaptists' and the Pelagians' opinions contrary to the premises, and every other man's opinion agreeable unto the said Anabaptists' or Pelagians' opinions in this behalf, for detestable heresies, and utterly to be condemned.

07. That men or children having the use of reason, and willing and desiring to be baptized, shall, by virtue of that holy sacrament, obtain the grace and remission of all their sins, if they shall come thereunto perfectly and truly repentant and contrite of all their sins before committed, and also perfectly and constantly confessing and believing all the articles of our faith, according as it was mentioned in the first article.

08. And finally, if they shall also have firm credence and trust in the promise of God adjoined to the said sacrament, that is to say, that in and by this said sacrament, which they shall receive, God the Father giveth unto them, for his Son Jesus Christ's sake, remission of all their sins and the grace of the Holy Ghost, whereby they be newly regenerated and made the very children of God, according to the saying of St John and the Apostle St Peter, *Delictorum paenitentiae agite, et baptizetur unusquisque vestrum in nomine Iesu Christi in remissionem peccatorum, et accipietis donum Spiritus Sancti,* that is to say, Do penance for your sins and be each of you baptized in the name of Jesus Christ, and you shall obtain remission of your sins, and shall receive the gift of the Holy Ghost.[3] And according also to the saying of St Paul, *Non ex operibus iustitiae quae fecimus nos, sed secundum suam misericordiam, salvos nos fecit per lavacrum regenerationis et renovationis Spiritus Sancti, quem effudit in nos opulente per Iesum Christum Servatorem nostrum, ut iustificati illius gratia haeredes efficiamur iuxta spem vitae aeternae;* that is to say, God hath not saved us for the works of justice which we have done, but of his mercy by baptism, and renovation of the Holy Ghost, whom he hath poured out upon us most plentifully, for the love of Jesus Christ our Saviour, to the intent that we, being justified by his grace, should be made the inheritors of everlasting life, according to our hope.[4]

03. The sacrament of penance

01. Thirdly, concerning the sacrament of penance, we will that all bishops and preachers shall instruct and teach our people committed by us unto their spiritual charge, that they ought and must most constantly believe, that that sacrament was instituted of Christ in the New Testament as a thing so necessary for man's salvation that no man, which after his baptism is fallen again, and hath committed deadly sin, can, without the same, be saved or attain everlasting life.

02. That like as such men which after baptism do fall again into sin, if they do not penance in this life, shall undoubtedly be damned; even so, whensoever the same men shall convert themselves from their naughty life and do such penance for the same as Christ requireth of them, they shall without doubt obtain remission of their sins and shall be saved.

03. That the sacrament of perfect penance which Christ requireth of such manner persons consisteth of three parts, that is to say, contrition, confession and the amendment of the former life, and a new obedient reconciliation unto the laws and will of God, that is to say, exterior acts in works of charity according as they be commanded of God, which be called in Scripture *fructus digni paenitentia*, the worthy fruits of penance.[5]

04. Furthermore, as touching contrition, which is the first part, we will that all bishops and preachers shall instruct and teach our people committed by us unto their spiritual charge, that the said contrition consisteth in two special parts, which must always be conjoined together, and cannot be dissevered; that is to say, the penitent and contrite man must first acknowledge the filthiness and abomination of his own sin, (unto which knowledge he is brought by hearing and considering of the will of God declared in his laws), and feeling and perceiving in his own conscience that God is angry and displeased with him for the same; he must also conceive not only great sorrow and inward shame that he hath so grievously offended God, but also great fear of God's displeasure towards him, considering he hath no works or merits of his own which he may worthily lay before God, as sufficient satisfaction for his sins; which done, then afterward with this fear, shame and sorrow must needs succeed and be conjoined the second part, that is to wit, a certain faith, trust and confidence of the mercy and goodness of God, whereby the penitent must conceive certain hope and faith that God will forgive him his sins, and repute him justified, and of the number of his elect children, not for the worthiness of any merit or work done by the penitent, but for the only merits of the blood and passion of our Saviour Jesus Christ.

05. That this certain faith and hope is gotten and also confirmed, and made more strong by the applying of Christ's words and promises of his grace and favour, contained in his Gospel, and the sacraments instituted by him in the New Testament; and therefore to attain this certain faith, the second part of penance is necessary, that is to say, confession to a priest, if it may be had; for the absolution given by the priest was instituted of Christ to apply the promises of God's grace and favour to the penitent. Wherefore, as touching confession, we will that all bishops and preachers shall instruct and teach our people, committed by us to their spiritual charge, that they ought and must certainly believe that the words of absolution pronounced by the priest, be spoken by authority given to him by Christ in the Gospel.

06. That they ought and must give no less faith and credence to the same words of absolution so pronounced by the ministers of the Church, than they would give unto the very words and voice of God himself if he should speak unto us out of heaven, according to the saying of Christ, *Quorumcunque remiseritis peccata, remittuntur eis; quorumcunque retinueritis retenta sunt*; that is to say, Whose sins soever ye do forgive, shall be forgiven; whose sins soever ye do retain, shall be retained.[6] And again, in another place Christ saith, *Qui vos audit, me audit, etc.*; that is to say, Whosoever heareth you, heareth me, etc.[7]

07. That in no wise they do contemn this auricular confession which is made unto the ministers of the Church, but that they ought to repute the same as a very expedient and necessary mean, whereby they may require and ask this absolution at the priest's hands, at such time as they shall find their consciences grieved with mortal sin, and have occasion so to do, to the intent they may thereby attain certain comfort and consolation of their consciences.

08. As touching the third part of penance, we will that all bishops and preachers shall instruct and teach our people committed by us to their spiritual charge, that although Christ and his death be sufficient oblation, sacrifice, satisfaction and recompense, for the which God the Father forgiveth and remitteth to all sinners not only their sin, but also eternal pain due for the same; yet all men truly penitent, contrite and confessed, must needs also bring forth the fruits of penance, that is to say, prayer, fastings, almsdeeds, and must make restitution or satisfaction in will and deed to their neighbours, in such things as they have done them wrong and injury in, and also must do all other good works of mercy and charity, and express their obedient will in the executing and fulfilling of God's commandment outwardly, when time, power and occasion shall be ministered unto them, or else they shall never be saved; for this is the express precept and commandment of God, *Agite fructus dignos paenitentia*; that is to say, Do you the worthy fruits of penance;[8] and St Paul saith, *Quemadmodum praebuistis membra vestra serva immunditiae et iniquitati ad aliam atque aliam iniquitatem; sic et nunc praebete membra vestra serva iustitiae ad sanctificationem, etc.*; that is to say, Like as in times past you have given and applied yourself and all the members of your body to all filthy living and wickedness, continually increasing the same, in like manner now you must give and apply yourself wholly to justice, increasing continually in purity and cleanness of life;[9] and in another place he saith, *Castigo corpus meum, et in servitutem redigo*, that is to say, I chastise and subdue my carnal body and the affections of the same, and make them obedient unto the spirit.[10]

09. That these precepts and works of charity be necessary works to our salvation, and God necessarily requireth that every penitent man shall perform the same, whensoever time, power and occasion shall be ministered unto him so to do.

10. That by penance and such good works of the same we shall not only obtain everlasting life, but also we shall deserve remission or mitigation of these present pains and afflictions in this world, according to the saying of St Paul, *Si nos ipsi iudicaremus, non iudicaremur a Domino*; that is to say, If we would correct and take punishment of ourselves, we should not be so grievously corrected of God;[11] and Zacharias the prophet saith, *Convertimini ad me et ego convertar ad vos*, that is to say, Turn yourselves unto me and I will turn again unto you,[12] and the prophet Isaiah saith, *Frangi esurienti panem tuum, et egenos vagosque induc in domum tuam. Cum videris nudum operi eum et carnem tuam ne despexeris; tunc erumpet quasi mane lumen tuum, et sanitas tua citius orietur, et anteibit faciem tuam iustitia tua, et gloria*

Dei colligit te; tunc invocabis et Dominus exaudiet te, clamabis et dicet: Ecce, adsum. Tunc orietur in tenebris lux tua et tenebrae tuae erunt sicut meridies, et requiem tibi dabit Dominus semper, et implebit splendoribus animam tuam, et deficient aquae, etc., that is to say, Break and deal thy bread unto the hungry, bring into thy house the poor man and such as want harborough; when thou seest a naked man and give him clothes to cover him with, and refuse not to succour the poor and needy, for he is thine own flesh. And if thou wilt thus do, then shall thy light glister out as bright as the sun in the morning, and thy health shall sooner arise unto thee, and thy justice shall go before thy face, and the glory of God shall gather thee up, that thou shalt not fall; and whensoever thou shalt call upon God, God shall hear thee; and whensoever thou shalt cry unto God, God shall say, Lo, here I am, ready to help thee. Then shall thy light overcome all darkness and thy darkness shall be as bright as the sun at noon days; and then God shall give unto thee continual rest, and shall fulfil thy soul with brightness, and shall deliver thy body from adversity; and then thou shalt be like a garden, that most plentifully bringeth forth all kinds of fruits, and like the well-spring that shall never want water.[13]

11. These things, and such other, should be continually taught and inculcated into the ears of our people, to the intent to stir and provoke them unto good works; and by the selfsame good works to exercise and confirm their faith and hope, and look for to receive at God's hand mitigation and remission of the miseries, calamities and grievous punishments, which God sendeth to men in this world for their sins.

04. The Sacrament of the Altar

Fourthly, as touching the sacrament of the altar, we will that all bishops and preachers shall instruct and teach our people committed by us unto their spiritual charge, that they ought and must constantly believe, that under the form and figure of bread and wine, which we there presently do see and perceive by outward senses, is verily, substantially and really contained and comprehended the very selfsame body and blood of our Saviour Jesus Christ, which was born of the Virgin Mary and suffered upon the cross for our redemption; and that under the same form and figure of bread and wine the very selfsame body and blood of Christ is corporally, really and in the very substance exhibited, distributed and received unto and of all them which receive the said sacrament; and that therefore the said sacrament is to be used with all due reverence and honour, and that every man ought first to prove and honour himself, and religiously to try and search his own conscience, before he shall receive the same, according to the saying of St Paul: *Quisquis ederit panem hunc aut biberit de poculo Domini indigne, reus erit corporis et sanguinis Domini; probet igitur seipsum homo, et sic de pane illo edat et de poculo illo bibat; nam qui edit aut bibet indigne iudicium sibi ipsi manducat et bibit, non diiudicans corpus Domini*; that is to say, Whosoever eateth this body of Christ unworthily, or drinketh of this blood of Christ unworthily, shall be guilty of the very body and blood of Christ; wherefore let every man first prove himself, and so let him eat of this bread and drink of this drink. For whosoever eateth it or drinketh it unworthily, he eateth and drinketh it to his own damnation; because he putteth no difference between the very body of Christ and other kinds of meat.[14]

05. Justification

01. As touching the order and cause of our justification, we will that all bishops and preachers shall instruct and teach our people committed by us to their spiritual charge, that this word *justification* signifieth remission of our sins and our acceptation or reconciliation into the grace and favour of God, that is to say, our perfect renovation in Christ.

02. That sinners attain this justification by contrition and faith joined with charity, after such sort and manner as we before mentioned and declared; not as though our contrition or faith, or any works proceeding thereof, can worthily merit or deserve to obtain the said justification; for the only mercy and grace of the Father, promised freely unto us for his Son's sake, Jesus Christ, and the merits of his blood and passion, be the only sufficient and worthy causes thereof; and yet that notwithstanding, to the attaining of the same justification, God requireth to be in us not only inward contrition, perfect faith and charity, certain hope and confidence, with all other spiritual graces and motions, which as we said before, must necessarily concur in remission of our sins, that is to say, our justification; but also he requireth and commandeth us, that after we be justified we must also have good works of charity and obedience towards God, in the observing and fulfilling outwardly of his laws and commandments; for although acceptation to everlasting life to be conjoined with justification, yet our good works be necessarily required to the attaining of everlasting life; and we being justified be necessarily bound, and it is our necessary duty to do good works, according to the saying of St Paul, *Debitores sumus non carni, ut secundum carnem vivamus. Nam si secundum carnem vixerimus, moriemur; sin autem spiritu facta corporis mortificaverimus, vivemus; etenim quicunque Spiritu Dei ducuntur, hi sunt filii Dei;* that is to say, We be not bound to live according to the flesh and to fleshly appetites; for if we live so, we shall undoubtedly be damned. And contrary, if we will mortify the deeds of our flesh, and live according to the Spirit, we shall be saved. For whosoever be led by the Spirit of God, they be children of God.[15] And Christ saith, *Si vis ad vitam ingredi, serva mandata*; that is to say, If ye will come to heaven, keep the commandments.[16] And St Paul, speaking of evil works, saith, *Qui talia agunt regnum Dei non possidebunt*; that is to say, Whosoever commit sinful deeds shall never come to heaven.[17] Wherefore we will that all bishops and preachers shall instruct and teach our people committed by us unto their spiritual charge, that God necessarily requireth of us to do good works commanded by him; and that not only outward and civil works, but also the inward spiritual motions and graces of the Holy Ghost; that is to say, to dread and fear God, to love God, to have firm confidence and trust in God, to invocate and call upon God, to have patience in all adversities, to hate sin, and to have certain purpose and will not to sin again, and such other like motions and virtues; for Christ saith, *Nisi abundaverit iustitia vestra plusquam Scribarum et Pharisaeorum, non intrabitis in regnum caelorum*; that is to say, We must not only do outward and civil good works, but also we must have these foresaid inward spiritual motions, consenting and agreeable to the law of God.[18]

Articles Concerning the Laudable Ceremonies used in the Church

06. And first of images

As touching images, truth it is that the same have been used in the Old Testament, and also for the great abuses of them sometime destroyed and put down; and in the New Testament they have been also allowed, as good authors do declare. Wherefore we will that all bishops and preachers shall instruct and teach our people committed by us unto their spiritual charge, how they ought and may use them. And first, that there may be attributed unto them, that they may be representers of virtue and good example, and that they also by occasion the kindlers and stirrers of men's minds, and make men oft to remember and lament their sins and offences, especially the images of Christ and our Lady; and that therefore it is meet that they should stand in our churches, and none otherwise to be esteemed; and to the intent the rude people should not from henceforth take such superstition, as in time past it is thought that the same hath used to do, we will that our bishops and preachers diligently shall teach them, and according to this doctrine reform their abuses, for else there might fortune idolatry to ensue, which God forbid. And as for censing of them, and kneeling and offering unto them, with other like worshippings, although the same hath entered by devotion and fallen to custom; yet the people ought to be diligently taught that they in no wise do it, nor think it meet to be done to the same images, but only to be done to God, and in his honour, although it be done before the images, whether it be of Christ, of the Cross, of our Lady or of any other saint beside.

07. Of honouring of saints

As touching the honouring of saints, we will that all bishops and preachers shall instruct and teach our people committed by us unto their spiritual charge, that saints now being with Christ in heaven be to be honoured of Christian people in earth; but not with that confidence and honour which are only due unto God, trusting to attain at their hands that which must be had only of God; but that they be thus to be honoured, because they be known the elect persons of Christ, because they be passed into godly life out of this transitory world, because they already do reign in glory with Christ; and most specially to laud and praise Christ in them for their excellent virtues which he planted in them, for example, of and by them to such as yet are in this world, to live in virtue and goodness, and also not to fear to die for Christ and his cause, as some of them did; and finally to take them, in that they may, to be advancers of our prayers and demands unto Christ. By these ways and such like, be saints to be honoured and had in reverence, and by none other.

08. Of praying to saints

As touching praying to saints, we will that all bishops and preachers shall instruct and teach our people committed by us unto their spiritual charge, that albeit grace, remission of sin and salvation cannot be obtained but of God only, by the mediation of our Saviour Christ, which is only sufficient Mediator for our sins; yet it is very laudable to pray to saints in heaven everlastingly living, whose charity is ever permanent, to be intercessors, and to pray for us and with us, unto Almighty God, after this manner: "All holy angels and saints in heaven pray for us and with us unto the Father, that for his dear Son Jesus Christ's sake, we may have grace of him and remission of our sins, with an earnest purpose, (not wanting ghostly strength), to observe and keep his holy commandments, and never to decline from the same again unto our lives' end"; and in this manner we may pray to our blessed Lady, to St John Baptist, to all and every of the Apostles or any other saint particularly, as our devotion doth serve us; so that it be done without any vain superstition, as to think that any saint is more merciful, or will hear us sooner than Christ, or that any saint doth serve for one thing more than another, or is patron of the same. And likewise we must keep holy-days unto God, in memory of him and his saints, upon such days as the Church hath ordained their memories to be celebrated; except they be mitigated and moderated by the assent and commandment of us, the Supreme Head, to the ordinaries, and then the subjects ought to obey it.

09. Of rites and ceremonies

As concerning rites and ceremonies of Christ's Church, as to have such vestments in doing God's service, as be and have been most part used, as sprinkling of holy water to put us in remembrance of our baptism, and the blood of Christ sprinkled for our redemption upon the Cross; giving of holy bread, to put us in remembrance of the sacrament of the altar, that all Christian men be one body mystical of Christ, as the bread is made of many grains, and yet but one loaf, and to put us in remembrance of the receiving of the holy sacrament and body of Christ, the which we ought to receive in right charity, which in the beginning of Christ's Church men did more often receive than they use nowadays to do; bearing of candles on Candlemas Day (02 February), in memory of Christ the spiritual light, of whom Simeon did prophesy, as is read in the Church that day; giving of ashes on Ash Wednesday, to put in remembrance every Christian man in the beginning of Lent and penance, that he is but ashes and earth, and thereto shall return, which is right necessary to be uttered from henceforth in our mother tongue always on the same day; bearing of palms on Palm Sunday, in memory of the receiving of Christ into Jerusalem, a little before his death, that we may have the same desire to receive him into our hearts; creeping to the cross and humbling ourselves to Christ on Good Friday before the cross, and there offering to Christ before the same, and kissing of it in memory of our redemption by Christ made upon the cross; setting up the sepulture of Christ, whose body after his death was buried; the hallowing of the font and other like exorcisms and benedictions by the ministers of Christ's Church; and all other like laudable customs, rites and ceremonies be not to be contemned and cast away, but to be used and continued as things good and laudable, to put us in remembrance of those spiritual things that they do signify; not suffering them to be forgot, or to be put in oblivion, but renewing them in our memories from time to time. But none of these ceremonies have power to remit sin, but only to stir and lift up our minds unto God, by whom only our sins be forgiven.

10. Of purgatory

Forasmuch as due order of charity requireth, and the Book of Maccabees,[19] and divers ancient authors plainly show, that it is a very good and charitable deed to pray for souls departed, and forasmuch also as such usage hath continued in the Church so many years, even from the beginning, we will that all bishops and preachers shall instruct and teach our people committed by us unto their spiritual charge, that no man ought to be grieved with the continuance of the same, and that it standeth with the very due order of charity, a Christian man to pray for souls departed, and to commit them in our prayers to God's mercy, and also to cause other to pray for them in masses and exequies, and to give alms to other to pray for them, whereby they may be relieved and holpen of some part of their pain; but forasmuch as the place where they be, the name thereof, and kind of pains there, also be to us uncertain by Scripture; therefore this with all other things we remit to Almighty God, unto whose mercy it is meet and convenient for us to commend them, trusting that God accepteth our prayers for them, referring the rest wholly to God, to whom is known their estate and condition.

Wherefore it is much necessary that such abuses be clearly put away, which under the name of purgatory hath been advanced, as to make men believe that through the Bishop of Rome's pardons souls might clearly be delivered out of purgatory, and all the pains of it, or that masses said at *Scala Caeli,** or otherwise, in any place, or before any image, might likewise deliver them from all their pain, and send them straight to heaven; and other like abuses.

[1] Jn 3:5
[2] Mk 16:16
[3] Ac 2:38
[4] Tt 3:6-7
[5] Mt 3:8
[6] Jn 20:23
[7] Lk 10:16
[8] Mt 3:8
[9] Ro 6:19
[10] I Co 9:27
[11] I Co 11:31
[12] Ze 1:3
[13] Is 58:7-11
[14] I Co 11:27-29
[15] Ro 8:12-14
[16] Mt 19:17
[17] Ga 5:21
[18] Mt 5:20. The English is not here a translation of the Latin, which reads: Except your justice exceed that of the Scribes and Pharisees, ye shall not enter into the kingdom of heaven.
[19] II Ma 12:39-45

* A name given to certain shrines, borrowed from the chapel of Scala Caeli (Ladder of Heaven) in Rome. They specialized in masses for the dead, etc.

17. THE FIRST HENRICIAN INJUNCTIONS, 1536

History

These were drawn up by Thomas Cromwell as an accompaniment to the Ten Articles. Their major purpose was to ensure that the doctrinal provisions of those Articles were adequately translated into Church practice at the parochial level. This involved a programme of religious instruction, which included the suppression of anything regarded as superstitious. Injunctions of this kind became a familiar feature of Tudor Church government, and they reflect perhaps better than any other type of document the progress and impact of the Reformation at the local level. From them we can learn how the Reformation was felt and applied, and what sort of resistance there was to it.

In the Name of God, Amen. In the year of our Lord God 1536, and of the most noble reign of our Sovereign Lord Henry VIII, King of England and France the twenty-eighth year, and the — day of — , I, Thomas Cromwell, knight, Lord Cromwell, Keeper of the Privy Seal of our said Sovereign Lord the King, and vicegerent unto the same, for and concerning all his jurisdiction ecclesiastical within this realm, visiting by the King's Highness's supreme authority ecclesiastical the people and clergy of this deanery of — by my trusty commissary — lawfully deputed and constituted for this part, have to the glory of Almighty God, to the King's Highness's honour, the public weal of this his realm, and increase of virtue in the same, appointed and assigned these Injunctions ensuing, to be kept and observed of the dean, parsons, vicars, curates and stipendiaries resident or having cure of souls, or any other spiritual administration within this deanery, under the pains hereafter limited and appointed.

01. The first is that the dean, parsons, vicars and others having cure of souls anywhere within this deanery shall faithfully keep and observe, and as far as in them may lie, shall cause to be observed and kept of other, all and singular laws and statutes of this realm made for the abolishing and extirpation of the Bishop of Rome's pretensed and usurped power and jurisdiction within this realm, and for the establishment and confirmation of the King's authority and jurisdiction within the same, as of the Supreme Head of the Church of England, and shall to the uttermost of their wit, knowledge and learning, purely, sincerely and without any colour or dissimulation declare, manifest and open for the space of one quarter of a year now next ensuing, once every Sunday, and after that at the leastwise

twice every quarter, in their sermons and other collations, that the Bishop of Rome's usurped power and jurisdiction, having no establishment nor ground by the law of God, was of most just causes taken away and abolished; and therefore they owe unto him no manner of obedience or subjection, and that the King's power is within his dominion the highest power and potentate under God, to whom all men within the same dominion by God's commandment owe most loyalty and obedience, afore and above all other powers and potentates in earth.

02. Item, whereas certain Articles were lately devised and put forth by the King's Highness's authority, and condescended upon by the prelates and clergy of this his realm, in Convocation, whereof part are necessary to be holden and believed for our salvation, and the other part do concern and touch certain laudable ceremonies, rites and usages of the Church meet and convenient to be kept and used for a decent and a politic order in the same; the said dean, parsons, vicars and other curates shall so open and declare in their said sermons and other collations the said Articles unto them that be under their cure, that they may plainly know and discern which of them be necessary to be believed and observed for their salvation; and which be not necessary, but only do concern the decent and politic order of the said Church, according to such commandment and admonition as has been given to them heretofore by authority of the King's Highness in that behalf.

03. Moreover that they shall declare unto all such as be under their cure the Articles likewise devised, put forth and authorized of late for and concerning the abrogation of certain superfluous holy days, according to the effect and purport of the same Articles, and persuade their parishioners to keep and observe the same inviolably, as things holily provided, decreed and established by common consent and public authority for the weal, commodity and profit of all this realm.

04. Besides this, to the intent that all superstition and hypocrisy, crept into divers men's hearts, may vanish away, they shall not set forth or extol any images, relics or miracles for any superstition or lucre, nor allure the people by any enticements to the pilgrimage of any saint, otherwise than is permitted in the Articles lately put forth by the authority of the King's Majesty and condescended upon by the prelates and clergy of this his realm in Convocation as though it were proper or peculiar to that saint to give this commodity or that, seeing all goodness, health and grace ought to be both asked and looked for only of God, as of the very author of the same, and of none other, for without him that cannot be given; but they shall exhort as well to the keeping of God's commandments and fulfilling of his works of charity, persuading them that they shall please God more by the true exercising of their bodily labour, travail or occupation, and providing for their families, than if they went about to the said pilgrimages; and that it shall profit more their soul's health, if they do bestow that on the poor and needy, which they would have bestowed upon the said images or relics.

05. Also in the same their sermons and other collations, the parsons, vicars and other curates abovesaid shall diligently admonish the fathers and mothers, masters and governors of youth, being within their cure, to teach or cause to be taught their children and servants, even from their infancy, their Paternoster, the Articles of our Faith [i.e. the Apostles' Creed, *ed.*], and the Ten Commandments in their mother tongue; and the same so taught, shall cause the said youth oft to repeat and understand; and to the intent this may be the more easily done, the said curates shall in their sermons deliberately and plainly recite oft the said Paternoster, the Articles of our Faith and the Ten Commandments, one clause or Article one day and another another day, till the whole be taught and learned by little; and shall deliver the same in writing, or show where printed books containing the same are to be sold, to them that can read or will desire the same; and thereto that the said fathers and mothers, masters and governors do bestow their children and servants, even from their childhood, either to learning or to some other honest exercise, occupation or husbandry, exhorting, counselling, and by all the ways and means they may, as well in their said sermons and collations, as other ways, persuading the said fathers, mothers, masters and other governors, being under their cure and charge, diligently to provide and foresee that the said youth be in no manner wise kept or brought up in idleness, lest at any time afterward they be driven, for lack of some mystery [i.e. trade, *ed.*] or occupation to live by, to fall to begging, stealing or some other unthriftiness; forasmuch as we may daily see through sloth and idleness divers valiant men fall, some to begging and some to theft and murder, which after, brought to calamity and misery, imputed great part thereof to their friends and governors which suffered them to be brought up so idly in their youth; where if they had been well educated and brought up in some good literature, occupation or mystery, they should, being rulers of their own family, have profited as well themselves, as divers other persons, to the great commodity and ornament of the common weal.

06. Also that the said parsons, vicars and other curates shall diligently provide that sacraments and sacramentals be duly and reverently ministered in their parishes; and if at any time it happen them other in any of the cases expressed in the statutes of this realm, or of special licence given by the King's Majesty, to be absent from their benefices, they shall leave their cures, not to a rude and unlearned person, but to an honest, well-learned and expert curate, that may teach the rude and unlearned of their cure wholesome doctrine, and reduce them to the right way that do err; and always let them see that neither they nor their vicars do seek more their own profit, promotion or advantage, than the profit of the souls that they have under their own cure, or the glory of God.

07. Also the said dean, parsons, vicars, curates and other priests shall in no wise, at any unlawful time, nor for any other cause than for their honest necessity, haunt or resort to any taverns or alehouses, and after their dinner or supper they shall not give themselves to drinking or riot, spending their time idly by day or by night, at tables or cardplaying, or any other unlawful game; but at such times as they shall have such leisure they shall read or hear somewhat of Holy Scripture, or shall occupy themselves with some other honest exercise, and that they always do those things which appertain to good congruence and honesty, with profit of the commonweal, having always in mind that they ought to excel all other in purity of life, and should be example to all other to live well and Christianly.

08. Furthermore, because the goods of the Church are called the goods of the poor, and at these days nothing is less seen than the poor to be sustained with the same, all parsons, vicars, pensionaries, prebendaries and other beneficed men within this deanery, not being resident upon their benefices, which may dispend yearly twenty pounds or above within this deanery or elsewhere, shall distribute hereafter yearly amongst their poor parishioners, or other inhabitants there, in the presence of the churchwardens or some other honest men of the parish, the fortieth part of the fruits and revenues of their said benefices, lest they be worthily noted of ingratitude, which, reserving so many parts to themselves, cannot vouchsafe to impart the fortieth portion thereof amongst the poor people of that parish, that is so fruitful and profitable unto them.

09. And to the intent that learned men may hereafter spring the more for the execution of the premises, every parson, vicar, clerk or beneficed man within this deanery, having yearly to dispend, in benefices and other promotions of the Church, an hundred pounds, shall give competent exhibition to one scholar, and for as many hundred pounds more as he may dispend, to so many scholars more shall give like exhibition in the University of Oxford or Cambridge, or some grammar school, which, after they have profited in good learning, may be partners of their patron's cure and charge, as well in preaching as otherwise in the execution of their offices, or may, when need shall be, otherwise profit the commonwealth with their counsel and wisdom.

10. Also that all parsons, vicars and clerks, having churches, chapels or mansions within this deanery, shall bestow yearly hereafter upon the same mansions or chancels of their churches, being in decay, the fifth part of their benefices, till they be fully repaired, and the same, so repaired, shall always keep and maintain in good state.

All which and singular Injunctions shall be inviolably observed of the said dean, parsons, vicars, curates, stipendiaries and other clerks and beneficed men, under the pain of suspension and sequestration of the fruits of their benefices, until they have done their duty according to these Injunctions.

18. THE SECOND HENRICIAN INJUNCTIONS, 1538

History

These were drawn up by Thomas Cromwell in furtherance of his educational and administrative reforms. Superstition of all kinds is strongly attacked, and an English Bible was to be placed in every parish church. Considering that it was only three years since the appearance of the first printed Bible in English, this marks a quite extraordinary progress. Also noticeable is the command to keep parish registers of births, marriages and deaths. This practice did not become general until the following reign, but Cromwell may justly be credited with the inspiration for a system of national record keeping, which was to remain exclusively in Church hands until 1837.

In the Name of God, Amen. By the authority and commission of the most excellent Prince Henry, by the grace of God King of England and France, Defender of the Faith, Lord of Ireland and in earth Supreme Head under Christ of the Church of England, I, Thomas, Lord Cromwell, Lord Privy Seal, vicegerent to the King's said Highness for all his jurisdictions ecclesiastical within this realm, do for the advancement of the true honour of Almighty God, increase of virtue and discharge of the King's Majesty, give and exhibit unto you these Injunctions following, to be kept, observed and fulfilled upon the pains hereafter declared.

01. First, that you shall truly observe and keep all and singular the King's Highness's injunctions given unto you heretofore in my name by his grace's authority, not only upon the pains therein expressed, but also in your default now after this second monition continued, upon further punishment to be straitly extended towards you by the King's Highness's arbitrament or his vicegerent aforesaid.

02. Item, that you shall provide on this side the feast Easter next coming (06 April 1539) one book of the whole Bible of the largest volume, in English, and the same set up in some convenient place within the said church that you have cure of, whereas your parishioners may most commodiously resort to the same and read it; the charges of which book shall be rateably borne between you, the parson and the parishioners aforesaid, that is to say, the one half by you and the other half by them.

03. Item, that you shall discourage no man privily or apertly from the reading or hearing of the said Bible, but shall expressly provoke, stir and exhort every person to read the same, as that which is the very lively Word of God, that every Christian man is bound to embrace, believe and follow if he look to be saved; admonishing them nevertheless, to avoid all contention and altercation therein, and to use an honest sobriety in the inquisition of the true sense of the same, and refer the explication of obscure places to men of higher judgement in Scripture.

04. Item, that you shall every Sunday and holyday through the year openly and plainly recite to your parishioners twice or thrice together, or oftener if need require, one particle or sentence of the Paternoster or Creed, in English, to the intent they may learn the same by heart, and so from day to day to give them one like lesson or sentence of the same, till they have learned the whole Paternoster or Creed, in English, by rote; and as they be taught every sentence of the same by rote, you shall expound and declare the understanding of the same unto them, exhorting all parents and householders to teach their children and servants the same, as they are bound in conscience to do, and that done, you shall declare unto them the Ten Commandments, one by one, every Sunday and holyday, till they be likewise perfect in the same.

05. Item, that you shall in confessions every Lent examine every person that comes to confession to you, whether they can recite the Articles of our Faith and the Paternoster in English, and here them say the same; particularly wherein if they be not perfect, you shall declare to the same that every Christian person ought to know the same before they should receive the blessed sacrament of the altar, and monish them to learn the same more perfectly by the next year following, or else like as they ought not to presume to come to God's board without perfect knowledge of the same; and if they do, it is to the great peril of their souls, so you shall declare unto them, that you look for other injunctions from the King's Highness by that time, to stay and repel all such from God's board, as shall be found ignorant in the premises; whereof you do thus admonish them, to the intent they should both eschew the peril of their souls and also the worldly rebuke that they might incur hereafter by the same.

06. Item, that you shall make or cause to be made in the said church, and every other cure you have, one sermon every quarter of the year at the least, wherein you shall purely and sincerely declare the very gospel of Christ, and in the same exhort your hearers to the works of charity, mercy and faith specially prescribed and commanded in Scripture, and not to repose their trust or affiance in any other works devised by men's fantasies beside Scripture; as in wandering to pilgrimages, offering of money, candles or tapers to images or relics, or kissing or licking the same, saying over a number of beads, not understood or minded on, or in suchlike superstition, for the doing whereof you not only have no promise of reward in Scripture, but contrariwise, great threats and maledictions of God, as things tending to idolatry and superstition, which of all other offences God Almighty does most detest and abhor, for that the same diminishes most his honour and glory.

07. Item, that such feigned images as you know in any of your cures to be so abused with pilgrimages or offerings of anything made thereunto, you shall for avoiding that most detestable offence of idolatry forthwith take down and delay, and shall suffer from henceforth no candles, tapers or images of wax to be set afore any image or picture, but only the light that commonly goeth across the church by the rood loft, the light before the sacrament of the altar, and the light about the sepulchre, which for the adorning of the church and divine service you shall suffer to remain; still admonishing your parishioners that images serve for none other purpose but as to be books of unlearned men that cannot know letters, whereby they might be otherwise admonished of the lives and conversation of them that the said images do represent; which images, if they abuse for any other intent than for such remembrances, they commit idolatry in the same to the great danger of their souls; and therefore the King's Highness, graciously tendering the weal of his subjects' souls, has in part already, and more will hereafter travail for the abolishing of such images as might be occasion of so great an offence to God, and so great a danger to the souls of his loving subjects.

08. Item, that not all in such benefices or cures as you have, whereupon you be not yourself resident, you shall appoint such curates in your stead, as both can by their ability, and will also promptly execute these Injunctions and do their duty; otherwise that you are bound in every behalf accordingly, and may profit their cure no less with good example of living, than with declaration of the Word of God; or else their lack and defaults shall be imputed unto you, who shall straitly answer for the same if they do otherwise.

09. Item, that you shall admit no man to preach within any your benefices or cures, but such as shall appear unto you to be sufficiently licensed thereunto by the King's Highness or his grace's authority, by the Archbishop of Canterbury, or the bishop of this diocese; and such as shall be so licensed you shall gladly receive to declare the Word of God, without any resistance or contradiction.

10. Item, if you have heretofore declared to your parishioners anything to the extolling or setting forth of pilgrimages, feigned relics or images, or any such superstition, you shall now openly, afore the same, recant and reprove the same, showing them, as the truth is, that you did the same upon no ground of Scripture, but as one being led and seduced by a common error and abuse crept into the Church, through the sufferance and avarice of such as felt profit by the same.

11. Item, if you do or shall know any man within your parish, or elsewhere, that is a letter (i.e. hinderer, *ed.*) of the Word of God to be read in English, or sincerely preached, or of the execution of these Injunctions, or a fautor (i.e. abettor, *ed.*) of the Bishop of Rome's pretensed power, now by the law of this realm justly rejected and extirped, you shall detect and present the same to the King's Highness, or his honourable council, or to his vicegerent aforesaid, or the justice of the peace next adjoining.

12. Item, that you and every parson, vicar or curate within this diocese shall for every church keep one book or register, wherein ye shall write the day and year of every wedding, christening and burying made within your parish for your time, and so every man succeeding you likewise; and also there insert every person's name that shall be so wedded, christened or buried; and for the safe keeping of the same book, the parish shall be bound to provide of their common charges one sure coffer with two locks and keys, whereof the one to remain with you, and the other with the wardens of every such parish wherein the said book shall be laid up; which book you shall every Sunday take forth and in the presence of the said wardens, or one of them, write and record in the same all the weddings, christenings and buryings made the whole week before, and that done, to lay up the book in the said coffer as before; and for every time that the same shall be omitted, the party that shall be in the fault thereof shall forfeit to the said church three shillings and fourpence, to be employed on the reparation of the same church.

13. Item, that you shall once every quarter of a year read these and the other former Injunctions given unto you by the authority of the King's Highness, openly and deliberately before all your parishioners, to the intent that both you may be the better admonished of your duty and your said parishioners the more incited to ensue the same for their part.

14. Item, forasmuch as by a law established, every man is bound to pay his tithes, no man shall, by colour of duty omitted by their curates, detain their tithes and so redub (i.e. repay, *ed.*) one wrong with another, or be his own judge; but shall truly pay the same as has been accustomed, to their parsons and curates, without any restraint or diminution; and such lack or default as they can justly find in their parsons and curates, to call for reformation thereof at their ordinaries' and other superiors' hands, who upon complaints and due proof thereof shall reform the same accordingly.

15. Item, that no parson shall from henceforth alter or change the order and manner of any fasting day that is commanded and indicted by the Church, nor of any prayer or divine service, otherwise than is specified in the said Injunctions, until such time as the same shall be so ordered and transposed by the King's Highness's authority, the eves of such saints whose holy days be abrogated only excepted, which shall be declared henceforth to be no fasting days; excepted also the commemoration of Thomas Becket, sometime Archbishop of Canterbury (29 December), which shall be clean omitted, and instead thereof the ferial service used.

16. Item, that the knelling of the Aves after service and certain other times, which has been brought in and begun by the pretence of the Bishop of Rome's pardon, henceforth be left and omitted, lest the people do hereafter trust to have pardon for the saying their Aves between the said knelling, as they have done in times past.

17. Item, where in times past men have used in divers places in their processions to sing *Ora pro nobis* to so many saints that they had no time to sing the good suffrages following, as *Parce nobis, Domine* and *Libera nos, Domine*, it must be taught and preached that better it were to omit *Ora pro nobis* and to sing the other suffrages.

All which and singular Injunctions I minister unto you and to your successors, by the King's Highness's authority to me committed in this part, which I charge and command you by the same authority to observe and keep, upon pain of deprivation, sequestration of the fruits, or such other coercion as (to) the King's Highness, or his vicegerent for the time being, shall be seen convenient.

19. THE THIRTEEN ARTICLES WITH THREE ADDITIONAL ARTICLES, 1538

History

These Articles were composed about 1538 by Archbishop Cranmer. They were discovered among his papers in the early nineteenth century, and were published in the Parker Society Edition of Cranmer's works (1846). Also discovered at that time, and published along with them, were three additional articles, which appear to have been composed at the same time and with the same purpose, though they are not part of the main collection. These Articles never had any official status, but they are of great interest because of what they reveal about Cranmer's links with Lutheranism. The original text is in Latin, and the English translation has been prepared for this edition. The three additional articles are printed together at the end.

Theology

The Thirteen Articles are the most clearly Lutheran document ever to be penned by an English churchman. The influence of the Wittenberg Articles is clearly apparent, but that of the Augsburg Confession is even greater. In many places, Cranmer's text is virtually identical to it, and it is obvious that he was adapting its provisions for English use. It is therefore extremely interesting to note that Cranmer omitted AC 06, which deals with the New Obedience, a doctrine which was of fundamental importance to Luther's understanding of the Gospel. Also of note is the fact that the articles on Penance (08), Rites and Ceremonies (11) and Civil Affairs (12) are extraordinarily long, reflecting concerns felt more deeply in England than on the Continent. It should also be noted that Cranmer only got as far as AC 17, which suggests that he probably broke off his labours before they were completed. This would tie in with the change in the King's policy which became apparent at about the same time. Lutheranism gave way to a revived form of Catholicism, though without the Pope, and these Articles were redundant. Of interest to us today is the fact that even at its height, Lutheran influence on Cranmer was far from being absolute. The Archbishop never felt that he was, or should become, a slavish imitator of the great Reformer, and this independence of mind was to remain characteristic of the English Church as it sought to come to terms with Protestant ideas from the Continent.

N.B. Where these Articles are virtually identical with the Augsburg Confession (1530) the text is printed in italics, and phrases which Cranmer later included in the Forty-two Articles (1553) are in bold type. Where the number of the corresponding article in the Augsburg Confession differs from the one in these Articles, it is indicated in parentheses.

01. De unitate Dei et trinitate personarum

De unitate essentiae divinae et de tribus personis, censemus decretum Nicaenae synodi verum, et sine ulla dubitatione credendum esse, videlicet, quod sit una essentia divina, quae et appellatur et est **Deus, aeternus, incorporeus, impartibilis, immensa potentia, sapientia, bonitate, creator et conservator omnium** rerum **visibilium** et **invisibilium**, et tamen tres sint personae eiusdem essentiae et potentiae, et coaeternae, **Pater, Filius et Spiritus Sanctus**; et nomine personae utimur ea significatione qua usi sunt in hac causa scriptores ecclesiastici, ut significet non partem aut qualitatem in alio, sed quod proprie subsistit. Damnamus omnes haereses contra hunc articulum exortas, ut Manichaeos, qui duo principia ponebant, bonum et malum: item Valentinianos, Arianos, Eunomianos, Mahometistas et omnes horum similes. Damnamus et Samosatenos, veteres et neotericos, qui cum tantum unam personam esse contendent, de Verbo et Spiritu Sancto astute et impie rhetoricantur, quod non sint personae distinctae, sed quod Verbum significet verbum vocale, et Spiritus motum in rebus creatum.

02. De peccato originali

Omnes homines, secundum naturam **propagati**, nascuntur cum peccato originali; hoc est, cum carentia **originalis iustitiae** debitae inesse, unde sunt filii irae, et deficiunt

01. The Unity of God and the Trinity of Persons

Concerning the unity of the divine essence and the three persons, we hold the decree of the Council of Nicaea to be true and without any doubt to be believed, viz. that there is one divine essence which is both called and is **God, eternal, incorporeal, indivisible, of immense power, wisdom and goodness, creator and preserver of all** things **visible** and **invisible, and yet there are three persons of the same essence** and power, coeternal, **Father, Son and Holy Spirit**; and we use the name Person in the same sence as it was used by the Church Fathers, i.e. as signifying not a part or a quality in another being, but what subsists in itself. We condemn all the heresies which have arisen against this article, e.g. the Manichees, who posited two principles, one good and one evil; likewise the Valentinians, Arians, Eunomians, Muslims and all like them. We also condemn the Adoptionists, ancient and modern, who argue that there is only one person, and cleverly and impiously prate that the Word and the Holy Spirit are not distinct persons, but that the Word is just a verbal utterance and the Spirit just a movement created in things.

02. Original Sin

All men, **engendered** according to nature, are born with original sin; that is, lacking the **original righteousness** which ought to be in them, and are therefore children of

cognitione Dei, metu Dei, fiducia erga Deum, etc. Et habent concupiscentiam, repugnantem legi Dei; estque hic morbus seu vitium originis vere peccatum, damnans et afferens nunc quoque aeternam mortem his qui non renascuntur per baptismum et Spiritum Sanctum. Damnamus Pelagianos, et alios, qui vitium originis negant esse peccatum, et ut extenuent gloriam meriti et beneficiorum Christi, disputant hominem viribus naturalibus sine Spiritu Sancto posse legi Dei satisfacere, et propter honesta opera rationis pronuntiari iustum coram Deo.

wrath, without any knowledge or fear of God or faith towards him, etc. And they have concupiscence, which is repugnant to the law of God. And this illness or original flaw is truly sin, condemning and now also bringing eternal death to those who are not born again by baptism and the Holy Spirit. We condemn the Pelagians and others who deny that the original flaw is sin, and in order to dissipate the glory of the merit and of the benefits of Christ, argue that man can fulfil the law of God in his natural strength, apart from the Holy Spirit, and be declared righteous before God on account of the good works of reason.

03. De duabus Christi naturis

03. The Two Natures of Christ

Item docemus, quod **Verbum**, hoc est, **Filius Dei, assumpserit humanam naturam in utero Beatae Mariae Virginis, ut** sint **duae naturae, divina et humana in unitate personae inseparabiliter coniunctae unus Christus vere Deus**, et vere homo, natus ex Virgine Maria, **vere passus, crucifixus, mortuus et sepultus, ut reconciliaret nobis Patrem**, et hostia esset non tentum pro culpa originis, sed etiam **pro omnibus actualibus hominum peccatis**. Item **descendit ad inferos, vere resurrexit** tertia die, deinde **ascendit ad caelos**, ut sedeat ad dexteram Patris et perpetuo regnet et dominetur omnibus creaturis, sanctificet credentes in ipsum, misso in corde eorum Spiritu Sancto, qui regat, consoletur, ac vivificet eos, ac defendat adversus Diabolum et vim peccati. Idem Christus palam est

We also teach that the **Word**, that is, the **Son** of God, **took unto him human nature in the womb of the** blessed Virgin Mary, so that there are **two natures, the divine and the human, inseparably joined together in unity of person; true God** and **true man**, born of the Virgin Mary; (who) **truly suffered, was crucified, dead and buried, that he might reconcile the Father unto us, and might be a sacrifice, not only for original guilt, but also for all actual sins of men**. The same also **descended into hell, and truly rose again** on the third day. Afterward **he ascended into heaven** to sit at the right hand of the Father, and reign for ever, and have dominion over all creatures; and to sanctify those who believe in him by sending the Holy Spirit into their hearts, to rule, comfort and quicken them, and

rediturus ut iudicet vivos et mortuos etc., iuxta Symbolum Apostolorum.

defend them against the Devil and the power of sin. The same Christ shall openly return to judge the living and the dead etc., as the Apostles' Creed states.

04. De iustificatione (AC 4/5)

04. Justification (AC 4/5)

Item de iustificatione docemus, quod ea proprie significat remissionem peccatorum et acceptationem seu reconciliationem nostram in gratiam et favorem Dei; hoc est, veram renovationem in Christo, et quod peccatores, licet non assequantur hanc iustificationem absque paenitentia, et bono ac propenso motu cordis quem Spiritus Sanctus efficit erga Deum et proximum, *non tamen propter dignitatem aut meritum paenitentiae aut ullorum operum seu meritorum suorum iustificantur, sed gratis propter Christum per fidem, cum credunt se in gratiam recipi, et peccata sua propter Christum remitti, qui sua morte pro nostris peccatis satisfecit. Hanc fidem imputat Deus pro iustitia coram ipso (Ro 3,4).* Fidem vero intelligimus non inanem et otiosam, sed eam "quae per dilectionem operatur". Est enim vera et Christiana fides, de qua hic loquimur, non sola notitia articulorum fidei, aut credulitas doctrinae Christianae dumtaxat historica; sed una cum illa notitia et credulitate, firma fiducia misericordiae Dei promissae propter Christum, qua videlicet certo persuademus ac statuimus eum etiam nobis misericordiam et propitium. Et haec fides vere iustificat, vere est salutifera, non ficta, mortua, aut hypocritica, sed necessario habet spem et

Likewise concerning justification, we teach that properly speaking, it signifies the forgiveness of sins and our acceptance, i.e. reconciliation into the grace and favour of God, that is, true renewal in Christ; and that sinners, although they cannot obtain this justification without penitence, and the right and proper movement of the heart towards God and (their) neighbour, which is the work of the Holy Spirit, *are yet not justified on account of any worth or merit of penitence or other works or merits of their own, but freely by faith on account of Christ, when they believe that they have been received into grace and that their sins have been forgiven on account of Christ, who by his death has made satisfaction for our sins. God reckons this faith as righteousness in his sight (Ro 3,4).* By faith, we do not mean something empty and useless, but rather that which "is worked through love". It is true and Christian faith of which we speak here, not merely knowledge of the articles of faith, or belief in Christian doctrine as historical fact; but alongside this knowledge and belief, a firm trust in the mercy of God promised on account of Christ, by which we boldly proclaim and declare that he himself is our mercy and sacrifice. And this faith truly justifies and

caritatem sibi individue coniunctas, ac etiam studium bene vivendi, et bene operatur pro loco et occasione. Nam bona opera ad salutem sunt necessaria, non quod de impio iustum faciunt, nec quod sunt pretium pro peccatis, aut causa iustificationis; sed quia necessum est, ut qui iam fide iustificatus est et reconciliatus Deo per Christum, voluntatem Dei facere studeat iuxta illud: "Non omnis qui dicit mihi Domine, Domine, intrabit regnum caelorum, sed qui facit voluntatem Patris mei, qui in caelis est". Qui vero haec opera facere non studet, sed secundum carnem vivit, neque veram fidem habet, neque iustus est, neque vitam aeternam (nisi ex animo resipiscat, et vere paeniteat) assequetur.

saves us. It is not feigned, dead or hypocritical, but of necessity has hope and love each joined to it, as well as a concern for right living, and it shows itself in the right time and place. For good works are necessary to salvation, not because they justify the ungodly, nor because they are a price paid for sin, or a cause of justification; but because it is necessary that one who is already justified by faith and reconciled to God through Christ, should strive to do God's will, as it is written: "Not everyone who says to me, Lord, Lord, will enter the kingdom of heaven, but he who does the will of my father, who is in heaven." One who does not strive to do such works, but who lives according to the flesh, does not have true faith, nor is he justified, nor will he obtain eternal life (unless he repents from the heart and is truly sorry).

(AC 5)

(AC 5)

Ut hanc fidem consequamur, institutum est ministerium docendi evangelii et porrigendi sacramenta. Nam per verbum et sacramenta tamquam per instrumenta donatur Spiritus Sanctus, qui fidem efficit, ubi et quando visum est Deo, in his qui audiunt evangelium, scilicet quod Deus non propter nostra merita sed propter Christum iustificet paenitentes, qui credunt se propter Christum in gratiam recipi. Damnamus Anabaptistas et alios, qui sentiunt Spiritum Sanctum contingere sine verbo externo hominibus per ipsorum praeparationes et opera.

For us to obtain this faith, the ministry of teaching the Gospel and administering the sacraments was instituted. For by the Word and sacraments, as by instruments, the Holy Spirit is given; who produces faith where and when it pleases God, in those that hear the Gospel, i.e. that God, not for our merits' sake, but for Christ's sake, justifies the penitent who believe that for Christ's sake they are received into grace. We condemn the Anabaptists and others, who believe that the Holy Spirit comes to men without any external word, through their own preparation and works.

05. De ecclesia (AC 7)

Ecclesia, praeter alias acceptationes in Scripturis duas habet praecipuas: unam, qua ecclesia accipitur pro congregatione omnium sanctorum et vere fidelium, qui Christo capiti vere credunt et sanctificantur Spiritu eius. Haec autem vivum est et vere sanctum Christi corpus mysticum, sed soli Deo cognitum, qui hominum corda solus intuetur. Altera acceptatio est qua ecclesia accipitur pro congregatione omnium qui baptizati sunt in Christo, et non palam abnegarunt Christum, nec iuste et per eius verbum sunt excommunicati. Ista ecclesiae acceptatio congruit eius statui in hac vita dumtaxat, in qua boni malis sunt admixti, et debet esse cognita ut possit audiri, iuxta illud: "Qui ecclesiam non audierit", etc. Cognoscitur autem per professionem evangelii et communionem sacramentorum. Haec est Ecclesia Catholica et Apostolica, quae non episcopatus Romani aut cuiusvis alterius ecclesiae finibus circumscribitur, sed universas totius Christianismi complectitur ecclesias, quae simul unam efficiunt Catholicam. In hac autem Catholica Ecclesia nulla particularis ecclesia, sive Romana fuerit sive quaevis alia, ex institutione Christi supra alias ecclesias eminentiam vel auctoritatem ullam vindicare potest. Est vero haec Ecclesia una, non quod in terris unum aliquot caput seu unum quendam vicarium sub Christo habeat aut habuerit unquam, (quod sibi iam diu pontifex Romanus divini iuris praetextu vindicavit, cum tamen revera divino iure nihil amplius illi sit concessum quam alii cuivis

05. The Church (AC 7)

In the Scriptures, the word "Church" has two main meanings, apart from others; one of which means the congregation of all the saints and true believers, who really believe in Christ the Head and are sanctified by his Spirit. This is the living and truly holy mystical body of Christ, but known only to God, who alone understands the hearts of men. The second meaning is that of the congregation of all who are baptized in Christ, who have not openly denied him nor been lawfully and by his Word excommunicated. This meaning of "Church" corresponds to its status in this life in that in it the good are mixed with the evil. It must be recognized in order to be heard, as it is written: "Whoever does not listen to the Church", etc. It is discerned by the proclamation of the Gospel and the fellowship of the sacraments. This is the Catholic and Apostolic Church which is not limited to the see of Rome or of any other church, but includes all the churches of Christendom, which together make up the one Catholic (Church). In this Catholic Church, no particular church, whether Roman or any other, can claim any primacy or authority, given by Christ's institution, over other churches. This Church is truly one, not because it has or has ever had a single head or vicar under Christ on earth (which is what the Roman pontiff has long claimed for himself under the pretext of divine right, when in fact no more is granted to him by divine right than to any other bishop.) But it is called

episcopo); sed ideo una dicitur, quia universi Christiani in vinculo pacis colligati unum caput Christum agnoscunt, cuius se profitentur esse corpus, unum agnoscunt Dominum, unam fidem, unum baptisma, unum Deum ac Patrem omnium.

Traditiones vero, et ritus, atque caeremoniae, quae vel ad decorum vel ordinem vel disciplinam ecclesiae ab hominibus sunt institutae, non omnino necesse est ut eaedem sint ubique aur prorsus similes. Hae enim et variae fuere, et variati possunt pro regionum et morum diversitate, ubi decus decensque ordo principibus rectoribus regionum videbuntur postulare; ita tamen ut nihil varietur aut instituatur contra Verbum Dei manifestum.

Et quamvis in ecclesia secundum posteriorem acceptionem *mali sunt bonis admixti, atque etiam ministeriis verbi et sacramentorum nonnunquam praesint;* tamen cum ministrent non suo sed Christi nomine, mandato et auctoritate, licet eorum ministerio uti, tam in verbo audiendo quam in recipiendis sacramentis, iuxta illud: "Qui vos audit, me audit". Nec per eorum malitiam minuitur effectus aut gratia donorum Christi rite accipientibus; *sunt enim efficacia propter promissionem et ordinationem Christi, etiamsi per malos exhibeantur.*

06. De baptismo (AC 9)

De baptismo dicimus, quod baptismus a Christo sit institutus, et *sit*

one because all Christians, joined in the bond of peace, recognize one Head, Christ, whose body they profess to be; they acknowledge one Lord, one faith, one baptism, one God and Father of all.

Traditions, and rites and ceremonies, which have been instituted by men either for decency, or order, or Church discipline, need not be identical everywhere, or even very similar. They have always been diverse, and may vary according to the differences of region and custom, when decency and good order are seen to be advocated by the princes and rulers of these regions, provided that nothing differ from, or be instituted which is contrary to, the plain Word of God.

And although *the evil are mixed together with the good* in the Church, as understood in the second sense, and even sometimes *preside over the ministry of the Word and sacraments,* yet when they minister not in their own but in Christ's name, we may use their ministry both in hearing the Word and in receiving the sacraments, as it is written: "Whoever hears you, hears me". Nor is the effect or the grace of the gifts of Christ, properly received, diminished by their wickedness; *for they are efficacious on account of the promise and ordination of Christ, even if they are manifested by evil men.*

06. Baptism (AC 9)

Concerning baptism, we say that it was instituted by Christ and *is*

necessarius ad salutem, et quod per baptismum offerantur remissio peccatorum et gratia Christi, infantibus et adultis. Et quod non debeat iterari baptismus. Et quod infantes debeant baptizari. Et quod infantes per baptismum consequantur remissionem peccatorum et gratiam, et sint filii Dei, quia promissio gratiae et vitae aeternae pertinet non solum ad adultos, sed etiam ad infantes. Et haec promissio per ministerium in ecclesia infantibus et adultis administrari debet. Quia vero infantes nascuntur cum peccato originis, habent opus remissione illius peccati, et illud ita remittitur ut reatus tollatur, licet corruptio naturae seu concupiscentia manet in hac vita, etsi incipit sanari, quia Spiritus Sanctus in ipsis etiam infantibus est efficax et eos mundat. Probamus igitur sententiam ecclesiae quae damnavit Pelagianos, quia negabant infantibus esse peccatum originis. *Damnamus et Anabaptistas qui negant infantes baptizandos esse.* De adultis vero docemus, quod ita consequuntur per baptismum remissionem peccatorum et gratiam, si baptizandi attulerint paenitentiam veram, confessionem articulorum fidei, et credant vere ipsis ibi donari remissionem peccatorum et iustificationem propter Christum, sicut Patrus ait in Actis: "Paenitentiam agite, et baptizetur unusquisque vestrum in nomine Iesu Christi in remissionem peccatorum, et accipietis donum Spiritus Sancti." (Ac 2:38)

necessary for salvation, and that through baptism forgiveness of sins and the grace of Christ are offered both to children and to adults. Baptism ought not to be repeated. Children ought to be baptized. Children receive forgiveness of sins and grace through baptism, and are children of God, because the promise of grace and eternal life does not pertain only to adults, but also to children. This promise ought to be given by the ministry in the Church both to children and to adults. For children are born with original sin, and need to have this sin forgiven, so that their guilt may be removed. Even though the corruption of nature called concupiscence remains in this life, it can begin to be healed because the Holy Spirit is effective even in children, and cleanses them. We therefore approve the judgement of the Church which condemned the Pelagians, who denied that children had original sin. *We also condemn the Anabaptists, who deny that children should be baptized.* Concerning adults, we teach that they receive forgiveness of sins and grace through baptism if, when being baptized, they are truly penitent, confess the articles of faith and truly believe that they will be granted forgiveness of sins and justification on account of Christ, as Peter says in Acts: "Do penitence and be baptized every one of you, in the name of Jesus Christ, for the forgiveness of sins, and you will receive the gift of the Holy Spirit." (Ac 2:38)

07. De eucharistia (AC 10)

De eucharistia constanter credimus et docemus, quod in sacramento corporis et sanguinis Domini, *vere, substantialiter et realiter adsint corpus et sanguis Christi* sub speciebus panis et vini. Et quod sub eisdem speciebus vere et realiter exhibentur et distribuuntur illis qui sacramentum accipiunt, sive bonis sive malis.

08. De paenitentia (AC 12)

Summam et ineffabilem suam erga peccatores clementiam et misericordiam Deus Opt. Max. apud prophetam declarans hisce verbis: "Vivo ego, dicit Dominus Deus, nolo mortem impii, set ut impius convertatur a via sua et vivet"(Ek 33:1), ut huius tantae clementiae ac misericordiae peccatores participes efficerentur, saluberrime instituit paenitentiam, quae sit omnibus resipiscentibus velut antidotum quoddam et efficax remedium adversus desperationem et mortem. Cuius quidem paenitentiae tantam necessitatem esse fatemur, ut quotquot a baptismo in mortalia peccata prolapsi sint, nisi in hac vita resipiscentes paenitentiam egerint, aeternae mortis iudicium effugere non poterint. Contra vero qui ad misericordiam Dei per paenitentiam tamquam ad asylum confugerint, quantiscumque peccatis obnoxii sunt, si ab illis serio conversi paenitentiam egerint, peccatorum omnium veniam ac remissionem indubie consequentur. Porro quon-

07. The Eucharist (AC 10)

Concerning the eucharist, we continue to believe and teach that in the sacrament of the body and blood of Christ, *the body and blood of Christ are truly, substantially and really present* under the forms of bread and wine. And that under these forms they are truly and really offered and administered to those who receive the sacrament, whether they be good or evil.

08. Penitence (AC 12)

The Most High God has declared his supreme and ineffable kindness and mercy towards sinners in these words of the prophet: "As I live, says the Lord God, I do not desire the death of the ungodly, but rather that the ungodly should turn from his way and live" (Ek 33:1). In order that sinners might share in this great kindness and mercy, he has most wholesomely instituted penitence, to be a kind of antidote and effective remedy against despair and death, for all who repent. So great, we say, is the need of such penitence, that those who have fallen into mortal sins after baptism, unless they repent in this life and do penitence, cannot escape the sentence of eternal death. But those who seek refuge in the mercy of God through penitence, however many sins they may be guilty of, if they seriously turn away from them and do penitence, they shall without doubt obtain pardon and remission for all their sins. Moreover, since sin is from ourselves, we judge it right to teach

iam peccare a nobis est et donum, valde utile et necessarium esse arbitramus docere, et cuius beneficium sit ut veram salutaremque paenitentiam agimus, et quaenam illa sit ac quibus ex rebus constet, de qua loquimur paenitentia. Dicimus itaque paenitentiae per quam peccator a morte animae resurgit, et denuo in gratiam cum Deo redit, Spiritum Sanctum auctorem esse et effectorem, nec quemquam posse sine huius arcano afflatu, peccata sua salutariter vel agnoscere vel odio habere, multo minus remissionem peccatorum a Deo sperare aut assequi. Qui quidem sacer Spiritus paenitentiae initium, progressum, et finem, caeteraque omnia quae veram paenitentiam perficiunt in anima peccatrice, hoc (quem docebimus) ordine ac modo operatur et efficit.

Principio, facit ut peccator per verbum terrores concipiat, dum sentit Deum irasci peccato, utque serio et ex corde doleat ac ingemiscat, quod Deum offenderit; quam peccati agnitionem, dolorem, et animi pavorem ob Deum offensum, sequitur peccati confessio, quae fit Deo dum rea conscientia peccatum suum Deo confitetur, et sese apud Deum accusat et damnat, et sibi petit ignosci. Ps 32:5 "Delictum meum cognitum tibi feci, et iniustitiam mean Domino, et tu remisisti impietatem peccati mei." Atque haec coram Deo confessio coniunctam habet certam fiduciam misericordiae divinae et remissionis peccatorum propter Christum, qua fiducia conscientia iam erigitur et pavore liberatur, ac certo statuit Deum sibi esse propitium, non merito aut dig-

that the gift is really useful and necessary, and what benefit it has, so that we might do true and saving penitence, as well as know what the penitence of which we speak means, and of what it consists. For we say that the Holy Spirit is the author and agent of that penitence whereby the sinner rises from the death of his soul and returns afresh into a state of grace with God. Nor can anyone either acknowledge his sins or hate them in a saving manner, without his secret breath, much less hope for or obtain forgiveness of his sins from God. It is this sacred Spirit who works and brings about the beginning, development and end of penitence, in this order and manner (which we shall expound), including everything else which perfects true penitence in the sinful soul.

First, he works so that the sinner, by (hearing) the Word, develops fears, as he realizes that God is angered by sin, so that he may be seriously sorry from the heart, and groan because he has offended God. The acknowledgement of sin, the grief and the fear of the mind because of an offended God, leads to confession of sin which is made to God when a guilty conscience confesses its sin to God, and accuses and condemns itself before God, asking to be forgiven. Ps 32:5 "I made my offence known to you, and my unrighteousness to the Lord, and you have put away the ungodliness of my sin." And this confession before God has joined to it a sure trust in the divine mercy and the forgiveness of sins on account of Christ, by which trust the conscience

nitate paenitentiae, aut suorum operum, sed ex gratuita misericordia propter Christum, qui solus est hostia, satisfactio, ac unica propitiatio pro peccatis nostris. Ad haec adest et certum animi propositum vitam totam in melius commutandi, ac studium faciendi voluntatem Dei et perpetuo abstinendi a peccatis. Nam vitae novitatem sive fructus dignos paenitentiae perfectionem necessario requirit Deus, iuxta illud, Ro 6:19 "Sicut exhibuistis membra vestra servire immunditiae et iniquitati, ad iniquitatem, ita nunc exhibete membra vestra servire iustitiae, in sanctificationem."

Atque haec quidem omnia, agnitionem peccati, odium peccati, dolorem pavoremque pro peccatis, peccati coram Deo confessionem, firmam fiduciam remissionis peccatorum propter Christum, una cum certo animi proposito postea semper a peccatis per Dei gratiam abstinendi et serviendi iustitiae, Spiritus Sanctus in nobis operatur et efficit, modo nos illius afflatui obsequamur, nec gratiae Dei nos ad paenitentiam invitanti repugnemus.

Caeterum cum has res quae paenitentiam efficiunt maxima pars Christiani populi ignoret, nec quomodo agenda sit vera paenitentia intelligat, nec ubi speranda sit remissio peccatorum norit, ut in his rebus omnibus melius instituatur et deceatur, non solum concionatores et pastores diligenter in publicis concionibus populum de hac re informare, et quid sit vera paen-

is aroused and delivered from fear, and clearly maintains that God is gracious to it, nor by any merit or value in penitence, or by its own works, but by the free mercy given on account of Christ, who alone is the sacrifice, satisfaction and only propitiation for our sins. In addition to these there is also present a real intention to lead a better life, and a desire to do God's will and for ever abstain from sinning. For God requires newness of life, i.e. fruits worthy of penitence, for the full perfection of penitence, as it says in Ro 6:19 "As you have presented your members to serve uncleanness and evil, so now present your members for the service of righteousness, for sanctification."

And all these things, the acknowledging of sin, the hatred of sin, the grief and fear for sins, the confession of sins before God, the firm trust in the forgiveness of sins for Christ's sake, together with a real intention to abstain from sin in future by the grace of God, and to do what is right, the Holy Spirit works and effects in us, so that we might respond to his inspiration and not reject the grace of God inviting us to penitence.

But as the greater part of Christ's people is ignorant of the things which bring about penitence, nor understands how true penitence should be made, nor where the forgiveness of sins is to be expected, in order for all these things to be better established and done it is not only necessary for the preachers and pastors to inform the people about this matter in public sermons, and to preach sincerely from Holy Writ

itentia, ex sacris litteris sincere praedicare debent, verum etiam valde utilem ac summe necessariam esse dicimus peccatorum confessionem, quae auricularis dicitur, et privatim fit ministris ecclesiae.

Quae sane confessio modis omnibus in ecclesia retinenda est et magni facienda, cum propter hominum imperitorum institutionem in Verbo Dei, et alia commoda non pauca (de quibus mox dicemus) tum praecipue propter absolutionis beneficium, hoc est remissionem peccatorum, quae in hac confessione confitentibus offertur et exhibetur per absolutionem et potestatem clavium, iuxta illud Christi, In. 20:23 "Quorum remiseritis peccata", etc. Cui absolutioni certo oportet credere. Est enim vox Evangelii, qua minister per verbum, non suo sed Christi nomine et auctoritate, remissionem peccatorum confitenti annuntiat et offert. Cui voci evangelii per ministrum sonanti, dum confitens certa fide credit et assentitur, illico conscientia eius fit certa de remissione peccatorum, et iam certo secum statuit Deum sibi propitium ac misericordem esse. Quae una profecto res Christianos omnes magnopere debet permovere, ut confessionem, in qua per absolutionem gratiae et remissionis peccatorum certitudo concipitur et confirmatur, modis omnibus et ament et amplectantur. Et in hac privata absolutione sacerdos potestatem habet absolvendi confitentem ab omnibus peccatis, etiam illis qui soliti sunt vocare casus reservati, ita tamen ut ille privatim absolutus, nihilominus pro man-

what true penitence is, but we say that the confession of sins which is called auricular, and is made in private to the ministers of the Church, is also really useful and extremely necessary.

This confession must be by all means retained in the Church, and made much of, for though there are many other suitable things (of which we shall soon speak) for men unskilled in the Word of God to learn, they ought first to have a clear understanding of the benefit of absolution, that is, the remission of sins, which is offered to those who confess in this way and is demonstrated through absolution and the power of the keys, as Christ says in Jn 20:23 "Whose sins you forgive, etc." It is certainly necessary to believe in this absolution. For it is the voice of the Gospel, with which the minister, by the Word, proclaims and offers forgiveness of sins to the one who confesses, not in his own name, but in the name and with the authority of Christ. When the penitent believes with a sure faith, and assents to this voice of the Gospel sounding from the minister, his conscience is assured of the remission of sins, and clearly accepts that God is gracious and merciful to him. This one thing accomplished should greatly move all Christians by all means to love and embrace confession, in which by the absolution of grace and the remission of sins, assurance is conceived and confirmed. And in this private absolution the priest has the power to absolve the penitent from all his sins, even from those customarily

ifestis criminibus (si in ius vocetur) publicis iudiciis subiaceat.

Accedunt huc et alia confessionis arcanae commoda, quorum unum est, quod indocti, ac imperiti homines nusquam commodius aut melius quam in confessione de doctrina Christiana institui possint, modo confessorem doctum et pium nacti fuerint. Nam cum animos attentos ac dociles in confessione efferunt, diligenter ad ea quae a sacerdote dicuntur animum advertunt. Quocirca et fides eorum explorari potest, et quid peccatum sit, quamque horrenda res sit, et quae sint peccatorum inter se discrimina, ac quam graviter contra peccata irascitur Deus, a doctis ac piis pastoribus seu confessoribus ex Verbo Dei doceri possunt ac informari. Multi enim, propterea quod haec ignorent, in conscientiis saepe graviter anguntur, illic trepidants timore, ubi timor non est, qui (ut Servator ait) "culicem excolantes, camelum deglutiunt"; in minimis levissimisque peccatis valde anxii, de maximis et gravissimis non perinde paenitentes. Sunt porro qui simili laborantes inscitia propter immodicum timorem et animi pusillanimitatem de peccatorum venia fere desperant. Contra sunt, qui per hypocrisim superbientes seipsos adversus Deum erigunt, quasi aut sine peccato sint, aut ipsos pro peccatis Deus nolit punire.

Iam quis nescit quam utilis et necessaria istiusmodi hominibus

called reserved cases, yet in such a way that the one privately absolved must still undergo public judgement for open crimes (if called into court).

To this may be added other useful features of secret confession, one of which is that unlearned and unskilled men will nowhere be better or more readily taught concerning Christian doctrine than in confession, provided they can find a learned and godly confessor. For when they bring attentive and obedient minds to confession, they listen carefully to what is said by the priest. In this way their faith can be tested, and they may be taught and instructed from the Word of God, by learned and godly pastors or confessors, what sin is, what a horrible thing it is, what the different types of sin are and how deeply God is angry with sin. For many, especially as they are ignorant of these things, are often deeply troubled in conscience, with fear where there is no reason to be afraid. As the Saviour says, they "strain at a gnat and swallow a camel". They are really anxious about the smallest and least important sins, and not at all repentant about the greatest and most serious. Moreover, there are those who because of similar ignorance are burdened with exaggerated fear and weakness of mind, and despair of obtaining any forgiveness for their sins. At the opposite extreme are those proud hypocrites, who stand up against God as if they are sinless, or as if God will not punish them for their sins.

For who does not know how useful and necessary this kind of confession

confessio sit, in qua hi Verbo Dei dure increpandi arguendique sunt, ut peccatores se agnoscant, atque intelligant, quam horribiliter Deus peccata puniat? Contra, illis qui nimio timore desperant, suavissima evangelii consolatio afferenda est. Ad haec in confessione ex Verbo Dei doceri homines possunt, non solum qua ratione Diaboli tentationes vincant, et carnem mortificent, ne ad priores vitae sordes postea relabantur, verum etiam quibus remediis peccata omnia fugiant, ut non regnent in ipsis. Praeterea illa animi humilitas qua homo homini propter Deum sese submittit, et pectoris sui arcana aperit, multarum profecto virtutum custos est et conservatrix. Quid quod pudor ille et erubescentia peccati quae ex confessione oritur, praeterquam quod animum a peccato ad Deum vere conversum indicat, etiam multos mortales a turpibus factis retrahit ac cohibet? Postremo, ut ille qui simpliciter et tamquam coram Deo peccata sua ministro ecclesiae confitetur, declarat se Verbum Dei timorem habere, ita hac animi humilitate discit Deum magis et timere et revereri, et innatam in corde superbiam reprimere, ut Dei voluntati facilius obsequatur et obtemperet. Iam vero, cum haec ita se habeant, nihil dubitamus, quin omnes viri boni hanc confessionem tot nominibus utilem ac necessariam, non solum in ecclesia retinendam esse, sed magno etiam in pretio habendam iudicent. Quod si qui sunt qui eam vel damnant, vel reiiciunt, hi profecto se et in Verbo Dei institutionem, et absolutionis beneficium, (quod in confessione datur) et alia

is to people, in which they are severely rebuked and castigated by the Word of God, to acknowledge that they are sinners, and to discover how horribly God punishes sins? On the other side, to those who despair from too much fear, the very sweet consolation of the Gospel is to be offered. In addition, people can be taught from the Word of God, not just how to overcome the temptations of the Devil, and mortify the flesh, so as not to fall back into their former evil ways, but also how to avoid all sins, so as not to be ruled by them. Moreover, that humility of mind by which one man submits to another on account of God, and opens the secrets of his heart, is the guardian and preserver of many further virtues. What is it if that shame and embarrassment for sin, which arises from confession, besides indicating that a mind has truly turned from sin to God, also brings many mortals back from evil deeds and restrains them? Finally, as he who simply, and as if before God, confesses his sins to a minister of the Church, declares that he has a fear towards the Word of God, so by this humility of mind he shows that he fears and reverences God all the more, and represses the innate pride in his heart, so as to respond more easily to the will of God and obey it. Indeed, in these circumstances we do not doubt that all good men judge that this confession, useful and necessary in so many ways, is not only to be retained in the Church, but also to be held in high esteem. For if there are some who condemn or reject it, they affect to neglect and

multa atque ingentia commoda Christianis valde utilia, negligere et contemnere ostendunt; nec animadvertunt se in orbem Christianum maximam peccandi licentiam invehere, et magnam in omne scelus ruendi occasionem praebere.

Quod vero, ad enumerationem peccatorum spectat, quemadmodum non probamus scrupulosam et anxiam, ne laqueam iniiciat hominum conscientiis, ita censemus segnem et supinam negligentiam in re tam salutari magnopere periculosam esse et fugiendam.

despise a teaching of the Word of God, the benefit of absolution (which is given in confession) and many other great advantages which are really useful for Christians. Nor do they realize that they are bringing into the Christian world the greatest licence to sin, and offering a great opportunity for falling into every kind of evil.

As concerns the listing of sins, although we do not approve of doing this in a scrupulous and anxious way which might ensnare the consciences of men, yet we think that a slack and lazy negligence in a matter of such importance for our salvation is very dangerous, and to be avoided.

09. De sacramentorum usu (AC 13)

09. The Use of the Sacraments (AC 13)

*Docemus, quod **sacramenta** quae per **Verbum Dei instituta** sunt, **non tantum sint notae professionis** inter Christianos, sed magis, **certa quaedam testimonia et efficacia signa gratiae**, et **bonae voluntatis Dei** erga **nos, per quae** Deus **invisibiliter operatur in nobis**, et suam gratiam in nos invisibiliter diffundit, siquidem ea rite susceperimus; quodque per ea **excitatur** et **confirmatur fides** in his qui eis utuntur. Porro docemus, quod ita utendum sit sacramentis, ut in adultis, praeter veram contritionem, necessario etiam debeat, accedere fides, quae credat praesentibus promissionibus, quae per sacramenta ostenduntur, exhibentur et praestantur. Neque enim in illis verum est, quod quidam dicunt, sacramenta conferre gratiam ex*

*We teach that **the sacraments** which have been **instituted by the Word of God** are **not only signs of profession** among Christians, but even more, **sure witnesses and effective signs of grace** and **of God's good will** toward us. **Through them**, God **works in us invisibly**, and pours his grace into us invisibly, if we receive them rightly, and **faith is also awakened through them and confirmed** in those who use them. Moreover we teach that the sacraments are to be so used that in the case of adults, besides true contrition, there must also be faith, which believes that the attendant promises which are offered by the sacraments are manifested and held forth. Nor is it true of them, as some say, that the sacraments confer grace "ex opere operato", apart from the good intention of the recipient, for in*

opere operato sine bono motu utentis, nam in ratione utentibus necessum est, ut fides etiam utentis accedat, per quam credat illis promissionibus, et accipiat res promissas, quae per sacramenta conferantur. De infantibus vero cum temerarium sit eos a misericordia Dei excludere, praesertim cum Christus in Evangelio dicat: "Sinite parvulos ad me venire, talium est enim regnum caelorum", et alibi: "Nisi quis renatus fuerit ex aqua et Spiritu Sancto, non potest intrare in regnum caelorum": cumque perpetua ecclesiae catholicae consuetudine, iam inde ab ipsis Apostolorum temporibus, receptum sit infantes debere baptizari in remissionem peccatorum et salutem, dicimus quod Spiritus Sanctus efficax sit in illis, et eos in baptismo mundet, quemadmodum supra in Articulo de baptismo dictum est.

respect of the recipients, it is necessary that the recipient's faith, by which he believes in the promises, should be present, so that he may receive the things promised, which are conferred by the sacraments. In the case of children, it would be presumptuous to exclude them from the mercy of God, especially as Christ says in the Gospel: "Let the little ones come to me, for of such is the kingdom of heaven" and elsewhere: "Unless a man be born again of water and the Holy Spirit, he cannot enter into the kingdom of heaven." Also, as it has always been accepted, by the perpetual custom of the Catholic Church since Apostolic times, that children ought to be baptized for the forgiveness of sins and salvation, we say that the Holy spirit is efficacious in them and cleanses them in baptism, as is said above in the Article on baptism.

10. De ministris Ecclesiae (AC 14)

10. The Ministers of the Church (AC 14)

De ministris Ecclesiae docemus, quod nemo debeat publice docere, aut sacramenta ministrare, nisi rite vocatus, et quidem ab his, penes quos in **Ecclesia**, iuxta Verbum Dei, et leges ac consuetudines uniuscuiusque regionis, ius est **vocandi** et admittendi. Et quod nullus ad Ecclesiae ministerium vocatus, etiamsi episcopus sit sive Romanus, sive quicunque alius, hoc sibi iure divino vindicare possit, ut publice docere, sacramenta ministrare, vel ullam ecclesiasticam functionem in aliena diocesi aut parochia exercere valeat; hoc est, nec episcopus in alterius

Concerning the ministers of the Church, we teach that no-one ought to teach publicly or administer the sacraments unless lawfully called by those in **the Church** who, according to the Word of God and the laws and customs of each country, have the right **to call** and ordain. No-one called to the ministry of the church, including the Roman or any other bishop, can claim for himself, as by divine right, the power to teach publicly, to administer the sacraments, or exercise any ecclesiastical function in another diocese or parish – i.e. neither a bishop in

episcopi diocesi, nec parochus in alterius parochia. Et demum quod militia ministri efficaciae sacramentorum nihil detrahat, ut iam supra docuimus in Articulo de ecclesia.

another diocese nor a parish priest in another parish. And furthermore, the conduct of the minister in no way detracts from the efficacy of a sacrament, as we taught above in the Article on the Church.

11. De ritibus ecclesiasticis (AC 15)

11. The Rites of the Church (AC 15)

Ritus, ceremoniae, et ordinationes ecclesiasticae humanitus institutae, quaecunque prosunt ad eruditionem, disciplinam, tranquillitatem, bonum ordinem, aut decorum in ecclesia, servandae sunt et amplectendae, ut stata festa, ieiunia, preces et his similia.

Church rites, ceremonies and ordinances instituted by men, if they contribute to learning, discipline, quietness, good order or decorum in the Church, are to be retained and embraced, e.g. statutory feasts, fasts, prayers and the like.

De quibus admonendi sunt homines quod non sunt illi cultus, quos Deus in Scriptura praecipit aut requirit, aut ipsa sanctimonia, sed quod ad illos cultus et ipsam sanctimoniam admodum utiles sunt, ac tum placent Deo, cum ex fide, caritate et oboedientia servantur. Sunt autem veri et genuini cultus, timor Dei, fides, dilectio, et caetera opera a Deo mandata. Ad quae consequenda et praestanda, quoties ritus et traditiones adiumentum adferunt diligenter servandae sunt, non tamquam res in Scripturis a Deo exactae, aut illis veris et genuinis cultibus aequandae, sed tamquam res Ecclesiae utiles, Deo gratae, et adminicula verae pietatis. Et quamvis ritus ac traditiones eiusmodi a Christianis observari debeant, propter causas quas ante diximus, tamen in illarum observatione ea libertatis Christianae ratio habenda est, ut nemo se illis ita teneri putet, quin eas possit omittere, modo adsit iusta violandi ratio et causa, et absit con-

Concerning these, people must be reminded that it is not the forms of worship which God teaches or requires in Scripture, or a pious appearance which matters. These forms of worship and piety are useful and pleasing to God only when they are kept in a spirit of faith, love and obedience. For true and genuine worship is fear of God, faith, love and other works commanded by God. In order to obtain and promote these things, whatever rites and traditions assist this purpose are to be diligently retained, not as things required by God in Scripture, or as substitutes for true and genuine worship, but as things useful to the Church, pleasing to God, and helpful to true godliness. And although such rites and traditions ought to be observed by Christians for the reasons we have stated, yet there must be a degree of Christian liberty in observing them, so that no-one should be so attached to them as to be unable to omit them, should there

temptus: nec per eiusmodi violationem proximi conscientia turbetur aut laedatur. Quod si eiusmodi ritus aut ordinationes alio animo ac consilio instituuntur, aut observantur, quam ut sint exercitia quaedam, admonitiones, et paedagogiae, quae excitent et conducant ad eas res in quibus sita est vera pietas et iustitia; nos talem institutionem et observationem omnino improbandam et reiiciendam esse dicimus. Non enim remissio peccatorum, iustificatio, et vera pietas tribuenda est eiusmodi ritibus et traditionibus, (nam remissionem peccatoris et iustificationem propter Christum gratis per fidem consequimur), sed hoc illis tribuendum est, quod quemadmodum nec sine legibus politicis civitas, ita nec sine ritibus ac traditionibus Ecclesiae ordo servari, confusio vitari, iuventus ac vulgus imperitum erudiri potest, quodque eiusmodi ritus et traditiones ad pietatem et spirituales animi motus non parum adminiculantur et prosunt. Quod si ullae traditiones aliquid praecipiunt contra Verbum Dei, vel quod sine peccato praestari non potest, nos eiusmodi traditiones, tamquam noxias et pestiferas, ab Ecclesia tollendas esse censemus: impias etiam opiniones et superstitiones quae Christi gloriam ac beneficium laedunt atque obscurant, quoties vel populi ignorantia ac simplicitate, vel prava doctrina aut negligentia pastorum, traditionibus ullis annectuntur et haerent, resacandas penitus et abolendas esse iudicamus. Praeterea etiam hoc docendi sunt homines, quod eiusmodi rituum ac traditionum

be just cause and reason for doing so, and not (merely) contempt for them. Nor should the conscience of a neighbour be disturbed or offended by an omission of this type. For if rites and observances of this kind are instituted or performed for reasons other than that they are exercises, reminders and lessons which arouse and lead us to those things in which true godliness and righteousness are found, then we say that such an institution and observance must be condemned and rejected. For forgiveness of sins, justification and true godliness are not to be attributed to rites and traditions of this kind (for we obtain the forgiveness of the sinner and justification freely by faith on account of Christ). Rather, this is to be attributed to them, that just as the state needs political laws, so the order of the Church cannot be served without rites and traditions, (so that) confusion may be avoided, youth and the ignorant masses may be instructed, and spiritually-minded persons may be helped to grow in piety by means of such rites and traditions. But if any of these traditions go against the Word of God, or if they cannot be observed without incurring sin, we say that traditions of this kind are harmful and pestiferous, and must be removed from the Church. We also judge that wicked ideas and superstitions which harm and obscure the glory and benefit of Christ must be thrown out and abolished, in so far as people are bound and cling to such traditions because of popular ignorance and simple-mindedness, or the corrupt

externa observatio Deo minime grata sit, nisi his, qui illis utuntur, animus adsit qui eas referat ad pietatem, propter quam institutae sunt. Ad haec, quod inter praecepta Dei, et ritus sive traditiones quae ab hominibus instituuntur, hoc discrimen habendum sit, nempe quod ritus sive traditiones humanitus institutae, mandatis ac praeceptis Dei (quae in Scripturis traduntur) cedere semper et postponi ubique debeant. Et nihilominus quoniam ordo et tranquillitas Ecclesiae absque ritibus et ceremoniis conservari non potest, docemus adeo utile esse et necessarium, Ecclesiam habere ritus et ceremonias, ut si ab Ecclesia tollerentur, ipsa illico Ecclesia et dissiparetur et labefactaretur.

Postremo ritus, ceremoniae, sive traditiones, de quibus antea diximus, non solum propter causas praedictas, verum etiam propter praeceptum Dei, qui iubet nos potestatibus oboedire, servandae sunt.

12. De rebus civilibus (AC 16)

Misera mortalium conditio peccato corrupta, praeceps ad iniquitatem et ad flagitia ruit, nisi salubri auctoritate retineatur, nec potest publica salus consistere, sine iusta gubernatione et oboedientia; quam ob rem benignissimus Deus ordinavit reges, principes ac gubernatores, quibus dedit auctoritatem non solum curandi ut populus iuxta divinae

teaching or neglect of their pastors. Moreover, people must be taught that the external observance of such rites and traditions is hardly pleasing to God, unless those who use them do so with a mind which leads them to godliness, for which cause they were instituted in the first place. In addition, between the commands of God and rites or traditions instituted by men, this distinction must be maintained – rites and traditions instituted by human beings must always give way and be placed after the commandments and precepts of God (which are handed down in Scripture). But at the same time, because the order and peace of the Church cannot be maintained without rites and ceremonies, we teach that it is useful and necessary for the Church to have rites and ceremonies, and that if they are removed from the Church, the Church itself will crumble and fall.

Finally, the rites, ceremonies or traditions of which we have spoken, are to be retained not only for the reasons given, but also because of the command of God, who orders us to obey the authorities.

12. Civil Affairs (AC 16)

The miserable condition of mortals is corrupted by sin, and heads straight for iniquity and disgrace, unless it is restrained by wholesoome authority, nor can public safety exist without just government and obedience, for which purpose the most merciful God has ordained kings, princes and governors, to whom he has given authority not

legis praescripta vivat, sed etiam legibus aliis reipublicae commodis, et iusta potestate eundem populum continendi ac regendi; hos autem in publicam salutem deputavit Deus, suos in terra ministros, et populi sui duces ac rectores, eisque subiecit universam cuiusvis sortis multitudinem reliquam. Atque ob eam causam multa ac diligenter de illis in Scripturis tradit. Primum quidem, ut ipsi caelestibus praeceptis erudiantur ad sapientiam et virtutem, quo sciant cuius sint ministri, et concessum a Deo iudicium et auctoritatem legitime atque salubriter exerceant, iuxta illud: "Erudimini qui iudicatis terram, servite Domino in timore". Deinde vero praecipit, atque illis in hoc ipsum auctoritatem dat, ut pro conditione reipublicae suae, salutares ac iustas leges (quoad pro virili possint) provideant atque legitime condant, per quas non solum equitas, iustitia, et tranquillitas in republica retineri, sed etiam pietas erga Deum promoveri possit; atque insuper ut legis Dei atque Christianae religionis tuendae curam habeant, quemadmodum Augustinus diserte fatetur, dicens: "In hoc reges, sicut eis divinitus praecipitur, Deo serviunt, in quantum reges sunt, si in suo regno bona iubeant, mala prohibeant, non solum quae pertinent ad humanam societatem, verum etiam quae ad divinam religionem". Proinde principum ac gubernatorum potestas et officium est, non solum pro sua et reipublicae incolumitate ac salute iusta bella suscipere, probos amplecti et fovere, in improbos animadvertere, pauperes tueri, afflictos et vim passos eripere,

only to ensure that a people should live according to the law of God, but also, by means of other laws suitable for the state, to order and rule the same people with lawful power. God has appointed them for the public good, as his ministers on earth, and as leaders and rulers of his people, and to them he has subjected the whole of the rest of mankind of whatever sort they may be. For this reason, Scripture frequently has much to say about them. First, that they should themselves be educated by the heavenly precepts in wisdom and virtue, that they might know whose ministers they are, and exercise the judgement and authority given to them by God legitimately and wholesomely, as it is written: "Be instructed, you who judge the earth; serve God in fear". God also teaches, and gives them authority for this very thing, that for the establishment of their state, they should provide and enact by statute, wholesome and just laws (as far as human power permits), by which not only equity, justice and peace may be preserved in the state, but also that piety towards God may be furthered. They are also, as stated above, to have responsibility for upholding the law of God and the Christian religion, as Augustine clearly says: "In this, kings, as they are divinely instructed, serve God, in so far as they are truly kings, if they command what is good in their kingdom, and forbid what is bad, not only in things pertaining to human society, but also in things pertaining to divine religion." Whence it is the duty and authority of princes and governors,

arcere iniurias, et ut ordo et concordia inter subditos conservetur, atque quod suum est cuique tribuatur curare; verum etiam prospicere, et (si causa ita postulaverit) etiam compellere, ut universi tam sacerdotes quam reliqua multitudo officiis suis rite et diligenter fungantur, omnem denique operam suam adhibere, ut boni and bene agendum invitentur, et improbi a malefaciendo cohibeantur. Et quamvis illi qui timore legum et poenarum corporalium cohibentur a peccando, aut in officio continentur, non eo ipso fiunt qui tales sunt, interim vel minus sint mali, vel saltem minus flagitiorum committant, viamque nonnunquam facilius inveniant ad pietatem, et reliquorum quies ac pietas minus turbetur, scandala et perniciosa exempla auferantur a Christianis coetibus, et apertis vitiis aut blasphemiis nomen Dei et religionis decus quam minimum dehonestetur.

Ad haec quia necessum est, ut auctoritatum principum, reipublicae atque rebus humanis summopere necessariam, populus tamquam Dei ordinationem agnoscat et revereatur; idcirco Deus Scripturis passim praecipit, omnes cuiuscunque in republica gradus aut conditionis fuerint, promptam et fidelem oboedientiam principibus praestent, idque non solum metu corporalis poenae, sed etiam propter Dei voluntatem;

not only to undertake just wars for the defence and safety of themselves and their state, to embrace and favour the just, censure the wicked, to protect the poor, to rescue the afflicted and suffering, to avenge wrongs, and so that order and harmony might be maintained among subjects, it is also his responsibility to assign to each one what is his. So also he must oversee (and if necessary) even compel, all priests and everyone else, to perform their duties properly, and exercise every effort to ensure that the good are encouraged to act well, and the wicked are restrained from evil-doing. And although those who are restrained from sin by the fear of the law and of corporal punishment, or are prevented by official means, do not thereby become what they should be, they are meanwhile less bad and commit fewer crimes than they might, and may more easily find the way to righteousness. Likewise the peace and godliness of the rest are less disturbed, scandals and bad examples are removed from Christian assemblies, and the name of God and the honour of religion are least dishonoured by open sins or blasphemies.

In addition, because it is necessary for God's people to acknowledge and respect the fact that the authority of princes is supremely necessary for the state and human affairs, God throughout the Scriptures ordains that everyone in the state, of whatever rank or condition, should give ready and faithful obedience to princes, and this not only for fear of corporal punishment, but also

quemadmodum Petrus diligenter monet: "Subditi (inquiens) estote omni humanae creaturae propter Deum, sive regi quasi praecellenti, dive ducibus, tamquam ab eo missis ad vindictam malefactorum, laudem vero bonorum, quia sic est voluntas Dei." Paulus vero in hunc modum: "Admone illos principibus et potestatibus subditos esse, magistratibus parere, ad omne opus bonum paratos esse, neminem blasphemare." Quod si malus princeps aut gubernator quicquam iniuste aut inique imperat subdito, quamvis ille potestate sua contra Dei voluntatem abutatur, ut animam suam laedat, nihilominus subditus debet eiusmodi imperium, quantumvis grave, pati ac sustinere, (nisi certo constat id esse peccatum), potius quam resistendo publicum ordinem aut quietem perturbare; quod si certo constet peccatum esse quod princeps mandat, tum subditus neque pareat neque reipublicae pacem quovismodo perturbet, sed pace servata incolumni, et causae ultione Deo relicta, vel ipsam potius mortem sustineat, quam quicquam contra Dei voluntatem et praeceptum perpetret.

because it is God's will, as Peter clearly reminds us: "Subjects (he says) must submit to every human creature for God's sake, whether to the king, as above all, or to lords, as to those sent by him for the punishment of evildoers and the praise of the good, for such is the will of God." Paul also likewise: "Remind them to be subject to princes and authorities, to obey the magistrates, to be ready for every good work, to blaspheme no-one." Even if a bad prince or governor should order the subject to do something wrong or unjust, and although he may be abusing his power, contrary to the will of God, to the hurt of his own soul; yet the subject must endure such rule and suffer it, however hard it may be, (unless it is clear that it is a sin), rather than disturb public order and peace by resisting. But if he is certain that what the prince commands is a sin, then the subject should neither obey nor disturb the peace of the state in any way, but keeping the peace, and leaving the vengeance to God, he should suffer even death itself, rather than do anything contrary to the will and commandment of God.

Porro quemadmodum de oboedientia principibus exhibenda Scriptura diligenter praecipit, ita etiam ut cetera officia alacriter illis praestemus, monet atque iubet; qualia sunt tributa, vectigalia, militiae labor, et his similia: quae populus, ex Dei praecepto, principibus pendere et praestare debet, propterea quod reipublicae absque stipendiis, prae-

Further, as Scripture speaks clearly about the obedience due to princes, so also it reminds us and requires us to perform willingly the other duties we owe them, such as taxes, tolls, military service and the like, which the people ought to offer and present to their princes by the command of God, especially as states cannot be defended or ruled without income,

sidiis, et magnis sumptibus neque defendi possunt neque regi. Est praeterea et honos principibus deferendus, iuxta Pauli sententiam, qui iubet, ut principibus honorem exhibeamus. Qui sane honos non in externa dumtaxat reverentia et observantia positus est, sed multo verius in animi iudicio et voluntate; nempe ut agnoscamus principes a deo ordinatos esse, et Deum per eos hominibus ingentia beneficia largiri: ad haec, ut principes propter Deum et metuamus et amemus, et ut ad omnem pro viribus gratitudinem illis praestandam parati simus: postremo ut Deum pro principibus precemur, uti servet eos, ac eorum mentes semper inflectat ad Dei gloriam et salutem reipublicae. Haec si fecerimus, vere principes honorabimus, iuxta Petri praeceptum: "Deum timete, regem honorificate."

Quae cum ita sint, non solum licet Christianis principibus ac gubernatoribus regna et ditiones possidere, atque dignitatibus et muneribus publicis fungi, quae publicam salutem spectant, et undecunque promovent vel tuentur, uti supra diximus; verum etiam, quando in eiusmodi functionibus respiciunt honorem Dei, et eodem dignitatem suam atque potestatem referunt, valde placent Deo, eiusque favorem ac gratiam ampliter demerentur. Sunt enim bona opera quae Deus praemiis magnificentissimis non in hac dumtaxat vita, sed multo magis in aeterna, cohonestat et coronat.

Licet insuper Christianis universis, ut singuli quique pro suo gradu ac conditione, iuxta divinas ac principum leges et honestas singularum

troops and great expenses. Moreover, there is an honour due to princes, as Paul says, who commands us to show honour to princes. This honour is not found in outward reverence and observance only, but much more in the judgement and will of the mind, so that we acknowledge that princes are ordained of God, and that through them God bestows huge benefits on mankind. In addition, we ought to fear and love princes for God's sake, and be ready to offer them every thanks we are capable of. Finally, we should pray to God for princes, that he might keep them and continually direct their minds to the glory of God and the safety of the state. If we do these things we shall honour princes, as Peter teaches: "Fear God, honour the king."

Therefore, it is not only right for Christian princes and governors to possess kingdoms and dominions, and to administer public dignities and offices, which concern public safety, and to advance or protect them in every way, as we said above, but also, when in functions of this kind they respect the honour of God and attribute their dignity and power to him, they are truly pleasing God, and merit his favour and grace fully. For these are good works which God will honour and crown with the most magnificent rewards, not only in this life, but much more in eternity.

It is further lawful for all Christians, each according to his own rank and condition, following the laws of God and of princes, and the honest

regionum consuetudines, talia munia atque officia obeant et exerceant, quibus mortalibus haec vita vel indiget, vel ornatur, vel conservatur; nempe ut victum quaerant ex honestis artibus, negotientur, faciant contractus, possideat proprium, res suas iure postulent, militent, copulentur legitimo matrimonio, praestent iurisiurandum, et huius-modi. Quae omnia, quemadmodum universis Christianis, pro sua cui-usque conditione ac gradu, divina iure licita sunt, ita cum pii subditi propter timorem Dei principibus ac gubernatoribus suis promptam atque debitam praestent oboedientiam, ceteraque student peragere, quae suum officium et reipublicae utilitas postulat, placent etiam ipsi magno-pere Deo, et bona faciunt opera, quibus Deus ingentia praemia promittit, et fidelissime largitur.

customs of particular countries, to occupy and exercise such offices and duties by which this mortal life either continues, or is graced or is pre-served, so that they may seek a living from honest trades, do business, make contracts, own property, conduct their affairs legally, serve in the army, marry according to law, take oaths and so on. All these things are lawful as of divine right, to all Christians, according to their condition and rank, so that when pious subjects offer prompt and due obedience to their princes and governors on account of the fear of God, and try to do the other things which their duty and the needs of the state require, they please God and do good works, for which God promises huge rewards, which he faithfully fulfils.

13. De corporum resurrectione et iudicio extremo (AC 17)

13. The Resurrection of the Body and the Last Judgement (AC 17)

Credendum firmiter et docendum censemus, quod in consummatione mundi Christus, sicut ipsemet apud Matthaeum affirmat, venturus est in gloria Patris sui cum angelis sanctis, et maiestate, ac potentia, sessurusque super sedem maiestatis suae; et quod in eodem adventu, summa celeritate, in momento temporis, ictu oculi, divina potentia sua suscitabit mortuos, sistetque in eisdem in quibus vixerunt corporibus ac carne coram tribunali suo cunctos homines, qui unquam ab exordio mundi fuerunt, aut postea unquam usque in illam diem futuri sunt. Et iudicabit exactissimo atque iustis-

We assert that it is to be firmly believed and taught that at the end of the world, Christ, as he himself says in Matthew, will come in the glory of his Father, with his holy angels, and in majesty and power, and will sit upon the throne of his majesty. At his coming, with great speed, in a moment of time, in the twinkling of an eye, he will raise the dead by his divine power, and place them in the same bodies and flesh in which they lived here below, before his judge-ment seat. All men, who have lived since the foundation of the world, and who will yet live up to that day, will be included in this. And God

simo iudicio singulos, et reddet unicuique secundum opera sua, quae in hac vita et corpore gessit: piis quidem ac iustis aeternam vitam et gloriam cum sanctis angelis; impiis vero et sceleratis aeternam mortem atque supplicium, cum Diabolo et praevaricatoribus angelis. Praeterea quod in illo iudicio perfecta et perpetua fiet separatio proborum ab improbis, et quod nullum erit postea terrenum regnum aut terrenarum voluptatem usus, qualia quidam errore decepti somniaverunt. Demum quod nullus post hoc iudicium erit finis tormentorum malis, qui tunc condemnabuntur ad supplicia, sicut nec ullus finis beatitudinis bonis, qui in illo die acceptabuntur ad gloriam.

will judge each one with the most exact and perfect judgement, and render to each according to his works, which he did in this life and body. To the godly and righteous he will give eternal life and glory with his holy angels; to the ungodly and wicked eternal death and punishment, with the Devil and the rebellious angels. Moreover in that judgement there will be a perfect and eternal separation of the just from the unjust, and that afterwards there will be no more earthly kingdom or enjoyment of earthly pleasures, as some deceived people have mistakenly imagined. Likewise, after this judgement there will be no end to the torments of the wicked, who will then be condemned to punishment, just as there will be no end of blessedness for the good, who on that day will be received into glory.

A. De missa privata

A. Private Mass

Lectiones sacras ac conciones in missa recitari, et precationes pro rebus vel in singulos vel etiam in universos necessariis fieri, et eucharistiam in missa populo exhiberi, non est dubium quin Paulus et reliqui Apostoli ecclesiis ordinaverunt. Quem morem, a primis Christianitatis incunabulis observatum, nullo nunc pacto abolendum, sed omni reverentia et religione in ecclesiam retinendum atque conservandum iudicamus. Nam lectiones illae permultum habent efficaciae ad excitandas hominum mentes, vel ac fidem, vel ad amorem ac timorem Dei et oboedientiam praeceptorum eius, maxime si populo satis

There is no doubt that Paul and the other Apostles ordained that there should be sacred lessons and homilies said in the mass, and prayers made for things necessary for individuals and for all, and that the eucharist should be shown to the people in the mass. Which custom, observed from the first beginnings of Christianity, we judge should not now be abolished by any accord, but should be retained and preserved with all reverence and piety in the Church. For these lessons are very effective in arousing the minds of men, either to faith, or to the love and fear of God and obedience to his commandments, especially if they

intelligantur, vel a concionatore docto et pio explicentur.

Siquidem et fides ex auditu est, et quid operis faciendum sit ut Deo placeas, non aliunde melius aut certius quam ex ipsius Verbo discas. Precationes autem, quae in communi coetu fiunt, promissiones a Christo quam amplissimas adiunctas habent; cum ait: "Si duo ex vobis consenserint super terram de omni re quacunque petierint, fiet illis a Patre meo qui in caelis est; ubi enim sunt duo vel tres congregati in nomine meo, ibi sum in medio eorum." Voluit igitur Christus, ut oraturi congregaremur, et nos ecclesiae totam sic inter se devinctam esse, ut haberet cor unum et animam unam, et invicem alii aliorum necessitatibus afficerentur, et pro illis communibus precibus Deum orarent, ratas fore promittens et sibi gratas huiusmodi precationes.

Praeterea ecclesiam convenire et iunctim Deo precari, valde etiam prodest ad exemplum. Ibi enim alii aliorum exemplis vel ignari docentur vel segnes excitantur, ut et ipsi credant et Deum invocent. Quam multos necessitatum publicarum vel nulla vel minima cura tangeret, nisi ibi admoneretur singulos debere affici publicis curis, et orare non solum pro ecclesia universa, ut liberetur ab erroribus, scandalis, disidiis, impiis cultibus, ut vera doctrina propagetur, ut veri cultus (pulsa superstitione) Deo praestentur, ut pax et tranquillitas Ecclesiae conservetur, sed etiam pro principum salute et felici guber-

are properly understood by the people, or are explained by a learned and godly preacher.

For if faith is by hearing, and you need to do something to please God, you could not do anything better or surer than to listen to his Word. Moreover, the prayers which are said in the common assembly contain the fullest promises of Christ, who said: "If two of you agree on earth about whatever they pray for, it will be granted to them by my Father in heaven, for where two or three are gathered together in my name, there am I in the midst of them." Therefore Christ willed that we should come together to pray, and that we should gather as churches. He wanted the whole Church to be so united that it would have one heart and soul, that everyone would be touched by each other's needs, and would pray to God for them in common prayers, setting out fixed prayers of this kind which were pleasing to him.

Moreover, for the Church to come together to pray to God sets an example. For by the example of others the ignorant may be taught, and the lazy aroused to believe and call upon God themselves. How many would have little or no interest in public needs if they were not there reminded that individuals should be affected by public concerns, and pray, not only for the universal Church, that it might be freed from errors, scandals, divisions, ungodly forms of worship, that true doctrine might be spread, that true forms of worship (rejecting superstition) might be offered to God, that the peace and quietness of the Church

natione, pro proventu frugum, contra pestilentiam et similibus! Huismodi precationes in missa et ceremoniis publicis censemus pie et necessario institutas esse, vel ob hoc quoque, ut assuescant homines in omnibus periculis Deum invocare, in illum fiduciam collocare, ab illo pendere, et auxilium petere et exspectare.

Sed precationes communes communi lingua fieri consentaneum foret; ut omnes astantes communiteret unanimiter orare Deum possint, tam mente quam spiritu. Ita enim oratio et Deo fieret acceptior, et hominibus haud dubie fructuosior, si populus intellecta sacerdotis verba, non minus animorum interius consensu, quam vocis exterius consono concentu approbaret. Nam, ut inquit Paulus: "Si orem lingua, spiritus meus orat, at mens mea fructu vacat."(I Co 14:14) Et iterum: "Si incertam vocem tuba dederit, quis apparabitur ad bellum? Sic et vos per linguam nisi significantem sermonem dederitis, quomodo intelligetur quod dicitur?" (I Co 14:9) Et mox ibidem: "Alioqui si benedixeris spiritu, is qui implet locum indocti quomodo dicturus est, Amen, ad tuam gratiarum actionem?" (I Co 14:16)

Peractis vero lectionibus, concionibus, et precationibus, populus corpus Christi quod pro nobis traditum est, et sanguinem eius qui pro nobis effusus est, in eucharistia sumebat, in memoriam videlicet mortis suae, uti ipse pridie passionis instituerat. Quo factum est, ut illi

might be preserved; but also for the safety of princes and good government, for the provision of food, against disease, and so on. We think that prayers of this type have been godly and necessarily introduced in the mass and in public ceremonies, partly also to accustom people to call on God in all dangers, to put their trust in him, to depend on him and to ask for, and expect his help.

But common prayers ought to be made in a common language, so that all those present may pray to God together, both in mind and spirit. For in this way prayer is more acceptable to God, and doubtless also more beneficial to men, if the people, understanding the words of the priest, agree with them no less by the inner consent of their mind than by the outward harmony of their voice. For as Paul says: "If I pray in a tongue, my spirit prays, but my mind is devoid of fruit," (I Co 14:14) and again: "If the trumpet gives an uncertain sound, who will appear for battle? So, if you speak in a tongue but do not produce meaningful speech, how will anyone understand what is being said?" (I Co 14:9) And soon afterwards again: "If you bless someone in the Spirit, how will he who sits in the place of the ignorant be able to say Amen to your prayer of thanksgiving?" (I Co 14:16)

After the lessons, homilies and prayers are over, the people would receive in the Eucharist the body of Christ, which was given for us, and his blood which was shed for us, in memory of his death, as he instituted the day before his passion. When this was done, they would regularly rise

veluti Christo incorporati et connati, et cum illo peccatis mortui, denuo in novae vitae emendationem saepissime resurgerent. Hodie vero adeo praevaluit Romani Antichristi tyrannis non solum adversus mundi monarchas, sed etiam contra veterem Ecclesiae morem et sinceram ac puram doctrinae Christianae religionem, ut quae sanctissime primitus fuerunt instituta, illa in sui suorumque gloriam ac commodum impurissime profanaverit.

Lectiones sacrae et precationes hodie apud sacerdotes manent, sed ea lingua ut a populo non intelligantur, et populus ipse quod precatur (quia peregrino sermone id facit) non intelligit. Conciones sacrae vel nullae vel rarissimae sunt; eucharistia a solo sumitur sacerdote, qui illa in turpissimum quaestum pro vivis ac defunctis applicat; populo Christiano vix in paschate datur, et ne tunc quidem integrum sacramentum. Ceterum quanto missa res est sacratior, tanto minus decet eam impiis opinionibus profanari, aut ad libidinem quorundam et quaestum in sinistrum usum converti. Damnanda est igitur impia illa opinio sententium usum sacramenti cultum esse a sacerdotibus applicandum pro aliis, vivis et defunctis, et mereri illis vitam aeternam et remissionem culpae et poenae, idque ex opere operato.

Talis siquidem doctrina ignota erat veteri Ecclesiae, et aliena est a Scripturis sacris, et subvertit rectam de fide iustificatione doctrinam, et parit alieni operis fiduciam. Christus

to the correction of new life, being incorporated into, and born again with Christ, and being dead with him to sin. Today the tyranny of the Roman Antichrist has corrupted these things for its own glory and convenience, having risen up not only against the monarchs of the world, but also against the ancient custom of the Church, and the pure practice of Christian doctrine, which was instituted in holiness at the beginning.

Sacred lessons and prayers still continue among the priests, but their language is not understood by the people, who pray without understanding because they do so in a foreign tongue. Sacred homilies are either non-existent or very rare; the Eucharist is received by the priest alone, who turns it into a most shameful plea on behalf of the living and the dead; the Christian people barely enters into the paschal act, and never receives the complete sacrament. But the more sacred the mass is, the less it should be profaned by impious opinions, nor should it be turned into some kind of licence or magic. Therefore the ungodly opinion of those who think that the sacrament can be received by the priest on behalf of others, living or dead, is to be condemned, as is the view that he can earn for them eternal life and the remission of guilt and punishment, and this moreover "ex opere operato".

Such a doctrine was unknown in the ancient Church, and is foreign to the sacred Scriptures, and undermines the right doctrine of justification by faith, and produces trust

autem, cum institueret hoc sacramentum, dixit: "Hoc facite in meam commemorationem," volens nimirum, ut ibi fieret in vera fide recordatio mortis ipsius, et beneficiorum quae nobis sua morte meruit. Quae beneficia per sacramentum applicantur sumenti, cum fidem tali recordatione exsuscitat. Non possunt autem aliis, quam sacramentum sumentibus, per sumentes applicari.

Sed quemadmodum unusquisque pro seipso tantum, et non pro alio baptizatur; ita et Eucharistia a Christo est instituta, ut illam nemo pro alio, sed pro sese quisque Christianus sumeret. Talis quippe est sacramentorum ratio et natura, ut signa sint visibilia, certa, et efficacia, per quae Deus invisibiliter in recte utentibus operatur; verum non nisi in ipsis tantum utentibus per illa operatur, nec aliis per alios, sive sacerdotes seu cuiuscunque ordinis aut conditionis fuerint, accommodari possunt. Qua re una animadversa ac perpensa, facile apparebit privatarum missarum applicationes et nundinationes non amplius esse ferendas. Nam cum teste Augustino, quaecumque sunt in missa praeter Eucharistiam nihil aliud sint quam laudes, gratiarum actiones, obsecrationes, et fidelium petitiones; Eucharistia autem non alii quam ipsi sumenti prosit aut applicari possit; reliqua vero, ut laudes, gratiarum actiones, obsecrationes, etc., tam a laicis quam a sacerdotibus afferri Deo possint et debeant; non erit iam amplius cur missas emere quisquam debebit.

in the work of another person. But Christ, when he instituted this sacrament, said: "Do this in memory of me," desiring above all that in true faith a memorial should be made of his death, and of the benefits which he earned for us by his death. These benefits are granted through the sacrament to the recipient, when he responds in faith to this memorial. They cannot be given to others through the recipients.

For just as everyone is baptized only for himself, and not for others, so the Eucharist was instituted by Christ so that no-one should take it on behalf of another but only each Christian for himself. For the logic and nature of a sacrament is this, that there are visible, sure and effective signs through which God works invisibly in those who rightly use them, and he works only in those who use them personally, not in those who want to be represented by others, whether they are priests or of whatever sort or condition they may be. Having considered and thoroughly examined this matter, it will easily appear that there is no further need to discuss the uses and activities connected with private masses. For if, as Augustine witnesses, the mass contains nothing besides the Eucharist except praises, thanksgivings, supplications and the petitions of the faithful, and if the Eucharist can benefit or be applied to no-one except the recipient, and if the other things like praises, thanksgivings, supplications and so on can and must be offered by both laity and priests, there will be no further reason why anyone will need to buy masses.

Porro, quia sine gratiarum actione recordatio mortis Christi rite non peragitur, ideo veteres hanc sacramenti perceptionem Eucharistiam appellarunt, quam et sacrificium nonnulli orthodoxi patres nominaverunt, quod videlicet in memoriam illius unici et semel peracti sacrificii fiat, non quod ipsum opus sit sacrificium applicabile vivis et mortuis in remissionem peccatorum. Id quod papisticum dumtaxat est figmentum; et quoniam ab hac tam impia opinione et quaestu inde proveniente missae privatae, illaeque porro magna parte satisfactoriae, in tentam multitudinem excreverunt, quarum nec mentionem nec exemplum ullum apud antiquiores invenimus, satisfactorias quidem prorsus abolendas, ceteras vero privatas vel in totum abrogandas, vel certe minuendas et reprimendas iudicamus; summam denique curam adhibendam, ut huius sacramenti verus ac genuinus usus ad gloriam Christi et Ecclesiae salutem restituatur.

Furthermore, since without thanksgiving, the memorial of Christ's death is not rightly celebrated, the ancients called the celebration of the sacrament "Eucharist", which was the name given to it by many orthodox Fathers, meaning that it was a memorial of that once-for-all, unique, perfect sacrifice, and not that it was itself a sacrifice applicable to both the living and the dead, for the forgiveness of sins. This papal notion is a fiction, and since it is from this ungodly opinion and practice that private masses, most of which are meant to be expiatory, derive and have multiplied enormously, though we have found no example or mention of them in the more ancient writers. We think that expiatory masses ought to be abolished, and that other private masses be either totally abrogated or else greatly restricted and controlled, and that the greatest care be taken to ensure that a true and genuine use of this sacrament be restored, to the glory of Christ and the salvation of the Church.

B. De veneratione sanctorum

Quamquam credimus et confitemur Deum omnis boni datorem ac largitorem esse, uti Iacobus testatur, dicens: "Omne datum optimum et omne donum perfectum desursum est descendens a Patre luminum," (Ja 1:17) et Christus apud Iohannem ait: "Quicquid petieritis Patrem in nomine meo, dabit vobis," (Jn 15:6) et Psal.: "Invoca me in die tribulationis," (Ps 50:15) etc. quibus Scripturae locis aperte docemur, quicquid

B. The Veneration of Saints

Although we believe and confess that God is the giver and provider of everything good, as James bears witness, saying: "Every good and every perfect gift comes from above from the Father of lights," (Ja 1:17) and Christ says in John: "Whatever you ask the Father in my name, he will give you," (Jn 15:16) and in the Psalms: "Call on me in the day of trouble," (Ps 50:15) etc., by which passages of Scripture we are clearly

ad corporis aut animi salutem pertinet, id a solo Deo petendum esse, et ab eo nobis dari, quoties in Christi nomine petimus: tamen cum iam inde ab exordio Ecclesiae receptum sit, sanctorum memorias et dies festos celebrare, valde utile ac necessarium putamus, eam de his rebus doctrinae formem tradere, quae Dei gloriam nulla in parte laedat aut imminuat, et tamen doceat perpetuam Ecclesiae consuetudinem in divorum memoriis ac festis celebrandis laudabilem esse, nec Scripturae sacrae adversari. Et cum non ignoramus in hanc quoque religionis Christianae partem, quae sanctorum venerationem continet, multos abusus ac superstitiones irrepsisse; curandum censemus, ut eo, quod vanum aut noxium est, improbato et reiecto, illud solum, quod utile ac verum est, retineatur ac probetur. Quod ut rectius et facilius fiat, docendum ducimus, quod sanctorum, qui corporibus exuti cum Christo vivunt, memoria in ecclesiis multis de causis utiliter habeatur.

Primum, quod nobis in mentem suggerit illa eximia Dei in sanctis opera, quae ut olim, dum per sanctos fierent, Dei potentiam et gloriam apud homines illustrabant, ita nunc vel sola recordatione ad Deum in sanctis laudandum nos invitant. Adde huc, quod in his sanctorum memoriis praeclarissima fidei, caritatis, patientiae et ceterarum virtutum exempla nobis proponuntur, quae nos exstimulent ad

taught that what pertains to the salvation of the body and the soul, we are to ask for of God alone, and be given them by him as often as we ask in the name of Christ; yet, as has been received from the foundation of the Church, we think it very useful and necessary to celebrate the memorials and feast days of the saints, and to hand down a form of doctrine concerning these things, which in no way hurts or offends the glory of God, yet teaches the constant custom of the Church in celebrating the memorials and feast days of saints is praiseworthy, and not opposed to sacred Scripture. And because we are not unaware that many abuses and superstitions have come into that part of the Christian religion which includes the veneration of saints, we think it necessary to ensure that whatever is meaningless or harmful be condemned and rejected, and that only that which is useful and true be retained and approved. In order to do this better and more easily, we think it ought to be taught that remembering the saints, who have cast off their bodies and live with Christ, is useful in the churches for many reasons.

First, because it calls to mind those outstanding works of God in the saints, which were once performed through them in order to illustrate God's power and glory among men, and which now call us to praise God in the saints by the simple remembrance of them. Add to this, that in these remembrances of the saints there are put before us the clearest examples of faith, love, patience and other virtues, which encourage us to

illorum imitationem: ut quemadmodum illi (He 11:33) "per fidem vicerunt regna, operati sunt iustitiam, adepti promissiones," ita nos illorum vestigiis insistentes, ad victoriae coronam, qua illi nunc ornantur, perveniamus. Quam sane sanctorum imitationem summum et maximum honorem esse arbitramur, quem Christus sit unicum illud et numeris omnibus perfectum vitae exemplar, quod imitari pro viribus omnes debemus, sunt tamen Christi beneficio et munere etiam in sanctis proposita nobis exempla, quae utiliter et multo cum fructu sequi possumus. Quos enim non animabit stupenda in tormentis martyrum constantia, ut omnia quantumvis aspera et dura propter Christi gloriam pati velint? Cui non Iosiae, Ezechiae, et aliorum piorum regum pietas, in vera Dei religione tuenda, et abolendis idololatricis cultibus, exemplo esse potest, ut illorum pietatem imitari pro viribus studeat? Iam vero et lapsus quoque et paenitentiae sanctorum, dum ex historiis cognoscuntur, magnam nobis utilitatem adferre poterunt. Nam cum Davidis, Petri, Magdalenae, et aliorum condonatos fuisse lapsus cognoscimus, quis dubitet quin et nostra peccata, nobis paenitentiam agentibus, Deus velit similiter condonare? Porro in sanctorum memoriis gratiae Deo agendae sunt, quod sanctis varia dona contulit, quibus illi insigniter Ecclesiae profuerunt, dum vel doctrinae vel vitae exemplo quam plurimos Christo lucrati sunt; quae Dei in sanctis dona non solum magnopere laudare oportet, sed etiam sanctos

imitate them, in so far as they "by faith conquered kingdoms, worked righteousness, claimed the promises," (He 11:33) so we following in their footsteps come to the crown of glory, with which they are now adorned. We consider that this imitation of the saints is the highest and greatest honour, even though Christ is the supreme and perfect example of life, which we ought all to imitate as far as we are able. Yet the examples offered to us in the saints are of value and benefit to us, which we may follow usefully and with much profit. For who will not be inspired by the great endurance of the martyrs in their torments, so as to desire to suffer verything, however hard and difficult, for the sake of the glory of Christ? To whom would the godliness of Josiah and Hezekiah and the other godly kings who preserved the true worship of God by abolishing idolatrous cults, not be an example to imitate as far as possible? Indeed, even the sins and penances of the saints, in so far as they are recorded, can be very helpful to us. For when we see how the sins of David, Peter, Mary Magdalene and others were forgiven, how can we doubt that God will also likewise forgive our sins if we do penance? Furthermore, in remembering the saints, thanks must be offered to God that he bestowed different gifts on the saints, by which they greatly advanced the Church, winning very many to Christ by the example either of their doctrine or of their life. It is not only right that we should greatly praise the gifts of God in the saints, but also offer praises for

ipsos, quia his donis bene usi sunt, laudibus attollere, amare, et suspicere, quemadmodum scribit Augustinus *De civit. Dei* 8: "Honoramus," inquit, "memorias martyrum tamquam sanctorum hominum Dei, qui usque ad mortem suorum corporum pro veritate certarunt – ut ea celebritate et Deo vero de illorum victoriis gratias agamus, et nos ad imitationem talium coronarum atque palmarum, eodem invocato in auxilium, ex eorum memoriae renovatione adhortemur." Et alibi: "Colimus... martyres eo cultu dilectionis et societatis, quo et in hac vita coluntur sancti homines Dei, quorum corda ad talem pro evangelica veritate passionem parata esse sentimus; sed illos tanto devotius quanto securius post incerta omnia superata: quanto etiam fidentiore laude praedicamus iam in vita feliciori victores, quam in ista adhuc usque pugnantes!" Et Basilius, in *Concione de Martyre Gordia:* "Sanctis non est opus additione ad gloriam, sed nobis eorum memoria opus est ad imitationem." Et alibi: "Hoc est martyrum encomium, adhortari Ecclesiam ad virtutis imitationem." Atque hactenus quidem de sanctorum veneratione, quae partim laudatione Dei in illis, partim in illorum imitatione constitit, diximus. Nunc vero ad alteram venerationis speciem veniamus, quae de sanctorum interpellatione tractat.

Est sane haec duplex, et vel sanctorum pro nobis ad Deum prec-

the saints themselves, who used the gifts so well, and love and admire them as Augustine writes in *The City of God* 8: "We honour," he says, "the memories of the martyrs as holy men of God, who contended for the truth even to the death of their bodies – so that by their fame we might give thanks to the true God for their victories, and be exhorted to imitate such crowns and rewards, by calling on the same God for help, by refreshing our memory of them." And elsewhere: "We venerate... the martyrs with the same veneration of love and fellowship with which holy men of God in this life are venerated, of whom we sense that their hearts are ready to suffer in a similar way for the truth of the Gospel, but we venerate them all the more devoutly and surely, in that all the uncertainties of this life have been overcome, just as we preach with a surer praise that those already in the happier life, rather than those who are still struggling in this one, have won the victory." And Basil, in his *Homily on the Martyr Gordias:* "The saints do not need anything to be added to their glory, but we need to remember them in order to imitate them." And elsewhere: "This is the praise of the martyrs, to exhort the Church to imitate their courage." And we have already said that the veneration of saints consists partly in praising God through them and partly in imitating them. Now let us come to another type of veneration, which concerns the intercession of the saints for us.

This is really a double issue, which involves both the prayers of the

ationes, vel nostram ad sanctos interpellationem significat. De priore dicimus, sanctos qui devicto peccato et morte in Christo obdormierunt, cum sunt unius atque eiusdem nobiscum corporis membra, nobis qui adhuc cum carne et mundo conflictamur, bene velle et bene precari. De posteriore vero, qua illorum opem imploramus, docemus, quod cum corporis et animi salus, remissio peccatorum, gratia, vita aeterna, et his similia solius Dei munera sint, nec a quoquam alio quam a solo Deo dari possint; quisquis pro his donis sanctos invocat et solicitat, et haec petit ab illis, quae nisi a solo Deo dari nequeunt, quasi ipsimet sancti haec petentibus largiri possent, is graviter sane errat, et Deum gloria sua spolians, creaturae eam tribuit.

Ceterum si sanctorum suffragia imploraverimus, et ab illis petierimus, ut nobiscum, et pro nobis, Deum precentur ac orent, ut illas res a Deo citius impetremus, quas nemo nisi Deus largiri potest; haec sane interpellatio tolerabilis est, et diuturno Catholicae Ecclesiae usu approbata et confirmata.

Neque enim periculum erit, ne Dei gloriam creaturis tribuamus, si modo populus doceatur, istud dumtaxat a sanctis petendum esse, ut sua apud Deum intercessione nos adiuvent. Quod caritatis officium cum in hac vita degentes, et cum carne et sanguine decertantes, alacriter praestiterunt, nihil ambigimus, quin nunc, cum Christo suo propius fruuntur, idem officium nobis

saints to God for us, and our intercessions to the saints. Of the former, we say that the saints who have overcome sin and in death sleep in Christ, because they are members of one and the same body as we are, who still struggle with the flesh and the world, desire our good and pray for it. Of the latter, by which we seek their assistance, we teach that because the salvation of the body and the soul, the forgiveness of sins, grace, eternal life and the like are solely in the gift of God, nor can be given by anyone other than by God, that anyone who prays to the saints and begs them for these gifts, and seeks them from the saints, as if they could bestow them on seekers, when he cannot obtain them except by the gift of God, makes a great mistake by depriving God of his glory and attributing it to a creature.

But if we cry out for the intercessions of the saints and ask them to pray and beseech God with us and for us, that we might more quickly obtain from God those things which no-one except God can bestow, then this form of intercession can be tolerated, and has long been approved and confirmed by the usage of the Catholic Church.

Nor will there be any danger of attributing the glory of God to creatures, provided that the people are taught that the saints may be asked only to assist us by making their own intercession to God. For since they willingly fulfilled the duty of love when they were still in this life, and contending with flesh and blood, we have no doubt that they will perform the same duty for us,

praestent.

Porro quoniam multi certis divis certorum morborum remedia, et aliarum rerum curam assignaverunt, et unum sanctum pro vitanda peste coluerunt, alium propter pecorum incolumitatem et salutem, alium ut res perditas citius invenirent, atque ita a certis divis res certas petierunt, quasi Deus hunc sanctum huic morbo curando, alium vero alii malo medendo, peculiariter praefecisset, et singulorum omnino tollatur, censemus populum docendum esse, ut in rebus tum prosperis tum adversis Deo, tamquam omnis boni et salutis auctori, suas preces offerat; sanctis vero non aliter utatur, quam ut intercessoribus pro nobis ad Deum, in quo nostra omnis spes ac fiducia ubique et semper collocanda est.

Quamquam non negamus quin, ad fidem et spem in Deum excitandum, possimus Deum velut admonere eorum miraculorum quae ad sanctorum preces iam olim ostendit, quibus admoniti maiori fide Dei beneficia petamus; veluti cum quis febre correptus Dominum orat, ut quemadmodum ad D. Petri preces eius socrum febricitantem sanitati restituit, ita velut nunc quoque febris ardores ab aegroto corpore de-pellere; sive cum oramus, ut Deus, qui Paulum in carcere cum collega Sila vinctum miraculo liberavit, idem nos e morborum aut pecc-atorum vinculis eripere dignetur.

now that they are enjoying their reward with Christ.

Furthermore, since many people have attributed the cures of certain diseases and a concern for other things to particular saints, and have venerated one saint in order to avoid the plague, another to obtain the safety and welfare of cattle, another to find more quickly things which they have lost, and thus asked for particular things from particular saints, as if God had put one saint in charge of curing this disease and another in charge of remedying another evil, thereby relieving himself of particular responsibility, we think that people must be taught to offer their prayers to God both in prosperity and in adversity, since he is the author of all good and salvation, and not to make use of the saints except as intercessors on our behalf before God, in whom all our hope and trust must always and everywhere be placed.

However we do not deny that we may, in order to arouse faith and hope in God, remind God of those miracles which he once performed at the bidding of the saints, so that being reminded of them we might pray for the benefits of God with greater faith, as when a man riddled with fever prays to the Lord that just as he healed Peter's sick mother-in-law at his behest, so also now he might chase the heat of the fever from his sick body, or when we pray that God, who miraculously delivered Paul from the prison where he was bound with his colleague Silas, might now be pleased to free us likewise from the chains of illnesses and sins.

C. De imaginibus

Quoniam imagines Christi et divorum illiteratis esse possunt vice librorum, dum velut scripti libri eos admoneant historiarum et rerum gestarum, censemus eas utiliter in templis Christianorum, aut alibi, statui ac poni posse. Quae quidem imagines, praeterquam quod illiteratis plurimum conducunt ad memoriam et intellectum historiae, etiam eruditis utilitatem adferunt: nam doctus interdum vehementius afficitur, dum conspicit Christi imaginem in cruce pendentem, quam dum illum legit crucifixum et passum.

Ceterum cum in imaginum usu graviter a populo peccatum sit, cum alii in templis posuerunt illarum rerum imagines, quarum nullum vel in sacris libris vel apud probatos auctores exstet testimonium: alii, neglectis Christi pauperibus, in supervacaneo statuarum ornatu ingentes sumptus fecerint, et hanc esse vel praecipuam pietatis partem falso sunt arbitrati; nonnulli (quod vehementer dolendum est) imagines quasdam collocata in ipsis fiducia coluerunt, eas virtutis ac numinis aliquid prae ceteris habere persuasi; alii imaginibus vota fecerunt, et illarum videndarum causa longas profectiones susceperunt, credentes Deum, in ipsius imaginis gratiam, in uno potius loco quam in alio exauditurum esse: has et alias harum similes opiniones ac iudicia praepostera, cum dissimulari non possit, quin plebs indocta de imaginibus habuerit; ut imagines ipsae in Ecclesia retineantur, et abusus omnes

C. Images

In so far as images of Christ and the saints can serve the illiterate instead of books, in instances where written books might remind them of their histories and deeds, we think that they may be usefully set up and placed in Christian churches or elsewhere. Such images, besides leading the illiterate above all to a remembrance and understanding of history, are also useful to the learned; for an educated person is all the more strongly affected when he sees the image of Christ hanging on the cross than when he reads that he suffered and was crucified.

But as people have greatly sinned in the use of images, since some have placed in churches images of things for which there is no evidence either in Scripture or in the standard authors, whilst others have neglected Christ's poor and spent huge sums on the outward decoration of statues, falsely deeming this to be the most important side of godliness, and some (which is greatly to be regretted) have venerated images to the point of putting their faith in them, being persuaded that they have some extraordinary power and holiness, while others have made offerings to images and undertaken long pilgrimages in order to see them, believing that God, thanks to the image, will hear them better in one place than in another; (and) since it is not possible to overlook these and other similar opinions and absurd beliefs, which an ignorant populace holds concerning images, we consider that in order for the images

ac superstitiones penitus tollantur, pastorum et concionatorum officium esse iudicamus, ut populum de his rebus melius instituant ac informent, utque verum imaginum usum esse doceant, intellectum et memoriam illarum rerum quas representant animis hominum suggerere atque subiicere, et intuentis animum nonnunquam exstimulare. In hunc finem imagines in templis positas fuisse nihil dubitamus; nempe ut imaginum aspectus nobis in memoriam revocaret illorum sanctorum virtutes et vitae exempla, quorum imagines intuemur; ut quoniam oculis subiecta magis movent quam audita, nos sanctorum virtutibus et exemplis, quae in ipsorum imaginibus repraesentantur, magis inflammaremur ad Deum in sanctis laudandum, ad nostra peccata deflenda, et Deum orandum ut sanctorum virtutes et vitam per illius gratiam imitari possimus.

Quod si quis, conspecto crucifixi signo, caput aperit aut inclinat, lignum illud non honorat, sed ad imaginis occasionem et aspectum veneratur Christum quem ea representat. Is honor, qui non statuis, sed Christo per statuae aspectum impenditur, et Deo placet, et ab idololatria procul est.

Ceterum vel imagines adorare, vel divinam aliquam vim aut numen illis tribuere, vel putare, quod Deus aut statuae alicuius gratiae aut loci, quia illic statua collocatur, invocantes citius sit exauditurus, vel ipsas sta-

themselves to be kept in the Church and all abuses and superstitions be completely removed, it is the duty of pastors and preachers to instruct and inform people better about these things, that they should teach the true purpose of the images, and that they should implant and secure the understanding and recollection of those things which they represent in the minds of men, arousing in no small way the minds of those who gaze upon them. We do not doubt that images were first placed in churches for this reason, so that the appearance of the images might call to mind the virtues of those saints and the examples of the lives of those on whose images we gaze, so that as things subject to the eyes move us more than things which are heard, we might be all the more encouraged by the virtues and examples of the saints, which are depicted in their images, to praise God in the saints, to weep for our sins, and to pray God that we might imitate the virtues of the saints and their life by his grace.

For if someone, seeing the crucifix, doffs his cap or inclines his head, he is not honouring the wood, but on meeting and seeing the image is venerating Christ, which it represents. This honour does not belong to the statue but to Christ, through the appearance of the statue, and is both pleasing to God, and far removed from idolatry.

But we greatly condemn these things and teach that Christians must not worship images, attribute any power or holiness to them, think that God, on account of any statue or the place where it may be set up, will

tuas lascive ac iuxta saeculi vanitates pingere aut formare, vel denique praeteritis et neglectis Christi pauperibus, quoties illis ex praecepto Dei subveniendum est, illas ornare, haec omnia et magnopere improbamus, et Christianis fugienda esse docemus.

hear those who call on him more readily, paint or sculpt these same statues immorally or according to the vanities of this age, or finally, decorate them while overlooking and neglecting Christ's poor, who are to be looked after according to the command of God.

20. THE ACT OF THE SIX ARTICLES, 1539

History

This Act was the first in what would turn out to be a long series of similar Acts designed to enforce uniformity in religion. It was passed by Parliament between 07 and 16 June 1539, and was inspired by the innate conservatism of the King, who was determined to protect traditional practices. Archbishop Cranmer opposed it, but eventually submitted, though Bishop Shaxton of Salisbury and Bishop Latimer of Worcester felt compelled to resign their sees because of it. It was highly unpopular with those of Protestant sympathies, who referred to it unofficially as "the bloody whip with six strings". The Act remained in force until the King's death (1547), but the severity of some of its provisions, notably 19 and 20, was soon relaxed.

Theology

The Six Articles are mainly concerned with ecclesiastical practices, and touch on few doctrinal matters other than predestination, which was now to be upheld on pain of death. The severity of the punishments, which included death for relatively minor offences, reflected the concern felt by many that the "old religion" was being overthrown, but it also demonstrates the essential hollowness of the opposition to reform. By compromising on superficial matters, and by pointing out the injustice suffered by those who went to their deaths for relatively minor offences, the Protestants were eventually able to promote their cause more quickly and more peacefully than might otherwise have been possible.

N.B. For this edition, the matters at issue, and the six articles dealing with them, are printed in bold type.

01. Where the King's most excellent Majesty is, by God's Law, Supreme Head immediately under him of this whole Church and Congregation of England, intending the conservation of this same Church and Congregation in a true, sincere and uniform doctrine of Christ's religion, calling also to his most blessed and gracious remembrance as well the great and quiet assurance, prosperous increase and other innumerable commodities, which have ever ensued, come and followed, of concord, agreement and unity in opinions, as also the manifold perils, dangers and inconveniences which have heretofore, in many places and regions, grown, sprung and arisen, of the diversities of minds and opinions especially of matters of Christian religion, and therefore desiring that such a unity might and should be charitably established in all things touching and concerning the same, as the same, so being established, might chiefly be to the honour of Almighty God, the very author and fountain of all true unity and sincere concord, and consequently redound to the common wealth of this his Highness's most noble realm, and of all his loving subjects, and other residents or inhabitants of or in the same; hath therefore caused and commanded that this his most High Court of Parliament, for sundry and many urgent causes and considerations, to be at this time summoned, and also a Synod and Convocation of all the archbishops, bishops and other learned men of the clergy of this his realm, to be in like manner assembled.

And for as much as in the said Parliament, Synod and Convocation, there were certain articles, matters and questions proponed and set forth touching Christian religion, that is to say:

First, whether in the most blessed sacrament of the altar remaineth after the consecration the substance of bread and wine or not;

Secondly, whether it be necessary by God's law that all men should be communicated with both kinds or not;

Thirdly, whether priests, (that is to say, men dedicated to God by priesthood), may by the law of God marry after, or not;

Fourthly, whether vows of chastity or widowhood made to God advisedly by man or woman, be by the law of God to be observed or not;

Fifthly, whether private masses stand with the law of God and be to be used and continued in the Church and Congregation of England, as things whereby good Christian people may and do receive both godly consolation and wholesome benefit or not;

Sixthly, whether auricular confession is necessary to be retained, continued, used and frequented in the Church, or not;

The King's most royal Majesty, most prudently pondering and considering, that by occasion of variable and sundry opinions and judgements of the said articles, great discord and variance has arisen, as well amongst the clergy of this his realm, as amongst a great number of vulgar people, his loving subjects of the same, and being in a full hope and trust that a full and perfect resolution of the said articles should make a perfect concord and unity generally amongst all his loving and obedient subjects, of his most excellent goodness, not only commanded that the said articles should deliberately and advisedly, by his said archbishops, bishops and other learned men of his clergy, be debated, argued and reasoned, and their opinions therein to be understood, declared and known, but also most graciously vouchsafed, in his own princely person, to descend and come into his said High Court of Parliament and Council, and there, like a prince of most high prudence and no less learning, opened and declared many things of high learning and great knowledge, touching the said articles, matters and questions, for a unity to be had in the same; whereupon, after a great and long, deliberate and advised disputation and consultation had and made concerning the said articles, as well by the consent of the King's Highness, as by the assent of the Lords spiritual and temporal, and other learned men of his clergy in their Convocation, and by the consent of the Commons in this present Parliament assembled, it was and is finally resolved, accorded and agreed in manner and form following, that is to say:

First, that in the most blessed sacrament of the altar, by the strength and efficacy of Christ's mighty word (it being spoken by the priest), is present really, under the form of bread and wine, the natural body and blood of our Saviour Jesus Christ, conceived of the Virgin Mary; and that after the consecration there remaineth no substance of bread and wine, nor any other substance, but the substance of Christ, God and man.

Secondly, that communion in both kinds is not necessary *ad salutem*, by the law of God, to all persons; and that it is to be believed, and not doubted of, but that in the flesh, under the form of bread, is the very blood; and with the blood, under the form of wine, is the very flesh; as well apart, as though they were both together;

Thirdly, that priests after the order of priesthood received, as afore, may not marry, by the law of God.

Fourthly, that vows of chastity or widowhood, by man or woman made to God advisedly, ought to be observed by the law of God; and that it exempts them from other liberties of Christian people, which without that they might enjoy.

Fifthly, that it is meet and necessary that private masses be continued and admitted in this the King's English Church and Congregation, as whereby good Christian people, ordering themselves accordingly, do receive both godly and goodly consolations and benefits; and it is agreeable also to God's law.

Sixthly, that auricular confession is expedient and necessary to be retained and continued, used and frequented in the Church of God.

For the which most godly study, travail and pain of his Majesty, and determination and resolution of the premises, his most humble and obedient subjects, the Lords spiritual and temporal and the Commons in this present Parliament assembled, not only render and give unto his Highness their most high and hearty thanks, and think themselves most bounden to pray for the long continuance of his Grace's most royal estate, but also being desirous that his most godly enterprise may be well accomplished, and brought to a full end and perfection, and so established that the same might be to the honour of God, and after to the common quiet, unity and concord to be had in the whole body of this realm for ever, most humbly beseech his royal Majesty, that the resolution and determination above written of the said articles may be established, and perpetually perfected, by authority of this present Parliament:

It is therefore ordained and enacted by the King our Sovereign Lord, the Lords spiritual and temporal, and the Commons in this present Parliament assembled, and by the authority of the same, that if any person or persons within this realm of England, or any other the King's dominions, after the twelfth of July next coming (12 July 1539), by word, writing, printing, ciphering or in any other wise do publish, preach, teach, say, affirm, declare, dispute, argue or hold any opinion, that in the blessed sacrament of the altar, under form of bread and wine, after the consecration thereof, there is not present really the natural body and blood of our Saviour Jesus Christ, conceived of the Virgin Mary; or that after the said consecration there remaineth any substance of bread and wine, or any other substance but the substance of Christ, God and man; or after the time above said, publish, preach, teach, say, affirm, declare, dispute, argue or hold opinion, that in the flesh under form of bread, is not the very blood of Christ, or that with the blood under form of wine is not the very flesh of Christ, as well apart as though they were both together, or by any of the means abovesaid or otherwise preach, teach, declare or affirm the said sacrament to be of other substance than is abovesaid, or by any means contempt, deprave or despise the said blessed sacrament, that then every such person and persons so offending, their aiders, comforters, counsellors, consenters and abettors therein, being thereof convicted in form underwritten, by the authority abovesaid, shall be deemed and adjudged heretics, and that every such offence shall be judged manifest heresy, and that every such offender and offenders shall therefore have and suffer judgement, execution, pain and pains of death by way of burning, without any abjuration, clergy or sanctuary to be therefore permitted, had, allowed, admitted, or suffered; and also shall therefore forfeit and lose to the King's Highness, his heirs and successors, all his or their honours, manors, castles, lands, tenancies, rents, revisions, services, possessions and all other his or their hereditaments, goods and chattels, terms and freeholds whatsoever they be, which any such offender or offenders shall have, at the time of any such offence or offences committed or done at any time after, as in cases of high treason.

02. And furthermore, be it enacted by the authority of this present Parliament, that if any person or persons, after the said twelfth day of July (12 July 1539), preach in any sermon or collation openly made to the King's people, or teach in any common school or to other congregation of people, or being called before such judges and according to such form of the law as hereafter shall be declared, do obstinately affirm, uphold, maintain or defend that the communion of the said blessed sacrament in both kinds, that is to say, in form of bread and also of wine, is necessary for the health of man's soul to be given or ministered to any person in both kinds, or that it is necessary so to be received or taken by any person, other than by priests being at mass and consecrating the same; or that any man, after the order of priesthood received as aforesaid, may marry or contract matrimony; or that private masses be not lawful or not laudable or should not be celebrated, had nor used in this realm, nor be not agreeable to the laws of God; or that auricular confession is not expedient and necessary to be retained and continued, used and frequented in the Church of God; or if any priest, after the said twelfth day of July (12 July 1539), or any other man or woman which advisedly hath vowed or after the said day advisedly do vow chastity or widowhood, do actually marry or contract matrimony with any person, that then all and every person and persons so preaching, teaching, obstinately affirming, upholding, maintaining or defending, or making marriage or contract of matrimony as above specified, be and shall be by authority above written, deemed and adjudged a felon and felons; and that every offender in the same being duly convicted or attainted by the laws underwritten, shall therefore suffer pains of death as in cases of felony without any benefit of clergy or privilege of Church or sanctuary to him or her to be allowed in that behalf, and shall forfeit all his or her lands and goods as in cases of felony; and that it shall be lawful to the patron or patrons, of any manner of benefice which any such offender at the time of his said conviction or attainder had, to present one other incumbent thereunto, as if the same person so convicted or attainted had been bodily deceased.

03. Also be it enacted by the authority aforesaid that if any person or persons, after the said twelfth of July (12 July 1539) by word, writing, printing, ciphering or otherwise than is above rehearsed, publish, declare or hold opinion that the said communion of the blessed sacrament in both kinds aforesaid is necessary for the health of man's soul to be given or ministered in both kinds, and so ought or should be given or ministered to any person, or ought or should be so in both kinds received or taken by any person other than by priests, being at mass and consecrating the same as is aforesaid; or that any man after the order of priesthood received as is aforesaid, may marry or may make contract of matrimony; or that any man or woman which advisedly hath made or shall make a vow to God of chastity or widowhood, may marry or may make contract of matrimony; or that private masses be not lawful or not laudable or should not be celebrated, had nor used, nor be agreeable to the laws of God; or that auricular confession is not expedient and necessary to be retained and continued, used and frequented in the Church of God; every person being for every such offence duly convicted and attainted, by the laws underwritten, shall forfeit and lose to the King our Sovereign Lord, all his goods and chattels for ever, and also the profits of all his lands, tenancies, annuities, fees and offices during his life, and all his benefices and spiritual promotions shall be utterly void; and also shall suffer imprisonment of his body at the will and pleasure of our said Sovereign Lord the King; and if any such person or persons, being once convicted of any of the offences mentioned in this article as is abovesaid, do afterwards eftsones [i.e. again, ed.] offend in any of the same and be thereof accused, indicted or presented and convicted again by the

authority of the laws underwritten, that then every such person and persons so being twice convicted and attainted of the said offences or of any of them, shall be adjudged a felon and felons; and shall suffer judgement, execution and pains of death, loss and forfeiture of lands and goods as in cases of felony, without any privilege of clergy or sanctuary to be in any wise permitted, admitted or allowed in that behalf.

04. Be it further enacted by the authority abovesaid, that if any person which is or hath been a priest, before this present Parliament or during the time of session of the same, hath married and hath made any contract of matrimony with any woman, or that any man or woman, which before the making of this Act advisedly hath vowed chastity or widowhood before this present Parliament or during the session of the same, hath married or contracted matrimony with any person; that then every such marriage and contract of matrimony shall be utterly void and of none effect; and that the ordinaries within whose dioceses or jurisdiction the person or persons so married or contracted is to be resident or abiding, shall from time to time make separation and divorces of the said marriages and contracts.

05. And further be it enacted by the authority abovesaid, that if any man which is or hath been a priest, as is aforesaid, at any time from and after the said twelfth day of July next coming (12 July 1539) do carnally keep or use any woman, to whom he is or hath been married, or with whom he hath contracted matrimony, or openly been conversant, nay kept company and familiarity with any such woman to the evil example of other persons, every such carnal use, copulation, open conversation, keeping of company and familiarity be and shall be deemed and adjudged felony, as well against the man as the woman; and that every such person so offending shall be inquired of, tried, punished, suffer, lose and forfeit all and every thing and things as other felons made and declared by this Act, and as in case of felony as is aforesaid.

06. And be it further enacted by authority abovesaid, that if any person or persons at any time hereafter contemn or contemptuously refuse, deny or abstain to be confessed, at the time commonly accustomed within this realm and Church of England, or contemn and contemptuously refuse, deny or abstain to receive the holy and blessed sacrament abovesaid at the time commonly used and accustomed for the same, that then every such offender being thereof duly convicted or attainted, by the laws underwritten, shall suffer such imprisonment and make such fine and ransom to the King our Sovereign Lord and his heirs as by his Highness or by his or their council shall be ordered or adjudged in that behalf; and if any such offender or offenders at any time or times after the said conviction or attainder so had, do eftsones (i.e. again, ed.) contemn or contemptuously refuse, deny or abstain to be confessed or to be communicated in manner and form above written, and be thereof duly convicted or attainted by the laws underwritten, that then every such offence shall be deemed and adjudged felony and the

offender or offenders therein shall suffer pains of death and lose and forfeit all his and their goods, lands and tenancies, as in cases of felony.

07. And for full and effectual execution of the premises before devised, ordered and enacted by this Act, be it further enacted by the authority of this present Parliament, that immediately after the said twelfth day of July next coming (12 July 1539), sundry commissions shall be made from time to time into every shire of this realm and Wales, and in and to such other places within the King's dominions as shall please his Majesty, to be directed to the archbishop or bishop of the diocese and to his chancellor or commissary, and to such other persons as shall be named by his Highness, or by such other as his Majesty at his pleasure shall appoint to name the same, which archbishop or bishop or his chancellor or commissary to be one, should hold and keep their sessions within the limits of their commission four several times of the year at the least, or oftener if they shall think it expedient by their discretions, and shall have power and authority by virtue of this Act and their said commission, as well to take information and accusation by the oaths and depositions of two able and lawful persons at the least, as to inquire by oaths of twelve men of all and singular the heresies, felonies, contempts and other offences above written, committed, done or perpetrated within the limits of their commission; and that every such accusation and information containing the matter, names and surnames and dwelling places of the offenders and the day, year, place and county when and wherein their offences were committed, shall be of as good force and effect in the law as if the matter therein contained had been presented by verdicts of twelve men.

08. And nevertheless it is further enacted that every of the said archbishops and bishops, and every of their chancellors, commissaries, archdeacons and other ordinaries, having any peculiar ecclesiastical jurisdiction within this realm or in Wales, or in any other the King's dominions, shall have full power and authority by virtue of this Act as well to inquire in their visitations and senys [possibly: synods, *ed.*], as there and elsewhere within their jurisdictions at any other time or place, to take accusations and informations as is aforesaid of the heresies, felonies, contempts and offences above mentioned, done, committed or perpetrated within the limits of their jurisdictions and authorities; and that every such accusation, information and presentment so taken or had as is aforesaid, shall be of as good force and effect as if the matter therein contained had been presented before the justices of peace in their sessions; and also that justices of peace in their sessions, and every steward, understeward or deputy of steward of any leet or lawday in their leet or lawday, shall have like power and authority by virtue of this Act to inquire by the oaths of twelve lawful men of all and singular the heresies, felonies, contempts and other offences above written, done, perpetrated or committed within the limits of their commissions and authorities.

09. And it is also enacted by the authority aforesaid, that every such person

or persons, after whom any presentment, information or accusation shall be made or taken as is aforesaid, shall examine the accusers what other witness were by and present at the time of doing and committing of the offence whereof the information, accusation or presentment shall be made, and how many others than the accusers have knowledge thereof; and shall have power and authority to bind by recognizance to be taken afore them, as well the said accusers as all such other persons whom the same accusers shall declare to have knowledge of the offences by them presented or informed, every of them in five pounds to the King our Sovereign Lord, to appear before the commissioners afore whom the offender or offenders shall be tried at the day of the trial of such offenders; and that all and singular indictments, presentments, accusations, informations and recognizances taken and had as is aforesaid, within twenty days next after the taking of the same shall be certified in due form by writing upon parchment by the taker or takers thereof under his or their seals, unto any one of the said commissioners to be appointed as is aforesaid, within the limits of whose commission the heresies, felonies, contempts and offences, whereof any such presentment, indictment, information or accusation shall be taken or had as is above written, shall be committed, done or perpetrated; and if any person or persons, which hereafter shall happen to take any such accusation, information, presentment or recognizances as is above said, do make default of the certificate thereof contrary to the form above rehearsed, that then every person and persons so offending shall forfeit to our Sovereign Lord the King for every such default ten pounds.

10. And it is further enacted by the authority abovesaid, that the said commissioners or three of them at the least, as is aforesaid by virtue of this Act, and their commission shall have full power and authority to make like process against every person and persons indicted, presented or accused in form as is above remembered, as is used and accustomed in case of felony, and that as well within the limits of their commission as into all other shires and places of the realm, Wales and other the King's dominions, as well within liberties as without, and the same process to be good and effectual in the law as in cases of felony; and upon the appearance of any of the offenders shall have full power and authority by virtue of this Act and the said commission to hear and determine the aforesaid heresies, felonies, contempts and other offences according to the laws of this realm and the effects of this Act.

11. And it is also enacted by the authority abovesaid, that every of the said commissioners, upon any such accusation, presentment or information, shall endeavour himself effectually, without affection, dread or corruption, to apprehend and take the offenders, and after the apprehension of any such offender or offenders, shall have full power and authority to let any person or persons so accused or presented upon sufficient sureties by their discretion to bail for their appearance, to be tried according to the tenor, form and effect of this Act.

12. And further it is enacted by the authority abovesaid that if any person or persons which hereafter shall be named and assigned to be commissioner or commissioners as is abovesaid, be accused, indicted or presented of or for any of the offences above written, that then all and every such commissioner or commissioners so accused, indicted and presented, shall be examined, put to answer and tried of and upon any such offence according to the tenor and effect of this Act, before such other person or persons as it shall please the King's Highness to name, assign and appoint by his grace's commission, to hear and determine the same.

13. And it is further enacted by authority abovesaid, that no person or persons which at any time hereafter shall be accused, indicted or presented, as is abovesaid, shall be admitted to the challenge of any person or persons, which shall be empanelled for the trial of his or their offence, for any matter or cause other than for malice or enmity, which challenge shall forthwith be tried in like manner as other challenges be used to be tried in cases of felony.

14. And it is further enacted by the authority abovesaid, that all foreign pleas triable by the country, which at any time hereafter shall be pleaded by any person or persons hereafter to be arraigned, or put to answer upon any accusation, indictment or presentment, of or for any of the offences above specified or of or for any of them, shall be tried before the same commissioners afore whom such person or persons shall be arraigned or put to answer, and by the jurors that shall try the said offence or offences without any further respite or delay.

15. And it is further enacted by the authority abovesaid, that all mayors, sheriffs, stewards, bailiffs of liberties, gaolers and other officers and ministers, of what name, degree or condition soever they be, and every of them, shall from time to time truly and diligently receive and serve all and all manner the process, precepts and commandments to them or any of them by the said commissioners or any of them to be made, given or directed touching or concerning the premises or any parcel thereof; and shall also from time to time be obedient and attendant unto the said commissioners for the time being for the due execution of this present Act or of anything therein contained.

16. And it is also enacted that every person which shall be named to be commissioner in the said commission, after that he hath knowledge thereof, shall effectually put his diligence and attendance in and about the execution of the said commission; and before he shall take upon him the execution of the said commission, shall take a corporal oath before the Lord Chancellor of England for the time being, or before him or them to whom the said Lord Chancellor shall direct the King's writ of *Dedimus potestatem* to take the same, the tenor of which oath hereafter ensueth: "Ye shall swear that ye to your cunning, wit and power shall truly and indifferently execute the authority to you given by the King's commission made for correction of heretics and other offenders mentioned in the same commission, without any favour, affection, corruption, dread or malice to be borne to any person or persons, as God you help and all saints." And in case that any of the said persons named to be commissioners refuse to take the said oath, or willingly absent or eloign (i.e. distance, *ed.*) himself from the taking of the said oath, then every such person so offending, and the same offence estreated and certified into the King's Exchequer by the said Lord Chancellor, or by him or them to whom any such writ of *Dedimus potestatem* as is aforesaid shall be directed, shall forfeit and lose to our said Sovereign Lord the King for every time so offending, five marks of lawful money.

17. And it is also enacted by the authority abovesaid, that the said commissioners and every of them, shall from time to time have full power and authority by virtue of this Act to take into his or their keeping or possession all and all manner of books, which be or have been or hereafter shall be set forth, read or declared within this realm or other the King's dominions, wherein is or be contained or comprised any clause, article, matter or sentence repugnant or contrary to the tenor, form or effect of this present Act, or any of the articles contained in the same; and the said commissioners, or three of them at the least, to burn or otherwise destroy the said books or any part of them, as unto the said commissioners or unto three of them at the least shall be thought expedient by their discretions.

18. And it is also enacted by the authority abovesaid, that every parson, vicar, curate or parish priest of every parish church within this realm or other the King's dominions, or his or their deputy, upon the Sunday next after the first day of September next ensuing (07 September 1539), and so from thenceforth once in every quarter of the year at the least, shall openly, plainly and distinctly read this present Act in the parish church where he is parson, vicar, curate, parish priest or deputy, unto his or their parishioners then assembled together to hear divine service; and that every such parson, vicar, curate, or parish priest making default of reading this Act, contrary to the form aforesaid, shall forfeit unto our said Sovereign Lord, his heirs or successors, for every such default, forty shillings sterling.

19. Saving to all and singular person and persons, bodies politic and corporate, their heirs and successors, and to the heirs and successors of every of them, other than all and singular such person and persons that shall be hereafter convicted or attainted of or for any of the offences or contempts above specified, their heirs and successors, and the heirs and successors of every of them, all such right, title, claim, interest, entry, possession, rents, reversions, fees, annuities, commons, offices, profits and demands whatsoever as they or any of them have, or then at the time of the said conviction or attainder had, shall have, of, in or to any honours, castles, lordships, manors, lands, tenancies, liberties, franchises, advowsons and other hereditaments, which any such person or persons being so convicted or attainted as is aforesaid, had or were entitled to have at the time of their offence or offences committed or at any time after, and that in as ample manner, form and condition to all intents, constructions and purposes as if this Act had never been had nor made; anything contained in this Act to the contrary in any wise notwithstanding. Provided always that the Lords shall not have nor claim any escheats of any offender or offenders that shall be judged to be burned by authority of this Act.

20. Be it also further enacted by the authority aforesaid, not giving advantage or detriment to any article aforesaid, that if any man, which is or hath been priest or hereafter shall be, at any time after the said twelfth day of July (12 July 1539), do carnally use and accustom any woman, or keep her as his concubine, as by paying for her board, maintaining her with money, array or any other gifts or means, to the evil example of other persons, that then every such offender being thereof duly convicted or attainted by the laws mentioned in this Act, shall forfeit and lose all his goods and chattels, benefices, prebends and other spiritual promotions and dignities, and also shall have and suffer imprisonment of his body at the King's will and pleasure; and that every of the said benefices, prebends and other promotions and dignities shall be to all intents and purposes utterly void as if the said offender had resigned or permuted; and if any such offender or offenders, at any time after the said conviction or attainder, eftsones [i.e. again, *ed.*] commit, do or perpetrate the said offences or any of them next afore rehearsed, and be thereof duly convicted or attainted by the laws aforesaid, that then all and every such offence and offences shall be deemed and adjudged felony, and the offender and offenders therein shall suffer pains of death and lose and forfeit all his and their goods, lands and tenancies as in cases of felony, without having any benefit of clergy or sanctuary.

21. And be it further enacted by the authority aforesaid, that those women with whom all or singular of the foresaid priests shall in any of the foresaid ways have to do with or carnally know as is aforesaid, shall have like punishment as the priest.

22. And because disputations and doubts might perhaps arise hereafter upon these words in this Act, that is to say, advisedly made to God, be it therefore provided and enacted by authority aforesaid, that these words in the Act, that is to say, advisedly made to God, for vows of chastity or widowhood, shall be alonely taken, expounded or interpreted to bind such person or persons and none other (saving priests) to and by the same, which at the time of any of their so vowing, being thereto admitted, were or shall be of the age of twenty-one years or above, and then did or do consent, submit themselves or condescend to the same, and continue or continued in observation of it any while after; unless any such person or persons do or can duly prove any unlawful coercion or compulsion done to them or any of them, for making of any such vow.

21. CRANMER'S PREFACE TO THE GREAT BIBLE, 1540

History

Within months of the final break with Rome, the Convocation of Canterbury petitioned the King to order "that the Holy Scripture should be translated into the vulgar English tongue by certain good and learned men, to be nominated by his Majesty, and should be delivered to the people for their instruction." But even before the King could accede to this request, Miles Coverdale managed to produce a complete English Bible, which incorporated most of William Tyndale's work (1535). Two years later, John Rogers, using the pseudonym of Thomas Matthew, produced the so-called Matthew Bible, which also relied heavily on Tyndale's work.

Given this situation, the King's advisers thought it best to use Coverdale, and gave him the authority to make a further revision of Matthew's Bible. In 1538 the Second Henrician Injunctions directed that a copy of the Bible in English (which would in effect be this revision) should be placed in every parish church by Easter (06 April) 1539.

The work itself was soon ready, and was sent to Paris late in 1538 for typesetting and printing. Unfortunately, it fell foul of the Inquisition there, just as the printing was nearly complete, and the whole operation had to be started over, this time on English soil. The result was that the Great Bible, as it came to be called, was not ready until April 1539, too late to meet the requirement of the Injunctions. A new order was therefore issued, extending the target date to All Saints' Day (01 November) 1539. Once again there were difficulties, though this time it was because demand for the edition was such that supplies were soon exhausted!

A second edition was soon needed, and was ready in April 1540. For this edition, Archbishop Thomas Cranmer provided a Preface, which soon became its hallmark. The Great Bible, or "Cranmer's Bible" as it now came to be called, went through a total of seven editions before further publication was suspended, at the end of 1541. An eighth edition came out in 1549, and ninth appeared in 1553, though as a result of Queen Mary's accession, most of it remained unsold. Copies were still available after her death, but by that time, the Great Bible had had its day. The tenth edition (1562) proved to be the last, because the Geneva Bible (1560) had effectively replaced it. A few years later (1568), the Bishops of the Church of England undertook their own revision of the Great Bible, but it never really caught on. Not until 1611 was there to be another version of the Scriptures appointed and authorized to be read in churches.

Theology

Cranmer's Preface to the Great Bible rapidly became a classic statement of the Reformation principle of *sola Scriptura*, as this applied to the Church of England. Cranmer drew on the patristic tradition, and in particular the work of the great exegete, John Chrysostom (d. 407), and the great theologian, Gregory of Nazianzus (d. 390), to explain to his readers how the Bible should be read for spiritual profit, as well as for intellectual stimulation. This combination of patristic theology and Reformation concerns became typical of the Anglican tradition, and in many ways served to distinguish it from other types of Protestantism.

N.B. The paragraph numbering has been supplied for ease of reference.

01. For two sundry sorts of people, it seemeth much necessary that something be said in the entry of this book, by the way of a preface or prologue; whereby hereafter it may be both the better accepted of them which hitherto could not well bear it, and also the better used of them which heretofore have misused it. For truly some there are that be too slow, and need the spur; some other seem too quick, and need more of the bridle: some lose their game by short shooting, some by overshooting: some walk too much on the left hand, some too much on the right. In the former sort be all they that refuse to read, or to hear read the Scripture in the vulgar tongues; much worse they that also let or discourage the other from the reading thereof. In the latter sort be they, which by their inordinate reading, undiscreet speaking, contentious disputing, or otherwise, by their licentious living, slander and hinder the Word of God most of all other, whereof they would seem to be greatest furtherers. These two sorts, albeit they be most far unlike the one to the other, yet they both deserve in effect like reproach. Neither can I well tell whether of them I may judge the more offender, him that doth obstinately refuse so godly and goodly knowledge, or him that so ungodly and so ungoodly doth abuse the same.

02. And as touching the former, I would marvel much that any man should be so mad as to refuse in darkness, light; in hunger, food; in cold, fire: for the Word of God is light: *lucerna pedibus meis Verbum tuum* (Thy Word is a light unto my feet;[1] food, *non in solo pane vivit homo, sed in omni Verbo Dei* (not on bread alone does man live, but in the whole Word of God);[2] fire, *ignem veni mittere in terram, et quid volo, nisi ut ardeat?* (I have come to put fire in the earth, and what do I desire, except that it burn?).[3] I would marvel (I say) at this, save that I consider how much custom and usage may do. So that if there were a people, as some write, *De Cimmeriis*, which never saw the sun by reason that they be situated far toward the North Pole, and be enclosed and overshadowed with high mountains; it is credible and like enough that if, by the power and will of God, the mountains should sink down and give place, that the light of the sun might have entrance to them, at the first some of them might be offended therewith. And the old proverb affirmeth, that after tillage of corn was first found, many delighted more to feed of mast and acorns, wherewith they had been accustomed, than to eat bread made of good corn. Such is the nature of custom, that it causeth us to bear all things well and easily, wherewith we have been accustomed, and to be offended with all things thereunto contrary. And therefore I can well think them worthy pardon, which at the coming abroad of Scripture doubted and drew back. But such as will persist still in their wilfulness, I must needs judge, not only foolish, froward and obstinate, but also peevish, perverse and indurate.

03. And yet, if the matter should be tried by custom, we might also allege custom for the reading of the Scripture in the vulgar tongues, and prescribe the more ancient custom. For it is not much above one hundred years ago, since Scripture hath not been accustomed to be read in the vulgar tongues within this realm; and many hundred years before that it was translated and read in the Saxons' tongue, which at that time was our mother's tongue; whereof there remaineth yet divers copies found lately in old abbeys, of such antique manners of writing and speaking, that few men now be able to read and understand them. And when this language waxed old and out of common usage, because folk should not lack the fruit of reading, it was again translated in the newer language. Whereof yet also many copies remain and be daily found.

04. But now to let pass custom, and to weigh, as wise men ever should, the thing in his own nature: let us here discuss, what availeth Scripture to be had and read of the lay and vulgar people. And to this question I intend here to say nothing but that was spoken and written by the noble doctor and most moral divine, St John Chrysostom, in his third sermon, *De Lazaro*: albeit I will be something shorter, and gather the matter into fewer words and less room than he doth there, because I would not be tedious. He exhorteth there his audience, that every man should read by himself at home in the mean days and time, between sermon and sermon, to the intent they might both more profoundly fix in their minds and memories that he had said before upon such texts, whereupon he had already preached; and also that they might have their minds the more ready and better prepared to receive and perceive that which he should say from thenceforth in his sermons, upon such texts as he had not yet declared and preached upon: therefore saith he there: "My common usage is to give you warning before, what matter I intend after to entreat upon, that you yourselves, in the mean days, may take the book in hand, read, weigh and perceive the sum and effect of the matter, and mark what hath been declared, and what remaineth yet to be declared: so that thereby your mind may be the more furnished, to hear the rest that shall be said. And that I exhort you," saith he, "and ever have and will exhort you, that ye (not only here in the church) give ear to that that is said by the preacher, but that also, when ye be at home in your houses, ye apply yourselves from time to time to the reading of Holy Scriptures, which thing also I never linn [i.e. cease, *ed.*] to beat into the ears of them that be my familiars, and with whom I have private acquaintance and conversation. Let no man make excuse and say," saith he, "'I am busied about matters of the commonwealth'; 'I bear this office or that'; 'I am a craftsman, I must apply mine occupation'; 'I have a wife, my children must be fed, my household must I provide for'; briefly, 'I am a man of the world, it is not for me to read the Scriptures, that belongeth to them that hath bidden the world farewell, which live in solitariness and contemplation, that hath been brought up and continually nosylled [i.e. nurtured, *ed.*] in learning and religion'".

05. To this answering, "What sayest thou, man?" saith he: "Is it not for thee to study and to read the Scripture, because thou art encumbered and distract with cures and business? So much the more it is behoveful for thee to have defence of Scriptures, how much thou art the more distressed in worldly dangers. They that be free and far from trouble and intermeddling of worldly things, liveth in safeguard and tranquillity, and in the calm, or within a sure haven. Thou art in the midst of the sea of worldly wickedness, and therefore thou needest the more of ghostly succour and comfort; they sit far from the strokes of battle, and far out of gunshot, and therefore they be but seldom wounded; thou that standest in the forefront of the host and nighest to thine enemies, must needs take now and then many strokes, and be grievously wounded. And therefore thou hast more need to have thy remedies and medicines at hand. Thy wife provoketh thee to anger, thy child giveth thee occasion to take sorrow and pensiveness, thine enemies lieth in wait for thee, thy friend (as thou takest him) sometime envieth thee, thy neighbour misreporteth thee, or pricketh quarrels against thee, thy mate or partner undermineth thee, thy lord judge or justice threateneth thee, poverty is painful unto thee, the loss of thy dear and well-beloved causeth thee to mourn; prosperity exalteth thee, adversity bringeth thee low. Briefly, so divers and so manifold occasions of cares, tribulations and temptations besetteth thee and besiegeth thee round about. Where canst thou have armour or fortress against thine assaults? Where canst thou have salve for thy sores, but of Holy Scripture? Thy flesh must needs be prone and subject to fleshly lusts, which daily walkest and art conversant amongst women, seest their beauties set forth to the eye, hearest their nice and wanton words, smellest their balm, civet and musk, with other like provocations and stirrings, except thou hast in a readiness wherewith to suppress and avoid them, which cannot elsewhere be had, but only out of the Holy Scriptures. Let us read and seek all remedies that we can, and all shall be little enough. How shall we then do, if we suffer and take daily wounds, and when we have done, will sit still and search for no medicines? Dost thou not mark and consider how the smith, mason or carpenter, or any other handy-craftsman, what need soever he be in, what other shift soever he make, he will not sell nor lay to pledge the tools of his occupation; for then how should he work his feat, or get a living thereby? Of like mind and affection ought we to be towards Holy Scripture; for as mallets, hammers, saws, chisels, axes and hatchets be the tools of their occupation, so be the books of the prophets and apostles, and all Holy Writ inspired by the Holy Ghost, the instruments of our salvation. Wherefore, let us not stick to buy and provide us the Bible, that is to say, the books of Holy Scripture. And let us think that to be a better jewel in our house than either gold or silver. For like as thieves be loth to assault a house where they know to be good armour and artillery; so wheresoever these holy and ghostly books be occupied, there neither the Devil nor none of his angels dare come near. And they that occupy them be in much safeguard, and having great consolation, and be the readier unto all goodness, the slower to all evil; and if they have done anything amiss, anon, even by the sight of the books, their consciences be admonished, and they wax sorry and ashamed of the fact.

06. Peradventure they will say unto me, "How and if we understand not that we read that is contained in the books?" What then? Suppose thou understand not the deep and profound mysteries of Scripture; yet can it not be but that much fruit and holiness must come and grow unto thee by the reading: for it cannot be that thou shouldest be ignorant in all things alike. For the Holy Ghost hath so ordered and attempered the Scriptures, that in them as well publicans, fishers and shepherds may find their edification, as great doctors their erudition: for those books were not made to vainglory, like as were the writings of the Gentile philosophers and rhetoricians, to the intent the makers should be had in admiration for their high styles and obscure manner of writing, whereof nothing can be understand (*sic*) without a master or an expositor. But the apostles and prophets wrote their books so that their special intent and purpose might be understanded and perceived of every reader, which was nothing but the edification or amendment of the life of them that readeth or heareth it. Who is that reading or hearing read in the Gospel "Blessed are they that be meek, blessed are they that be merciful, blessed are they that be of clean heart", and such other like places, can perceive nothing, except he have a master to teach him what it meaneth? Likewise the signs and miracles with all other histories of the doings of Christ or his apostles, who is there of so simple wit and capacity, but he may be able to perceive and understand them? These be but excuses and cloaks for the rain, and coverings of their own idle slothfulness. "I cannot understand it". What marvel? How shouldest thou understand, if thou wilt not read nor look upon it? Take the books into thine hands, read the whole story, and that thou understandest keep it well in memory; thou that understandest not, read it again and again: if thou can neither so come by it, counsel with some other that is better learned. Go to thy curate and preacher; show thyself to be desirous to know and learn: and I doubt not but God, seeing thy diligence and readiness (if no man else teach thee), will himself vouchsafe with his Holy Spirit to illuminate thee, and to open unto thee that which was locked from thee.

07. "Remember the eunuch of Candace, Queen of Ethiopia, which, albeit he was a man of a wild and barbarous country, and one occupied with worldly cures and businesses, yet riding in his chariot, he was reading the Scripture. Now consider, if this man passing in his journey, was so diligent as to read the Scripture, what thinkest thou of like was he wont to do sitting at home? Again, he that letted not to read, albeit he did not understand, what did he then, trowest [i.e. believest, *ed.*] thou, after that, when he had learned and gotten understanding? For that thou may well know that he understood not what he read, hearken what Philip there saith unto him: 'Understandest thou what thou readest?' And he, nothing ashamed to confess his ignorance, answereth, 'How should I understand, having nobody to show me the way?' Lo, when he lacked one to show him the way and to expound to him the Scriptures, yet did he read; and therefore God the rather provided for him a guide of the way, that taught him to understand it. God perceived his willing and toward mind; and therefore he sent him a teacher by and by. Therefore let no man be negligent about his own health and salvation: though thou have not Philip always when thou wouldest, the Holy Ghost, which then moved and stirred up Philip, will be ready and not to fail thee if thou do thy diligence accordingly. All these things be written to us to our edification and amendment, which be born towards the latter end of the world. The reading of Scriptures is a great and strong bulwark or fortress against sin; the ignorance of the same is the greater ruin and destruction of them that will not know it. That is the thing that bringeth in heresies, that it is that causeth all corrupt and perverse living; that it is that bringeth all things out of good order."

08. Hitherto, all that I have said, I have taken and gathered out of the foresaid sermon of this holy doctor, St John Chrysostom. Now if I should in like manner bring forth what the selfsame doctor speaketh in other places, and what other doctors and writers say concerning the same purpose, I might seem to you to write another Bible rather than to make a Preface to the Bible. Wherefore, in few words to comprehend the largeness and utility of the Scripture, how it containeth fruitful instruction and erudition for every man; if any things be necessary to be learned, of the Holy Scripture we may learn it. If falsehood shall be reproved, thereof we may gather wherewithal. If anything be to be corrected and amended, if there need any exhortation or consolation, of the Scripture we may well learn. In the Scriptures be the fat pastures of the soul; therein is no venomous meat, no unwholesome thing; they be the very dainty and pure feeding. He that is ignorant shall find there what he should learn. He that is a perverse sinner shall there find his damnation to make him to tremble for fear. He that laboureth to serve God shall find there his glory, and the promissions of eternal life, exhorting him more diligently to labour. Herein may princes learn how to govern their subjects; subjects obedience, love and dread to their princes; husbands, how they should behave them unto their wives; how to educate their children and servants; and contrary the wives, children and servants may know their duty to their husbands, parents and masters. Here may all manner of persons, men, women, young, old, learned, unlearned, rich, poor, priests, laymen, lords, ladies, officers, tenants, and mean men, virgins, wives, widows, lawyers, merchants, artificers, husbandmen, and all manner of persons, of what estate or condition soever they be, may in this book learn all things what they ought to believe, what they ought to do, and what they should not do, as well concerning Almighty God, as also concerning themselves and all other. Briefly, to the reading of the Scripture none can be enemy, but that either be so sick that they love not to hear of any medicine, or else that be so ignorant that they know not Scripture to be the most healthful medicine.

09. Therefore, as touching this former part, I will here conclude and take it as a conclusion sufficiently determined and approved, that it is convenient and good the Scripture to be read of all sorts and kinds of people, and in the vulgar tongue, without further allegations and probations for the same; which shall not need, since that this one place of John Chrysostom is enough and sufficient to persuade all of them that be not frowardly and perversely set in their own wilful opinion; specially now that the King's Highness, being Supreme Head next under Christ of this Church of England, hath approved with his royal assent the setting forth hereof, which only to all true and obedient subjects ought to be a sufficient reason for the allowance of the same, without farther delay, reclamation or resistance, although there were no Preface nor other reason herein expressed.

10. Therefore now to come to the second and latter part of my purpose. There is nothing so good in this world, but it may be abused, and turned from fruitful and wholesome to hurtful and noisome. What is there above better than the sun, the moon, the stars? Yet was there that took occasion by the great beauty and virtue of them to dishonour God, and to defile themselves with idolatry, giving the honour of the living God and Creator of all things to such things as he had created. What is there here beneath better than fire, water, meats, drinks, metals of gold, silver, iron and steel? Yet we see daily great harm and much mischief done by every one of these, as well for lack of wisdom and providence of them that suffer evil, as by the malice of them that worketh the evil. Thus to them that be evil of themselves everything setteth forward and increaseth their evil, be it of his own nature a thing never so good; like as contrarily, to them that studieth and endeavoureth themselves to goodness, everything prevaileth them and profiteth unto good, be it of his own nature a thing never so bad. As St Paul saith: *His qui diligant Deum, omnia cooperantur in bonum* (To them that love God, everything works together for good);[4] even as out of most venomous worms is made treacle, the most sovereign medicine for the preservation of man's health in time of danger. Wherefore I would advise you all, that cometh to the reading or hearing of this book, which is the Word of God, the most precious jewel, and most holy relic that remaineth upon

earth, that ye bring with you the fear of God, and that ye do it with all due reverence, and use your knowledge thereof, not to vainglory of frivolous disputation, but to the honour of God, increase of virtue and edification both of yourselves and other.

11. And to the intent that my words may be the more regarded, I will use in this part the authority of St Gregory Nazianzene, like as in the other I did of St John Chrysostom. It appeareth that in his time there were some (as I fear me, there be also now at these days a great number) which were idle babblers and talkers of the Scripture out of season and all good order, and without any increase of virtue or example of good living. To them he writeth all his first book, *De theologia* [*Orat.* 27, *ed.*]; whereof I shall briefly gather the whole effect, and recite it here unto you. "There be some," saith he, "whose not only ears and tongues, but also their fists, be whetted and ready bent all to contention and unprofitable disputation; whom I would wish, as they be vehement and earnest to reason the matter with tongue, so they were also ready and practive to do all good deeds. But forasmuch as they, subverting the order of all godliness, have respect only to this thing, how they may bind and loose subtle questions, so that now every market-place, every alehouse and tavern, every feast-house, briefly, every company of men, every assembly of women, is filled with such talk; since the matter is so," saith he, "and that our faith and holy religion of Christ beginneth to wax nothing else, but as it were a sophistry or a talking-craft, I can no less do but say something thereunto. It is not fit," saith he, "for every man to dispute the high questions of divinity, neither is it to be done at all times, neither in every audience must we discuss every doubt; but we must know when, to whom, and how far we ought to enter into such matters."

12. "First, it is not for every man, but it is for such as be of exact and exquisite judgements, and such as have spent their time before in study and contemplation; and such as before have cleansed themselves as well in soul and body, or at the least, endeavoured themselves to be made clean. For it is dangerous," saith he, "for the unclean to touch that thing that is most clean; like as the sore eye taketh harm by looking upon the sun. Secondarily, not at all times, but when we be reposed and at rest from all outward dregs and trouble, and when that our heads be not encumbered with other worldly and wandering imaginations: as if a man should mingle balm and dirt together. For he that shall judge and determine such matters and doubts of Scriptures, must take his time when he may apply his wits thereunto, that he may thereby the better see and discern what is truth. Thirdly, where, and in what audience? There and among those that be studious to learn, and not among such as have pleasure to trifle with such matters as with other things of pastime, which repute for their chief delicates the disputation of high questions, to show their wits, learning and eloquence in reasoning of high matters."

13. "Fourthly, it is to be considered how far to wade in such matters of difficulty. No further," saith he, "but as every man's own capacity will serve him; and again, no further than the weakness or intelligence of the other audience may bear. For like as too great noise hurteth the ear, too much meat hurteth a man's body, too heavy burdens hurteth the bearers of them, too much rain doth more hurt than good to the ground; briefly, in all things too much is noyous [i.e. harmful, *ed.*]; even so weak wits and weak consciences may soon be oppressed with over-hard questions. I say not this to dissuade men from the knowledge of God, and reading or studying of the Scripture. For I say that it is as necessary for the life of man's soul, as for the body to breathe. And if it were possible so to live, I would think it good for a man to spend all his life in that, and to do no other thing. I commend the law which biddeth to meditate and study the Scriptures always, both night and day, and sermons and preachings to be made both morning, noon and eventide; and God to be lauded and blessed in all times, to bedward, from bed, in our journeys and all our other works. I forbid not to read, but I forbid to reason. Neither forbid I to reason so far as is good and godly. But I allow not that this is done out of season, and out of measure and good order. A man may eat too much of honey, be it never so sweet, and there is time for everything; and that thing that is good is not good, if it be ungodly done; even as a flower in winter is out of season and as a woman's apparel becometh not a man, neither contrarily, the man's the woman; neither is weeping convenient at a bridal, neither laughing at burial. Now if we can observe and keep that is comely and timely in all other things, shall not we then the rather do the same in the Holy Scriptures? Let us not run forth as it were wild horse, that can suffer neither bridle in their mouths nor sitter on their backs. Let us keep us in our bounds, and neither let us go too far on the one side, lest we return into Egypt, neither too far over the other, lest we be carried away to Babylon. Let us not sing the song of our Lord in a strange land; that is to say, let us not dispute the Word of God at all adventures, as well where it is not to be reasoned as where it is, and as well in the ears of them that be not fit therefore as of them that be. If we can in no wise forbear but that we must needs dispute, let us forbear thus much at the least, to do it out of time and place convenient. And let us entreat of those things which be holy holily; and upon those things that be mystical, mystically; and not to utter the divine mysteries in the ears unworthy to hear them; but let us know what is comely as well in our silence and talking, as in our garments' wearing, in our feeding, in our gesture, in our goings and in all our other behaving. This contention and debate about Scriptures and doubts thereof (specially when such as pretend to be the favourers and students thereof cannot agree within themselves) dost most hurt to ourselves, and to the furthering of the cause and quarrels that we would have furthered above all things. And we in this," saith he, "be not unlike to them that, being mad, set their own houses on fire, and that slay their own children, or beat their own parents. I marvel much," saith he, "to recount whereof cometh all this desire of vainglory, whereof cometh all this tongue-itch, that we have so much delight to talk and clatter? And wherein is our communication? Not in the commendations and virtuous and good deeds of hospitality, of love between Christian brother and brother, of love between man and wife, of virginity and chastity, and of alms towards the poor; not in psalms and godly songs, not in lamenting for our sins, not in repressing the affections of the body, not in prayers to God. We talk of Scripture, but in the meantime we subdue not our flesh by fasting, waking and weeping; we make not this life a meditation of death; we do not strive to be lords of our appetites and affections; we go not about to pull down our proud and high minds, to abate our fumish and rancorous stomachs, to restrain our lusts and bodily delectations, our undiscreet sorrows, our lascivious mirth, our inordinate looking, our insatiable hearing of vanities, our speaking without measure, our inconvenient thoughts, and briefly, to reform our life and manners. But all our holiness consisteth in talking. And we pardon each other from all good living, so that we may stick fast together in argumentation; as though there were no more ways to heaven but this alone, the way of speculation and knowledge (as they take it); but in very deed it is rather the way of superfluous contention and sophistication."

14. Hitherto have I recited the mind of Gregory Nazianzene in that book which I spake of before. The same author saith also in another place (*Orat.* 39), that "the learning of a Christian man ought to begin of the fear of God, to end in matters of high speculation; and not contrarily, to begin with speculation, and to end in fear. For speculation," saith he, "either high cunning or knowledge, if it be not stayed with the bridle of fear to offend God, is dangerous and enough to tumble a mean headlong down the hill. Therefore," saith he, "the fear of God must be the first beginning, and as it were an ABC, or an introduction to all them that shall enter to the very true and most fruitful knowledge of Holy Scriptures. Where as is the fear of God, there is," saith he, "the keeping of the commandments, there is the cleansing of the flesh, which flesh is a cloud before the soul's eye, and suffereth it not purely to see the beam of the heavenly light. Where as is the cleansing of the flesh, there is the illumination of the Holy Ghost, the end of all our desires, and the very light whereby the verity of Scriptures is seen and perceived." This is the mind and almost the words of Gregory Nazianzene, doctor of the Greek Church, of whom St Jerome saith, that unto his time the Latin Church had no writer able to be compared and to make an even match with him.

15. Therefore, to conclude this latter part, every man that cometh to the reading of this holy book ought to bring with him first and foremost this fear of Almighty God, and then next a firm and stable purpose to reform his own self according thereunto; and so to continue, proceed, and prosper from time to time, showing himself to be a sober and fruitful hearer and learner. Which if he do, he shall prove at the length well able to teach, though not with his mouth, yet with his living and good example, which is sure the

most lively and most effectuous form and manner of teaching. He that otherwise intermeddleth with this Book, let him be assured at once he shall make account therefore, when he shall have said to him, as it is written in the prophet David, *Peccatori dicit Deus etc.* (Ps. 50:16-23): "Unto the ungodly saith God, Why dost thou preach my laws, and takest my testament in thy mouth? Whereas thou hatest to be reformed, and hast been partakers with advoutrers [i.e. adulterers, *ed.*]. Thou hast let thy mouth speak wickedness, and with thy tongue thou hast set forth deceit. Thou sattest and spakest against thy brother; and hast slandered thine own mother's son. These things hast thou done, and I held my tongue, and thou thoughtedst (wickedly) that I am even such a one as thyself. But I will reprove thee, and set before thee the things that thou hast done. O consider this, ye that forget God; lest I pluck you away, and there be none to deliver you. Whoso offereth me thanks and praise, he honoureth me: and to him that ordereth his conversation right will I show the salvation of God."

God save the King.

[1] Ps. 119:105   [2] Mt 4:4   [3] Lk 12:49   [4] Ro 8:28

Cranmer's Reformation:

The Reign of Edward VI

(1547-1553)

22. THE EDWARDIAN INJUNCTIONS, 1547

History

Following the death of Henry VIII (28 January 1547), the forces of change were quick to seize control. Within a few months they were preparing a widespread reformation of the Church. The Injunctions were drawn up by the Duke of Somerset as Lord Protector, and by Archbishop Cranmer, and published on 31 July 1547. Many of them reflect provisions which were made earlier in the Henrician Injunctions of 1536 and 1538. In some respects they were quickly superseded by events, but it is remarkable how many of their provisions remained in force, not least the compulsory registration of births, marriages and deaths, which continued unaltered until 1837, when provision was made for civil as well as ecclesiastical registration.

Theology

The injunctions consolidated the reforms made under Henry VIII and gave notice that further changes were in the offing. Though not a theological document as such, they paved the way for the radical reforms which soon followed.

N.B. Where an injunction recapitulates one made under Henry VIII, the reader is referred to the earlier text by a note in parentheses, immediately following the number of the injunction given here. The first and second injunctions of Henry VIII are distinguished by Roman numerals.

Injunctions given by the most excellent Prince Edward the VI by the Grace of God King of England, France and Ireland, Defender of the Faith, and in earth under Christ, of the Church of England and of Ireland the Supreme Head, To all and singular his loving subjects, as well of the clergy as of the laity.

The King's most royal Majesty, by the advice of his most dear uncle the Duke of Somerset, Lord Protector of all his realms, dominions and subjects, and governor of his most royal Person, and the residue of his most honourable council, intending the advancement of the true honour of Almighty God, the suppression of idolatry and superstition throughout all his realms and dominions, and to plant true religion to the extirpation of all hypocrisy, enormities and abuses, as to his duty appertaineth, doth minister unto his loving subjects these godly injunctions hereafter following, whereof part were given unto them heretofore by the authority of his most beloved father, King Henry VIII of most famous memory, and part are now ministered and given by his Majesty. All which injunctions, his Highness willeth and commandeth his said loving subjects, by his supreme authority, obediently to receive and truly to observe and keep, every man in their offices, degrees and states, as they will avoid his displeasure and the pains in the same injunctions hereafter expressed.

01. (I, 01) The first is that all deans, archdeacons, parsons, vicars and other ecclesiastical persons shall faithfully keep and observe, and as far as in them may be, shall cause to be observed and kept of other, all and singular laws and statutes made as well for the abolishing and extirpation of the Bishop of Rome, his pretended and usurped power and jurisdiction, as for the establishment and confirmation of the King's authority, jurisdiction and supremacy of the Church of England and Ireland. And furthermore, all ecclesiastical persons, having cure of soul, shall to the uttermost of their wit, knowledge and learning, purely and sincerely, and without any colour or dissimulation, declare, manifest and open, four times every year at the least, in their sermons and other collations, that the Bishop of Rome's usurped power and jurisdiction, having no establishment nor ground by the law of God, was of most just causes taken away and abolished, and that therefore no manner of obedience or subjection within his realms and dominions is due unto him. And that the King's power within his realms and dominions is the highest power under God, to whom all men within the same realms and dominions, by God's laws owe most loyalty and obedience, afore and above all other powers and potentates in earth.

Besides this, to the intent that all superstition and hypocrisy crept into men's hearts, may vanish away, they shall not set forth or extol any images, relics or miracles, for any superstition or lucre, nor allure the people by any enticements, to the pilgrimage of any saint or image, but reproving the same, they shall teach that all goodness, health and grace ought to be both asked and looked for only of God, as of the very author and giver of the same, and of none other.

02. (II, 06) Item, that they, the persons above rehearsed, shall make or cause to be made in their churches, and every other cure they have, one sermon, every quarter of the year at the least, wherein they shall purely and sincerely declare the Word of God, and in the same, exhort their hearers to the works of faith, mercy and charity specially prescribed and commanded in Scripture, and that works devised by men's fantasies, besides Scripture, as wandering to pilgrimages, offering of money, candles or tapers to relics, or images, or kissing and licking of the same, praying upon beads, or such like superstition, have not only no promise of reward in Scripture, for doing of them, but contrariwise, great threats and maledictions of God, for that they be things tending to idolatry and superstition, which of all other offences God Almighty doth most detest and abhor, for that the same diminish his honour and glory.

03. (II, 07) Item, that such images as they know in any of their cures to be or have been so abused with pilgrimage or offerings, or anything made thereunto, or shall be hereafter censed unto, they (and none other private persons) shall for the avoiding of that most detestable offence of idolatry, forthwith take down or cause to be taken down, and destroy the same, and shall suffer from henceforth no torches, nor candles, tapers or images of wax to be set afore any image or picture, but only two lights upon the high altar before the sacrament, which for the signification that Christ is the very true light of the world, they shall suffer to remain still, admonishing their parishioners that images serve for no other purpose but to be a remembrance, whereby men may be admonished, of the holy lives and conversation of them that the said images do represent, which images, if they do abuse for any other intent, they commit idolatry in the same, to the great danger of their souls.

04. (II, 04) Item. That every holy day throughout the year, when they have no sermon, they shall immediately after the Gospel openly and plainly recite to their parishioners, in the pulpit, the *Paternoster*, the *Credo* and the Ten Commandments in English, to the intent that the people may learn the same by heart, exhorting all parents and householders to teach their children and servants the same, as they are bound by the law of God and in conscience to do.

05. (I, 05) Item. That they shall charge fathers and mothers, masters and governors, to bestow their children and servants, even from their childhood, either to learning or to some honest exercise, occupation or husbandry, exhorting and counselling, and by all the ways and means they may, as well in their sermons and collations as otherwise, persuading their said fathers and mothers, masters and other governors, diligently to provide and foresee that the youth be in no manner or wise brought up in idleness, lest at any time afterwards, for lack of some craft, occupation or other honest means to live by, they be driven to fall to begging, stealing or some other unthriftiness; forasmuch as we may daily see, through sloth and idleness, divers valiant men fall, some to begging and some to theft and murder, which after brought to calamity and misery, do blame their parents, friends and governors, which suffered them to be brought up so idly in their youth, where, if they had been well brought up in good learning, some occupation or craft, they should (being rulers of their own households) have profited as well themselves, as divers other persons, to the great commodity and ornament of the commonwealth.

06. (I, 06) Also that the said parsons, vicars and other curates shall diligently provide that the sacraments be duly and reverently ministered in their parishes. And if at any time it happen them in any of the cases expressed in the statutes of this realm, or of special licence given by the King's Majesty, to be absent from their benefices, they shall leave their cure, not to a rude and unlearned person, but to an honest, well-learned and expert curate, that can by his ability teach the rude and unlearned of their cure wholesome doctrine, and reduce them to the right way that do err, and which will also execute their injunctions, and do their duty otherwise as they are bound to do in every behalf, and accordingly may and will profit their cure, no less with good example of living than with the declaration of the Word of God, or else their lack and default shall be imputed unto them, who shall straightly answer for the same, if they do otherwise. And always let them see that neither they nor their curates do seek more their own profit, promotion or advantage than the profit of the souls that they have under their cure, or the glory of God.

07. (II, 02) Also that they shall provide within three months next after this visitation, one book of the whole Bible, of the largest volume, in English. And within one twelve-months next after the said visitation, the Paraphrasis of Erasmus also in English upon the Gospels, and the same set up in some convenient place, within the said church that they have cure of, whereas their parishioners may most commodiously resort unto the same and read the same. The charges of which books have been ratably borne, between the Parson or proprietary, and the parishioners aforesaid, that is to say, the one half by the Parson or proprietary and the other half by the parishioners. And they shall discourage no man (authorized and licenced thereto) from the reading of any part of the Bible, either in Latin or in English, but shall rather conform and exhort every person to read the same, as the very lively Word of God, and the special food of man's soul, that all Christian persons are bound to embrace, believe and follow, if they look to be saved; whereby they may the better know their duties to God, to their Sovereign Lord the King and their neighbour, ever gently and charitably exhorting them, and in his Majesty's name, straightly charging and commanding them, that in the reading thereof, no man to reason or contend, but quietly to hear the reader.

08. (I, 07) Also, the said ecclesiastical persons shall in no wise at any unlawful time, nor for any other cause than their honest necessity, haunt or resort to any taverns or alehouses. And after their dinner and supper, they shall not give themselves to drinking or riot, spending their time idly, by day or by night, at dice, cards or tables playing, or any other lawful game, but at all times as they shall have leisure, they shall hear or read somewhat of Holy Scripture, or shall occupy themselves with some other honest exercise, and that they always do the things which appertain to honesty, with endeavour to profit the common weal, having always in mind that they ought to excel all others in purity of life and should be examples to the people, to live well and Christianly.

09. (II, 05) Item, that they shall in confessions every Lent, examine every person that cometh to confession to them, whether they can recite the articles of their faith, the *Paternoster* and the Ten Commandments in English, and hear them say the same particularly wherein, if they be not perfect, they shall declare then that every Christian person ought to know the said things

before they should receive the blessed sacrament of the altar, and (ad)monish them to learn the said necessary things more perfectly, or else they ought not to presume to come to God's board, without perfect knowledge and will to observe the same, and if they do, it is to the great peril of their souls, and also to the worldly rebuke, that they might incur hereafter by the same.

10. (II, 09) Item, that they shall admit no man to preach within any of their cures, but such as shall appear unto them to be sufficiently licensed thereunto by the King's Majesty, the Lord Protector's grace, the Archbishop of Canterbury, the Archbishop of York in his province or the bishop of the diocese. And such as shall be so licensed they shall gladly receive to declare the Word of God, without any resistance or contradiction.

11. (II, 10) Also, if they have heretofore declared to their parishioners anything to the extolling or setting forth of pilgrimages, relics or images, or lighting of candles, kissing, kneeling or decking of the same images, or any such superstition, they shall now openly, before the same, recant and reprove the same, showing them, as the truth is, that they did the same upon no ground of Scripture, but were led and seduced by a common error and abuse crept into the Church, through the sufferance and avarice of such as felt profit by the same.

12. (II, 11) Also, if they do or shall know any man within their parish, or elsewhere, that is a letter (i.e. hinderer, *ed.*) of the Word of God to be read in English, or sincerely preached, or of the execution of these the King's Majesty's Injunctions, or a fautor (i.e. abettor, *ed.*) of the Bishop of Rome's pretended power, now by the laws of this realm justly rejected, extirped and taken away utterly, they shall detect and present the same to the King or his council, or to the justice of peace next adjoining.

13. (II, 12) Also, that the parson, vicar or curate and parishioners of every parish within this realm shall in their churches and chapels keep one book or register, wherein they shall write the day and year of every wedding, christening and burial made within their parish for their time, and so every man succeeding them likewise; and also therein shall write every person's name that shall be so wedded, christened or buried; and for the safe keeping of the same book, the parish shall be bound to provide of their common charges one sure coffer with two locks and keys, whereof the one to remain with the parson, vicar or curate and the other with the wardens of every parish church or chapel wherein the said book shall be laid up; which book you shall every Sunday take forth and in the presence of the said wardens, or one of them, write and record in the same all the weddings, christenings and burials made the whole week before, and that done, to lay up the book in the said coffer as before; and for every time that the same shall be omitted, the party that shall be in the fault thereof shall forfeit to the said church three shillings and fourpence, to be employed to the poor men's box of that parish.

14. (I, 08) Furthermore, because the goods of the Church are called the

goods of the poor, and at these days nothing is less seen than the poor to be sustained with the same, all parsons, vicars, pensionaries, prebendaries and other beneficed men within this deanery, not being resident upon their benefices, which may dispend yearly twenty pounds or above, either within this deanery or elsewhere, shall distribute hereafter among their poor parishioners, or other inhabitants there, in the presence of the churchwardens or some other honest men of the parish, the fortieth part of the fruits and revenues of this said benefice, lest they be worthily noted of ingratitude, which, reserving so many parts to themselves, cannot vouchsafe to impart the fortieth portion thereof among the poor people of that parish, that is so fruitful and profitable unto them.

15. (I, 09) And to the intent that learned men may hereafter spring the more for the execution of the premises, every parson, vicar, clerk or beneficed man within this deanery, having yearly to dispend, in benefices and other promotions of the Church, an hundred pounds, shall give competent exhibition to one scholar, and for as many hundred pounds more as he may dispend, to so many scholars more shall give like exhibition in the University of Oxford or Cambridge, or some grammar school, which, after they have profited in good learning, may be partners of their patron's cure and charge, as well in preaching as otherwise in the execution of their offices, or may, when need shall be, otherwise profit the commonwealth with their counsel and wisdom.

16. (I, 10) Also that all proprietaries, parsons, vicars and clerks, having churches, chapels or mansions within this deanery, shall bestow yearly hereafter upon the same mansions or chancels of their churches, being in decay, the fifth part of that their benefices, till they be fully repaired, and the same, so repaired, shall always keep and maintain in good estate.

17. (II, 13) Also, that the said parsons, vicars and clerks shall once every quarter of the year read these Injunctions given unto them openly and deliberately before all their parishioners, to the intent that both they may be the better admonished of their duty and their said parishioners the more moved to follow the same for their part.

18. (II, 14) Also, forasmuch as by a law established, every man is bound to pay his tithes, no man shall, by colour of duty omitted by their curates, detain their tithes and so redouble and requite one wrong with another, or be his own judge; but shall truly pay the same as he hath been accustomed, to their parsons, vicars and curates, without any restraint or diminution; and such lack or default as they can justly find in their parsons and curates, to call for reformation thereof at their ordinaries' and other superiors' hands, who upon complaint and due proof thereof shall reform the same accordingly.

19. (II, 15) Also, that no parson shall from henceforth alter or change the order and manner of any fasting day that is commanded, nor of common prayer or divine service, otherwise than is specified in these Injunctions,

until such time as the same shall be otherwise ordered and transposed by the King's authority.

20. Also that every parson, vicar, curate, chantry priest and stipendiary, being under the degree of Bachelor of Divinity, shall provide and have of his own, within three months after this visitation, the New Testament both in Latin and in English, with Paraphrasis upon the same of Erasmus, and diligently study the same, conferring the one with the other. And the bishops and other ordinaries by themselves, or their officers, in their synods and visitations, shall examine the said ecclesiastical persons, how they have profited in the study of Holy Scripture.

21. Also in the time of high mass, within every church, he that sayeth or singeth the same shall read, or cause to be read, the Epistle and Gospel of that mass in English and not in Latin, in the pulpit, or in such convenient place as the people may hear the same. And also every Sunday and holy day they shall plainly and distinctly read, or cause to be read, one chapter of the New Testament in English, in the said place at Mattins, immediately after the lessons, and at Evensong, after *Magnificat*, one chapter of the Old Testament. And to the intent the premises may be more conveniently done, the King's Majesty's pleasure is that when nine lessons should be read in the church, three of them shall be omitted and left out, with their responses. And at Evensong time, the responses with all the memories shall be left off, for that purpose.

22. Also, because those persons which be sick or in peril of death be oftentimes put in despair by the craft and subtlety of the devil who is then most busy, and specially with them that lack the knowledge, sure persuasion and steadfast belief that they may be made partakers of the great and infinite mercy which Almighty God of his most bountiful goodness and mere liberality, without our deserving, hath offered freely to all persons that put their full trust and confidence in him; Therefore, that this damnable device of despair may be clearly taken away and firm belief and steadfast hope surely conceived of all their parishioners, being in any danger, they shall learn, and have always in a readiness, such comfortable places and sentences of Scripture as do set forth the mercy, benefits and goodness of Almighty God, towards all penitent and believing persons, that they may at all times, when necessity shall require, promptly comfort their flock with the lively Word of God, which is the only stay of man's conscience.

23. Also, to avoid all contention and strife which heretofore hath arisen among the King's Majesty's subjects, in sundry places of his realms and dominions, by reason of fond courtesy and challenging of places in processions, and also that they may the more quickly hear that which is said or sung, to their edifying; they shall not from henceforth in any parish church, at any time use any procession about the church or churchyard, or other place, but immediately before high mass the priest, with others of the choir, shall kneel in the midst of the church and sing or say, plainly and distinctly,

the Litany, which is set forth in English, with all the suffrages following, and none other procession or litany to be had or used but the said Litany in English, adding nothing thereto but as the King's grace shall hereafter appoint; and in cathedral or collegiate churches the same shall be done in such places as our commissaries in our visitation shall appoint. And in the time of the Litany, of the high mass, of the sermon, and when the priest readeth the Scripture to the parishioners, no manner of persons, without a just and urgent cause, shall depart out of the church, and all ringing and knolling of bells shall be utterly forborne for that time, to be rung or knolled before the sermon.

24. Also, like as the people be commonly occupied on the workday, with bodily labour for their bodily sustenance, so was the holy day at the first beginning godly instituted and ordained, that the people should that day give themselves wholly to God. And whereas in our time, God is more offended than pleased, more dishonoured than honoured upon the holy day, because of idleness, pride, drunkenness, quarrelling and brawling, which are most used in such days, people nevertheless persuading themselves sufficiently to honour God on that day, if they hear mass and service, though they understand nothing to their edifying; therefore all the King's loving and faithful subjects shall from henceforth celebrate and keep their holy date, according to God's holy will and pleasure, that is, in hearing the Word of God read and taught in private and public prayers, in acknowledging their offences to God, and amendment of the same; in reconciling themselves charitably to their neighbours, where displeasure hath been; in oftentimes receiving the communion of the very body and blood of Christ; in visiting of the poor and sick; in using all soberness and godly conversation. Yet notwithstanding all parsons, vicars and curates shall teach and declare unto their parishioners that they may with a safe and quiet conscience in the time of harvest, labour upon the holy and festival days, and save that thing which God hath sent. And if for any scrupulosity or grudge of conscience men should superstitiously abstain from working upon those days, that then they should grievously offend and displease God.

25. Also, forasmuch as variance and contention is a thing which most displeaseth God and is most contrary to the blessed communion of the body and blood of our Saviour Christ, curates shall in no wise admit to the receiving thereof any of their cure and flock who hath maliciously and openly contended with his neighbour, unless the same do first charitably and openly reconcile himself again, remitting all rancour and malice, whatsoever controversy hath been between them, and nevertheless, their just titles and rights, they may charitably prosecute before such as have authority to hear the same.

26. Also that every dean, archdeacon, master of collegiate church, master of hospital and prebendary, being priest, shall preach by himself personally twice every year at the least, either in the place where he is entitled, or in

some church where he hath jurisdiction, or else which is to the said place appropriate or united.

27. Also, that they should instruct and teach in their cures that no man ought obstinately and maliciously break and violate the laudable ceremonies of the Church, by the King commanded to be observed, and as yet not abrogated. And on the other side, that whosoever doth superstitiously abuse them, doth the same to the great peril and danger of his soul's health; as in casting holy water upon his bed, upon images or other dead things; or bearing about him holy bread, or St John's Gospel; or making crosses of wood upon Palm Sunday, in time of reading of the Passion, or keeping of private holy days, as bakers, brewers, smiths, shoemakers and such others do, or ringing of the holy bells, or blessing with the holy candle, to the intent thereby to be discharged of the burden of sin, or to drive away devils, or to put away dreams and fantasies, or in putting trust and confidence of health and salvation in the same ceremonies when they be only ordained, instituted and made to put us in remembrance of the benefits which we have received by Christ. And if he use them for any other purpose, he grievously offendeth God.

28. Also that they shall take away, utterly extinct and destroy all shrines, covering of shrines, all tables and candlesticks, trundles or rolls of ware, pictures, paintings and all other monuments of feigned miracles, pilgrimages, idolatry and superstition, so that there remain no memory of the same in walls, glasses, windows or elsewhere within their churches or houses. And they shall exhort all their parishioners to do the like within their several houses. And that the churchwardens, at the common charge of the parishioners in every church, shall provide a comely and honest pulpit, to be set in a convenient place within the same, for the preaching of God's Word.

29. Also, they shall provide and have within three months after this visitation, a strong chest with a hole in the upper part thereof, to be provided at the cost and charge of the parish, having three keys, whereof one shall remain in the custody of the parson, vicar or curate, and the other two in the custody of the churchwardens, or any other two honest men to be appointed by the parish from year to year. Which chest you shall set and fashion near to the high altar, to the intent the parishioners should put into it their oblation and alms, for their poor neighbours. And the parson, vicar and curate shall diligently from time to time, and specially when men make their testaments, call upon, exhort and move their neighbours to confer and give (as they may well spare) to the said chest, declaring unto them, whereas heretofore they have been diligent to bestow much substance otherwise than God commanded upon pardons, pilgrimages, trentals, decking of images, offering of candles, giving to friars and upon other like blind devotions, they ought at this time to be much more ready to help the poor and needy, knowing that to relieve the poor is a true worshipping of God, required earnestly upon pain of everlasting damnation; and that also, whatsoever is

given for their comfort is given to Christ himself and is so accepted of him, that he will mercifully reward the same with everlasting life. The which alms and devotion of the people, the keepers of the keys shall at all times convenient take out of the chest and distribute the same in the presence of the whole parish, one sixth of them to be truly and faithfully delivered to their most needy neighbours, and if they be provided for, then to the reparation of highways next adjoining. And also the money which riseth of fraternities, guilds and other flocks of the Church (except by the King's Majesty's authority it be otherwise appointed) shall be put into the said chest and converted to the said use, and also the rents of lands, the profit of cattle and money given or bequeathed to the finding of torches, lights, tapers and lamps, shall be converted to the said use, saving that it shall be lawful for them to bestow part of the said profits upon the reparation of the church if great need require, and whereas the parish is very poor and not able otherwise to repair the same.

30. And forasmuch as priests be public ministers of the Church and upon the holy days ought to apply themselves to the common administration of the whole parish, they shall not be bound to go to women lying in childbed, except in time of dangerous sickness, and not to fetch any corpse before it is brought to the churchyard, and if the woman be sick or the corpse brought to the church, the priest shall do his duty accordingly in visiting the woman and burying the dead person.

31. Also to avoid the detestable sin of simony, because buying and selling of benefices is execrable before God, therefore all such persons as buy any benefices or come to them by fraud or deceit, shall be deprived of such benefices and be made unable at any time after, to receive any other spiritual promotion. And such as do sell them, or by any colour do bestow them for their own gain and profit, shall lose their right and title of patronage and presentment for that time and the gift thereof for that vacation shall appertain to the King's Majesty.

32. Also because through lack of preachers in many places of the King's realms and dominions the people continue in ignorance and blindness, all parsons, vicars and curates shall read in their churches every Sunday one of the homilies which are and shall be set forth for the same purpose, by the King's authority in such sort as they shall be appointed to do, in the preface of the same.

33. Also, whereas many indiscreet persons do at this date uncharitably contemn and abuse priests and ministers of the Church, because some of them (having small learning) have of long time favoured fantasies rather than God's truth; yet forasmuch as their office and function is appointed of God, the King's Majesty willeth and chargeth all his loving subjects that from henceforth they shall use them charitably and reverently, for their office and ministration's sake, and especially all such as labour in the setting forth of God's Holy Word.

34. Also, that all manner of persons which understand not the Latin tongue shall pray upon none other primer but upon that which was lately set forth in English, by the authority of King Henry VIII of most famous memory. And that no teacher of youth shall teach any other than the said Primer. And all those which have no knowledge of the Latin tongue shall pray upon none other Latin Primer but upon that which is likewise set forth by the same authority. And that all graces to be said at dinner and supper shall be always said in the English tongue. And that none other grammar shall be taught in any school or other place within the King's realms and dominions but only that which is set forth by the said authority.

35. Item, that all chantry priests shall exercise themselves in teaching youth to read and write, and bringing them up in good manners and other virtuous exercises.

36. Item, when any sermon or homily shall be had, the Prime and Hours shall be omitted.

The Form of Bidding the Common Prayers

You shall pray for the whole congregation of Christ's Church and specially for this Church of England and Ireland; wherein first, I commend to your devout prayers the King's most excellent Majesty, Supreme Head immediately under God of the spiritualty and temporalty of the same Church, and for Queen Katherine dowager, and also for my Lady Mary and my Lady Elizabeth, the King's sisters.

Secondly, you shall pray for my Lord Protector's grace, with all the rest of the King's Majesty's council, for all the lords of this realm and for the clergy and the commons of the same, beseeching Almighty God to give every of them in his degree grace to use themselves in such wise as may be to God's glory, the King's honour and the weal of this realm.

Thirdly, you shall pray for all them that be departed out of this world in the faith of Christ, that they with us and we with them at the Day of Judgement may rest, both body and soul, with Abraham, Isaac and Jacob in the Kingdom of Heaven.

All which and singular Injunctions the King's Majesty ministereth unto his clergy and their successors and to all other his loving subjects, straightly charging and commanding them to observe and keep the same, upon pain of deprivation, sequestration of fruits of benefices, suspension, excommunication and such other coercion as to ordinaries or others having ecclesiastical jurisdiction, whom His Majesty hath appointed for due execution of the same, shall be seen convenient, charging and commanding them to see these Injunctions observed and kept of all persons, being under their jurisdiction, as they will answer to his Majesty for the contrary. And his Majesty's pleasure is that every justice of peace (being required) shall assist the ordinaries, and every of them, for the due execution of the said Injunctions.

23. THE SACRAMENT ACT, 1547
(1 Edward VI c.1)

History

In November 1547, Convocation agreed that Communion should thenceforth be received in both kinds, and the following Act, whose official title is "An Act against Revilers, and for Receiving in Both Kinds" was passed by Parliament. The inclusion of two separate sections helped to secure the passage of the Act without difficulty, since those who might have objected to receiving in both kinds could not easily oppose sanctions against blasphemers. This Act was repealed by Mary I with effect from 20 December 1553, but reinstated by Elizabeth I in 1559.

Theology

Reception in both kinds was a major element in the Reformer's doctrine of the Eucharist. It had been the universal custom of the early Church, and continued into the Middle Ages in the West, but it gradually died out, possibly because of fear of plague. By the early fifteenth century it had disappeared, and attempts to reintroduce it were regarded as heretical. Its most famous proponent was the Czech reformer Jan Hus, who was burnt at the stake for his beliefs in 1415. The controversy was known as the *Utraquist* dispute, from the Latin expression *sub utraque specie* (under each kind). The official Catholic position was that Christ was fully received under one kind, and that therefore reception in both kinds was unnecessary. The Reformers (rightly) scoffed at this reasoning, and restored the cup to the laity.

01. The King's most excellent majesty, minding the governance and order of his most loving subjects to be in most perfect unity and concord in all things, and in especial in the true faith and religion of God, and wishing the same to be brought to pass with all clemency and mercy on his Highness's part towards them, as his most princely serenity and majesty has already declared by evident proofs, to the intent that his most loving subjects, provoked by clemency and goodness of their prince and king, shall study, rather for love than for fear, to do their duties, first to Almighty God and then to his Highness and the commonwealth, nourishing concord and love amongst themselves; yet considers and perceives that in a multitude all be not on that sort, that reason and the knowledge of their duties can move them from offence, but many which had need have some bridle of fear, and that the same be men most contentious and arrogant for the most part, or else most blind and ignorant: by the means of which sort of men, many things well and godly instituted, and to the edification of many, be perverted and abused, and turned to their own and others' great loss and hindrance, and sometime to extreme destruction, the which does appear in nothing more or sooner than in matters of religion, and in the great and high mysteries thereof, as in the most comfortable sacrament of the body and blood of our Saviour Jesus Christ, commonly called the sacrament of the altar, and in Scripture, the supper and table of the Lord, the communion and partaking of the body and blood of Christ:

Which sacrament was instituted of no less author than of our Saviour, both God and man, when at his last supper, amongst his apostles, he did take the bread into his holy hands and did say: *Take you and eat; this is my body which is given and broken for you.* (I Co 11:24) And taking up the chalice or cup, did give thanks and say: *This is my blood of the new testament, which is shed for you and for many, for the remission of sins,* (I Co 11:25) that whensoever we should do the same, we should do it in the remembrance of him, and to declare and set forth his death and most glorious passion until his coming. Of the which bread whosoever eateth, or of the which cup whosoever drinketh unworthily, eateth and drinketh condemnation and judgement to himself, making no difference of the Lord's body; the institution of which sacrament being ordained by Christ, as is beforesaid, and the said words spoken of it here before rehearsed, being of eternal, infallible and undoubted truth:

Yet the said sacrament (all this notwithstanding) has been of late marvellously abused by such manner of men before rehearsed, who of wickedness, or else of ignorance and want of learning, for certain abuses heretofore committed of some, in misusing thereof, having condemned in their hearts and speech the whole thing, and contemptuously depraved, despised or reviled the same most holy and blessed sacrament, and not only disputed and reasoned unreverently and ungodly of that most high mystery, but also in their sermons, preachings, readings, lectures, communications, arguments, talks, rhymes, songs, plays or jests, name or call it by such vile and unseemly words as Christian ears do abhor to hear rehearsed.

For reformation whereof, be it enacted by the King's Highness, with the assent of the Lords spiritual and temporal, and of the Commons, in this present Parliament assembled, and by the authority of the same, that whatsoever person or persons, from and after the first day of May next coming (01 May 1548), shall deprave, despise or contemn the said most blessed sacrament, in contempt thereof, by any contemptuous words, or by any words of depraving, despising or reviling, or what person or persons shall advisedly, in any other wise, contemn, despise or revile the said most blessed sacrament, contrary to the effects and declaration abovesaid; that then he or they shall suffer imprisonment of his or their bodies, and make fine and ransom at the King's will and pleasure.

02. And for full and effectual execution of the premises before devised, ordained and enacted by this Act, be it furthermore enacted by the authority

of this present Parliament, that immediately after the first day of May next coming (01 May 1548), the justices of peace, or three of them at the least, whereof one of them to be of the *quorum*, in every shire of this realm, and Wales, and all other places within the King's dominions shall have full power and authority by virtue of this Act, as well to take information and accusation by the oaths and depositions of two able, honest and lawful persons at the least, and after such accusation or information so had, to inquire by the oaths of twelve men, in every of their four quarter sessions yearly to be holden, of all and singular such accusations or informations to be had or made of any of the offences abovesaid, to be committed or done after the said first day of May, within the limits of their commission; and that upon every such accusation and information, the offender and offenders shall be inquired of, and indicted before the said justices of peace, or three of them at the least, as is aforesaid, of the said contempts and offences, by the verdict of twelve honest and indifferent men, if the matter of the said accusation and information shall seem to the said jury good and true.

03. And it is also further enacted by the authority aforesaid, that the said justices of peace, or three of them at the least, as is aforesaid, before whom any such presentment, information and accusation shall be made or taken as is aforesaid, shall examine the accusers, what other witnesses were by and present at the time of doing and committing of the offence, whereof the information, accusation and presentment shall be made, and how many others than the accusers have knowledge thereof, and shall have full power and authority by their discretions to bind, by recognizance to be taken before them, as well the said accusers, as all such other persons whom the said accusers shall declare to have knowledge of the offences by them presented and informed, every of them in five pounds to the King, to appear before the said justices of peace, before whom the offender or offenders shall be tried, at the day of the trial and deliverance of such offenders.

04. And it is further enacted by the authority aforesaid, that the said justices of peace, or three of them at the least, as is abovesaid, by virtue of this Act, shall have full power and authority to make process against every person and persons so indicted, by two *capias* ("let you seize") and an exigent, and by *capias utlagatum* ("let you seize the outlaw"), as well within the limits of their commission as into all other shires and places of this realm, Wales and other the King's dominions, as well within liberties as without, and the same process to be good and effectual in the law to all intents, constructions and purposes, and upon the appearance of any of the offenders, shall have full power and authority by virtue of this Act and the commission of peace, to determine the contempts and offences aforesaid according to the laws of this realm and the effects of this Act: and that the said justices of peace, or three of them at the least as is abovesaid, shall have full power and authority to let any such person or persons, so indicted, upon sufficient sureties, by their discretions, to bail for their appearance to be tried, according to the tenor, form and effect of this Act.

05. Provided always, and be it enacted, that the said justices of peace, or three of them at the least, at their quarter sessions, where any offender or offenders shall be or stand indicted of any of the contempts or offences abovesaid, shall direct and award one writ, in the King's name, to the bishop of the diocese where the said offence or offences be supposed to be committed or done, willing and requiring the said bishop to be in his own person, or by his chancellor, or other his sufficient deputy learned, at the quarter sessions in the said county to be holden, when and where the said offender shall be arraigned and tried, appointing to them in the said writ the day and place of the said arraignment; which writ shall be of this form:

Rex etc. Episcopo L. salutem. Praecipimus tibi quod tu, Cancellarius tuus, vel alius deputatus tuus sufficienter eruditus, sitis cum iusticiariis nostris ad pacem in comitatu nostro B. conservandam assignatis apud D. tali die, ad sessionem nostram, ad tunc et ibidem tenendam ad dandum consilium et advisamentum eisdem iusticiariis nostris ad pacem, super arranamentum et deliberationem offendentium contra formam statuti concernentis sacrosanctum sacramentum altaris.

(The King, etc. to Bishop N. We command thee that thou, thy chancellor, or another deputy of thine who is sufficiently learned, be present at X, with our justices appointed to preserve the peace in our county Y, on such day as our session is to be held then and there, in order to give counsel and advice to those our justices of the peace, about the arraignment and trial of offenders against the form of the Act concerning the sacrosanct sacrament of the altar).

06. Provided always, and be it enacted by the authority aforesaid, that no person or persons shall be indicted of any of the contempts or offences abovesaid, but only of such contempts or offences as shall be done or perpetrated within three months next after the said offence or offences so committed or done.

07. And be it further enacted by the authority aforesaid that in all trials, for any such offenders, before the said justices, as is aforesaid, the person or persons being complained on and arraigned, shall be admitted to purge or try his or their innocency by as many or more witnesses in number, and of as good honesty and credence, as the witnesses be which deposed against him or them or any of them.

08. And forasmuch as it is more agreeable, both to the first institution of the said sacrament of the most precious body and blood of our Saviour Jesus Christ, and also more conformable to the common use and practice both of the apostles and of the primitive Church, by the space of 500 years and more after Christ's ascension, that the said blessed sacrament should be ministered to all Christian people under both kinds of bread and wine, than under the form of bread only, and also it is more agreeable to the first institution of Christ, and to the usage of the apostles and the primitive Church, that the people being present should receive the same with the priest, than that the priest should receive it alone; therefore be it enacted by our said Sovereign Lord the King, with the consent of the Lords spiritual and temporal, and the Commons, in this present Parliament assembled, and by the authority of the same, that the said most blessed sacrament be hereafter commonly delivered and ministered unto the people within the Church of England and Ireland, and other the King's dominions, under both the kinds, that is to say, of bread and wine, except necessity otherwise require:

And also that the priest which shall minister the same shall, at the least one day before, exhort all persons which shall be present likewise to resort and prepare themselves to receive the same.

And when the day prefixed comes, after a godly exhortation by the minister made (wherein shall be further expressed the benefit and comfort promised to them which worthily receive the said holy sacrament, and the danger and indignation of God threatened to them which shall presume to receive the same unworthily, to the end that every man may try and examine his own conscience before he shall receive the same), the said minister shall not, without lawful cause, deny the same to any person that will devoutly and humbly desire it; any law, statute, ordinance or custom contrary thereunto in any wise notwithstanding; not condemning hereby the usage of any Church out of the King's Majesty's dominions.

24. THE ELECTION OF BISHOPS ACT, 1547 (1 Edward VI, c. 2)

History

The procedure for the election of bishops was laid down in 1534, as part of the final break with Rome. However, the theory that the Church should be completely subordinated to the state gained ground, particularly among the laity as represented in Parliament, and as soon as Henry was dead a new procedure was devised for episcopal appointments. It was enacted in 1547 and repealed, along with other such legislation, by Mary I, with effect from 20 December 1553. It was not renewed by Elizabeth I, who preferred to return to the earlier legislation of 1534. The full title of the Act is: "An Act for the election of Bishops, and what Seals and Style they and other Spiritual Persons exercising Jurisdiction Ecclesiastical shall use".

Theology

The theology of this Act can best be described as "erastian", from the name of the Swiss theologian Thomas Erastus (1524-1583). It is the belief that the Church should be directly controlled by the secular power. The Church of England has always faced the accusation that the princes of this world have more say in its affairs than the Word of God, and it must be admitted that there is some justification for this charge. However, there are degrees of erastianism, and this Act represents an extreme form of it to which the Church has not subsequently returned.

01. Forasmuch as the elections of the archbishop and bishops by the deans and chapters within the King's Majesty's realms of England and Ireland at this present time be as well to the long delay as to the great costs and charges of such persons as the King's Majesty giveth any archbishopric or bishopric unto; and whereas the said elections be in very deed no elections, but only by a writ of *congé d'élire* have colours, shadows or pretences of elections, serving nevertheless to no purpose and seeing also derogatory and prejudicial to the King's prerogative royal, to whom only appertaineth the collation and gift of all archbishoprics and bishoprics and suffragan bishops within his Highness's said realms of England and Ireland, Wales and other his dominions and marches; for a due reformation hereof, be it therefore enacted by the King's Highness, with the assent of the Lords spiritual and temporal and the Commons in this present Parliament assembled and by the authority of the same, that from thenceforth no such *congé d'élire* be granted, nor election of any archbishop or bishop by the dean and chapter made, but that the King may by his letters patent at all times when any archbishopric or bishopric be void, confer the same to any person whom the King shall think meet; the which collation so by the King's letters patent made and delivered to the person to whom the King shall confer the same archbishopric or bishopric, or to his sufficient proctor and attorney, shall stand to all intents, constructions and purposes to as much and the same effect as though *congé d'élire* had been given, the election duly made and the same confirmed; and that upon the said person to whom the said archbishopric, bishopric or suffraganship is so conferred, collated or given, may be consecrated and sew his livery or outerlemain and do other things as well as if the said ceremonies and elections had been done and made.

02. Provided alway and be it enacted by the authority aforesaid that every such person to whom any collation or gift of any archbishopric, bishopric or suffraganship shall be given or collated by the King, his heirs or successors, shall pay, do and yield to all and every person all such fees, interests and duties as of old time have been accustomed to be done; anything in this Act or in any other to the contrary hereof in any wise notwithstanding.

03. And whereas the archbishops and bishops and other spiritual persons in this realm do use to make and send out their summons and citations and other processes in their own names, and in such form and manner as was used in the time of the usurped power of the Bishop of Rome, contrary to the form and order of the summons and process of the common law used in this realm, seeing that all authority of jurisdiction spiritual and temporal is derived and deducted from the King's Majesty, as Supreme Head of the churches and realms of England and Ireland, and so justly acknowledged by the clergy of the said realms, and that all courts ecclesiastical within the said two realms be kept by no other power and authority other, foreign or within the realm, but by the authority of his most excellent Majesty, be it therefore further enacted by the authority aforesaid that all summons and citations or other process ecclesiastical in all suits and causes of instance between party and party, in all causes of correction, in all causes of bastardy or bigamy, or inquiry *de iure pronatus* (legally "originating"), probates of testaments and commissions of administration of persons deceased, and all aquittance of and upon accounts made by the executors, administrators or collectors of goods of any dead person, be from the first day of July next following (01 July 1547) made in the name and with the style of the King, as it is in writs original or judicial at the common law, and that the test thereof be in the name of the archbishop or bishop or other having ecclesiastical jurisdiction, who hath the commission and grant of the authority ecclesiastical immediately from the King's Highness; and that his commissary, official or substitute exercising jurisdiction under him shall put his name in the citation or process after the test.

04. Furthermore be it enacted by authority aforesaid that all manner of person or persons who hath the exercise of ecclesiastical jurisdiction shall have from the first day of July before expressed in their seals of office, the

King's Highness's arms, decently set with certain characters under the arms for the knowledge of the diocese, and shall use no other seal of jurisdiction but wherein his Majesty's arms be engraven; upon pain that if any person shall use ecclesiastical jurisdiction after the day before expressed in this realm of England, Wales and other his dominions or territories, and not send or make out the citation or process in the King's name, or use any seal of jurisdiction other than before limited, that every such offender shall incur and run in the King's Majesty's displeasure and indignation, and suffer imprisonment at his Highness's will and pleasure.

05. Provided always that no more or other fees be taken or paid for the seal and writing of any citations or other process than was heretofore accustomed.

06. Provided also and be it enacted by the authority aforesaid that the Archbishop of Canterbury for the time being shall use his own seal and in his own name in all faculties and dispensations, according to the tenor of an Act thereof made; and that the said archbishops and bishops shall make, admit, order and reform their chancellors, officials, commissaries, advocates, proctors and other their officers, ministers and substitutes and commissions to the suffragan bishops in their own names, under their own seals, in such manner and form as they have heretofore used, and shall certify to the court of tenths their certificates under their own name and seals as heretofore they have used, and according to the statute in that case made and provided; and likewise shall make collations, presentations, gifts, institutions and inductions of benefices, letters of orders or dimissories under their own names and seals as they have heretofore accustomed; anything in this Act contained to the contrary notwithstanding.

07. Provided always and be it enacted by the authority aforesaid that all process hereafter to be made or awarded by any ecclesiastical person or persons for the trial of any plea or matter depending, or that hereafter shall depend in any of the King's courts of record at the common law, and limited by the laws and customs of this realm to the spiritual courts to try the same, that the certificate of the same after the trial thereof shall be made in the King's name for the time being, and with the style of the same King, and under the seal of the bishop graved with the King's arms with the name of the bishop or spiritual officer being to the test of the same process and certificate, and to every of them.

25. THE ACT OF UNIFORMITY, 1549
(2 and 3 Edward VI c. 1)

History

This Act came into force on Whitsunday (09 June) 1549 and remained the law of the land until it was superseded in 1552. The Act itself was formally repealed by Mary I on 20 December 1553. A notable feature of this Act is that punishments for offenders are much less severe than those found in the Act of Six Articles, which suggests that the government of the day had learned that religious persecution usually backfires in the end.

Theology

This Act is important chiefly because it established the First Prayer Book of Edward VI as the only legal form of worship. The Book, which had been composed by Archbishop Cranmer, was intended to be a statement of Protestant doctrine, especially on the key issue of justification by faith, though it retained enough Catholic ceremonial not to give undue offence to traditionalists. In the end the fact that Catholics could continue to use it in good conscience scandalized Protestant opinion, and forced Cranmer to write a new, and much more unambiguously Protestant Prayer Book.

01. Where of long time there hath been had in this realm of England and in Wales divers forms of common prayer, commonly called the service of the Church; that is to say, the Use of Sarum, of York, of Bangor, and of Lincoln; and besides the same now of late much more divers and sundry forms and fashions have been used in the cathedral and parish churches of England and Wales, as well concerning the Matins, or Morning Prayer and the Evensong, as also concerning the Holy Communion, commonly called the Mass, with divers and sundry rites and ceremonies concerning the same, and in the administration of other sacraments of the Church; and as the doers and executors of the said rites and ceremonies, in other form than of late years they have been used, were pleased therewith, so other, not using the same rites and ceremonies, were thereby greatly offended. And albeit the King's Majesty, with the advice of his most entirely beloved uncle the Lord Protector and other of his Highness's council, hath heretofore divers times essayed to stay innovations or new rites concerning the premises; yet the same hath not had such good success as his Highness required in that behalf;

Whereupon his Highness by the most prudent advice aforesaid, being pleased to bear with the frailty and weakness of his subjects in that behalf, of his great clemency hath not been only content to abstain from punishment of those that have offended in that behalf, for that his Highness taketh that they did it of a good zeal; but also to the intent a uniform quiet and godly order should be had concerning the premises, hath appointed the Archbishop of Canterbury, and certain of the most learned and discreet bishops, and other learned men of this realm, to consider and ponder the premises; and thereupon having as well eye and respect to the most sincere and pure Christian religion taught by the Scripture, so to the usages in the primitive Church, should draw and make one convenient and meet order, rite and fashion of common and open prayer and administration of the sacraments, to be had and used in his Majesty's realm of England, and in Wales; the which at this time, by the aid of the Holy Ghost, with one uniform agreement is of them concluded, set forth and delivered to his Highness, to his great comfort and quietness of mind, in a book entitled, *The Book of Common Prayer and Administration of the Sacraments, and other Rites and Ceremonies of the Church, after the use of the Church of England.*

Wherefore the Lords spiritual and temporal and the Commons in this present Parliament assembled, considering as well the most godly travail of the King's Highness, of the Lord Protector, and other of his Highness's council, in gathering and collecting the said archbishop, bishops and learned men together, as the godly prayers, orders, rites and ceremonies in the said book mentioned, and the considerations of altering those things which be altered, and retaining those things which be retained in the said book, but also the honour of God and great quietness, which by the grace of God shall ensue upon the one and uniform rite and order in such common prayer and rites and external ceremonies to be used throughout England and in Wales, at Calais and the marches of the same, do give to his Highness most hearty and lowly thanks for the same; and humbly pray that it may be ordained and acted by his Majesty, with the assent of the Lords and Commons in this present Parliament assembled, and by authority of the same, that all and singular person and persons that have offended concerning the premises, other than such person and persons as now be and remain in ward in the Tower of London, or in the Fleet, may be pardoned thereof; and that all and singular ministers in any cathedral or parish church or other place within this realm of England, Wales, Calais and the marches of the same, or other the King's dominions, shall from and after the feast of Pentecost next coming (09 June 1549), be bound to say and use the Matins, Evensong, celebration of the Lord's Supper, commonly called the Mass, and administration of each of the sacraments, and all their common and open prayer, in such order and form as is mentioned in the said book, and none other or otherwise.

02. And albeit that the same be so godly and good, that they give occasion to every honest and comfortable man most willingly to embrace them, yet lest any obstinate person who willingly would disturb so godly order and quiet in this realm should not go unpunished, that it may also be ordained

and enacted by the authority aforesaid that if any manner of parson, vicar or other whatsoever minister, that ought or should sing or say common prayer mentioned in the said book, or minister the sacraments, shall after the said feast of Pentecost next coming (09 June 1549) refuse to use the said common prayers, or to minister the sacraments in such cathedral or parish church or other places as he should use or minister the same, in such order and form as they be mentioned and set forth in the said book; or shall use, wilfully or obstinately standing in the same, any other rite, ceremony, order, form or manner of Mass openly or privily, or Matins, Evensong, administration of the sacraments, or other open prayer than is mentioned and set forth in the said book (open prayer in and throughout this Act, is meant that prayer which is for other to come unto or hear, either in common churches or private chapels or oratories, commonly called the service of the Church); or shall preach, declare or speak anything in the derogation or depraving of the said book, or anything therein contained, or of any part thereof, and shall be thereof lawfully convicted according to the laws of this realm, by verdict of twelve men, or by his own confession, or by the notorious evidence of the facts, shall lose and forfeit to the King's Highness, his heirs and successors, for his first offence, the profit of such one of his spiritual benefices or promotions as it shall please the King's Highness to assign or appoint, coming and arising in one whole year next after his conviction; and also that the same person so convicted shall for the same offence suffer imprisonment by the space of six months, without bail or mainprize; and if any such person, once convicted of any offence concerning the premises, shall after his first conviction eftsones (i.e. again, *ed.*) offend, and be thereof in form aforesaid lawfully convicted, that then the same person shall for his second offence suffer imprisonment by the space of one whole year, and also shall therefore be deprived *ipso facto* of all his spiritual promotions; and that it shall be lawful to all patrons, donors and grantees of all and singular the same spiritual promotions to present to the same any other able clerk, in like manner and form as though the party so offending were dead; and that if any such person or persons, after he shall be twice convicted in form aforesaid, shall offend against any of the premises the third time shall suffer imprisonment during his life; and if the person that shall offend or be convicted in form aforesaid, concerning any of the premises, shall not be beneficed nor have any spiritual promotion, that then the same person so offending and convicted shall for the first offence suffer imprisonment during six months without bail or mainprize; and that if any such person not having any spiritual promotion after his first conviction shall eftsones offend in anything concerning the premises, and shall in form aforesaid be lawfully convicted, that then the same person shall for his second offence suffer imprisonment during his life.

03. And it is ordained and enacted by the authority abovesaid that if any person or persons whatsoever, after the said feast of Pentecost next coming (09 June 1549), shall in any interludes, plays, songs, rhymes or by other open

words declare or speak anything in the derogation, depraving or despising of the same book or of anything therein contained, or any part thereof, or shall by open fact, deed, or by open threatenings, compel or cause, or otherwise procure or maintain any parson, vicar or other minister in any cathedral or parish church, or in any chapel or other place, to sing or say any common or open prayer, or to minister any sacrament otherwise or in any other manner or form than is mentioned in the said book; or that by any of the said means shall unlawfully interrupt or let (i.e. hinder, *ed.*) any parson, vicar or other ministers in any cathedral or parish church, chapel or any other place, to sing or say common or open prayer, or to minister the sacraments or any of them in any such manner and form as is mentioned in the said book, that then every person being thereof lawfully convicted in form abovesaid shall forfeit to the King our Sovereign Lord, his heirs and successors for the first offence, ten pounds; and if any person or persons, being once convicted of any such offence, eftsones offend against any of the premises and shall in form aforesaid be thereof lawfully convicted, that then the same person so offending and convicted shall for the second offence forfeit to the King our Sovereign Lord, his heirs and successors, twenty pounds; and if any persons, after he in form aforesaid shall be twice convicted of any offence concerning any of the premises, shall offend the third time and be thereof in form lawfully convicted, that then every person so offending and convicted shall for his third offence forfeit to our Sovereign Lord the King all his goods and chattels, and shall suffer imprisonment during his life; and if any person or persons, that for his first offence concerning the premises shall be convicted in form aforesaid, does not pay the sum to be paid by virtue of his conviction in such manner and form as the same ought to be paid, within six weeks next after his conviction, that then every person so convicted and so not paying the same shall for the same first offence, instead of the said ten pounds, suffer imprisonment by the space of three months, without bail or mainprize; and if any person or persons that for his second offence concerning the premises shall be convicted in form aforesaid do not pay the sum to be paid by virtue of his conviction in such manner and form as the same ought to be paid, within six weeks next after his said second conviction, that then every person so convicted and not so paying the same, shall for the same second offence, instead of the said twenty pounds, suffer imprisonment during six months without bail or mainprize.

04. And it is ordained and enacted by the authority aforesaid that all and every justice of *oyer* and *determiner* or justices of assize, shall have full power and authority, in every of their open and general sessions, to inquire, hear and determine all and all manner of offences that shall be committed or done contrary to any article contained in this present Act, within the limit of the commission to them directed, and to make process for the execution of the same as they do against any person being indicted before them of trespass, or lawfully convicted thereof.

05. Provided always and be it enacted by the authority aforesaid, that all and every archbishop and bishop shall or may, at all time and times at his liberty and pleasure, join and associate himself by virtue of this Act to the said justices of *oyer* and *determiner* or to the said justices of assize, at every of the said open and general sessions to be holden in any place within his diocese, for and to the inquiry, hearing and determining of the offence aforesaid.

06. Provided always that it shall be lawful to any man that understandeth the Greek, Latin and Hebrew tongue, or other strange tongue, to say and have the said prayers, heretofore specified, of Matins and Evensong in Latin, or any such other tongue, saying the same privately, as they do understand. And for the further encouraging and learning in the tongues in the Universities of Cambridge and Oxford, to use and exercise in their common and open prayer, the Matins, Evensong, Litany and all other prayers (the Holy Communion, commonly called the Mass, excepted) prescribed in the said book in Greek, Latin or Hebrew, anything in this present Act notwithstanding.

07. Provided also that it shall be lawful for all men, as well in churches, chapels, oratories or other places, to use openly any psalm or prayer taken out of the Bible at any due time, not letting or omitting thereby the Service, or any part thereof mentioned in the said book.

08. Provided also and be it enacted by the authority aforesaid, that the books concerning the said services shall at the costs and charges of the parishioners of every parish and cathedral church be attained and gotten before the feast of Pentecost next following (09 June 1549), or before; and that all such parish and cathedral churches, or other place where the said books shall be attained (i.e. obtained, *ed.*) and gotten before the said feast of Pentecost, shall within three weeks next after the said books so attained and gotten use the said service and put the same in use according to this Act.

09. And be it further enacted by the authority aforesaid, that no person or persons shall be at any time hereafter impeached or otherwise molested of or for any of the offences above mentioned hereafter to be committed or done contrary to this Act, unless he or they so offending be thereof indicted at the next general sessions to be holden before any such justices of *oyer* or *determiner* or justices of assize, next after any offence committed or done contrary to the tenor of this Act.

10. Provided always and be it ordered and enacted by the authority aforesaid that all and singular Lords in the Parliament for the third offence above mentioned shall be tried by their peers.

11. Provided always and be it ordered and enacted by the authority aforesaid that the mayor of London and all other mayors, bailiffs and other head officers, of all and singular cities, boroughs and towns corporate within this realm, Wales, Calais and the marches of the same to the which justices of assize do not commonly repair, shall have full power and authority by virtue of this Act to inquire, hear and determine the offences above said and every of them, yearly within fifteen days after the feasts of Easter and St Michael the Archangel (29 September), in like manner and form as justices of assize and *oyer* and *determiner* may do.

12. Provided always and be it ordained and enacted by the authority aforesaid that all singular archbishops and bishops, and every of their chancellors, commissaries, archdeacons and other ordinaries, having any peculiar ecclesiastical jurisdiction, shall have full power and authority by virtue of this Act as well to inquire in their visitations and synods, and elsewhere within their jurisdiction at any other time or place to take accusations and informations, of all and every the things above mentioned, done, committed or perpetrated within the limits of their jurisdictions and authority, and to punish the same by admonition, excommunication, sequestration or deprivation, or other censures and process, in like form as heretofore hath been used in like cases by the King's ecclesiastical laws.

13. Provided always and be it enacted that whatsoever person offending in the premises shall for the first offence receive punishment of the ordinary, having a testimonial thereof under the said ordinary's seal, shall not for the same offence eftsones be convened before the justices; and likewise receiving for the said first offence punishment by the justices, he shall not for the same offence eftsones receive punishment of the ordinary; anything contained in this Act to the contrary notwithstanding.

26. THE PREFACE TO THE BOOK OF COMMON PRAYER, 1549

History

Fundamental to the work of reformation was the provision of a public liturgy which could teach the new doctrine and incidentally help congregations to worship in their own language. This need was met in the first Book of Common Prayer, which established the principle of uniformity in worship throughout England. The 1549 Book encountered a number of criticisms, most of which suggested that it did not go far enough in reforming the services of the Church, and Archbishop Cranmer produced a radical revision of it in 1552. The intentions of the Book remained much the same however, as the similarity of the Prefaces indicates.

The section **Of Ceremonies** was printed at the end of the 1549 Book but was annexed to the Preface in 1552. Both (in their 1552 form) are now included with the Preface to the 1662 Book.

Theology

The Preface is the most concise and articulate argument in favour of a truly common prayer for all members of the Church of England. It is a defence of the Reformation, particularly in the alterations which were made to the ceremonial practices of the Church, and also a defence of set forms of prayer, on the ground that everything ought to be done decently and in order, with the full knowledge and consent of the congregation.

Concerning the Service of the Church

There was never anything by the wit of man so well devised or so sure established, which in continuance of time hath not been corrupted, as among other things, it may plainly appear by the common prayers in the Church, commonly called Divine Service. The first original and ground whereof if a man would search out by the ancient Fathers, he shall find that the same was not ordained but of a good purpose and for a great advancement of godliness. For they so ordered the matter that the whole Bible (or the greatest part thereof) should be read over once every year; intending thereby that the clergy, and especially such as were ministers in the congregation, should (by often reading and meditation in God's Word) be stirred up to godliness themselves, and be more able to exhort others by wholesome doctrine, and to confute them that were adversaries to the truth; and further that the people (by daily hearing of Holy Scripture read in the Church) might continually profit more and more in the knowledge of God and be the more inflamed with the love of his true religion.

But these many years passed, this godly and decent order of the ancient Fathers hath been so altered, broken and neglected by planting in uncertain stories and legends, with multitude of responds, verses, vain repetitions, commemorations and synodals, that commonly, when any book of the Bible was begun, after three or four chapters were read out, all the rest were unread. And in this sort the Book of Isaiah was begun in Advent and the Book of Genesis in Septuagesima, but they were only begun and never read through; after like sort were other books of Holy Scripture used. And moreover, whereas St Paul would have such language spoken to the people in the Church as they might understand and have profit by hearing the same, the service in this Church of England these many years hath been read in Latin to the people, which they understand not, so that they have heard with their ears only and their heart, spirit and mind have not been edified thereby. And furthermore, notwithstanding that the ancient Fathers have divided the Psalms into seven portions, whereof every one was called a Nocturn; now of late time a few of them have been daily said, and the rest utterly omitted. Moreover, the number and hardness of the rules called the *Pie*, and the manifold changings of the service, was the cause that to turn the book only was so hard and intricate a matter, that many times there was more business to find out what should be read than to read it when it was found out.

These inconveniences therefore considered, here is set forth such an order whereby the same shall be redressed. And for a readiness in this matter, here is drawn out a calendar for that purpose which is plain and easy to be understood, wherein (so much as may be) the reading of Holy Scripture is so set forth that all things shall be done in order without breaking one piece from another. For this cause be cut off anthems, responds, invitatories and such like things as did break the continual course of the reading of the Scripture.

Yet because there is no remedy, but that of necessity there must be some rules, therefore certain rules are here set forth which, as they are few in number, so they are plain and easy to be understood. So that here you have an order for prayer and for the reading of the Holy Scripture much agreeable to the mind and purpose of the old Fathers, and a great deal more profitable and commodious than that which of late was used. It is more profitable because here are left out many things whereof some are untrue, some uncertain, some vain and superstitious, and nothing is ordained to be read but the very pure Word of God, the Holy Scriptures, or that which is agreeable to the same, and that in such a language and order as is most easy and plain for the understanding both of the readers and hearers. It is also more commodious, both for the shortness thereof and for the plainness of the order, and for that the rules be few and easy.

And whereas heretofore there hath been great diversity in saying and singing in churches within this realm, some following Salisbury Use, some Hereford Use, and some the Use of Bangor, some of York, some of Lincoln; now from henceforth all the whole realm shall have but one Use.

And forasmuch as nothing can be so plainly set forth, but doubts may arise in the use and practice of the same; to appease all such diversity (if any arise) and for the resolution of all doubts, concerning the manner how to understand, do and execute the things contained in this Book; the parties that so doubt, or diversely take anything, shall alway resort to the bishop of the diocese, who by his discretion shall take order for the quieting and appeasing of the same; so that the same order be not contrary to anything contained in this book. And if the bishop of the diocese be in doubt, then he may send for the resolution thereof to the bishop.

Though it be appointed that all things shall be read and sung in the church in the English tongue, to the end that the congregation may be thereby edified, yet it is not meant but that when men say Morning and Evening Prayer privately, they may say the same in any language that they themselves do understand.

1549 version:

Neither that any man shall be bound to the saying of them, but such as from time to time in cathedral and collegiate churches, and chapels to the same annexed, shall serve the congregation.

1552 version:

And all priests and deacons are to say daily the Morning and Evening Prayer either privately or openly, not being let by sickness or some other urgent cause.

And the curate that ministereth in every parish church or chapel, being at home and not being otherwise reasonably hindered, shall say the same in the parish church or chapel where he ministereth, and shall cause a bell to be tolled thereunto a convenient time before he begin, that the people may come to hear God's Word and to pray with him.

Of Ceremonies, why some be abolished and some retained

Of such ceremonies as be used in the church and have had their beginning by the institution of man, some at the first were of godly intent and purpose devised, and yet at length turned to vanity and superstition; some entered the church by undiscreet devotion, and such a zeal as was without knowledge, and for because they were winked at in the beginning, they grew daily to more and more abuses, which not only for their unprofitableness but also because they have much blinded the people and obscured the glory of God, are worthy to be cut away and clean rejected; other there be which, although they have been devised by man, yet it is thought good to reserve them still, as well for a decent order in the church (for the which they were first devised) as because they pertain to edification, whereunto all things done in the church (as the Apostle teacheth) ought to be referred.

And although the keeping or omitting of a ceremony, in itself considered, is but a small thing, yet the wilful and contemptuous transgression and breaking of a common order and discipline is no small offence before God, *Let all things be done among you*, saith Saint Paul, *in a seemly and due order*; the appointment of the which order pertaineth not to private men, therefore no man ought to take in hand, nor presume to appoint or alter any public or common order in Christ's Church, except he be lawfully called and authorized thereunto.

And whereas in this our time the minds of men are so diverse that some think it a great matter of conscience to depart from a piece of the least of their ceremonies, they be so addicted to their old customs; and again on the other side, some be so new-fangled that they would innovate all things and so despise the old that nothing can like them, but that is new; it was thought expedient, not so much to have respect how to please and satisfy either of these parties, as how to please God and profit them both. And yet lest any man should be offended, whom good reason might satisfy, here be certain causes rendered, why some of the accustomed ceremonies be put away and some retained and kept still.

Some are put away because the great excess and multitude of them hath so increased in these latter days that the burden of them was intolerable; whereof Saint Augustine in his time complained that they were grown to such a number that the estate of Christian people was in worse case concerning that matter than were the Jews. And he counselled that such yoke and burden should be taken away as time would serve quietly to do it. But what would Saint Augustine have said if he had seen the ceremonies of late days used among us, whereunto the multitude used in his time was not to be compared? This our excessive multitude of ceremonies was so great and many of them so dark that they did more confound and darken than declare and set forth Christ's benefits unto us. And besides this, Christ's Gospel is not a ceremonial law (as much of Moses' law was), but it is a religion to serve God, not in bondage of the figure or shadow but in the freedom of the Spirit, being content only with those ceremonies which do serve to a decent order and godly discipline and such as be apt to stir up the dull mind of man to the remembrance of his duty to God, by some notable and special signification whereby he might be edified. Furthermore, the most weighty cause of the abolishment of certain ceremonies was that they were so far abused, partly by the superstitious blindness of the rude and unlearned and partly by the unsatiable avarice of such as sought more their own lucre than the glory of God, that the abuses could not well be taken away, the thing remaining still.

But now as concerning those persons which peradventure will be offended for that some of the old ceremonies are retained still; if they consider that without some ceremonies it is not possible to keep any order or quiet discipline in the church, they shall easily perceive just cause to reform their judgements. And if they think much that any of the old do remain and would rather have all devised anew, then such men granting some ceremonies convenient to be had, surely where the old may be well used, there they cannot reasonably reprove the old only for their age without bewraying of their own folly. For in such a case they ought rather to have reverence unto them for their antiquity, if they will declare themselves to be more studious of unity and concord than of innovations and new-fangledness, which (as much as may be with the true setting forth of Christ's religion) is always to be eschewed. Furthermore, such shall have no just cause with the ceremonies reserved to be offended. For as those be taken away which were most abused and did burden men's consciences without a cause, so the other that remain are retained for a discipline and order which (upon just causes) may be altered and changed, and therefore are not to be esteemed equal with God's law. And moreover, they be neither dark nor dumb ceremonies but are so set forth that every man may understand what they do mean, and to what use they do serve. So that it is not like that they in time to come should be abused as other have been. And in these our doings we condemn no other nations, nor prescribe anything but to our own people only; for we think it convenient that every country should use ceremonies as they shall think best to the setting forth of God's honour and glory and to the reducing of the people to a most perfect and godly living, without error or superstition; and that they should put away other things which from time to time they perceive to be most abused, as in men's ordinances it often chanceth diversely in divers countries.

27. THE PREFACE TO THE ORDINAL, 1549

History

As the Church of England developed its vernacular liturgy, it became necessary to provide a series of services for the ordination of bishops, priests and deacons. Appended to the Book of Common Prayer, these services, known collectively as the Ordinal, are one of the basic formularies of the Church, along with the Prayer Book, the Homilies and the Articles of Religion. The Ordinal itself was substantially modified in 1552, though the Preface was left unchanged. On the other hand, the 1662 Preface is somewhat different, whilst the services themselves are close to those of 1552.

Theology

The theology of the Ordinal, much of which is contained in the Preface, has been of major importance in the history of Anglicanism. The assertion is made that the threefold order of bishops, priests and deacons is both biblical and patristic in origin, and in the 1662 version, recognition is refused to ministers who have not been ordained by a bishop. This requirement was not strictly observed in the seventeenth century, as can be seen by the admission of Huguenot ministers to the Church of England without reordination, but that is no longer the case. In the twentieth century insistence on this rule has often prevented the reunion of Anglican with other Protestant Churches, and in some cases, notably that of the Church of South India (1947), has prevented the full recognition of ministerial order by the Anglican Communion.

N.B. In this edition, the 1549 text is combined with that of 1662. Words present in the former but dropped in the latter are in italics; words absent in the former but added to the latter are in bold type.

It is evident unto all men diligently reading Holy Scripture and ancient authors, that from the Apostles' time there *hath* **have** been these orders of ministers in Christ's Church – bishops, priests and deacons. Which offices were evermore had in such reverend estimation that no man *by his own private authority* might presume to execute any of them, except that he were first called, tried, examined and known to have such *equalities* **qualities** as *were* **are** requisite for the same; and also by public prayer, with imposition of hands, **were** approved and admitted thereunto **by lawful authority**. And therefore, to the intent that these orders may be continued and reverently used and esteemed in *this* **the** Church of England, *it is requisite that* no man (*not being at this present bishop, priest nor deacon*) shall *execute any of them* **be accounted or taken to be a lawful bishop, priest or deacon in the Church of England, or suffered to execute any of the said functions,** except he be called, tried, examined and admitted **thereunto,** according to the form hereafter following, **or hath had formerly episcopal consecration or ordination.**

And none shall be admitted a deacon, except he be *twenty-one* **full twenty-three** years of age *at the least* **unless he have a faculty.** And every man which is to be admitted a priest shall be full twenty-four years *old* **of age, unless being over twenty-three years of age, he have a faculty.** And every man which is to be ordained or consecrated bishop shall be *fully* **full** thirty years of age.

And the bishop, knowing either by himself or by sufficient testimony, any person to be a *man* **person** of virtuous conversation and without crime, and after examination and trial finding him *learned in the Latin tongue* **to possess the qualifications required by law** and sufficiently instructed in Holy Scripture, *may upon a Sunday or holiday* **on the Sundays immediately following the ember weeks* or on the feast of St Michael and All Angels (29 September), or of St Thomas the Apostle (21 December) or on such other days as shall be provided by Canon** in the face of the Church, admit him a deacon in such manner and form as hereafter followeth.

---

* The third Sunday in Advent, the second Sunday in Lent, the Sunday following St Peter's Day (29 June) and the Sunday following St Michael and All Angels (29 September).

28. ACT TO TAKE AWAY
ALL POSITIVE LAWS AGAINST THE
MARRIAGE OF PRIESTS
(2-3 Edward VI, c. 21)

History

The marriage of priests had been disapproved of in the Western Church at least since the time of Pope Gregory I (590-604) but it had not been finally outlawed until 1123. After the Reformation in Germany, Martin Luther declared that Roman legislation against clerical marriage was unbiblical, and he himself took a wife. This provoked considerable opposition from the laity, partly because it went against popular feeling, but more because it was seen as a breach of the vow of celibacy which all monks, nuns and secular clergy were obliged to take.

In England, clerical marriage came in by stealth, with the Archbishop of Canterbury, Thomas Cranmer, among the "offenders". However, Henry VIII would not accept it, and in 1539 Cranmer and the other married clergy were obliged to forgo their wives. After the accession of Edward VI this situation could be legally altered, but clerical marriage continued to seem an anomaly to many people. Convocation approved of it in December 1547, as did the House of Commons, but because of opposition in the Lords it was not until February 1549 that Parliament enacted this legislation. This statute was repealed by Mary I in 1553 and was not reinstated by Elizabeth I, who also disapproved of married clergy. However, she was forced to make some provision for them, and did so in the twenty-ninth of her Injunctions.

The provisions of this Act were not reinstated in statute law until 1603, since when clerical marriage has been generally accepted within the Church of England.

01. Although it were not only better for the estimation of priests and other ministers in the Church of God, to live chaste, sole and separate from the company of women and the bond of marriage, but also thereby they might the better intend to the administration of the Gospel, and be less intricated and troubled with the charge of household, being free and unburdened from the care and cost of finding wife and children, and that it were most to be wished that they would willingly and of theirselves endeavour themselves to a perpetual chastity and abstinence from the use of women:

Yet forasmuch as the contrary has rather been seen, and such uncleanness of living and other great inconveniences not meet to be rehearsed, have followed of compelled chastity, and of such laws as have prohibited those (such persons) the godly use of marriage; it were better and rather to be suffered in the commonwealth that those which could not contain, should after the counsel of Scripture, live in holy marriage, than feignedly abuse with worse enormity outward chastity or single life:

Be it therefore enacted by our sovereign lord the king, with the assent of the Lords spiritual and temporal, and the Commons in this present Parliament assembled, and by the authority of the same, that all and every law and laws positive, canons, constitutions and ordinances heretofore made by the authority of man only, which do prohibit or forbid marriage to any ecclesiastical or spiritual person or persons, of what estate, condition or degree they be, or by what name or names soever they be called, which by God's law may lawfully marry, in all and every article, branch, and sentence, concerning only the prohibition for the marriage of the persons aforesaid, shall be utterly void and of none effect; and that all manner of forfeitures, pains, penalties, crimes or actions which were in the said laws contained, and the same did follow, concerning the prohibition for the marriage of the persons aforesaid, be clearly and utterly void, frustrate and of none effect, to all intents, constructions and purposes, as well concerning marriages heretofore made by any of the ecclesiastical or spiritual persons aforesaid, as also such which hereafter shall be duly and lawfully had, celebrated and made betwixt the persons which by the laws of God may lawfully marry.

02. Provided alway, and be it enacted by the authority aforesaid, that this Act, or anything therein contained, shall not extend to give liberty to any person to marry without asking in the church, or without any other ceremony being appointed by the order prescribed and set forth in the book entitled, *The Book of Common Prayer and Administration of the Sacraments*, anything above mentioned to the contrary in any wise notwithstanding.

03. Provided also, and be it enacted by the authority aforesaid, that this Act, or anything therein contained, shall not extend to alter, change, revoke, repeal or otherwise to disannul any decree, judgement, sentence or divorce heretofore had or made, but that all and every such decree, judgement, sentence and divorce shall remain and be of such like force, effect, strength and degree, to all intents, constructions and purposes as they were in before the making of this Act, and as though this Act had never been had nor made; this Act or anything therein contained to the contrary in any wise notwithstanding.

29. THE ACT OF UNIFORMITY 1552
(5 and 6 Edward VI c. 1)

History
This Act became law on All Saints' Day (01 November) 1552, but was repealed by Mary I on 20 December 1553.

Theology
This Act introduced the Second Prayer Book of Edward VI, which was a much more Protestant form of worship than the 1549 Book had been. After being suppressed under Mary I, the Book was slightly modified in 1559, and again in 1662, since when it has remained the official Prayer Book of the Church of England. The Act is also noteworthy for the fact that it compelled weekly Church attendance for the first time, a feature which was to be retained in the 1559 Act of Uniformity.

01. Where there hath been a very godly order set forth by authority of Parliament for common prayer and administration of the sacraments, to be used in the mother tongue within the Church of England, agreeable to the Word of God and the primitive Church, very comfortable to all good people desiring to live in Christian conversation and most profitable to the estate of this realm, upon the which the mercy, favour and blessing of Almighty God is in no wise so readily and plenteously poured as by common prayers, due using of the sacraments and often preaching of the Gospel with the devotion of the hearers:

And this notwithstanding, a great number of people in divers parts of this realm, following their own sensuality and living either without knowledge or due fear of God, do wilfully and damnably before Almighty God abstain and refuse to come to their parish churches and other places where common prayer, administration of the sacraments and preaching of the Word of God is used upon the Sundays and other days ordained to be holy days.

For reformation hereof, be it enacted by the King our Sovereign Lord, with the assent of the Lords and Commons in this present Parliament assembled and by the authority of the same, that from and after the feast of All Saints next coming (01 November 1552), all and every person and persons inhabiting within this realm, or any other the King's Majesty's dominions shall diligently and faithfully, having no lawful or reasonable excuse to be absent, endeavour themselves to resort to their parish church or chapel accustomed, or upon reasonable let [i.e. hindrance, *ed.*] thereof, to some usual place where common prayer and such service of God shall be used in such time of let, upon every Sunday, and other days ordained and used to be kept as holy days, and then and there to abide orderly and soberly during the time of the common prayer, preachings, or other service of God there to be used and ministered, upon pain of punishment by the censures of the Church.

02. And for the due execution hereof, the King's most excellent Majesty, the Lords temporal and all the Commons in this present (Parliament) assembled, doth in God's name earnestly require and charge all the archbishops, bishops and other ordinaries, that they shall endeavour themselves to the uttermost of their knowledge, that the due and true execution hereof may be had throughout their dioceses and charges, as they will answer before God for such evils and plagues wherewith Almighty God may justly punish his people for neglecting this good and wholesome law.

03. And for their authority in this behalf be it further likewise enacted by the authority aforesaid that all and singular the same archbishops, bishops and all other their officers exercising ecclesiastical jurisdiction as well in place exempt as not exempt within their dioceses, shall have full power and authority by this Act to reform, correct and punish by censures of the Church, all and singular persons which shall offend, within any of their jurisdictions or dioceses, after the said feast of All Saints next coming (01 November 1552) against this Act and Statute; any other law, statute, privilege, liberty or provision heretofore made, had or suffered to the contrary notwith-standing.

04. And because there hath arisen in the use and exercise of this aforesaid common service in the Church, heretofore set forth, divers doubts for the fashion and manner of the ministration of the same, rather by the curiosity of the minister, and mistakers, than of any other worthy cause:

Therefore, as well for the more plain and manifest explanation hereof, as for the more perfection of the said order of common service, in some places where it is necessary to make the same prayers and fashion of service more earnest and fit to stir Christian people to the true honouring of Almighty God, the King's most excellent Majesty, with the assent of the Lords and Commons in this present Parliament assembled, and by the authority of the same, hath caused the foresaid order of common service, entitled The Book of Common Prayer, to be faithfully and godly perused, explained and made fully perfect, and by the foresaid authority hath annexed and joined it, so explained and perfected, to this present Statute: adding also a form and manner of making and consecrating archbishops, bishops, priests and deacons, to be of like force, authority and value as the same like aforesaid book, entitled, The Book of Common Prayer, was before, and to be accepted, received, used and esteemed in like sort and manner, and with the same clauses of provisions and exceptions, to all intents, constructions and purposes as by the Act of Parliament made in the second year of the King's Majesty's reign was ordained and limited, expressed and appointed for the uniformity of service and administration of the sacraments throughout the realm, upon such several pains as in the said Act of Parliament is expressed.

And the said former Act to stand in full force and strength, to all intents and constructions, and to be applied, practised and put in use to and for the establishing of the Book of Common Prayer, now explained and hereunto annexed, and also the said form of making of archbishops, bishops, priests and deacons hereunto annexed as it was for the former book.

05. And by the authority aforesaid it is now further enacted that if any manner of person or persons inhabiting and being within this realm, or any other the King's Majesty's dominions, shall after the said feast of All Saints (01 November 1552) willingly and wittingly hear and be present at any other manner or form of common prayer, of administration of the sacraments, of making of ministers in the churches, or of any other rites contained in the book annexed to this Act, than is mentioned and set forth in the said book, or that is contrary to the form of sundry provisions and exceptions contained in the foresaid former Statute, and shall be thereof convicted according to the laws of this realm, before the justices of assize, justices of *oyer* and *determiner*, justices of peace in their sessions, or any of them, by the verdict of twelve men, or by his or their own confession or otherwise, shall for the first offence suffer imprisonment for six months, without bail or mainprize, and for the second offence, being likewise convicted as is abovesaid, imprisonment for one whole year; and for the third offence, imprisonment during his or their lives.

06. And for the more knowledge to be given hereof, and better observation of this law, be it enacted by the authority aforesaid, that all and singular curates shall upon one Sunday every quarter of the year during one whole year next following the foresaid feast of All Saints next coming (01 November 1552), read this present Act in the church at the time of the most assembly, and likewise once in every year following; at the same time declaring unto the people, by the authority of the Scripture, how the mercy and goodness of God hath in all ages been showed to his people in their necessities and extremities, by means of hearty and faithful prayers made to Almighty God, especially where people be gathered together with one faith and mind, to offer up their hearts by prayer, as the best sacrifices that Christian men can yield.

30. THE FORTY-TWO ARTICLES, 1553
THE THIRTY-EIGHT ARTICLES, 1563
THE THIRTY-NINE ARTICLES, 1571

History

The Forty-two Articles of Religion were composed by Archbishop Cranmer after considerable discussion and debate, which reached back into the early years of the reign of Edward VI. In their final form, they were promulgated on 19 June 1553, and clergy were instructed to subscribe to them. However, the sudden death of the King on 06 July 1553 meant that this instruction was never carried out, and the Articles were dropped. They were reintroduced in a revised form in 1563 (1562 by the Old Style), and again in 1571, with further instructions that the clergy must subscribe to them. The 1571 revision remains an official doctrinal statement of the Church of England, and is printed in editions of the Book of Common Prayer (1662).

Theology

The theology of the Articles is uncompromisingly Protestant, and even Calvinist in tone. When Cranmer produced the 1553 edition, it was the most advanced systematization of Protestant theology then in existence anywhere. The 1563 revision removed some articles which were felt to be no longer matters of controversy, and clarified various points in several others. At the last minute Article 29 (in the 1571 revision) was omitted, because it was thought that it would offend Lutherans, with their doctrine of consubstantiation. By 1571 the prospect of union with the Lutheran churches had faded, and the Article was reinstated. The Protestant character of the Articles was challenged by John Henry Newman in his notorious Tract XC (1841), but the strong reaction to his thesis played a major part in his departure from the Church of England four years later. Since that time, the Articles have been regarded as one of the principal bulwarks of Protestantism within the Church.

N.B. For this edition, the following procedure has been adopted:

1. The Latin text of 1553 is printed alongside the English text. All spellings have been modernized.

2. Portions of the 1553 text which were deleted in 1563 and 1571 are indicated in bold type.

3. Additions which were made to the 1563 and 1571 texts are indicated in parentheses.

4. Where the numbering of the Articles differs in 1563 and/or 1571, this is indicated

in parentheses. Where the number refers only to the revision of 1571, it is underlined.

Occasionally it will be noticed that changes were made to the English text (and less frequently to the Latin) without affecting the other language. When an Article presents special features not covered by the above provisions, a note is appended to it to explain them.

Articuli de guibus in synodo Londineusi Anno Domini MDLII ad tollendam opinionum dissensionem et consensum verae religionis firmandum, inter episcopos et alios eruditos viros convenerat.

Articles agreed upon by the bishops and other learned men in the synod at London, in the year of our Lord God MDLII (1552) for the avoiding of controversy in opinions and the establishment of a godly concord in certain matters of religion.

(Articuli de guibus in synodo Londinensi Anno Domini, iuxta ecclesiae Anglicanae computationem, MDLXII, ad tollendam opinionum dissensionem, et firmandum in vera religione consensum, inter archiepiscopos episcoposque utriusque provinciae, nec non etiam universum clerum conveniti).

(Articles whereupon it was agreed by the archbishops and bishops of both provinces and the whole cleargy, in the convocation holden at London in the year of our Lord God 1562, according to the computation of the Church of England, for the avoiding of the diversities of opinions, and for the stablishing of consent touching true religion).

01. *De fide in sacrosanctam Trinitatem*

01. *Of Faith in the Holy Trinity*

Unus est vivus et verus Deus, aeternus, incorporeus, impartibilis, impassibilis, immensae potentiae, sapientiae, ac bonitatis, creator et conservator omnium, tum visibilium tum invisibilium. Et in unitate huius divinae naturae tres sunt personae, eiusdem essentiae, potentiae, ac aeternitatis. Pater, Filius et Spiritus Sanctus.

There is but one living and true God, everlasting, without body, parts or passions, of infinite power, wisdom and goodness, the maker and preserver of all things both visible and invisible. And in Unity of this Godhead there be three persons, of one substance, power and eternity, the Father, the Son and the Holy Ghost.

02. *Verbum Dei, verum hominem esse factum.*

02. *That (Of) the Word or Son of God, which was made Very Man*

Filius qui est Verbum Patris, (ab aeterno a Patre genitus verus et aeter-

The Son, which is the Word of the Father, (begotten from everlasting of

nus Deus, ac Patri consubstantialis), in utero Beatae Virginis ex illius substantia naturam humanam assumpsit: ita ut duae naturae, divina et humana, integre atque perfecte in unitate personae, fuerint insepara- biliter coniunctae: ex quibus est unus Christus, verus Deus et verus Homo: qui vere passus est, crucifixus, mortuus et sepultus, ut Patrem nobis reconciliaret, essetque hostia non tantum pro culpa originis, verum etiam pro omnibus actualibus hominum peccatis.[1]

the Father, the very and eternal God, of one substance with the Father), took man's nature in the womb of the Blessed Virgin, of her substance: so that two whole and perfect natures, that is to say the Godhead and manhood, were joined together in one Person, never to be divided, whereof is one Christ, very God and very Man, who truly suffered, was crucified, dead and buried, to reconcile his Father to us and to be a sacrifice **for all sin of man, both original and actual** (not only for original guilt but also for all actual sins of men).

03. De descensu Christi ad inferos

03. Of the going down of Christ into Hell

Quemadmodum Christus pro nobis mortuus est et sepultus, ita est etiam credendus ad inferos descendisse. **Non corpus usque ad resurr- ectionem in sepulchro iacuit, Spir- itus ab illo emissus, cum spiritibus qui in carcere sive in inferno detinebantur fuit, illisque prae- dicavit, quemadmodum testatur Petri locus.**

As Christ died **and was buried for us** (for us, and was buried), so also it is to be believed, that he went down into hell. **For the body lay in the sepulchre until the resur- rection, but his Ghost departing from him, was with the ghosts that were in prison, or in Hell, and did preach to the same, as the place of St Peter doth testify.**

04. Resurrectio Christi

04. (Of) the Resurrection of Christ

Christus vere a mortuis resurrexit suumque corpus cum carne, ossibus, omnibusque ad integritatem hum- anae naturae pertinentibus, recepit, cum quibus in caelum ascendit, ibique residet, quoad extremo die ad iudicandos homines **revertatur** (reversurus sit).

Christ did truly arise again from death, and took again his body, with flesh, bones and all things apper- taining to the perfection of man's nature, wherewith he ascended into heaven, and there sitteth, until he return to judge (all) men at the last day.

---

[1] The Latin text of the last phrase in this Article is the same in both versions; only the English translation was altered, to make it more accurate.

(05. De Spiritu Sancto)

(Spiritus Sanctus a Patre et Filio procedens, eiusdem est cum Patre et Filio essentiae, maiestatis, et gloriae verus ac aeternus Deus).

05. (06) *Divinae Scripturae doctrina sufficit ad salutem*

Scriptura sacra continet omnia quae sunt ad salutem necessaria, ita ut quicquid in ea nec legitur neque inde probari potest, **licet interdum a fidelibus, ut pium et conducibile ad ordinem et decorum admittatur, attamen a quoquam non exigendum est,** (non sit a quoquam exigendum), ut tanquam articulis fidei credatur, et ad **salutis** necessitatem (salutis) requiri putetur.

(Sacrae Scripturae nomine eos Canonicos libros Veteris et Novi Testamenti intelligimus, de quorum auctoritate in Ecclesia nunquam dubitandum est.

Catalogus librorum sacrae canonicae Scripturae Veteris Testamenti (1563)
  Genesis
  Exodus
  Leviticus
  Numeri
  Deuteronomium
  Iosue
  Iudicum
  Ruth
  2 Samuelis

(05. Of the Holy Ghost)

(The Holy Ghost, proceeding from the Father and the Son, is of one substance, majesty and glory with the Father and the Son, very and eternal God).

05. The Doctrine of Holy Scripture is sufficient to Salvation
(06. *Of the Sufficiency of the Holy Scriptures for Salvation*)

Holy Scripture containeth all things necessary to salvation: so that whatsoever is **neither** (not) read therein, nor may be proved thereby, **although it be sometime received of the faithful, as godly and profitable for an order and comeliness: yet no man ought to be constrained to believe it** (is not to be required of any man, that it should be believed) as an article of the faith, **or repute it** (or be thought) requisite **to the necessity of** (as necessary to) salvation.

(In the name of Holy Scripture we do understand those canonical books of the Old and New Testament, of whose authority was never any doubt in the Church.

Of the names and number of the Canonical Books (1571)
  Genesis
  Exodus
  Leviticus
  Numbers
  Deuteronomy
  Joshua
  Judges
  Ruth
  The first book of Samuel

	The second book of Samuel
2 Regum	The first book of Kings
	The second book of Kings
2 Paralipomenon	The first book of Chronicles
	The second book of Chronicles
2 Esdrae	The first book of Esdras (Ezra)
	The second book of Esdras (Nehemiah)
Hester	Esther
Iob	Job
Psalmi	Psalms
Proverbia	Proverbs
Ecclesiastes	Ecclesiastes
Cantica	Song of Solomon
Prophetae maiores	4 Prophets the greater
Prophetae minores	12 Prophets the less

Alios autem libros, ut ait Hieronymus, legit quidem Ecclesia ad exempla virae et formandos mores, illos tamen ad dogmata confirmanda non adhibet, ut sunt:

And the other books as Hierome (Jerome) saith, the Church doth read for example of life and instruction of manners, but yet doth it not apply them to establish any doctrine. Such are these following:

Tertius et quartus Esdrae	The third book of Esdras
	The fourth book of Esdra
Tobias	Tobias (Tobit)
Iudith	Judith
	The rest of the book of Esther
Sapientia	Wisdom
Iesus filius Sirach	Jesus the son of Sirach
	Baruch
	Song of the Three Children
	Susanna
	Bel and the Dragon
	Prayer of Manasses
Libri Machabaeorum 2	The first book of Maccabees
	The second book of Maccabees

Novi Testamenti libros omnes, ut vulgo recepti sunt, recipimus et habemus pro canonicis.)

All the books of the New Testament as they are commonly received, we do receive and account them for canonical.)

06. *(07) Vetus Testamentum **non est reiiciendum**[1]*

06. *(07) Of the Old Testament **is not to be refused**[1]*

---

[1] Though this Article was substantially rewritten in 1563, a good deal of the original phrasing was retained. This has been underlined here for purposes of comparison.

Testamentum Vetus, quasi Novo contrarium sit, non est repudiandum, sed retinendum, quandoquidem tam in veteri quam in novo per Christum qui unicus est Mediator Dei et hominum, Deus et homo, aeterna vita humano generi est proposita. Quare non sunt audienda, qui veteres tantum in promissiones temporarias sperasse confingunt.

(Testamentum Vetus Novo contrarium non est, quandoquidem tam in veteri quam novo, per Christum, qui unicus est Mediator Dei et hominum, Deus et homo, aeterna vita humano generi est proposita. Quare male sentiunt, qui veteres tantum in promissiones temporarias sperasse confingunt. Quamquam Lex a Deo datur per Mosen, quoad ceremonias et ritus, Christianos non astringat, neque civilia eius praecepta in aliqua Republica necessario recipi debeant, nihilominus tamen ab oboedientia mandatorum, quae Moralia vocantur, nullus quantumvis Christianus est solutus.)

07. *(08) Symbola tria*

Symbola tria, Niceni, Athanasii, et quod vulgo Apostolorum appellatur, omnino recipienda sunt (et credenda). Nam firmissimis divinarum Scripturarum testimoniis probari sunt.

08. *(09) Peccatum originale*

Peccatum originis non est, ut fabul-

The Old Testament is not to be put away as though it were contrary to the New, but to be kept still: for both in the old and new Testaments, everlasting life is offered to mankind by Christ, who is the only mediator between God and man, being both God and man. Wherefore they are not to be heard, which feign that the old Fathers did look only for transitory promises.

(The Old Testament is not contrary to the New, for both in the old and new Testament everlasting life is offered to mankind by Christ, who is the only Mediator between God and man, being both God and man. Wherefore they are not to be heard which feign that the old Fathers did look only for transitory promises. Although the law given from God by Moses, as touching ceremonies and rites, do not bind Christian men, nor the civil precepts thereof, ought of necessity to be received in any commonwealth; yet notwithstanding, no Christian man whatsoever is free from the obedience of the commandments which are called Moral.)

07. *(08) (Of) the Three Creeds*

The three Creeds, Nicene Creed, Athanasius' Creed, and that which is commonly called the Apostles' Creed, ought throughly to be received (and believed), for they may be proved by most certain warrants of Holy Scripture.

08. *(09) Of Original, or Birth Sin*

Original sin standeth not in the fol–

antur Pelagiani **et hodie Anabaptistae repetunt,** in imitatione Adami situm, sed est vitium et depravatio naturae cuiuslibet hominis ex Adamo naturaliter propagati, qua fit ut ab originali iustitia quam longissime distet, ad malum sua natura propendeat et caro semper adversus spiritum concupiscat; unde in unoquoque nascentium, iram Dei et damnationem meretur. Manet etiam in renatis haec naturae depravatio, qua fit ut affectus carnis, Graece phronema sarkos, quod alii sapientiam, alii sensum, alii affectum, alii studium **vocant** (interpretantur), legi Dei non subiiciatur. Et quamquam renatis et credentibus nulla propter Christum est condemnatio, peccati tamen in sese rationem habere concupiscentiam fatetur Apostolus.

lowing of Adam, as the Pelagians do vainly talk, **which also the Anabaptists do nowadays renew,** but it is the fault and corruption of the nature of every man, that naturally is engendered of the offspring of Adam, whereby man is very far gone from **his former** (original) righteousness, **which he had at his creation** and is of his own nature **given** (enclined) to evil, so that the flesh **desireth** (lusteth) always contrary to the spirit, and therefore in every person born into this world, it deserveth God's wrath and damnation. And this infection of nature doth remain, yea in them that are **baptized** (regenerated), whereby the lust of the flesh, called in Greek phronema sarkos, which some do expound the wisdom, some sensuality, some the affection, and some the desire of the flesh, is not subject to the Law of God. And although there is no condemnation for them that believe and are baptized, yet the Apostle doth confess that concupiscence and lust hath of itself the nature of sin.

09. *(10) De libero arbitrio*

(Ea est hominis post lapsum Adae conditio, ut sese naturalibus suis viribus et bonis operibus ad fidem et invocationem Dei convertere ac praeparare non possit, quare) absque gratia Dei, quae per Christum est, nos praeveniente, ut velimus, et co-operante dum volumus, ad pietatis opera facienda, quae Deo grata sint et accepta, nihil valemus.

09. *(10) Of Free Will*

(The condition of man after the fall of Adam is such that he cannot turn and prepare himself by his own natural strength and good works to faith and calling upon God; wherefore) we have no power to do good works pleasant and acceptable to God, without the grace of God by Christ preventing us, that we may have a good will, and working in (with) us, when we have that good will.

10. *De gratia*

Gratia Christi, seu Spiritus Sanctus, qui per eum datur, cor lapideum aufert et dat cor carneum. Atque licet ex nolentibus quae recta sunt volentes faciat, et ex colentibus prava, nolentes reddat, voluntati nihilominus violentiam nullam infert. Et nemo hac de causa, cum peccaverit, seipsum excusare potest, quasi nolens aut coactus peccaverit, ut eam ob causam accusari non mereatur aut damnari.

11. *De hominis iustificatione*[1]

Iustificatio ex sola fide Iesu Christi, eo sensu quo in Homelia de iustificatione explicatur, est certissima et saluberrima Christianorum doctrina.
(Tantum propter meritum Domini ac Servatoris nostri Iesu Christi per fidem, non propter opera et merita nostra, iusti coram Deo reputamur; quare <u>sola fide</u> nos iustificari, <u>doctrina est saluberrima</u>, ac consolationis plenissima, ut <u>in Homelia de iustificatione</u> hominis fusius <u>explicatur</u>.)

(12. *De bonis operibus*)

(Bona opera quae sunt fructus fidei et iustificatos sequuntur, quamquam peccata nostra expiari et divini iudicii severitatem ferre non possunt, Deo tamen grata sunt et accepta in Christo, atque ex vera et viva fide

10. *Of Grace*

The Grace of Christ, of the Holy Ghost by him given, doth take away the stony heart and giveth an heart of flesh. And although those that have no will to good things, he maketh them to will, and those that would evil things, he maketh them not to will the same; yet nevertheless he enforceth not the will. And therefore no man when he sinneth can excuse himself, as not worthy to be blamed or condemned, by alleging that he sinned unwillingly or under compulsion.

11. *Of the Justification of Man*[1]

Justification by only faith in Jesus Christ, in that sense, as is declared in the Homily of Justification, is a most certain and wholesome doctrine for Christian men.
(We are accounted righteous before God only for the merit of our Lord and Saviour Jesus Christ by faith, and not for our own works or deservings. Wherefore, that we are justified <u>by faith only</u>, is a <u>most wholesome doctrine,</u> and very full of comfort, as more largely is expressed <u>in the Homily of Justification</u>.)

(12. *Of Good Works*)

(Albeit that good works, which are the fruits of faith, and follow after justification, cannot put away our sins, and endure the severity of God's judgement; yet are they pleasing and acceptable to God in

---

[1] Words underlined in the 1563 text have been taken over from 1553.

necessario profluunt, ut plane ex illis, aeque fides viva cognosci possit, atque arbor ex fructu iudicari.)

Christ, and do spring out necessarily of a true and lively faith, in so much that by them a lively faith may be as evidently known, as a tree discerned by the fruit.)

12. *(13) Opera ante iustificationem*

Opera quae fiunt ante gratiam Christi, et Spiritus eius afflatum, cum ex fide Iesu Christi non prodeant, minime Deo grata sunt. Neque gratiam, ut multa vocant, de congruo merentur; imo cum non sint facta ut Deus illa fieri voluit et praecepit, peccati rationem habere non dubitamus.

12. *(13) (Of) Works before Justification*

Works done before the grace of Christ, and the inspiration of his Spirit, are not pleasant to God, forasmuch as they spring not of faith in Jesu Christ, neither do they make men meet to receive grace, or as the School authors say, deserve grace of congruity; **but because** (yet rather for that) they are not done as God hath willed and commanded them to be done, we doubt not but they have the nature of sin.

13. *(14) Opera supererogationis*

Opera quae supererogationis appellant, non possunt sine arrogantia et impietate praedicari, nam illis declarant homines non tantum se Deo reddere quae tenentur, sed plus in eius gratiam facere quam deberent; cum aperte Christus dicat: "Cum feceritis omnia quaecunque praecepta sunt vobis, dicite: Servi inutiles sumus".

13. *(14) (Of) Works of Supererogation*

Voluntary works besides, over and above God's commandments, which they call works of supererogation, cannot be taught without arrogance and **iniquity** (impiety). For by them men do declare that they do not only render unto God as much as they are bound to do, but that they do more for his sake than of bounden duty is required; whereas Christ saith plainly: "When ye have done all that are commanded (to) you, say: We be unprofitable servants".

14. *(15) Nemo praeter Christum est sine peccato*

Christus in nostrae naturae veritate

14. *No man is without sin, but Christ alone*
(15. *Of Christ alone without Sin*)

Christ in the truth of our nature, was

per omnia similis factus est nobis, excepto peccato, a quo prorsus erat immunis, tum in carne tum in spiritu. Venit, ut agnus absque macula esset, qui mundi peccata per immolationem sui semel factam, tolleret; et peccatum, ut inquit Ioannes, in eo non erat. Sed nos reliqui, etiam baptizati, et in Christo regenerati, in multis tamen offendimus omnes; et si dixerimus quia peccatum non habemus, nos ipsos seducimus, et veritas in nobis non est.

made like unto us in all things, sin only except, from which he was clearly void, both in his flesh and in his spirit. He came to be the lamb without spot, who by the sacrifice of himself once made, should take away the sins of the world; and sin, as St John saith, was not in him. But all we the rest, although baptized and born again in Christ, yet offend in many things, and if we say we have no sin, we deceive ourselves and the truth is not in us.

15. De peccato in Spiritum Sanctum (16. De lapsis post baptismum)

15. Of Sin against the Holy Ghost (16. Of Sin after Baptism)

Non omne peccatum mortale post baptismum voluntarie perpetratum, est peccatum in Spiritum Sanctum et irremissibile. Proinde lapsis a baptismo in peccata, locus paenitentiae non est negandus. Post acceptum Spiritum Sanctum, possumus a gratia data recedere atque peccare, denuoque per gratiam Dei resurgere ac resipiscere. Ideoque illi damnandi sunt, qui se quamdiu hic vivant, amplius non posse peccare affirmant, aut vere resipiscentibus paenitentiae locum denegant.

(Not) every deadly sin willingly committed after baptism is **not** sin against the Holy Ghost, and unpardonable. Wherefore **the place for penitentes** (the grant of repentance) is not to be denied to such as fall into sin after baptism. After we have received the Holy Ghost, we may depart from grace given and fall into sin, and by the grace of God we may (a)rise again and amend our lives. And therefore they are to be condemned, which say they can no more sin as long as they live here, or deny the place **for penitentes** (of forgiveness) to such as truly repent **and amend their lives.**

16. *Blasphemia in Spiritum Sanctum*

16. *Blasphemy against the Holy Ghost*

Blasphemia in Spiritum Sanctum est cum quis verborum Dei manifeste perceptam veritatem, ex malitia et obfirmatione animi, conviciis insectatur, et hostiliter insequitur. Atque huiusmodi, quia

Blasphemy against the Holy Ghost is when a man of malice and stubbornness of mind doth rail upon the truth of God's Word manifestly perceived, and being enemy thereunto persecuteth the

maledicto sunt obnoxii, gravissimo sese astringunt sceleri. Unde peccati hoc genus irremissibile a Domino appellatur, et affirmatur.

same. And because such be guilty of God's curse, they entangle themselves with a most grievous and heinous crime, whereupon this kind of sin is called and affirmed of the Lord, unpardonable.

17. *De praedestinatione et electione*

Praedestinatio ad vitam est aeternum Dei propositum, quo ante iacta mundi fundamenta suo consilio, nobis quidem occulto, constanter decrevit eos quos (in Christo) elegit ex hominum genere, a maledicto et exitio liberare, atque ut vasa in honorem efficta, per Christum ad aeternam salutem adducere; unde qui tam praeclaro Dei beneficio sunt donati, illi Spiritu eius opportuno tempore operante, secundum propositum eius vocantur, vocationi per gratiam parent; iustificantur gratis; adoptantur in filios unigeniti Iesu Christi imagini efficiuntur conformes; in bonis operibus sancte ambulant, et demum ex Dei misericordia pertingunt ad sempiternam felicitatem.

Quemadmodum praedestinationis et electionis nostrae in Christo pia consideratio, dulcis, suavis et ineffabilis consolationis plena est vere piis et his qui sentiunt in se vim Spiritus Christi, facta carnis et membra quae adhuc sunt super terram mortificantem, animumque ad caelestia et superna rapientem, tum quia fidem nostram de aeterna

17. *Of Predestination and Election*

Predestination to life is the everlasting purpose of God, whereby before the foundations of the world were laid, he hath constantly decreed by his **own judgement** (counsel) secret to us, to deliver from curse and damnation those whom he hath chosen (in Christ) out of mankind, and to bring them (by Christ) to everlasting salvation **by Christ**, as vessels made to honour. **Whereupon such as have** (Wherefore they which be indued with) so excellent a benefit of God **given unto them** be called according to God's purpose by his Spirit, working in due season; they through grace obey the calling; they be justified freely; they be made sons (of God) by adoption; they be made like the image of his only begotten Son Jesus Christ; they walk religiously in good works and at length by God's mercy, they attain to everlasting felicity.

As the godly consideration of predestination, and our election in Christ is full of sweet, pleasant and unspeakable comfort to godly persons, and such as feel in themselves the working of the Spirit of Christ, mortifying the works of the flesh and their earthly members, and drawing up their mind to high and heavenly things, as well because it

salute consequenda per Christum plurimum stabilit atque confirmat, tum quia amorem nostrum in Deum vehementer accendit; ita hominibus curiosis, carnalibus, et Spiritu Christi destitutis, ob oculos perpetuo versari praedestinationis Dei sententiam, perniciosissimum est praecipitium, unde illos Diabolus protrudit, vel in desperationem, vel in aeque perniciosam impurissime vitae securitatem.

Deinde **licet praedestinationis decreta sunt nobis ignota,** promissiones **tamen** divinas sic amplecti oportet, ut nobis in sacris litteris generaliter propositae sunt; et Dei volutas in nostris actionibus ea sequenda est, quam in Verbo Dei habemus diserte revelatam.

18. *Tantum in nomine Christi speranda est aeterna salus*

Sunt **et** illi anathematizandi qui dicere audent, unumquemque in lege aut secta quam profitetur esse servandum, modo iuxta illam et lumen naturae accurate vixerit: cum sacrae litterae tantum Iesu Christi nomen praedicent in quo salvos fieri homines oporteat.

19. *Omnes obligantur ad moralia legis praecepta servanda*

Lex a Deo data per Mosen, licet

doth greatly (e)stablish and confirm their faith of eternal salvation to be enjoyed through Christ, as because it doth fervently kindle their love towards God; so for curious and carnal persons, lacking the Spirit of Christ, to have continually before their eyes the sentence of God's predestination, is a most dangerous downfall, whereby the Devil **may** (doth) thrust them either into desperation, or into a recklessness of most unclean living, no less perilous than desperation.

Furthermore, **although the decrees of predestination are unknown to us, yet** we must receive God's promises in such wise as they be generally set forth to us in Holy Scripture; and in our doings that will of God is to be followed which we have, expressly declared to us in the Word of God.

18. *We must trust to obtain eternal Salvation only by the Name of Christ*
(18. *Of obtaining eternal Salvation, only by the Name of Christ)*

They also are to be had accursed **and abhorred** that presume to say that every man shall be saved by the law or sect which he professeth, so that he be diligent to frame his life according to that law, and the light of nature. For Holy Scripture doth set out unto us only the name of Jesus Christ, whereby men must be saved.

19. *All Men are bound to keep the Moral Commandments of the Law*

The Law which was given of God

quoad ad caeremonias et ritus Christianos non astringat, neque civilia eius praecepta in aliqua Republica necessario recipi debeant, nihilominus ab oboedientia mandatorum quae moralia vocantur, nullus quantumvis Christianus est solutus. Quare illi non sunt audiendi, qui sacras literas tantum infirmis datas esse perhibent, et Spiritum perpetuo iactant, a quo sibi quae praedicant suggeri asserunt, quamquam cum sacris literis apertissime pugnent.

by Moses, although it bind not Christian men as concerning the ceremonies and rites of the same; neither is it required that the civil precepts and orders of it should of necessity be received in any commonwealth; yet no man (be he never so perfect a Christian) is exempt and loosed from the obedience of these commandments, which are called moral. Wherefore they are not to be hearkened unto, who affirm that Holy Scripture is given only to the weak, and do boast themselves continually of the Spirit, of whom they say they have learned such things as they teach, although the same be most evidently repugnant to the Holy Scripture.

20. *(19) De ecclesia*

Ecclesia Christi visibilis est coetus fidelium in quo Verbum Dei purum praedicatur et sacramenta quoad ea quae necessario exiguntur, iuxta Christi institutum recte administrantur.

Sicut erravit Ecclesia Hierosolymitana, Alexandrina et Antiochena, ita et erravit Ecclesia Romana, non solum quoad agenda (et caeremoniarum ritus), verum in his etiam quae credenda sunt.

20. *(19) Of the Church*

The visible Church of Christ is a congregation of faithful men in which the pure Word of God is preached and the sacraments be duly administered, according to Christ's ordinance in all those things that of necessity are requisite to the same.

As the Church of Jerusalem, Alexandria and Antioch have erred, so also the Church of Rome hath erred, not only in their living (and manner of ceremonies), but also in matters of **their** faith.

21. *(20) De ecclesiae auctoritate*

(Habet Ecclesia ritus statuendi ius, et in fidei controversiis auctoritatem, quamvis) Ecclesiae non licet quicquam instituere, quod Verbo Dei

21. *(20) Of the Authority of the Church*

(The Church hath power to decree rites and ceremonies, and authority in controversies of faith; and yet) it is not lawful for the Church to ordain

scripto adversetur, neque unum Scripturae locum sic exponere potest, ut alteri contradicat. Quare licet Ecclesia sit divinorum librorum testis et conservatrix, attamen ut adversus eos nihil decernere, ita praeter illos nihil credendum de necessitate salutis debet obtrudere.

anything that is contrary to God Word written, neither may it so expound one place of Scripture that it is repugnant to another. Wherefore, although the Church be a witness and a keeper of Holy Writ; yet as it ought not to decree anything against the same, so besides the same, ought it not to enforce anything to be believed for necessity of salvation.

22. (21) De auctoritate conciliorum generalium

22. (21) Of the Authority of General Councils

Generalia concilia sine iussu et voluntate principum congregari non possunt; et ubi convenerint, quia ex hominibus constant qui non omnes Spiritu et verbis Dei reguntur, et errare possunt et interdum errarunt, etiam in his quae ad normam pietatis pertinent; ideo quae ab illis constituuntur, ut ad salutem necessaria, neque robur habent neque auctoritatem, nisi ostendi possunt e sacris literis esse desumpta.

General councils may not be gathered together without the commandment and will of princes. And when they be gathered together, forasmuch as they shall be an assembly of men, whereof all be not governed with the Spirit and Word of God, they may err, and sometimes have erred, **not only in worldly matters, but also** (even) in things pertaining unto God. Wherefore things ordained by them as necessary to salvation have neither strength nor authority, unless it may be declared that they be taken out of Holy Scripture.

23. (22) De purgatorio

23. (22) Of Purgatory

Scholasticorum doctrina (Romanensium) de purgatorio, de indulgentiis, de veneratione et adoratione tum imaginum tum reliquiarum, nec non de invocatione sanctorum, res est futilis, inaniter conficta, et nullis Scripturarum testimoniis innititur, imo Verbo Dei **perniciose** contradicit.

The (Romish) doctrine **of School-authors** concerning purgatory, pardons, worshipping and adoration as well of images as of relics, and also invocation of saints, is a fond thing vainly invented, and grounded upon no warrant(y) of Scripture, but rather repugnant to the Word of God.

24. *(23) Nemo in ecclesia ministret nisi vocatus*

24. No man may minister in the Congregation except he be called
(23. *Of ministering in the Congregation*)

Non licet cuiquam sumere sibi munus publice praedicandi, aut administrandi sacramenta in Ecclesia, nisi prius fuerit ad haec obeunda legitime vocatus et missus. Atque illos legitime vocatos et missos existimare debemus, qui per homines, quibus potestas vocandi ministros atque mittendi in vineam Domini publice concessa est in Ecclesia, cooptati fuerint et asciti in hoc opus.

It is not lawful for any man to take upon him the office of public preaching, or ministering the sacraments in the congregation, before he be lawfully called and sent to execute the same. And those we ought to judge lawfully called and sent, which be chosen, and called to this work by men, who have public authority given unto them in the congregation, to call and send ministers into the Lord's vineyard.

25. (24) *Agendum est in ecclesia lingua quae sit populo nota*

25. Men must speak in the Congregation in such Tongue as the People understandeth
(24. *Of speaking in the Congregation in such a Tongue as the People understandeth*)

Decentissimum est et Verbo Dei maxime congruit, ut nihil in Ecclesia publice legatur aut recitetur lingua populo ignota, idque Paulus fieri vetuit, nisi adesset qui interpretaretur.

It is most seemly and most agreeable to the Word of God, that in the congregation nothing be openly read or spoken in a tongue unknown to the people, the which thing St Paul did forbid, except some were present that should declare the same.

(Lingua populo non intellecta publicas in Ecclesia preces peragere, aut sacramenta administrare, Verbo Dei et primitivae Ecclesiae consuetudine plane repugnat.)

(It is a thing plainly repugnant to the Word of God and the custom of the primitive Church to have public prayer in the Church, or to minister the sacraments in a tongue not understanded of the people.)

26. (25) *De sacramentis*[1]

26. (25) *Of the Sacraments*[1]

Dominus noster Iesus Christus

Our Lord Jesus Christ hath knit

---

[1] The underlined passages were included both in 1553 (as in bold type) and in 1563/1571, when they were relegated to the concluding paragraph. Note also that the concluding paragraph of 1553 became the opening paragraph of 1563/1571.

sacramentis numero paucissimis, observatu facillimis, significatione praestantissimis, societatem novi populi colligavit, sicuti est baptismus et coena Domini.

Sacramenta non instituta sunt a Christo ut spectarentur aut circumferrentur, sed ut rite illis uteremur; et in his dumtaxat qui digne percipiunt, salutarem habent effectum, idque non ex opere, ut quidam loquuntur, operato; quae vox ut peregrina est et sacris literis ignota, sed parit sensum minime pium sed admodum superstitiosum; qui vero indigne percipiunt, damnationem, ut inquit Paulus, sibi ipsis acquirunt.

Sacramenta per Verbum Dei (a Christo) instituta non tantum sunt notae professionis Christianorum, sed certa quaedam potius testimonia, et efficacia signa gratiae atque bonae in nos voluntatis Dei, per quae invisibiliter ipse in nobis operatur, nostramque fidem in se non solum excitat, verum etiam confirmat.

(Duo a Christo Domino nostro in Evangelio instituta sunt sacramenta, scilicet baptismus et coena Domini.

Quinque illa vulgo nominata sacramenta, scilicet, confirmatio, paenitentia, ordo, matrimonium et extrema unctio, pro sacramentis evangelicis habenda non sunt, ut quae partim a prava Apostolorum imitatione profluxerunt, partim vitae status sunt in Scripturis quidem probati, sed sacramentorum eandem cum baptismo et coena Domini

together a company of new people with sacraments, most few in number, most easy to be kept, most excellent in signification, as is baptism and the Lord's supper.

The sacraments were not ordained of Christ to be gazed upon, or to be carried about, but that we should rightly use them. And in such only as worthily receive the same, they have an wholesome effect and operation, and yet not that of the work wrought, as some men speak, which word, as it is strange, and unknown to Holy Scripture; so it engendereth no godly, but a very superstitious sense. But they that receive the sacraments unworthily purchase to themselves damnation, as St Paul saith.

Sacraments ordained by the Word of God (of Christ), be not only badges or tokens of Christian men's profession; but rather they be certain sure witnesses and effectual signs of grace towards us, by the which he doth work invisibly in us, and doth not only quicken, but also strengthen and confirm our faith in him.

(There are two sacraments ordained of Christ our Lord in the Gospel, that is to say, baptism and the supper of the Lord.

Those five, commonly called sacraments, that is to say, confirmation, penance, orders, matrimony and extreme unction, are not to be counted for sacraments of the Gospel, being such as have grown partly of the corrupt following of the Apostles, partly are states of life allowed in the Scriptures; but yet have not like nature of sacraments

rationem non habentes; quomodo nec paenitentia, ut quae signum aliquod visibile seu caeremoniam a Deo institutam non habeat.

(Sacramenta non instituta sunt a Christo ut spectarentur aut circumferrentur, sed ut rite illis uteremur; et in his dumtaxat qui digne percipiunt, salutarem habent effectum qui vero indigne percipiunt, damnationem, ut inquit Paulus, sibi ipsis acquirunt.)

with baptism and the Lord's supper, for that they have not any visible sign or ceremony ordained of God.

(The sacraments were not ordained of Christ to be gazed upon or to be carried about; but that we should duly use them. And in such only as worthily receive the same, they have a wholesome effect or operation; but they that receive them unworthily, purchase to themselves damnation, as St Paul saith.)

27. (26) *Ministrorum malitia non tollit efficaciam institutionum divinarum*

27. The Wickedness of the Ministers doth not take away the effectual Operation of God's Ordinances
(26. *Of the Unworthiness of the Ministers, which hinder not the Effect of the Sacraments*)

Quamvis in Ecclesia visibili bonis mali sunt semper admixti, atque interdum ministerio verbi et sacramentorum administrationi praesint, tamen cum non suo sed Christi nomine agant, eiusque mandato et auctoritate ministrent, illorum ministerio uti licet, cum in Verbo Dei audiendo, tum in sacramentis percipiendis; neque per illorum malitiam effectus institutionum Christi tollitur, aut gratia donorum Dei minuitur quoad eos, qui fide et rite sibi oblata percipiunt, quae propter institutionem Christi et promissionem efficacia sunt, licet per malos administrentur. Ad Ecclesiae tamen disciplinam pertinet, ut in **eos** (malos ministros) inquiratur, accusenturque ab iis, qui eorum flagitia noverint, atque tandem iusto convicti iudicio, deponantur.

Although in the visible Church the evil be ever mingles with the good, and sometime the evil have chief authority in the ministration of the Word and sacraments; yet forasmuch as they do not the same in their own name but **do minister by Christ's** (in Christ's, and do minister by his) commission and authority; we may use their ministry both in hearing the Word of God, and in the receiving (of) the sacraments. Neither is the effect of **God's** (Christ's) ordinances taken away by their wickedness, nor the grace of God's gifts diminished from such as by faith and rightly (do) receive the sacraments ministered unto them, which be effectual because of Christ's institution and promise, although they be ministered by evil men. Nevertheless it appertaineth to the discipline of the Church, that inquiry be made of **such** (evil ministers), and that they be accused by those that have knowledge of their offences, and finally, being found guilty by just judgement, be deposed.

28. (27) *De baptismo*

Baptismus non est tantum **signum** professionis (signum) ac discriminis nota, qua Christiani a non Christianis discernuntur, sed etiam est signum regenerationis, per quod tamquam per instrumentum recte baptismum suspicientes, ecclesiae **inferuntur (inseruntur)**, promissiones de remissione peccatorum atque adoptione nostra in filios Dei per Spiritum Sanctum visibiliter obsignantur, fides confirmatur, et vi divinae invocationis, gratia augetur. **Mos Ecclesiae baptizandi parvulos est laudandus et** (Baptismus parvulorum) omnino in Ecclesia retinendus (est, ut qui cum Christi institutione optime congruat.)

28. (27) *Of Baptism*

Baptism is not only a sign of profession and mark of difference, whereby Christian men are discerned from other that be not christened; but **it** is also a sign **and seal of our** (of regeneration or) new birth, whereby as by an instrument, they that receive baptism rightly are grafted into the Church; the promises of (the) forgiveness of sin, and (of) our adoption to be the sons of God, (by the Holy Ghost), are visibly signed and sealed; faith is confirmed; and grace increased by virtue of prayer unto God. **The custom of the Church to christen young children is to be commended and** (The baptism of young children is) in any wise to be retained in the Church (as most agreeable with the institution of Christ.)

29. (28) *De coena Domini*

Coena Domini non est tantum signum mutuae benevolentiae Christianorum inter sese, verum potius est sacramentum nostrae per mortem Christi redemptionis. Atque adeo rite, digne et cum fide sumentibus panis quem frangimus est communicatio corporis Christi; similiter poculum benedictionis est communicatio sanguinis Christi.

Panis et vini transubstantiatio in

29. (28) *Of the Lord's Supper*

The Supper of the Lord is not only a sign of the love Christians ought to have among themselves to one another; but rather it is a sacrament of our redemption by Christ's death. Insomuch that to such as rightly, worthily and with faith receive the same, the bread which we break is a communion (partaking) of the body of Christ, (and) likewise the cup of blessing is a communion (partaking) of the blood of Christ.

Transubstantiation, or the change

eucharistia, ex sacris literis probari non potest, sed apertis Scripturae verbis adversatur, (sacramenti naturam evertit), et multarum superstitionum dedit occasionem.

Quum naturae humanae veritas requiret, ut unius eiusdemque hominis corpus in multis locis simul esse non posset, sed in uno aliquo et definito loco esse oporteat, idcirco Christi corpus, in multis et diversis locis, eodem tempore praesens esse non potest. Et quoniam, ut tradunt Sacrae literae, Christus in caelum fuit sublatus, et ibi usque ad finem saeculi est permansurus, non debet quisquam fidelium carnis eius et sanguinis realem et corporalem, ut loquuntur, praesentiam in eucharistia vel credere vel profiteri.

(Corpus Christi datur, accipitur, et manducatur in coena, tantum caelesti et spirituali ratione. Medium autem quo corpus Christi accipitur et manducatur in coena fides est.)

Sacramentum eucharistiae ex institutione Christi non servabatur, circumferebatur, elevabatur, nec adorabatur.

of the substance of bread and wine into the substance of Christ's body and blood (in the supper of the Lord), cannot be proved by Holy Writ, but is repugnant to the plain words of Scripture, (overthroweth the nature of a sacrament), and hath given occasion to many superstitions.

Forasmuch as the truth of man's nature requireth, that the body of one and the selfsame man cannot be at one time in diverse places, but must needs be in one certain place; therefore the body of Christ cannot be present at one time in many and diverse places. And because, as Holy Scripture doth teach, Christ was taken up into heaven, and there shall continue until the end of the world, a faithful man ought not either to believe or openly to confess the real and bodily presence, as they term it, of Christ's flesh and blood, in the sacrament of the Lord's supper.

(The body of Christ is given, taken and eaten in the supper only after an heavenly and spiritual manner; and the mean whereby the body of Christ is received and eaten in the supper is faith.)

The sacrament of the Lord's supper was not **commanded** by Christ's ordinance **to be kept** (reserved), carried about, lifted up **nor** (or) worshipped.

(*29. Of the Wicked which do not eat the Body of Christ in the Use of the Lord's Supper)*[1]

---

[1] This Article appears only in 1571. The Latin text printed here was extant in 1563, but was not included in the printed version of the Articles. Because of the insertion of a new Article 29 in 1571, the numbering of the Articles differs by one from both 1553 and 1563 from this point on. The 1571 number is given immediately after the 1563 number, thus: 29/30, etc.

Impii, et fide viva destituti, licet carnaliter et visibiliter, ut Augustinus loquitur, corporis et sanguinis Christi sacramentum dentibus premant, nullo tamen modo Christi participes efficiuntur. Sed potius tantae rei sacramentum seu symbolum, ad iudicium sibi manducant et bibunt.

The wicked, and such as be void of a lively faith, although they do carnally and visibly press with their teeth, as St Augustine saith, the sacrament of the body and blood of Christ; yet in no wise are they partakers of Christ, but rather to their condemnation do eat and drink the sign or sacrament of so great a thing.

(29/30. *De utraque specie*)

(29/30. *Of both kinds*)

Calix Domini laicis non est denegandus; utraque enim pars dominici sacramenti ex Christi institutione et praecepto, omnibus Christianis ex aequo administrari debet.

The cup of the Lord is not to be denied to the laypeople. For both the parts of the Lord's sacrament, by Christ's ordinance and commandment, ought to be ministered to all Christian men alike.

30/31. *De unica Christi oblatione in cruce perfecta*

30. *Of the perfect Oblation of Christ made upon the Cross*
(30/31. *Of the one Oblation of Christ finished upon the Cross*)

Oblatio Christi semel facta, perfecta est redemptio, propitiatio et satisfactio pro omnibus peccatis totius mundi, tam originalibus quam actualibus; neque praeter illam unicam est ulla alia pro peccatis expiatio. Unde missarum sacrificia, quibus vulgo dicebatur, sacerdotem offerre Christum in remissionem poenae aut culpae pro vivis et defunctis, (blasphema) figmenta sunt, et perniciosae imposturae.

The offering of Christ (once) made **once for ever**, is the perfect redemption, **the pacifying of God's displeasure** (propitiation), and satisfaction for all the sins of the whole world, both original and actual, and there is none other satisfaction for sin but that alone. Wherefore the sacrifices of masses, in the which it was commonly said that the priest(s) did offer Christ for the quick and the dead, to have remission of pain or **sin** (guilt), were **forged** (blasphemous) fables and dangerous deceits.

31. *Caelibatus ex Verbo Dei praecipitur nemini*
(31/32. *De coniugio sacerdotum*)

31. *The State of single Life is commanded to no Man by the Word of God*
(31/32. *Of the Marriage of Priests*)

Episcopis, presbyteris et diaconis **non est mandatum** (nullo mandato divino praeceptum est) ut **aut** caelibatum voveant; **neque iure divino coguntur matrimonio abstinere** (aut a matrimonio abstineant. Licet igitur etiam illis, ut caeteris omnibus Christianis, ubi hoc ad pietatem magis facere iudicaverint, pro suo arbitratu matrimonium contrahere.)

Bishops, priests and deacons are not commanded (by God's law) to vow the (e)state of single life, **without** (or to abstain from) marriage, **neither by God's law are they compelled to abstain from matrimony.** (Therefore it is lawful also for them, as for all other Christian men, to marry at their own discretion, as they shall judge the same to serve better to godliness.)

32/33. *Excommunicati vitati sunt*

32. *Excommunicate persons are to be avoided*
(32/33. *Of excommunicate Persons, how they are to be avoided*)

Qui per publicam Ecclesiae denuntiationem rite ab unitate Ecclesiae praecisus (est) et excommunicatus, is ab universa fidelium multitudine, donec per paenitentiam publice reconciliatus fuerit arbitrio iudicis competentis, habendus est tamquam ethnicus et publicanus.

That person, which by open denunciation of the Church is rightly cut off from the unity of the Church and excommunicate(d), ought to be taken of the whole multitude of the faithful as an heathen and publican, until he be openly reconciled by penance, and received into the Church by a judge that hath authority thereto.

33/34. *Traditiones ecclesiasticae*

33. *Traditions of the Church*
(33/34. *Of the Traditions of the Church*)

Traditiones atque caeremonias easdem non omnino necessarium est esse ubique aut prorsus consimiles. Nam (et) variae **et** semper fuerunt et mutari possunt pro regionum, (temporum) et morum diversitate; modo nihil contra **Dei** Verbum (Dei) instituatur.

It is not necessary that traditions and ceremonies be in all places one or utterly like, for at all times they have been diverse, and may be changed according to the diversity of countries (times) and men's manners, so that nothing be ordained against God's Word.

Traditiones et caeremonias ecclesiasticas, quae cum Verbo Dei non pugnant et sunt auctoritate publica

Whosoever through his private judgement willingly and purposely doth openly break the traditions and

institutae atque probatae, quisquis privato consilio volens et data opera publice violaverit, is, ut qui peccat in publicum ordinem Ecclesiae, quique laedit auctoritatem magistratus, et qui infirmorum fratrum conscientias vulnerat, publice, ut caeteri timeant, arguendus est.

(Quaelibet ecclesia particularis, sive nationalis, auctoritatem habet instituendi, mutandi, aut abrogandi caeremonias aut ritus ecclesiasticos, humana tantum auctoritate institutos, modo omnia ad aedificationem fiant.)

ceremonies of the Church, which be not repugnant to the Word of God and be ordained and approved by common authority, ought to be rebuked openly, that other may fear to do the like, as **one** (he) that offendeth against the common order of the Church, and hurteth the authority of the magistrate, and woundeth the consciences of the weak brethren.

(Every particular or national church hath authority to ordain, change and abolish ceremonies, or rites of the Church ordained only by man's authority, so that all things be done to edifying.)

34/35. Homiliae

Homiliae nuper Ecclesiae Anglicanae per iniunctiones regias traditae atque commendatae, piae sunt atque salutares, doctrinamque ab omnibus amplectendam continent; quare populo diligenter, expedite clareque recitandae sunt.

(Tomus secundus Homiliarum, quarum singulos titulos huic Articulo subiunximus, continet piam et salutarem doctrinam, et his temporibus necessarium, non minus quam prior tomus homiliarum quae editae sunt tempore Edwardi sexti. Itaque eas in ecclesiis per ministros diligenter et clare, ut a populo intelligi possint, recitandas esse iudicamus.

01. De recto Ecclesiae usu
02. Adversus idololatriae pericula
03. De reparandis ac purgandis ecclesiis
04. De bonis operibus; de ieiunio
05. In gulae atque ebrietatis vitia

34/35. (Of) Homilies

The homilies of late given, and set out by the King's authority, be godly and wholesome, containing doctrine to be received of all men, and therefore are to be read to the people diligently, distinctly and plainly.

(The second Book of Homilies, the several titles whereof we have joined under this Article, doth contain a godly and wholesome doctrine, and necessary for these times, as doth the former book of homilies, which were set forth in the time of King Edward the Sixth; and therefore we judge them to be read in churches by the ministers diligently and distinctly, that they may be understanded of the people.

01. Of the right use of the Church
02. Against peril of idolatry
03. Of repairing and keeping clean of churches
04. Of good works, first of fasting
05. Against gluttony and drunkenness

06. In nimis sumptuosos vestuium apparatus

06. Against excess of apparel

07. De oratione sive precatione

07. Of prayer

08. De loco et tempore orationi destinatis

08. Of the place and time of prayer

09. De publicis precibus ac sacramentis, idiomate vulgari omnibusque noto, habendis

09. That common prayers and sacraments ought to be ministered in a known tongue

10. De sacrosancta verbi divini auctoritate

10. Of the reverent estimation of God's Word

11. De eleemosina

11. Of almsdoing

12. De Christi nativitate

12. Of the nativity of Christ

13. De Dominica passione

13. Of the passion of The Lord

14. De resurrectione Christi

14. Of the resurrection of Christ

15. De digna corporis et sanguinis dominici in coena Domini participatione

15. Of the worthy receiving of the sacrament of the body and blood of Christ the Lord in the Lord's supper

16. De donis Spiritus Sancti

16. Of the gifts of the Holy Ghost

17. In diebus, qui vulgo rogationum dicti sunt, concio

17. For the rogation days

18. De matrimonii statu

18. Of the state of matrimony

19. De paenitentia[1]

19. Of repentance[1]

20. De otio seu socordia)

20. Against idleness

21. Against rebellion)

35. *De libro precationum et caeremoniarum Ecclesiae Anglicanae*

(35/36. *De episcoporum et ministrorum consecratione*)

Liber qui nuperrime auctoritate regis et Parliamenti Ecclesiae Anglicanae traditus est, continend modum et formam orandi, et sacramenta administrandi in Ecclesia Anglicana; similiter et libellus eadem auctoritate editus de ordinatione ministrorum Ecclesiae, quoad doctrinae veritatem, pii sunt, et salutari doctrinae Evangelii in nullo repugnant sed congruunt, et

35. *Of the Book of Prayers and Ceremonies of the Church of England*

(35/36. *Of Consecration of Bishops and Ministers*)

The book which of very late time was given to the Church of England by the King's authority, and the Parliament, containing the manner and form of praying and ministering the sacraments in the Church of England, likewise also the Book of Ordering ministers of the Church, set forth by the foresaid authority are godly, and in no point repugnant to the wholesome doctrine of the Gospel,

[1] The order of Homilies 19 and 20 was reversed in 1571, and number 21 added.

eandem non parum promovent et illustrant, atque ideo ab omnibus Ecclesiae Anglicanae fidelibus membris, et maxime a ministris Verbi cum omni promptitudine animorum et gratiarum actione, recipiendi, approbandi, et populo Dei commendandi sunt.

(Libellus de consecratione archiepiscoporum et episcoporum, et de ordinatione presbyterorum et diaconorum aeditus nuper temporibus Edwardii Sexti, et auctoritate Parliamenti illis ipsis temporibus confirmatus, omnia ad eiusmodi consecrationem et ordinationem necessaria continet, et nihil habet quod ex se sit aut superstitiosum aut impium. Itaque quicunque iuxta ritus illius libri consecrati aut ordinati sunt ab annon secundo praedicti Edwardi, usque ad hoc tempus, aut in posterum iuxta eosdem ritus consecrabuntur aut ordinabuntur rite, ordine, atque legitime, statuimus esse et fore consecratos et ordinatos.)

36/37. *De civilibus magistratibus*

Rex Angliae est supremum caput in terris, post Christum, Ecclesiae Anglicanae et Hibernicae.

(Regia maiestas in hoc Angliae regno ac caeteris euis dominiis, iure summam habet potestatem, ad quam omnium statuum huius regni, sive illi ecclesiastici sunt sive non, in omnibus causis suprema gubernatio pertinet, et nulli externae iurisdictioni est subiecta, nec esse debet.

but agreeable thereunto, furthering and beautifying the same not a little, and therefore of all faithful members of the Church of England, and chiefly of the ministers of the Word, they ought to be received, and allowed with all readiness of mind and thanksgiving, and to be commended to the people of God.

(The book of consecration of archbishops and bishops, and ordering of priests and deacons, lately set forth in the time of Edward the Sixth, and confirmed at the same time by authority of Parliament, doth contain all things necessary to such consecration and ordering; neither hath it anything that of itself is superstitious or ungodly. And therefore, whosoever are consecrate or ordered according to the rites of that book, since the second year of the aforenamed King Edward, unto this time, or hereafter shall be consecrated or ordered according to the same rites we decree all such to be rightly, orderly and lawfully consecrated and ordered.)

(36/37. *Of (the) Civil Magistrates*

The King of England is supreme head in earth, next under Christ, of the Church of England and Ireland.

(The Queen's Majesty hath the chief power in this realm of England, and other her dominions, unto whom the chief government of all estates of this realm, whether they be ecclesiastical or civil, in all causes doth appertain, and is not, nor ought to be subject to any foreign jurisdiction.

Cum regiae maiestati summam gubernationem tribuimus, quibus titulis intelligimus animos quorundam calumniatorum offendi; non damus regibus nostris aur Verbi Dei aut sacramentorum administrationem quod etiam iniunctiones ab Elizabetha Regina nostra nuper aeditae, apertissime testantur; sed cum tantum praerogativum quam in Sacris Scripturis a Deo ipso omnibus piis principibus videmus semper fuisse attributam, hoc est, ut omnes status atque ordines fidei suae a Deo commissos, sive illi ecclesiastici sint, sive civiles, in officio contineant, et contumaces ac delinquentes, gladio civili coerceant.)

Romanus Pontifex nullam habet iurisdictionem in hoc Regno Angliae. **Magistratus civilis est a Deo ordinatus atque probatus, quamobrem illi, non solum propter iram sed etiam propter conscientiam, oboediendum est.**

Leges civiles possunt Christianos propter capitalia et gravia crimina morte punire. Christianis licet (et) ex mandato magistratus arma portare et iusta bella administrare.

37/38. *Christianorum bona non sunt communia*

Facultates et bona Christianorum non sunt communia, quoad ius et possessionem, ut quidam Anabaptistae falso iactant; debet tamen quisque de his quae possidet pro facultatum ratione, pauperibus eleemosynas benigne distribuere.

Where we attribute to the Queen's Majesty the chief government, by which titles we understand the minds of some slanderous folk to be offended; we give not to our princes the ministering either of God's Word or of sacraments, the which thing the injunctions also lately set forth by Elizabeth our Queen doth most plainly testify; but that only prerogative which we see to have been given always to all godly princes in Holy Scriptures by God himself, that is, that they should rule all estates and degrees committed to their charge by God, whether they be ecclesiastical or temporal, and restrain with the civil sword the stubborn and evil doers.)

The Bishop of Rome hath no jurisdiction in this realm of England. **The civil magistrate is ordained and allowed of God; wherefore we must obey him, not only for fear of punishment but also for conscience sake.**

The **civil** laws (of the realm) may punish Christian men with death for heinous and grievous offences. It is lawful for **Christians** (Christian men), at the commandment of the magistrate, to wear weapons and to serve in (the) **lawful** wars.

37/38. *(Of) Christian Men's Goods, (which) are not common*

The riches and goods of Christians are not common, as touching the right title and possession of the same, as certain Anabaptists do falsely boast; notwithstanding, every man ought of such things as he possesseth, liberally to give alms to the poor, according to his ability.

38/39. *Licet Christianis iurare*

38. Christian Men may take an Oath

(38/39. *Of a Christian Man's Oath*)

Quemadmodum iuramentum vanum et temerarium a Domino nostro Iesu Christo et **ab** Apostolo eius Iacobo, Christianis hominibus interdictum esse fatemur; ita Christianam religionem minime prohibere censemus, quin iubente magistratu, in causa fidei et caritatis iurare liceat, modo id fiat iuxta Prophetae doctrinam, in iustitia, in iudicio et veritate.

As we confess that vain and rash swearing is forbidden Christian men by our Lord Jesus Christ, and **his Apostle** James (his Apostle); so we judge that Christian religion doth not prohibit, but that a man may swear when the magistrate requireth, in a cause of faith and charity, so it be done, according to the Prophet's teaching, in justice, judgement and truth.

39. Resurrectio mortuorum nondum est facta

39. The Resurrection of the Dead is not yet brought to pass

Resurrectio mortuorum non adhuc facta est, quasi tantum ad animam pertineat, qui per Christi gratiam a morte peccatorum excitetur, sed extremo die quoad omnes qui obierunt, expectanda est; tunc enim vita defunctis, ut Scripturae manifestissime testantur, propria corpora, carnes et ossa restituentur, ut homo integer, prout vel recte vel perdite vixerit, iuxta sua opera, sive praemia sive poenas reportet.

The resurrection of the dead is not as yet brought to pass, as though it only belonged to the soul, which by the grace of Christ is raised from the death of sin, but it is to be looked for at the last day; for then, as Scripture doth most manifestly testify, to all that be dead in their own bodies, flesh and bone shall be restored that the whole man may, according to his works, have other reward, or punishment, as he hath lived virtuously or wickedly.

40. Defunctorum animae neque cum corporibus intereunt, neque otiose dormiunt

40. The Souls of them that depart this Life do neither die with the Bodies, nor sleep idly

Qui animas defunctorum praedicant usque ad diem iudicii absque omni sensu dormire, aut illas asserunt una cum corporibus mori, et extrema die cum illis excitandas, ab orthodoxa fide,

They which say that the souls of such as depart hence do sleep, being without all sense, feeling or perceiving until the day of judgement, or affirm that the souls die with the bodies, and at the last

quae nobis in sacris literis traditur, prorsus dissentiunt.

day shall be raised up with the same, do utterly dissent from the right belief declared unto us in Holy Scripture.

41. Millenarii

Qui Millenariorum fabulam revocare conantur, sacris literis adversantur, et in Iudaica deliramenta sese praecipitant.

41. Heretics called Millenarii

They that go about to renew the fable of heretics called Millenarii be repugnant to Holy Scripture, and cast themselves headlong into a Jewish dotage.

42. Non omnes tandem servandi sunt

Hi quoque damnatione digni sunt, qui conantur hodie perniciosam opinionem instaurare, quod omnes, quantumvis impii, servandi sunt tandem, cum definito tempore a iustitia divina poenas de admissis flagitiis lucerunt.

42. All Men shall not be saved at the length

They also are worthy of condemnation, who endeavour at this time to restore the dangerous opinion that all men, be they never so ungodly, shall at length be saved, when they have suffered pains for their sins a certain time appointed by God's justice.

The Latin declaration following Article 42 was appended to the Articles in 1563; the English translation has been prepared for this edition.

Hos Articulos fidei Christianae continentes in universum novemdecim paginas in autographo, quod asservatur apud reverendissimum in Christo patrem Dominum Matthaeum Cantuariensem Archiepiscopum, totius Angliae primatem et metropolitanum, archiepiscopi et episcopi utriusque provinciae Regni Angliae, in sacra provinciali synodo legitime congregati, unanimi assensu recipiunt et profitentur, et ut veros atque orthodoxos, manuum suarum subscriptionibus approbant, vicesimo nono die mensis Ianuarii, Anno Domini, secundum computationem

These Articles of the Christian faith, containing in all nineteen pages in the original, which is kept by the most reverend father in Christ, Matthew Archbishop of Canterbury, Primate of All England and Metropolitan, the archbishops and bishops of each province of the realm of England, gathered lawfully in the holy provincial synod, receive with one voice and confess, and by the subscription of their own hands approve as true and orthodox, the twenty-ninth day of the month of January, in the Year of our Lord, according to the reckoning of the

Ecclesiae Anglicanae, millesimo quingenesimo sexagesimo secundo; universusque clerus inferioris domus, eosdem etiam unanimiter et recepit et professus est, ut ex manuum suarum subscriptionibus patet, quas obtulit et deposuit apud eundem reverendissimum quinto die Februarii, Anno praedicto.

Quibus omnibus Articulis, serenissima princeps Elizabeth, Dei gratia Angliae, Franciae et Hiberniae regina, fidei defensor etc., per seipsam diligenter prius lectis et examinatis, regium suum assensum praebuit.

Church of England, one thousand five hundred and sixty-two (29 January 1562). And the whole clergy of the lower house has likewise received and confessed them with one voice, as is clear from the subscriptions of their own hands, which (subscriptions the clergy) have presented and deposited with the same most reverend (Archbishop of Canterbury), the fifth day of February in the aforesaid year (05 February 1562).

To all which Articles, the most sovereign princess Elizabeth, by the grace of God of England, France and Ireland, Queen, Defender of the Faith etc., having herself carefully read and examined them beforehand, has given her royal assent.

In 1571 the following declaration, in English only, was appended to the Articles:

This book of Articles before rehearsed is again approved, and allowed to be holden and executed within the realm, by the assent and consent of our Sovereign Lady Elizabeth, by the grace of God, of England, France and Ireland Queen, defender of the Faith etc. Which Articles were deliberately read and confirmed again by the subscription of the hands of the archbishop and bishops of the upper house, and by the subscription of the whole clergy of the nether house in their Convocation, in the year of our Lord God, 1571.

Reaction and Recovery

(1553-1559)

31. THE MARIAN INJUNCTIONS, 1554

History

Upon her accession to the throne on 18 July 1553, Mary I set about dismantling the Reformation as far as she could. The legislation of Edward VI was largely repealed during her first Parliament, which sat in the autumn of 1553. The following year, Parliament repealed all anti-Papal legislation which had been enacted since 1529. England was officially reconciled with Rome on 29 November 1554, and remained so at least until Mary's death on 17 November 1558. Her Injunctions, issued on 04 March 1554, indicate the kind of counter-reformation she had in mind, and her wishes were apparently carried out as far as they could be in the circumstances.

Theology

Mary wanted to return the Church of England to the position it had occupied in 1529. She abolished all reference to the Royal Supremacy, and ordered an investigation of heresy among the clergy. In practice, it seems that most of those who were deprived of their livings suffered because they had married, which shows that clerical celibacy was still a particularly sensitive issue among the traditionalists. The "sacramentaries" she castigated were people of Protestant, especially Zwinglian, views of the Eucharist. Mary was particularly concerned to put a stop to Protestant propaganda which was evidently spreading beyond her control, and which was soon to become even more vicious as the persecution of the Reformers became bloody.

01. That every bishop and his officers, with all other having ecclesiastical jurisdiction, shall with all speed and diligence, and all manner of ways to them possible, put in execution all such canons and ecclesiastical laws heretofore in the time of King Henry VIII used within this realm of England, and the dominions of the same, not being direct and expressly contrary to the laws and statutes of this realm.

02. That no bishop or any his officer, or other person aforesaid, hereafter in any of their ecclesiastical writings in process, or other extra-judicial acts, do use to put in this clause or sentence: *regia auctoritate fulcitus* (sanctioned by royal authority).

03. That no bishop or any his officers or other person aforesaid, do hereafter exact or demand in the admission of any person to any ecclesiastical promotion, order or office, any oath touching the primacy or succession, as of late, in few years past, has been accustomed and used.

04. That every bishop and his officers, with all other persons aforesaid, have a vigilant eye and use special diligence and foresight, that no person be admitted or received to any ecclesiastical function, benefice or office, being a sacramentary, infected or defamed with any notable kind of heresy or other great crime; and that the said bishop do stay and cause to be stayed, as much as lieth in him, that benefices and ecclesiastical promotions do not notably decay, or take hindrance, by passing or confirming of unreasonable leases.

05. That every bishop and all other persons aforesaid do diligently travail for the repressing of heresies and notable crimes, especially in the clergy, duly correcting and punishing the same.

06. That every bishop and all other persons aforesaid do likewise travail for the condemning and repressing of corrupt and naughty opinions, unlawful books, ballads and other pernicious and hurtful devices, engendering hatred among the people and discord among the same; and that schoolmasters, preachers and teachers do exercise and use their offices and duties without teaching, preaching or setting forth any evil or corrupt doctrine; and that, doing the contrary, they may be, by the bishop and his said officers, punished and removed.

07. That every bishop and all the other persons aforesaid, proceeding summarily, and with all celerity and speed, may and shall deprive, or declare deprived, and amove, according to their learning and discretion, all such persons from their benefices and ecclesiastical promotions who, contrary to the state of their order and the laudable custom of the Church, have married and used women as their wives, or otherwise notably and slanderously disordered or abused themselves; sequestering also, during the said process, the fruits and profits of the said benefices and ecclesiastical promotions.

08. That the said bishop and all other persons aforesaid, do use more lenity and clemency with such as have married, whose wives be dead, than with others whose women do yet remain in life; and likewise such priests as, with the consents of their wives or women, openly in the presence of the bishop do profess to abstain, to be used the more favourably; in which case, after penance effectually done, the bishop, according to his discretion and wisdom, may, upon just consideration, receive and admit them again to their former administration, so it be not in the same place; appointing them such a portion to live upon, to be paid out of their benefice, whereof they be deprived, by discretion of the said bishop, or his officers, as they shall think they may be spared of the said benefice.

09. That every bishop and all persons aforesaid, do foresee that they suffer not any religious man, having solemnly professed chastity, to continue with his woman or wife; but that all such persons, after deprivation of their benefice or ecclesiastical promotion, be also divorced every one from his said woman, and due punishment otherwise taken for the offence therein.

10. That every bishop and all other persons aforesaid do take order and direction with the parishioners of every benefice where priests do want [i.e. are lacking, *ed.*], to repair to the next parish for divine service; or to appoint for a convenient time, till other better provision may be made, one curate to serve (alternately) in divers parishes, and to allot to the said curate for his labour some portion of the benefice that he so serves.

11. That all and all manner of processions of the Church be used, frequented and continued after the old order of the Church, in the Latin tongue.

12. That all such holy days and fasting days be observed and kept, as were observed and kept in the latter time of Henry VIII.

13. That the laudable and honest ceremonies which were wont to be used, frequented and observed in the Church be also hereafter used, frequented and observed.

14. That children be christened by the priest, and confirmed by the bishops, as heretofore hath been accustomed and used.

15. Touching such persons as were heretofore promoted to any orders after the new sort and fashion of order, considering they were not ordered in very deed, the bishop of the diocese finding otherwise sufficiency and ability in these men, may supply that thing which wanted in them before; and then, according to his discretion, admit them to minister.

16. That by the bishop of the diocese, a uniform doctrine be set forth by homilies or otherwise, for the good instruction and teaching of all people; and that the said bishop and other persons aforesaid, do compel the parishioners to come to their several churches and there devoutly to hear divine service, as of reason they ought.

17. That they examine all schoolmasters and teachers of children, and finding them suspect in any wise, to remove them and place Catholic men in their rooms, with a special commandment to instruct their children, so as they may be able to answer the priest at the Mass and so help the priest to Mass as has been accustomed.

18. That the said bishop and all other persons aforesaid have such regard, respect and consideration of and for the setting forth of the premises with all kind of virtue, godly living and good example, with repressing also and keeping under of vice and unthriftiness, as they and every of them may be sen to favour the restitution of true religion; and also to make an honest account and reckoning of their office and cure to the honour of God, our good contentation, and the profit of this realm and dominions of the same.

32. THE ACT OF SUPREMACY, 1559
(1 Elizabeth I, c.1)

History

Upon succeeding to the throne in 1558, Queen Elizabeth I was forced to come to a quick settlement of Church affairs. The death of Cardinal Pole, on the same day as Mary I, made things easier for her, but she was still forced to tread warily. The bishops were Marian appointees, and opposed to a restored Protestantism. On the other hand, many in the House of Commons, and the returning exiles, wanted a more thoroughgoing change than even Edward VI had introduced.

Elizabeth compromised by restoring the Church of England to what was essentially its pre-1553 Protestantism, with certain minor modifications designed to placate the extremists. Historians still debate whether she got what she wanted, or was forced to accept a settlement not altogether to her liking, but either way, she defended it for the remainder of her reign, and it became the classical expression of Anglican erastianism.

A small part of the Act is still on the statute book, though most of it has been repealed by recent legislation. The process of repeal can be outlined as follows:

1640 Act for Repeal, etc.: Section 08 (end)
1846 Religious Disabilities Act: Section 14 (part)
1863 Statute Law Revision Act: Sections 09, 17, 20, 23, 24
1871 Promissory Oaths Act: Sections 10-13
1888 Statute Law Revision Act: Section 08 (preamble)
1948 Statute Law Revision Act: Sections 06, 16
1948 Criminal Justice Act: Section 18
1967 Criminal Law Act: Section 15
1969 Statute Law Revision Act: Sections 01-05, 07, 14 (rest), 21, 22

N.B. The portions of the Act which are still in force are indicated in this edition in **bold type**.

An Act restoring to the Crown the ancient Jurisdiction over the State Ecclesiastical and Spiritual, and abolishing all Foreign Power repugnant to the same.

01. Most humbly beseech your most excellent Majesty, your faithful and obedient subjects, the Lords spiritual and temporal, and the Commons, in this your present Parliament assembled, that where in time of the reign of your most dear father, of worthy memory, King Henry VIII, divers good laws and statutes were made and established, as well for the utter extinguishment and putting away of all usurped and foreign powers and authorities out of this your realm, and other your Highness's dominions and countries, as also for the restoring and uniting to the imperial crown of this realm the ancient jurisdictions, authorities, superiorities and pre-eminences to the same of right belonging and appertaining, by reason whereof we, your most humble and obedient subjects, from the five and twentieth year of the reign of your said dear father (1533-34), were continually kept in good order, and were disburdened of divers great and intolerable charges and exactions before that time unlawfully taken and exacted by such foreign power and authority as before that was usurped, until such time as all the said good laws and statutes, by one Act of Parliament made in the first and second years of the reigns of the late King Philip and Queen Mary (1554), your Highness's sister, intituled *An Act repealing all statutes, articles and provisions made against the See Apostolic of Rome since the twentieth year of King Henry VIII* (1529), and also for the establishment of all spiritual and ecclesiastical possessions and hereditaments conveyed to the laity, were all clearly repealed and made void, as by the same *Act of repeal* more at large does and may appear; by reason of which *Act of repeal*, your said humble subjects were eftsones [i.e. again, *ed.*] brought under an usurped foreign power and authority, and do yet remain in that bondage, to the intolerable charges of your loving subjects, if some redress, by the authority of this your High Court of Parliament, with the assent of your Highness, be not had and provided:

May it therefore please your Highness, for the repressing of the said usurped foreign power and the restoring of the rites, jurisdictions and pre-eminences appertaining to the imperial crown of this your realm, that it may be enacted by the authority of this present Parliament, that the said Act made in the said first and second years of the late King Philip and Queen Mary (1554), and all and every branch, clauses and articles therein contained (other than such branches, clauses and sentences as hereafter shall be excepted) may, from the last day of this session of Parliament (08 May 1559), be repealed, and shall from thenceforth be utterly void and of none effect.

02. And that also for the reviving of divers of the said good laws and statutes made in the time of your said dear father, it may also please your Highness, that one Act and statute made in the twenty-third year of the reign of the said late King Henry VIII (1531-32), intituled, *An Act that no person shall be cited out of the diocese wherein he or she dwells, except in certain cases*;

And one other Act made in the twenty-fourth year of the reign of the said late King (1532-33), intituled, *An Act that appeals in such cases as have been used to be pursued to the see of Rome shall not be from henceforth had nor used, but within this realm*;

And one other Act made in the twenty-fifth year of the said late King (1533-34), concerning restraint of payment of annates and firstfruits of archbishoprics and bishoprics to the See of Rome;

And one other Act in the said twenty-fifth year (1533-34), intituled, *An Act concerning the submission of the clergy to the King's Majesty*;

And also one Act made in the said twenty-fifth year (1533-34), intituled, *An Act restraining the payment of annates or firstfruits to the Bishop of Rome, and of the electing and consecrating of archbishops and bishops within this realm;*

And one other Act made in the said twenty-fifth year (1533-34), intituled, *An Act concerning the exoneration of the King's subjects from exactions and impositions heretofore paid to the See of Rome, and for having licenses and dispensations within this realm, without suing further for the same*;

And one other Act made in the twenty-sixth year of the said late King (1534-35), intituled, *An Act for nomination and consecration of suffragans within this realm*;

And also one other Act made in the twenty-eighth year of the reign of the said late King (1536-37), intituled, *An Act for the release of such as have obtained pretended licenses and dispensations from the See of Rome*;

And all and every branches, words and sentences in the said several Acts and statutes contained, by authority of this present Parliament, from and at all times after the last day of this session of Parliament (08 May 1559), shall be revived, and shall stand and be in full force and strength, to all intents, constructions and purposes.

And that the branches, sentences and words of the said several Acts, and every of them, from thenceforth shall and may be judged, deemed and taken to extend to your Highness, your heirs and successors, as fully and largely as ever the same Acts, or any of them, did extend to the said late King Henry VIII, your Highness's father.

03. And that it may also please your Highness, that it may be enacted by the authority of this present Parliament, that so much of one Act or statute made in the thirty-second year of the reign of your said dear father King Henry VIII (1540-41), intituled, *An Act concerning precontracts of marriages, and touching degrees of consanguinity*, as in the time of the late King Edward VI, your Highness's most dear brother, by one other Act or statute, was not repealed; and also one Act made in the thirty-seventh year of the reign of the said late King Henry VIII (1545-46), intituled, *An Act that doctors of the civil law, being married, may exercise ecclesiastical jurisdiction*; and all and every branches and articles in the said two Acts last mentioned, and not repealed in the time of the said late King Edward VI, may from thenceforth likewise stand and be revived, and remain in their full force and strength, to all intents and purposes; anything contained in the said Act of repeal aforementioned, or any other matter or cause to the contrary notwithstanding.

04. And that it may also please your Highness, that it may be further enacted by the authority aforesaid, that all other laws and statutes, and the branches and clauses of any Act or statute, repealed and made void by the said Act of repeal, made in the time of the said late King Philip and Queen Mary, and not in this present Act specially mentioned and revived, shall stand, remain and be repealed and void, in such like manner and form as they were before the making of this Act; anything herein contained to the contrary notwithstanding.

05. And that it may also please your Highness, that it may be enacted by the authority aforesaid, that one Act and statute made in the first year of the reign of the late King Edward VI, your Majesty's most dear brother, intituled, *An Act against such persons as shall unreverently speak against the Sacrament of the Body and Blood of Christ, commonly called the sacrament of the altar, and for the receiving thereof under both kinds,* and all and every branches, clauses and sentences therein contained, shall and may be likewise, from the last day of this session of Parliament (08 May 1559), be revived, and from thenceforth shall and may stand, remain and be in full force, strength and effect, to all intents, constructions and purposes, in such like manner and form as the same was at any time in the first year of the reign of the said late King Edward VI (1547); any law, statute or other matter to the contrary in any wise notwithstanding.

06. And that also it may please your Highness, that it may be further established and enacted by the authority aforesaid, that one Act and statute made in the first and second years of the said late King Philip and Queen Mary (1554), intituled, *An Act for the reviving of three statutes made for the punishment of heresies,* and also the said three statutes mentioned in the said Act, and by the same Act revived, and all and every branches, articles, clauses and sentences contained in the said several Acts and statutes, and every of them, shall be from the last day of this session of Parliament (08 May 1559) deemed and remain utterly repealed, void and of none effect, to all intents and purposes; anything in the said several Acts or any of them contained, or any other matter or cause to the contrary notwithstanding.

07. And to the intent that all usurped and foreign power and authority, spiritual and temporal, may for ever be clearly extinguished, and never to be used or obeyed within this realm, or any other your Majesty's dominions or countries, may it please your Highness that it may be further enacted by the authority aforesaid, that no foreign prince, person, prelate, state or potentate, spiritual or temporal, shall at any time after the last day of this session of Parliament (08 May 1559), use, enjoy or exercise any manner of power, jurisdiction, superiority, authority, pre-eminence or privilege, spiritual or ecclesiastical, within this realm, or within any other your Majesty's dominions or countries that now be, or hereafter shall be, but from thenceforth the same shall be clearly abolished out of this realm, and all other your Highness's dominions for ever; any statute, ordinance, custom, constitutions or any other matter or cause whatsoever to the contrary in any wise notwithstanding.

08. And that also it may likewise please your Highness, that it may be established and enacted by the authority aforesaid, **that such jurisdictions, privileges, superiorities and pre-eminences, spiritual and ecclesiastical, as by any spiritual or ecclesiastical power or authority have heretofore been, or may lawfully be exercised or used for the visitation of the ecclesiastical state and persons, and for reformation, order and correction of the same, and of all manner of errors, heresies, schisms, abuses, offences, contempts and enormities, shall for ever, by authority of this present Parliament, be united and annexed to the imperial crown of this realm.**

And that your Highness, your heirs and successors, kings or queens of this realm, shall have full power and authority by virtue of this Act, by letters patent under the great seal of England, to assign, name, and authorize, when and as often as your Highness, your heirs and successors, shall think meet and convenient, and for such and so long time as shall please your Highness, your heirs or successors, such person or persons being natural-born subjects to your Highness, your heirs or successors, as your Majesty, your heirs or successors, shall think meet, to exercise, use, occupy and execute under your Highness, your heirs and successors, all manner of jurisdictions, privileges and pre-eminences, in any wise touching or concerning any spiritual or ecclesiastical jurisdiction, within these your realms of England and Ireland, or any other your Highness's dominions or countries; and to visit, reform, redress, order, correct and amend all such errors, heresies, schisms, abuses, offences, contempts and enormities whatsoever, which by any manner spiritual or ecclesiastical power, authority or jurisdiction, can or may lawfully be reformed, ordered, redressed, corrected, restrained or amended, to the pleasure of Almighty God, to the increase of virtue and the conservation of the peace and unity of this realm, and that such person or persons so to be named, assigned, authorized and appointed by your Highness, your heirs or successors, after the said letters patent to him or them made and delivered, as is aforesaid, shall have full power and authority, by virtue of this Act, and of the said letters patent, under your Highness, your heirs and successors, to exercise, use, and execute all the premises, according to the tenor and effect of the said letters patent; any matter or cause to the contrary in any wise notwithstanding.

09. And for the better observation and maintenance of this Act, may it please your Highness that it may be further enacted by the authority aforesaid, that all and every archbishop, bishop, and all and every other ecclesiastical person, and other ecclesiastical officer and minister, of what estate, dignity, pre-eminence or degree soever he or they be or shall be, and all and every temporal judge, justice, mayor and other lay and temporal officer and minister, and every other person having your Highness's fee or wages, within this realm, or any your Highness's dominions, shall make, take and receive a corporal oath upon the Evangelist, before such person or persons as shall please your Highness, your heirs or successors, under the great seal of England to assign and name, to accept and to take the same according to the tenor and effect hereafter following, that is to say:

"I, A. B., do utterly testify and declare in my conscience, that the Queen's Highness is the only Supreme Governor of this realm, and of all other her Highness's dominions and countries, as well in all spiritual or ecclesiastical things or causes, as temporal, and that no foreign prince, person, prelate, state or potentate has, or ought to have, any jurisdiction, power, superiority, pre-eminence or authority ecclesiastical or spiritual, within this realm; and therefore I do utterly renounce and forsake all foreign jurisdictions, powers, superiorities and authorities, and do promise that from henceforth I shall bear faith and true allegiance to the Queen's Highness, her heirs and lawful successors, and to my power shall assist and defend all jurisdictions, pre-eminences, privileges and authorities granted or belonging to the Queen's Highness, her heirs and successors, or united and annexed to the imperial crown of this realm. So help me God, and by the contents of this book."

10. And that it may be also enacted, that if any such archbishop, bishop or other ecclesiastical officer or minister, or any of the said temporal judges, justiciaries or other lay officer or minister, shall peremptorily or obstinately refuse to take or receive the said oath, that then he so refusing shall forfeit and lose, only during his life, all and every ecclesiastical and spiritual promotion, benefice and office, and every temporal and lay promotion and office, which he has solely at the time of such refusal made; and that the whole title, interest and incumbency, in every such promotion, benefice and other office, as against such person only so refusing, during his life, shall clearly cease and be void, as though the party so refusing were dead.

And that also all and every such person and persons so refusing to take the said oath, shall immediately after such refusal be from thenceforth, during his life, disabled to retain or exercise any office or other promotion which he, at the time of such refusal, has jointly, or in common, with any other person or persons.

And that all and every person and persons, that at any time hereafter shall be preferred, promoted or collated to any archbishopric or bishopric, or to any other spiritual or ecclesiastical benefice, promotion, dignity, office or ministry, or that shall be by your Highness, your heirs or successors, preferred or promoted to any temporal or lay office, ministry or service within this realm, or in any your Highness's dominions, before he or they shall take upon him or them to receive, use, exercise, supply or occupy any such archbishopric, bishopric, promotion, dignity, office, ministry or service, shall likewise make, take and receive the said corporal oath before mentioned, upon the Evangelist, before such persons as have or shall have authority to admit any such person to any such office, ministry or service, or else before such person or persons as by your Highness, your heirs or successors, by commission under the great seal of England, shall be named, assigned or appointed to minister the said oath.

11. And that it may likewise be further enacted by the authority aforesaid, that if any such person or persons, as at any time hereafter shall be promoted, preferred or collated to any such promotion spiritual or ecclesiastical, benefice, office or ministry, or that by your Highness, your heirs or successors, shall be promoted or preferred to any temporal or lay office, ministry or service, shall and do peremptorily and obstinately refuse to take the same oath so to him to be offered; that then he or they so refusing shall presently be judged disabled in the law to receive, take or have the same promotion spiritual or ecclesiastical, the same temporal office, ministry or service within this realm, or any other your Highness's dominions, to all intents, constructions and purposes.

12. And that it may be further enacted by the authority aforesaid, that all and every person and persons temporal, suing livery or *ouster le main* out of the hands of your Highness, your heirs or successors, before his or their livery or *ouster le main* sued forth and allowed, and every temporal person or persons doing any homage to your Highness, your heirs or successors, or that shall be received into service with your Highness, your heirs or successors, shall make, take and receive the said corporal oath before mentioned, before the Lord Chancellor of England, or the Lord Keeper of the great seal for the time being, or before such person or persons as by your Highness, your heirs or successors, shall be named and appointed to accept or receive the same.

And that also all and every person and persons taking orders, and all and every other person and persons which shall be promoted or preferred to any degree of learning in any university within this your realm or dominions, before he shall receive or take any such orders, or be preferred to any such degree of learning, shall make, take and receive the said oath by this Act set forth and declared as is aforesaid, before his or their ordinary, commissary, chancellor or vice-chancellor, or their sufficient deputies in the said university.

13. Provided always, and that it may be further enacted by the authority aforesaid, that if any person, having any estate of inheritance in any temporal office or offices, shall hereafter obstinately and peremptorily refuse to accept and take the said oath as is aforesaid, and after, at any time during his life, shall willingly require to take and receive the said oath, and so do take and accept the same oath before any person or persons that shall have lawful authority to minister the same; that then every such person, immediately after he has so received the same oath, shall be vested, deemed and judged in like estate and possession of the said office, as he was before the said refusal, and shall and may use and exercise the said office in such manner and form as he should or might have done before such refusal, anything in this Act contained to the contrary in any wise notwithstanding.

14. And for the more sure observation of this Act, and the utter extinguishment of all foreign and usurped power and authority, may it please your Highness, that it may be further enacted by the authority aforesaid, that if any person or persons dwelling or inhabiting within this your realm, or in any other your Highness's realms or dominions, of what estate, dignity or degree soever he or they be, after the end of thirty days next after the determination of this session of the present Parliament (i.e. by 07 June 1559), shall by writing, printing, teaching, preaching, express words, deed or act, advisedly, maliciously and directly affirm, hold, stand with, set forth, maintain or defend the authority, pre-eminence, power or jurisdiction, spiritual or ecclesiastical, of any foreign prince, prelate, person, state or potentate whatsoever, heretofore claimed, used or usurped within this realm, or any dominion or country being within or under the power, dominion or obeisance of your Highness, or shall advisedly, maliciously and directly put in ure or execute anything for the extolling, advancement, setting forth, maintenance or defence of any such pretended or usurped jurisdiction, power, pre-eminence or authority, or any part thereof; that then every such person and persons so doing and offending, their abettors, aiders, procurers and counsellors, being thereof lawfully convicted and attainted, according to the due order and course of the common laws of this realm, for his or their first offence shall forfeit and lose unto your Highness, your heirs and successors, all his and their goods and chattels, as well real as personal.

And if any such person so convicted or attainted shall not have or be worth of his proper goods and chattels to the value of twenty pounds, at the time of his conviction or attainder, that then every such person so convicted and attainted, over and besides the forfeiture of all his said goods and chattels, shall have and suffer imprisonment by the space of one whole year, without bail or mainprize.

And that also all and every the benefices, prebends and other ecclesiastical promotions and dignities whatsoever, of every spiritual person so offending, and being attainted, shall immediately after such attainder be utterly void to all intents and purposes, as though the incumbent thereof were dead; and that the patron and donor of every such benefice, prebend, spiritual promotion and dignity, shall and may lawfully present unto the same, or give the same, in such manner and form as if the said incumbent were dead.

And if any such offender or offenders, after such conviction or attainder, do eftsones [i.e. again, ed.] commit or do the said offences, or any of them, in manner and form aforesaid, and be thereof duly convicted and attainted, as is aforesaid; that then every such offender and offenders shall for the same second offence incur into the dangers, penalties and forfeitures ordained and provided by the statute of Provision and *Praemunire*, made in the sixteenth year of the reign of King Richard II (1393).

And if any such offender or offenders, at any time after the said second conviction and attainder, do the third time commit and do the said offences, or any of them, in manner and form aforesaid, and be thereof duly convicted and attainted, as is aforesaid; that then every such offence or offences shall be deemed and adjudged high treason, and that the offender and offenders therein, being thereof lawfully convicted and attainted, according to the laws of this realm, shall suffer pains of death, and other penalties, forfeitures and losses, as in cases of high treason by the laws of this realm.

15. And also that it may likewise please your Highness, that it may be enacted by the authority aforesaid, that no manner of person or persons shall be molested or impeached for any of the offences aforesaid, committed or perpetrated only by preaching, teaching or words, unless he or they be thereof lawfully indicted within the space of one half-year next after his or their offences so committed; and in case any person or persons shall fortune to be imprisoned for any of the said offences committed by preaching, teaching or words only, and be not thereof indicted within the space of one half-year next after his or their such offence so committed and done, that then the said person so imprisoned shall be set at liberty, and be no longer detained in prison for any such cause or offence.

16. Provided always, and be it enacted by the authority aforesaid, that this Act, or anything therein contained, shall not in any wise extend to repeal any clause, matter or sentence contained or specified in the said Act of repeal made in the said first and second years of the reigns of the said late King Philip and Queen Mary (1554), as does in any wise touch or concern any matter or case of *Praemunire*, or that does make or ordain any matter or cause to be within the case of *Praemunire*; but that the same, for so much only as touches or concerns any case or matter of *Praemunire*, shall stand and remain in such force and effect as the same was before the making of this Act, anything in this Act contained to the contrary in any wise notwithstanding.

17. Provided also, and be it enacted by the authority aforesaid, that this Act, or anything therein contained, shall not in any wise extend or be prejudicial to any person or persons for any offence or offences committed or done, or hereafter to be committed or done, contrary to the tenor and effect of any Act or statute now revived by this Act, before the end of thirty days next after the end of the session of this present Parliament (i.e. by 07 June 1559); anything in this Act contained or any other matter or cause to the contrary notwithstanding.

18. And if it happen that any peer of this realm shall fortune to be indicted of and for any offence that is revived or made *Praemunire* or treason by this Act, that then he so being indicted shall have his trial by his peers, in

such like manner and form as in other cases of treason has been used.

19. Provided always, and be it enacted as is aforesaid, that no manner of order, Act, or determination, for any manner of religion or cause ecclesiastical, had or made by the authority of this present Parliament, shall be accepted, deemed, interpreted or adjudged at any time hereafter, to be any error, heresy, schism or schismatical opinion; any order, decree, sentence, constitution or law, whatsoever the same be, to the contrary notwithstanding.

20. Provided always, and be it enacted by the authority aforesaid, that such person or persons to whom your Highness, your heirs or successors, shall hereafter, by letters patent, under the great seal of England, give authority to have or execute any jurisdiction, power or authority spiritual, or to visit, reform, order or correct any errors, heresies, schisms, abuses or enormities by virtue of this Act, shall not in any wise have authority or power to order, determine or adjudge any matter or cause to be heresy, but only such as heretofore have been determined, ordered or adjudged to be heresy by the authority of the canonical Scriptures, or by the first four general Councils, or any of them, or by any other general Council wherein the same was declared heresy by the express and plain words of the said canonical Scriptures, or such as hereafter shall be ordered, judged or determined to be heresy by the High Court of Parliament of this realm, with the assent of the clergy in their Convocation; anything in this Act contained to the contrary notwithstanding.

21. And be it further enacted by the authority aforesaid, that no person or persons shall be hereafter indicted or arraigned for any the offences made, ordained, revived or adjudged by this Act, unless there be two sufficient witnesses or more, to testify and declare the said offences whereof he shall be indicted or arraigned; and that the said witnesses, or so many of them as shall be living and within this realm at the time of the arraignment of such person so indicted, shall be brought forth in person, face to face, before the party so arraigned, and there shall testify and declare what they can say against the party so arraigned, if he require the same.

22. Provided also, and be it enacted by the authority aforesaid, that if any person or persons shall hereafter happen to give any relief, aid or comfort, or in any wise be aiding, helping, or comforting to the person or persons of any that shall hereafter happen to be an offender in any matter or case of *Praemunire* or treason, revived or made by this Act, that then such relief, aid or comfort given shall not be judged or taken to be any offence, unless there be two sufficient witnesses at the least, that can and will openly testify and declare that the person or persons that so gave such relief, aid or comfort, had notice and knowledge of such offence committed and done by the said offender, at the time of such relief, aid, or comfort so to him given or ministered; anything in this Act contained, or any other matter or cause to the contrary in any wise notwithstanding.

23. And where one pretended sentence has heretofore been given in the Consistory of Paul's before certain judges delegate, by the authority legatine of the late Cardinal Pole, by reason of a foreign usurped power and authority, against Richard Chetwood, Esq., and Agnes his wife, by the name of Agnes Woodhall, at the suit of Charles Tyrrell, gentleman, in a cause of matrimony solemnized between the said Richard and Agnes, as by the same pretended sentence more plainly doth appear, from which sentence the said Richard and Agnes have appealed to the court of Rome, which appeal does there remain, and yet is not determined; may it therefore please your Highness that it may be enacted by the authority aforesaid, that if sentence in the said appeal shall happen to be given at the said court of Rome for and in the behalf of the said Richard and Agnes, for the reversing of the said pretended sentence, before the end of threescore days next after the end of this session of this present Parliament (i.e. by 07 July 1559), that then the same shall be judged and taken to be good and effectual in the law, and shall and may be used, pleaded and allowed in any court or place within this realm; anything in this Act or any other Act or statute contained to the contrary notwithstanding.

And if no sentence shall be given at the court of Rome in the said appeal for the reversing of the said pretended sentence before the end of the said threescore days, that then it shall and may be lawful for the said Richard and Agnes, and either of them, at any time hereafter, to commence, take, sue and prosecute their said appeal from the said pretended sentence, and for the reversing of the said pretended sentence, within this realm, in such like manner and form as was used to be pursued, or might have been pursued, within this realm, at any time since the twenty-fourth year of the reign of the said late King Henry VIII (1532-33), upon any sentences given in the court or courts of any archbishop within this realm.

And that such appeal as so hereafter shall be taken or pursued by the said Richard Chetwood and Agnes, or either of them, and the sentence that herein or thereupon shall hereafter be given, shall be judged to be good and effectual in the law to all intents and purposes; any law, custom, usage, canon, constitution or any other matter or cause to the contrary notwithstanding.

24. Provided also and be it enacted by the authority aforesaid, that where there is the like appeal now depending in the said court of Rome between one Robert Harcourt, merchant of the staple, and Elizabeth Harcourt, otherwise called Elizabeth Robins, of the one part, and Anthony Fydell, merchant-stranger, on the other part, that the said Robert, Elizabeth and Anthony, and every of them, shall and may, for the prosecuting and trying of their said appeal, have and enjoy the like remedy, benefit and advantage, in like manner and form as the said Richard and Agnes, or any of them, has, may or ought to have and enjoy; this Act or anything therein contained to the contrary in any wise notwithstanding.

33. THE ACT OF UNIFORMITY, 1559
(1 Elizabeth I, c. 2)

History

Soon after ascending the throne, Elizabeth I moved to ensure that the Church of England would be established along the same lines as it had been at the close of the reign of Edward VI. The Act of Uniformity which came into effect on 24 June 1559 repealed all Mary's anti-Protestant legislation. Well over half the text of the Act of Uniformity of 1549 is repeated *verbatim*, and parts of the 1552 Act are incorporated as well. One point worth noticing is that the Edwardian provision for the continued use of Latin in the universities and other places where it was understood is not repeated in this Act. The Act remained in force until 1640, when the breakdown of the 1559 Settlement led to civil war.

Theology

The 1559 Act enjoined a Settlement which was clearly Protestant, though somewhat less radical than that of 1552. A number of minor concessions were made to traditionalist sensibilities, in the hope that those of Catholic sympathies might be reconciled to the new order. Most Protestants accepted the apparent compromise, recognizing the difficult political situation at the beginning of the new reign, though many hoped for further reform later. In this they were to be disappointed, and as time went on a "Puritan" party emerged to make the case for a more thorough and consistent Reformation. Elizabeth I consistently opposed their demands, and encouraged conformist theologians to develop an apologetic for the 1559 Settlement, calling it the middle way (*via media*) between Geneva and Rome.

01. Where at the death of our late Sovereign Lord King Edward the Sixth, there remained one uniform order of common service and prayer and of the administration of sacraments, rites and ceremonies in the Church of England, which was set forth in one book entitled the *Book of Common Prayer and Administration of Sacraments and Other Rites and Ceremonies in the Church of England*, authorized by Act of Parliament holden in the fifth and sixth years of our said late Sovereign Lord King Edward the Sixth, intitled *An Act for the Uniformity of Common Prayer and Administration of the Sacraments*, the which was repealed and taken away by Act of Parliament in the first year of the reign of our late Sovereign Lady Queen Mary, to the great decay of the due honour of God and discomfort to the professors of the truth of Christ's religion:

Be it therefore enacted by the authority of this present Parliament that the said Statute of Repeal and everything therein contained, only concerning the said Book and Service, Administration of Sacraments, Rites and Ceremonies contained or appointed in or by the said Book, shall be void and of none effect from and after the feast of the nativity of St John Baptist next coming (24 June 1559), and that the said Book, with the Order of Service and of the Administration of Sacraments, Rites and Ceremonies, with the alterations and additions therein added and appointed by this statute, shall stand and be from and after the said feast of the nativity of St John Baptist in full force and effect according to the tenor and effect of this statute, anything in the aforesaid statute of repeal to the contrary notwithstanding.

02. And further be it enacted by the Queen's Highness with the assent of the Lords and Commons in this present Parliament assembled, and by the authority of the same, that all and singular ministers in any cathedral or parish church or other place within this realm of England, Wales, and the marches of the same, or other the Queen's dominions, shall from and after the feast of the nativity of St John Baptist next coming (24 June 1559), be bound to say and use the Matins, Evensong, celebration of the Lord's Supper, and administration of each of the sacraments, and all their common and open prayer, in such order and form as is mentioned in the said book so authorized by Parliament in the said fifth and sixth year of the reign of King Edward the Sixth, with one alteration or addition of certain lessons to be used on every Sunday in the year, and the form of the Litany altered and corrected, and two sentences only added in the delivery of the sacrament to the communicants, and none other or otherwise; and that if any manner of parson, vicar or other whatsoever minister, that ought or should sing or say common prayer mentioned in the said book, or minister the sacraments, shall after the said feast of the nativity of St John Baptist next coming (24 June 1559) refuse to use the said common prayers, or to minister the sacraments in such cathedral or parish church or other places as he should use to minister the same, in such order and form as they be mentioned and set forth in the said book; or shall use, wilfully or obstinately standing in the same, any other rite, ceremony, order, form or manner of Mass openly or privily, or Matins, Evensong, administration of the sacraments, or other open prayer than is mentioned and set forth in the said book (open prayer in and throughout this Act, is meant that prayer which is for other to come unto or hear, either in common churches or private chapels or oratories, commonly called the service of the Church); or shall preach, declare or speak anything in the derogation or depraving of the said book, or anything therein contained, or of any part thereof, and shall be thereof lawfully convicted according to the laws of this realm, by verdict of twelve men, or by his own confession, or by the notorious evidence of the fact, shall lose and forfeit to the Queen's Highness, her heirs and successors, for his first offence, the profit of all his spiritual benefices or promotions coming and arising in one whole year next after his conviction; and also that the same person so convicted shall for the same offence suffer imprisonment by the space of six months, without bail or mainprize; and if any such person, once convicted of any offence concerning the premises, shall after his first conviction eftsones [i.e. again, *ed.*] offend, and be thereof in form aforesaid lawfully convicted, that then the same person shall for his second offence suffer imprisonment by the space of one whole year, and also shall therefore be deprived *ipso facto* of all his spiritual promotions; and that it shall be lawful to all patrons, donors and grantees of all and singular the same spiritual promotions to present to the same any other able clerk, in like manner and form as though the party so offending were dead; and that if any such person or persons, after he shall be twice convicted in form aforesaid, shall offend against any of the premises the third time shall be deprived *ipso facto* of all his spiritual promotions and also shall suffer imprisonment during his life; and if the person that shall offend or be convicted in form aforesaid, concerning any of the premises, shall not be beneficed nor have any spiritual promotion, that then the same person so offending and convicted shall for the first offence suffer imprisonment during one whole year next after his conviction without bail or mainprize; and that if any such person not having any spiritual promotion after his first conviction shall eftsones offend in anything concerning the premises, and shall in form aforesaid be lawfully convicted, that then the same person shall for his second offence suffer imprisonment during his life.

03. And it is ordained and enacted by the authority abovesaid that if any person or persons whatsoever, after the said feast of the nativity of St John Baptist next coming (24 June 1559), shall in any interludes, plays, songs, rhymes or by other open words declare or speak anything in the derogation, depraving or despising of the same book or of anything therein contained, or any part thereof, or shall by open fact, deed, or by open threatenings, compel or cause, or otherwise procure or maintain any parson, vicar or other minister in any cathedral or parish church, or in any chapel or other place, to sing or say any common or open prayer, or to minister any sacrament otherwise or in any other manner or form than is mentioned in the said book; or that by any of the said means shall unlawfully interrupt or let [i.e. hinder, *ed.*] any parson, vicar or other ministers in any cathedral or parish church, chapel or any other place, to sing or say common or open prayer, or to minister the sacraments or any of them in any such manner and form as is mentioned in the said book, that then every person being thereof lawfully convicted in form abovesaid shall forfeit to the Queen our Sovereign Lady, her heirs and successors for the first offence, a hundred marks; and if any person or persons, being once convicted of any such offence, eftsones offend against any of the last recited offences and shall in form aforesaid be thereof lawfully convicted, that then the same person so offending and convicted shall for the second offence forfeit to the Queen our Sovereign Lady, her heirs and successors, four hundred marks; and if any persons, after he in form aforesaid shall be twice convicted of any offence concerning any of the last recited offences, shall offend the third time and be thereof in form lawfully convicted, that then every person so offending and convicted shall for his third offence forfeit to our Sovereign Lady the Queen all his goods and chattels, and shall suffer imprisonment during his life; and if any person or persons, that for his first offence concerning the premises shall be convicted in form aforesaid, does not pay the sum to be paid by virtue of his conviction in such manner and form as the same ought to be paid, within six weeks next after his conviction, that then every person so convicted and so not paying the same shall for the same first offence, instead of the said sum, suffer imprisonment by the space of six months, without bail or mainprize; and if any person or persons that for his second offence concerning the premises shall be convicted in form aforesaid do not pay the sum to be paid by virtue of his conviction in such manner and form as the same ought to be paid, within six weeks next after his said second conviction, that then every person so convicted and not so paying the same, shall for the same second offence, instead of the said sum, suffer imprisonment during twelve months without bail or mainprize; and that from and after the said feast of the nativity of St John Baptist next coming (24 June 1559), all and every person and persons inhabiting within this realm or any other the Queen's Majesty's dominions, shall diligently and faithfully, having no lawful or reasonable excuse to be absent, endeavour themselves to resort to their parish church, or chapel accustomed, or upon reasonable let thereof to some usual place where common prayer and such service of God shall be used in such time of let, upon every Sunday and other days ordained and used to be kept as Holy Days, and then and there to abide orderly and soberly during the time of the common prayer, preachings or other service of God there to be used and ministered; upon pain or punishment by the censures of the Church, and also upon pain that every person so offending shall forfeit for every such offence twelve pence, to be levied by the churchwardens of the parish where such offence shall be done, to the use of the poor of the same parish, of the goods, lands and tenements of such offender by way of distress.

04. And for the due execution hereof, the Queen's most excellent Majesty, the Lords temporal and all the Commons in this present (Parliament) assembled, doth in God's name earnestly require and charge all the archbishops, bishops and other ordinaries, that they shall endeavour themselves to the uttermost of their knowledge, that the due and true execution hereof may be had throughout their dioceses and charges, as they will answer before God for such evils and plagues wherewith Almighty God may justly punish his people for neglecting this good and wholesome law. And for their authority in this behalf, be it further likewise enacted by the authority aforesaid, that all and singular the same archbishops, bishops and all other their officers exercising ecclesiastical jurisdiction, as well in place exempt as not exempt within their dioceses, shall have full power and authority by this Act to reform, correct and punish by censures of the Church, all and singular persons which shall offend, within any of their jurisdictions or dioceses, after the said feast of the nativity of St John Baptist next coming (24 June 1559) against this Act and Statute; any other law, statute, privilege, liberty or provision heretofore made, had or suffered to the contrary notwithstanding.

05. And it is ordained and enacted by the authority aforesaid that all and every justice of *oyer* and *determiner* or justices of assize, shall have full power and authority, in every of their open and general sessions, to inquire, hear and determine all and all manner of offences that shall be committed or done contrary to any article contained in this present Act, within the limit of the commission to them directed, and to make process for the execution of the same as they do against any person being indicted before them of trespass, or lawfully convicted thereof.

06. Provided always and be it enacted by the authority aforesaid, that all and every archbishop and bishop shall or may, at all time and times at his liberty and pleasure, join and associate himself by virtue of this Act to the said justices of *oyer* and *determiner* or to the said justices of assize, at every of the said open and general sessions to be holden in any place within his diocese, for and to the inquiry, hearing and determining of the offence aforesaid.

07. Provided also and be it enacted by the authority aforesaid, that the books concerning the said services shall at the costs and charges of the parishioners of every parish and cathedral church be attained and gotten before the feast of the nativity of St John Baptist next following (24 June 1559); and that all such parish and cathedral churches, or other place where the said books shall be attained [i.e. obtained, *ed.*] and gotten before the said feast of the nativity of St John Baptist, shall within three weeks next after the said books so attained and gotten use the said service and put the same in use according to this Act.

08. And be it further enacted by the authority aforesaid, that no person or persons shall be at any time hereafter impeached or otherwise molested of or for any of the offences above mentioned hereafter to be committed or done contrary to this Act, unless he or they so offending be thereof indicted at the next general sessions to be holden before any such justices of *oyer* or *determiner* or justices of assize, next after any offence committed or done contrary to the tenor of this Act.

09. Provided always and be it ordered and enacted by the authority aforesaid that all and singular Lords in the Parliament for the third offence above mentioned shall be tried by their peers.

10. Provided always and be it ordered and enacted by the authority aforesaid that the mayor of London and all other mayors, bailiffs and other

head officers, of all and singular cities, boroughs and towns corporate within this realm, Wales, and the marches of the same to the which justices of assize do not commonly repair, shall have full power and authority by virtue of this Act to inquire, hear and determine the offences above said and every of them, yearly within fifteen days after the feasts of Easter and St Michael the Archangel (29 September), in like manner and form as justices of assize and *oyer* and *determiner* may do.

11. Provided always and be it ordained and enacted by the authority aforesaid that all singular archbishops and bishops, and every of their chancellors, commissaries, archdeacons and other ordinaries, having any peculiar ecclesiastical jurisdiction, shall have full power and authority by virtue of this Act as well to inquire in their visitations and synods, and elsewhere within their jurisdiction at any other time or place to take accusations and informations, of all and every the things above mentioned, done, committed or perpetrated within the limits of their jurisdictions and authority, and to punish the same by admonition, excommunication, sequestration or deprivation, or other censures and process, in like form as heretofore hath been used in like cases by the Queen's ecclesiastical laws.

12. Provided always and be it enacted that whatsoever person offending in the premises shall for the first offence receive punishment of the ordinary, having a testimonial thereof under the said ordinary's seal, shall not for the same offence eftsones be convened before the justices; and likewise receiving for the said first offence punishment by the justices, he shall not for the same offence eftsones receive punishment of the ordinary; anything contained in this Act to the contrary notwithstanding.

13. Provided always and be it enacted that such ornaments of the Church and of the ministers thereof shall be retained and be in use as was in the Church of England by authority of Parliament in the second year of the reign of King Edward the Sixth, until other order shall be therein taken by the Queen's Majesty, with the advice of her commissioners appointed and authorized under the great seal of England for ecclesiastical causes, or of the metropolitan of this realm; and also that if there shall happen any contempt or irreverence to be used in the ceremonies or rites of the Church by the misusing of the orders appointed in this Book, the Queen's Majesty may by the like advice of the said commissioners or metropolitan ordain and publish such further ceremonies or rites as may be most for the advancement of God's glory, the edifying of his Church and the due reverence of Christ's holy mysteries and sacraments.

14. And be it further enacted by the authority aforesaid that all laws, statutes and ordinances wherein or whereby any other service, administration of sacraments or common prayer is limited, established or set forth to be used within this realm or any other the Queen's dominions or countries, shall from henceforth be utterly void and of none effect.

34. THE ELIZABETHAN INJUNCTIONS, 1559

History

These Injunctions repeat most of those of Edward VI. To facilitate comparison with them, the corresponding numbers of the Edwardian Injunctions are printed in parentheses immediately after the numbers in this text. Phrases which were altered or added in 1559 are indicated in italics, except for such obvious changes as the substitution of the word "Queen" for "King" etc.

Theology

The Injunctions reveal the essentially Protestant character of Elizabeth's religious policy, and their implementation became a cornerstone of her Settlement of the Church. As time went on, they came to be regarded as a bulwark of conservative orthodoxy against the rising trend of Puritanism, and many of their provisions fell into disuse as more radical positions were adopted by many ministers. Charles I (1625-1649) tried to revive them as the basis for an agreed conformity within the Church of England, but his attempt failed – a clear indication of how far ecclesiastical opinion had moved in the direction of Puritanism since the early days of the Protestant Settlement.

Injunctions given by the Queen's Majesty, as well to the clergy as to the laity of this realm.

The Queen's most royal Majesty, by the advice of her most honourable council, intending the advancement of the true honour of Almighty God, the suppression of superstition throughout all her Highness's realms and dominions, and to plant true religion to the extirpation of all hypocrisy, enormities and abuses, as to her duty appertaineth, doth minister unto her loving subjects these godly injunctions hereafter following. All which injunctions, her Highness willeth and commandeth her said loving subjects obediently to receive and truly to observe and keep, every man in their offices, degrees and states, as they will avoid her Highness's displeasure and the pains of the same hereafter expressed.

01. (01a) The first is that all deans, archdeacons, parsons, vicars and other ecclesiastical persons shall faithfully keep and observe, and as far as in them may be, shall cause to be observed and kept of other, all and singular laws and statutes made *for the restoring to the Crown the ancient jurisdiction*

over the state ecclesiastical, and abolishing of all foreign power repugnant to the same. And furthermore, all ecclesiastical persons, having cure of soul, shall to the uttermost of their wit, knowledge and learning, purely and sincerely, and without any colour or dissimulation, declare, manifest and open, four times every year at the least, in their sermons and other collations, that *all* usurped *and foreign* power, having no establishment nor ground by the law of God, was of most just causes taken away and abolished, and that therefore no manner of obedience or subjection within her Highness's realms and dominions is due unto *any such foreign power.* And that the Queen's power within her realms and dominions is the highest power under God, to whom all men within the same realms and dominions, by God's laws owe most loyalty and obedience, afore and above all other powers and potentates in earth.

02. (01b) Besides this, to the intent that all superstition and hypocrisy crept into men's hearts, may vanish away, they shall not set forth or extol any images, relics or miracles, for any superstition or lucre, nor allure the people by any enticements, to the pilgrimage of any saint or image, but reproving the same, they shall teach that all goodness, health and grace ought to be both asked and looked for only of God, as of the very author and giver of the same, and of none other.

03. (02) Item, that they, the persons above rehearsed, shall *preach* in their churches, and every other cure they have, one sermon, every quarter of the year at the least, wherein they shall purely and sincerely declare the Word of God, and in the same, exhort their hearers to the works of faith, mercy and charity specially prescribed and commanded in Scripture, and that works devised by men's fantasies, besides Scripture, as wandering to pilgrimages, offering of money, candles or tapers to relics, or images, or kissing and licking of the same, praying upon beads, or such like superstition, have not only no promise of reward in Scripture, for doing of them, but contrariwise, great threats and maledictions of God, for that they be things tending to idolatry and superstition, which of all other offences God Almighty doth most detest and abhor, for that the same diminish his honour and glory.

04. (32) Item, that they the persons above rehearsed shall preach in their own persons once in every quarter of the year at the least, one sermon, being licensed specially thereunto, as is specified hereafter, or else shall read some homily prescribed to be used by the Queen's authority every Sunday at the least, unless some other preacher sufficiently licensed, as hereafter chance to come to the parish for the same purpose of preaching.

05. (04) Item, that every holy day throughout the year, when they have no sermon, they shall immediately after the Gospel openly and plainly recite to their parishioners, in the pulpit, the *Paternoster*, the Creed and the Ten Commandments in English, to the intent that the people may learn the same by heart, exhorting all parents and householders to teach their children and servants the same, as they are bound by the law of God and in conscience to do.

06. (07) Also that they shall provide within three months next after this visitation, one book of the whole Bible, of the largest volume, in English. And within one twelve-months next after the said visitation, the Paraphrasis of Erasmus also in English upon the Gospels, and the same set up in some convenient place, within the said church that they have cure of, whereas their parishioners may most commodiously resort unto the same and read the same, *out of the time of common service*. The charges of which books have been ratably borne, between the Parson or proprietary, and the parishioners aforesaid, that is to say, the one half by the Parson or proprietary and the other half by the parishioners. And they shall discourage no man (authorized and licensed thereto) from the reading of any part of the Bible, either in Latin or in English, but shall rather conform and exhort every person to read the same, as the very lively Word of God, and the special food of man's soul, that all Christian persons are bound to embrace, believe and follow, if they look to be saved; whereby they may the better know their duties to God, to their Sovereign Lady the Queen and their neighbour, ever gently and charitably exhorting them, and in her Majesty's name, straightly charging and commanding them, that in the reading thereof, no man to reason or contend, but quietly to hear the reader.

07. (08) Also, the said ecclesiastical persons shall in no wise at any unlawful time, nor for any other cause than their honest necessity, haunt or resort to any taverns or alehouses. And after their dinner and supper, they shall not give themselves to drinking or riot, spending their time idly, by day or by night, at dice, cards or tables playing, or any other lawful game, but at all times as they shall have leisure, they shall hear or read somewhat of Holy Scripture, or shall occupy themselves with some other honest exercise, and that they always do the things which appertain to honesty, with endeavour to profit the common weal, having always in mind that they ought to excel all others in purity of life and should be examples to the people, to live well and Christianly.

08. (10) Also, that they shall admit no man to preach within any of their cures, but such as shall appear unto them to be sufficiently licensed thereunto by the Queen's Majesty, the Archbishop of Canterbury, the Archbishop of York in *either their provinces* or the bishop of the diocese, *or by the Queen's Majesty's visitors*. And such as shall be so licensed they shall gladly receive to declare the Word of God, without any resistance or contradiction. *And that no other be suffered to preach out of his own cure or parish than such as shall be licensed, as is above expressed.*

09. (12) Also, if they do or shall know any man within their parish, or elsewhere, that is a letter (i.e. hinderer, *ed.*) of the Word of God to be read in English, or sincerely preached, or of the execution of these the Queen's Majesty's Injunctions, or a fautor (i.e. abettor, *ed.*) of *any usurped and foreign* power, now by the laws of this realm justly rejected, extirped and taken away utterly, they shall detect and present the same to the Queen or her council, *or to the ordinary* or to the justice of peace next adjoining.

10. (13) Also, that the parson, vicar or curate and parishioners of every parish within this realm shall in their churches and chapels keep one book or register, wherein they shall write the day and year of every wedding, christening and burial made within their parish for their time, and so every man succeeding them likewise; and also therein shall write every person's name that shall be so wedded, christened or buried; and for the safe keeping of the same book, the parish shall be bound to provide of their common charges one sure coffer with two locks and keys, whereof the one to remain with the parson, vicar or curate and the other with the wardens of every parish church or chapel wherein the said book shall be laid up; which book you shall every Sunday take forth and in the presence of the said wardens, or one of them, write and record in the same all the weddings, christenings and burials made the whole week before, and that done, to lay up the book in the said coffer as before; and for every time that the same shall be omitted, the party that shall be in the fault thereof shall forfeit to the said church three shillings and fourpence, to be employed *the one half* to the poor men's box of that parish, *the other half towards the repair of the church.*

11. (14) Furthermore, because the goods of the Church are called the goods of the poor, and at these days nothing is less seen than the poor to be sustained with the same, all parsons, vicars, pensionaries, prebendaries and other beneficed men within this deanery, not being resident upon their benefices, which may dispend yearly twenty pounds or above, either within this deanery or elsewhere, shall distribute hereafter among their poor parishioners, or other inhabitants there, in the presence of the churchwardens or some other honest men of the parish, the fortieth part of the fruits and revenues of this said benefice, lest they be worthily noted of ingratitude, which, reserving so many parts to themselves, cannot vouchsafe to impart the fortieth portion thereof among the poor people of that parish, that is so fruitful and profitable unto them.

12. (15) And to the intent that learned men may hereafter spring the more for the execution of the premises, every parson, vicar, clerk or beneficed man within this deanery, having yearly to dispend, in benefices and other promotions of the Church, an hundred pounds, shall give competent exhibition to one scholar, and for as many hundred pounds more as he may dispend, to so many scholars more shall give like exhibition in the University of Oxford or Cambridge, or some grammar school, which, after they have profited in good learning, may be partners of their patron's cure and charge, as well in preaching as otherwise in the execution of their offices, or may, when need shall be, otherwise profit the commonwealth with their counsel and wisdom.

13. (16) Also that all proprietaries, parsons, vicars and clerks, having churches, chapels or mansions within this deanery, shall bestow yearly hereafter upon the same mansions or chancels of their churches, being in decay, the fifth part of that their benefices, till they be fully repaired, and the same, so repaired, shall always keep and maintain in good estate.

14. (17) Also, that the said parsons, vicars and clerks shall once every quarter of the year read these Injunctions given unto them openly and deliberately before all their parishioners, to the intent that both they may be the better admonished of their duty and their said parishioners the more moved to follow the same for their part.

15. (18) Also, forasmuch as by a law established, every man is bound to pay his tithes, no man shall, by colour of duty omitted by their curates, detain their tithes and so redouble and requite one wrong with another, or be his own judge; but shall truly pay the same as he hath been accustomed, to their parsons, vicars and curates, without any restraint or diminution; and such lack or default as they can justly find in their parsons and curates, to call for reformation thereof at their ordinaries' and other superiors' hands, who upon complaint and due proof thereof shall reform the same accordingly.

16. (20) Also that every parson, vicar, curate, chantry priest and stipendiary, being under the degree of *a Master of Arts*, shall provide and have of his own, within three months after this visitation, the New Testament both in Latin and in English, with Paraphrasis upon the same of Erasmus, and diligently study the same, conferring the one with the other. And the bishops and other ordinaries by themselves, or their officers, in their synods and visitations, shall examine the said ecclesiastical persons, how they have profited in the study of Holy Scripture.

17. (22b) Also, that this *vice of* damnable despair may be clearly taken away and firm belief and steadfast hope surely conceived of all their parishioners, being in any danger, they shall learn, and have always in a readiness, such comfortable places and sentences of Scripture as do set forth the mercy, benefits and goodness of Almighty God, towards all penitent and believing persons, that they may at all times, when necessity shall require, promptly comfort their flock with the lively Word of God, which is the only stay of man's conscience.

18. (23) Also, to avoid all contention and strife which heretofore hath arisen among the Queen's Majesty's subjects, in sundry places of her realms and dominions, by reason of fond courtesy and challenging of places in processions, and also that they may the more quickly hear that which is said or sung, to their edifying; they shall not from henceforth in any parish church, at any time use any procession about the church or churchyard, or other place, but immediately before high mass the priest, with others of the choir, shall kneel in the midst of the church and sing or say, plainly and distinctly, the Litany, which is set forth in English, with all the suffrages following, and none other procession or litany to be had or used but the said Litany in English, adding nothing thereto but as the Queen's grace shall hereafter appoint; and in cathedral or collegiate churches the same shall be done in such places as our commissaries in our visitation shall appoint. And in the time of the Litany, of the *common prayer*, of the sermon, and when the priest readeth the Scripture to the parishioners, no manner of persons, without a just and urgent cause, *shall use any walking in the church, nor* shall depart out of the church, and all ringing and knolling of bells shall be utterly forborne for that time, to be rung or knolled before the sermon. *But yet for the retaining of the perambulation of the circuits of parishes, they shall once in the year at the time accustomed, with the curate and the substantial men of the parish, walk about their parishes as they were accustomed, and at their return to the church make their common prayers.*

19. Provided that the curate in their said common perambulations used heretofore in the days of rogations, at certain convenient places shall admonish the people to give thanks to God in the beholding of God's benefits for the increase and abundance of his fruits upon the face of the earth, with the saying the 103rd Psalm, *Benedic anima mea*, or such like, at which time also the same minister shall inculcate these or such sentences: *Cursed be he which translateth the bounds and doles of his neighbour* or such other order of prayers as shall be hereafter appointed.

20. (24b) Item, all the Queen's faithful and loving subjects shall from henceforth celebrate and keep their holy date, according to God's holy will and pleasure, that is, in hearing the Word of God read and taught in private and public prayers, in acknowledging their offences to God, and amendment of the same; in reconciling themselves charitably to their neighbours, where displeasure hath been; in oftentimes receiving the communion of the very body and blood of Christ; in visiting of the poor and sick; in using all soberness and godly conversation. Yet notwithstanding all parsons, vicars and curates shall teach and declare unto their parishioners that they may with a safe and quiet conscience in the time of harvest, labour upon the holy and festival days, and save that thing which God hath sent. And if for any scrupulosity or grudge of conscience men should superstitiously abstain from working upon those days, that then they should grievously offend and displease God.

21. (25) Also, forasmuch as variance and contention is a thing which most displeaseth God and is most contrary to the blessed communion of the body and blood of our Saviour Christ, curates shall in no wise admit to the receiving thereof any of their cure and flock who hath maliciously and openly contended with his neighbour, unless the same do first charitably and openly reconcile himself again, remitting all rancour and malice, whatsoever controversy hath been between them, and nevertheless, their just titles and rights, they may charitably prosecute before such as have authority to hear the same.

22. (27a) Also, that they shall instruct and teach in their cures that no man ought obstinately and maliciously break and violate the laudable ceremonies of the Church, commanded *by public authority* to be observed.

23. (28a) Also that they shall take away, utterly extinct and destroy all shrines, covering of shrines, all tables and candlesticks, trundles or rolls of ware, pictures, paintings and all other monuments of feigned miracles, pilgrimages, idolatry and superstition, so that there remain no memory of

the same in walls, glasses, windows or elsewhere within their churches or houses. And they shall exhort all their parishioners to do the like within their several houses.

24. (28b) And that the churchwardens, at the common charge of the parishioners in every church, shall provide a comely and honest pulpit, to be set in a convenient place within the same, for the preaching of God's Word.

25. (29) Also, they shall provide and have within three months after this visitation, a strong chest with a hole in the upper part thereof, to be provided at the cost and charge of the parish, having three keys, whereof one shall remain in the custody of the parson, vicar or curate, and the other two in the custody of the churchwardens, or any other two honest men to be appointed by the parish from year to year. Which chest you shall set and fashion *in a most convenient place*, to the intent the parishioners should put into it their oblation and alms, for their poor neighbours. And the parson, vicar and curate shall diligently from time to time, and specially when men make their testaments, call upon, exhort and move their neighbours to confer and give (as they may well spare) to the said chest, declaring unto them, whereas heretofore they have been diligent to bestow much substance otherwise than God commanded upon pardons, pilgrimages, trentals, decking of images, offering of candles, giving to friars and upon other like blind devotions, they ought at this time to be much more ready to help the poor and needy, knowing that to relieve the poor is a true worshipping of God, required earnestly upon pain of everlasting damnation; and that also, whatsoever is given for their comfort is given to Christ himself and is so accepted of him, that he will mercifully reward the same with everlasting life. The which alms and devotion of the people, the keepers of the keys shall at all times convenient take out of the chest and distribute the same in the presence of the whole parish, one sixth of them to be truly and faithfully delivered to their most needy neighbours, and if they be provided for, then to the reparation of highways next adjoining. And also the money which riseth of fraternities, guilds and other flocks of the Church (except by the Queen's Majesty's authority it be otherwise appointed) shall be put into the said chest and converted to the said use, and also the rents of lands, the profit of cattle and money given or bequeathed to *obits and dirges, or to* the finding of torches, lights, tapers and lamps, shall be converted to the said use, saving that it shall be lawful for them to bestow part of the said profits upon the reparation of the church if great need require, and whereas the parish is very poor and not able otherwise to repair the same.

26. (31) Also to avoid the detestable sin of simony, because buying and selling of benefices is execrable before God, therefore all such persons as buy any benefices or come to them by fraud or deceit, shall be deprived of such benefices and be made unable at any time after, to receive any other spiritual promotion. And such as do sell them, or by any colour do bestow them for their own gain and profit, shall lose their right and title of patronage and presentment for that time and the gift thereof for that vacation shall appertain to the Queen's Majesty.

27. (32) Also because through lack of preachers in many places of the Queen's realms and dominions the people continue in ignorance and blindness, all parsons, vicars and curates shall read in their churches every Sunday one of the homilies which are and shall be set forth for the same purpose, by the Queen's authority in such sort as they shall be appointed to do, in the preface of the same.

28. (33) Also, whereas many indiscreet persons do at this date uncharitably contemn and abuse priests and ministers of the Church, because some of them (having small learning) have of long time favoured fantasies rather than God's truth; yet forasmuch as their office and function is appointed of God, the Queen's Majesty willeth and chargeth all her loving subjects that from henceforth they shall use them charitably and reverently, for their office and ministration's sake, and especially all such as labour in the setting forth of God's Holy Word.

29. Item, although there be no prohibition by the Word of God, nor any example of the primitive Church, but that the priests and ministers of the Church may lawfully, for the avoiding of fornication, have an honest and sober wife, and that for the same purpose, the same was by Act of Parliament in time of our dear brother King Edward the Sixth made lawful, whereupon a great number of the clergy of this realm were then married, and so yet continue, yet because there hath grown offence and some slander to the Church by lack of discreet and sober behaviour in many ministers of the Church, both in choosing of their wives and in indiscreet living with them, the remedy whereof is necessary to be sought. It is thought therefore very necessary that no manner of priest or deacon shall hereafter take to his wife any manner of woman, without the advice and allowance first had upon good examination by the bishop of the same diocese, and two justices of the peace of the same shire, dwelling next to the place where the same woman hath made her most abode before her marriage, nor without the good will of the parents of the said woman, if she have any living, or two of the next of her kinfolks, or for lack of knowledge of such, of her master or masters where she serveth. And before he shall be contracted in any place, he shall make a good and certain proof thereof to the minister, or to the congregation assembled for that purpose, which shall be upon some holy day where divers may be present. And if any shall do otherwise, that then they shall not be permitted to minister either the Word or the Sacraments of the Church, nor shall be capable of any ecclesiastical benefice. And for the manner of marriages of any bishops, the same shall be allowed and approved by the metropolitan of the province, and also by such commissioners as the Queen's Majesty shall thereunto appoint. And if any master or dean or any head of any college shall purpose to marry, the same shall not be allowed, but by such to whom the visitation of the same doth properly belong, who shall in

any wise provide that the same tend not to the hindrance of their house.

30. Item, her Majesty being desirous to have the prelacy and clergy of this realm to be had as well in outward reverence as otherwise regarded for the worthiness of their ministries, and thinking it necessary to have them known to the people in all places and assemblies, both in the Church and without, and thereby to receive the honour and estimation due to the special ministers and messengers of Almighty God, willeth and commandeth that all archbishops and bishops, and all other that be called to preaching or ministry of the sacraments, or that be admitted into any vocation ecclesiastical, or into any society of learning in either of the universities or elsewhere, shall use and wear such seemly habits, garments and such square caps as were most commonly and orderly received in the latter year of the reign of King Edward the Sixth, not thereby meaning to attribute any holiness or special worthiness to the said garments, but as St Paul writeth: *Omnia decenter et secundum ordinem fiant* (I Co 14:40) (Let all things be done decently and in order).

31. Item, that no man shall wilfully and obstinately defend or maintain any heresies, errors or false doctrine, contrary to the faith of Christ and his Holy Scripture.

32. Item, that no persons shall use charms, sorcery, enchantments, witch-crafts, soothsaying or any like devilish device, nor shall resort at any time to the same for counsel or help.

33. Item, that no person shall, neglecting their own parish church, resort to any other church in time of common prayer or preaching, except it be by the occasion of some extraordinary sermon, in some parish of the same town.

34. Item, that no innholders or alehouse keepers shall use to sell meat or drink in the time of common prayer, preaching, reading of the Homilies or Scriptures.

35. Item, that no persons keep in their houses any abused images, table, pictures, paintings, and other monuments of feigned miracles, pilgrimages, idolatry or superstition.

36. Item, that no man shall willingly let or disturb the preacher in time of his sermon, or let or discourage any curate or minister to sing or say the divine service now set forth, nor mock or jest at the ministers of such service.

37. Item, that no man shall talk or reason of the Holy Scriptures, rashly or contentiously, nor maintain any false doctrine or error, but shall commune of the same when occasion is given, reverently, humbly, and in the fear of God, for his comfort and better understanding.

38. Item, that no man, woman nor child shall be otherwise occupied in the time of the service than in quiet attendance, to hear, mark and understand that is read, preached and ministered.

39. Item, that every schoolmaster and teacher shall teach the grammar set forth by King Henry the Eighth of noble memory, and continued in the time of King Edward the Sixth, and none other.

40. Item, that no man shall take upon him to teach, but such as shall be allowed by the ordinary, and found meet, as well for his learning and dexterity in teaching as for sober and honest conversation, and also for right understanding of God's true religion.

41. Item, that all teachers of children shall stir and move them to the love and due reverence of God's true religion, now truly set forth by public authority.

42. Item, that they shall accustom their scholars reverently to learn such sentences of Scriptures as shall be most expedient to enduce them to all godliness.

43. Item, forasmuch as in these latter days many have been made priests, being children, and otherwise utterly unlearned, so that they could read to say Mattins and Mass, the ordinaries shall not admit any such to any cure or spiritual function.

44. Item, every parson, vicar and curate shall upon every holy day and every second Sunday in the year, hear and instruct all the youth of the parish for half an hour at the least, before Evening Prayer, in the Ten Commandments, the Articles of the Belief, and in the Lord's Prayer, and diligently examine them and teach the Catechism set forth in the Book of Public Prayer.

45. Item, that the ordinaries do exhibit unto our visitors their books, or a true copy of the same, containing the causes why any person was imprisoned, famished or put to death for religion.

46. Item, that in every parish three or four discreet men which tender God's glory and his true religion shall be appointed by the ordinaries, diligently to see that all the parishioners duly resort to their church upon all Sundays and holy days, and there to continue the whole time of the godly service. And all such as shall be found slack or negligent in resorting to the church, having no great nor urgent cause of absence, they shall straightly call upon them and after due monition, if they amend not, they shall denounce them to the ordinary.

47. Item, that the churchwardens of every parish shall deliver unto our visitors the inventories of vestments, copes or other ornaments, plate, books and specially of grails, couchers, legends, processionals, hymnals, manuals, portuals and such like, appertaining to their church.

48. Item, that weekly upon Wednesdays and Fridays, not being holy days, the curate at the accustomed hours of service shall resort to church and cause warning to be given to the people by knolling of the bell, and say the Litany and prayers.

49. Item, because divers collegiate and some parish churches heretofore, there hath been livings appointed for the maintenance of men and children, to use singing in the church, by means whereof the laudable science of music hath been had in estimation and preserved in knowledge, the Queen's Majesty neither meaning in any wise the decay of anything that might conveniently tend to the use and continuance of the said science, neither to have the same in any part so abused in the church, that thereby the common prayer should be the worse understood of the hearers, willeth and commandeth that first, no alteration be made of such alignments of living, as heretofore hath been appointed to the use of singing or music in the church, but that the same to remain. And that there be a modest and distinct song so used, in all parts of the common prayers in the church, that the same may be as plainly understanded as if it were read without singing. And yet nevertheless, for the comforting of such as delight in music, it may be permitted that in the beginning or in the end of common prayers, either at morning or evening, there may be sung an hymn or suchlike song, to the praise of Almighty God, in the best sort of melody and music that may be conveniently devised, having respect that the sentence of the hymn may be understanded and perceived.

50. Item, because in all alterations and specially in rites and ceremonies, there happeneth discord among the people, and thereupon slanderous words and railings whereby charity, the knot of all Christian society, is loosed. The Queen's Majesty being most desirous of all other earthly things, that her people should live in charity both towards God and man, and therein abound in good works, willeth and straightly commandeth all manner her subjects to forbear all vain and contentious disputations in matters of religion, and not to use in despite or rebuke of any person, these convicious words: Papist, or Papistical heretic, schismatic or sacramentary, or any suchlike words of reproach. But if any manner of person shall deserve the accusation of such, that first he be charitably admonished thereof. And if that shall not amend him, then to denounce the offenders to the ordinary or to some higher power having authority to correct the same.

51. Item, because there is a great abuse in the printers of books, which for courteousness chiefly, regard not what they print, so they may have gain, whereby ariseth great disorder by publication of unfruitful, vain and infamous books and papers, the Queen's Majesty straightly chargeth and commandeth that no manner of person shall print any manner of book or paper, of what sort, nature, or in what language soever it be, except the same be first licensed by her Majesty by expert words in writing, or by six of her Privy Council, or be perused and licensed by the Archbishops of Canterbury and York, the Bishop of London, the chancellors of both universities, the bishop being ordinary, and the archdeacon also of the place where any such shall be printed, or by two of them, whereof the ordinary of the place to be always one. And that the names of such as shall allow the same to be added in the end of every such work, for a testimony of the allowance thereof. And because many pamphlets, plays and ballets be oftentimes printed, wherein regard would be had that nothing therein should be either heretical, seditious or unseemly for Christian ears, her Majesty likewise commandeth that no manner of person shall enterprise to print any such, except the same be to him licensed by such her Majesty's commissioners, or three of them, as be appointed in the City of London to hear and determine divers causes ecclesiastical, tending to the execution of certain statutes, made the last Parliament for uniformity of order in religion. And if any shall sell or utter any manner of books or papers, being not licensed as is abovesaid; that the same party shall be punished by order of the said commissioners as to the quality of the fault shall be thought meet. And touching all other books of matters of religion or policy or governance that hath been printed, either on this side the seas or on the other side, because the diversity of them is great, and that there needeth good consideration to be had of the particularities thereof, her Majesty referreth the prohibition or permission thereof to the order which her said commissioners within the City of London shall take and notify. According to the which, her Majesty straightly commandeth all manner her subjects, and specially the wardens and company of stationers, to be obedient.

Provided that these orders do not extend to any profane authors and works in any language that hath been heretofore commonly received or allowed in any of the universities or schools, but the same may be printed and used, as by good order they were accustomed.

52. Item, although Almighty God is at all times to be honoured with all manner of reverence that may be devised, yet of all other times, in time of common prayer the same is most to be regarded. Therefore it is to be necessarily received, that in time of the Litany, and of all other collects and common supplications to Almighty God, all manner of people shall devoutly and humbly kneel upon their knees, and give ear thereunto. And that whensoever the name of Jesus shall be in any lesson, sermon or otherwise in the church pronounced, that due reverence be made of all persons, young and old, with lowliness of curtsy, and uncovering of heads of the men kind, as thereunto doth necessarily belong, and heretofore hath been accustomed.

53. Item, that all ministers and readers of public prayers, chapters and homilies shall be charged to read leisurely, plainly and distinctly, and also such as are but mean readers, shall peruse over before once or twice the chapters or homilies, to the intent they may read to the better understanding of the people, and the more encouragement to godliness.

The Admonition to Simple Men deceived by Malicious

The Queen's Majesty being informed that in certain places of this realm, sundry of her native subjects, being called to ecclesiastical ministry in the Church, be by sinister persuasion and perverse construction induced to find some scruple in the form of an oath which by an Act of the last Parliament is prescribed to be required of divers persons, for the recognition of their allegiance to her Majesty, which certainly neither was ever meant, nor by any equity of words or good sense can be thereof gathered, would that all her loving subjects should understand that nothing was, is or shall be meant or intended by the same oath, to have any other duty, allegiance or bond required by the same oath than was acknowledged to be due to the most noble kings of famous memory, King Henry the Eighth, her Majesty's father, or King Edward the Sixth, her Majesty's brother.

And further, her Majesty forbiddeth all manner her subjects to give ear or credit to such perverse and malicious persons, which most sinisterly and maliciously labour to notify her loving subjects, how by the words of the said oath it may be collected that the Kings or Queens of this realm, possessors of the Crown, may challenge authority and power of ministry of divine offices in the Church, wherein her said subjects be much abused by such evil disposed persons. For certainly her Majesty neither doth, nor ever will challenge any other authority than that was challenged, and lately used by the said noble kings of famous memory, King Henry the Eighth and King Edward the Sixth, which is and was of ancient time due to the imperial Crown of this realm. That is under God, to have the sovereignty and rule over all manner of persons born within these her realms, dominions and countries, of what estate either ecclesiastical or temporal so ever they be, so as no other foreign power shall or ought to have any superiority over them. And if any person that hath conceived any other sense of the form of the said oath, shall accept the same oath with this interpretation, sense or meaning, her Majesty is well pleased to accept every such in that behalf, as her good and obedient subjects, and shall acquit them of all manner penalties contained in the said Act against such as shall peremptorily, or obstinately refuse to take the same oath.

For the Tables in the Church

Whereas her Majesty understandeth that in many and sundry parts of the realm, the altars of the churches be removed and tables placed for ministration of the Holy Sacrament, according to the form of the law therefor provided, and in some other places the altars be not yet removed, upon opinion conceived of some other order therein to be taken of her Majesty's visitors. In the order whereof, saving for an uniformity, there seemeth no matter of great moment, so that the sacrament be duly and reverently ministered, yet for observation of one uniformity throughout the whole realm, and for the better imitation of the law in that behalf, it is ordered that no altar be taken down but by oversight of the curate of the church and the churchwardens, or one of them at the least, wherein no riotous or disordered manner to be used, and that the Holy Table in every church be decently made, and set in the place where the altar stood, and there commonly covered as thereto belongeth, and as shall be appointed by the visitors, and so to stand, saving when the communion of the sacrament is to be distributed, at which time the same shall be so placed in good sort within the chancel, as whereby the minister may be more conveniently heard of the communicants, in his prayer and ministration, and the communicants also, more conveniently and in more number communicate with the said minister, and after the communion done, from time to time the same Holy Table to be placed where it stood before.

Item, where also it was in the time of King Edward the Sixth used to have the sacramental bread of common fine bread, it is ordered for the more reverence to be given to these holy mysteries, being the sacraments of the body and blood of our Saviour Jesus Christ, that the same sacramental bread be made and formed plain, without any figured thereupon, of the same fineness and fashion round, though somewhat bigger in compass and thickness, as the usual bread and water heretofore named singing cakes, which served for the use of the private mass.

The form of Bidding Prayers to be used generally in this uniform sort

Ye shall pray for Christ's holy, catholic Church, that is, for the whole congregation of Christian people, dispersed throughout the whole world, and specially for the Church of England and Ireland. And herein I require you most specially to pray for the Queen's most excellent Majesty, our Sovereign Lady Elizabeth, Queen of England, France and Ireland, Defender of the Faith, and Supreme Governor of this realm, as well in causes ecclesiastical as temporal.

You shall also pray for the ministers of God's Holy Word and Sacraments, as well archbishops and bishops, as other pastors and curates.

You shall also pray for the Queen's most honourable Council, and for all the nobility of this realm, that all and every of these in their calling, may serve truly and painfully, to the glory of God and edifying of his people, remembering the account that they must make.

Also you shall pray for the whole Commons of this realm, that they may live in true faith and fear of God, in humble obedience and brotherly charity one to the other.

Finally, let us pray God for all those which are departed out of this life in the faith of Christ, and pray unto God that we may have grace so to direct our lives after their good example, that after this life, we with them may be made partakers of the glorious resurrection, in the life everlasting.

And this done, show the holy days and fasting days.

All which and singular Injunctions, the Queen's Majesty ministereth unto her clergy, and to all other her loving subjects, straightly charging and commanding them to observe and keep the same, upon pain of deprivation, sequestration of fruits and benefices, suspension, excommunication and such other coercion as to ordinaries or to other having ecclesiastical jurisdiction, whom her Majesty hath appointed, or shall appoint, for the due execution of the same, shall be seen convenient. Charging and commanding them to see these Injunctions observed and kept of all persons, being under their jurisdiction, as they will answer to her Majesty for the contrary. And her Highness's pleasure is that every justice of peace (being required) shall assist the ordinaries, and every of them, for the due execution of the said Injunctions.

35. THE ELEVEN ARTICLES, 1559

History

These Articles were drawn up in 1559 or 1560 and approved by Archbishop Matthew Parker for the subscription of the clergy. The intention was to make them as close to the Forty-two Articles (1553) as possible, though in fact they bear little relation to that document. Clergy were expected to subscribe to these Articles twice a year, as well as when they were presented to a living. They were effectively replaced by the Thirty-eight Articles in 1563.

Theology

The Articles are clearly Protestant, though it is obvious that the main emphasis is on the recognition of Royal Supremacy. It was this, more than anything else, which Elizabeth was keen to secure, so that the other elements of her religious policy could be implemented without serious objections.

Forasmuch as it appertaineth to all Christian men, but especially to the ministers and the pastors of the Church, being teachers and instructors of others, to be ready to give a reason of their faith when they shall be thereunto required; I for my part, now appointed your parson, vicar or curate, having before my eyes the fear of God, and the testimony of my conscience, do acknowledge for myself, and require you to assent to the same.

01. First, that there is but one living and true God, of infinite power, wisdom and goodness, the Maker and Preserver of all things; and that in unity of this Godhead there be three Persons, of one substance, of equal power and eternity, the Father, Son and the Holy Ghost.

02. I believe also whatsoever is contained in the holy canonical Scriptures, in the which Scriptures are contained all things necessary to salvation, by the which also errors and heresies may sufficiently be reproved and convicted, and all doctrine and articles necessary to salvation established. I do also most firmly believe and confess all the articles contained in the three Creeds, the Nicene Creed, Athanasius' Creed, and our common Creed, called the Apostles' Creed; for these do briefly contain the principal articles of our faith, which are at large set forth in the Holy Scriptures.

03. I do acknowledge also that church to be the spouse of Christ, wherein the Word of God is truly taught, the sacraments orderly ministered according to Christ's institution, and the authority of the keys duly used; and that every such particular church hath authority to institute, to change, to clean put away ceremonies and other ecclesiastical rites, as they be superfluous, or be absurd, and to constitute other making more to seemliness, to order or edification.

04. Moreover I confess that it is not lawful for any man to take upon him any office or ministry, either ecclesiastical or secular, but such only as are lawfully thereunto called by their high authorities, according to the ordinances of this realm.

05. Furthermore, I do acknowledge the Queen's Majesty's prerogative and superiority of government of all estates and in all causes, as well ecclesiastical as temporal, within this realm, and other her dominions and countries, to be agreeable to God's Word, and of right to appertain to her highness in such sort, as is in the late act of Parliament expressed, and since by Her Majesty's injunctions declared and expounded.

06. Moreover, touching the Bishop of Rome, I do acknowledge and confess that by the Scriptures and the Word of God he hath no more authority than other bishops have in their provinces and dioceses; and therefore, the power which he now challengeth, that is, to be supreme head of the universal Church of Christ, and to be above all emperors, kings and princes, is an usurped power, contrary to the Scriptures and Word of God, and contrary to the example of the primitive Church, and therefore is for most just causes taken away and abolished in this realm.

07. Furthermore, I do grant and confess that the Book of Common Prayer and administration of the holy sacraments, set forth by the authority of Parliament, is agreeable to the Scriptures, and that it is catholic, apostolic and most for the advancing of God's glory and the edifying of God's people, both for that it is in a tongue that may be understood of the people, and also for the doctrine and form of ministration contained in the same.

08. And although in the administration of baptism there is neither exorcism, oil, salt, spittle or hallowing of the water now used, and for that they were of late years abused and esteemed to be necessary, where they pertain not to the substance and necessity of the sacrament, that they be reasonably abolished, and yet the sacrament full and perfectly ministered to all intents and purposes, agreeable to the institution of our Saviour Christ.

09. Moreover I do not only acknowledge that private masses were never used amongst the fathers of the primitive Church, I mean, public ministration and receiving of the sacrament by the priest alone, without a just number of communicants, according to Christ's saying: *Take ye and eat ye*, (I Co 11:24) etc., but also that the doctrine that maintaineth the mass to be a propitiatory sacrifice for the quick and the dead, and a mean to deliver souls out of purgatory, is neither agreeable to Christ's ordinance nor grounded upon doctrine apostolic, but contrariwise most ungodly and most injurious to the precious redemption of our Saviour Christ, and his only sufficient sacrifice offered once for ever upon the altar of the cross.

10. I am of that mind also, that the holy communion or sacrament of the body and blood of Christ, for the due obedience to Christ's institution, and to express the virtue of the same, ought to be ministered unto the people under both kinds; and that it is avouched by certain fathers of the Church to be a plain sacrilege, to rob them of the mystical cup, for whom Christ hath shed his most precious blood, seeing he himself hath said: *Drink ye all of this*; (I Co 11:25) considering also that in the time of the ancient doctors of the Church, as Cyprian, Jerome, Augustine, Gelasius and others, six hundred years after Christ and more, both the parts of the sacrament were ministered to the people.

11. Last of all, as I do utterly disallow the extolling of images, relics and feigned miracles, and also all kind of expressing God invisible in the form of an old man, or the Holy Ghost in the form of a dove, and all other vain worshipping of God, devised by man's fantasies, besides or contrary to the Scriptures, as wandering on pilgrimages, setting up of candles, praying upon beads, and such like superstition; which kinds of works have no promise of reward in Scripture, but contrariwise threatenings and maledictions; so I do exhort all men to the obedience of God's law and to the works of faith, as charity, mercy, pity, alms, devout and frequent prayer with the affection of the heart, and not with the mouth only, godly abstinence and fasting, charity, obedience to the rulers, and superior powers, with such like works and godliness of life commanded by God in his Word, which as St Paul saith: *hath promises both of this life and of the life to come*, (I Ti 4:8) and are works only acceptable in God's sight.

These things above rehearsed, though they be appointed by common order, yet I do without all compulsion, with freedom of mind and conscience, from the bottom of my heart, and upon most sure persuasion, acknowledge to be true and agreeable to God's Word; and therefore I exhort you all, of whom I have cure, heartily and obediently to embrace and receive the same, that we all joining together in unity of spirit, faith and charity, may also at length be joined together in the Kingdom of God, and that through the merits and death of our Saviour Jesus Christ, to whom with the Father and the Holy Ghost be all glory and empire now and for ever. Amen.

The Progress of Protestantism

(1560-1625)

36. THE PREFACE TO THE GENEVA BIBLE, 1560

History

Soon after the accession of Mary I a number of prominent English Protestants found it advisable to leave the country. Some of them made their way to Geneva, where they were made welcome by John Calvin and his followers. One of these exiles, William Whittingham, married into Calvin's family, and it was he who later took the initiative in Bible translation.

Working under the direction of the greatest Greek and Hebrew scholars of the day, Whittingham and his associates, who may have included Miles Coverdale and John Knox, proceeded to revise the work of the predecessors. In particular, they produced a fresh translation of those parts of the Old Testament which Tyndale had not reached. The result was a version which for quality, far outstripped its rivals in the field.

The Geneva Bible appeared in 1560, at a propitious moment in British history. The translators hoped that it would replace the Great Bible in England, but this desire was thwarted by the outspoken Calvinism of the marginal notes which accompanied the text. The English bishops felt obliged to produce their own version of the Great Bible, without such notes, which appeared in 1568. Unfortunately, this Bishops' Bible was inferior to the Geneva version, and it never really caught on. The Geneva Bible became and remained the popular text, read and studied by all classes of the population. In Scotland, it received official sanction, and did much to spread the use of standard English in that country.

The last edition of the Geneva Bible was printed in 1644, by which time the Authorized (King James) Version had replaced both it and the Bishops' Bible.

Theology

The Geneva Bible was famous, or notorious, for its Calvinist theology, but this was mostly contained in the marginal notes, which directed the reader to consider the application of various texts to particular points of theological dispute. In the text itself, the versions Calvinism can mostly be seen is its preference for words like *congregation* and *elder* instead of *church* and *priest*. Church politics, as much as anything else, made it the Bible of Puritanism, though it never achieved official status as such. By the time the Puritans were in control of the government it was on the way out, and it did not resurface as the Bible of Dissent after the Restoration.

To the most virtuous and noble Queen Elizabeth, Queen of England, France and Ireland, etc., Your humble subjects of the English Church at Geneva, with grace and peace from God the Father through Christ Jesus our Lord.

How hard a thing it is, and what great impediments let, to enterprise any worthy act, not only daily experience sufficiently showeth (most noble and virtuous Queen), but also that notable proverb doth confirm the same, which admonisheth us that all things are hard which are fair and excellent. And what enterprise can there be of greater importance, and more acceptable unto God, or more worthy of singular commendation, than the building of the Lord's temple, the house of God, the Church of Christ, whereof the Son of God is the head and perfection?

When Zerubbabel went about to build the material temple, according to the commandment of the Lord, what difficulties and stays daily arose to hinder his worthy endeavours, the books of Ezra and Esdras plainly witness; how that not only he and the people of God were sorely molested with foreign adversaries (whereof some maliciously warred against them and corrupted the King's officers, and others craftily practised under pretence of religion) but also at home with domestical enemies, as false prophets, crafty worldlings, faint-hearted soldiers and oppressors of their brethren, who as well by false doctrine and lies as by subtle counsel, cowardice and extortion, discouraged the hearts almost of all, so that the Lord's work was not only interrupted and left off for a long time, but scarcely at the length with great labour and danger after a sort brought to pass.

Which thing when we weigh aright, and consider earnestly how much greater charge God hath laid upon you in making you a builder of his spiritual temple, we cannot but partly fear, knowing the craft and force of Satan our spiritual enemy and the weakness and inability of this our nature; and partly be fervent in our prayers toward God that he would bring to perfection this noble work which he hath begun by you, and therefore we endeavour ourselves by all means to aid, and to bestow our whole force under your grace's standard, whom God hath made as our Zerubbabel for the erecting of this most excellent temple, and to plant and maintain his holy Word to the advancement of his glory, for your own honour and salvation of your soul, and for the singular comfort of that great flock which Christ Jesus the great shepherd hath bought with his precious blood, and committed unto your charge to be fed both in body and soul.

Considering therefore how many enemies there are, which by one means or other, as the adversaries of Judah and Benjamin went about to stay the building of that temple, so labour to hinder the course of this building (whereof some are Papists, who under pretence of favouring God's Word, traitorously seek to erect idolatry and to destroy your Majesty; some are worldlings, who as Demas have forsaken Christ for the lord of this world; others are ambitious prelates, who as Amaziah and Diotrephes can abide none but themselves, and as Demetrius may practise sedition to maintain their errors) we persuaded ourselves that there was no way so expedient and necessary for the preservation of the one, and destruction of the other, as to present unto your Majesty the Holy Scriptures faithfully and plainly translated according to the languages wherein they were first written by the Holy Ghost. For the Word of God is an evident token of God's love and our assurance of his defence, wheresoever it is obediently received; it is the trial of the spirits, and as the prophet saith, it is a fire and hammer to break the stony hearts of them that resist God's mercies offered by the preaching of the same (Je 23:29). Yea it is sharper than any two-edged sword to examine the very thoughts and to judge the affections of the heart, and to discover whatsoever lieth hid under hypocrisy and would be secret from the face of God and his Church. So that this must be the first foundation and groundwork, according whereunto the good stones of this building must be framed, and the evil tried out and rejected.

Now as he that goeth about to lay a foundation surely, first taketh away such impediments as might justly either hurt, let or deform the work; so it is necessary that your grace's zeal appear herein, that neither the crafty persuasion of man, neither worldly policy, or natural fear dissuade you to root it out, cut down and destroy these weeds and impediments which do not only deface your building, but utterly endeavour, yea and threaten the ruin thereof. For when the noble Josiah enterprised the like kind of work, among other notable and many things, he destroyed not only, with utter confusion, the idols with their appurtenances, but also burnt (in sign of detestation) the idolatrous priests' bones upon their altars, and put to death the false prophets and sorcerers, to perform the words of the law of God; and therefore the Lord gave him good success and blessed him wonderfully, so long as he made God's Word his line and rule to follow, and enterprised nothing before he had enquired at the mouth of the Lord.

And if these zealous beginnings seem dangerous and to breed disquietness in your dominions, yet by the story of King Asa it is manifest that the quietness and peace of the kingdoms standeth in the utter abolishing of idolatry, and in advancing of true religion; for in his days Judah lived in rest and quietness for the space of five and thirty years, till at length he began to be cold in the zeal of the Lord, feared the power of man, imprisoned the prophet of God and oppressed the people; then the Lord sent him wars and at length took him away by death.

Wherefore great wisdom, not worldly, but heavenly, here is required, which your grace must earnestly crave of the Lord, as did Solomon, to whom God gave an understanding heart to judge his people aright, and to discern between good and bad. For if God for the furnishing of the old temple gave the Spirit of wisdom and understanding to them that should be the workmen thereof, as to Bezaleel, Aholiab and Hiram; how much more will he indue your grace and other godly princes and chief governors with a principal spirit, that you may procure and command things necessary for this most holy temple, foresee and take heed of things that might hinder it, and abolish and destroy whatsoever might impair and overthrow the same?

Moreover the marvellous diligence and zeal of Jehoshaphat, Josiah and Hezekiah are by the singular providence of God left as an example to all godly rulers to reform their countries and to establish the Word of God with all speed, lest the wrath of the Lord fall upon them for the neglecting thereof. For these excellent kings did not only embrace the Word promptly and joyfully, but also procured earnestly and commanded the same to be taught, preached and maintained through all their countries and dominions, binding them and all their subjects both great and small with solemn protestations and covenants before God to obey the word, and to walk after the ways of the Lord. Yea and in the days of King Asa it was enacted that whosoever would not seek the Lord God of Israel, should be slain, whether he were small or great, man or woman. And for the establishing hereof and performance of this solemn oath, as well priests and judges were appointed and placed through all the cities of Judah to instruct the people in the true knowledge and fear of God, and to minister justice according to the Word, knowing that, except God by his Word did reign in the hearts and souls, all man's diligence and endeavours were of none effect, for without this Word we cannot discern between justice and injury, protection and oppression, wisdom and foolishness, knowledge and ignorance, god and evil. Therefore the Lord, who is the chief governor of his Church, willeth that nothing be attempted before we have inquired thereof at his mouth. For seeing he is our God, of duty we must give him this pre-eminence, that of ourselves we enterprise nothing but that which he hath appointed, who only knoweth all things and governeth them as may best serve to his glory and our salvation. We ought not therefore to prevent him, or do anything without his Word, but as soon as he hath revealed his will, immediately to put it in execution.

Now as concerning the manner of this building, it is not according to man, nor after the wisdom of the flesh, but of the Spirit, and according to the Word of God, whose ways are divers from man's ways. For if it was not lawful for Moses to build the material tabernacle after any other sort than God had showed him by a pattern, neither to prescribe any other ceremonies and laws than such as the Lord had expressly commanded; how can it be lawful to proceed in this spiritual building any other ways, than Jesus Christ the Son of God, who is both the foundation, head and chief cornerstone thereof, hath commanded by his Word? And forasmuch as he hath established and left an order in his Church for the building up of his body, appointing some to be apostles, some prophets, others evangelists, some pastors and teachers, he signifieth that every one according as he is placed in this body which is the Church, ought to enquire of his ministers concerning the will of the Lord, which is revealed in his Word. For they are, saith Jeremiah, as the mouth of the Lord (Je 15:19); yea, and he promiseth to be with their mouth, and that their lips shall keep knowledge, and that the truth and the law shall be in their mouth. For it is their office chiefly to understand the Scriptures and teach them. For this cause the people of Israel in matters of difficulty used to ask the Lord either by the prophets or by the means of the high priest, who bare urim and thummim, which were tokens of light and knowledge, of holiness and perfection, which should be in the high priest. Therefore when Jehoshaphat took this order in the Church of Israel, he appointed Amariah to be the chief concerning the Word of God, because he was most expert in the law of the Lord and could give counsel and govern according unto the same. Else there is no degree or office which may have that authority and privilege to decide concerning God's Word, except withal he have the Spirit of God, and sufficient knowledge and judgement to define according thereunto. And as everyone is indued of God with greater gifts, so ought he to be herein chiefly heard, or at least that without the express word none be heard; for he that hath not the Word speaketh not by the mouth of the Lord. Again, what danger it is to do anything, seem it never so godly or necessary, without consulting with God's mouth, the examples of the Israelites, deceived hereby through the Gibeonites; and of Saul, whose intention seemed good and necessary, and of Josiah also, who for great considerations was moved for the defence of true religion and his people, to fight against Pharaoh Necho King of Egypt, may sufficiently admonish us.

Last of all (most gracious Queen) for the advancement of this building and rearing up of the work, two things are necessary; first, that we have a lively and steadfast faith in Christ Jesus, who must dwell in our hearts as the only means and assurance of our salvation; for he is the ladder that reacheth from the earth to heaven; he lifteth up his Church and setteth it in the heavenly places; he maketh us lively stones and buildeth us upon himself; he joineth us to himself as the members and body to the head; yea he maketh himself and his Church one Christ. The next is that our faith bring forth good fruits, so that our godly conversation may serve us as a witness to confirm our election, and be an example to all others to walk as appertaineth to the vocation whereunto they are called; lest the Word of God be evil spoken of, and this building be stayed to grow up to a just height, which cannot be without the great provocation of God's just vengeance and discouraging of many thousands through all the world, if they should see that our life were not holy and agreeable to our profession. For the eyes of all that fear God in all places behold your countries as an example to all that believe, and the prayers of all the godly at all times are directed to God for the preservation of your Majesty. For considering God's wonderful mercies toward you at all seasons, who hath pulled you out of the mouth of the lions, and how that from your youth you have been brought up in the Holy Scriptures, the hope of all men is so increased that they cannot but look that God should bring to pass some wonderful work by your grace to the universal comfort of his Church. Therefore even above strength you must show yourself strong and bold in God's matters; and though Satan lay all his power and craft together to hurt and hinder the Lord's building, yet be you assured that God will fight from heaven against this great dragon, the ancient serpent, which is called the devil and Satan, till he have accomplished the whole work and made his Church glorious to himself, without spot or wrinkle. For albeit all other kingdoms and monarchies, as the Babylonians, Persians, Grecians and Romans have fallen and taken end; yet the Church of Christ even under the cross hath from the beginning of the world been victorious, and shall be everlastingly. Truth it is, that sometime it seemeth to be shadowed with a cloud or driven with a stormy persecution, yet suddenly the beams of Christ the sun of justice shine and bring it to light and liberty. If for a time it lie covered with ashes, yet it is quickly kindled again by the wind of God's Spirit, though it seem drowned in the sea, or parched and pined in the wilderness, yet God giveth ever good success, for he punisheth the enemies and delivereth his, nourisheth them and still preserveth them under his wings. This Lord of lords and King of kings who hath ever defended his, strengthen, comfort and preserve your Majesty, that you may be able to build up the ruins of God's house to his glory, the discharge of your conscience, and to the comfort of all them that love the coming of Christ Jesus our Lord.

From Geneva, 10 April 1560.

To our beloved in the Lord, the brethren of England, Scotland, Ireland, etc. Grace, mercy and peace, through Christ Jesus.

Besides the manifold and continual benefits which Almighty God bestoweth upon us, both corporal and spiritual, we are especially bound (dear brethren) to give him thanks without ceasing for his great grace and unspeakable mercies, in that it hath pleased him to call us unto this marvellous light of his Gospel, and mercifully to regard us after so horrible backsliding and falling away from Christ to Antichrist, from light to darkness, from the living God to dead and dumb idols, and that after so cruel murther of God's saints, as alas hath been among us, we are not altogether cast off, as were the Israelites and many others for the like, or not so manifest wickedness, but received again to grace with most evident signs and tokens of God's especial love and favour. To the intent therefore that we may not be unmindful of these great mercies, but seek by all means (according to our duty) to be thankful for the same, it behoveth us so to walk in his fear and love, that all the days of our life we may procure the glory of his holy name. Now forasmuch as this thing chiefly is attained by the knowledge and practising of the Word of God (which is the light to our paths, the key of the kingdom of heaven, our comfort in affliction, our shield and sword against Satan, the school of all wisdom, the glass wherein we behold God's face, the testimony of his favour, and the only food and nourishment of our souls) we thought that we could bestow our labours and study in nothing which could be more acceptable to God and comfortable to his Church than in the translating of the Holy Scriptures into our native tongue; the which thing, albeit that divers heretofore have endeavoured to achieve, yet considering the infancy of those times and the imperfect knowledge of the tongues, in respect of this ripe age and clear light which God hath now revealed, the translations required greatly to be perused and reformed. Not that we vindicate anything to ourselves above the least of our brethren (for God knoweth with what fear and trembling we have been now, for the space of two years and more day and night occupied herein) but being earnestly desired and by divers, whose learning and godliness we reverence, exhorted and also encouraged by the ready wills of such, whose hearts God likewise touched, not to spare any charges for the furtherance of such a benefit and favour of God toward his Church (though the time then was most dangerous and the persecution sharp and furious) we submitted ourselves at length to their godly judgements, and seeing the great opportunity and occasions which God presented unto us in this Church, by reason of so many godly and learned men, and such diversities of translations in divers tongues; we undertook this great and wonderful work (with all reverence, as in the presence of God, as intreating the Word of God, whereunto we think ourselves insufficient), which now God according to his divine providence and mercy hath directed to a most prosperous end. And this we may with good conscience protest, that we have in every point and word, according to the measure of that knowledge which it pleased Almighty God to give us, faithfully rendered the text, and in all hard places most sincerely expounded the same. For God is our witness that we have by all means endeavoured to set forth the purity of the Word and right sense of the Holy Ghost for the edifying of the brethren in faith and charity.

Now as we have chiefly observed the sense, and laboured always to restore it to all integrity, so have we most reverently kept the propriety of the words, considering that the apostles who spake and wrote to the Gentiles in the Greek tongue, rather constrained them to the lively phrase of the Hebrew than enterprised far by mollifying their language to speak as the Gentiles did. And for this and other causes we have in many places reserved the Hebrew phrases, notwithstanding that they may seem somewhat hard in their ears that are not well practised, and also delight in the sweet-sounding phrases of the Holy Scriptures. Yet lest either the simple should be discouraged, or the malicious have any occasion of just cavillation, seeing some translations read after one sort and some after another, whereas all may serve to good purpose and edification, we have in the margin noted that diversity of speech or reading which may also seem agreeable to the mind of the Holy Ghost and proper for our language with this mark: '.

Again whereas the Hebrew speech seemed hardly to agree with ours, we have noted it in the margin after this sort: ", using that which was more intelligible. And albeit that many of the Hebrew names be altered from the old text and restored to the true writing and first original, whereof they have their signification, yet in the usual names little is changed for fear of troubling the simple readers. Moreover, whereas the necessity of the sentence required anything to be added (for such is the grace and propriety of the Hebrew and Greek tongues, that it cannot but either by circumlocution, or by adding the verb or some word, be understand (*sic*) of them that are not well practised therein) we have put it in the text with another kind of letter, that it may easily be discerned from the common letter. As touching the division of the verses, we have followed the Hebrew examples, which have so even from the beginning distinct them. Which thing as it is most profitable for memory, so doth it agree with the best translations and is most easy to find out both by the best concordances, and also by the quotations which we have diligently herein perused and set forth by this star: *. Besides this, the principal matters are noted and distinguished by this mark: ¶. Yea and the arguments both for the book and for the chapters with the number of the verse are added, that by all means the reader might be holpen. For the which cause also we have set over the head of every page some notable word or sentence which may greatly further as well for memory, as for the chief point of the page. And considering how hard a thing it is to understand the Holy Scriptures, and what errors, sects and heresies grow daily for lack of the true knowledge thereof, and how many are discouraged (as they pretend) because they cannot attain to the true and simple meaning of the same, we have also endeavoured both by the diligent reading of the best commentaries, and also by the conference with the godly and learned brethren, to gather brief annotations upon all the hard places, as well for the understanding of such words as are obscure, and for the declaration of the text, as for the application of the same as may most appertain to God's glory and the edification of his Church. Furthermore, whereas certain places in the books of Moses, of the Kings and Ezekiel, seemed so dark that by no description they could be made easy to the simple reader, we have to set them forth with figures and notes for the full declaration thereof, that they which cannot by judgement, being holpen by the annotations noted by the letters a b c etc., and attain thereunto, yet by the perspective, and as it were by the eye may sufficiently know the true meaning of all such places. Whereunto also we have added certain maps of cosmography which necessarily serve for the perfect understanding and memory of divers places and countries, partly described, and partly by occasion touched, both in the Old and New Testament. Finally, that nothing might lack which might be bought by labours, for the increase of knowledge and the furtherance of God's glory, we have adjoined two more profitable tables, the one serving for the interpretation of the Hebrew names and the other containing all the chief and principal matters of the whole Bible; so that nothing (as we trust) that any could justly desire, is omitted. Therefore, as brethren that are partakers of the same hope and salvation with us, we beseech you, that this rich pearl and inestimable treasure may not be offered in vain, but as sent from God or the people of God, for the increase of his kingdom, the comfort of his Church, and discharge of our conscience, whom it hath pleased him to raise up for this purpose, so you would willingly receive the Word of God, earnestly study it and in all your life practise it, that you may now appear indeed to be the people of God, not walking any more according to this world, but in the fruits of the Spirit, that God in us may be fully glorified through Christ Jesus our Lord, who liveth and reigneth for ever. Amen. From Geneva, 10 April 1560.

37. THE PREFACE TO THE RHEIMS NEW TESTAMENT, 1582

History

The rapid progress of Protestantism, due in no small measure to the widespread circulation of the vernacular Scriptures, finally persuaded the Roman Catholic Church that it too, needed a Bible in the language of the people. Needless to say, the existing Protestant translations were all held to be full of heresy and error, and none of them was remotely acceptable to Catholics. Instead, Catholic exiles at Reims (Rheims) undertook to produce their own translation, based on the Latin Vulgate.

The Rheims New Testament reflected its Latin origins in much of its vocabulary and phraseology, and large parts of it were unintelligible, even to contemporaries. Catholic apologists have spared no effort to defend the translators, and it is true that in some ways – notably in their use of the definite article – they were more accurate than their Protestant counterparts. But technical excellence of this kind could not outweigh the enormous defects of their translation, and the Rheims New Testament never became the household version that the Geneva Bible did.

Theology

The Preface is of great interest as a statement of Catholic opposition to the Reformers' pretensions, and it gives us a flavour of the continuing opposition which the Protestants had to face. Bible translation was always to some extent a theological enterprise, but seldom more so than in the Catholic response to the Reformers. At stake was nothing less than the source of Christian truth, and the right of the Church to interpret it according to tradition. The Catholics of the sixteenth century were committed, not merely to a defence of the patristic heritage (something which they shared in large measure with Anglicans) but also – and at that time more important – to the specifically Latin tradition represented by the Vulgate, which to them was the Authorized Version of the Holy Bible. Not until after the Second Vatican Council (1962-65) did the Roman Church break away from this inheritance, and make a truly ecumenical approach to the Bible and to Christian theology possible.

The main target of the translators' attacks was Théodore de Bèze (1519-1605), usually known as Beza, who was Calvin's successor at Geneva and by common consent, the leading Biblical exegete of his time. Ironically, the attacks made on him only serve to increase his reputation as a scholar who could rise above the prejudices of his age. It is also interesting to note that the English Catholics who prepared the Rheims translation targeted the Puritans in England as their real enemies, a sure sign of the great influence which they were beginning to wield within the national church.

N.B. For this edition, the paragraphs have been numbered for ease of reference.

The Preface to the reader, treating of these three points:
(01.) of the translation of Holy Scriptures into the vulgar tongues, and
namely into English
(02.) of the causes why this New Testament is translated according to the
ancient vulgar Latin text
(03.) and of the manner of translating the same.

01. The Holy Bible long since translated by us into English, and the Old Testament lying by us for lack of good means to publish the whole in such sort as a work of so great charge and importance requireth, we have yet through God's goodness at length fully finished for thee (most Christian reader) all the New Testament, which is the principal, most profitable and comfortable piece of Holy Writ, and as well for all other institution of life and doctrine, as specially for deciding the doubts of these days, more proper and pregnant than the other part not yet printed.

Translation of the Scriptures into the vulgar tongues, not absolutely necessary or profitable, but according to the time

02. Which translation we do not for all that publish, upon erroneous opinion of necessity, that the Holy Scriptures should always be in our mother tongue, or that they ought, or were ordained by God, to be read indifferently of all, or could be easily understood of everyone that readeth or heareth them in a known language, or that they were not often through man's malice or infirmity, pernicious and much hurtful to many; or that we generally and absolutely deemed it more convenient in itself, and more agreeable to God's Word and honour, or edification of the faithful, to have them turned into vulgar tongues, than to be kept and studied only in the ecclesiastical learned languages; not for these nor any such like causes do we translate this sacred book, but upon special consideration of the present time, state and condition of our country, unto which divers things are either necessary, or profitable and medicinable now, that otherwise in the peace of the Church were neither much requisite, nor perchance wholly tolerable.

The Church's wisdom and moderation concerning vulgar translation

03. In this matter, to mark only the wisdom and moderation of holy Church and the governors thereof on the one side, and the indiscreet zeal of the popular, and their factious leaders on the other, is a high point of prudence. These later, partly of simplicity, partly of curiosity, and specially of pride and disobedience, have made claim in this case for the common people, with plausible pretences many, but good reasons none at all. The other, to whom Christ hath given charge of our souls, the dispensing of God's mysteries and treasures (among which Holy Scripture is no small store) and the feeding his family in season with food fit for every sort, have neither of old nor of late ever wholly condemned all vulgar versions of Scripture, nor have at any time generally forbidden the faithful to read the same; yet they have not by public authority prescribed, commanded or authentically ever recommended any such interpretation to be indifferently used of all men.

The Scriptures in the vulgar languages of divers nations

04. The Armenians say they have the Psalter and some other pieces translated by St John Chrysostom into their language, when he was banished among them. And George the Patriarch, in writing his life, signifieth no less. The Slavonians affirm they have the Scriptures in their vulgar tongue, turned by St Jerome, and some would gather so much by his own words in his epistle to Sophronius, but the place indeed proveth it not. Ulfilas (Wulfila) surely gave the Scriptures to the Goths in their own tongue, and that before he was an Arian.

Ancient Catholic translations of the Bible into the Italian, French and English tongue

05. It is almost three hundred years since James, Archbishop of Genoa, is said to have translated the Bible into Italian. More than two hundred years ago, in the days of Charles V the French King, was it put forth faithfully in French, the sooner to shake out of the deceived people's hands the false heretical translations of the sect called Waldenses.

An ancient provincial constitution in England concerning English translations

06. In our own country, notwithstanding the Latin tongue was ever (to use Venerable Bede's words) common to all the provinces of the same for meditation or study of Scriptures (*Historia I, I*), and no vulgar translation commonly used or occupied of the multitude, yet they were extant in English even before the troubles that Wycliffe and his followers raised in our Church, as appeareth as well by the testimony of Malmesbury, recording that Venerable Bede translated divers parts into the vulgar tongue of his time, and by some pieces yet remaining, as by a provincial constitution of Thomas Arundel, Archbishop of Canterbury in a council holden at Oxford. Where straight provision was made that no heretical version set forth by Wycliffe, or his adherents, should be suffered, nor any other in or after his time be published or permitted to be read, being not approved and allowed by the diocesan before; alleging St Jerome for the difficulty and danger of interpreting the Holy Scripture out of one tongue into another, though by learned and Catholic men. So also it is there insinuated that neither the translations set forth before that heretic's time, nor other afterward being approved by the lawful ordinaries, were ever in our country wholly forbidden, though they were not (to say the truth) in quiet and better times (much less when the people were prone to alteration, heresy or novelty) either hastily admitted, or ordinarily read of the vulgar, but used only or specially of some devout religious and contemplative persons, in reverence, secrecy and silence, for their spiritual comfort.

The like Catholic and vulgar translations in many countries, since Luther's time

07. Now since Luther's revolt also, divers learned Catholics, for the more speedy abolishing of a number of false and impious translations put forth by sundry sects, and for the better preservation or reclaim of many good souls endangered thereby, have published the Bible in the several languages of almost all the principal provinces of the Latin Church, no other books in the world being so pernicious as heretical translations of the Scriptures, poisoning the people under colour of divine authority, and not many other remedies being more sovereign against the same (if it be used in order, discretion and humility) than the true, faithful and sincere interpretation opposed thereunto.

The Church's order and determination concerning the reading of Catholic translations of the Bible in vulgar tongues

08. Which causeth the holy Church not to forbid utterly any Catholic translation, though she allow not the publishing or reading of any absolutely and without exception or limitation; knowing by her divine and most sincere wisdom how, where, when and to whom these her Master's and Spouse's gifts are to be bestowed to the most good of the faithful; and therefore neither generally permitteth that which must needs do hurt to the unworthy, nor absolutely condemneth that which may do much good to the worthy. Whereupon, the order which many a wise man wished for before, was taken by the deputies of the late famous Council of Trent in this behalf, and confirmed by supreme authority, that the Holy Scriptures, though truly and Catholicly translated into vulgar tongues, yet may not be indifferently read of all men, nor of any other than such as have express licence thereunto of their lawful ordinaries, with good testimony from their curates or confessors, that they be humble, discreet and devout persons, and likely to take much good and no harm thereby. Which prescript, though in these days of ours it cannot be so precisely observed, as in other times and places where there is more due respect of the Church's authority, rule and discipline; yet we trust all wise and godly persons will use the matter in the meanwhile, with such moderation, meekness and subjection of heart, as the handling of so sacred a book, the sincere senses of God's truth therein, and the holy canons, councils, reason and religion do require.

The Holy Scriptures never read of all persons indifferently, at their pleasure

09. Wherein, though for due preservation of this divine work from abuse and profanation, and for the better bridling of the intolerable insolency of proud, curious and contentious wits, the governors of the Church, guided by God's Spirit, as ever before, so also upon more experience of the malady of this time than before, have taken more exact order both for the readers and translations in these later ages, than of old; yet we must not imagine that in the primitive Church, either everyone that understood the learned tongues wherein the Scriptures were written, or other languages into which they were translated, might without reprehension read, reason, dispute, turn and toss the Scriptures; or that our forefathers suffered every schoolmaster, scholar or grammarian that had a little Greek or Latin, straight to take in hand the holy Testament; or that the translated Bibles into the vulgar tongues were in the hands of every husbandman, artificer, apprentice, boys, girls, mistress, maid, man; that they were sung, played, alleged, of every tinker, taverner, rhymer, minstrel; that they were for table talk, for ale benches, for boats and barges, and for every profane person and company. No, in those better times men were neither so ill, nor so curious of themselves, so to abuse the blessed book of Christ; neither was there any such easy means before printing was invented, to disperse the copies into the hands of every man, as now there is.

Where and in whose hands the Scriptures were in the primitive Church

10. They were then in libraries, monasteries, colleges, churches, in bishops' priests' and some other devout principal laymen's houses and hands; who used them with fear and reverence, and specially such parts as pertained to good life and manners, not meddling, but in pulpit and schools (and that moderately, too) with the hard and high mysteries and places of greater difficulty.

How the laity of those days did read them, with what humility and religion, and information of life and manners

11. The poor ploughman could then, in labouring the ground, sing the hymns and psalms either in known or unknown languages, as they heard them in the holy Church, though they could neither read nor know the sense, meaning and mysteries of the same. Such holy persons of both sexes to whom St Jerome in divers epistles to them commendeth the reading and meditation of Holy Scriptures, were diligent to search all the godly histories and imitable examples of chastity, humility, obedience, clemency, poverty, penance, renouncing the world; they noted specially the places that did breed the hatred of sin, fear of God's judgement, delight in spiritual cogitations; they referred themselves in all hard places to the judgement of the ancient fathers and their masters in religion, never presuming to contend, control, teach or talk of their own sense and fantasy, in deep questions of divinity. Then the virgins did meditate upon the places and examples of chastity, modesty and demureness; the married, on conjugal faith and continency; the parents, how to bring up their children in faith and fear of God; the Prince, how to rule; the subject, how to obey; the Priest, how to teach; the people, how to learn.

The Fathers sharply reprehend as an abuse, that all indifferently should read, expound and talk of the Scriptures

12. Then the scholar taught not his master, the sheep controlled not the pastor, the young student set not the doctor to school, nor reproved their fathers or error and ignorance. Or if any were in those better days (as in all times of heresy such must needs be) that had itching ears, tickling tongues and wits, curious and contentious disputers, hearers and talkers, rather than doers of God's Word; such the Fathers did ever sharply reprehend, counting them unworthy and unprofitable readers of the Holy Scriptures. St Jerome, in his epistle to Paulinus (*Ep. 53,7*), after declaration that no handicraft is so base, nor liberal science so easy that can be had without a master (which St Augustine also affirmeth, *De util. cred. 7*) nor that men presume in any occupation to teach that which they never learned, "Only", saith he, "the art of Scripture is that which every man challengeth; this the chatting old wife, this the doting old man, this the brabling sophister, this on every hand, men presume to teach before they learn it." Again: "Some with poise of lofty words devise of Scripture matters among women; othersome (fie upon it!) learn of women what to teach men; and lest that be not enough, by facility of tongue or rather audacity, teach that to others which they understand never a whit themselves. To say nothing of such as be of my faculty; who stepping from secular learning to Holy Scriptures, and able to tickle the ears of the multitude with smooth tale, think all they speak to be the law of God." This he wrote then, when this malady of arrogancy and presumption in divine matters was nothing so outrageous as now it is.

The Scriptures must be delivered in measure and discretion, according to each man's need and capacity

13. St Gregory Nazianzene made an oration of the moderation that was to be used in these matters; where he saith that some in his time thought themselves to have all the wisdom in the world, when they could once repeat two or three words, and them ill couched together, out of Scriptures; but he there divinely discourseth of the orders and differences of degrees; how in Christ's mystical body some are ordained to learn, some to teach; that all are not apostles, all doctors, all interpreters, all of tongues and knowledge, not all learned in Scriptures and divinity; that the people went not up to talk with God in the mountain, but Moses, Aaron and Eleazar; nor they neither, but by the difference of their callings; that they that rebel against this ordinance are guilty of the conspiracy of Korah and his accomplices; that in Scripture there is both milk for babes and meat for men, to be dispensed, not according to everyone's greediness of appetite or wilfulness, but as is most meet for each one's necessity and capacity; that as it is a shame for a bishop or priest to be unlearned in God's mysteries, so for the common people it is oftentimes profitable to salvation, not to be curious, but to follow their pastors in sincerity and simplicity; whereof excellently saith St Augustine: "*Fidei simplicitate et sinceritate lactati nutriamur in Christo: et cum parvi sumus, maiorum cibos non appetamus,*" that is: "Being fed with the simplicity and sincerity of faith, as it were with milk, so let us be nourished in Christ, and when we are little ones, let us not covet the meats of the elder sort." (*De agone Christ. 33,35*). Who in another place testifieth that the Word of God cannot be preached, nor certain mysteries uttered to all men alike, but are to be delivered according to the capacities of the hearers; as he proveth both by St Paul's example, who gave not to every sort strong meat, but milk to many, as being not spiritual, but carnal and not capable; and by our Lord's also, who spake to some plainly and to others in parables, and affirmed that he had many things to utter which the hearers were not able to bear. (*De dono persever. 16,40; De Gen. ad Litt. 7,9; Hom. in Ioh. 18,5*).

How much more may we gather, that all things that be written, are not for the capacity and diet of every of the simple readers, but that very many mysteries of Holy Writ be very far above their reach, and may and ought to be (by as great reason) delivered them in measure and mean most meet for them? Which indeed can hardly be done, when the whole book of the Bible lieth before every man in his mother tongue, to make choice of what he list (i.e. wishes, *ed.*)

The Jews' law for not reading certain books of Holy Scripture until a time

14. For which cause the said Gregory Nazianzene wisheth the Christians had as good a law as the Hebrews of old had (*De moderat. in disp. serv.*); who, as St Jerome also witnesseth, took order among themselves that none should read the *Cantica Canticorum* (Song of Songs), nor certain other pieces of hardest Scriptures till they were thirty years of age (*In Ezech. Prol.*). And truly there is no cause why men should be more loth to be ordered and moderated in this point by God's Church and their pastors, than they are in the use of the holy sacraments; for which as Christ hath appointed priests and ministers at whose hands we must receive them, and not be our own carvers; so hath he given us doctors, prophets, expounders, interpreters, teachers and preachers, to take the law and our faith at their mouths; because our faith and religion cometh not to us properly or principally by reading of Scriptures, but (as the Apostle saith, Ro 10:17) by hearing of the preachers lawfully sent; though reading in order and humility, much confirmeth and advanceth the same. Therefore this holy book of the Scriptures is called of St Ambrose *Liber sacerdotalis* (The Book of Priests), at whose hands and disposition we must take and use it (*Ad Grat.* 1, 2).

The popular objections of withholding the Scriptures from the people answered

15. The wise will not here regard what some wilful people do mutter, that the Scriptures are made for all men, and that it is of envy that the priests do keep the holy book from them. Which suggestion cometh of the same serpent that seduced our first parents, who persuaded them that God had forbidden them that tree of knowledge, lest they should be as cunning as himself, and like unto the Highest (Gn 3:5).

Why the Church permitteth not everyone at their pleasure to read the Scripture

16. No, no, the Church doth it to keep them from blind ignorant presumption and from that which the Apostle calleth *falsi nominis scientiam*, "knowledge falsely so called" (I Ti 6:20); and not to embar them from the true knowledge of Christ. She would have all wise, but *usque ad sobrietatem*, "Unto sobriety", as the Apostle speaketh (Ro 12:3); she knoweth the Scriptures be ordained for every state, as meats, elements, fire, water, candle, knives, sword and the like; which are as needful (most of them) for children as old folks, for the simple as the wise; but yet would mar all, if they were at the guiding of other than wise men, or were in the hands of everyone, for whose preservation they be profitable.

The Holy Scriptures to carnal men and heretics, are as pearls to swine

17. She forbiddeth not the reading of them in any language, envieth no man's commodity, but giveth order how to do it to edification and not destruction; how to do it without casting "the holy to dogs" or "pearls to hogs" (Mt 7:6); (see St John Chrysostom, *Hom. 24 in Matt.* declaring these hogs and dogs to be carnal men and heretics, that take no good of the holy mysteries, but thereby do both hurt themselves and others); how to do it agreeably to the sovereign sincerity, majesty and depth of mystery contained in the same. She would have the presumptuous heretic, notwithstanding he allege them never so fast, flying as it were through the whole Bible, and quoting the Psalms, Prophets, Gospels, Epistles, never so readily for his purpose, as Vincentius Lirinensis (Vincent of Lérins) saith such men's fashion is; yet she would, according to Tertullian's rule, have such mere usurpers quite discharged of all occupying and possession of the holy Testament, which is her old and only right of inheritance, and belongeth not to heretics at all (*De praes. haer. 15-19*), whom Origen called *Scripturarum fures*, "thieves of the Scriptures" (*In Rom. 2.*). She would have the unworthy repelled, the curious repressed, the simple measured, the learned humbled, and all sorts so to use them or abstain from them, as is most convenient for everyone's salvation; with this general admonition, that none can understand the meaning of God in the Scriptures except Christ open their sense (Lk 24:27, 45), and make them partakers of his Holy Spirit in the unity of his mystical body; and for the rest, she committeth it to the pastor of every province and people, according to the difference of time, place and persons, how and in what sort the reading of the Scriptures is more or less to be procured or permitted.

St Chrysostom's exhortations to the reading of Holy Scriptures, and when the people is to be so exhorted

18. Wherein, the variety of circumstances causeth them to deal diversely; as we see by St Chrysostom's people of Constantinople, who were so delicate, dull, worldly and so much given to dice, cards, specially stage plays or theatres (as St Gregory Nazianzene witnesseth; *De laud. Ath.*) that the Scriptures and all holy lections of divine things were loathsome unto them; whereby their holy bishop was forced in many of his sermons to cry out against their extreme negligence and contempt of God's Word, declaring that not only hermits and religious (as they alleged for their excuse) but secular men of all sorts might read the Scriptures, and often have more need thereof in respect of themselves than the other that live in more purity and contemplation; further insinuating that though divers things be high and hard therein, yet many godly histories, lives, examples, and precepts of life and doctrine be plain; and finally, that when the Gentiles were so cunning and diligent to impugn their faith, it were not good for Christians to be simple or negligent in the defence thereof, as (in truth) it is more requisite for a Catholic man in these days when our adversaries be industrious to impeach our belief, to be skilful in Scriptures, than at other times when the Church had no such enemies (*Hom. in Matt. 2,5*).

St Chrysostom maketh nothing for the popular and licentious reading of Scriptures used among the Protestants nowadays

19. To this sense said St Chrysostom divers things, not as a teacher in school, making exact and general rules to be observed in all places and times, but as a pulpit man, agreeably to that audience and his people's default.

Every simple artificer among them readeth much more the deepest and hardest questions of Holy Scripture, than the moral parts

20. Not making it therefore (as some perversely gather of his words) a thing absolutely needful for every poor artificer to read or study Scriptures, nor any whit favouring the presumptuous, curious and contentious jangling and searching of God's secrets reproved by the foresaid fathers, much less approving the excessive pride and madness of these days, when every man and woman is become not only a reader but a teacher, controller, and judge of doctors, Church, Scriptures and all; such as either contemn or easily pass over all the moral parts, good examples and precepts of life (by which as well the simple as learned might be much edified) and only in a manner, occupy themselves in dogmatical, mystical, high and hidden secrets of God's counsels, as of predestination, reprobation, election, prescience, forsaking of the Jews, vocation of the Gentiles and other incomprehensible mysteries, "Languishing about questions" (I Ti 6:4) of only faith, fiducy, new phrases and figures, "ever learning" but "never coming to knowledge" (II Ti 3:7), reading and tossing in pride of wit, conceit of their own cunning, and upon presumption of I can tell what spirit, such books especially and epistles, as St Peter foretold that the unlearned and instable would deprave to their own damnation (II Pe 3:16).

They presuppose no difficulties, which all the learned Fathers felt to be in the Scriptures

21. They delight in none more than the Epistle to the Romans, the *Cantica*

Canticorum (Song of Songs), the Apocalypse, which have in them as many mysteries as words. They find no difficulty in the sacred book clasped with seven seals (Re 5:1); they ask for no expositor with the holy eunuch (Ac 8:27ff.), they feel no such depth of God's science in the Scriptures, as St Augustine did, when he cried out: "*Mira profunditas eloquiorum tuorum, mira profunditas (Deus meus) mira profunditas: horror est intendere in eam, horror honoris, et tremor amoris*", that is: "O wonderful profoundness of thy words; wonderful profoundness, my God, wonderful profoundness; it maketh a man quake to look on it, to quake for reverence, and to tremble for the love thereof." (*Conf. 12,14, 7*). They regard not that which the same doctor affirmeth, that the depth and profundity of wisdom, not only in the words of Holy Scripture, but also in the matter and sense, is so wonderful, that, live a man never so long, be he of never so high a wit, never so studious, never so fervent to attain the knowledge thereof, yet when he endeth, he shall confess he doth but begin (*Ep. 137, 3*). They feel not, with St Jerome, that the text hath a hard shell to be broken before we come to the kernel (*Ep. 58, 9*). They will not stay themselves in only reading the sacred Scriptures thirteen years together, with St Basil and St Gregory Nazianzene, before they expound them, nor take the care (as they did) never otherwise to interpret them, than by the uniform consent of their forefathers and tradition apostolic.

Manners and life nothing amended; but much worse, since this licentious tossing of Holy Scriptures

22. If our new ministers had had this cogitation and care that these and all other wise men have, and ever had, our country had never fallen to this miserable state in religion, and that under pretence, colour and countenance of God's Word; neither should virtue and good life have been so pitifully corrupted in time of such reading, toiling, trembling and translating the book of our life and salvation; whereof the more precious the right and reverent use is, the more pernicious is the abuse and profanation of the same; which every man of experience by these few years prove, and by comparing the former days and manners to these of ours, may easily try.

Look whether your men be more virtuous, your women more chaste, your children more obedient, your servants more trusty, your maids more modest, your friends more faithful, your laity more just in dealing, your clergy more devout in praying; whether there be more religion, fear of God, faith and conscience in all states now, than of old, when there was not so much reading, chatting and jangling of God's Word, but much more sincere dealing, doing and keeping the same. Look whether through this disorder, women teach not their husbands, children their parents, young fools their old and wise fathers, the scholars their masters, the sheep their pastor, and the people the priest.

Scriptures as profanely cited as heathen poets

23. Look whether the most chaste and sacred sentences of God's Holy Word be not turned of many into mirth, mockery, amorous ballets and detestable letters of love and lewdness; their delicate times, tunes and translations much increasing the same.

Scriptures erroneously expounded according to every wicked man's private fantasy

24. This fall of good life and profaning the divine mysteries, everybody seeth; but the great corruption and decay of faith hereby none see but wise men, who only know that were the Scriptures never so truly translated, yet heretics and ill men that follow their own spirit, and know nothing but their private fantasy, and not the sense of the holy Church and doctors, must needs abuse them to their damnation; and that the curious, simple and sensual men which have no taste of the things that be of the Spirit of God, may of infinite places take occasion of pernicious errors. For though the latter or text (in Mk 10:18) have no error, yet (saith St Ambrose) the Arian, or (as we may now speak) the Calvinian interpretation hath errors (*Ad Gratianum 2,1*). And Tertullian saith: "The sense adulterated is as perilous as the style corrupted" (*De praes. haer. 17*). St Hilary also speaketh thus: "Heresy riseth about the understanding, not about the writing; the fault is in the sense, not in the word." (*De trin. 2,1*). And St Augustine saith that many hold the Scriptures as they do the sacraments: "*ad speciem et non ad salutem*; to the outward show and not to salvation." (*De bapt. cont. Donat. 3,19*).

All heretics pretend Scriptures

25. Finally, all sect-masters and ravening wolves, yea the devils themselves pretend Scriptures, allege Scriptures, and wholly shroud themselves in Scriptures, as in the wool and fleece of the simple sheep, whereby the vulgar, in these days of general disputes, cannot but be in extreme danger of error, though their books were truly translated, and were truly in themselves God's own Word indeed.

The Scriptures have been falsely and heretically translated into the vulgar tongues, and sundry other ways sacrilegiously abused, and so given to the people to read

26. But the case now is more lamentable, for the Protestants, such as St Paul calleth: "*ambulantes in astutia*; walking in deceitfulness" (II Co 4:2), have so abused the people, and many other in the world, not unwise, that by their false translations they have, instead of God's Law and Testament, and for Christ's written will and word, given them their own wicked writing and fantasies, most shamefully in all their versions, Latin, English and other tongues, corrupting both the letter and sense by false translation, adding, detracting, altering, transposing, pointing, and all other guileful means; specially where it serveth for the advantage of their private opinions, for which they are bold also, partly to disauthorize quiet, partly to make doubtful, divers whole books allowed for canonical Scripture by the universal Church of God this thousand years and upward; to alter all the authentical and ecclesiastical words used since our Christianity into new profane novelties of speeches agreeable to their doctrine; to change the titles of works, to put out the names of the authors, to charge the very Evangelist with following untrue translation (Lk 1:78; Beza), to add whole sentences proper to their sect, into their Psalms in metre, even into the very Creed in rhyme. All which the poor deceived people say and sing as though they were God's own Word, being indeed through such sacrilegious treachery made the Devil's word.

All this their dealing is noted (as occasion serveth) in the annotations upon this Testament; and more at large in a book lately made purposely of that matter, called "A Discovery, etc."

27. To say nothing of their intolerable liberty and licence to change the accustomed callings of God, angels, men, places and things used by the Apostles and all antiquity, in Greek, Latin and all other languages of Christian nations, into new names, sometimes falsely, and always ridiculously and for ostentation taken from the Hebrews; to frame and fine the phrases of Holy Scriptures after the form of profane writers, sticking not, for the same to supply, add, alter or diminish as freely as if they translated Livy, Vergil or Terence.

Calvin complaineth of the new delicate translators, namely, Castalion; himself and Beza being as bad or worse

28. Having no religious respect to keep either the majesty or sincere simplicity of that venerable style of Christ's spirit, as St Augustine speaketh, which kind the Holy Ghost did choose of infinite wisdom to have the divine mysteries rather uttered in, than any other more delicate, much less in that meretricious manner of writing that sundry of these new translators do use; of which sort Calvin himself and his pew-fellows, so much complain, that they profess Satan to have gained more by these new interpreters (their number, levity of spirit, and audacity increasing daily) than he did before by keeping the word from the people. And for a pattern of this mischief, they give Castalion, adjuring all their churches and scholars to beware of his translation, as one that hath made a very sport and mockery of God's Holy Word. So they charge him themselves (and the Zwinglians of Zürich, whose translations Luther therefore abhorred) handling the matter with no more fidelity, gravity or sincerity than the others; but rather with much more falsification, or (to use the Apostle's words) *cauponation* and *adulteration* of God's Word (II Co 2:17), than they, besides many wicked glosses, prayers, confessions of faith, containing both blasphemous errors and plain contradictions to themselves and among themselves, all privileged and authorized to be joined to the Bible, and to be said and sung of the poor people, and to be believed as articles of faith and wholly consonant to God's Word.

The purpose and commodity of setting forth this Catholic edition

29. We therefore, having compassion to see our beloved countrymen, with extreme danger of their souls, to use only such profane translations and erroneous men's mere fantasies, for the pure and blessed word of truth, much also moved thereunto by the desires of many devout persons; have set forth for you (benign readers) the New Testament to begin withal, trusting that it may give occasion to you, after diligent perusal thereof, to lay away at least such their pure versions as hitherto you have been forced to occupy. How well we have done it, we must not be judges, but refer all to God's Church and our superiors in the same. To them we submit ourselves, and this, and all other our labours, to be in part or in the whole, reformed, corrected, altered or quite abolished; most humbly desiring pardon if through our ignorance, temerity or other human infirmity, we have anywhere mistaken the sense of the Holy Ghost. Further promising, that if hereafter we espy any of our own errors, or if any other, either friend of good will or adversary for desire of reprehension, shall open unto us the same; we will not (as Protestants do) for defence of our estimation, or of pride and contention, by wrangling words wilfully persist in them, but be most glad to hear of them, and in the next edition or otherwise to correct them; for it is truth that we seek for, and God's honour, which being had either by good intention or by occasion, all is well.

The religious care and sincerity observed in this translation

30. This we profess only, that we have done our endeavour with prayer, much fear and trembling, lest we should dangerously err in so sacred, high and divine a work; that we have done it with all faith, diligence and sincerity; that we have used no partiality for the disadvantage of our adversaries, nor no more licence than is sufferable in translating of Holy Scriptures; continually keeping ourselves as near as is possible to our text and to the very words and phrases which by long use are made venerable, though to some profane or delicate ears they may seem more hard and barbarous, as the whole style of Scripture doth lightly to such at the beginning; acknowledging with St Jerome, that in other writings it is enough to give in translation, sense for sense, but that in Scriptures, lest we miss the sense, we must keep the very words (*Ad Pammach. Ep. 101,2*). We must, saith St Augustine, speak according to a set rule, lest licence of words breed some wicked opinion concerning the things contained under the words (*De civit. Dei 10,12*).

The ancient Fathers kept religiously the very barbarisms of the vulgar Latin text

31. Whereof our holy Fathers and ancient doctors had such a religious care that they would not change the very barbarisms or incongruities of speech which by long use had prevailed in the old readings or recitings of Scriptures, as *neque nubent, neque nubentur* (Mt 22:30), in Tertullian (*Adv. Marc. 4,38*); St Hilary (*In. Mt. 22*) and in all the Fathers. *Qui me confusus fuerit, confundar et ego sum*, in St Cyprian (*Ep. 63,7*). *Talis enim nobis decebat sacerdos* (which was an older translation than the vulgar Latin that now is) in St Ambrose (*De fuga saec.3*), and St Jerome himself, who otherwise corrected the Latin translation that was used before his time, yet keepeth religiously (as himself professeth, *Praef. in 4 Evan. ad Damasum*) these and the like speeches. *Nonne vos magis pluris estis illis?* (Mt 6:26) and *Filius hominis non venit ministrari, sed ministrare* (Mt 20:28; cf. Mk 10:45), and *neque nubent neque nubentur* (Lk 10:33), in his commentaries upon these places; and, *Non capit prophetam perire extra Hierusalem*, in his commentaries on Joel 2 (*sub finem*). And St Augustine, who is most religious in all these phrases, counteth it a special pride and infirmity in those that have a little learning in tongues, and none in things, that they easily take offence of the simple speeches or solecisms in the Scriptures (*De doct. Christ. 2,13*). See also the same holy father (*De doct. Christ. 3,3* and *Tract. 2 in Evan. Ioh.*) But of the manner of our translation, more anon.

Now though the text thus truly translated, might sufficiently in the sight of the learned, and all indifferent men, both control the adversaries' corruptions and prove that the Holy Scripture, whereof they have made so great vaunts, make nothing for their new opinions, but wholly for the Catholic Church's belief and doctrine, in all the points of difference betwixt us; yet knowing that the good and simple may easily be seduced by some few obstinate persons of perdition (whom we see given over into a reprobate sense, to whom the Gospel, which in itself is the odour of life to salvation, is made the odour of death to damnation, over whose eyes for sin and disobedience God suffereth a veil or cover to lie, whilst they read the New Testament, even as the Apostle saith the Jews have till this day, in reading of the Old (II Co 3:13-16), that as the one sort cannot find Christ in the Scriptures, read they never so much, so the other cannot find the Catholic Church nor her doctrine there neither) and finding by experience this saying of St Augustine to be most true: "If the prejudice of any erroneous persuasion preoccupate the mind, whatsoever the Scripture hath contrary, men take it for a figurative speech." (*De doct. Christ. 3,10,15*).

Of the Annotations, why they were made and what matter they contain

32. For these causes, and somewhat to help the faithful reader in the difficulties of divers places, we have also set forth reasonable Annotations, thereby to show the studious reader in most places pertaining to the controversies of this time, both the heretical corruptions and false deductions, and also the Apostolic tradition, the expositions of the holy Fathers, the decrees of the Catholic Church and most ancient Councils; which means, whosoever trusteth not, for the sense of Holy Scriptures, but had rather follow his private judgement or the arrogant spirit of these sectaries, he shall worthily through his own wilfulness be deceived; beseeching all men to look with diligence, sincerity and indifferency, into the case that concerneth no less than everyone's eternal salvation or damnation.

Heresies make Catholics more diligent to search and find the senses of Holy Scripture for repelling the same

33. Which if he do, we doubt not but he shall to his great contentment, find the Holy Scriptures most clearly and invincibly to prove the articles of Catholic doctrine against our adversaries, which perhaps he had thought before this diligent search, either not to be consonant to God's Word, or at least not contained in the same, and finally he shall prove this saying of St Augustine to be most true. "*Multi sensus, etc.*; Many senses of Holy Scriptures lie hidden, and are known to some few of greater understanding; neither are they at any time avouched more commodiously and acceptably than at such times, when the care to answer heretics doth force men thereunto. For then, even they that be negligent in matters of study and learning, shaking off sluggishness, are stirred up to diligent hearing, that the adversaries may be repelled. Again, how many senses of Holy Scriptures, concerning Christ's Godhead, have been avouched against Photinus; how many of his Manhood, against Mani; how many of the Trinity, against Sabellius; how many of the unity in Trinity, against the Arians, Eunomians,

Macedonians; how many, of the Catholic Church dispersed throughout the whole world, and of the mixture of good and bad in the same until the end of the world, against the Donatists and Luciferians (i.e. followers of Lucifer of Cagliari, *ed.*) and others of the like error; how many against all other heretics, which it were too long to rehearse? Of which senses and expositions of Holy Scripture the approved authors and avouchers should otherwise not be known at all, or not so well known as the contradictions of proud heretics have made them." (*Ennar. in Ps. 67; 1, 39*).

Thus he saith of such things as not seeming to be in Holy Scriptures to the ignorant or heretics, yet indeed be there. But in other points doubted of, that indeed are not decided by Scripture, he giveth us this goodly rule to be followed in all, as he exemplifieth in one. "Then do we hold, " saith he, "the verity of the Scriptures, when we do that which now hath seemed good to the Universal Church, which the authority of the Scriptures themselves doth commend; so that, forasmuch as the Holy Scripture cannot deceive, whosoever is afraid to be deceived with the obscurity of questions, let him therein ask counsel of the same Church, which the Holy Scripture most certainly and evidently showeth and pointeth unto." (*Contra Crescon. 13, 33*).

Many causes why this New Testament is translated according to the ancient vulgar Latin text

34. Now to give thee also intelligence in particular, most gentle reader, of such things as it behoveth thee specially to know concerning our translation – we translate the old vulgar Latin text, not the common Greek text, for these causes:

01. *It is most ancient.* It is so ancient that it was used in the Church of God above 1300 years ago, as appeareth by the Fathers of those times.
02. *Corrected by St Jerome.* It is that (by the common received opinion, and by all probability) which St Jerome afterward corrected according to the Greek, by the appointment of Damasus, then Pope, as he maketh mention in his preface before the four evangelists, unto the said Damasus, and *In catalogo (in fine)* and *Ep. 102.*
03. *Commended by St Augustine.* Consequently it is the same which St Augustine so commendeth and alloweth in an epistle to St Jerome. (*Ep. 71*).
04. *Used and expounded by the Fathers.* It is that which for the most part ever since hath been used in the Church's service, expounded in sermons, alleged and interpreted in the commentaries and writings of the ancient Fathers of the Latin Church.
05. *Only authentical, by the holy Council of Trent.* The holy Council of Trent, for these and many other important considerations, hath declared and defined this only of all other Latin translations to be authentical, and so only to be used and taken in public lessons, disputations,

preachings, and expositions, and that no man presume upon any pretence to reject or refuse the same.

06. *Most grave, least partial.* It is the gravest, sincerest, of greatest majesty, least partiality, as being without all respect of controversies and contentions, specially these of our time, as appeareth by those places which Erasmus and others at this day translate much more to the advantage of the Catholic cause.

07. *Precise in following the Greek.* It is so exact and precise according to the Greek, both the phrase and the word, that delicate heretics therefore reprehend it of rudeness. And that it followeth the Greek far more exactly that the Protestants' translations, beside infinite other places, we appeal to these (Tt 3:14): *"Curent bonis operibus praeesse, proistasthai.* English Bible, 1577: "to maintain good works". And He 10:20: *"Viam nobis initiavit, enekainisen.* English Bible: "he prepared". So in these words, *iustificationes, traditiones, idola, etc.* In all which they come not near the Greek, but avoid it of purpose.

08. *Preferred by Beza himself.* The adversaries themselves, namely Beza, prefer it before all the rest (*In praefat. NT 1556*). And again he saith that the old interpreter translated very religiously (*Annot. in Lc 1:1*).

09. *All the rest misliked of the sectaries themselves, each reprehending another.* In the rest, there is such diversity and dissension, and no end of reprehending one another, and translating every man according to his fantasy, that Luther said: If the world should stand any long time, we must receive again (which he thought absurd) the Decrees of the Councils, for preserving the unity of faith, because of so divers interpretations of the Scripture. And Beza, (in the place above-mentioned) noteth the itching ambition of his fellow translators, that had much rather disagree and dissent from the best, than seem themselves to have said or written nothing. And Beza's translation itself being so esteemed in our country, that the Geneva English Testaments be translated according to the same, yet sometime goeth so wide from the Greek, and from the meaning of the Holy Ghost, that themselves which protest to translate it, dare not follow it. For example (Lk 3:36), they have put the words: "The son of Canaan", which he wittingly and wilfully left out; and (Ac 1:14) they say: "With the women", agreeably to the vulgar Latin, where he saith *cum uxoribus*, with their wives.

10. *It is truer than the vulgar Greek text itself.* It is not only better than all other Latin translations, but than the Greek text itself, in those places where they disagree.

The ancient Fathers for proof thereof, and the adversaries themselves

35. The proof hereof is evident, because most of the ancient heretics were

Grecians, and therefore the Scriptures in Greek were corrupted by them, as the ancient Fathers often complain. Tertullian noteth the Greek text which is at this day (I Co 15:47) to be an old corruption of Marcion the heretic, and the truth to be as in our vulgar Latin: "*Secundus homo de coelo coelestis*; the second man from heaven, heavenly." So read other ancient Fathers, and Erasmus thinketh it must needs be so, and Calvin himself followeth it (*Inst. 2,13,2*). Again, St Jerome noteth that the Greek text (I Co 7:33) which is at this day, is not the Apostolical verity or the true text of the Apostle, but that which is in the vulgar Latin: "*Qui cum uxore est, solicitus est quae sunt mundi, quomodo placeat uxori, et divisus est*. He that is with a wife is careful of worldly things, how he may please his wife, and is divided or distracted." The ecclesiastical history called the tripartite, noteth the Greek text that now is (I Jn 4:3) to be an old corruption of the ancient Greek copies, by the Nestorian heretics, and the true reading to be as in our vulgar Latin: "*omnis spiritus qui solvit IESUM, ex Deo non est*; Every spirit that dissolveth JESUS, is not of God"; and Beza confesseth that Socrates in his *Ecclesiastical History* readeth so in the Greek: *pan pneuma ho lyei ton Iesoun Christon*, etc.

The Calvinists themselves often forsake the Greek as corrupt, and translate according to the ancient vulgar Latin text

36. But the proof is more pregnant out of the adversaries themselves. They forsake the Greek text as corrupted and translate according to the vulgar Latin, namely Beza and his scholars the English translators of the Bible, in these places. He 9:1, saying: The first covenant, for that which is in the Greek: The first tabernacle. Where they put *covenant*, not as of the text, but in another letter, as to be understood according to the vulgar Latin, which most sincerely leaveth it out altogether, saying: "*Habuit quidem et prius iustificationes* etc.; The former also indeed had justifications." Again, Ro 11:21 they translate not according to the Greek text: *Tempori servientes*; serving the time, which Beza saith must needs be a corruption; but according to the vulgar Latin: *Domino servientes*, serving our Lord. Again, Re 11:2, they translate not the Greek text, *Atrium quod intra templum est*, the court which is within the temple; but clean contrary, according to the vulgar Latin, which Beza saith is the true reading, *Atrium quod est foris templum*, the court which is without the temple. Only in this last place, one English Bible, of the year 1562 (the last edition of the Great Bible, ed.), followeth the error of the Greek. Again, II Ti 2:14, they add *but* more than is in the Greek, to make the sense more commodious and easy, according as it is in the vulgar Latin. Again, Ja 5:12, they leave the Greek and follow the vulgar Latin, saying: lest you fall into condemnation. "I doubt not" saith Beza, "but this is the true and sincere reading, and I suspect the corruption in the Greek

came thus", etc. It were infinite to set down all such places, where the adversaries, specially Beza, follow the old vulgar Latin and the Greek copy agreeable thereunto, condemning the Greek text that now is, of corruption.

Superfluities in the Greek, which Erasmus calleth trifling and rash additions

37. Again, Erasmus the best translator of all the later, by Beza's judgement, saith that the Greek sometime hath superfluities corruptly added to the text of Holy Scripture, as Mt 6:13 to the end of the *Pater Noster*, these words: because thine is the kingdom, the power and the glory, for ever-more. Which he calleth *nugas*, trifles rashly added to our Lord's prayer, and reprehendeth Valla for blaming the old vulgar Latin because it hath it not. Likewise Ro 11:6, these words in the Greek, and not in the vulgar Latin: "But if of works, it is not now grace; otherwise the work is no more a work." And Mk 10:29, these words, *or wife*, and suchlike. Yea the greek text in these superfluities condemneth itself, and justifieth the vulgar Latin exceedingly; as being marked throughout in a number of places, that such and such words are superfluous, in all which places our vulgar Latin hath no such thing, but is agreeable to the Greek, which remaineth after the superfluities be taken away. For example, that before mentioned in the end of the *Pater Noster*, hath a mark of superfluity in the Greek text thus", and Mk 6:11 these words: "Amen, I say unto you, it shall be more tolerable for the land of Sodom and Gomorrah in the day of judgement than for that city"; and Mt 20:22, these words: "And be baptized with the baptism that I am baptized with?" which is also superfluously repeated again (v. 23), and suchlike places exceeding many; which being noted superfluous in the Greek, and being not in the vulgar Latin, prove the Latin in those places to be better, truer and more sincere than the Greek.

The vulgar Latin translation agreeth with the best Greek copies, by Beza's own judgement

38. Whereupon we conclude of these premises that it is no derogation to the vulgar Latin text, which we translate, to disagree from the Greek text, whereas it may notwithstanding be not only as good, but also better. And this the adversary himself, their greatest and latest translator of the Greek, doth avouch against Erasmus in behalf of the old vulgar Latin translation, in these notorious words: "How unworthy and without cause," saith he, "doth Erasmus blame the old interpreter as dissenting from the Greek? He dissented, I grant, from those Greek copies which he had gotten, but we have found, not in one place, that same interpretation which he blameth, is grounded upon the authority of other Greek copies, and those most ancient.

Yea in some number of places we have observed that the reading of the Latin text of the old interpreter, though it agree not sometime with our Greek copies, yet it is much more convenient, for that it seemed he followed some better and truer copy." (*Praef. in NT 1556*). Thus for Beza. In which words he unwittingly, but most truly, justifieth and defendeth the old vulgar translation against himself and all other cavillers that accuse the same, because it is not always agreeable to the Greek text.

When the Fathers say that the Latin text must yield to the Greek, and be corrected by it, they mean the true and uncorrupted Greek text

39. Whereas it was translated out of other Greek copies (partly extant, partly not extant at this day) either as good and as ancient, such as St Augustine speaketh of, calling them: "*doctiores et diligentiores*; the more learned and diligent Greek copies," whereunto the Latin translations that fail in any place, must needs yield (*De doct. Christ. 2,15*). And if it were not too long to exemplify and prove this, which would require a treatise by itself, we could show by many and most close examples throughout the New Testament, these sundry means of justifying the old translation.

The vulgar Latin translation is many ways justified by most ancient Greek copies, and the Fathers

40. First, if it agree with the Greek text (as commonly it doth, and in the greatest places concerning the controversies of our time, it doth most certainly) so far the adversaries have not to complain; unless they will complain of the Greek also, as they do (Ja 4:2 and I Pe 3:21), where the vulgar Latin followeth exactly the Greek text, saying *occiditis*, and *quod vos similes formae*, etc. But Beza in both places correcteth the Greek text also as false.

If it disagree here and there from the Greek text, it agreeth with another Greek copy set in the margin, whereof see examples in the foresaid Greek Testaments of Robert Stevens and Crispin throughout, namely II Pe 1:10: "*Satagite ut per bona opera certam vestram vocationem faciatis, dia ton agathon ergon.* And Mk 8:7: *Et ipsos benedixit, eulogesas auta.*

If these marginal Greek copies be thought less authentical than the Greek text, the adversaries themselves tell us the contrary, who in their translations often follow the marginal copies and forsake the Greek text; as in the examples above mentioned (Ro 11; Re 11: II Ti 2; Ja 5, etc.) it is evident.

If all Erasmus' Greek copies have not that which is in the vulgar Latin, Beza had copies which have it, and those most ancient (as he saith) and better. And if all Beza's copies fail in this point and will not help us, Gagney, the French King's preacher, and he that might command in all the King's libraries, he found Greek copies that have just according to the vulgar Latin; and that in such place as would seem otherwise less probable, as Ja 3:5: "*Ecce quantus ignis quam magnam silvam incendit*; Behold how much fire, what a great wood it kindleth." A man would think it must be as in the Greek text: "A little fire, what a great wood it kindleth!" But an approved ancient Greek copy, alleged by Gagney, hath as it is in the vulgar Latin. And if Gagney's copies also fail sometime, there Beza and Crispin supply Greek copies fully agreeable to the vulgar Latin, as Ju 5: "*Scientes semel omnia, quoniam Iesus*, etc." and v.19: "*Segregant semetipsos.*" Likewise, Ep 2:2: "*Quod elegerit vos primitias*"; *aparchas* in some Greek copies. Gagney and II Co 9:2: "*Vestra aemulatio, ho hymon zelos.*" So hath one Greek copy (Beza).

The Greek Fathers

41. If all their copies be not sufficient, the ancient Greek fathers had copies and expounded them agreeable to our vulgar Latin, as I Ti 6:20: "*Profanas vocum novitates*" – so readeth St John Chrysostom and expoundeth it against heretical and erroneous novelties. Yet now we know no Greek copy that readeth so. Likewise Jn 10:29: *Pater meus quod mihi dedit maius omnibus est.* So readeth St Cyril of Alexandria and expoundeth it (*In Ioh. 7,10*). Likewise 1 Jn 4:3: *omnis spiritus qui solvit IESUM, ex Deo non est.* So readeth St Irenaeus (*Adv. haer. 3,18*), St Augustine (*Tract. 6:14 in Ioh.*), St Leo (*Ep. 10:5*), besides Socrates in his *Ecclesiastical History* (7, 22), and the *Tripartite* (12,4), who say plainly that this was the old and true reading of this place in Greek. And in what Greek copy extant at this day is there this text (Jn 5:2): *Est autem Hierosolymis probatica piscina?* And yet St John Chrysostom, St Cyril and Theophylact read so in the Greek, and Beza saith it is the better reading. And so is the Latin text of the Roman Mass Book justified, and eight other Latin copies that read so. For our vulgar Latin here is according to the Greek text, "*super probatica*", and Ro 5:17: *Donationis et iustitiae.* So readeth Theodoret in Greek. And Lk 2:14 Origen and St John Chrysostom read: *Hominibus bonae voluntatis*, and Beza liketh it better than the Greek text that now is.

Where there is no such sign of any ancient Greek copy in the fathers, yet these later interpreters tell us that the old interpreter did follow some other Greek copy, as Mk 7:3: *Nisi crebro laverint.* Erasmus thinketh that he did read in the Greek *pyknei*, "often"; and Beza and others commend his conjecture, yea and the English Bibles are so translated. Whereas now it is *pygmei*, which signifieth the length of the arm up to the elbow. And who would not think that the Evangelist should say: "The Pharisees wash often, because otherwise they eat not" rather than thus: "Unless they wash up to the elbow, they eat not"?

The Latin Fathers

42. If all such conjectures, and all the Greek Fathers help us not, yet the Latin Fathers with great consent will easily justify the old vulgar translation, which for the most part they follow and expound, as Jn 7:39: *Nondum erat spiritus datus*. So readeth St Augustine (*De trin. 4,20; Quaest. 83,62; Tract. in Ioh. 52, 8*); Leo (*Ser. 2 de Pent.*). Whose authority were sufficient, but indeed Didymus, also a Greek doctor, readeth so (*De Sp. Sanct. 2,33*), translated by St Jerome, and a Greek copy in the Vatican, and the Syriac New Testament. Likewise Jn 21:22: *Sic eum volo manere*; so readeth St Ambrose (*Ps. 45 and Ps. 118 Resh*); St Augustine (*Hom. in Ioh. 124,1*) and the Venerable Bede (*In Ioh. 21*) upon St John's Gospel.

And lastly, if some other Latin Fathers of ancient time read otherwise, either here or in other places, not all agreeing with the text of our vulgar Latin, the cause is the great diversity and multitude that was then of Latin copies (whereof St Jerome complaineth), till this one vulgar Latin grew only into use. Neither doth their divers reading make more for the Greek than for the vulgar Latin, differing oftentimes from both, as when St Jerome in this last place readeth: *Si sic eum volo manere* (*Adv. Iovin. 1,26*), it is according to no Greek copy now extant. And if yet there be some doubt that the readings of some Greek or Latin Fathers, differing from the vulgar Latin, be a check or condemnation to the same; let Beza, that is, let the adversary himself, tell us his opinion in this case also. "Whosoever," saith he, "shall take upon him to correct these things" (speaking of the vulgar Latin translation) "out of the ancient Fathers' writings, either Greek or Latin, unless he do it very circumspectly and advisedly, he shall surely corrupt all rather than amend it, because it is not to be thought that as often as they cited any place, they did always look into the book or number every word." As if he should say: "We may not by and by think that the vulgar Latin is faulty and to be corrected, when we read otherwise in the Fathers either Greek or Latin, because they did not always exactly cite the words, but followed some commodious and godly sense thereof."

The few and small faults negligently crept into the vulgar Latin translation

43. Thus then we see that by all means the old vulgar Latin translation is approved good, and better than the Greek text itself, and that there is no cause why it should give place to any other text, copies or readings. Marry, if there be any faults evidently crept in by those that heretofore wrote or copied out the Scriptures (as there be some) them we grant no less, than we would grant faults nowadays committed by the printer, and they are exactly noted of Catholic writers, namely in all Plantin's Bibles set forth by the divines of Louvain; and the holy Council of Trent willeth that the vulgar

Latin text be in such points throughly mended, and so to be most authentical. Such faults as these, *in fide* for *in fine*; *praescientiam* for *praesentiam*; *suscipiens* for *suspiciens*; and such like very rare, which are evident corruptions made by the copyists, or grown by the similitude of words. These being taken away, which are no part of those corruptions and differences before talked of, we translate that text which is most sincere, and in our opinion, and as we have proved, incorrupt. The adversaries contrary, translate that text, which themselves confess both by their writings and doings, to be corrupt in a number of places and more corrupt than our vulgar Latin, as is before declared.

The Calvinists confessing the Greek to be most corrupt, yet translate that only, and hold that only for authentical Scripture

44. And if we would here stand to recite the places in the Greek which Beza pronounceth to be corrupted, we should make the reader to wonder how they can either so plead otherwise for the Greek text, as though there were no other truth of the New Testament but that; or how they translate only that (to deface, as they think, the old vulgar Latin) which themselves so shamefully disgrace, more than the vulgar Latin, inventing corruptions where none are, nor can be, in such universal consent of all both Greek and Latin copies. For example, Mt 10:2: "The first Simon, who is called Peter". I think, saith Beza, this word *protos*, "first", hath been added to the text of some that would establish Peter's primacy. Again, Lk 22:20: The chalice, *that is shed for you*. It is most likely (saith he) that these words, being sometime but a marginal note, came by corruption out of the margin into the text. Again, Ac 7:43: Figures which they made, *to adore them*. It may be suspected (saith he) that these words, as many other, have crept by corruption into the text out of the margin. And I Co 15:57: He thinketh the Apostle said not *nikos* (victory), as it is in all Greek copies, but *neikos* (contention). And Ac 13:20 – he calleth it a manifest error, that in the Greek it is 400 years for 300. And Ac 7:16, he reckoneth up a whole catalogue of corruptions, namely Mk 12:42: *ho esti kodrantes*; which is a farthing; and Ac 8:26: *hauté estin éremos*; this is a desert. And Ac 7:16, the name of Abraham, and such like. All which he thinketh to have been added or altered into the Greek text by corruption.

They standing precisely upon the Hebrew of the Old, and Greek text of the New Testament, must of force deny the one of them

45. But among other places he laboureth exceedingly to prove a great corruption (Ac 7:14) where it is said (according to the Septuagint, that is, the Greek text of the Old Testament) that Jacob went down into Egypt with 75 souls. And Lk 3:36, he thinketh these words *tou kainan*, which was of Canaan, to be so false that he leaveth them clean out in both his editions of the New Testament (1556; 1565); saying that he is bold so to do by the authority of Moses. Whereby he will signify that it is not in the Hebrew text of Moses or of the Old Testament, and therefore it is false in the Greek of the New Testament. Which consequence of theirs (for it is common among them and concerneth all Scriptures), if it were true, all places of the Greek text of the New Testament, cited out of the Old according to the Septuagint, and not according to the Hebrew (which they know are very many) should be false; and so by tying themselves only to the Hebrew in the Old Testament, they are forced to forsake the Greek of the New; or if they will maintain the Greek of the New, they must forsake sometime the Hebrew in the Old; but this argument shall be forced against them elsewhere.

They say the Greek is more corrupt than we will grant them

46. By this little, the reader may see what gay patrons they are of the Greek text, and how little cause they have in their own judgements to translate it, or vaunt of it as in derogation of the vulgar Latin translation, and how easily we might answer them in a word why we translate not the Greek; forsooth because it is so infinitely corrupted. But the truth is, we do by no means grant it so corrupted as they say, though in comparison we know it less sincere and incorrupt than the vulgar Latin, and for that cause and others before alleged, we prefer the said Latin and have translated it.

We prefer not the vulgar Latin text as making more for us. The Greek text maketh for us more than the vulgar Latin

47. If there yet remain one thing which perhaps they will say, when they cannot answer our reasons aforesaid; to wit, that we prefer the vulgar Latin before the Greek text, because the Greek maketh more against us; we protest that, as for other causes we prefer the Latin, so in this respect of making for us or against us, we allow the Greek as much as the Latin, yea in sundry places more than the Latin, being assured that they have not one, and that we have many advantages in the Greek more than in the Latin, as by the Annotations of this New Testament shall evidently appear; namely in all such places where they dare not translate the Greek, because it is for us and against them, as when they translate *dikaiomata* "ordinances" and not "justifications", and that of purpose as Beza confesseth; Lk 1:6, *paradoseis*, "ordinances" or "instructions" and not "traditions", in the better part. II Th

2:15, *presbyterous*, "elders" and not "priests"; *eidola*, "images" rather than "idols".

For the real presence. And especially when St Luke in the Greek so maketh for us (the vulgar Latin being indifferent for them and us) that Beza saith it is a corruption crept out of the margin into the text. What need these absurd devices and false dealings with the Greek text, if it made for them more than for us, yea if it made not for us against them?

For fasting. But that the Greek maketh more for us, see I Co 7:5. In the Latin, *Defraud not one another, but for a time, that you give yourselves to prayer*; in the Greek, *to fasting and prayer*. Ac 10:30, in the Latin Cornelius saith: *From the fourth day past until this hour I was praying in my house, and behold a man, etc.*; in the Greek, *I was fasting and praying*.

For free will. I Jn 5:18 in the Latin: *We know that everyone which is born of God sinneth not, but the generation of God preserveth him, etc.;* in the Greek: *but he that is born of God preserveth himself.*

Against only faith. Re 22:14, in the Latin: *Blessed are they that wash their garments in the blood of the Lamb, etc.*; in the Greek: *Blessed are they that do his commandments.*

Against special assurance of salvation. Ro 8:38. *Certus sum, etc.* I am sure that neither *death nor life, nor other creature is able to separate us from the charity of God*. As though he were assured, or we might and should assure ourselves of our predestination; in the Greek *pepeismai; I am probably persuaded that neither death nor life, etc.*

For the sacrifice of Christ's body and blood. In the Evangelists about the sacrifice and blessed sacrament, in the Latin thus: *This is my blood that shall be shed for you* (Lk 22:20); and in St Paul, *This is my body which shall be betrayed or delivered for you* (I Co 11:24); both being referred to the time to come and to the sacrifice on the cross; in the Greek, *This is my blood which is shed for you*, and *my body which is broken for you*; both being referred to that present time when Christ gave his body and blood at his supper, then shedding the one and breaking the other, that is sacrificing it sacramentally and mystically. Lo these and the like our advantages in the Greek, more than in the Latin.

The Protestants condemning the old vulgar translation as making for us condemn themselves

48. But is the vulgar translation for all this papistical and therefore do we follow it? (For so some of them call it, and say it is the worst of all other.) If it be, the Greek (as you see) is more, and so both Greek and Latin and consequently the Holy Scripture of the New Testament is papistical. Again, if the vulgar Latin be papistical, papistry is very ancient and the Church of God for so many hundred years wherein it hath used and allowed this translation, hath been papistical. But wherein is it papistical? Forsooth in these phrases and speeches: *Paenitentiam agite* (Mt 3:2, etc.); *Sacramentum hoc magnum est* (Ep 5:32); *Ave, gratia plena* (Lk 1:28); *Talibus hostiis promeretur Deus* (He 13:16), and such like. First, doth not the Greek say the same? See the annotations upon these places. Secondly, could he translate these things papistically or partially, or rather prophetically so long before they were in controversy? Thirdly, doth he not say for *paenitentiam agite*, in another place, *paenitemini*; and doth he not translate other mysteries, by the word *sacramentum*, as Re 17:5: *sacramentum mulieris*; and as he translateth one word *gratia plena*, so doth he not translate the very like word *plenus ulceribus*, which themselves do follow also? Is this also papistry?

It is void of all partiality

49. When he said (He 10:29): *Quanto deteriora merebitur supplicia*, etc., and they like it well enough, might he not have said according to the same Greek word: *Vigilate ut mereamini fugere ista omnia et stare ante filium hominis* (Lk 21:36) and *Qui merebuntur saeculum illud et resurrectionem ex mortuis*, etc. (Lk 20:35), and *Tribulationes quas sustinetis ut mereamini regnum Dei, pro quo et patimini* (II Th 1:5). Might he not (we say) if he had partially affected the word "merit", have used it in all these places, according to his and your own translation of the same Greek word (He 10:29)? Which he doth not, but in all these places saith simply: *Ut digni habeamini*, and *Qui digni habebuntur*. And how can it be judged papistical or partial, when he saith *Talibus hostiis promeretur Deus* (He 13:16)? Was Primasius, also St Augustine's scholar, a papist for using this text, and all the rest that have done the like? Was St Cyprian a papist, for using so often this speech: *promereri Dominum iustis operibus, paenitentia, etc.*? (*Ep. 14,18*). Or is there any difference, but that St Cyprian useth it as a deponent, more Latinly; the other as a passive, less finely? Was it papistry, to say *senior* for *presbyter*, *ministrantibus* for *sacrificantibus*, or *liturgiam celebrantibus* (Ac 13:2), *simulacris* for *idolis* (I Th 1:9; I Jn 5:21), *fides tua te salvum fecit* sometime for *sanum fecit* (Mt 9:22, etc.)? Or shall we think he was a Calvinist for translating thus, as they think he was a papist, when any word soundeth for us?

The papistry thereof (as they term it) is in the very sentences of the Holy Ghost, more than in the translation

50. Again, was he a papist in these kinds of words only, and was he not in whole sentences? As *Tibi dabo claves*, etc. *Quidquid solveris in terra, erit solutum et in coelis;* and *Quorum remiseritis peccata, remittuntur eis* (Mt 16:19); and, *Tunc reddet unicuique secundum opera sua* (Ro 2:6); and *Nunquid poterit fides salvare eum? Ex operibus iustificatur homo et non ex fide tantum* (Ja 2:24); and *Nubere volunt, damnationem habentes quia* *primam fidem irritam fecerunt* (I Ti 5:11f.); and, *Mandata eius gravia non sunt*; and *Aspexerit in remunerationem* (He 11:26). Are all these and such like papistical translations because they are most plain for the Catholic faith which they call papistry? Are they not word for word as in the Greek, and the very words of the Holy Ghost? And if in these there be no accusation of papistical partiality, why in the other? Lastly, are the ancient fathers, General Councils, the churches of all the west part, that use all these speeches and phrases now so many hundred years, are they all papistical? Be it so, and let us in the name of God follow them, speak as they speak, translate as they translated, interpret as they interpreted, because we believe as they believed. And thus far for defence of the old vulgar Latin translation, and why we translated it before all others.

The manner of this translation and what hath been observed therein

51. In this our translation, because we wish it to be most sincere, as becometh a Catholic translation, and have endeavoured so to make it; we are very precise and religious in following our copy, the old vulgar approved Latin; not only in sense, which we hope we always do, but sometime in the very words and phrases, which may seem to the vulgar reader and to common English ears not yet acquainted therewith, rudeness or ignorance; but to the discreet reader that deeply weigheth and considereth the importance of sacred words and speeches, and how easily the voluntary translator may miss the true sense of the Holy Ghost, we doubt not but our consideration and doing therein shall seem reasonable and necessary; yea and that all sorts of Catholic readers will in short time think that familiar, which at the first may seem strange, and will esteem it more when they shall otherwise be taught to understand it, than if it were the common known English.

Certain words not English nor as yet familiar in the English tongue

52. *Amen.* For example, we translate often thus, *Amen, amen, I say unto you.* Which as yet seemeth strange, but after a while it will be as familiar as *Amen* in the end of all prayers and psalms, and even as when we end with *Amen*, it soundeth far better than *so be it*, so in the beginning, *Amen, amen* must needs by use and custom sound far better than *verily, verily.* Which indeed, doth not express the asseveration and assurance signified in this Hebrew word; besides that is the solemn and usual word of our Saviour to express a vehement asseveration, and therefore is not changed, neither in the Syriac nor Greek nor vulgar Latin Testament, but is preserved and used of the Evangelists and Apostles themselves, even as Christ spake it, *propter sanctiorem auctoritatem*, as St Augustine saith of this and of *Alleluia, for* *the more holy and sacred authority thereof* (*De doct. Christ. 2,11*).

Alleluia. And therefore do we keep the word *alleluia* (Re 19:4) as it is both in Greek and Latin, yea and in all the English translations, though in their Books of Common Prayer they translate it, *Praise ye the Lord.*

Paraskeve. Again, if hosanna, raca, Belial and such like be untranslated in the English Bibles, why may we not say *Corbanna* and *Paraskeve*, specially when they, Englishing this later thus, *the preparation of the Sabbath*, put three words more into the text than the Greek word doth signify (Mt 27:62). And others saying thus, after the day of *preparing*, make a cold translation and short of the sense; as if they should translate the Sabbath, *the resting*, for *Paraskeve* is as solemn a word for the Sabbath eve as *Sabbath* is for the Jews' seventh day; and now among Christians much more solemner, taken for Good Friday only. These words then we thought it far better to keep in the text and to tell their signification in the margin or in a table for that purpose, than to disgrace both the text and them with translating them.

Pasche. Azymes. Such are also these words, the *Pasche*, the feast of *azymes*, the bread of *proposition*. Which they translate the *passover*, the feast of *sweet bread* (more familiarly, *unleavened bread, ed.*), the *shewbread*. But if *Pentecost* (Ac 2:1) be yet untranslated in their Bibles and seemeth not strange, why should not *Pasche* and *azymes* so remain also, being solemn feasts, as pentecost was? Or why should they English one rather than the other? Specially whereas *Passover* at the first was as strange as *Pasche* may seem now, and perhaps as many now understand *Pasche* as *Passover*. And as for *azymes*, when they English it as the feast of *sweet bread*, it is a false interpretation of the word and nothing expresseth that which belongeth to the feast, concerning unleavened bread. And as for their term of *shewbread*, it is very strange and ridiculous.

Neophyte. Again, if *Proselyte* be a received word in the English Bibles (Mt 23:15; Ac 2:11), why may we not be bold to say *Neophyte* (I Ti 3:6)? Specially when they, translating it into English, do falsely express the signification of the word thus, *a young scholar*. Whereas it is a peculiar word to signify them that were lately baptized, as *cathechumenus* signifieth the newly instructed in faith not yet baptized, who is also a young scholar rather than the other; and many that have been old scholars may be *neophytes*, by deferring baptism. And if *phylacteries* be allowed for English (Mt 23:5), we hope that *didrachms* also, *prepuce, paraclete* and such like will easily grow to be current and familiar. And in good sooth there is in all these such necessity, that they cannot be conveniently translated, as when St Paul saith, *concisio, non circumcisio* (Ph 3:2), how can we but follow his very words and allusion? And how is it possible to express *evangelizo*, but as we do, *evangelize*? For *Evangelium* being the Gospel, what is *evangelizo*, or *to evangelize*, but to show the glad tidings of the Gospel, of the time of grace of all Christ's benefits? All which signification is lost by translating as the English Bibles do, *I bring you good tidings* (Lk 2:10).

Therefore we say *depositum* (I Ti 6:20) and *he exinanited* himself (Ph 2:7) and, You have *reflourished* (Ph 4:10) and to *exhaust* (He 9:28), because we cannot possibly attain to express these words fully in English and we think much better, that the reader, staying at the difficulty of them, should take an occasion to look in the table following, or otherwise to ask the full meaning of them, than by putting some usual English words that express them not, so to deceive the reader.

Catholic terms proceeding from the very text of Scripture

53. Sometime also we do it for another cause, as when we say, *The advent of our Lord*, and, *Imposing of hands*, because one is a solemn time, the other a solemn action in the Catholic Church; to signify to the people that these and suchlike names come out of the very Latin text of the Scripture. So did *penance, doing penance, chalice, priest, deacon, traditions, altar, host* and the like (which we exactly keep as Catholic terms) proceed even from the very words of Scripture.

Certain hard speeches and phrases

54. Moreover, we presume not in hard places to mollify the speeches or phrases, but religiously keep them word for word, and point for point, for fear of missing or restraining the sense of the Holy Ghost to our fantasy, as Ep 6:12: *Against the spiritual of wickedness in the celestials*. And, *What to me and thee, woman?* (Jn 2:4), whereof, see the Annotation upon this place. And I Pe 2:2: *As infants even now born, reasonable, milk without guile desire ye*. We do so place *reasonable* of purpose, that it may be indifferent both to infants going before, as in our Latin text; or to milk that followeth after, as in other Latin copies and in the Greek.

The Protestants' presumptuous boldness and liberty in translating

55. Jn 3:8 we translate: *The spirit breatheth where he will, etc.*, leaving it indifferent to signify either the Holy Ghost, or wind, which, the Protestants translating "wind", take away the other sense more common and usual in the ancient fathers. We translate Lk 8:23: *They were filled*, not adding of our own, *with water*, to mollify the sentence, as the Protestants do, and 22:20: *This is the chalice, the New Testament, etc.*, not *This chalice is the New Testament*. Likewise Mk 13:19: *Those days shall be such tribulation*, etc. not as the adversaries: *In those days*, both our text and theirs being otherwise. Likewise Ja. 4:6: *And giveth greater grace*, leaving it indifferent to the *Scripture*, or to the *Holy Ghost*, both going before. Whereas the adversaries do too boldly and presumptuously add, saying: *The Scripture* giveth, taking away the other sense, which is far more probable. Likewise (He 12:21) we translate: *So terrible was it which was seen, Moses said*, etc. Neither doth Greek or Latin permit us to add *that* Moses said, as the Protestants presume to do. So we say: *Men brethren* (Ac 1:16; 2:29), *a widow woman* (Lk 4:26), *a woman a sinner* (Lk 7:37), *James of Alphaeus*, and the like. Sometime also we follow of purpose the Scripture's phrase, as: *The hell of fire*, according to Greek and Latin, which we might say perhaps, *The fiery hell*, by the Hebrew phrase in such speeches, but not *hellfire*, as commonly it is translated. Likewise Lk 4:36: What *word* is this, that in power and authority he commandeth the unclean spirits? As also Lk 2:15: Let us pass over, and see the *word* that is done, where we might say *thing*, by the Hebrew phrase, but there is a certain majesty and more signification in these speeches, and therefore both Greek and Latin keep them, although it is no more the Greek or Latin phrase than it is the English. And why should we be squeamish at new words or phrases in the Scripture, which are necessary, when we do easily admit and follow new words coined in court and in courtly or other secular writings?

The Greek added often in the margin for many causes

56. We add the Greek in the margin for divers causes. Sometime when the sense is hard, then the learned reader may consider of it and see if he can help himself better than by our translation, as Lk 11 (*sic*: Lk 12:29?): *Nolite extolli; me meteorizesthe*; and again: *Quod superest date eleemosynam, ta enonta* (Lk 11:40f.). Sometime to take away the ambiguity of the Latin or English, as Lk 11:17: *Et domum supra domum cadet*, which we must needs English, *and house upon house shall fall*. By the Greek the sense is not, one house shall fall upon another, but if one house rise upon itself, that is, against itself, it shall perish, according as he speaketh of a kingdom divided against itself, in the words before. And Ac 14:12: *Sacerdos Iovis qui erat*, in the Greek, *qui* is referred to Jupiter. Sometime to satisfy the reader that might otherwise conceive the translation to be false, as Ph 4:6: *But in everything by prayer*, etc., *en panti proseuchei*, not *in all prayer*, as in the Latin it may seem. Sometime when the Latin neither doth, nor can reach to the signification of the Greek word, we add the Greek also as more significant. *Illi soli servies*, him only shalt thou serve, *latreuseis*. And Ac 6:5: Nicholas, a *stranger* of Antioch, *proselytos*. And Ro 9:4: the service, *he latreia*. And Ep 1:10: To *perfite, instaurare omnia in Christo, anakephalaiosasthai*. And: Wherein he hath gratified us, *echaritosen* (Ep 1:6) and Ep 6:11: Put on the armour, *panoplian*, and a number the like. Sometime, when the Greek hath two senses and the Latin but one, we add the Greek. II Co 1:4: By the exhortation wherewith we also are exhorted, the Greek signifieth also *consolation*, etc.; and II Co 10:15: But having hope of your faith increasing, to be, etc., where the Greek may also signify, *as* or *when* your faith increaseth. Sometime for advantage of the Catholic cause, when the Greek maketh for us more than the Latin, as: *seniores, presbyterous*; *Ut digni habeamini, hina axiothete* (II Th 1:5); *Qui effundetur, to ekchynomenon* (Lk 22:20); *praecepta, paradoseis* (II Th 2:14); and Jn 21:15: *poimaine; pasce et rege*. And sometime to show the false translation of the heretic, as when Beza saith: *Hoc poculum in meo sanguine qui; to poterion en toi emoi haimati to ekchynomenon* (Lk 22:20) and *Quem oportet coelo contineri; hon dei ouranon dechesthai* (Ac 3:21). Thus we use the Greek divers ways, and esteem of it as it is worthy, and take all commodities thereof for the better understanding of the Latin, which being a translation, cannot always attain to the full sense of the principal tongue, as we see in all translations.

The Latin text sometime noted in the margin

57. Item, we add the Latin word sometime in the margin, when either we cannot fully express it, as Ac 8:2: They took order for Stephen's funeral, *curaverunt Stephanum* and: All take not this word, *non omnes capiunt* (Mt 19:11) or when the reader might think, it cannot be as we translate, as Lk 8:23: A storm of wind descended into the lake and *they were filled*, and *complebantur*; and Jn 5:6, when Jesus knew that he had now a long time, *quia iam multum tempus haberet*, meaning, in his infirmity.

In the beginning of books, Matthew, Paul etc., not St Matthew, St Paul, etc.

58. This precise following of our Latin text, in neither adding nor diminishing, is the cause why we say not in the title of books, in the first page, St Matthew, St Paul; because it is so neither in Greek nor Latin, though in the tops of the leaves following, where we may be bolder, we add St Matthew, etc. to satisfy the reader. Much unlike to the Protestants our adversaries, which make no scruple to leave out the name of Paul in the title of the Epistle to the Hebrews, though it be in every Greek book which they translate. And their most authorized English Bibles leave out *Catholic* in the title of St James' Epistle and the rest, which were famously known in the primitive Church by the name of *Catholicae Epistulae* (Eusebius, *Hist. eccl. 51, 2, 22*).

Another reading in the margin

59. Item, we give the reader in places of some importance, another reading in the margin, specially when the Greek is agreeable to the same, as Jn 4 (*sic*; 5:24): *transiet de morte ad vitam*. Other Latin copies have, *transiit*, and so it is in the Greek.

The pointing something altered

60. We bind not ourselves to the points of any one copy, print or edition of the vulgar Latin, in places of no controversy, but follow the pointing most agreeable to the Greek and to the Fathers' commentaries. As Cl 1:10: *Ambulantes digni Deo, per omnia placentes*. Walking worthy of God, in all things p ing. *Axios tou Kyriou eis pasan areskeian* (Ep 1:17). We point thus: *Deus Domini nostri Iesu Christi, pater gloriae*, as in the Greek and St John Chrysostom, and St Jerome both in text and commentaries. Which the Catholic reader specially must mark, lest he find fault, when he seeth our translation disagree in such places from the pointing of his Latin Testament.

The margin reading sometime preferred before the text

61. We translate sometime the word that is in the Latin margin, and not that in the text, when by the Greek or the fathers we see it is a manifest fault of the writers heretofore, that mistook one word for another. As *in fine*, not *in fide* (I Pe 3:8); *praesentiam*, not *praescientiam* (II Pe 1:16); *latuerunt*, not *placuerunt* (He 13:2).

Thus we have endeavoured by all means to satisfy the indifferent reader and to help his understanding every way, both in the text and by Annotations; and withal to deal most sincerely before God and man, in translating and expounding the most sacred text of the holy Testament. Farewell good reader, and if we profit the any whit by our poor pains, let us for God's sake be partakers of thy devout prayers, and together with humble and contrite heart call upon our Saviour Christ to cease these troubles and storms of his dearest spouse; in the meantime comforting ourselves with this saying of St Augustine: *That heretics, when they receive power corporally to afflict the Church, do exercise her patience; but when they oppugn her only by their evil doctrine or opinion, then they exercise her wisdom* (*De civit. Dei 18,51*).

38. ARCHBISHOP WHITGIFT'S ARTICLES, 1583

History

The consecration of John Whitgift as Archbishop of Canterbury (1583-1604) marked the beginning of the persecution of the Puritan element within the Church of England. These Articles were intended to weed Puritan ministers of Presbyterian convictions out of the Church. By about 1585 most of the moderate Puritans had abandoned Presbyterianism and become reconciled to the Church of England, at least for the duration of Elizabeth's reign. Persecutions after that date largely concerned the more radical Separatists, often collectively known as "Brownists", after Robert Browne, one of their leaders. "Brownists" were disliked by Presbyterians as much as by Episcopalians, and they were still being attacked at the time of the Westminster Assembly of Divines (1643-1646).

These Articles were only haphazardly enforced during Elizabeth's reign, but they were incorporated as Canon 36 of the Canons of 1604, after which subscription to them was regularly insisted upon.

Note that Whitgift made no distinction between the Thirty-eight Articles of 1563 (1562 according to the Old Style) and the Thirty-nine Articles of 1571; it is the latter text which is meant here, though it is the earlier one which is referred to by name.

Theology

Whitgift shared the strong Calvinist theology of the Puritans, but disagreed radically with their proposals for the reform of the Church along Presbyterian lines. He engaged in lengthy debates with Thomas Cartwright, the leading Presbyterian, and did everything he could to defend the 1559 Settlement. Elizabeth I regarded him as her most valuable servant in ecclesiastical affairs, and fully supported him in his efforts to destroy the Presbyterian movement.

... that none be permitted to preach, read, catechize, minister the sacraments or to execute any other ecclesiastical function, by what authority soever he be admitted thereunto, unless he first consent and subscribe to these articles following, before the ordinary of the diocese wherein he preacheth, readeth, catechizeth or ministreth the sacraments, viz.:

1. That Her Majesty, under God, hath and ought to have the sovereignty and rule over all manner of persons born within her realms and dominions and countries, of what estate ecclesiastical or temporal soever they may be. And that none other foreign power, prelate, state or potentate hath or ought

to have any jurisdiction, power, superiority, pre-eminence or authority ecclesiastical or temporal within Her Majesty's said realms, dominions and countries.

2. That the Book of Common Prayer, and of ordering bishops, priests and deacons, containeth nothing in it contrary to the Word of God. And that the same may be lawfully used; and that he himself will use the form of the said book prescribed, in public prayer and administration of the sacraments, and none other.

3. That he alloweth the book of Articles of Religion, agreed upon by the archbishops and bishops in both provinces, and the whole clergy in the Convocation holden at London in the year of Our Lord 1562, and set forth by Her Majesty's authority. And that he believeth all the articles therein contained to be agreeable to the Word of God.

39. THE LAMBETH ARTICLES, 1595

History

These articles were originally drawn up by Dr William Whitaker, Regius Professor of Divinity in the University of Cambridge and a leading Puritan. After some modifications, they were approved by the Archbishops of Canterbury and York, as well as by a number of other bishops who met at Lambeth Palace on 20 November 1595. Queen Elizabeth withheld her approval of the Articles, largely because she disapproved of action taken by her Archbishops without her permission. They were taken over by the Church of Ireland and included in the Irish Articles (1615), but they faded from view in the reign of Charles I (1625-1649). The text of the Articles is in Latin; the English version has been prepared for this edition.

Theology

The Articles were intended to be a supplement to the Thirty-nine Articles (1571), and they express a Calvinistic doctrine of predestination. This met with considerable opposition in England, from what is usually (though inaccurately) known as the Arminian party, named after the Dutch theologian, Jacob Arminius (1560-1609).

01. Deus ab aeterno praedestinavit quosdam ad vitam, et quosdam ad mortem reprobavit.

01. From eternity God has predestined some men to life and condemned others to death.

02. Causa movens aut efficiens praedestinationis ad vitam non est praevisio fidei, aut perseverantiae, aut bonorum operum, aut ullius rei, quae insit in personis praedestinatis, sed sola voluntas beneplaciti Dei.

02. The moving or efficient cause of predestination to life is not the foresight of faith or of perseverance, or of good works, or of anything inherent in the persons predestined, but only the will of God's good pleasure.

03. Praedestinatorum praefinitus at certus numerus est qui nec augeri nec minui potest.

03. There is a predetermined and fixed number of predestinate which cannot be increased or diminished.

04. Qui non sunt praedestinati ad salutem necessario propter peccata sua damnabuntur.

04. Those not predestined to salvation will necessarily be condemned because of their sins.

05. Vera, viva et iustificans fides, et Spiritus Dei sanctificans non ex-

05. A true, living and justifying faith, which the Holy Spirit sanctifies,

tinguitur, non excidit, non evanescit in electis, aut finaliter aut totaliter.

cannot be extinguished, nor can it fall away or disappear in the elect, either finally or totally.

06. Homo vere fidelis, id est, fide iustificante praeditus, certus est plerophoria fidei, de remissione peccatorum suorum et salute sempiterna sua per Christum.

06. The true believer, i.e. one who possesses justifying faith, is certain, by the full assurance of faith, of the forgiveness of his sins and of eternal salvation through Christ.

07. Gratia salutaris non tribuitur, non communicatur, non conceditur universis hominibus, qua servari possint, si voluerint.

07. Saving grace is not granted, communicated or given to all men, so that they might be saved by it if they wished to be.

08. Nemo potest venire ad Christum nisi datum ei fuerit, et nisi Pater eum traxerit. Et omnes homines non trahuntur a Patre, ut veniant ad Filium.

08. No-one can come to Christ unless it is given to him (to come), and unless the Father draws him. And not all men are drawn by the Father to come to the Son.

09. Non est positum in arbitrio aut potestate uniuscuiusque hominis servari.

09. It is not placed in the will or power of any and every man to be saved.

40. THE PREFACE TO THE DOUAY OLD TESTAMENT, 1609

History

This was the second part of the Catholic translation of the Bible begun at Reims. The English College which had been founded there was transferred to Douai (Douay) shortly after the New Testament was completed, but difficulties of organization delayed the production of the Old Testament for many years. In general however, it is fair to say that the advantages and defects of the Rheims New Testament reappear in the Old Testament produced at Douai, in spite of the lapse of time.

The Douay-Rheims translation, taken together, is now usually known as the Douay Bible, and was officially imposed on English-speaking Catholics as the only vernacular translation permitted for use. However, its defects soon made themselves felt, and many revisions were attempted. The most successful of these were the ones made by Bishop Richard Challoner (1691-1781), who was a convert from Protestantism, and therefore familiar with the Authorized (King James) Version. His revisions, which were made between 1749 and 1772 removed most of the unintelligible Latinisms and replaced them by phraseology taken from the Authorized Version. It is in this form that the Douay Bible has survived until the present day, although, like the Authorized Version, its use has declined in recent years, particularly since the appearance of *The Jerusalem Bible* in 1966.

Theology

The anti-Protestant polemic characteristic of the Rheims New Testament is continued in this Old Testament Preface. Perhaps the only difference to note is that between 1582 and 1609 the fortunes of English Catholicism had declined dramatically, thanks to the failure of the Spanish Armada (1588) and the Gunpowder Plot (1605). In the seventeenth century, the foreign character of Catholicism became much more marked, and religious dissension in England, though still very lively, became largely a matter of disputes within the Protestant camp, rather than arguments with Rome, as had been the case during most of the sixteenth century.

There is no doubt that this Preface, and especially its concluding sections, reflects an atmosphere of persecution, with little hope of immediate deliverance. The emphasis is very much on patient endurance, and there is open recognition that few are heeding the call to sacrifice themselves, if necessary, for the sake of the cause.

N.B. For this edition, paragraphs have been numbered for easy reference.

To the right well-beloved English reader, grace and glory in Jesus Christ everlasting.

The cause of delay in setting forth this English Bible

01. At last through God's goodness (most dearly beloved) we send you here the greater part of the Old Testament, as long since you received the New, faithfully translated into English. The residue is in hand to be finished, and your desire thereof shall not now (God prospering our intention) be long frustrate. As for the impediments which hitherto have hindered this work, they all proceeded (as many do know) of one general cause, our poor estate in banishment. Wherein expecting better means, greater difficulties rather ensued. Nevertheless you will hereby the more perceive our fervent good will, ever to serve you, in that we have brought forth this Tome, in these hardest times, of above forty years, since this college was most happily begun. Wherefore we nothing doubt, but you our dearest, for whom we have dedicated our lives, will both pardon the long delay which we could not well prevent, and accept now this fruit of our labours, with like good affection, as we acknowledge them due, and offer the same unto you.

Why and how it is allowed to have Holy Scriptures in vulgar tongues

02. If any demand why it is now allowed to have the Holy Scriptures in vulgar tongues, which generally is not permitted, but in the three sacred only; for further declaration of this and other like points, we remit you to the Preface before the New Testament. Only here, as by an epitome, we shall repeat the sum of all that is there more largely discussed.

Scriptures being hard are not to be read of all

03. To this first question therefore we answer that both just reason and highest authority of the Church judge it not absolutely necessary, nor always convenient that Holy Scriptures should be in vulgar tongues. For being as they are, hard to be understood, even by the learned, reason doth dictate to reasonable men, that they were not written, nor ordained to be read indifferently of all men.

Many take harm by reading Holy Scriptures

04. Experience also teacheth that through ignorance, joined often with pride and presumption, many reading Scriptures have erred grossly, by misunderstanding God's Word. Which, though it be most pure in itself, yet the sense being adulterated is as perilous (saith Tertullian) as the style corrupted (*De praes. haer. 17*). St Ambrose observeth that where the text is true, the Arians' interpretation hath errors (*De fide ad Grat. 2,1,16*). St Augustine also teacheth that heresies and perverse doctrines, entangling souls, and throwing them down headlong into the depth, do not otherwise spring up, but when good (or true) Scriptures are not well (and truly) understood, and when that which in them is not well understood, is also rashly and boldly avouched (*Hom. in Ioh. 18,1*). For in the same cause St Jerome utterly disallowed that all sorts of men and women, old and young, presumed to read and talk of the Scriptures, whereas no artisan nor tradesman dare presume to teach any faculty which he hath not first learned (*Ep. 53,7*).

Reading of Scriptures moderated

05. Seeing therefore that dangers and hurts happen in many, the careful chief pastors in God's Church have always moderated the reading of Holy Scriptures, according to persons, times and other circumstances; prohibiting some and permitting some, to have and read them in their mother tongue.

Scriptures translated into divers tongues

06. So St John Chrysostom translated the Psalms and some other parts of Holy Scriptures for the Armenians when he was there in banishment. The Slavonians and Goths say they have the Bible in their languages. It was translated into Italian by an Archbishop of Genoa. Into French in the time of King Charles V, especially because the Waldensian heretics had corruptly translated it, to maintain their errors. We had some parts in English translated by Venerable Bede, as Malmesbury witnesseth. And Thomas Arundel, Archbishop of Canterbury, in a council holden at Oxford, straightly ordained that no heretical translation set forth by Wycliffe and his accomplices, nor any other vulgar edition should be suffered till it were approved by the ordinary of the diocese, alleging St Jerome's judgement of the difficulty and danger in translating Holy Scriptures out of one tongue into another. And therefore it must needs be much more dangerous, when ignorant people read also corrupted translations.

A calumnious suggestion of Lutherans

07. Now since Luther and his followers have pretended that the Catholic Roman faith and doctrine should be contrary to God's written Word and that the Scriptures were not suffered in vulgar languages, lest the people could see the truth, and withal these new masters corruptly turning the Scriptures into divers tongues, as might best serve their own opinions;

against this false suggestion and practice, Catholic pastors have, for one special remedy, set forth true and sincere translations in most languages of the Latin Church. But so, that people must read them with licence of their spiritual superior, as in former times they were in like sort limited. Such also of the laity, yea and of the meaner learned clergy, as were permitted to read Holy Scriptures, did not presume to interpret hard places, nor high mysteries, much less to dispute and contend; but leaving the discussion thereof to the more learned, searched rather, and noted the godly and imitable examples of good life, and so learned more humility, obedience, hatred of sin, fear of God, zeal of religion and other virtues. And thus Holy Scriptures may be rightly used in any tongue, "to teach, to argue, to correct, to instruct in justice, that the man of God may be perfect, and (as St Paul addeth) instructed to every good work" (II Ti 3:16f.), when men labour rather to be "doers of God's will and word, than readers or hearers only, deceiving themselves" (Ja 1:22).

Why we translate the old Latin text

08. But here another question may be proposed: Why we translate the Latin text, rather than the Hebrew or Greek, which Protestants prefer, as the fountain tongues wherein Holy Scriptures were first written?

More pure than the Hebrew or Greek now extant

09. To this we answer, that if indeed those first pure editions were now extant, or if such as be extant were more pure than the Latin, we would also prefer such fountains before the rivers, in whatsoever they should be found to disagree. But the ancient best learned fathers and doctors of the Church do much complain and testify to us that both the Hebrew and the Greek editions are foully corrupted by Jews and heretics, since the Latin was truly translated out of them whilst they were more pure. And that the same Latin hath been far better conserved from corruptions. So that the old Vulgate Latin edition hath been preferred and used for the most authentical above a thousand and three hundred years. For by this very term St Jerome calleth that version the Vulgate, or common, which he conferred with the Hebrew of the Old Testament and with the Greek of the New; which he also purged from faults committed by writers, rather amending than translating it. Though in regard of this amending, St Gregory calleth it the new version of St Jerome (*Moral. in Hiob 20,24*); who nevertheless in another place calleth the selfsame the old Latin edition, judging it most worthy to be followed. St Augustine calleth it the Italian. St Isidore witnesseth that St Jerome's version was received and approved by all Christian Churches (*De off. 1,12*). Sophronius, also a most learned man, seeing St Jerome's edition so much esteemed, not only of the Latins but also of the Grecians, turned the Psalter and Prophets out

of the same Latin into Greek. Of latter times what shall we need to recite other most learned men? St Bede, St Anselm, St Bernard, St Thomas Aquinas, St Bonaventure and the rest? Who all uniformly allege this only text as authentical. In so much that all other Latin editions, which St Jerome saith were in his time almost innumerable, are as it were fallen out of all divines' hands, and grown out of credit and use. If moreover, we consider St Jerome's learning, piety, diligence and sincerity, together with the commodities he had of best copies, in all languages then extant, and of other learned men with whom he conferred; and if we so compare the same with the best means that hath been since, surely no man of indifferent judgement will match any other edition with St Jerome's, but easily acknowledge with the whole Church, God's particular providence in this great doctor, as well for expounding as most especially for the true text and edition of Holy Scriptures.

His edition free from partiality

10. Neither do we flee unto this old Latin text for more advantage. For besides that it is free from partiality, as being most ancient of all Latin copies, and long before the particular controversies of those days began; the Hebrew also and the Greek when they are truly translated, yea and Erasmus his Latin, in sundry places, prove more plainly the Catholic Roman doctrine than this which we rely upon. So that Beza and his followers take also exception against the Greek, when Catholics allege it against them.

Preferred before all other editions by Beza

11. Yea the same Beza preferreth the old Latin version before all others and freely testifieth that the old interpreter translated religiously.

None yet in England allowed for sufficient

12. What then do our countrymen that refuse this Latin, but deprive themselves of the best, and yet all this while have set forth none that is allowed by all Protestants, for good or sufficient.

What is done in this edition

13. How well this is done the learned may judge, when by mature conference they shall have made trial thereof. And if anything be mistaken, we will (as still we promise) gladly correct it. Those that translated it about thirty years since were well known to the world to have been excellent in the tongues, sincere men, and great divines.

Divers readings resolved upon, and none left in the margin

14. Only one thing we have done touching the text, whereof we are especially to give notice. That whereas heretofore in the best Latin editions there remained many places differing in words, some also in sense, as in long process of time, the writers erred in their copies; now lately, and by the care and diligence of the Church, those divers readings were maturely and judiciously examined and conferred with sundry the best written and printed books, and so resolved upon, that all which before were left in the margin are either restored into the text or else omitted, so that now none such remain in the margin. For which cause we have again conferred this English translation, and conformed it to the most perfect Latin edition.

They touched not present controversies

15. Where yet by the way we must give the vulgar reader to understand, that very few or none of the former varieties touched controversies of this time; so that this recognition is no way suspicious of partiality, but is merely done for the more secure conservation of the true text; and more ease and satisfaction of such as otherwise should have remained more doubtful.

Why some words are not translated into vulgar English

16. Now for the strictness observed in translating some words, or rather the not translating of some, which is in more danger to be disliked, we doubt not but the discreet learned reader, deeply weighing and considering the importance of sacred words, and how easily the translator may miss the sense of the Holy Ghost, will hold that which is here done for reasonable and necessary.

Some Hebrew words not translated into Latin nor Greek

17. We have also the example of the Latin and Greek, where some words are not translated, but left in Hebrew, as they were first spoken and written; which seeing they could not or were not convenient to be translated into Latin or Greek, how much less could they, or was it reason to turn them into English?

More authority in sacred tongues

18. St Augustine also yieldeth a reason, exemplifying in the words *amen* and *alleluia*, for the more sacred authority thereof; which doubtless is the cause why some names of solemn feasts, sacrifices and other holy things are reserved in sacred tongues, Hebrew, Greek or Latin.

Some words cannot be turned into English

19. Again for necessity, English not having a name, or sufficient term, we either keep the word as we find it, or only turn it to our English termination, because it would otherwise require many words in English, to signify one word of another tongue. In which cases, we commonly put the explication in the margin.

Protestants leave some words untranslated

20. Briefly, our apology is easy against English Protestants, because they also reserve some words in the original tongues, not translated into English, as *Sabbath, ephod, Pentecost, proselyte,* and some others. The sense whereof is indeed as soon learned as if they were turned so near as is possible into English. And why then may we not say *prepuce, phase* or *Pasch, azymes, breads of proposition, holocaust* and the like? Rather than as Protestants translate them: *foreskin, Passover, the feast of sweet breads, shewbreads, burnt offerings,* etc. By which terms, whether they be truly translated into English or no, we will pass over. Sure it is, an Englishman is still to seek what they mean, as if they remained in Hebrew or Greek.

Corruptions in Protestants' translations of Holy Scriptures

21. It more importeth that nothing be wittingly and falsely translated for advantage of doctrine in matter of faith. Wherein as we dare boldly avouch the sincerity of this translation, and that nothing is here either untruly or obscurely done of purpose, in favour of Catholic Roman religion, so we cannot but complain and challenge English Protestants, for corrupting the text contrary to the Hebrew and Greek, which they profess to translate for the more show and maintaining of their peculiar opinions against Catholics, as is proved in the *Discovery of manifold corruptions.*

Of purpose against Catholic doctrine

22. For example, we shall put the reader in memory of one or two. Gn 4:7, whereas (God speaking to Cain) the Hebrew words in grammatical construction may be translated either thus: *Unto thee also pertaineth the lust THEREOF and thou shalt have dominion over IT,* or thus: *Also unto thee HIS desire shall be subject, and thou shalt rule over HIM;* though the coherence of the text require the former and in the Bibles printed (1552 and 1577) Protestants did so translate it, yet in the year 1579 and 1603 they translate it the other way, rather saying that Abel was subject to Cain, and that Cain by God's ordinance had dominion over his brother Abel, than that concupiscence or lust of sin is subject to man's will, or that man hath power of free will, to resist (by God's grace) temptation of sin. But as we hear in a new edition (which we have not yet seen) they translate it almost as the first.

Against Melchizedek's sacrifice

23. In like sort Gn 14:18. The Hebrew particle *waw*, which St Jerome and all antiquity translated *enim* (for), Protestants will by no means admit it, because (besides other arguments) we prove thereby Melchizedek's sacrifice. And yet themselves translate the same, as St Jerome doth (Gn 20:3) saying: *for she is a man's wife*, etc.

And against holy images

24. Again, Gn 31:19. The English Bibles (1552 and 1577) translate *theraphim* "images". Which the edition of 1603 correcting, translateth "idols". And the marginal Annotation well proveth that it ought to be so translated.

This edition dedicated to all that understand English

25. With this then we will conclude, most dear (we speak to you all that understand our tongue, whether you be of contrary opinions in faith, or of mundane fear participate with another congregation, or profess with us the same Catholic religion) to you all we present this work, daily beseeching God Almighty, the divine wisdom, eternal goodness, to create, illuminate and replenish your spirits with his grace, that you may attain eternal glory, every one in his measure, in those many mansions prepared and promised by our Saviour in his Father's house. Not only to those which first received and followed his divine doctrine, but to all that should afterwards believe in him and keep the same precepts.

Christ redeemed all but all are not saved

26. For there is one God, one also Mediator of God and men, Man Christ Jesus, who gave himself a redemption for all. Whereby appeareth his will that all should be saved. Why then are all not saved? The Apostle addeth that they must first come to the knowledge of the truth, because without faith it is impossible to please God.

True faith first necessary

27. This groundwork therefore of our creation in Christ by true faith, St Paul laboured most seriously by word and writing, to establish in the hearts of all men. In this he confirmed the Romans by his Epistle, commending their faith as already received, and renowned in the whole world. He preached the same faith to many nations, amongst others, to the learned Athenians. Where it seemed to some as absurd as strange, in so much that they scornfully called him a *word-sower*, and a preacher of new gods (Ac 17:18).

The twelve Apostles were first reapers before they were sowers. St Paul at first a sower, or seminary Apostle

28. But St Augustine alloweth the term for good, which was reproachfully spoken of the ignorant. And so distinguishing between reapers and sowers in God's Church, he teacheth that whereas the other Apostles reaped in the Jews that which the patriarchs and prophets had sown, St Paul sowed the seed of Christian religion in the Gentiles. And so in respect of the Israelites to whom they were first sent, calleth the other Apostles *messores*, reapers, and St Paul being specially sent to the Gentiles, *seminatorem*, a sower, or seminary Apostle.

Pastoral cures and Apostolical missions

29. Which two sorts of God's workmen are still in the Church, with distinct offices of pastoral cures and Apostolical missions; the one for the perpetual government of Catholic countries; the other for conversion of such as either have not received Christian religion, or are relapsed. As at this time in our country, for the divers sorts of pretended religions, these divers spiritual works are necessary to teach and feed all Britain's people.

New doctrine is falsely called the Gospel

30. Because some in error of opinions preach another Gospel, whereas in verity there is no other Gospel. They preach indeed new doctrines which cannot save.

The seduced and externally conformable are punished with the authors of iniquity

31. Others follow them, believing falsehood. But when the blind lead the blind (not the one only, but) both fall into the ditch (Mt 15:14). Others conform themselves in external show, fearing them that can punish and kill the body. But our Lord will bring such as decline unto (unjust) obligations, and them that work iniquity (Ps 124:5). The relics and final flock of Catholics in our country have great sadness and sorrow of heart, not so much for our own affliction, for that is comfortable, but for you our brethren and kinsmen in flesh and blood. Wishing, with our own temporal damage whatsoever, your salvation.

Grace in the New Testament more abundant than in the Old

32. Now is the acceptable time, now are the days of salvation (II Co 6:2), the time of grace by Christ, whose days many kings and prophets desired to see (Lk 10:24); they saw them (in spirit) and rejoiced. But we are made partakers of Christ and his mysteries, so that ourselves neglect not his heavenly riches; if we receive and keep the beginning of his substance firm unto the end; that is, the true Catholic faith; building thereon good works by his grace, without which we cannot think a good thought, by which we can do all things necessary to salvation. But if we hold not fast this ground, all the building faileth.

Both wicked works and omission of good works are damnable

33. Or if, confessing to know God in words, we deny him in deeds; committing works of darkness (Tt 1:16), or omitting works of mercy, when we may do them to our distressed neighbours (Mt 25:31f.); briefly, if we have not charity, the form and perfection of all virtues, all is lost and nothing worth (I Co 13). But if we build upon firm ground, gold, silver and precious stones, such building shall abide and make our vocation sure by good works, as St Peter speaketh (II Pe 1:10). These (saith St Paul) are the heirs of God, co-heirs of Christ (Ro 8:17).

Innumerable saved by Christ

34. Neither is the number of Christ's blessed children counted, as of the Jews, an hundred forty-four thousand, of every tribe of Israel twelve thousand signed (Re 7:4); but a most great multitude of Catholic Christians which no man can number, of all nations and tribes and peoples and tongues, standing before the throne of the Lamb, clothed in white robes and palms (of triumph) in their hands, having overcome temptations in the virtuous race of good life.

They are more happy that suffer persecution for the truth

35. Much more those which also endure persecution for the truth's sake shall receive most copious great rewards in heaven. For albeit the passions of time (in themselves) are not condign to the glory to come that shall be revealed in us; yet our tribulation, which presently is momentary and light, worketh (through grace) above measure exceedingly an eternal weight of glory (Ro 8:18; cf. II Co 4:8f.)

English Catholics most happy in this age

36. What shall we therefore meditate of the especial prerogative of English Catholics at this time? For to you it is given for Christ, not only that you believe in him, but also that you suffer for him. A little now, if you must be made pensive in divers temptations, that the probation of your faith, much more precious than gold which is proved by the fire (I Pe 1:6f.), may be found unto praise and glory and honour in the revelation of Jesus Christ. Many of you have sustained the spoil of your goods with joy, knowing that you have a better and permanent substance. Others have been deprived of your children, fathers, mothers, brothers, sisters and nearest friends, in ready resolution also, some with sentence of death, to lose your own lives. Others have had trials of reproaches, mockeries and stripes. Others of bands, prisons and banishments.

The due praise of martyrs and other glorious saints exceedeth mortal tongues

37. The innumerable renowned late English martyrs and confessors, whose happy souls for confessing true faith before men, are now most glorious in heaven, we pass here with silence; because their due praise, requiring longer discourse, yea rather angels, than English tongues, far surpasseth the reach of our conceits. And so we leave it to your devout meditation. They now secure for themselves and solicitous for us their dearest clients, incessantly (we are well assured) intercede before Christ's divine Majesty for our happy consummation, with the conversion of our whole country.

Patience necessary to the end of man's life

38. To you therefore (dearest friends mortal) we direct this speech, admonishing ourselves and you, in the Apostles' words, that for so much as we have not yet resisted temptations to (last) blood (and death itself) patience is still necessary for us, that doing the will of God, we may receive the promise. So we repine not in tribulation but ever love them that hate us, pitying their case and rejoicing in our own.

Persecution profitable

39. For neither can we see during this life how much good they do us, nor know how many of them shall be (as we heartily desire they all may be) saved; our Lord and Saviour having paid the same price by his death, for them and for us. Love all therefore, pray for all. Do not lose your confidence, which hath a great remuneration. For yet a little and very little while, he that is to come will come, and he will not slack.

Confession of faith before men necessary to salvation

40. Now the just liveth by faith, believing with heart to justice, and confessing with mouth to salvation. But he that withdraweth himself shall not please Christ's soul. Attend to your salvation, dearest countrymen. You that are far off, draw near, put on Christ. And you that are within Christ's fold, keep your standing, persevere in him to the end. His grace dwell and remain in you, that glorious crowns may be given you. Amen.

From the English College at Douai, the Octave of All Saints, 1609 (08 November 1609).

The God of patience and comfort give you to be of one mind, one towards one another in Jesus Christ; that of one mind, with one mouth you may glorify God.

41. THE PREFACE TO THE AUTHORIZED (KING JAMES) VERSION, 1611

History

With the accession of James VI of Scotland (1567-1625) to the throne of England in 1603, pressures for further reform of the Church, which had been growing in the 1590s, came to the surface. A conference was held at Hampton Court in January 1604, which attempted to resolve these, but it met with little success. In spite (or more probably because) of the King's Presbyterian upbringing, he was not prepared to see the Church of England move towards a type of Reformation similar to that of Scotland. One exception to this general rule however, was his decision to accept a proposal, put forward by a leading Puritan, Dr John Reynolds of Corpus Christi College, Oxford, that a new translation of the Bible be prepared for general use. Since 1568 there had been an uneasy co-existence between the Bishops' Bible, read in church but generally unloved, and the Geneva Bible, with its many marginal notes proclaiming a strident Calvinism. James particularly objected to these, and insisted that any new translation must appear without notes to "guide" the reader!

The King took a personal interest in the work, which eventually involved 47 different translators. He ordered that the Bishops' Bible be used as the basis of the new translation, but this scarcely limited the freedom of the translators, who worked from the best Hebrew and Greek manuscripts then available and were free to consult any translation they chose. In the case of the Old Testament, the Hebrew text available in 1611 was not substantially different from that in use today, but things are very different in the case of the Greek New Testament. King James' men used the edition of Robert Estienne (1550), which came out in Holland in 1633 with the notation *Textus Receptus* ("Received Text"), a title which it has borne ever since. However, subsequent manuscript discovery has revealed that this Received Text is quite different in many places from the Greek original, and this has made the Authorized Version out of date scientifically, as well as linguistically.

The Authorized Version did not immediately establish itself as the classic English text of the Bible, but by about 1640 it was well on the way to acquiring that position, among Puritans as well as conformists to the Church of England. There was no serious attempt to revise or replace it until 1881, when the so-called Revised Version appeared. That failed to catch on, largely because of its wooden and pedantic rendering of the original texts, and it was not until the 1960s that the Authorized Version faced serious competition from modern translations. It is now falling into disuse, though its status as a literary classic remains unchallenged, and on this score at least, none of the modern versions produced so far can hope to rival it.

Theology

The theology of the Authorized Version represents Anglicanism at its moderate best. It is neither Papist nor Puritan, but seeks to represent the classic *via media*, retaining "churchy" words like *bishop*, but rejecting terms like *penance* which had acquired an unacceptable theological sense. Perhaps the best witness to its relative objectivity is the fact that all English-speaking Christians, even Roman Catholics, eventually came under its sway and used it to support very different theological and ecclesiological positions.

N.B. The paragraph numbering in the Preface ("The Translators to the Reader") is that of the original document.

Epistle Dedicatory

To the most High and Mighty Prince James by the Grace of God, King of Great Britain, France, and Ireland, Defender of the Faith, etc, the translators of the Bible wish grace, mercy and peace, through Jesus Christ our Lord

Great and manifold were the blessings, most dread Sovereign, which Almighty God, the Father of all mercies, bestowed upon us the people of England, when first he sent your Majesty's royal person to rule and reign over us. For whereas it was the expectation of many, who wished not well unto our Zion, that upon the setting of that bright occidental star, Queen Elizabeth of most happy memory, some thick and palpable clouds of darkness would so have overshadowed this land that men should have been in doubt which way they were to walk, and that it should hardly be known who was to direct the unsettled state; the appearance of your Majesty, as of the sun in his strength, instantly dispelled those supposed and surmised mists and gave unto all that were well affected exceeding cause of comfort; especially when we beheld the government established in your Highness, and your hopeful seed, by an undoubted title, and this also accompanied with peace and tranquillity at home and abroad.

But among all our joys, there was no one that more filled our hearts, than the blessed continuance of the preaching of God's sacred Word among us; which is that inestimable treasure, which excelleth all the riches of the earth; because the fruit thereof extendeth itself, not only to the time spent in this transitory world, but directeth and disposeth men unto that eternal happiness which is above in heaven.

Then not to suffer this to fall to the ground, but rather to take it up, and to continue it in that state, wherein the famous predecessor of Your Highness did leave it: nay, to go forward with the confidence and resolution of a Man in maintaining the truth of Christ, and propagating it far and near, is that which hath so bound and firmly knit the hearts of all your Majesty's loyal and religious people unto you, that your very name is precious among them: their eye doth behold you with comfort, and they bless You in their hearts, as that sanctified person, who, under God, is the immediate author of their true happiness. And thus their contentment doth not diminish or decay, but every day increaseth and taketh strength when they observe, that the zeal of your Majesty toward the house of God doth not slack or go backward, but is more and more kindled, manifesting itself abroad in the farthest parts of Christendom, by writing in defence of the truth, (which hath given such a blow unto that man of sin, as will not be healed,) and every day at home, by religious and learned discourse, by frequenting the house of God, by hearing the Word preached, by cherishing the teachers thereof, by caring for the Church, as a most tender and loving nursing Father.

There are infinite arguments of this right Christian and religious affection in Your Majesty; but none is more forcible to declare it to others than the vehement and perpetual desire of accomplishing and publishing of this work, which now with all humility we present unto your Majesty. For when your Highness had once out of deep judgement apprehended how convenient it was, that out of the Original Sacred Tongues, together with comparing of the labours, both in our own, and other foreign languages, of many worthy men who went before us, there should be one more exact translation of the Holy Scriptures into the English tongue; your Majesty did never desist to urge and to excite those to whom it was commended, that the work might be hastened, and that the business might be expedited in so decent a manner, as a matter of such importance might justly require.

And now at last, by the mercy of God, and the continuance of our labours, it being brought unto such a conclusion, as that we have great hopes that the Church of England shall reap good fruit thereby; we hold it our duty to offer it to your Majesty, not only as to our King and Sovereign, but as to the principal mover and author of the work, humbly craving of your most sacred Majesty, that since things of this quality have ever been subject to the censures of ill-meaning and discontented persons, it may receive approbation and patronage from so learned and judicious a prince as your Highness is, whose allowance and acceptance of our labours shall more honour and encourage us, than all the calumniations and hard interpretations of other men shall dismay us. So that if, on the one side, we shall be traduced by popish persons at home or abroad, who therefore will malign us, because we are poor instruments to make God's holy truth to be yet more and more known unto the people, whom they desire still to keep in ignorance and darkness; or if, on the other side, we shall be maligned by self-conceited brethren, who run their own ways, and give liking unto nothing, but what is framed by themselves, and hammered on their anvil we may rest secure, supported within by the truth and innocency of a good conscience, having walked the ways of simplicity and integrity, as before the Lord; and sustained without by the powerful protection of your Majesty's grace and favour, which will ever give countenance to honest and Christian endeavours against bitter censures and uncharitable imputations.

The Lord of heaven and earth bless your Majesty with many and happy days, that, as his heavenly hand hath enriched your Highness with many singular and extraordinary graces, so you may be the wonder of the world in this latter age for happiness and true felicity, to the honour of that great GOD, and the good of his Church, through Jesus Christ our Lord and only Saviour.

The Translators to the Reader

01. The best things have been calumniated.

Zeal to promote the common good, whether it be by devising anything ourselves, or revising that which hath been laboured by others, deserveth certainly much respect and esteem, but yet findeth but cold entertainment in the world. It is welcomed with suspicion instead of love, and with emulation instead of thanks: and if there be any hole left for cavil to enter, (and cavil, if it do not find a hole, will make one) it is sure to be misconstrued, and in danger to be condemned. This will easily be granted by as many as know history, or have any experience. For, was there ever anything projected, that savoured any way of newness or renewing, but the same endured many a storm of gain-saying, or opposition? A man would think that civility, wholesome laws, learning and eloquence, synods, and Church maintenance, (that we speak of no more things of this kind) should be as safe as a sanctuary, and out of the danger of the dart, as they say, that no man would lift up the heel, no, nor dog move his tongue against the motioners of them. For by the first, we are distinguished from brute beasts led with sensuality: By the second, we are bridled and restrained from outrageous behaviour, and from doing of injuries, whether by fraud or by violence: By the third, we are enabled to inform and reform others, by the light and feeling that we have attained unto ourselves: Briefly, by the fourth being brought together to a parley face to face, we sooner compose our differences then by writings, which are endless: And lastly, that the Church be sufficiently provided for, is so agreeable to good reason and conscience, that those mothers are holden to be less cruel, that kill their children as soon as they are born, than those nursing fathers and mothers (wheresoever they be) that withdraw from them who hang upon their breasts (and upon whose breasts again themselves do hang to receive the spiritual and sincere milk of the word) livelihood and support fit for their estates. Thus it is apparent, that these things which we speak of, are of most necessary use, and therefore, that none, either without absurdity can speak against them, or without note of wickedness, can spurn against them.

Yet for all that, the learned know that certain worthy men have been brought to untimely death for none other fault, but for seeking to reduce their countrymen to good order and discipline: and that in some Commonwealths it was made a capital crime, once to motion the making of a new law for the abrogating of an old, though the same were most pernicious: And that certain, which would be counted pillars of the State, and patterns of virtue and prudence, could not be brought for a long time to give way to good letters and refined speech, but bare themselves as averse from them, as from rocks, or boxes of poison: And fourthly, that he was no babe, but a great clerk, that gave forth (and in writing to remain to posterity) in passion peradventure, but yet he gave forth, that he had not seen any profit to come by any synod, or meeting of the clergy, but rather the contrary: And lastly, against Church maintenance and allowance, in such sort, as the ambassadors and messengers of the great King of kings should be furnished, it is not unknown what a fiction or fable (so it is esteemed, and for no better by the reporter himself, though superstitious) was devised: Namely, that at such time as the professors and teachers of Christianity in the Church of Rome, then a true Church, were liberally endowed, a voice forsooth was heard from heaven, saying; Now is poison poured down into the Church, etc. Thus not only as oft as we speak, as one saith, but also as oft as we do anything of note or consequence, we subject ourselves to everyone's censure, and happy is he that is least tossed upon tongues: for utterly to escape the snatch of them it is impossible. If any man conceit, that this is the lot and portion of the meaner sort only, and that princes are privileged by their high estate, he is deceived. As the sword devoureth as well one as the other, as it is in Samuel, nay as the great commander charged his soldiers in a certain battle, to strike at no part of the enemy, but at the face; And as the king of Syria commanded his chief captains to fight neither with small nor great, save only against the King of Israel: so it is too true, that envy striketh most spitefully at the fairest, and at the chiefest. David was a worthy prince, and no man to be compared to him for his first deeds, and yet for as worthy an act as ever he did, (even for bringing back the Ark of God in solemnity) he was scorned and scoffed at by his own wife. Solomon was greater than David though not in virtue, yet in power: and by his power and wisdom he built a Temple to the LORD, such a one as was the glory of the land of Israel, and the wonder of the whole world. But was that his magnificence liked of by all? We doubt of it. Otherwise, why do they lay it in his son's dish, and call unto him for easing of the burden, Make, say they, the grievous servitude of thy Father, and his sore yoke, lighter. Belike he had charged them with some levies, and troubled them with some carriages; Hereupon they raise up a tragedy, and wish in their heart the temple had never been built. So hard a thing it is to please all, even when we please God best, and do seek to approve ourselves to everyone's conscience.

02. The highest personages have been calumniated.

If we all descend to later times, we shall find many the like examples of such kind, or rather unkind acceptance. The first Roman Emperor did never do a more pleasing deed to the learned, nor more profitable to posterity, for conserving the record of times in true supputation, then when he corrected the calendar, and ordered the year according to the course of the Sun: and yet this was imputed to him for novelty, and arrogancy, and procured to him great obloquy. So the first christened Emperor (at the leastwise that openly professed the faith himself, and allowed others to do the like) for strengthening the empire at his great charges, and providing for the Church, as he did, got for his labour the name Pupillus, as one who would say, a wasteful prince, that had need of a Guardian, or overseer. So the best christened Emperor, for the love that he bare unto peace, thereby to enrich both himself and his subjects, and because he did not seek war but find it, was judged to be no man at arms (though indeed he excelled in feats of chivalry, and showed so much when he was provoked) and condemned for giving himself to his ease, and to his pleasure. To be short, the most learned Emperor of former times, (at the least, the greatest politician) what thanks had he for cutting off the superfluities of the laws, and digesting them into some order and method? This, that he hath been blotted by some to be an epitomist, that is, one that extinguished worthy whole volumes, to bring his abridgements into request. This is the measure that hath been rendered to excellent princes in former times, even *Cum bene facerent, male audire.* (For their good deeds to be evil spoken of.) Neither is there any likelihood, that envy and malignity died, and were buried with the ancient. No, no, the reproof of Moses taketh hold of most ages: You are risen up in your fathers' stead, an increase of sinful men. What is that that hath been done? That which shall be done, and there is no new thing under the sun, saith the wise man: and St Stephen, As your fathers did, so do you.

03. His Majesty's constancy notwithstanding calumniation, for the survey of the English translations.

This, and more to this purpose, his Majesty that now reigneth (and long, and long may he reign, and his offspring forever, himself and children, and children's children always) knew full well, according to the singular wisdom given unto him by God, and the rare learning and experience that he hath attained unto; namely, that whosoever attempteth any thing for the public (specially if it pertain to religion, and to the opening and clearing of the Word of God) the same setteth himself upon a stage to be gloated upon by every evil eye, yea, he casteth himself headlong upon pikes, to be gored by every sharp tongue. For he that meddleth with men's religion in any part, meddleth with their custom, nay, with their freehold; and though they find no content in that which they have, yet they cannot abide to hear of altering. Notwithstanding his royal heart was not daunted or discouraged for this or that colour, but stood resolute, as a statue immoveable, and an anvil not easy to be beaten into plates, as one saith; he knew who had chosen him to be a soldier, or rather a captain, and being assured that the course which he intended, made much for the glory of God, and the building up of his Church, he would not suffer it to be broken off for whatsoever speeches or practices. It doth certainly belong unto Kings, yea, it doth specially belong unto them, to have care of religion, yea, to know it aright, yea, to profess it zealously, yea, to promote it to the uttermost of their power. This is their glory before all nations which mean well, and this will bring unto them a far most excellent weight of glory in the day of the Lord Jesus. For the Scripture saith not in vain, Them that honour me, I will honour, neither was it a vain word that Eusebius delivered long ago, that piety towards God was the weapon, and the only weapon that both preserved Constantine's person, and avenged him of his enemies.

04. The praise of the Holy Scriptures.

But now what piety without truth? What truth (what saving truth) without the Word of God? What Word of God (whereof we may be sure) without the Scripture? The Scriptures we are commanded to search, Jn 5:39; Is 8:20. They are commended that searched and studied them, Ac 17:11, and 8:28-29. They are reproved that were unskillful in them, or slow to believe them, Mt 22:29, Lk 24:25. They can make us wise unto salvation, 2 Ti 3:15. If we be ignorant, they will instruct us; if out of the way, they will bring us home; if out of order, they will reform us; if in heaviness, comfort us; if dull, quicken us; if cold, inflame us. *Tolle, lege; Tolle, lege*, Take up and read, take up and read the Scriptures, (for unto them was the direction) it was said unto St Augustine by a supernatural voice, Whatsoever is in the Scriptures, believe me, saith the same St Augustine, is high and divine; there is verily truth and a doctrine most fit for the refreshing and renewing of men's minds, and truly so tempered that everyone may draw from thence that which is sufficient for him, if he come to draw with a devout and pious mind, as true religion requireth. Thus St Augustine. And St Jerome, *Ama Scripturas et amabit te sapientia, etc*. (Love the Scriptures, and wisdom will love thee.) And St Cyril against Julian: Even boys that are bred up in the Scriptures become most religious, etc. But what mention we three or four uses of the Scripture, whereas whatsoever is to be believed or practised, or hoped for, is contained in them? Or three or four sentences of the Fathers, since whosoever is worthy the name of a Father, from Christ's time downward, hath likewise written not only of the riches, but also of the perfection of the Scripture? I adore the fullness of the Scripture, saith Tertullian against Hermogenes. And again, to Apelles, a heretic of the like stamp, he saith, I do not admit that which thou bringest in (or concludest) of thine own (head or store, *de tuo*) without Scripture. So Saint Justin Martyr before him; We must know by all means, saith he, that it is not lawful (or possible) to learn (anything) of God or of right piety, save only out of the prophets, who teach us by divine inspiration. So Saint Basil after Tertullian, It is a manifest falling away from the faith and a fault of presumption, either to reject any of those things that are written, or to bring in (upon the head of them, *epeisagein*) any of those things that are not written. We omit to cite to the same effect, St Cyril, Bishop of Jerusalem in his fourth *Cathechesis*, St Jerome against Helvidius, Saint Augustine, in his third book against the letters of Petilian, and in very many other places of his works. Also we forbear to descend to later Fathers, because we will not weary the reader. The Scripture then being acknowledged to be so full and so perfect, how can we excuse ourselves of negligence, if we do not study them, of curiosity, it we be not content with them? Men talk much of *eiresione*, how many sweet and goodly things it had hanging on it; of the philosophers' stone, that it turneth copper into gold: of cornucopia, that it had all things necessary for food in it, of panaces the herb, that it was good for all diseases: of catholicon the drug, that it is instead of all purges: of Vulcan's armour, that it was an armour of proof against all thrusts, and all blows, etc. Well, that which they falsely or vainly attributed to these things for bodily good, we may justly and with full measure ascribe unto the Scripture, for spiritual. It is not only an armour, but also a whole armour of weapons, both offensive, and defensive; whereby we may save ourselves, and put the enemy to flight. It is not an herb, but a tree, or rather a whole paradise of trees of life, which bring forth fruit every month, and the fruit thereof is for meat, and the leaves for medicine. It is not a pot of Manna, or a cruse of oil, which were for memory only, or for a meal's meat or two, but as it were a shower of heavenly bread, sufficient for a whole host, be it never so great; and as it were a whole cellar full of oil vessels, whereby all our necessities may be provided for, and our debts discharged. In a word, it is a panary of wholesome food against fenowed [i.e. mouldy, musty, *ed.*] traditions; a physician's shop (Saint Basil called it) of preservatives against poisoned heresies; a pandect of profitable laws against rebellious spirits; a treasure of most costly jewels, against beggarly rudiments; Finally, a fountain of most pure water springing up unto everlasting life. And what marvel? The original thereof being from heaven, not from earth; the author being God, not man; the indicter, the Holy Spirit, not the wit of the Apostles or Prophets; the penmen such as were sanctified from the womb, and endued with a principal portion of God's Spirit; the matter, verity, piety, purity, uprightness; the form, God's Word, God's testimony, God's oracles, tbe Word of truth, the Word of salvation, etc., the effects, light of understanding, stableness of persuasion, repentance from dead works, newness of life, holiness, peace, joy in the Holy Ghost; lastly, the end and reward of the study thereof, fellowship with the saints, participation of the heavenly nature, fruition of an inheritance immortal, undefiled, and that never shall fade away: Happy is the man that delighteth in the Scripture, and thrice happy that meditateth in it day and night.

05. Translation necessary.

But how shall men meditate in that, which they cannot understand? How shall they understand that, which is kept close in an unknown tongue? As it is written, Except I know the power of the voice, I shall be to him that speaketh a barbarian, and he that speaketh shall be a barbarian to me. The Apostle excepteth no tongue; not Hebrew the ancientest, not Greek the most copious, not Latin the finest. Nature taught a natural man to confess, that all of us in those tongues which we do not understand, are plainly deaf; we may turn the deaf ear unto them. The Scythian counted the Athenian, whom he did not understand, barbarous: so the Roman did the Syrian, and the Jew, (even Saint Jerome himself calleth the Hebrew tongue barbarous, belike because it was strange to so many) so the Emperor of Constantinople called the Latin tongue barbarous, though Pope Nicholas do storm at it: so the Jews long before Christ, called all other nations *Lognazim*, which is little better than barbarous. Therefore as one complaineth, that always in the Senate of Rome there was one or other that called for an interpreter, so lest the Church be driven to the like exigent, it is necessary to have translations in a readiness. Translation it is that openeth the window, to let in the light; that breaketh the shell, that we may eat the kernel; that putteth aside the curtain, that we may look into the most holy place; that removeth the cover of the well, that we may come by the water, even as Jacob rolled away the stone from the mouth of the well, by which means the flocks of Laban were watered. Indeed without translation into the vulgar tongue, the unlearned are but like children at Jacob's well (which was deep) without a bucket, or something to draw with: or as that person mentioned by Isaiah, to whom when a sealed book was delivered, with this motion. Read this, I pray thee, he was fain to make this answer, I cannot, for it is sealed.

06. The translation out of the Hebrew into Greek.

While God would be known only in Jacob, and have his name great in Israel, and in none other place, while the dew lay on Gideon's fleece only, and all the earth besides was dry; then for one and the same people, which spake all of them the language of Canaan, that is, Hebrew, one and the same original in Hebrew was sufficient. But when the fullness of time drew near that the Sun of Righteousness, the Son of God should come into the world, whom God ordained to be a reconciliation through faith in his blood, not of the Jews only, but also of the Greek, yea, of all them that were scattered abroad; then lo, it pleased the Lord to stir up the spirit of a Greek prince, (Greek for descent and language) even of Ptolemy Philadelphus King of Egypt, to procure the translating of the Book of God out of Hebrew into Greek. This is the translation of the seventy interpreters, commonly so called (i.e. the Septuagint), which prepared the way for our Saviour among the

Gentiles by written preaching, as Saint John Baptist did among the Jews by vocal. For the Grecians being desirous of learning, were not wont to suffer books of worth to lie moulding in kings' libraries, but had many of their servants, ready scribes, to copy them out, and so they were dispersed and made common. Again, the Greek tongue was well known, and made familiar to most inhabitants in Asia, by reason of the conquests that there the Grecians had made, as also by the colonies, which thither they had sent. For the same causes also it was well understood in many places of Europe, yea, and of Africa too. Therefore the Word of God being set forth in Greek, becometh hereby like a candle set upon a candlestick, which giveth light to all that are in the house, or like a proclamation sounded forth in the market place, which most men presently take knowledge of; and therefore the language was fittest to contain the Scriptures, both for the first preachers of the Gospel to appeal unto for witness, and for the learners also of those times to make search and trial by. It is certain, that that translation was not so sound and so perfect, but that it needed in many places correction; and who had been so sufficient for this work as the Apostles or Apostolic men? Yet it seemed good to the Holy Ghost and to them, to take that which they found, (the same being for the greatest part true and sufficient) rather then by making a new, in that new world and green age of the Church, to expose themselves to many exceptions and cavillations, as though they made a translation to serve their own turn, and therefore bearing witness to themselves, their witness not to be regarded. This may be supposed to be some cause, why the translation of the Seventy was allowed to pass for current. Notwithstanding though it was commended generally, yet it did not fully content the learned, no not of the Jews. For not long after Christ, Aquila fell in hand with a new translation, and after him Theodotion, and after him Symmachus: yea, there was a fifth and a sixth edition, the authors whereof were not known. These with the Seventy made up the Hexapla, and were worthily and to great purpose compiled together by Origen. Howbeit the edition of the Seventy went away with the credit, and therefore not only was placed in the midst by Origen (for the worth and excellency thereof above the rest, as Epiphanius gathereth) but also was used by the Greek Fathers for the ground and foundation of their Commentaries. Yea, Epiphanius above named doth attribute so much unto it, that he holdeth the authors thereof not only for interpreters, but also for prophets in some respect: and Justinian the Emperor enjoining the Jews his subjects to use specially the translation of the Seventy, rendereth this reason thereof, because they were as it were enlightened with prophetical grace. Yet for all that, as the Egyptians are said of the prophet to be men and not God, and their bones flesh and not spirit: so it is evident (and Saint Jerome affirmeth as much) that the Seventy were interpreters, they were not prophets; they did many things well, as learned men; but yet as men they stumbled and fell, one while through oversight, another while through ignorance, yea, sometimes they may be noted to add to the original, and sometimes to take from it; which made the Apostles to leave them many times, when they left the Hebrew, and to deliver the sense thereof according to the truth of the word, as the Spirit gave them utterance. This may suffice touching the Greek translations of the Old Testament.

07. The translating of the Scripture into the vulgar tongues.

There were also within a few hundred years after Christ, translations many into the Latin tongue: for this tongue also was very fit to convey the Law and the Gospel by, because in those times very many countries of the West, yea, of the South, East, and North, spake or understood Latin, being made provinces to the Romans. But now the Latin translations were too many to be all good, for they were infinite (*Latini interpres nullo modo numerari possunt*, saith Saint Augustine). Again, they were not out of the Hebrew fountain (we speak of the Latin translations of the Old Testament) but out of the Greek stream, therefore the Greek being not altogether clear, the Latin derived from it, must needs be muddy. This moved St Jerome a most learned father, and the best linguist, without controversy, of his age, or of any that went before him, to undertake the translating of the Old Testament, out of the very fountains themselves, which he performed with that evidence of great learning, judgement, industry and faithfulness, that he hath for ever bound the Church unto him, in a debt of special remembrance and thankfulness.

08. Translation out of Hebrew and Greek into Latin.

Now though the Church were thus furnished with Greek and Latin translations, even before the faith of Christ was generally embraced in the empire: (for the learned know that even in St Jerome's time, the consul of Rome and his wife were both ethnics [i.e. pagans, *ed.*], and about the same time the greatest part of the Senate also) yet for all that the godly-learned were not content to have the Scriptures in the language which themselves understood, Greek and Latin, (as the good lepers were not content to fare well themselves, but acquainted their neighbours with the store that God had sent, that they also might provide for themselves) but also for the behoof and edifying of the unlearned, which hungered and thirsted after righteousness, and had souls to be saved as well as they, they provided translations into the vulgar for their countrymen, insomuch that most nations under heaven did shortly after their conversion, hear Christ speaking unto them in their mother tongue, not by the voice of their minister only, but also by the written word translated. If any doubt hereof, he may be satisfied by examples enough, if enough will serve the turn. First Saint Jerome saith,

Multarum gentium linguis Scriptura ante translata, docet falsa esse qua addita sunt, etc., i.e. The Scripture being translated before in the languages of many nations, doth show that those things that were added (by Lucian or Hesychius) are false. So St Jerome in that place. The same St Jerome elsewhere affirmeth, that he, the time was, had set forth the translation of the Seventy, *sua lingua hominibus*, i.e. for his countrymen of Dalmatia. Which words not only Erasmus doth understand to purport, that Saint Jerome translated the Scripture into the Dalmatian tongue, but also Sixtus Senensis, and Alphonsus a Castro (that we speak of no more) men not to be excepted against by them of Rome, do ingenuously confess as much. So St John Chrysostom that lived in St Jerome's time giveth evidence with him: The doctrine of St John (saith he) did not in such sort (as the philosophers did) vanish away: but the Syrians, Egyptians, Indians, Persians, Ethiopians and infinite other nations, being barbarous people, translated it into their own (mother) tongue and have learned to be (true) philosophers, he meaneth Christians. To this may be added Theodoret, as next unto him, both for antiquity, and for learning. His words be these, Every country that is under the sun is full of these words, (of the Apostles and Prophets) and the Hebrew tongue (he meaneth the Scriptures in the Hebrew tongue) is turned not only into the language of the Grecians, but also of the Romans and Egyptians, and Persians and Indians, and Armenians and Scythians, and Sarmatians, and briefly into all the languages that any nation useth. So he in like manner, Ulfilas (Wulfila) is reported by Paulus Diaconus and Isidore (and before them by Sozomen) to have translated the Scriptures into the Gothic tongue: John, Bishop of Seville by Vasseus, to haw turned them into Arabic, about the year of our Lord 717: Bede by Cisterciensis [i.e. St Bernard, *ed.*], to have turned a great part of them into Saxon: Ethnard by Trithemius, to have abridged the French Psalter, as Bede had done the Hebrew, about the year 800: King Alfred by the same Cisterciensis, to have turned the Psalter into Saxon: Methodius by Aventinus (printed at Ingolstadt) to have turned the Scriptures into Slavonian: Valdo, Bishop of Friesing, by Beatus Rhenanus, to have caused about that time, the Gospels to be translated into Dutch rhyme, yet extant in the library of Corbinian: Valdus, by divers to have turned them himself, or to have gotten them turned into French, about the year 1160: Charles, the fifth of that name, surnamed The Wise, to have caused them to be turned into French, about 200 years after Valdus his time, of which translation there may be many copies yet extant, as witnesseth Beroaldus. Much about that time, even in our King Richard the Second's days, John Trevisa translated them into English, and many English Bibles in written hand are yet to be seen with divers, translated, as it is very probable, in that age. So the Syrian translation of the New Testament is in most learned men's libraries, of Widminstodius his setting forth; and the Psalter in Arabic is with many, of Augustinus Nebiensis setting forth. So Postel affirmeth, that in his travail he saw the Gospels in the Ethiopian tongue. And Ambrose

Thesius allegeth the Psalter of the Indians, which he testifieth to have been set forth by Potken in Syrian characters. So that to have the Scriptures in the mother tongue, is not a quaint conceit lately taken up, either by the Lord Cromwell in England, or by the Lord Radziwill in Poland, or by the Lord Ungnadius in the Emperor's dominion, but hath been thought upon, and put in practice of old, even from the first times of the conversion or reformation of any nation; no doubt, because it was esteemed most profitable to cause faith to grow in men's hearts the sooner, and to make them to be able to say with the words of the Psalm, As we have heard, so we have seen.

09. The unwillingness of our chief adversaries, that the Scriptures should be divulged in the mother tongue, etc.

Now the Church of Rome would seem at the length to bear a motherly affection towards her children, and to allow them the Scriptures in their mother tongue: but indeed it is a gift, not deserving to be called a gift, an unprofitable gift: they must first get a licence in writing before they may use them, and to get that, they must approve themselves to their confessor, that is, to be such as are, if not frozen in the dregs, yet soured with the leaven of their superstition. Howbeit, it seemed too much to Clement VIII that there should be any Licence granted to have them in the vulgar tongue, and therefore he overruleth and frustrateth the grant of Pius IV. So much are they afraid of the light of the Scripture, (*Lucifugae Scripturarum*: fleers of the light of Scripture, as Tertullian speaketh) that they will not trust the people with it, no not as it is set forth by their own sworn men, no not with the Licence of their own Bishops and Inquisitors. Yea, so unwilling they are to communicate the Scriptures to the people's understanding in any sort, that they are not ashamed to confess, that we forced them to translate it into English against their wills. This seemeth to argue a bad cause, or a bad conscience, or both. Sure we are, that it is not he that hath good gold, that is afraid to bring it to the touchstone, but he that hath the counterfeit; neither is it the true man that shunneth the light, but the malefactor, lest his deeds should be reproved: neither is it the plain-dealing merchant that is unwilling to have the weights, or the meteyard brought in place, but he that useth deceit. But we will let him alone for this fault, and return to translation.

10. The speeches and reasons, both of our brethren and of our adversaries, against this work.

Many men's mouths have been open a good while, (and yet are not stopped) with speeches about the translation so long in hand, or rather perusals of translations made before: and ask what may be the reason, what the necessity of the employment: Hath the Church been deceived, say they, all this while? Hath her sweet bread been mingled with leaven, her silver with dross, her wine with water, her milk with lime? (*Lacte gypsum male miscetur*, saith St Irenaeus). We hoped that we had been in the right way, that we had had the oracles of God delivered unto us, and that though all the world had cause to be offended and to complain, yet that we had none. Hath the nurse holden out the breast, and nothing but wind in it? Hath the bread been delivered by the Fathers of the Church, and the same proved to be *lapidosus*, as Seneca speaketh? What is it to handle the word of God deceitfully, if this be not? Thus certain brethren. Also the adversaries of Judah and Jerusalem, like Sanballat in Nehemiah, mock, as we hear, both at the work and workmen, saying: What do these weak Jews, etc.; will they make the stones whole again out of the heaps of dust which are burnt? Although they build, yet if a fox go up, he shall even break down their stony wall. Was their translation good before? Why do they now mend it? Was it not good? Why then was it obtruded to the people? Yea, why did the Catholics (meaning popish Romanists), always go in jeopardy, for refusing to go to hear it? Nay, if it must be translated into English, Catholics are fittest to do it. They have learning, and they know when a thing is well, they can *manum de tabula* (i.e. size a thing up, *ed.*). We will answer them both briefly: and the former, being brethren, thus, with St Jerome: *Damnamus veteres? minime, sed post priorum studio in domo Domini, quod possumus laboramus*. That is: Do we condemn the ancient? In no case, but after the endeavours of them that were before us, we take the best pains we can in the house of God. As if he said, Being provoked by the example of the learned that lived before my time, I have thought it my duty, to essay whether my talent in the knowledge of the tongues, may be profitable in any measure to God's Church, lest I should seem to have laboured in them in vain, and lest I should be thought to glory in men, (although ancient,) above that which was in them. Thus St Jerome may be thought to speak.

11. A satisfaction to our brethren.

And to the same effect say we, that we are so far off from condemning any of their labours that travailed before us in this kind, either in this land or beyond sea, either in King Henry's time, or King Edward's (if there were any translation, or correction of a translation in his time) or Queen Elizabeth's of ever renowned memory, that we acknowledge them to have been raised up of God, for the building and furnishing of his Church, and that they deserve to be had of us and of posterity in everlasting remembrance. The judgement of Aristotle is worthy and well known: If Timotheus had not been, we had not had much sweet music, but if Phrynis (Timotheus his master) had not been, we had not had Timotheus. Therefore blessed be they, and most honoured be their name, that break the ice, and give the onset upon that which helpeth forward to the saving of souls. Now what can be more available thereto, than to deliver God's book unto God's people in a tongue which they understand? Since of an hidden treasure, and of a fountain that is sealed, there is no profit, as Ptolemy Philadelphus wrote to the rabbis or masters of the Jews, as witnesseth Epiphanius: and as St Augustine saith: A man had rather be with his dog than with a stranger (whose tongue is strange unto him.) Yet for all that, as nothing is begun and perfected at the same time, and the later thoughts are thought to be the wiser: so if we building upon their foundation that went before us, and being holpen by their labours, do endeavour to make that better which they left so good; no man, we are sure, hath cause to mislike us; they, we persuade ourselves, if they were alive, would thank us. The vintage of Abiezer that strake the stroke; yet the gleaning of grapes of Ephraim was not to be despised. See Jg 8:2. Joash the king of Israel did not satisfy himself, till he had smitten the ground three times; and yet he offended the prophet for giving over then. Aquila, of whom we spake before, translated the Bible as carefully, and as skillfully as he could; and yet he thought good to go over it again, and then it got the credit with the Jews, to be called *kat'akribeian*, that is, accurately done, as Saint Jerome witnesseth. How many books of profane learning have been gone over again and again, by the same translators, by others? Of one and the same book of Aristotle's *Ethics*, there are extant not so few as six or seven several translations. Now if this cost may be bestowed upon the gourd, which affordeth us a little shade, and which today nourisheth, but tomorrow is cut down; what may we bestow, nay, what ought we not to bestow upon the vine, the fruit whereof maketh glad the conscience of man, and the stem whereof abideth for ever? And this is the Word of God, which we translate. What is the chaff to the wheat, saith the Lord? *Tanti vitreum, quanti verum margaritum*? (saith Tertullian) if a toy of glass be of that reckoning with us, how ought we to value the true pearl? Therefore let no man's eye be evil, because his Majesty's is good; neither let any be grieved, that we have a prince that seeketh the increase of the spiritual wealth of Israel (let Sanballats and Tobiahs do so, which therefore do bear their just reproof) but let us rather bless God from the ground of our heart, for working this religious care in him, to have the translations of the Bible maturely considered and examined. For by this means it cometh to pass, that whatsoever is sound already (and all is sound for substance, in one or other of our editions, and the worst of ours far better than their authentic vulgar) the same will shine as gold more brightly, being rubbed and polished; also, if anything be halting, or superfluous, or not so agreeable to the original, the same may be corrected, and the truth set in place. And what can the King command to be done, that will bring him more true honour than this? And wherein could they that have been set a work, approve their duty to the King, yea their obedience to God, and love to his saints more, than by yielding their service, and all that is within them, for the furnishing of the work? But besides all this, they were the principal motives of it, and therefore ought least to quarrel it: for the very historical truth is, that upon the importunate petitions of the Puritans, at his Majesty's coming to this Crown, the Conference at Hampton Court having been appointed for hearing their complaints: when by force of reason they were put from all other grounds, they had recourse at the last, to this shift, that they could not with good conscience subscribe to the Communion book, since it maintained the Bible as it was there translated, which was, as they said, a most corrupted translation. And although this was judged to be but a very poor and empty shift; yet even hereupon did his Majesty begin to bethink himself of the good that might ensue by a new translation, and presently after gave order for this translation which is now presented unto thee. Thus much to satisfy our scrupulous brethren.

12. An answer to the imputations of our adversaries.

Now to the latter we answer; that we do not deny, nay we affirm and avow, that the very meanest translation of the Bible in English, set forth by men of our profession (for we have seen none of theirs of the whole Bible as yet) containeth the Word of God, nay, is the Word of God. As the King's speech which he uttered in Parliament, being translated into French, Dutch, Italian, and Latin, is still the King's speech, though it be not interpreted by every translator with the like grace, nor peradventure so fitly for phrase, nor so expressly for sense, everywhere. For it is confessed, that things are to take their denomination of the greater part; and a natural man could say, *Verbum ubi multa nitent in carmine, non ego paucis offendor maculis, etc.* A man may be counted a virtuous man, though he have made many slips in his life, (else, there were none virtuous, for in many things we offend all) also a comely man and lovely, though he have some warts upon his hand, yea, not only freckles upon his face, but also scars. No cause therefore why the word translated should be denied to be the word, or forbidden to be current, notwithstanding that some imperfections and blemishes may be noted in the setting forth of it. For what ever was perfect under the sun, where Apostles or Apostolic men, that is, men indued with an extraordinary measure of God's Spirit, and privileged with the privilege of infallibility, had not their hand? The Romanists therefore in refusing to hear, and daring to burn the Word translated, did no less than despite the Spirit of grace, from whom originally it proceeded, and whose sense and meaning, as well as man's weakness would enable, it did express. Judge by an example or two. Plutarch writeth, that after that Rome had been burnt by the Gauls, they fell soon to build it again: but doing it in haste, they did not cast the streets, nor proportion the houses in such comely fashion, as had been most sightly and convenient; was Catiline therefore an honest man, or a good patriot, that sought to bring it to a combustion? Or Nero a good prince, that did indeed set it on fire? So, by the story of Ezra, and the prophecy of Haggai it may be gathered, that the temple built by Zerubbabel after the return from

Babylon, was by no means to be compared to the former built by Solomon (for they that remembered the former, wept when they considered the latter) notwithstanding, might this latter either have been abhorred and forsaken by the Jews, or profaned by the Greeks? The like we are to think of translations. The translation of the Seventy dissenteth from the original in many places, neither doth it come near it for perspicuity, gravity, majesty; yet which of the Apostles did condemn it? Condemn it? Nay, they used it, (as it is apparent, and as St Jerome and most learned men do confess) which they would not have done, nor by their example of using it, so grace and commend it to the Church, if it had been unworthy the appellation and name of the Word of God. And whereas they urge for their second defence of their vilifying and abusing of the English Bibles, or some pieces thereof, which they meet with, for that heretics (forsooth) were the authors of the translations, (heretics they call us by the same right that they call themselves catholics, both being wrong) we marvel what divinity taught them so. We are sure Tertullian was of another mind: *Ex personis probamus fidem, an ex fide personas?* So we try men's faith by their person? We should try their persons by their faith. Also St Augustine was of another mind: for he lighting upon certain rules made by Tyconius a Donatist, for the better understanding of the word, was not ashamed to make use of them, yea to insert them into his own book, with giving commendation to them so far forth as they were worthy to be commended, as is to be seen in St Augustine's third book *De doctrina Christiana*. To be short, Origen, and the whole Church of God for certain years, were of another mind: for they were so far from treading under foot, (much more from burning) the translation of Aquila a proselyte, that is, one that had turned Jew; of Symmachus, and Theodotion, both Ebionites, that is, most vile heretics, that they joined them together with the Hebrew original, and the translation of the Seventy, (as hath been before signified out of Epiphanius) and set them forth openly to be considered of and perused by all. But we weary the unlearned, who need not know so much, and trouble the learned, who know it already.

Yet before we end we must answer a third cavil and objection of theirs against us, for altering and amending our translation so oft; wherein truly they deal hardly, and strangely with us. For to whom ever was it imputed for a fault (by such as were wise) to go over that which he had done, and to amend it where he saw cause? St Augustine was not afraid to exhort St Jerome to a *palinodia* or recantation; the same St Augustine was not ashamed to retractate, we might say, revoke, many things that had passed him, and doth even glory that he seeth his infirmities. If we will be sons of the truth, we must consider what it speaketh, and trample upon our own credit, yea, and upon other men's too, if either be any way an hindrance to it. This to the cause: then to the persons we say, that of all men they ought to be most silent in this case. For what varieties have they, and what alterations have they made, not only of their Service books, Portesses and Breviaries, but also of their Latin translation? The Service Book supposed to be made by St Ambrose (*Officium Ambrosianum*) was a great while in special use and request: but Pope Hadrian calling a Council with the aid of Charles the Emperor, abolished it, yea, burnt it, and commanded the Service Book of St Gregory universally to be used. Well, *Officium Gregorianum* gets by this means to be in credit, but doth it continue without change or altering? No, the very Roman Service was of two fashions, the New fashion, and the Old, (the one used in one church, the other in another) as is to be seen in Pamelius a Romanist, his Preface, before *Micrologus*. The same Pamelius reporteth out of Radulphus de Rivo, that about the year of our Lord 1277, Pope Nicholas III removed out of the churches of Rome, the more ancient books (of service) and brought into use the missals of the Friars Minorites, and commanded them to be observed there; insomuch that about an hundred years after, when the above-named Radulphus happened to be at Rome, he found all the books to be new, (of the new stamp.) Neither was there this chopping and changing in the more ancient times only, but also of late: Pius V himself confesseth, that every bishopric almost had a peculiar kind of service, most unlike to that which others had: which moved him to abolish all other Breviaries, though never so ancient, and privileged, and published by Bishops in their Dioceses, and to establish and ratify that only which was of his own setting forth, in the year 1568. Now, when the father of their Church, who gladly would heal the sore of the daughter of his people softly and sleightly, and make the best of it, findeth so great fault with them for their odds and jarring; we hope the children have no great cause to vaunt of their uniformity. But the difference that appeareth between our translations, and our often correcting of them, is the thing we are specially charged with; let us see therefore whether they themselves be without fault this way, (if it be to be counted a fault, to correct) and whether they be fit men to throw stones at us: *O tandem maior pareas insani minori*: they that are less sound themselves, ought not to object infirmities to others. If we should tell them that Valla, Stapulensis, Erasmus, and Vives found fault with their vulgar translation, and consequently wished the same to be mended, or a new one to be made, they would answer peradventure, that we produced their enemies for witnesses against them; albeit, they were in no other sort enemies, than as St Paul was to the Galatians, for telling them the truth: and it were to be wished, that they had dared to tell it them plainlier and oftener. But what will they say to this, that Pope Leo X allowed Erasmus translation of the New Testament, so much different from the vulgar, by his Apostolic Letter and Bull; That the same Leo exhorted Pagninus to translate the whole Bible, and bare whatsoever charges were necessary for the work? Surely, as the Apostle reasoneth to the Hebrews, that if the former law had been sufficient, there had been no need of the latter: so we may say, that if the old vulgar had been at all points allowable, to small purpose had labour and charges been undergone, about framing of a new. If they say, it was one pope's private opinion, and that he consulted only himself; then we are able to go further with them, and to aver that more of their chief men of all sorts, even their own Trent-champions Paiva and Vega, and their own inquisitor Hieronymus ab Oleastro, and their own Bishop Isidorus Clarius, and their own Cardinal Thomas a Vio Cajetan, do either make new translations themselves, or follow new ones of other men's making, or note the vulgar interpreter for halting; none of them fear to dissent from him, nor yet to except against him. And call they this an uniform tenor of text and judgement about the text, so many of their worthies disclaiming the now received conceit? Nay, we will yet come nearer the quick: doth not their Paris edition differ from the Louvain, and Hentenius, his from them both, and yet all of them allowed by authority? Nay, doth not Sixtus V confess that certain Catholics (he meaneth certain of his own side) were in such an humour of translating the Scriptures into Latin that Satan, taking occasion by them, though they thought of no such matter, did strive what he could, out of so uncertain and manifold a variety of translations, so to mingle all things, that nothing might seem to be left certain and firm in them, etc.? Nay further, did not the same Sixtus ordain by an inviolable decree, and that with the counsel and consent of his cardinals, that the Latin edition of the Old and New Testament which the Council of Trent would have to be authentic, is the same without controversy which he then set forth, being diligently corrected and printed in the printing house of the Vatican? Thus Sixtus in his Preface before his Bible. And yet Clement VIII his immediate successor, to account of, publisheth another edition of the Bible, containing in it infinite differences from that of Sixtus, (and many of them weighty and material) and yet this must be authentic by all means. What is to have the faith of our glorious Lord Jesus Christ with Yea and Nay, if this be not? Again, what is sweet harmony and consent, if this be? Therefore as Demaratus of Corinth advised a great king, before he talked of the dissensions among the Grecians, to compose his domestic broils: (for at that time his queen and his son and heir were at deadly feud with him) so all the while that our adversaries do make so many and so various editions themselves, and do jar so much about the worth and authority of them, they can with no show of equity challenge us for changing and correcting.

13. The purpose of the translators, with their number, furniture, care, etc.

But it is high time to leave them, and to show in brief what we proposed to ourselves, and what course we held in this our perusal and survey of the Bible. Truly (good Christian reader) we never thought from the beginning, that we should need to make a new translation, nor yet to make of a bad one a good one, (for then the imputation of Sixtus had been true in some sort, that our people had been fed with gall of dragons instead of wine, with whey instead of milk;) but to make a good one better, or out of many good ones, one principal good one, not justly to be excepted against; that hath been our endeavour, that our mark. To that purpose there were many chosen, that were greater in other men's eyes then in their own, and that sought the truth rather than their own praise. Again, they came or were thought to come to the work, not *exercendi causa* (as one saith) but *exercitati*, that is, learned, not to learn: For the chief overseer and *ergodioktes* under his Majesty, to whom not only we, but also our whole Church was much bound, knew by his own wisdom, which thing also Nazianzene taught so long ago, that it is a preposterous order to teach first and to learn after, yea that *to en pithoi keramian manthanein*, to learn and practise together, is neither commendable for the workman nor safe for the work. Therefore such were thought upon, as could say modestly with St Jerome: *Et Hebraeum sermonem ex parte didicimus, et in Latino paene ab ipsis incunabulis etc. detriti sumus.* (Both we have learned the Hebrew tongue in part, and in the Latin we have been exercised almost from our very cradle.) Saint Jerome maketh no mention of the Greek tongue, wherein yet he did excel, because he translated not the Old Testament out of Greek, but out of Hebrew. And in what sort did these assemble? In the trust of their own knowledge, or of their sharpness of wit, or deepness of judgement, as it were in an arm of flesh? At no hand. They trusted in him that hath the key of David, opening and no man shutting; they prayed to the Lord the Father of our Lord, to the effect that St Augustine did: O let thy Scriptures be my pure delight, let me not be deceived in them, neither let me deceive by them. In this confidence, and with this devotion did they assemble together; not too many, lest one should trouble another; and yet many, lest many things haply might escape them. If you ask what they had before them, truly it was the Hebrew text of the Old Testament, the Greek of the New. These are the two golden pipes, or rather conduits, where through the olive branches empty themselves into the gold. St Augustine calleth them precedent, or original tongues; St Jerome, fountains. The same St Jerome affirmeth, and Gratian hath not spared to put into his Decree, That as the credit of the old books (he meaneth of the Old Testament) is to be tried by the Hebrew volumes, so of the New by the Greek tongue, he meaneth by the original Greek. If truth be to be tried by these tongues, then whence should a translation be made, but out of them? These tongues therefore, the Scriptures we say in those tongues, we set before us to translate, being the tongues wherein God was pleased to speak to his Church by his Prophets and Apostles. Neither did we run over the work with that posting haste that the Septuagint did, if that be true which is reported of them, that they finished it in seventy-two days; neither were we barred or hindered from going over it again, having once done it, like Saint Jerome, if that be true which himself reporteth, that he could no sooner write anything, but presently it was caught from him, and published, and he could not have leave to mend it: neither, to be short, were we the first that fell in hand with translating the Scripture into English, and consequently destitute of former helps, as it is written of Origen, that he was the first in a manner, that put his hand to write commentaries upon the Scriptures, and therefore no marvel, if he overshot himself many times. None of these things: the work hath not been huddled up in seventy-two days, but hath cost the workmen, as light as it seemeth, the pains of twice seven times seventy-two days and more: matters of such weight and consequently destitute of former helps, as it is written of business of moment a man feareth not the blame of convenient slackness. Neither did we think much to consult the translators or commentators, Chaldee, Hebrew, Syrian, Greek or Latin, no nor the Spanish, French, Italian, or Dutch; neither did we disdain to revise that which we had done, and to bring back to the anvil that which we had hammered: but having and using as great helps as were needful, and fearing no reproach for slowness, nor coveting praise for expedition, we have at the length, through the good hand of the Lord upon us, brought the work to that pass that you see.

14. Reasons moving us to set diversity of senses in the margin, where there is great probability for each.

Some peradventure would have no variety of senses to be set in the margin, lest the authority of the Scriptures for deciding of controversies by that show of uncertainty, should somewhat be shaken. But we hold their judgement not to be so sound in this point. For though, Whatsoever things are necessary are manifest, as St John Chrysostom saith, and as St Augustine: In those things that are plainly set down in the Scriptures all such matters are found that concern faith, hope and charity. Yet for all that it cannot be dissembled, that partly to exercise and whet our wits, partly to wean the curious from loathing of them for their everywhere-plainness, partly also to stir up our devotion to crave the assistance of God's Spirit by prayer, and lastly, that we might be forward to seek aid of our brethren by conference, and never scorn those that be not in all respects so complete as they should be, being to seek in many things ourselves, it hath pleased God in his divine providence, here and there to scatter words and sentences of that difficulty and doubtfulness, not in doctrinal points that concern salvation (for in such it hath been vouched that the Scriptures are plain) but in matters of less moment, that fearfulness would better beseem us than confidence, and if we will resolve, to resolve upon modesty with St Augustine, (though not in this same case altogether, yet upon the same ground) *Melius est dubitare de occultis, quam litigare de incertis*, (it is better to make doubt of those things which are secret, then to strive about those things that are uncertain.) Then be many words in the Scriptures, which be never found there but once, (having neither brother nor neighbour, as the Hebrews speak) so that we cannot be holpen by conference of places. Again, then be many rare names of certain birds, beasts and precious stones, etc. concerning which the Hebrews themselves are so divided among themselves for judgement, that they may seem to have defined this or that, rather because they would say something, than because they were sure of that which they said, as Saint Jerome somewhere saith of the Septuagint. Now in such a case, doth not a margin do well to admonish the reader to seek further, and not to conclude or dogmatize upon this or that peremptorily? For as it is a fault of incredulity, to doubt of those things that are evident: so to determine of such things as the Spirit of God hath left (even in the judgement of the judicious) questionable, can be no less then presumption. Therefore as Saint Augustine saith, that variety of translations is profitable for the finding out of the sense of the Scriptures: so diversity of signification and sense in the margin, when the text is not so clear, must needs do good, yea, is necessary as we are persuaded. We know that Sixtus V expressly forbiddeth, that any variety of readings of their vulgar edition, should be put in the margin (which though it be not altogether the same thing to that we have in hand, yet it looketh that way) but we think he hath not all of his own side his favourers, for this conceit. They that are wise, had rather have their judgements at liberty in differences of readings, then to be captivated to one, when it may be the other. If they were sure that their high Priest had all laws shut up in his breast, as Paul II bragged, and that he were as free from error by special privilege, as the dictators of Rome were made by law inviolable, it were another matter; then his word were an oracle, his opinion a decision. But the eyes of the world are now open, God be thanked, and have been a great while, they find that he is subject to the same affections and infirmities that others be, that his body is subject to wounds, and theretore so much as he proveth, not as much as he claimeth, they grant and embrace.

15. Reasons inducing us not to stand curiously upon an identity of phrasing.

Another thing we think good to admonish thee of (gentle reader) that we have not tied ourselves to an uniformity of phrasing, or to an identity of words, as some peradventure would wish that we had done, because they observe, that some learned men somewhere, have been as exact as they could that way. Truly, that we might not vary from the sense of that which we had translated before, if the word signified the same thing in both places (for, there be some words that be not of the same sense everywhere) we were especially careful, and made a conscience, according to our duty. But, that we should express the same notion in the same particular word; as for example, if we translate the Hebrew or Greek word once by *purpose*, never to call it *intent*; if one where *journeying*, never *travelling*; if one where *think*, never *suppose*; if one where *pain*, never *ache*; if one where *joy*, never *gladness*, etc. Thus to mince the matter, we thought to favour more of curiosity than wisdom, and that rather it would breed scorn in the Atheist, then bring profit to the godly reader. For is the kingdom of God become words or syllables? Why should we be in bondage to them if we may be free, use one precisely when we may use another no less fit, as commodiously? A godly Father in the primitive time showed himself greatly moved, that one of newfangledness called *krabbaton skimpous*, the difference be little or none; and another reporteth, that he was much abused for turning *cucurbita* (to which reading the people had been used) into *hedera*. Now if this happen in better times, and upon so small occasions, we might justly fear hard censure, if generally we should make verbal and unnecessary changings. We might also be charged (by scoffers) with some unequal dealing toward a great number of good English words. For as it is written of a certain great philosopher, that he should say, that those logs were happy that were made images to be worshipped; for their fellows, as good as they, lay for blocks behind the fire; so if we should say, as it were, unto certain words, Stand up higher, have a place in the Bible always, and to others of like quality, Get ye hence, be banished for ever, we might be taxed peradventure with St James his words, namely, To be partial in ourselves, and judges of evil thoughts. Add hereunto, that niceness in words was always counted the next step to trifling, and so was to be curious about names too: also that we cannot follow a better pattern for elocution than God himself; therefore he using divers words, in his Holy Writ, and indifferently for one thing in nature: we, if we will not be superstitious, may use the same liberty in our English versions out of Hebrew and Greek, for that copy or store that he hath given us. Lastly, we have on the one side avoided the scrupulosity of the Puritans, who leave the old ecclesiastical words, and betake them to other, as when they put *washing* for *baptism*, and *congregation* instead of *church*: as also on the other side, we have shunned the obscurity of the papists, in their *azymes, tunic, rational, holocausts, prepuce, Pasche*, and a number of such like, whereof their late translation is full, and that of purpose to darken the sense, that since they must needs translate the Bible, yet by the language thereof, it may be kept from being understood. But we desire that the Scripture may speak like itself, as in the language of Canaan, that it may be understood even of the very vulgar.

Many other things we might give thee warning of (gentle reader) if we had not exceeded the measure of a Preface already. It remaineth, that we commend thee to God, and to the Spirit of his grace, which is able to build further than we can ask or think. He removeth the scales from our eyes, the veil from our hearts, opening our wits, that we may understand his Word, enabling our hearts, yea correcting our affections, that we may love it above gold and silver, yea that we may love it to the end. Ye are brought unto fountains of living water which ye digged not; do not cast earth into them with the Philistines, neither prefer broken pits before them with the wicked

Jews. Others have laboured, and you may enter into their labours; O receive not so great things in vain! O despise not so great salvation! Be not like swine to tread under foot so precious things, neither yet like dogs to tear and abuse holy things. Say not to our Saviour with the Gergasites, Depart out of our coasts, neither yet with Esau, Sell your birthright for a mess of pottage. If light be come into the world, love not darkness more than light: if food, if clothing be offered, go not naked, starve not yourselves. Remember the advice of Nazianzene: It is a grievous thing (or dangerous) to neglect a great fair, and to seek to make markets afterwards. Also the encouragement of St John Chrysostom: It is altogether impossible, that he that is sober and watchful should at any time be neglected. Lastly, the admonition and menacing of St Augustine: They that despise God's will inviting them shall feel God's will taking vengeance of them. It is a fearful thing to fall into the hands of the living God: but a blessed thing it is, and will bring us to everlasting blessedness in the end, when God speaketh unto us, to hearken; when he setteth his Word before us, to read it; when he stretcheth out his hand and calleth, to answer, Here am I; here we are to do thy will, O God. The Lord work a care and conscience in us to know him and serve him, that we may be acknowledged of him at the appearing of our Lord Jesus Christ, to whom with the Holy Ghost, be all praise and thanksgiving. Amen.

42. THE IRISH ARTICLES, 1615

History

In the early stages of the Reformation, it appears that the Irish clergy, or at least those who lived in areas controlled by the king's government, generally followed their English brethren in accepting the various reforms which were proposed. The Eleven Articles (1559) were adopted by the Irish in 1566, and the same conditions of subscription were imposed. It is unclear to what extent the Thirty-eight or Thirty-nine Articles were able to displace them. At a synod in Dublin (1615), the Church of Ireland, under the influence of James Ussher, who later became Archbishop of Armagh, adopted these Articles. They incorporated the Lambeth Articles (1595), although without acknowledgement. It is not known to what extent clergy were expected to subscribe to them, though it seems that they were increasingly ignored in favour of the English Thirty-nine Articles. This was certainly true of the Convocation of 1635, when the king tried to impose Laudian views and policies on the Irish Church. The settlement of 1662, confirmed by the union of the Churches of England and Ireland in 1801 (dissolved in 1871), finally relegated these Articles to the history books, and they no longer have any authority in the Church of Ireland.

Theology

The Articles have a distinctly Calvinist flavour, and form a kind of bridge between the Thirty-nine Articles (1571) and the Westminster Confession (1647). They retain most of the substance of the earlier document, but add matters which had become pressing in the seventeenth century. They may have been intended, along with the little-known Scots Confession of 1616, as a preliminary to a joint confession of the three national Churches of the British Isles, a project which was finally realised, under very different circumstances, at Westminster in 1647. It is interesting to note that they begin, not with the doctrine of God, but with that of Holy Scripture, a change of method which is unique among purely Anglican documents of this kind, and which is a measure of the influence which contemporary Calvinism exercised on their composition.

01. Of the Holy Scripture and the Three Creeds

01. The ground of our religion and the rule of faith and all saving truth is the Word of God, contained in the Holy Scriptures.

02. By the name of Holy Scripture we understand all the canonical books of the Old and New Testament, viz:

Of the Old Testament:

The five books of Moses
Joshua
Judges
Ruth
The first and second of Samuel
The first and second of Kings
The first and second of Chronicles
Ezra
Nehemiah
Esther
Job

Psalms
Proverbs
Ecclesiastes
The Song of Solomon
Isaiah
Jeremiah, his Prophecy and Lamentation
Ezekiel
Daniel
The 12 lesser Prophets

Of the New Testament:

The Gospels according to:
  Matthew
  Mark
  Luke
  John
Acts of the Apostles
Epistle of St Paul to the Romans
Corinthians (2)
Galatians
Ephesians
Philippians

Colossians
Thessalonians (2)
Timothy (2)
Titus
Philemon
Hebrews
Epistle of St James
St Peter (2)
St John (3)
St Jude
Revelation of St John

All which we acknowledge to be given by the inspiration of God, and in that regard to be of most certain credit and highest authority.

03. The other books, commonly called Apocryphal, did not proceed from such inspiration and therefore are not of sufficient authority to establish any point of doctrine, but the Church doth read them as books containing many worthy things for example of life and instruction of manners.

Such are these following:

The third book of Esdras
The fourth book of Esdras
The book of Tobias (Tobit)
The book of Judith
Additions to the book of Esther
The book of Wisdom
The book of Jesus, son of Sirach, called Ecclesiasticus

Baruch, with the Epistle of Jeremiah
The Song of the Three Children
Susanna
Bel and the Dragon
The Prayer of Manasses
The first book of Maccabees
The second book of Maccabees

04. The Scriptures ought to be translated out of the original tongues into all languages for the common use of all men; neither is any person to be discouraged from reading the Bible in such a language as he doth understand, but seriously exhorted to read the same with great humility and reverence, as a special means to bring him to the true knowledge of God, and of his own duty.

05. Although there be some hard things in the Scripture (especially such as have proper relation to the times in which they were first uttered, and prophecies of things which were afterwards to be fulfilled), yet all things that are necessary to be known unto everlasting salvation are clearly delivered therein; and nothing of that kind is spoken under dark mysteries in one place, which is not in other places spoken more familiarly and plainly, to the capacity of learned and unlearned.

06. The Holy Scriptures contain all things necessary to salvation, and are able to instruct sufficiently in all points of faith that we are bound to believe, and all good duties that we are bound to practise.

07. All and every the Articles contained in the Nicene Creed, the Creed of Athanasius and that which is commonly called the Apostles' Creed, ought firmly to be received and believed, for they may be proved by most certain warrant of Holy Scripture.

02. Of Faith in the Holy Trinity

08. There is but one living and true God, everlasting, without body, parts or passions, of infinite power, wisdom and goodness, the maker and preserver of all things, both visible and invisible. And in unity of this Godhead there be three persons of one and the same substance, power and eternity: the Father, the Son and the Holy Ghost.

09. The essence of the Father doth not beget the essence of the Son, but the Person of the Father begetteth the Person of the Son, by communicating his whole essence to the person begotten from eternity.

10. The Holy Ghost, proceeding from the Father and the Son, is of one substance, majesty and glory with the Father and the Son, very and eternal God.

03. Of God's Eternal Decree, and Predestination

11. God from all eternity did by his unchangeable counsel ordain whatsoever in time should come to pass; yet so, as thereby no violence is offered to the wills of the reasonable creatures, and neither the liberty nor the contingency of the second causes is taken away, but established rather.

12. By the same eternal counsel God hath predestinated some unto life and reprobated some unto death; of both which there is a certain number, known only to God, which can neither be increased nor diminished.

13. Predestination to life is the everlasting purpose of God, whereby, before the foundations of the world were laid, he hath constantly decreed in his secret counsel to deliver from curse and damnation, those whom he hath chosen in Christ out of mankind, and to bring them by Christ unto everlasting salvation, as vessels made to honour.

14. The cause moving God to predestinate unto life is not the foreseeing of faith, or perseverance of good works, or of anything which is in the person predestinated, but only the good pleasure of God himself. For all things being ordained for the manifestation of his glory, and his glory being to appear both in the works of his mercy and of his justice; it seemed good to his heavenly wisdom to choose out a certain number towards whom he would extend his undeserved mercy, leaving the rest to be spectacles of his justice.

15. Such as are predestinated unto life be called according unto God's purpose (his Spirit working in due season) and through grace they obey the calling, they be justified freely, they be made sons of God by adoption, they be made like the image of his only begotten Son Jesus Christ, they walk religiously in good works, and at length, by God's mercy, they attain to everlasting felicity. But such as are not predestinated to salvation shall finally be condemned for their sins.

16. The godlike consideration of predestination and our election in Christ is full of sweet, pleasant and unspeakable comfort to godly persons, and such as feel in themselves the working of the Spirit of Christ, mortifying the works of the flesh and their earthly members, and drawing up their minds to high and heavenly things; as well because it doth greatly confirm and establish their faith of eternal salvation to be enjoyed through Christ, as because it doth fervently kindle their love towards God; and on the contrary side, for curious and carnal persons, lacking the Spirit of Christ, to have continually before their eyes the sentence of God's predestination, is very dangerous.

17. We must receive God's promises in such wise as they be generally set forth unto us in Holy Scripture, and in our doings, that will of God is to be followed which we have, expressly declared unto us, in the Word of God.

04. Of the Creation and Government of All Things

18. In the beginning of time, when no creature had any being, God by his Word alone, in the space of six days, created all things, and afterwards by his providence doth continue, propagate and order them according to his own will.

19. The principal creatures are angels and men.

20. Of angels, some continued in that holy state wherein they were created and are by God's grace for ever established therein; others fell from the same and are reserved in chains of darkness unto the judgement of the great day.

21. Man being at the beginning created according to the image of God (which consisted especially in the wisdom of his mind and the true holiness of his free will) had the covenant of the Law ingrafted in his heart; whereby God did promise unto him everlasting life, upon condition that he performed entire and perfect obedience unto his commandments, according to that measure of strength wherewith he was endued in his creation, and threatened death unto him if he did not perform the same.

05. Of the Fall of Man, Original Sin and the State of Man before Justification

22. By one man sin entered into the world and death by sin; and so death went over all men, forasmuch as all have sinned.

23. Original sin standeth not in the imitation of Adam (as the Pelagians dream) but is the fault and corruption of the nature of every person that naturally is engendered and propagated from Adam; whereby it cometh to pass that man is deprived of original righteousness and by nature is bent unto sin. And therefore, in every person born into the world, it deserveth God's wrath and damnation.

24. This corruption of nature doth remain even in those that are regenerated, whereby the flesh always lusteth against the spirit and cannot be made subject to the law of God. And howsoever for Christ's sake there be no condemnation to such as are regenerate and do believe; yet doth the Apostle acknowledge that in itself this concupiscence hath the nature of sin.

25. The condition of man after the fall of Adam is such that he cannot turn and prepare himself by his own natural strength and good works to faith and calling upon God. Wherefore we have no power to do good works, pleasing and acceptable unto God, without the grace of God preventing us, that we may have a good will, and working with us when we have that good will.

26. Works done before the grace of Christ and the inspiration of his Spirit are not pleasing to God forasmuch as they spring not of faith in Jesus Christ, neither do they make men meet to receive grace, or (as School Authors say) deserve grace of congruity; yea rather, for that they are not done in such sort as God hath willed and commanded them to be done, we doubt not but they are sinful.

27. All sins are not equal but some are far more heinous than others; yet the very least is of its own nature mortal, and without God's mercy maketh the offender liable unto everlasting damnation.

28. God is not the author of sin; howbeit he doth not only permit, but also by his providence govern and order the same, guiding it in such sort by his infinite wisdom, as it turneth to the manifestation of his own glory and to the good of his elect.

06. Of Christ, the Mediator of the Second Covenant

29. The Son, which is the Word of the Father, begotten from everlasting of the Father, the true and eternal God, of one substance with the Father, took man's nature in the womb of the Blessed Virgin, of her substance; so that two whole and perfect natures, that is to say, the Godhead and Manhood, were inseparably joined in one person, making one Christ, very God and very man.

30. Christ, in the truth of our nature, was made like unto us in all things, sin only excepted, from which he was clearly void, both in his life and in his nature. He came as a lamb without spot, to take away the sins of the world by the sacrifice of himself once made, and sin (as St John saith) was not in him. He fulfilled the law for us perfectly; for our sakes he endured most grievous torments immediately in his soul, and most painful sufferings in his body. He was crucified and died to reconcile his father unto us, and to be a sacrifice not only for original guilt, but also for all our actual transgressions. He was buried and descended into hell, and the third day rose from the dead and took again his body, with flesh, bones and all things appertaining to the perfection of man's nature; wherewith he ascended into heaven and there sitteth at the right hand of his Father until he return to judge all men at the last day.

07. Of the Communicating of the Grace of Christ

31. They are to be condemned that presume to say that every man shall be saved by the law or sect which he professeth, so that he be diligent to frame his life according to that law, and the light of nature. For Holy Scripture doth set out unto us only the name of Jesus Christ whereby men must be saved.

32. None can come unto Christ unless it be given unto him, and unless the Father draw him. And all men are not so drawn by the Father that they may come unto the Son. Neither is there such a sufficient measure of grace vouchsafed unto every man, whereby he is enabled to come unto everlasting life.

33. All God's elect are in their time inseparably united unto Christ by the effectual and vital influence of the Holy Ghost, derived from him as from the head, unto every true member of his mystical body. And being thus made one with Christ, they are truly regenerated and made partakers of him and all his benefits.

08. Of Justification and Faith

34. We are accounted righteous before God only for the merit of our Lord and Saviour Jesus Christ, applied by faith; and not for our own works or merits. And this righteousness, which we so receive of God's mercy and Christ's merits, embraced by faith, is taken, accepted and allowed of God, for our perfect and full justification.

35. Although this justification be free unto us, yet it cometh not so freely unto us that there is no ransom paid therefore at all. God showed his great mercy in delivering us from our former captivity, without requiring of any ransom to be paid or amends to be made on our parts, which thing by us had been impossible to be done. And whereas all the world was not able of themselves to pay any part towards their ransom, it pleased our heavenly Father of his infinite mercy, without any desert of ours, to provide for us the most precious merits of his own Son, whereby our ransom might be fully paid, the law fulfilled, and his justice fully satisfied. So that Christ is now the righteousness of all them that truly believe in him. He for them paid their ransom by his death. He for them fulfilled the Law in his life. That now in him and by him, every true Christian man may be called a fulfiller of the Law, forasmuch as that which our infirmity was not able to effect, Christ's justice hath performed. And thus the justice and mercy of God do embrace each other; the grace of God not shutting out the justice of God in the matter of our justification, but only shutting out the justice of man (that is to say, the justice of our own works) from being any cause of deserving our justification.

36. When we say that we are justified by faith only, we do not mean that the said justifying faith is alone in man, without true repentance, hope, charity and the fear of God (for such a faith is dead and cannot justify), neither do we mean that this our act to believe in Christ, or this our faith in Christ, which is within us, doth of itself justify us, or deserve our justification unto us, (for that were to account ourselves to be justified by the virtue or dignity of something that is within ourselves); but the true understanding and meaning thereof is that although we hear God's Word and believe it, although we have faith, hope, charity, repentance and the fear of God within us and add never so many good works thereunto; yet we must renounce the merit of all our said virtues, of faith, hope, charity and all our other virtues, and good deeds, which we either have done, shall do or can do, as things that be far too weak and imperfect, and insufficient to deserve remission of our sins and our justification; and therefore we must trust only in God's mercy and the merits of his most dearly beloved Son, our only Redeemer, Saviour and Justifier Jesus Christ. Nevertheless, because faith doth directly send us to Christ for our justification, and that by faith given us of God we embrace the promise of God's mercy, and the remission of our sins, (which thing none other of our virtues or works properly doth); therefore the Scripture useth to say that *faith without works*, and the ancient fathers of the Church to the same purpose, that *only faith* doth justify us.

37. By justifying faith we understand not only the common belief of the Articles of Christian religion, and a persuasion of the truth of God's Word

in general, but also a particular application of the gratuitous promises of the Gospel, to the comfort of our own souls; whereby we lay hold of Christ, with all his benefits, having an earnest trust and confidence in God, that he will be merciful unto us for his only Son's sake. So that a true believer may be certain, by the assurance of faith, of the forgiveness of his sins, and of his everlasting salvation by Christ.

38. A true and lively justifying faith, and the sanctifying Spirit of God, is not extinguished, nor vanisheth away in the regenerate, either finally or totally.

09. Of Sanctification and Good Works

39. All that are justified are likewise sanctified, their faith being always accompanied with true repentance and good works.

40. Repentance is a gift of God whereby a godly sorrow is wrought in the heart of the faithful, for offending God their merciful Father by their former transgressions, together with a constant resolution for the time to come to cleave unto God, and to lead a new life.

41. Albeit that good works, which are fruits of faith, and follow after justification, cannot make satisfaction for our sins, and endure the severity of God's judgement; yet are they pleasing to God, and accepted of him in Christ, and do spring from a true and lively faith, which by them is to be discerned, as a tree by the fruit.

42. The works which God would have his people to walk in are such as he hath commanded in his Holy Scripture, and not such works as men have devised out of their own brain, of a blind zeal and devotion, without the warrant of the Word of God.

43. The regenerate cannot fulfil the Law of God perfectly in this life. For in many things we offend all, and if we say we have no sin we deceive ourselves, and the truth is not in us.

44. Not every heinous sin willingly committed after baptism is sin against the Holy Ghost and unpardonable. And therefore to such as fall into sin after baptism, place for repentance is not to be denied.

45. Voluntary works besides, over and above God's commandments, which they call works of supererogation, cannot be taught without arrogance and impiety. For by them men do declare that they do not only render unto God as much as they are bound to do, but that they do more for his sake than of bounden duty is required.

10. Of the Service of God

46. Our duty towards God is to believe in him, to fear him and to love him with all our heart, with all our mind and with all our soul and with all our strength; to worship him and to give him thanks, to put our whole trust in him, to call upon him, to honour his holy name and his Word, and to serve him truly all the days of our life.

47. In all our necessities we ought to have recourse unto God by prayer, assuring ourselves that whatsoever we ask of the Father in the name of his Son (our only mediator and intercessor) Christ Jesus, and according to his will, he will undoubtedly grant it.

48. We ought to prepare our hearts before we pray and understand the things that we ask when we pray, that both our hearts and voices may together sound in the ears of God's Majesty.

49. When Almighty God smiteth us with affliction, or some great calamity hangeth over us, or any other weighty cause so requireth, it is our duty to humble ourselves in fasting, to bewail our sins with a sorrowful heart and to addict ourselves to earnest prayer, that it might please God to turn his wrath from us, or supply us with such graces as we greatly stand in need of.

50. Fasting is a withholding of meat, drink and all natural food, with other outward delights, from the body, for the determined time of fasting. As for those abstinences which are appointed by public order of our state, for eating of fish and forebearing of flesh at certain times and days appointed, they are no ways meant to be religious fasts, nor intended for the maintenance of any superstition in the choice of meats, for provision of things tending to the better preservation of the commonwealth.

51. We must not fast with this persuasion in mind, that our fasting can bring us to heaven, or ascribe holiness in the outward work wrought. For God alloweth not our fast for the work's sake (which of itself is a thing merely indifferent), but chiefly respecteth the heart, how it is affected therein. It is therefore requisite that first before all things we cleanse our hearts from sin, and then direct our fast to such ends as God will allow to be good; that the flesh may thereby be chastised, the spirit may be more fervent in prayer, and that our fasting may be a testimony of our humble submission to God's Majesty, when we acknowledge our sins unto him, and are inwardly touched with sorrowfulness of heart, bewailing the same in the affliction of our bodies.

52. All worship devised by man's fantasy, besides or contrary to the Scripture (as wandering on pilgrimages, setting up of candles, stations and jubilees, pharisaical sects and feigned religions, praying upon beads and suchlike superstition) hath not only no promise of reward in Scripture, but contrariwise, threatenings and maledictions.

53. All manner of expressing God the Father, the Son and the Holy Ghost in an outward form is utterly unlawful. As also all other images devised or made by man to the use of religion.

54. All religious worship ought to be given to God alone, from whom all goodness, health and grace ought to be both asked and looked for, as from the very author and giver of the same, and from none other.

55. The name of God is to be used with all reverence and holy respect, and therefore all vain and rash swearing is to be utterly condemned. Yet notwithstanding upon lawful occasions, an oath may be given and taken according to the Word of God, justice, judgement and truth.

56. The first day of the week, which is the Lord's Day, is wholly to be dedicated unto the service of God, and therefore we are bound therein to rest from our common and daily business, and to bestow that leisure upon holy exercises, both public and private.

11. Of the Civil Magistrate

57. The King's Majesty under God hath the sovereign and chief power within his realms and dominions, over all manner of persons of what estate, either ecclesiastical or civil, soever they be; so as no other foreign power hath or ought to have any superiority over them.

58. We do profess that the supreme government of all estates within the said realms and dominions, in all causes, as well ecclesiastical as temporal, doth of right appertain to the King's Highness. Neither do we give unto him hereby the administration of the Word and Sacraments, or the power of the keys; but that prerogative only, which we see to have been always given unto all godly princes in Holy Scripture by God himself; that is, that he should contain all estates and degrees committed to his charge by God, whether they be ecclesiastical or civil, within their duty, and restrain the stubborn and evil doers with the power of the civil sword.

59. The Pope, neither of himself nor by any authority of the Church or See of Rome, or by any other means with any other, hath any power or authority to depose the King, or to dispose any of his kingdoms or dominions, or to authorize any other prince to invade or annoy him in his countries, or to discharge any of his subjects of their allegiance and obedience to his Majesty, or to give license or leave to any of them to bear arms, raise tumult, or to offer any violence or hurt to his royal person, state or government, or to any of his subjects within his Majesty's dominions.

60. That princes which be excommunicated or deprived by the Pope may be deposed or murdered by their subjects, or any other whatsoever, is impious doctrine.

61. The laws of the realm may punish Christian men with death for heinous and grievous offences.

62. It is lawful for Christian men, at the commandment of the magistrate, to bear arms and to serve in just wars.

12. Of our Duty towards our Neighbours

63. Our duty towards our neighbours is to love them as ourselves, and to do to all men as we would they should do to us; to honour and obey our superiors, to preserve the safety of men's persons, as also their chastity, goods and good names, to bear no malice nor hatred in our hearts, to keep our bodies in temperance, soberness and chastity, to be true and just in all our doings, not to covet other men's goods, but labour truly to get our own living, and to do our duty in that estate of life unto which it pleaseth God to call us.

64. For the preservation of the chastity of men's persons, wedlock is commanded unto all men that stand in need thereof. Neither is there any prohibition by the Word of God, but that the ministers of the Church may enter into the state of matrimony, they being nowhere commanded by God's Law either to vow the estate of single life or to abstain from marriage. Therefore it is lawful also for them, as well as for all other Christian men, to marry at their own discretion, as they shall judge the same to serve better unto godliness.

65. The riches and goods of Christians are not common, as touching the right, title and possession of the same, as certain Anabaptists falsely affirm. Notwithstanding, every man ought of such things as he possesseth, liberally to give alms to the poor, according to his ability.

66. Faith given is to be kept, even with heretics and infidels.

67. The popish doctrine of equivocation and mental reservation is most ungodly and tendeth plainly to the subversion of all human society.

13. Of the Church and Outward Ministry of the Gospel

68. There is but one Catholic Church (out of which there is no salvation) containing the universal company of all the saints that ever were, are or shall be, gathered together in one body, under one head Christ Jesus; part whereof is already in heaven triumphant, part as yet militant, here upon earth. And because this Church consisteth of all those, and those alone, which are elected by God unto salvation, and regenerated by the power of his Spirit, the number of whom is known only unto God himself; therefore it is called Catholic or universal, and the Invisible Church.

69. But particular and visible churches (consisting of those who make profession of the faith of Christ and live under the outward means of salvation) be many in number; wherein the more or less sincerely, according to Christ's institution, the Word of God is taught, the sacraments are administered and the authority of the keys is used, the more or less pure are such churches to be accounted.

70. Although in the visible Church the evil be ever mingled with the good, and sometimes the evil have chief authority in the ministration of the Word and Sacraments; yet, forasmuch as they do not the same in their own name, but in Christ's, and minister by his commission and authority, we may use their ministry both in hearing the Word and in receiving the Sacraments. Neither is the effect of Christ's ordinance taken away by their wickedness, nor the grace of God's gifts diminished from such as by faith and rightly do receive the sacraments ministered unto them; which are effectual because of Christ's institution and promise, although they be ministered by evil men. Nevertheless, it appertaineth to the discipline of the Church that inquiry be made of evil ministers, and that they be accused by those that have knowledge of their offences, and finally being found guilty, by just judgement be deposed.

71. It is not lawful for any man to take upon him the office of public preaching or ministering the sacraments in the Church unless he be first lawfully called and sent to execute the same. And those we ought to judge lawfully called and sent, which be chosen and called to this work by men who have public authority given them in the Church, to call and send ministers into the Lord's vineyard.

72. To have public prayer in the Church, or to administer the sacraments in a tongue not understood of the people is a thing plainly repugnant to the Word of God and the custom of the primitive Church.

73. That person which by public denunciation of the Church is rightly cut off from the unity of the Church and excommunicate, ought to be taken of the whole multitude of the faithful as a heathen and publican, until by repentance he be openly reconciled and received into the Church by the judgement of such as have authority in that behalf.

74. God hath given power to his ministers not simply to forgive sins (which prerogative he hath reserved only to himself) but in his name to declare and pronounce unto such as truly repent and unfeignedly believe his Holy Gospel, the absolution and forgiveness of sins. Neither is it God's pleasure that his people should be tied to make a particular confession of all their known sins unto any mortal man; howsoever any person grieved in his conscience, upon any special cause, may well resort unto any godly and learned minister, to receive advice and comfort at his hands.

14. Of the Authority of the Church, General Councils and Bishop of Rome

75. It is not lawful for the Church to ordain anything that is contrary to God's Word, neither may it so expound one place of Scripture that it be repugnant to another. Wherefore, although the Church be a witness and a keeper of Holy Writ, yet as it ought not to decree anything against the same, so besides the same ought it not enforce anything to be believed upon necessity of salvation.

76. General Councils may not be gathered together without the commandment and will of princes, and when they be gathered together (forasmuch as they be an assembly of men not always governed with the Spirit and Word of God) they may err, and sometimes have erred even in things pertaining to the rule of piety. Wherefore things ordained by them, as necessary to

salvation, have neither strength nor authority, unless it may be shown that they be taken out of Holy Scriptures.

77. Every particular church hath authority to institute, to change and clean to put away ceremonies and other ecclesiastical rites, as they be superfluous or abused; and to constitute other, making more to seemliness, to order or edification.

78. As the Churches of Jerusalem, Alexandria and Antioch have erred, so also the Church of Rome hath erred, not only in those things which concern matters of practice and point of ceremonies, but also in matters of faith.

79. The power which the Bishop of Rome now challengeth to be Supreme Head of the universal Church of Christ and to be above all emperors, kings and princes, is a usurped power, contrary to the Scriptures and Word of God, and contrary to the example of the primitive Church; and therefore is for most just causes taken away and abolished within the King's Majesty's realms and dominions.

80. The Bishop of Rome is so far from being the supreme head of the universal church of Christ that his works and doctrine do plainly discover him to be "that man of sin" foretold in the Holy Scriptures, "whom the Lord shall consume with the spirit of his mouth, and abolish with the brightness of his coming."

15. Of the State of the Old and New Testament

81. In the Old Testament the commandments of the Law were more largely, and the promises of Christ more sparingly and darkly propounded, shadowed with a multitude of types and figures, and so much the more generally and obscurely delivered as the manifesting of them was further off.

82. The Old Testament is not contrary to the New. For both in the Old and New Testament everlasting life is offered to mankind by Christ, who is the only Mediator between God and man, being both God and man. Wherefore they are not to be heard, which feign that the old Fathers did look only for transitory promises. For they looked for all benefits of God the Father through the merits of his Son Jesus Christ, as we now do; only they believed in Christ which should come, we in Christ already come.

83. The New Testament is full of grace and truth, bringing joyful tidings unto mankind, that whatsoever formerly was promised of Christ is now accomplished; and so instead of the ancient types and ceremonies, exhibiteth the things themselves, with a large and clear declaration of all the benefits of the Gospel. Neither is the ministry thereof restrained any longer to one circumcised nation, but is indifferently propounded unto all people, whether they be Jews or Gentiles. So that there is now no nation which can truly complain that they be shut forth from the communion of saints and the liberties of the people of God.

84. Although the Law given from God by Moses as touching ceremonies and rites be abolished, and the civil precepts thereof be not of necessity to be received in any commonwealth; yet notwithstanding, no Christian man whatsoever is freed from the obedience of the commandments which are called moral.

16. Of the Sacraments of the New Testament

85. The Sacraments ordained by Christ be not only badges or tokens of Christian men's profession, but rather certain, sure witnesses and effectual or powerful signs of grace and God's good will towards us, by which he doth work invisibly in us, and not only quicken but also strengthen and confirm our faith in him.

86. There be two sacraments ordained of Christ our Lord in the Gospel, that is to say, Baptism and the Lord's Supper.

87. Those five which by the Church of Rome are called sacraments, to wit, Confirmation, Penance, Orders, Matrimony and Extreme Unction, are not to be accounted sacraments of the Gospel, being such as have partly grown from corrupt imitation of the Apostles, partly are states of life allowed in the Scriptures, but yet have not like nature of sacraments with Baptism and the Lord's Supper, for that they have not any visible sign or ceremony ordained of God, together with a promise of saving grace annexed thereunto.

88. The sacraments were not ordained of Christ to be gazed upon, or to be carried about, but that we should duly use them. And in such only as worthily receive the same, they have a wholesome effect and operation; but they that receive them unworthily thereby draw judgement upon themselves.

17. Of Baptism

89. Baptism is not only an outward sign of our profession and a note of difference whereby Christians are discerned from such as are no Christians, but much more a sacrament of our admission into the Church, sealing unto us our new birth (and consequently our justification, adoption and sanctification) by the communion which we have with Jesus Christ.

90. The baptism of infants is to be retained in the Church as agreeable to the Word of God.

91. In the administration of baptism, exorcism, oil, salt, spittle and superstitious hallowing of the water are for just causes abolished, and without them the sacrament is fully and perfectly administered, to all intents and purposes, agreeable to the institution of our Saviour Christ.

18. Of the Lord's Supper

92. The Lord's Supper is not only a sign of the mutual love which Christians ought to bear one towards another, but much more a sacrament of our preservation in the Church, sealing unto us our spiritual nourishment and continual growth in Christ.

93. The change of the substance of bread and wine into the substance of the body and blood of Christ, commonly called Transubstantiation, cannot be proved by Holy Writ, but is repugnant to plain testimonies of the Scripture, overthroweth the nature of a sacrament, and hath given occasion to most gross idolatry and manifold superstitions.

94. In the outward part of the Holy Communion the body and blood of Christ is in a most lively manner represented, being not otherwise present with the visible elements than things signified and sealed are present with the signs and seals, that is to say, symbolically and relatively. But in the inward and spiritual part the same body and blood is really and substantially presented unto all those that believe in his name. And unto such as in this manner do worthily testify and with faith repair unto the Lord's table, the body and blood of Christ is not only signified and offered, but also truly exhibited and communicated.

95. The body of Christ is given, taken and eaten in the Lord's Supper only after an heavenly and spiritual manner, and the mean whereby the body of Christ is thus received and eaten is faith.

96. The wicked, and such as want a lively faith, although they do carnally and visibly (as St Augustine speaketh) press with their teeth the sacrament of the body and blood of Christ, yet in no wise are they made partakers of Christ, but rather to their condemnation do eat and drink the sign or sacrament of so great a thing.

97. Both the parts of the Lord's sacrament, according to Christ's institution and the practice of the ancient Church, ought to be ministered unto God's people, and it is plain sacrilege to rob them of the mystical cup, for whom Christ hath shed his most precious blood.

98. The sacrament of the Lord's Supper was not by Christ's ordinance reserved, carried about, lifted up or worshipped.

99. The sacrifice of the mass, wherein the priest is said to offer up Christ for obtaining the remission of pain or guilt for the quick and the dead, is neither agreeable to Christ's ordinance nor grounded upon doctrine apostolic, but contrariwise most ungodly and most injurious to that all-sufficient sacrifice of our Saviour Christ, offered once for ever upon the cross, which is the only propitiation and satisfaction for all our sins.

100. Private mass, that is the receiving of the Eucharist by the priest alone, without a competent number of communicants, is contrary to the institution of Christ.

19. Of the State of the Souls of Men, after they be Departed out of this Life; together with the General Resurrection and the Last Judgement

101. After this life is ended, the souls of God's children be presently received into heaven, there to enjoy unspeakable comforts; the souls of the wicked are cast into hell, there to endure endless torments.

102. The doctrine of the Church of Rome, concerning *limbus patrum, limbus puerorum*, purgatory, prayer for the dead, pardons, adorations of images and relics and also invocation of saints, is vainly invented without all warrant of Holy Scripture, yea and is contrary unto the same.

103. At the end of this world the Lord Jesus shall come in the clouds with the glory of his Father, at which time, by the almighty power of God, the living shall be changed and the dead shall be raised; and all shall appear both in body and soul before his judgement seat, to receive according to that which they have done in their bodies, whether good or evil.

104. When the last judgement is finished, Christ shall deliver up the kingdom to his Father and God shall be all in all.

20. The Decree of the Synod

(105.) If any minister, of what degree or quality soever he be, shall publicly teach any doctrine contrary to these Articles agreed upon, if, after due admonition, he do not conform himself and cease to disturb the peace of the Church, let him be silenced and deprived of all spiritual promotions he doth enjoy.

43. THE CANONS OF THE SYNOD OF DORT, 1619

History

The Synod of Dort (Dordrecht) was called in 1618 to debate the Articles put forward in 1612 by the Remonstrants, a group of Dutch theologians who followed the teachings of Jacob Arminius (1560-1609), and rejected the strict Calvinism of the majority of Dutch divines at that time. The appearance of these Articles set off a storm in the Dutch Reformed Church, which reverberated across Protestant Europe. In response to an invitation from Holland, James I (1603-1625) sent a delegation from the Church of England to the Synod of Dort, which condemned the Articles, and propounded what has since become the classical, "Calvinist" understanding of grace and salvation. The Canons of Dort were never officially ratified by the Church of England, but they came to represent what the "Calvinist" party within the Church stood for. During the reign of James I this party was in the ascendant, and the Canons of Dort were very nearly ratified in 1625. But the King's death changed matters, and Charles I (1625-1649) was not prepared to endorse Calvinism in this form.

The Synod of Dort had little effect on the Church of England, but it marked the beginning of a special relationship between Dutch and British Protestants which eventually culminated in the reign of William III of Orange as King of England (1689-1702). William secured a Protestant settlement of the Church which remains the basis of the constitution of the United Kingdom to this day. The Latin text of the Canons is published in P. Schaff, *The Creeds of Christendom*, New York, 1931, pp. 550-580. This English edition has been prepared from that text, incorporating the parts of it given in translation by Schaff (*ibid.* pp. 581-597).

Theology

The Remonstrant Articles of 1612 taught the following five points as being "agreeable to the Word of God":

1. *That God, by an eternal, unchangeable purpose in Jesus Christ his Son, before the foundation of the world, has determined, out of the fallen, sinful race of men, to save in Christ, for Christ's sake, and through Christ, those who, through the grace of the Holy Spirit, shall believe on his Son Jesus, and shall persevere in this faith and obedience of faith, through this grace, even to the end; and on the other hand, to leave the incorrigible and unbelieving in sin and under wrath, and to condemn them as alien to Christ, according to the word of the Gospel*

(Jn 3:36): "He who believes on the Son has everlasting life, and he who does not believe the Son shall not see life, but the wrath of God abides in him", and according to other passages of Scripture also.

2. *That according to this, Jesus Christ, the Saviour of the world, died for all men and for every man, so that he has obtained for them all, by his death on the cross, redemption and the forgiveness of sins; yet that no-one actually enjoys this forgiveness of sins except the believer, according to the word of the Gospel (Jn 3:16): "God so loved the world that he gave his only-begotten Son, that whoever believes in him should not perish, but have everlasting life." And in I Jn 2:2: "And he is the propitiation for our sins, and not for ours only, but also for the sins of the whole world."*

3. *That man does not have saving grace of himself, nor of the energy of his free will, inasmuch as he, in the state of apostasy and sin, can of and by himself neither think, will, nor do anything that is truly good (such as saving faith essentially is); but that it is needful that he be born again of God in Christ, through his Holy Spirit, and renewed in understanding, inclination or will, and all his powers, in order that he may rightly understand, think, will and effect what is truly good, according to the Word of Christ (Jn 15:5): "Without me you can do nothing."*

4. *That this grace of God is the beginning, continuance and accomplishment of all good, even to this extent, that the regenerate man himself, without prevenient or assisting, awakening, following and co-operative grace, can neither think, will, nor do good, nor withstand any temptation to evil; so that all good deeds or movements, that can be conceived, must be ascribed to the grace of God in Christ. But as respects the mode of the operation of this grace, it is not irresistible, inasmuch as it is written concerning many, that they have resisted the Holy Spirit (Ac 7 and elsewhere in many places).*

5. *That those who are incorporated into Christ by a true faith, and have thereby become partakers of his life-giving Spirit, have thereby full power to strive against Satan, sin, the world and their own flesh, and to win the victory; it being well understood that it is ever through the assisting grace of the Holy Spirit, and that Jesus Christ assists them through his Spirit in all temptations, extends to them his hand, and if only they are ready for the conflict, and desire his help, and are not inactive, keeps them from falling, so that they, by no craft or power of Satan, can be misled nor plucked out of Christ's hands, according to the Word of Christ (Jn 10:28): "Neither shall any man pluck them out of my hand". But whether they are capable, through negligence, or forsaking again the first beginnings of their life in Christ, of again returning to this present evil world, of turning away from the holy doctrine which was delivered to them, of losing a good conscience, of becoming devoid of grace, that must be more particularly determined out of Holy Scripture, before we ourselves can teach it with the full persuasion of our minds.*

It was to counter these arguments that the Synod of Dort convened and established what has since become the classical, "Calvinist" understanding of grace and salvation. Within the Church of England there were many who were sympathetic to the Remonstrants, but to call them an "Arminian party" would be going too far. Only later, in the eighteenth century, is it really possible to speak of "Arminians" as opposed to Calvinists. Anglican Arminianism is best represented by John Wesley and the Methodists, while its Calvinist counterpart is usually associated with Wesley's contemporary, George Whitefield, and the Evangelical tradition within the Church of England.

Preface

In the name of our Lord and Saviour Jesus Christ, Amen.

Among the many consolations which our Lord and Saviour Jesus Christ has given to the Church militant in this wretched pilgrimage, that is justly celebrated, which he left to it when he was about to go to the Father, his sanctuary in heaven, saying: *I am with you always, even to the end of the world.* The truth of this most sweet promise shines in the Church of every age, when from the beginning it was assailed not only by the open violence of its enemies and the impiety of heretics, but also by the covert cleverness of seducers, so that if the Lord had ever deprived the Church of the saving defence of his presence, it would either have been oppressed by the power of tyrants or been seduced into error by the deception of impostors. But the Good Shepherd himself, who continually loves his flock for which he laid down his life, has always miraculously put down, often by his outstretched right arm, the raging fever of the persecutors, and has thwarted and dissipated the tortuous ways of the seducers and their deceptive counsels, by both which activities he demonstrates that he is most present in the Church. An illustrious record of this exists in the histories of pious emperors, kings and princes, whom the Son of God has so often raised up in defence of his Church, whom he has set ablaze with the holy zeal of his house, and by whose work he has not only quelled the furor of tyrants, but also obtained for the Church the remedies of holy synods, when it was torn apart by false teachers who were corrupting religion in their different ways. In these activities the faithful servants of Christ have by their common prayers, counsels and labours for the Church and the truth of God stood fast, opposing themselves with valour against the servants of Satan, even if they turned themselves into angels of light; they have endured the planting of errors and discord and preserved the Church in the harmony of true religion, and have transmitted the true worship of God to their descendants undiluted.

By a similar blessing, our faithful Saviour has borne witness to his gracious presence with the Dutch Church, which has been afflicted now for many years. For this Church, delivered by the powerful hand of God from the tyranny of the Roman Antichrist and the horrible idolatry of Popery, and so often miraculously protected in the dangers of everyday warfare, and flourishing in the harmony of true doctrine and discipline, to the praise of

God, to the admirable increase of the state and to the joy of the whole Reformed world, has Jacob Arminius and his party, calling themselves Remonstrants, tried by various errors, some new, some old, at first secretly and then openly. And having thoroughly disturbed the Church by scandalous divisions and dissensions, they had brought matters to such a pass that had the mercy of our Saviour not intervened at the right moment, they would have set a flourishing Church on fire with horrible disagreements and schisms. But blessed be the Lord for ever, who after hiding his face from us (who have provoked his wrath and indignation in many ways), has borne witness to the whole world that he has not forgotten his Covenant, nor spurned the desires of his servants. For when scarcely any hope of salvation appeared to the human eye, he inspired this mind in the illustrious and powerful States General of the Dutch federation, that by the counsel and direction of the illustrious and strong Prince of Orange, the right means, which were used by the Apostles and which have proved their worth in the long history of the Church since their time, and which have already been used with good effect in the Dutch Church, should be used to avoid these oppressive evils, and that they should by their own authority convene a synod of all the provinces represented (i.e. in the States-General, ed.) at Dordrecht, with theologians sent to it by the favour of the most high and mighty King of Great Britain, James, and by the most illustrious princes, counts and republics, so that by the convocation of so many serious theologians, and by the common judgement of so many theologians of the Reformed Church, these doctrines of Arminius and his party might be condemned accurately, and from the Word of God alone; true doctrine might be established and the false rejected, and harmony, peace and tranquillity might be restored to the Dutch Churches by the blessing of God. For this is God's blessing, in which the Dutch Churches rejoice, humbly acknowledging and gratefully proclaiming the mercies of their faithful Saviour.

Therefore this esteemed synod (by the authority of the supreme magistrate over all others in the Dutch churches, for averting the wrath of God and imploring his gracious aid, by the proclamation and celebration of prayers and fasting), gathered together at Dordrecht in the Lord's name, fired with love for the majesty of God and the salvation of the Church, and after calling upon the name of God, bound by sacred oath to use only Holy Scripture as the norm for making its judgements, and that in the discerning and judging of this case, to exercise a good and honest conscience, has acted with such care and patience, as to induce the principal defenders of these (sc. false, ed.) doctrines, who have been called to appear before it, to accept its opinion of the above named five chapters of doctrine, and the reasons for them, which are to be more fully expounded. But since they have rejected the summons of the synod, or (which amounts to the same thing) refused to answer its questions, and since they have paid no attention either to the warnings of the synod or to the entreaties of the Delegates to the most generous and comprehensive States-General, or above all to the commands of these same high and mighty Delegates of the States-General, the synod had been obliged to embark on another course, by the command of its Lords and by the custom already long ago adopted in the ancient synods, and on the basis of documents, confessions and declarations, some of which have appeared previously and some of which are presented here for the first time, to begin an examination of the five points of doctrine. And as by the special grace of God, the greatest diligence, faith and conscientiousness, agreement has been achieved on each and every point, this synod, to the glory of God and mindful of the integrity of saving truth, the quietness of consciences, and the peace and safety of the Dutch church, following its decision, has ordered it to be published, together with which its opinion, agreeable to the Word of God, concerning the aforementioned five points of doctrine, is set out, and false opinions contrary to the Word of God are rejected.

01. Of Divine Predestination

01. As all men have sinned in Adam, lie under the curse, and are obnoxious to eternal death, God would have done no injustice by leaving them all to perish, and delivering them over to condemnation on account of sin, according to the words of the Apostle (Ro 3:19): *that every mouth may be stopped, and all the world may become guilty before God*; (v. 23): *for all have sinned and come short of the glory of God*; and Ro 6:23: *for the wages of sin is death.*

02. But *in this the love of God was manifested, that he sent his only-begotten Son into the world; that whosoever believeth on him should not perish, but have everlasting life* (I Jn 4:9; Jn 3:16).

03. And that men may be brought to believe, God mercifully sends the messengers of these most joyful tidings to whom he will, and at what time he pleaseth; by whose ministry men are called to repentance and faith in Christ crucified. *How then shall they call on him in whom they have not believed? And how shall they believe in him of whom they have not heard? And how shall they hear without a preacher? And how shall they preach, except they be sent?* (Ro 10:14-15).

04. The wrath of God abideth upon those who believe not this Gospel, but such as receive it, and embrace Jesus the Saviour by a true and living faith, are by him delivered from the wrath of God and from destruction, and have the gift of eternal life conferred upon them.

05. The cause or guilt of this unbelief, as well as of all other sins, is nowise in God, but in man himself; whereas faith in Jesus Christ and salvation through him is the free gift of God, as it is written: *By grace are ye saved through faith, and that not of yourselves, it is the gift of God* (Ep 2:8), and *Unto you it is given in the behalf of Christ, not only to believe on him*, etc. (Ph 1:29).

06. That some receive the gift of faith from God and others do not receive it proceeds from God's eternal decree. *For known unto God are all his works from the beginning of the world* (Ac 15:18; Ep 1:11). According to which decree he graciously softens the hearts of the elect, however obstinate, and inclines them to believe; while he leaves the non-elect in his just judgement to their own wickedness and obduracy. And herein is especially displayed the profound, the merciful, and at the same time the righteous discrimination between men, equally involved in ruin; or that decree of election and reprobation, revealed in the Word of God, which, though men of perverse, impure and unstable minds wrest it to their own destruction, yet to holy and pious souls affords unspeakable consolation.

07. Election is the unchangeable purpose of God whereby, before the foundation of the world, he hath out of mere grace, according to the sovereign good pleasure of his own will, chosen from the whole human race, which had fallen through their own fault, from their primitive state of rectitude, into sin and destruction, a certain number of persons to redemption in Christ, whom he from eternity appointed the Mediator and head of the elect, and the foundation of salvation.

This elect number, though by nature neither better nor more deserving than others, but with them involved in one common misery, God hath decreed to give to Christ to be saved by him and effectually to call and draw them to his communion by his Word and Spirit; to bestow upon them true faith, justification and sanctification; and having powerfully preserved them in the fellowship of his Son, finally to glorify them for the demonstration of his mercy, and for the praise of the riches of his glorious grace, as it is written: *According as he hath chosen us in him before the foundation of the world, that we should be holy and without blame before him in love; having predestinated us unto the adoption of children by Jesus Christ to himself, according to the good pleasure of his will, to the praise of the glory of his grace wherein he hath made us accepted in the Beloved* (Ep 1:4-6). And elsewhere: *Whom he did predestinate, them he also called, and whom he called, them he also justified, and whom he justified, them he also glorified* (Ro 8:30).

08. There are not various decrees of election, but one and the same decree respecting all those who shall be saved both under the Old and New Testament; since the Scripture declares the good pleasure, purpose and counsel of the divine will to be one, according to which he hath chosen us from eternity, both to grace and glory, to salvation and the way of salvation, which he hath ordained that we should walk therein.

09. This election was not founded upon foreseen faith, and the obedience of faith, holiness or any other good quality or disposition in man, as the prerequisite, cause or condition on which it depended; but men are chosen to faith and to the obedience of faith, holiness, etc. Therefore election is the fountain of every saving good; from which proceed faith, holiness and the other gifts of salvation, and finally eternal life itself, as its fruits and effects, according to that of the Apostle. *He hath chosen us* (not because we were, but) *that we should be holy and without blame before him in love* (Ep 1:4).

10. The good pleasure of God is the sole cause of this gracious election, which doth not consist herein that God, foreseeing all possible qualities of human actions, elected certain of these as a condition of salvation, but that he was pleased out of the common mass of sinners to adopt some certain persons as a peculiar people to himself, as it is written: *For the children being not yet born, neither having done any good or evil*, etc., *it was said* (namely, to Rebecca), *the elder shall serve the younger, as it is written: Jacob have I loved, but Esau have I hated* (Ro 9:11-13) and *As many as were ordained to eternal life believed* (Ac 13:48).

11. And as God himself is most wise, unchangeable, omniscient and omnipotent, so the election made by him can neither be interrupted nor changed, recalled nor annulled; neither can the elect be cast away, not their number diminished.

12. The elect, in due time, though in various degrees and in different measures, attain the assurance of this their eternal and unchangeable election, not by inquisitively prying into the secret and deep things of God, but by observing in themselves, with a spiritual joy and holy pleasure, the infallible fruits of election pointed out in the Word of God; such as a true faith in Christ, filial fear, a godly sorrow for sin, a hungering and thirsting after righteousness, etc.

13. The sense and certainty of this election afford to the children of God additional matter for daily humiliation before him, for adoring the depth of his mercies and rendering grateful returns of ardent love to him who first manifested so great love towards them. The consideration of this doctrine of election is so far from encouraging remissness in the observance of the divine commands, or from sinking men into carnal security, that these, in the just judgement of God, are the usual effects of rash presumption or of idle and wanton trifling with the grace of election, in those who refuse to walk in the ways of the elect.

14. As the doctrine of divine election by the most wise counsel of God was declared by the Prophets, by Christ himself, and by the Apostles, and is clearly revealed in the Scriptures both of the Old and New Testament, so it is still to be published in due time and place in the Church of God, for which it was peculiarly designed, provided it be done with reverence, in the spirit of discretion and piety, for the glory of God's most holy name, and for enlivening and comforting his people, without vainly attempting to investigate the secret ways of the Most High.

15. What peculiarly tends to illustrate and recommend to us the eternal and unmerited grace of election is the express testimony of Sacred Scripture, that not all, but some only are elected, while others are passed by in the eternal decree; whom God, out of his sovereign, most just, irreprehensible and unchangeable good pleasure, hath decreed to leave in the common misery into which they have wilfully plunged themselves, and not to bestow upon them saving faith and the grace of conversion; but permitting them in his just judgement to follow their own way; at last, for the declaration of his justice, to condemn and punish them for ever, not only on account of their unbelief, but also for all their other sins. And this is the decree of reprobation which by no means makes God the author of sin (the very thought of which is blasphemy), but declares him to be an awful, irreprehensible and righteous judge and avenger.

16. Those who do not yet experience a lively faith in Christ, an assured confidence of soul, peace of conscience, an earnest endeavour after filial obedience, and glorying in God through Christ, efficaciously wrought in them, and do nevertheless persist int he use of the means which God hath appointed for working these graces in us, ought not to be alarmed at the mention of reprobation, nor to rank themselves among the reprobate, but diligently to persevere in the use of means, and with ardent desires devoutly and humbly to wait for a season of richer grace. Much less cause have they to be terrified by the doctrine of reprobation, who, though they seriously desire to be turned to God, to please him only, and to be delivered from the body of death, cannot yet reach that measure of holiness and faith to which they aspire; since a merciful God has promised that he will not quench the smoking flax nor break the bruised reed. But this doctrine is justly terrible to those who, regardless of God and of the Saviour Jesus Christ, have wholly given themselves up to the cares of the world and the pleasures of the flesh, so long as they are not seriously converted to God.

17. Since we are to judge of the will of God from his Word, which testifies that the children of believers are holy, not by nature, but in virtue of the covenant of grace, in which they together with the parents are comprehended, godly parents have no reason to doubt of the election and salvation of their children whom it pleaseth God to call out of this life in their infancy.

18. To those who murmur at the free grace of election, and just severity of reprobation, we answer with the Apostle: *Nay but, O man, who art thou that repliest against God?* (Ro 9:20), and quote the language of our Saviour: *Is it not lawful for me to do what I will with mine own?* (Mt 20:15). And therefore with holy adoration of these mysteries, we exclaim in the words of the Apostle: *O the depth of the riches both of the wisdom and knowledge of God! How unsearchable are his judgements, and his ways past finding out! For who hath known the mind of the Lord, or who hath been his counsellor? Or who hath first given to him, and it shall be recompensed unto him again? For of him, and through him and to him are all things: to whom be glory for ever. Amen.* (Ro 11:33-36).

Rejection of Errors

The synod rejects the errors of those who teach that:

01. "The Will of God concerning the salvation of those who will believe

and persevere in faith and in the obedience of faith is the full and complete decree of election to salvation, nor is anything else concerning this decree revealed in the Word of God." For these men do harm to the simple and openly contradict Holy Scripture, which testifies that God does not only will to save those who will believe, but also that he has elected certain particular men from eternity, and given them faith and perseverance in Christ ahead of others in time, as it is written: *I have made thy name manifest unto those men whom thou hast given me* (Jn 17:6). And: *As many as were ordained to eternal life believed* (Ac 13:48). And *He chose us before the foundations of the world were laid, that we should be holy*, etc. (Ep 1:4).

02. "The election of God to eternal life is many-sided; there is one which is general and indefinite and another which is particular and definite. The first of these is incomplete, revocable, not peremptory but conditional. The other is complete, irrevocable, peremptory and absolute. Also, there is one election to justifying faith without peremptory election to salvation." For this is an idea of the mind invented apart from the Scriptures which corrupts the doctrine of election and dissolves the golden chain of salvation. *Whom he predestined, those he also called; and whom he called, those he also justified; and whom he justified, those he also glorified* (Ro 8:30).

03. "The good pleasure and will of God, which Scripture records in the doctrine of election, does not consist in the fact that God has elected some men and not others, but in the fact that God, out of all possible conditions (among which the works of the Law are included), or out of the order of all things, has elected an act of faith, worthless in itself, and the imperfect obedience of faith as a condition of salvation; and has graciously counted it as perfect obedience, and worth the prize of eternal life." For by this pernicious error God's good pleasure and Christ's merit are undermined, and men are called away from the truth of free justification and the simplicity of the Scriptures by useless questions; and this is the sign of a false Apostle. *God has called us with a holy calling, not by works but by his will and grace, which was given to us in Christ Jesus before all ages.* (II Ti 1:9).

04. "This condition is necessary for election to faith, that a man must make right use of the light of nature, be honest, meek, humble and disposed to eternal life, as if election were somehow dependent on this kind of thing." For they know Pelagius, and as false teachers scarcely conceal their imitation of the Apostle, who wrote: *For once we all lived in the passions of our flesh, following the desires of body and mind, and so we were by nature children of wrath, like the rest of mankind. But God, who is rich in mercy, out of the great love with which he loved us, even when we were dead through our trespasses, made us alive together with Christ (by grace you have been saved), and raised us up with him, and*

made us sit with him in the heavenly places in Christ Jesus. For by grace you have been saved through faith; and this is not your own doing, it is the gift of God – not because of works, lest any man should boast." (Ep 2:3-9).

05. "The election of particular persons to salvation is incomplete and not peremptory, and comes about because of foreseen faith, repentance, holiness and piety begun and for a certain space of time continued. It becomes complete and peremptory by the final perseverance of foreseen faith, repentance, holiness and piety, and this is the gracious and evangelical dignity by which the one who is elect is better off than the one who is not. But faith, the obedience of faith, holiness, piety and perseverance are not the fruits or the effects of immutable election to glory, but conditions and causes fully required in advance, and foreseen, even appointed, without which there can be no election." This is completely contrary to Scripture, which throughout implants these and other similar sayings in our ears and hearts: *Election is not of works, but of him who calls* (Ro 9:11). *As many as were ordained to eternal life believed* (Ac 13:48). *He chose us in himself, that we might be holy* (Ep 1:4). *You did not choose me, but I chose you* (Jn 15:16). *If of grace, then not by works* (Ro 11:6). *In this is love, not that we loved God, but that he loved us and sent his Son* (I Jn 4:10).

06. "Not all election to salvation is immutable, but some of the elect, notwithstanding any decree of God, may perish and perish in eternity." By this crass error they make God mutable, and undermine the comfort which pious persons derive from the unchangeableness of their election, and contradict the Holy Scriptures which teach: *It is not possible to deceive the elect* (Mt 24:24). *Christ will not lose those who have been given to him by the Father* (Jn 6:39). *Whom God predestined, he called and justified and also glorified* (Ro 8:30).

07. "Of the immutable election to glory there is no fruit in this life, no indication and no certainty, except what is mutable and contingent." Apart from the fact that it is absurd to say that certainty is uncertain, they are contradicted by the experience of the saints, who with the Apostle rejoice at the sense of their election, who celebrate this blessing of God, who rejoice with the disciples according to the teaching of Christ, *because their names are written in heaven* (Lk 10:20) and who lastly oppose the sense of election to the fiery weapons of diabolical temptations, asking: *Who will bring any charge against God's elect?* (Ro 8:33).

08. "Out of the just measure of his will, God does not abandon anyone who has fallen in Adam and who lives in the common state of sin and damnation, nor does he withhold from them the knowledge of the grace necessary for faith and conversion." It is written: *He has mercy on those whom he wills, and he hardens those whom he wills* (Ro 9:18). And: *To*

you it is given to know the mysteries of the kingdom of heaven, but to them it is not given (Mt 13:11). And: *I glorify thee, Father, Lord of heaven and earth, because thou hast hidden these things from the wise and learned, and revealed them unto babes, for Father, it hath pleased thee to do this* (Mt 11:25-26).

09. "The reason why God sends the Gospel to one nation and not to another is not because this is his sole will and pleasure, but because this nation is better and more worthy than one to whom the Gospel has not been given." For Moses, addressing the people of Israel, claims: *Behold, to the Lord your God belong heaven and the heaven of heavens, the earth with all that is in it; yet the Lord set his heart in love upon your fathers and chose their descendants after them, you above all peoples, as at this day* (De 10:14-15). And Christ: *Woe to thee, Chorazin, woe to thee, Bethsaida, for if the things which have been done in you had been done in Tyre and Sidon, they would have repented in sackcloth and ashes* (Mt 11:21).

02. Of the Death of Christ and the Redemption of Men Thereby

01. God is not only supremely merciful, but also supremely just. And his justice requires (as he hath revealed himself in his Word), that our sins committed against his infinite majesty should be punished, not only with temporal but with eternal punishments, both in body and soul; which we cannot escape unless satisfaction be made to the justice of God.

02. Since therefore, we are unable to make that satisfaction in our own persons, or to deliver ourselves from the wrath of God, he hath been pleased of his infinite mercy to give his only-begotten Son for our surety, who was made sin and became a curse for us, and in our stead, that he might make satisfaction to divine justice on our behalf.

03. The death of the Son of God is the only and most perfect sacrifice and satisfaction for sin; is of infinite worth and value, abundantly sufficient to expiate the sins of the whole world.

04. This death derives its infinite value and dignity from these considerations because the person who submitted to it was not only really man and perfectly holy, but also the only-begotten Son of God, of the same eternal and infinite essence with the Father and the Holy Spirit, which qualifications were necessary to constitute him a Saviour for us, and because it was attended with a sense of the wrath and curse of God due to us for sin.

05. Moreover the promise of the Gospel is that whosoever believeth in Christ crucified shall not perish, but have everlasting life. This promise, together with the command to repent and believe, ought to be declared and published to all nations, and to all persons promiscuously and without distinction, to whom God out of his good pleasure sends the Gospel.

06. And whereas many who are called by the Gospel do not repent nor believe in Christ, but perish in unbelief; this is not owing to any defect or insufficiency in the sacrifice offered by Christ upon the cross, but is wholly to be imputed to themselves.

07. But as many as truly believe and are delivered and saved from sin and destruction through the death of Christ, are indebted for this benefit solely to the grace of God given them in Christ from everlasting, and not to any merit of their own.

08. For this was the sovereign counsel and most gracious will and purpose of God the Father, that the quickening and saving efficacy of the most precious death of his Son should extend to all the elect, for bestowing upon them alone the gift of justifying faith, thereby to bring them infallibly to salvation; that is, it was the will of God that Christ, by the blood of the cross, whereby he confirmed the new covenant, should effectually redeem out of every people, tribe, nation and language, all those and those only, who were from eternity chosen to salvation, and given to him by the Father; that he should confer upon them faith, which together with all the other saving gifts of the Holy Spirit, he purchased for them by his death; should purge them from all sin, both original and actual, whether committed before or after believing; and having faithfully preserved them even to the end, should at last bring them free from every spot and blemish to the enjoyment of glory in his own presence for ever.

09. This purpose proceeding from everlasting love towards the elect, has from the beginning of the world to this day, been powerfully accomplished, and will henceforward still continue to be accomplished, notwithstanding all the ineffectual opposition of the gates of hell; so that the elect in due time may be gathered together into one and that there never may be wanting a Church composed of believers, the foundation of which is laid in the blood of Christ, which may steadfastly love and serve him as their Saviour, who as a bridegroom for his bride, laid down his life for them upon the cross, and which may celebrate his praises here and through all eternity.

Rejection of Errors

The synod rejects the errors of those who teach that:

01. "Because God the Father sent his Son to death on the cross, without a certain or definite plan to save anyone in particular, so that the necessity, utility and value of the death of Christ can stand complete and whole, fully worked out and perfect, ready to be accepted, though the redemption thus gained is not applied to any individual by the act of Christ itself." This assertion is injurious to the wisdom of God the Father and the merit of Jesus Christ, and is contrary to Scripture. For thus says the Saviour: *I lay down my life for the sheep and I know them* (Jn

10:15,27). And concerning the Saviour, the prophet Isaiah says: *When he makes himself an offering for sin, he shall see his offspring, he shall prolong his days; the will of the Lord shall prosper in his hand* (Is 53:10). Lastly, it overturns an Article of Faith, by which we believe the Church.

02. "The death of Christ did not bring about a new covenant sealed by his blood, but simply satisfied the justice of the Father, so as to make possible a new covenant with men, whether of grace or of works." This is repugnant to Scripture, which teaches that Christ *has become the author and mediator of a new* (i.e. of a better) *covenant* (He 7:22). And: *A will takes effect only in death* (He 9:15,17).

03. Christ, by his satisfaction has not certainly merited salvation and faith, by which this satisfaction of Christ is effectively applied to salvation, for anyone, but has only acquired for the Father the power, or the full will, to act again among men, and to prescribe new conditions, of whatever kind he might wish, whose accomplishment depends on man's free will, and may be so done that either no-one or everyone might fulfil them." For these people think too little of the death of Christ, they do not recognize the firstfruits or the benefit imparted by it, and they call the Pelagian error back from hell.

04. "The new covenant of grace, which God the Father has established with men on the basis of the death of Christ, does not consist of the fact that by faith, which apprehends the merit of Christ, we are justified and saved before God; but in this, that God, having taken away the demand of perfect obedience under the Law, reckons this faith and the imperfect obedience of faith as if it were perfect obedience under the Law, and considers it worthy of the free gift of eternal life." For these people contradict Scripture: *They are freely justified by his grace, by the redemption made in Jesus Christ, whom God gave as a satisfaction through faith in his blood* (Ro 3:24-25). And with the impious Socinus, they introduce a new and strange kind of justification, against the entire consensus of the Church.

05. "All men are assumed into a state of reconciliation and the grace of the covenant, so that no-one is liable to damnation because of original sin, or will be condemned, but all are immune from the guilt of that sin." This opinion is repugnant to Scripture, which says that: *we are by nature children of wrath* (Ep 2:3).

06. "There is no distinction between reception and application, so that God, as far as he is able, wishes to confer the same benefits equally on all men, which are acquired by the death of Christ. However, some become partakers of the forgiveness of sins and of eternal life, before others do; the difference depending entirely on their own free will, which may accept grace given indifferently and not by a special gift of mercy, working effectively in them, so that they might apply this grace to themselves ahead of others." For these, though they pretend to put

forward this distinction in a sane way, in fact are trying to poison people with the dangerous venom of Pelagianism.

07. "Christ could not, should not and did not die for those whom God most loves, and has chosen for eternal life, since there is not need for Christ to die for them." These people contradict the Apostle, who says: *Christ loved me and gave himself for me* (Ga 2:20). And also: *Who is it who would lay any charge against God's elect? God is the only one who justifies, Who shall condemn? Christ is the one who has died* (especially for them)" (Ro 8:33-34). And they contradict the Saviour who affirms: *I lay down my life for the sheep* (Jn 10:15). And: *This is my commandment, that you love one another as I have loved you. Greater love hath no man than this, that a man lay down his life for his friends*" (Jn 15:12-13).

03/04. Of the Corruption of Man, his Conversion to God and the Manner thereof

01. Man was originally formed after the image of God. His understanding was adorned with a true and saving knowledge of his Creator and of spiritual things. His heart and will were upright, all his affections pure, and the whole man was holy; but revolting from God by the instigation of the Devil, and abusing the freedom of his own will, he forfeited these excellent gifts, and on the contrary entailed of himself blindness of mind, horrible darkness, vanity and perverseness of judgement; became wicked, rebellious and obdurate in heart and will, and impure in all his affections.

02. Man after the fall begat children in his own likeness. A corrupt stock produced a corrupt offspring. Hence all the posterity of Adam, Christ only excepted, have derived corruption from their original parent, not by imitation, as the Pelagians of old asserted, but by the propagation of a vicious nature in consequence of a just judgement of God.

03. Therefore all men are conceived in sin and are by nature children of wrath, incapable of any saving good, prone to evil, dead in sin and in bondage thereto; and without the regenerating grace of the Holy Spirit, they are neither able nor willing to return to God, to reform the depravity of their nature, nor to dispose themselves to reformation.

04. There remain however, in man since the fall, the glimmerings of natural light, whereby he retains some knowledge of God, of natural things, and of the difference between good and evil, and discovers some regard for virtue, good order in society, and for maintaining an orderly external deportment. But so far is this light of nature from being sufficient to bring him to a saving knowledge of God and to true conversion, that he is incapable of using it aright even in things natural and civil. Nay farther, this light, such as it is, man in various ways renders wholly polluted, and holds it back in unrighteousness; by doing which he becomes inexcusable before God.

05. In the same light are we to consider the law of the Decalogue, delivered by God to his peculiar people the Jews, by the hands of Moses. For though it discovers the greatness of sin, and more and more convinces man thereof, yet as it neither points out a remedy nor imparts strength to extricate him from misery, and thus being weak through the flesh leaves the transgression under the curse, man cannot by this law obtain saving grace.

06. What therefore, neither the light of nature nor the law could do, that God performs by the operation of his Holy Spirit through the word or ministry of reconciliation; which is the glad tidings concerning the Messiah, by means whereof it hath pleased God to save such as believe, as well under the Old as under the New Testament.

07. This mystery of his will God discovered to but a small number under the Old Testament; under the New, he reveals himself to many, without any distinction of people. The cause of this dispensation is not to be ascribed to the superior worth of one nation above another, nor to their making a better use of the light of nature, but results wholly from the sovereign good pleasure and unmerited love of God. Hence they to whom so great and so gracious a blessing is communicated, above their desert, or rather notwithstanding their demerits, are bound to acknowledge it with humble and grateful hearts, and with the apostle to adore, not curiously to pry into the severity and justice of God's judgements displayed in others, to whom this grace is not given.

08. As many as are called by the Gospel are unfeignedly called; for God hath most earnestly and truly declared in his Word what will be acceptable to him, namely, that all who are called should comply with the invitation. He moreover seriously promises eternal life and rest to as many as shall come to him, and believe on him.

09. It is not the fault of the Gospel, nor of Christ offered therein, nor of God, who calls men by the Gospel and confers upon them various gifts, that those who are called by the ministry of the Word refuse to come and be converted. The fault lies in themselves; some of whom when called, regardless of their danger, reject the Word of life; others, though they receive it, suffer it not to make a lasting impression on their heart; therefore their joy, arising only from a temporary faith, soon vanishes and they fall away; while others choke the seed of the Word by perplexing cares and the pleasures of this world, and produce no fruit. This our Saviour teaches in the parable of the sower (Mt 13).

10. But that others who are called by the Gospel obey the call and are converted, is not to be ascribed to the proper exercise of freewill, whereby one distinguishes himself above others equally furnished with grace sufficient for faith and conversion (as the proud heresy of Pelagius maintains); but it must be wholly ascribed to God, who, as he hath chosen his own from eternity in Christ, so he calls them effectually in time, confers upon them faith and repentance, rescues them from the power of darkness, and translates them into the kingdom of his own Son, that they may show forth the praises of him who hath called them out of darkness into his marvellous light; and may glory not in themselves but in the Lord, according to the testimony of the Apostles in various places.

11. But when God accomplishes his good pleasure in the elect, or works in them true conversion, he not only causes the Gospel to be externally preached to them, and powerfully illuminates their minds by his Holy Spirit, that they may rightly understand and discern the things of the Spirit of God, but by the efficacy of the same regenerating Spirit he pervades the inmost recesses of the man; he opens the closed and softens the hardened heart, and circumcises that which was uncircumcised; infuses new qualities into the will, which, though heretofore dead, he quickens; from being evil, disobedient and refractory, he renders it good, obedient and pliable; actuates and strengthens it, that like a good tree, it may bring forth the fruits of good actions.

12. And this is the regeneration so highly celebrated in Scripture and denominated a new creation; a resurrection from the dead, a making alive, which God works in us without our aid. But this is nowise effected merely by the external preaching of the Gospel, by moral suasion or such a mode of operation that, after God has performed his part, it still remains in the power of man to be regenerated or not, to be converted or to continue unconverted; but it is evidently a supernatural work, most powerful, and at the same time most delightful, astonishing, mysterious and ineffable; not inferior in efficacy to creation or the resurrection from the dead, as the Scripture inspired by the author of this work declares; so that all in whose hearts God works in this marvellous manner are certainly, infallibly and effectually regenerated, and do actually believe. Whereupon the will thus renewed is not only actuated and influenced by God, but in consequence of this influence becomes itself active. Wherefore also, man is himself rightly said to believe and repent, by virtue of that grace received.

13. The manner of this operation cannot be fully comprehended by believers in this life. Notwithstanding which, they rest satisfied with knowing and experiencing that by this grace of God they are enabled to believe with the heart and to love their Saviour.

14. Faith is therefore to be considered as the gift of God, not on account of its being offered by God to man, to be accepted or rejected at his pleasure, but because it is in reality conferred, breathed and infused into him; not even because God bestows the power or ability to believe, and then expects that man should, by the exercise of his own freewill, consent to the terms of salvation, and actually believe in Christ; but because he who works in man both to will and to do, and indeed all things in all, produces both the will to believe and the act of believing also.

15. God is under no obligation to confer this grace upon any, for how can he be indebted to man, who had no previous gift to bestow as a foundation for such recompense? Nay, who has nothing of his own but sin and falsehood.

He therefore, who becomes the subject of this grace owes eternal gratitude to God, and gives him thanks for ever. Whoever is not made partaker thereof is either altogether regardless of these spiritual gifts and satisfied with his own condition, or is in no apprehension of danger, and vainly boasts the possession of that which he has not. With respect to those who make an external profession of faith and lead regular lives, we are bound, after the example of the Apostle, to judge and speak of them in the most favourable manner; for the secret recesses of the heart are unknown to us. And as to others who have not yet been called, it is our duty to pray for them to God, who calleth those things which be not as though they were. But we are in no wise to conduct ourselves towards them with haughtiness, as if we had made ourselves to differ.

16. But as man by the fall did not cease to be a creature endowed with understanding and will, nor did sin, which pervaded the whole race of mankind, deprive him of the human nature, but brought upon him depravity and spiritual death; so also this grace of regeneration does not treat men as senseless stocks and blocks, nor take away their will and its properties, neither does violence thereto; but spiritually quickens, heals, corrects and at the same time sweetly and powerfully bends it, that where carnal rebellion and resistance formerly prevailed, a ready and sincere spiritual obedience begins to reign; in which the true and spiritual restoration and freedom of our will consist. Wherefore, unless the admirable author of every good work wrought in us, man could have no hope of recovering from his fall by his own freewill, by the abuse of which, in a state of innocence, he plunged himself into ruin.

17. As the almighty operation of God, whereby he prolongs and supports this our natural life, does not exclude, but requires the use of means, by which God of his infinite mercy and goodness hath chosen to exercise his influence; so also the before-mentioned supernatural operation of God, by which we are regenerated, in no wise excludes or subverts the use of the Gospel, which the most wise God hath ordained to be the seed of regeneration and food of the soul. Wherefore as the Apostles and the teachers who succeeded them piously instructed the people concerning this grace of God, to his glory and the abasement of all pride, and in the meantime however, neglected not to keep them by the sacred precepts of the Gospel, in the exercise of the Word, the sacraments and discipline; so, even to this day, be it far from either instructors or instructed to presume to tempt God in the Church by separating what he of his good pleasure hath most intimately joined together. For grace is conferred by means of admonitions, and the more readily we perform our duty, the more eminent usually is this blessing of God working in us, and the more directly is his work advanced; to whom alone all glory, both of means and their saving fruit and efficacy, is for ever due. Amen.

Rejection of Errors

The synod rejects the errors of those who teach that:

01. "It is not correct to say that original sin sufficed by itself to condemn the entire human race, or bring upon it temporal and eternal punishments." These people contradict the Apostle, who says in Ro 5:12: *Through one man sin came into the world, and through sin death, and so death came upon all men, in whom all have sinned.* And v. 16: *Sin entered through one unto condemnation.* Again, Ro 6:23: *The wages of sin is death.*

02. "Spiritual gifts, or good habits and virtues like goodness, holiness and righteousness, could have had no place in the will of man when it was first created, and therefore have not been separated from it in the Fall." This goes against the description of the image of God, which the Apostle outlines in Ep 4:24, where he describes it on the basis of righteousness and holiness, which are located above all in the will.

03. "Spiritual gifts are not separated from man's will by spiritual death, since the will is in no way corrupt in itself, but only hindered by the darkness of the mind and the disorder of the affections. Take away these hindrances and the free ability innate in the will returns, so that whatever good may be proposed to it, it may wish, if it so chooses, or not wish, if it so chooses." This is a novelty and an error, and produces a glorification of powers of freewill, against what the prophet Jeremiah (17:9) says: *The heart is deceitful above all things, and wicked.* And the Apostle also says (Ep 2:3): *Among whom* (i.e. wicked men), *we also once walked in the lusts of our flesh, doing the will of the flesh and the mind.*

04. "The unregenerate man is not properly nor fully dead in his sins, or destitute of all power to do spiritual good, but he is able to hunger and thirst after righteousness or life, and to offer the sacrifice of a contrite and burdened heart, which is acceptable to God." These people are opposed by the open testimonies of Scripture. Ep 2:1, 5: *You were dead in trespasses and sins.* And Gn 6:5 and 8:21: *The imagination of the thoughts of the heart of man is everyday evil.* In addition, it belongs to the regenerate, and to those who are called blessed, to hunger and thirst after freedom from misery and after life, and to offer to God the sacrifice of a contrite heart (Ps 51:19; Mt 5:6).

05. "The corrupt and animal man may by common grace, which is the light of nature, or else by means of gifts left after the Fall, as much as possible, by using them well, obtain greater grace, even evangelical and saving grace, and gradually obtain his salvation. And in this way God, for his part, takes care to show himself to all men sufficiently and effectively, for the purpose of revealing Christ to all men, by whatever means are necessary to the revelation of Christ, to faith and repentance." That this

is false, Scripture witnesses by the experience of every age. Ps 147:19-20: *He shows his words to Jacob, his statutes and ordinances to Israel. He has not done this for any other nation, and has not made his ordinances known to them.* Ac 14:16: *In past generations God allowed all nations to walk in their own ways.* Ac 16:6-7: *They were prevented* (i.e. Paul and his fellows) *by the Holy Spirit from preaching the Word of God in Asia.* And: *When they came into Mysia, they tried to go on to Bithynia, but the Spirit did not allow them.*

06. "In the true conversion of a man it is not possible for new qualities, habits or gifts to be imparted to him by God against his will, and even the faith by which we are first converted and by which we are called believers, is not a quality or gift imparted by God. It is only an act of man, nor can it be called a gift except with respect to the power it conveys to come to faith." These people contradict Holy Scripture which bears witness that God imparts the new qualities of faith, obedience and the feelings of his love into our hearts. Je 31:33: *I will put my law in their mind, and I will write it on their heart.* Is 44:3: *I will pour out waters over the thirsty, and streams over the parched; I will pour out my Spirit over all your seed.* Ro 5:5: *The love of God is poured out in our hearts by the Holy Spirit, who is given to us.* They also go against the constant practice of the Church, which prays with the prophet: *Convert me Lord, and I shall be converted* (Je 31:18).

07. "The grace by which we are converted to God is nothing other than gentle persuasion, or (as others explain it) the most noble way of acting for the conversion of man, and the one most comfortable to human nature. There is nothing to prevent a lesser, or only moral grace from making animal men spiritual, for God does not produce the consent of the will by any other than moral means, and the efficacy of the divine operation consists in this, that it is greater than the work of Satan, for God promises eternal blessings, whereas those of Satan are merely temporal." This is totally Pelagian, and completely contrary to Scripture, which above all else recognizes that the holy Spirit's mode of action in the conversion of men is by far the more effective and divine. Ek 36:26: *I will give you my heart, and I will put a new spirit within you, and I will take out the heart of stone, and I will give you a heart of flesh.*

08. "In the regeneration of a man, God does not employ those powers of his omnipotence by which he turns the man's will to faith and conversion in a powerful and infallible way, but allowing for all the operations of grace which God uses to convert a man, the man concerned may nevertheless by his own acts resist God and the Spirit who intends his regeneration and wishes to regenerate him, so as to hinder his regeneration and even to remain in a position to decide whether to be regenerated or not." This is nothing other than to remove any effect of the grace of God in our lives, and to subject the acts of an all-powerful

God to the will of men, and this against the teaching of the Apostles: *We believe because of the effectiveness of the great power of God* (Ep 1:19). And: *May God fulfil every good resolve and work of faith by his power in us* (II Th 1:11). And: *His divine power has given us all things, which pertain to life and holiness* (II Pe 1:3).

09. "Grace and freewill are partial causes working together to initiate conversion, nor in the order of causation does grace precede the effect of the will." That is, "God does not effectively tend a man towards conversion before he exercises his own will, for it is the will of man which initiates and determines conversion." For the Church long ago condemned this doctrine from the Apostle, when attacking the Pelagians (Ro 9:16): *It is not of him who wills, or of him who strives, but of God who has mercy.* And I Co 4:7: *Who sees anything different in you?* And: *What do you have which you did not receive?* Likewise (Ph 2:13): *It is God who works in you to will and to do his good pleasure.*

05. Of the Perseverance of the Saints

01. Whom God calls according to his purpose, to the communion of his Son our Lord Jesus Christ, and regenerates by the Holy Spirit, he delivers also from the dominion and slavery of sin in this life; though not altogether from the body of sin and from the infirmities of the flesh, so long as they continue in this world.

02. Hence spring daily sins of infirmity, and hence spots adhere to the best works of the saints, which furnish them with constant matter for humiliation before God, and flying for refuge to Christ crucified; for mortifying the flesh more and more by the spirit of prayer and by holy exercises of piety; and for pressing forward to the goal of perfection, till being at length delivered from this body of death, they are brought to reign with the Lamb of God in heaven.

03. By reason of these remains of indwelling sin and the temptations of sin and of the world, those who are converted could not persevere in a state of grace if left to their own strength. But God is faithful, who having conferred grace, mercifully confirms and powerfully preserves them therein, even to the end.

04. Although the weakness of the flesh cannot prevail against the power of God, who confirms and preserves true believers in a state of grace, yet converts are not always so influenced and actuated by the Spirit of God as not in some particular instances sinfully to deviate from the guidance of divine grace, so as to be seduced by, and to comply with, the lusts of the flesh; they must therefore be constant in watching and prayer, that they be not led into temptation. When these are neglected they are not only liable to be drawn into great and heinous sins by Satan, the world and the flesh, but sometimes by the righteous permission of God actually fall into these evils. This the lamentable fall of David, Peter and other saints described in Holy Scriptures, demonstrates.

05. By such enormous sins however, they very highly offend God, incur a deadly guilt, grieve the Holy Spirit, interrupt the exercise of faith, very grievously wound their consciences, and sometimes lose the sense of God's favour for a time, until on their returning into the right way by serious repentance, the light of God's fatherly countenance again shines upon them.

06. But God, who is rich in mercy, according to his unchangeable purpose of election, does not wholly withdraw the Holy Spirit from his own people, even in their melancholy falls; nor suffer them to proceed so far as to lose the grace of adoption and forfeit the state of justification, or to commit the sin unto death; nor does he permit them to be totally deserted, and to plunge themselves into everlasting destruction.

07. For in the first place, in these falls he preserves in them the incorruptible seed of regeneration from perishing or being totally lost; and again, by his Word and Spirit, he certainly and effectually renews them to repentance, to a sincere and godly sorrow for their sins, that they may seek and obtain remission in the blood of the mediator, may again experience the favour of a reconciled God, through faith adore his mercies, and henceforward more diligently work out their own salvation with fear and trembling.

08. Thus it is not in consequence of their own merits or strength, but of God's free mercy, that they do not totally fall from faith and grace, nor continue and perish finally in their backslidings; which, with respect to themselves is not only possible, but would undoubtedly happen; but with respect to God, it is utterly impossible, since his counsel cannot be changed nor his promise fail, neither can the call according to his purpose be revoked, not the merit, intercession and preservation of Christ be rendered ineffectual, nor the sealing of the Holy Spirit be frustrated or obliterated.

09. Of this preservation of the elect to salvation, and of their perseverance in the faith, true believers for themselves may and do obtain assurance according to the measure of their faith, whereby they arrive at the certain persuasion that they ever will continue true and living members of the Church, and that they experience forgiveness of sins and will at last inherit eternal life.

10. This assurance however is not produced by any peculiar revelation contrary to, or independent of the Word of God, but springs from faith in God's promises which he has most abundantly revealed in his Word for our comfort; from the testimony of the Holy Spirit, witnessing with our spirit, that we are children and heirs of God (Ro 8:16); and lastly, from a serious and holy desire to preserve a good conscience, and to perform good works. And if the elect of God were deprived of this solid comfort, that they shall finally obtain the victory, and of this infallible pledge or earnest of eternal glory, they would be of all men the most miserable.

11. The Scripture moreover testifies that believers in this life have to struggle with various carnal doubts, and that under grievous temptations they are not always sensible of this full assurance of faith and certainty of persevering. *But God, who is the Father of all consolation, does not suffer them to be tempted above that they are able, but will with the temptation make a way to escape, that they may be able to bear it* (1 Co 10:13); and by the Holy Spirit again inspires them with the comfortable assurance of persevering.

12. This certainty of perseverance however, is so far from exciting in believers a spirit of pride, or of rendering them carnally secure, that on the contrary, it is the real source of humility, filial reverence, true piety, patience in every tribulation, fervent prayers, constancy in suffering and in confessing the truth, and of solid rejoicing in God; so that the consideration of this benefit should serve as an incentive to the serious and constant practice of gratitude and good works, as appears from the testimonies of Scripture and the examples of the saints.

13. Neither does renewed confidence of persevering produce licentiousness or a disregard to piety in those who are recovered from backsliding; but it renders the Lord, which he hath ordained, that they who walk therein may maintain an assurance of persevering; lest by abusing his fatherly kindness, God should turn away his gracious countenance from them (to behold which is to the godly dearer than life, the withdrawing whereof is more bitter than death), and they in consequence thereof should fall into more grievous torments of conscience.

14. And as it hath pleased God, by the preaching of the Gospel, to begin this work of grace in us, so he preserves, continues and perfects it by the hearing and reading of his Word, by meditation thereon, and by the exhortations, threatenings and promises thereof, as well as by the use of the sacraments.

15. The carnal mind is unable to comprehend this doctrine of the perseverance of the saints and the certainty thereof, which God hath most abundantly revealed in his Word, for the glory of his name and the consolation of pious souls, and which he impresses upon the hearts of the faithful. Satan abhors it; the world ridicules it; the ignorant and hypocrite abuse, and heretics oppose it. But the spouse of Christ hath always most tenderly loved and constantly defended it, as an inestimable treasure; and God, against whom neither counsel nor strength can prevail, will dispose her to continue this conduct to the end. NOW TO THIS ONE GOD, FATHER, SON AND HOLY SPIRIT, BE HONOUR AND GLORY FOR EVER. AMEN.

Rejection of Errors

The synod rejects the errors of those who teach:

01. "The perseverance of true believers is not the effect of election, or the

gift of God imparted by the death of Christ, but is the ground of a new covenant, which a man may choose before his election and justification (as they say), by his own freewill." For Holy Scripture testifies that perseverance follows from election and is given to the elect on the strength of the death, resurrection and intercession of Christ. Ro 11:7: *The election obtained it but the rest were hardened.* And Ro 8:32-35: *He who did not spare his own Son but gave him up for us all, will he not also give us all things with him? Who shall bring any charge against God's elect? It is God who justifies; who is to condemn? It is Christ Jesus who died, yea, who was raised from the dead, who is at the right hand of God, who intercedes for us. Who shall separate us from the love of Christ?*

02. "God has given the believer sufficient strength to persevere, and prepared him to keep them in himself as much as necessary. Yet given all these things, which are necessary for persevering in faith, God does not want to interfere in preserving faith, but everything hangs on a decision of the will to persevere or not as it chooses." This statement obviously contains Pelagianism, and while it wishes to set men free makes them blasphemers, against the perpetual consensus of evangelical doctrine, which rejects anything by which man may glory and ascribes the praise of this benefit to the grace of God alone. It also goes against the witness of the Apostle: *It is God who will sustain you to the end, guiltless in the day of our Lord Jesus Christ* (I Co 1:8).

03. "True regenerate believers not only can depart finally and completely from justifying faith, from grace and from salvation, but in fact it is not at all rare for them to do so, and to perish everlastingly." For this opinion makes void the grace of justification and regeneration, and the perpetual care of Christ, against the express words of the Apostle Paul in Ro 5:8-9: *If Christ died for us while we were yet sinners, how much more, now that we have been justified by his blood, shall we be preserved from wrath through him.* And they go against the Apostle John (Jn 3:9): *Everyone who is born of God gives no place to sin; for his seed remains in him and he cannot sin, because he is born of God.* They even go against the words of Jesus Christ (Jn 10:28-29): *I give eternal life to my sheep and they will not perish in eternity, nor will anyone take them out of my hand; my Father, who has given them to me, is greater than all, nor can anyone take them out of my Father's hand.*

04. "True regenerate believers can sin even unto death, or against the Holy Spirit." In I Jn 5:16-17 the Apostle refers to those who have committed mortal sin and forbids us to pray for them, adding immediately (v. 18): *We know that whoever is born of God does not sin* (i.e. this type of sin), *but whoever is born of God preserves himself, and the evil one does not touch him.*

05. "It is impossible to have any certainty of future perseverance in this

life, apart from special revelation." By this teaching the solid consolation of true believers in this life is taken away, and the doubting of the Papists is brought back into the Church. For Holy Scripture constantly refers to this certainty, not as the result of special or extraordinary revelation, but from signs proper to the sons of God, and the most faithful promises of God. The Apostle Paul writes in Ro 8:39: *No created thing can separate us from the love of God, which is in Christ Jesus our Lord.* And John writes (I Jn 3:24): *Whoever keeps his commandments abides in him and he in them, and by this we know that he is in us, by the Spirit which is given us.*

06. "The doctrine concerning perseverance and the certainty of faith, by its nature and inclination, is an aid to the flesh and harmful to piety, good morals, prayers and other holy exercises. Therefore it is praiseworthy to doubt it." These people demonstrate that they have no knowledge of the effectiveness of divine grace and of the operation of the indwelling Holy Spirit, and they contradict what the apostle John expressly affirms (I Jn 3:2-3): *My beloved, now we are children of God, but it is not yet clear what we shall be. However, we know that when he shall be revealed, we shall be like him, because we shall see him as he is. And whoever has this hope in him purifies himself, even as he is pure.* Moreover, they are refuted by the examples of the saints of both the Old and the New Testaments, who had assurance of their perseverance and salvation, but were nevertheless diligent in prayers and other pious exercises.

07. "The faith of those who believe for a time is no different, apart from length, from justifying and saving faith." For Christ himself (Mt 13:20; Lk 8:13) gives us three ways of distinguishing temporary from true believers, when he says that the former receive the seed in stony ground, the latter in good ground, or in a good heart; the former lack roots, the latter have firm roots; the former bear no fruit, the latter continue to bear fruit in different measure, but without ceasing.

08. "It is not absurd for a man, having lost his earlier regeneration, to return and be born again several times." Those who hold this doctrine deny the incorruptibility of the divine seed, by which we are born again. This goes against the testimony of the Apostle Peter (I Pe 1:23): *Born again not of corruptible seed, but of incorruptible.*

09. "Christ never prayed for an infallible perseverance of believers in faith." These contradict Christ himself, who said (Lk 22:32): *I prayed for thee, Peter, that thy faith fail not.* John the Evangelist also testifies (Jn 17:20), that Christ prayed not only for the Apostles but for all believers, e.g. v. 11: *Holy Father, keep them in thy name* and v. 15: *I do not pray that thou take them out of the world, but that thou keep them from evil.*

Conclusion

And this is the perspicuous, simple and ingenuous declaration of the orthodox doctrine respecting the five articles which have been controverted in the Dutch churches, and the rejection of the errors with which they have for some time been troubled. This doctrine the synod judges to be drawn from the Word of God and to be agreeable to the confession of the Reformed Churches. Whence it clearly appears that some, whom such conduct by no means became, have violated all truth, equity and charity, in wishing to persuade the public:

> "That the doctrine of the Reformed Churches concerning predestination and the points annexed to it, by its own genius and necessary tendency, leads off the minds of men from all piety and religion; that it is an opiate administered by the flesh and the devil; and the stronghold of Satan, where he lies in wait for all, and from which he wounds multitudes, and mortally strikes through many with the darts both of despair and security; that it makes God the author of sin, unjust, tyrannical, hypocritical; that it is nothing more than an interpolated Stoicism, Manichaeism, Libertinism, Turkism [i.e. Islam, *ed.*]; that it renders men carnally secure, since they are persuaded by it that nothing can hinder the salvation of the elect, let them live as they please; and therefore, that they may safely perpetrate every species of the most atrocious crimes; and that if the reprobate should ever perform truly all the works of the saints, their obedience would not in the least contribute to their salvation; that the same doctrine teaches that God, by a mere arbitrary act of his will, without the least respect or view to any sin, has predestinated the greatest part of the world to eternal damnation, and has created them for this very purpose; that in the same manner in which the election is the fountain and cause of faith and good works, reprobation is the cause of unbelief and impiety; that many children of the faithful are torn, guiltless, from their mothers' breasts, and tyrannically plunged into hell; so that neither baptism nor the prayers of the Church at their baptism can at all profit them"

and many other things of the same kind which the Reformed Churches not only do not acknowledge, but even detest with their whole soul.

Wherefore this synod of Dordrecht, in the name of the Lord, conjures as many as piously call upon the name of our Saviour Jesus Christ to judge of the faith of the Reformed Churches, not from the calumnies which on every side are heaped upon it, nor from the private expressions of a few among ancient and modern teachers, often dishonestly quoted, or corrupted and wrested to a meaning quite foreign to their intention; but from the public confessions of the Churches themselves, and from this declaration of the orthodox doctrine, confirmed by the unanimous consent of all and each of the members of the whole synod. Moreover, the synod warns calumniators themselves to consider the terrible judgement of God which awaits them, for bearing false witness against the confessions of so many churches, for distressing the consciences of the weak, and for labouring to render suspected the society of the truly faithful.

Finally, this synod exhorts all their brethren in the Gospel of Christ to conduct themselves piously and religiously in handling this doctrine, both in the universities and churches; to direct it, as well in discourse as in writing, to the glory of the Divine name, to holiness of life, and to the consolation of afflicted souls; to regulate, by the Scripture, according to the analogy of faith, not only their sentiments but also their language, and to abstain from all those phrases which exceed the limits necessary to be observed in ascertaining the genuine sense of the Holy Scriptures, and may furnish insolent sophists with a just pretext for violently assailing, or even vilifying the doctrine of the Reformed Churches.

May Jesus Christ, the Son of God, who, seated at the Father's right hand, gives gifts to men, sanctify us in the truth; bring to the truth those who err; shut the mouths of the calumniators of sound doctrine, and endue the faithful ministers of his Word with the spirit of wisdom and discretion, that all their discourses may tend to the glory of God and the edification of those who hear them. Amen.

The Protestant Schism

and the Final Settlement

(1625-1700)

44. THE KING'S DECLARATION, 1628

History

It was part of Charles I's ecclesiastical policy to favour the anti-Calvinist elements, though he must have known that they were a minority in the Church as a whole. As a first step towards overthrowing Calvinism, he tried to prevent discussion of the issues which had arisen out of the Synod of Dort. To do this, he issued a declaration, stating that the Thirty-nine Articles (1571) were henceforth to be the Church's official doctrinal statement. The declaration survived the many vicissitudes of the king's ecclesiastical policy, and it is still printed with the Articles in the Book of Common Prayer (1662), though many of its provisions are clearly no longer in force.

Theology

The declaration was a compromise move, in that the Thirty-nine Articles could be accepted by both Calvinists and their opponents. This was because they had been composed before the outbreak of the controversy, and therefore did not take a specific position on the matters of dispute. It was still possible to affirm the doctrine of Predestination (Article 17) in a way acceptable to Calvinists, but at the same time the Calvinists could not impose their particular understanding of the doctrine as this had been elaborated at the Synod of Dort. Because it was clearly intended to be a restraint on Calvinism, only the anti-Calvinists were happy with it, and its presence in the Book of Common Prayer (1662) was intended to reinforce Anglican rejection of pure Calvinism.

Being by God's ordinance, according to our just title, Defender of the Faith and Supreme Governor of the Church within these our dominions, we hold it most agreeable to this our kingly office and our own religious zeal, to conserve and maintain the Church committed to our charge in unity of true religion and in the bond of peace; and not to suffer unnecessary disputations, altercations or questions to be raised which may nourish faction both in the Church and commonwealth. We have therefore, upon mature deliberation, and with the advice of so many of our bishops as might conveniently be called together, thought fit to make this declaration following:

That the Articles of the Church of England (which have been allowed and authorized heretofore, and which our clergy generally have subscribed unto) do contain the true doctrine of the Church of England agreeable to God's Word; which we do therefore ratify and confirm, requiring all our loving subjects to continue in the uniform profession thereof, and prohibiting the least difference from the said Articles, which to that end we command to be new printed, and this our declaration to be published therewith.

That we are Supreme Governor of the Church of England, and that if any difference arise about the external policy, concerning the injunctions, canons and other constitutions whatsoever thereto belonging, the clergy in their convocation is to order and settle them, having first obtained leave under our broad seal so to do; and we approving their said ordinances and constitutions, providing that none be made contrary to the laws and customs of the land.

That out of our princely care that the churchmen may do the work which is proper unto them, the bishops and clergy, from time to time in convocation, upon their humble desire, shall have licence under our broad seal to deliberate of, and to do all such things as, being made plain by them, and assented unto by us, shall concern the settled continuance of the doctrine and discipline of the Church of England now established; from which we will not endure any varying or departing in the least degree.

That for the present, though some differences have been ill raised, yet we take comfort in this, that all clergymen within our realm have always most willingly subscribed to the Articles established; which is an argument to us that they all agree in the true, usual, literal meaning of the said Articles; and that even in those curious points in which the present differences lie, men of all sorts take the Articles of the Church of England to be for them; which is an argument again, that none of them intend any desertion of the Articles established.

That therefore in these both curious and unhappy differences which have for so many hundred years, in different times and places, exercised the Church of Christ, we will that all further curious search be laid aside, and these disputes shut up in God's promises, as they be generally set forth to us in the Holy Scriptures and the general meaning of the Articles of the Church of England according to them. And that no man hereafter shall either print or preach to draw the Article aside any way, but shall submit to it in the plain and full meaning thereof; and shall not put his own sense or comment to be the meaning of the Article, but shall take it in the literal and grammatical sense.

That if any public reader in either of our universities, or any head or master of a college, or any other person respectively in either of them, shall affix any new sense to any Article or shall publicly read, determine or hold any public disputation, or suffer any such to be held either way, in either the universities or colleges respectively; or if any divine in the universities shall preach or print anything either way, other than is already established in Convocation with our royal assent; he, or they the offenders shall be liable to our displeasure, and the Church's censure in our commission ecclesiastical, as well as any other; and we will see there shall be due execution upon them.

45. THE SOLEMN LEAGUE AND COVENANT, 1643

History

The Solemn League and Covenant was based on a Scottish document of the same name, which had been voluntarily subscribed by a large section of the Scottish people in 1638. In August 1643, as part of the union between Scotland and the Parliamentary forces in the Civil War, this document was revised and submitted to both the Scottish Estates and the Westminster Assembly. The Estates agreed to it on 17 August 1643, as did the Assembly, with minor alterations. This revised text was then sent to the House of Commons, where it was approved on 25 September 1643 and to the House of Lords, which gave its assent on 15 October. On 05 February 1644 it was imposed on all Englishmen over the age of eighteen.

More than any other document, the Solemn League and Covenant was the charter of the Commonwealth of England. It remained in force until the Restoration in 1660, and repudiation of it was made a condition for rehabilitation under Charles II.

A solemn league and covenant for reformation and defence of religion, the honour and happiness of the king, and the peace and safety of the three kingdoms of England, Scotland and Ireland.

We noblemen, barons, knights, gentlemen, citizens, burgesses, ministers of the Gospel, and commons of all sorts in the kingdoms of England, Scotland and Ireland, by the providence of God living under one king and being of one reformed religion; having before our eyes the glory of God and the advancement of the kingdom of our Lord and Saviour Jesus Christ, the honour and happiness of the king's majesty and his posterity, and the true public liberty, safety and peace of the kingdoms, wherein everyone's private condition is included; and calling to mind the treacherous and bloody plots, conspiracies, attempts and practices of the enemies of God against the true religion and professors thereof in all places, especially in these three kingdoms, ever since the reformation of religion, and how much their rage, power and presumption are of late, and at this time increased and exercised, whereof the deplorable estate of the Church and kingdom of Ireland, the distressed estate of the Church and kingdom of England and the dangerous estate of the Church and kingdom of Scotland are present and public testimonies: we have (now at last), after other means of supplication, remonstrance, protestations and sufferings, for the preservation of ourselves and our religion from utter ruin and destruction, according to the commendable practice of these kingdoms in former times, and the example of God's people in other nations, after mature deliberation, resolved and determined to enter into a mutual and solemn league and covenant, wherein we all subscribe, and each one of us for himself, with our hands lifted up to the most high God, do swear:

01. That we shall sincerely, really and constantly, through the grace of God, endeavour in our several places and callings, the preservation of the reformed religion in the Church of Scotland, in doctrine, worship, discipline and government, against our common enemies; the reformation of religion in the kingdoms of England and Ireland, in doctrine, worship, discipline and government, according to the Word of God and the example of the best reformed churches; and we shall endeavour to bring the churches of God in the three kingdoms to the nearest conjunction and uniformity in religion, confession of faith, form of church government, directory for worship and catechizing, that we, and our posterity after us may, as brethren live in faith and love, and the Lord may delight to dwell in the midst of us.

02. That we shall in like manner, without respect of persons, endeavour the extirpation of popery, prelacy (that is, church government by archbishops, bishops, their chancellors and commissaries, deans, deans and chapters, archdeacons and all other ecclesiastical officers depending on that hierarchy), superstition, heresy, schism, profaneness and whatsoever shall be found to be contrary to sound doctrine and the power of godliness, lest we partake in other men's sins and thereby be in danger to receive of their plagues; and that the Lord may be one, and his name one in the three kingdoms.

03. We shall, with the same sincerity, reality and constancy, in our several vocations, endeavour with our estates and lives mutually to preserve the rights and privileges of the Parliaments, and the liberties of the kingdoms, and to preserve and defend the king's majesty's person and authority, in the preservation and defence of the true religion and liberties of the kingdoms, that the world may bear witness with our consciences of our loyalty, and that we have no thoughts or intentions to diminish his majesty's just power and greatness.

04. We shall also with all faithfulness endeavour the discovery of all such as have been or shall be incendiaries, malignants or evil instruments, by hindering the reformation of religion, dividing the king from his people, or one of the kingdoms from another, or making any faction or parties among the people, contrary to the league and covenant, that they may be brought to public trial and receive condign punishment, as the degree of their offences shall require or deserve, or the supreme judicatories of both kingdoms respectively, or others having power from them for that effect, shall judge convenient.

05. And whereas the happiness of a blessed peace between these kingdoms, denied in former times to our progenitors, is by the good providence of God granted unto us, and hath been lately concluded and settled by both Parliaments: we shall each one of us, according to our places and interest, endeavour that they may remain conjoined in a firm peace and union to all posterity, and that justice may be done upon the wilful opposers thereof, in manner expressed in the precedent articles.

06. We shall also, according to our places and callings, in this common cause of religion, liberty and peace of the kingdom, assist and defend all those that enter into this league and covenant, in the maintaining and pursuing thereof; and shall not suffer ourselves, directly or indirectly, by whatsoever combination, persuasion or terror, to be divided and withdrawn from this blessed union and conjunction, whether to make defection to the contrary part, or give ourselves to a detestable indifferency or neutrality in this cause, which so much concerneth the glory of God, the good of the kingdoms, and the honour of the king; but shall all the days of our lives zealously and constantly continue therein, against all opposition, and promote the same according to our power, against all lets and impediments whatsoever; and what we are not able ourselves to suppress or overcome we shall reveal and make known, that it may be timely prevented or removed: all which we shall do in the sight of God.

And because these kingdoms are guilty of many sins and provocations against God and his Son Jesus Christ, as is too manifest by our present distresses and dangers, the fruits thereof: we profess and declare, before God and the world, our unfeigned desire to be humbled for our sins and for the sins of these kingdoms; especially that we have not as we ought valued the inestimable benefit of the Gospel; that we have not laboured for the purity and power thereof; and that we have not endeavoured to receive Christ in our hearts, nor to walk worthy of him in our lives, which are the causes of other sins and transgressions so much abounding amongst us, and our true and unfeigned purpose, desire and endeavour, for ourselves and all others under our power and charge, both in public and in private, in all duties we owe to God and man, to amend our lives, and each one to go before another in the example of a real reformation, that the Lord may turn away his wrath and heavy indignation and establish these churches and kingdoms in truth and peace. And this covenant we make in the presence of Almighty God, the searcher of all hearts, with a true intention to perform the same, as we shall answer at that great day when the secrets of all hearts shall be disclosed; most humbly beseeching the Lord to strengthen us by his Holy Spirit for this end, and to bless our desires and proceedings with such success as may be a deliverance and safety to his people, and encouragement to the Christian churches groaning under or in danger of the yoke of antichristian tyranny, to join in the same or like association and covenant, to the glory of God, the enlargement of the kingdom of Jesus Christ, and the peace and tranquillity of Christian kingdoms and commonwealths.

46. THE WESTMINSTER CONFESSION OF FAITH, 1647

History

On the outbreak of the Civil War in 1642, the Parliamentary forces lost little time in embarking on the great project of a union of the Churches of England, Scotland and Ireland by means of a single Confession of Faith. An assembly of divines was convened at Westminster in 1643, and deliberated for three years. Initially there were attempts to revise the Thirty-nine Articles (1571), which at that time were the most widely accepted statement of faith in the British Isles. But these attempts were eventually abandoned, and a new document took their place. It was approved in principle by Parliament on 04 December 1646, and after appropriate Scripture proofs were added, it was authorized for printing on 29 April 1647. The Westminster Confession, as it came to be called, remained the official doctrinal statement of the three Churches until the Restoration (1660), when it was rescinded, along with other Commonwealth legislation. However, in 1690 it once again became the official Confession of the Church of Scotland, a position which it still retains.

Theology

The Westminster Confession ranks with the Thirty-nine Articles as the main confessional statement of the British Reformation, and its influence has been even greater. It has become the foundational document of Presbyterian churches worldwide, and (in slightly modified forms) has been accepted by Congregationalists and many Baptists as well. The Anglican Communion has never accorded it official recognition, though many Low Church (Evangelical) Anglicans regard it as the best expression of the Calvinist faith they hold. The majority of the divines at the assembly came from the Church of England, and by and large it was their contributions which prevailed in the deliberations. The Confession's influence on Anglican Reformed thought has continued to be very great, and most modern confessional theology among Anglicans, as well as other Evangelicals is deeply indebted to it.

The Confession follows a pattern which differs substantially from the Thirty-nine Articles, but is fairly close to the Irish Articles of 1615. Of particular note is the primacy given to the place of Holy Scripture, and the transposition of the doctrines of election and predestination, which were initially regarded as dependent on the doctrine of salvation, to a place where they became factors controlling even the work of creation. It is also noteworthy how the sixteenth-century preoccupations with Church order and the ministry have virtually disappeared; in particular, nothing is said about episcopacy or about presbyterian government, even though they were major issues in dispute at the time. The Westminster Confession deserves to recover its forgotten place in the history of the English Church, and to be studied carefully in the context of the theological debates of its time, even if it can no longer be regarded as an official statement of Anglican theology.

01. Of the Holy Scripture

01. Although the light of nature and the works of creation and providence do so far manifest the goodness, wisdom and power of God, as to leave men inexcusable,[1] yet are they not sufficient to give that knowledge of God and of His will which is necessary unto salvation.[2] Therefore it pleased the Lord at sundry times, and in diverse manners, to reveal Himself, and to declare that His will unto His Church,[3] and afterwards, for the better preserving and propagating of the truth, and for the more sure establishment and comfort of the Church against the corruption of the flesh, and the malice of Satan and of the world, to commit the same wholly unto writing,[4] which maketh the Holy Scripture to be most necessary,[5] those former ways of God's revealing Himself unto His people being now ceased.[6]

02. Under the name of Holy Scripture or the Word of God written are now contained all the books of the Old and New Testament, which are these:

Of the Old Testament:

Genesis	II Chronicles	Daniel
Exodus	Ezra	Hosea
Leviticus	Nehemiah	Joel
Numbers	Esther	Amos
Deuteronomy	Job	Obadiah
Joshua	Psalms	Jonah
Judges	Proverbs	Micah
Ruth	Ecclesiastes	Nahum
I Samuel	The Song of Songs	Habakkuk
II Samuel	Isaiah	Zephaniah
I Kings	Jeremiah	Haggai
II Kings	Lamentations	Zechariah
I Chronicles	Ezekiel	Malachi

Of the New Testament:

The Gospels according to	Galatians	The Epistle to
Matthew	Ephesians	the Hebrews
Mark	Philippians	The Epistle of James
Luke	Colossians	The first and second
John	Thessalonians I	Epistles of Peter
The Acts of the Apostles	Thessalonians II	The first, second and
Paul's Epistles to the	To Timothy I	third Epistles of John
Romans	To Timothy II	The Epistle of Jude
Corinthians I	To Titus	The Revelation of John
Corinthians II	To Philemon	

All of which are given by inspiration of God to be the rule of faith and life.[7]

03. The books commonly called Apocrypha, not being of divine inspiration, are no part of the canon of the Scripture, and therefore are of no authority in the Church of God, nor to be any otherwise approved or made use of, than other human writings.[8]

04. The authority of the holy Scripture for which it ought to be believed and obeyed, dependeth not upon the testimony of any man or Church, but wholly upon God (who is truth itself) the author thereof, and therefore it is to be received, because it is the Word of God.[9]

05. We may be moved and induced by the testimony of the Church to an high and reverent esteem of the Holy Scripture.[10] And the heavenliness of the matter, the efficacy of the doctrine, the majesty of the style, the consent of all the parts, the scope of the whole (which is to give all glory to God), the full discovery it makes of the only way of man's salvation, the many other incomparable excellencies and the entire perfection thereof, are arguments whereby it doth abundantly evidence itself to be the Word of God; yet notwithstanding, our full persuasion and assurance of the infallible truth and divine authority thereof is from the inward work of the Holy Spirit bearing witness by and with the Word in our hearts.[11]

06. The whole counsel of God concerning all things necessary for His own glory, man's salvation, faith and life, is either expressly set down in Scripture or by good and necessary consequence may be deduced from Scripture; unto which nothing at any time is to be added, whether by new revelations of the Spirit or traditions of men.[12] Nevertheless, we acknowledge the inward illumination of the Spirit of God to be necessary for the saving understanding of such things as are revealed in the Word,[13] and that there are some circumstances concerning the worship of God, and government of the Church, common to human actions and societies, which are to be ordered by the light of nature and Christian prudence, according to the general rules of the Word, which are always to be observed.[14]

07. All things in Scripture are not alike plain in themselves, nor alike clear unto all,[15] yet those things which are necessary to be known, believed and observed for salvation are so clearly propounded and opened in some place of Scripture or other, that not only the learned, but the unlearned, in a due use of the ordinary means, may attain unto a sufficient understanding of them.[16]

08. The Old Testament in Hebrew (which was the native language of the people of God of old), and the New Testament in Greek (which at the time of the writing of it was most generally known to the nations), being immediately inspired by God, and by His singular care and providence kept pure in all ages, are therefore authentical;[17] so as in all controversies of religion the Church is finally to appeal unto them[18]. But because these original tongues are not known to all the people of God who have right unto, and interest in the Scriptures, and are commanded, in the fear of God, to read and search them[19], therefore they are to be translated into the vulgar language of every nation unto which they come,[20] that, the Word of God dwelling plentifully in all, they may worship Him in an acceptable manner,[21] and through patience and comfort of the Scriptures, may have hope.[22]

09. The infallible rule of interpretation of Scripture is the Scripture itself, and therefore, where there is a question about the true and full sense of any Scripture (which is not manifold, but one), it must be searched and known by other places that speak more clearly.[23]

10. The supreme judge by which all controversies of religion are to be determined, and all decrees of councils, opinions of ancient writers, doctrines of men and private spirits are to be examined, and in whose sentence we are to rest, can be no other but the Holy Spirit speaking in the Scripture.[24]

02. Of God and the Holy Trinity

01. There is but one only[25] living and true God,[26] who is infinite in being and perfection,[27] a most pure spirit,[28] invisible,[29] without body, parts[30] or passions,[31] immutable,[32] immense,[33] eternal,[34] incomprehensible,[35] almighty,[36] most wise,[37] most holy,[38] most free,[39] most absolute,[40] working all things according to the counsel of His own immutable and most righteous will,[41] for His own glory,[42] most loving,[43] gracious, merciful, longsuffering, abundant in goodness and truth, forgiving iniquity, transgression and sin,[44] the rewarder of them that diligently seek Him,[45] and withal most just and terrible in His judgements,[46] hating all sin,[47] and who will by no means clear the guilty.[48]

02. God hath all life,[49] glory,[50] goodness,[51] blessedness,[52] in and of Himself; and is alone in and unto Himself all-sufficient, not standing in need of any creatures which He hath made[53] nor deriving any glory from them,[54] but only manifesting His own glory in, by, unto and upon them. He is the alone fountain of all being, of whom, through whom and to whom are all things,[55] and hath most sovereign dominion over them, to do by them, for them, or upon them whatsoever Himself pleaseth.[56] In His sight all things are open and manifest,[57] His knowledge is infinite, infallible and independent upon the creature,[58] so as nothing is to Him contingent or uncertain.[59] He is most holy in all His counsels, in all His works and in all His commands.[60] To Him is due from angels and men and every other creature, whatsoever worship service or obedience He is pleased to require of them.[61]

03. In the unity of the Godhead there be three Persons, of one substance power and eternity – God the Father, God the Son and God the Holy Ghost.[62] The Father is of none, neither begotten nor proceeding; the Son is eternally begotten of the Father;[63] the Holy Ghost eternally proceeding from the Father and the Son.[64]

03. Of God's Eternal Decree

01. God from all eternity did, by the most wise and holy counsel of His own will, freely and unchangeably ordain whatsoever comes to pass;[65] yet so, as thereby neither is God the author of sin[66] nor is violence offered to the will of the creatures, nor is the liberty or contingency of second causes taken away, but rather established.[67]

02. Although God knows whatsoever may or can come to pass upon all supposed conditions,[68] yet hath He not decreed anything because He foresaw it as future, or as that which would come to pass upon such conditions.[69]

03. By the decree of God, for the manifestation of His glory, some men and angels[70] are predestinated unto everlasting life and others foreordained to everlasting death.[71]

04. These angels and men, thus predestinated and foreordained, are particularly and unchangeably designed, and their number so certain and definite that it cannot be either increased or diminished.[72]

05. Those of mankind that are predestinated unto life, God, before the foundation of the world was laid, according to His eternal and immutable purpose, and the secret counsel and good pleasure of His will, hath chosen in Christ unto everlasting glory,[73] out of His mere free grace and love, without any foresight of faith or good works, or perseverance in either of them, or any other thing in the creature, as conditions or causes moving Him thereunto,[74] and all to the praise of His glorious grace.[75]

06. As God hath appointed the elect unto glory so hath He, by the eternal and most free purpose of His will, foreordained all the means thereunto.[76] Wherefore they who are elected, being fallen in Adam, are redeemed by Christ,[77] are effectually called unto faith in Christ by His Spirit working in due season, are justified, adopted, sanctified[78] and kept by His power, through faith, unto salvation.[79] Neither are any other redeemed by Christ, effectually called, justified, adopted, sanctified and saved, but the elect only.[80]

07. The rest of mankind was pleased, according to the unsearchable counsel of His own will, whereby He extendeth or withholdeth mercy, as He pleaseth, for the glory of His sovereign power over His creatures, to pass by; and to ordain them to dishonor and wrath for their sin to the praise of His glorious justice.[81]

08. The doctrine of this high mystery of predestination is to be handled with special prudence and care,[82] that men, attending to the will of God revealed in His Word, and yielding obedience thereunto, may, from the certainty of their effectual vocation, be assured of their eternal election.[83] So shall this doctrine afford matter of praise, reverence and admiration of God,[84] and of humility, diligence and abundant consolation to all that sincerely obey the Gospel.[85]

04. Of Creation

01. It pleased God the Father, Son and Holy Ghost,[86] for the manifestation of the glory of His eternal power, wisdom and goodness,[87] in the beginning to create, or make of nothing, the world, and all things therein, whether visible or invisible, in the space of six days, and all very good.[88]

02. After God had made all other creatures, He created man, male and female,[89] with reasonable and immortal souls,[90] endued with knowledge, righteousness and true holiness, after His own image;[91] having the law of God written in their hearts[92] and power to fulfil it;[93] and yet under a possibility of transgressing, being left to the liberty of their own will, which was subject unto change.[94] Beside this law written in their hearts they received a command not to eat of the tree of the knowledge of good and evil,[95] which while they kept, they were happy in their communion with God, and had dominion over the creatures.[96]

05. Of Providence

01. God the great Creator of all things, doth uphold,[97] direct, dispose and govern all creatures, actions and things[98] from the greatest even to the least,[99] by His most wise and holy providence,[100] according to His infallible foreknowledge[101] and the free and immutable counsel of His own will,[102] to the praise of the glory of His wisdom, power, justice, goodness and mercy.[103]

02. Although in relation to the foreknowledge and decree of God, the first cause, all things come to pass immutably and infallibly,[104] yet by the same providence He ordereth them to fall out according to the nature of second causes, either necessarily, freely or contingently.[105]

03. God in His ordinary providence maketh use of means,[106] yet is free to work without,[107] above[108] and against them[109] at His pleasure.

04. The almighty power, unsearchable wisdom and infinite goodness of God so far manifest themselves in His providence that it extendeth itself even to the first fall, and all other sins of angels and men,[110] and that not by a bare permission,[111] but such as hath joined it with a most wise and powerful bounding,[112] and otherwise ordering and governing of them in a manifold dispensation, to His own holy ends;[113] yet so, as the sinfulness thereof proceedeth only from the creature and not from God, who being most holy and righteous, neither is nor can be the author or approver of sin.[114]

05. The most wise, righteous and gracious God doth oftentimes leave for a season His own children to manifold temptations, and the corruption of their own hearts, to chastise them for their former sins or to discover unto them the hidden strength of corruption and deceitfulness of their hearts, that they may be humbled;[115] and to raise them to a more close and constant dependence for their support upon Himself and to make them more watchful against all future occasions of sin, and for sundry other just and holy ends.[116]

06. As for those wicked and ungodly men whom God as a righteous judge, for former sins doth blind and harden;[117] from them He not only withholdeth His grace whereby they might have been enlightened in their understandings, and wrought upon in their hearts,[118] but sometimes also withdraweth the gifts that they had,[119] and exposeth them to such objects as their corruption makes occasions of sin;[120] and withal gives them over to their own lusts, the temptations of the world and the power of Satan,[121] whereby it comes to pass that they harden themselves even under those means which God useth for the softening of others.[122]

07. As the providence of God doth in general reach to all creatures, so after a most special manner it taketh care of His Church and disposeth all things to the good thereof.[123]

06. Of the Fall of Man of Sin and of the Punishment thereof

01. Our first parents, being seduced by the subtlety and temptation of Satan, sinned in eating the forbidden fruit.[124] This their sin, God was pleased, according to His wise and holy counsel, to permit, having purposed to order it to His own glory.[125]

02. By this sin they fell from their original righteousness and communion with God[126] and so became dead in sin,[127] and wholly defiled in all the parts and faculties of soul and body.[128]

03. They being the root of mankind, the guilt of this sin was imputed;[129] and the same death in sin and corrupted nature conveyed to all their posterity descending from them by ordinary generation.[130]

04. From this original corruption whereby we are utterly indisposed, disabled and made opposite to all good,[131] and wholly inclined to all evil,[132] do proceed all actual transgressions.[133]

05. This corruption of nature during this life doth remain in those that are regenerated[134] and although it be through Christ pardoned and mortified, yet both itself and all the motions thereof are truly and properly sin.[135]

06. Every sin, both original and actual, being a transgression of the righteous law of God and contrary thereunto,[136] doth in its own nature bring guilt upon the sinner,[137] whereby he is bound over to the wrath of God[138] and curse of the law,[139] and so made subject to death[140] with all miseries spiritual,[141] temporal,[142] and eternal.[143]

07. Of God's Covenant with Man

01. The distance between God and the creature is so great that although reasonable creatures do owe obedience unto Him as their Creator, yet they could never have any fruition of Him as their blessedness and reward but by some voluntary condescension on God's part which He hath been pleased to express by way of covenant.[144]

02. The first covenant made with man was a covenant of works[145] wherein life was promised to Adam, and in him to his posterity,[146] upon condition of perfect and personal obedience.[147]

03. Man by his fall, having made himself incapable of life by that covenant, the Lord was pleased to make a second,[148] commonly called the covenant of grace, wherein He freely offereth unto sinners life and salvation by Jesus Christ, requiring of them faith in Him that they may be saved,[149] and promising to give unto all those that are ordained unto eternal life His Holy Spirit, to make them willing and able to believe.[150]

04. This covenant of grace is frequently set forth in Scripture by the name of a testament, in reference to the death of Jesus Christ the Testator and to the everlasting inheritance, with all things belonging to it, therein bequeathed.[151]

05. This covenant was differently administered in the time of the law and in the time of the gospel;[152] under the law it was administered by promises, prophecies, sacrifices, circumcision, the paschal lamb, and other types and ordinances delivered unto the people of the Jews, all fore-signifying Christ to come;[153] which were for that time sufficient and efficacious, through the operation of the Spirit, to instruct and build up the elect in faith in the promised Messiah,[154] by whom they had full remission of sin and eternal salvation, and is called the Old Testament.[155]

06. Under the gospel, when Christ the substance[156] was exhibited, the ordinances in which this covenant is dispensed are the preaching of the Word and the administration of the sacraments of baptism and the Lord's Supper,[157] which though fewer in number and administered with more simplicity and less outward glory, yet in them, it is held forth in more fullness, evidence and spiritual efficacy[158] to all nations, both Jews and Gentiles,[159] and is called the New Testament.[160] There are not therefore two covenants of grace, differing in substance, but one and the same, under various dispensations.[161]

08. Of Christ the Mediator

01. It pleased God in His eternal purpose to choose and ordain the Lord Jesus, His only begotten Son, to be the mediator between God and man,[162] the Prophet,[163] Priest,[164] and King,[165] the Head and Saviour of His Church,[166] the heir of all things[167] and judge of the world,[168] unto whom He did from all eternity give a people, to be His seed[169] and to be by Him in time redeemed, called, justified, sanctified and glorified.[170]

02. The Son of God, the second person in the Trinity, being very and eternal God, of one substance and equal with the Father, did, when the fullness of time was come, take upon Him man's nature[171] with all the essential properties and common infirmities thereof, yet without sin;[172] being conceived by the power of the Holy Ghost in the womb of the Virgin Mary, of her substance.[173] So that two whole, perfect and distinct natures, the Godhead and the manhood, were inseparably joined together in one person, without conversion, composition or confusion.[174] Which person is very God and very man, yet one Christ, the only mediator between God and man.[175]

03. The Lord Jesus, in His human nature thus united to the divine, was sanctified and anointed with the Holy Spirit above measure,[176] having in Him all the treasures of wisdom and knowledge,[177] in whom it pleased the Father that all fullness should dwell;[178] to the end that being holy, harmless, undefiled and full of grace and truth,[179] He might be thoroughly furnished to execute the office of a mediator, and surety.[180] Which office He took not unto Himself, but was thereunto called by His Father,[181] who put all power and judgement into His hand, and gave Him commandment to execute the same.[182]

04. This office the Lord Jesus did most willingly undertake,[183] which that He might discharge, He was made under the law[184] and did perfectly fulfill it,[185] endured most grievous torments immediately in His soul[186] and most painful sufferings in His body,[187] was crucified and died,[188] and was buried, and remained under the power of death, yet saw no corruption.[189] On the third day He arose from the dead[190] with the same body in which He suffered,[191] with which also He ascended into heaven, and there sitteth at the right hand of His Father,[192] making intercession,[193] and shall return to judge men and angels at the end of the world.[194]

05. The Lord Jesus, by His perfect obedience and sacrifice of Himself, which He through the eternal Spirit once offered up unto God, hath fully satisfied the justice of His Father[195] and purchased not only reconciliation, but an everlasting inheritance in the kingdom of heaven, for all those whom the Father hath given unto Him.[196]

06. Although the work of redemption was not actually wrought by Christ till after His incarnation, yet the virtue, efficacy and benefits thereof were communicated unto the elect, in all ages successively from the beginning of the world, in and by those promises, types and sacrifices wherein He was revealed, and signified to be the seed of the woman which should bruise the serpent's head, and the Lamb slain from the beginning of the world, being yesterday and today the same, and for ever.[197]

07. Christ, in the work of mediation, acts according to both natures, by each nature doing that which is proper to itself,[198] yet by reason of the unity of the person that which is proper to one nature is sometimes in Scripture attributed to the person dominated by the other nature.[199]

08. To all those for whom Christ hath purchased redemption He doth certainly and effectually apply and communicate the same,[200] making intercession for them[201] and revealing unto them, in and by the Word, the mysteries of salvation;[202] effectually persuading them by His Spirit to believe and obey, and governing their hearts by His Word and Spirit,[203] overcoming all their enemies by His almighty power and wisdom, in such manner and ways as are most consonant to His wonderful and unsearchable dispensation.[204]

09. Of Free-Will

01. God hath endued the will of man with that natural liberty, that it is neither forced nor, by any absolute necessity of nature, determined to good or evil.[205]

02. Man in his state of innocency had freedom and power to will and to do that which was good and well pleasing to God,[206] but yet mutably, so that he might fall from it.[207]

03. Man, by his fall into a state of sin, hath wholly lost all ability of will to any spiritual good accompanying salvation,[208] so as a natural man, being altogether averse from that good,[209] and dead in sin,[210] is not able by his own strength, to convert himself, or to prepare himself thereunto.[211]

04. When God converts a sinner and translates him into the state of grace, He freeth him from his natural bondage under sin,[212] and by His grace alone enables him freely to will and to do that which is spiritually good,[213] yet so as by that reason of his remaining corruption, he doth not perfectly, nor only will that which is good, but doth also will that which is evil.[214]

05. The will of man is made perfectly and immutably free to good alone in the state of glory only.[215]

10. Of Effectual Calling

01. All those whom God hath predestinated unto life, and those only, He is pleased in His appointed and accepted time, effectually to call[216] by his Word and Spirit,[217] out of that state of sin and death in which they are by nature, to grace and salvation by Jesus Christ,[218] enlightening their minds spiritually and savingly to understand the things of God,[219] taking away their heart of stone and giving unto them a heart of flesh,[220] renewing their wills and by His almighty power, determining them to that which is good,[221] and effectually drawing them to Jesus Christ,[222] yet so as they come most freely, being made willing by His grace.[223]

02. This effectual call is of God's free and special grace alone, not from anything at all foreseen in man,[224] who is altogether passive therein, until, being quickened and renewed by the Holy Spirit,[225] he is thereby enabled to answer this call and to embrace the grace offered and conveyed in it.[226]

03. Elect infants, dying in infancy, are regenerated and saved by Christ, through the Spirit,[227] who worketh when, where and how He pleaseth;[228] so also are all other elect persons who are incapable of being outwardly called by the ministry of the Word.[229]

04. Others, not elected, although they may be called by the ministry of the Word,[230] and may have some common operations of the Spirit,[231] yet they never truly come unto Christ, and therefore cannot be saved;[232] much less can men not professing the Christian religion be saved in any other way whatsoever, be they never so diligent to frame their lives according to the light of nature, and the laws of that religion they do profess.[233] And to assert and maintain that they may is very pernicious, and to be detested.[234]

11. Of Justification

01. Those whom God effectually calleth He also freely justifieth,[235] not by infusing righteousness into them, but by pardoning their sins and by accounting and accepting their persons as righteous, not for anything wrought in them or done by them, but for Christ's sake alone, nor by imputing faith itself, the act of believing, or any other evangelical obedience to them, as their righteousness, but by imputing the obedience and satisfaction of Christ unto them,[236] they receiving and resting on Him and His righteousness by faith, which faith they have not of themselves, it is the gift of God.[237]

02. Faith, thus receiving and resting on Christ and His righteousness is the alone instrument of justification;[238] yet it is not alone in the person justified but is ever accompanied with all other saving graces and is no dead faith, but worketh by love.[239]

03. Christ by His obedience and death did fully discharge the debt of all those that are thus justified and did make a proper, real and full satisfaction to His Father's justice in their behalf.[240] Yet inasmuch as He was given by the Father for them[241] and His obedience and satisfaction accepted in their stead,[242] and both freely, not for anything in them; their justification is only of free grace,[243] that both the exact justice and rich grace of God might be glorified in the justification of sinners.[244]

04. God did from all eternity decree to justify all the elect,[245] and Christ did in the fullness of time die for their sins and rise again for their justification;[246] nevertheless they are not justified until the Holy Spirit doth in due time actually apply Christ unto them.[247]

05. God doth continue to forgive the sins of those that are justified[248] and although they can never fall from the state of justification,[249] yet they may by their sins fall under God's fatherly displeasure and not have the light of His countenance restored unto them until they humble themselves, confess their sins, beg pardon and renew their faith and repentance.[250]

06. The justification of believers under the old testament was in all these respects one and the same with the justification of believers under the new testament.[251]

12. Of Adoption

01. All those that are justified, God vouchsafeth in and for His only Son Jesus Christ to make partakers of the grace of adoption,[252] by which they are taken into the number and enjoy the liberties and privileges of the children of God,[253] have His name put upon them,[254] receive the Spirit of adoption,[255] have access to the throne of grace with boldness,[256] are enabled to cry, Abba, Father,[257] are pitied,[258] protected,[259] provided for[260] and chastened by Him as by a Father,[261] yet never cast off,[262] but sealed to the day of redemption[263] and inherit the promises,[264] as heirs of everlasting salvation.[265]

13. Of Sanctification

01. They who are once effectually called and regenerated, having a new heart and a new spirit created in them, are further sanctified, really and personally, through the virtue of Christ's death and resurrection,[266] by His Word and Spirit dwelling in them;[267] the dominion of the whole body of sin is destroyed[268] and the several lusts thereof are more and more weakened and mortified,[269] and they more and more quickened and strengthened in all saving graces,[270] to the practice of true holiness, without no man shall see the Lord.[271]

02. This sanctification is throughout in the whole man,[272] yet imperfect in this life, there abiding still some remnants of corruption in every part,[273] whence ariseth a continual and irreconcilable war, the flesh lusting against the Spirit, and the Spirit against the flesh.[274]

03. In which war, although the remaining corruption for a time may much prevail,[275] yet through the continual supply of strength from the sanctifying Spirit of Christ, the regenerate part doth overcome,[276] and so the saints grow in grace,[277] perfecting holiness in the fear of God.[278]

14. Of Saving Faith

01. The grace of faith whereby the elect are enabled to believe to the saving of their souls[279] is the work of the Spirit of Christ in their hearts[280] and is ordinarily wrought by the ministry of the Word,[281] by which also, and by the administration of the sacraments and prayer, it is increased and strengthened,[282]

02. By this faith a Christian believeth to be true whatsoever is revealed in the Word, for the authority of God Himself speaking therein,[283] and acteth differently upon that which each particular passage thereof containeth, yielding obedience to the commands,[284] trembling at the threatenings[285] and embracing the promises of God for this life and that which is to come.[286] But the principal acts of saving faith are accepting, receiving and resting upon Christ alone for justification, sanctification and eternal life, by virtue of the covenant of grace.[287]

03. This faith is different in degrees, weak or strong,[288] may be often and many ways assailed and weakened, but gets the victory,[289] growing up in many to the attainment of a full assurance through Christ,[290] who is both the author and finisher of our faith.[291]

15. Of Repentance Unto Life

01. Repentance unto life is an evangelical grace,[292] the doctrine whereof is to be preached by every minister of the Gospel, as well as that of faith in Christ.[293]

02. By it a sinner, out of the sight and sense not only of the danger but also of the filthiness and odiousness of his sins, as contrary to the holy nature and righteous law of God, and upon the apprehension of His mercy in Christ to such as are penitent, so grieves for and hates his sins as to turn from them all unto God,[294] purposing and endeavouring to walk with Him in all the ways of His commandments.[295]

03. Although repentance is not to be rested in, as any satisfaction for sin, or any cause of the pardon thereof,[296] which is the act of God's free grace in Christ,[297] yet it is of such necessity to all sinners that none may expect pardon without it.[298]

04. As there is no sin so small but it deserves damnation,[299] so there is no sin so great that it can bring damnation upon those who truly repent.[300]

05. Men ought not to content themselves with a general repentance, but it is every man's duty to endeavor to repent of his particular sins, particularly.[301]

06. As every man is bound to make private confession of his sins to God, praying for the pardon thereof,[302] upon which, and the forsaking of them, he shall find mercy;[303] so he that scandalizeth his brother or the Church of Christ ought to be willing, by a private or public confession, and sorrow for his sin, to declare his repentance to those that are offended[304] who are thereupon to be reconciled to Him, and in love to receive Him.[305]

16. Of Good Works

01. Good works are only such as God hath commanded in His Holy Word[306] and not such as, without the warrant thereof, as devised by men out of blind zeal, or upon any pretence of good intention.[307]

02. These good works done in obedience to God's commandments are the fruits and evidences of a true and lively faith,[308] and by them believers manifest their thankfulness,[309] strengthen their assurance,[310] edify their brethren,[311] adorn the profession of the Gospel,[312] stop the mouths of the adversaries[313] and glorify God,[314] whose workmanship they are, created in Christ Jesus thereunto,[315] that having their fruit unto holiness they may have the end, eternal life.[316]

03. Their ability to do good works is not at all of themselves, but wholly from the Spirit of Christ.[317] And that they may be enabled thereunto, beside the graces they have already received, there is required an actual influence of the same Holy Spirit to work in them to will and to do of His good pleasure,[318] yet are they not hereupon to grow negligent as if they were not bound to perform any duty unless upon a special motion of the Spirit, but they ought to be diligent in stirring up the grace of God that is in them.[319]

04. They who, in their obedience attain to the greatest height which is possible in this life are so far from being able to supererogate and to do more than God requires, as that they fall short of much which in duty they are bound to do.[320]

05. We cannot by our best works merit pardon of sin or eternal life at the hand of God by reason of the great disproportion that is between them and the glory to come, and the infinite distance which is between us and God, whom by them, we can neither profit nor satisfy for the debt of our former sins,[321] but when we have done all we can, we have done but our duty and are unprofitable servants,[322] and because as they are good they proceed from His Spirit,[323] and as they are wrought by us they are defiled and mixed with so much weakness and imperfection that they cannot endure the severity of God's judgement.[324]

06. Notwithstanding, the persons of believers being accepted through Christ, their good works also are accepted in Him,[325] not as though they were in this life wholly unblameable and unreprovable in God's sight[326] but that He, looking upon them in His Son, is pleased to accept and reward that which is sincere, although accompanied with many weaknesses and imperfections.[327]

07. Work done by unregenerate men, although for the matter of them they may be things which God commands and of good use both to themselves and others,[328] yet because they proceed not from an heart purified by faith[329] nor are done in a right manner according to the Word,[330] nor to a right end, the glory of God,[331] they are therefore sinful and cannot please God or make a man meet to receive grace from God;[332] and yet their neglect of them is more sinful and displeasing unto God.[333]

17. Of the Perseverance of the Saints

01. They whom God has accepted in His Beloved, effectually called and sanctified by His Spirit, can neither totally nor finally fall away from the state of grace, but shall certainly persevere therein to the end, and be eternally saved.[334]

02. This perseverance of the saints depends not upon their own free will but upon the immutability of the decree of election flowing from the free and unchangeable love of God the Father,[335] upon the efficacy of the merit and intercession of Jesus Christ,[336] the abiding of the Spirit and of the seed of God within them,[337] and the nature of the covenant of grace,[338] from all which ariseth also the certainty and infallibility thereof.[339]

03. Nevertheless, they may, through the temptations of Satan and of the world, the prevalency of corruption remaining in them and the neglect of the means of their preservation, fall into grievous sins[340] and for a time continue therein;[341] whereby they incur God's displeasure[342] and grieve His Holy Spirit,[343] come to be deprived of some measure of their graces and comforts,[344] have their hearts hardened[345] and their consciences wounded,[346] hurt and scandalize others[347] and bring temporal judgements upon themselves.[348]

18. Of the Assurance of Grace and Salvation

01. Although hypocrites and other unregenerate men may vainly deceive themselves with false hopes and carnal presumptions of being in the favour of God and estate of salvation[349] (which hope of theirs shall perish),[350] yet such as truly believe in the Lord Jesus and love Him in sincerity, endeavoring to walk in all good conscience before Him, may in this life be certainly assured that they are in the state of grace,[351] and may rejoice in the hope of the glory of God, which hope shall never make them ashamed.[352]

02. This certainty is not a bare conjectural and probable persuasion grounded upon a fallible hope,[353] but an infallible assurance of faith founded upon the divine truth of the promises of salvation,[354] the inward evidence of those graces unto which these promises are made,[355] the testimony of the Spirit of adoption witnessing with our spirits that we are the children of God,[356] which Spirit is the earnest of our inheritance whereby we are sealed to the day of redemption.[357]

03. This infallible assurance doth not so belong to the essence of faith, but that a true believer may wait long and conflict with many difficulties before he be partaker of it,[358] yet being enabled by the Spirit to know the things which are freely given him of God, he may, without extraordinary revelation, in the right use of ordinary means, attain thereunto.[359] And therefore it is the duty of everyone to give all diligence to make his calling and election sure,[360] that thereby his heart may be enlarged in peace and joy in the Holy Ghost, in love and thankfulness to God and in strength and cheerfulness in the duties of obedience,[361] the proper fruits of this assurance, so far is it from inclining men to looseness.[362]

04. True believers may have the assurance of their salvation diverse ways shaken, diminished and intermitted, as by negligence in preserving of it, by falling into some special sin which woundeth the conscience and grieveth the Spirit, by some sudden or vehement temptation, by God's withdrawing the light of His countenance and suffering even such as fear Him to walk in darkness and to have no light,[363] yet are they never utterly destitute of that seed of God and life of faith, that love of Christ and the brethren, that sincerity of heart and conscience of duty out of which by the operation of the Spirit, this assurance may in due time be revived,[364] and by the which in the mean time, they are supported from utter despair.[365]

19. Of the Law of God

01. God gave to Adam a law as a covenant of works, by which He bound him and all his posterity to personal, entire, exact and perpetual obedience, promised life upon the fulfilling, and threatened death upon the breach of it, and endued him with power and ability to keep it.[366]

02. This law, after his fall, continued to be a perfect rule of righteousness and as such, was delivered by God upon Mount Sinai in ten commandments and written in two tables,[367] the four first commandments containing our duty towards God, and the other six our duty to man.[368]

03. Beside this law commonly called moral, God was pleased to give to the people of Israel as a church under age, ceremonial laws containing several typical ordinances, partly of worship, prefiguring Christ, His graces, actions, sufferings and benefits,[369] and partly holding forth diverse instructions of moral duties.[370] All which ceremonial laws are now abrogated under the new testament.[371]

04. To them also as a body politic, He gave sundry judicial laws which expired together with the state of that people, not obliging any other now further than the general equity thereof may require.[372]

05. The moral law doth forever bind all, as well justified persons as others, to the obedience thereof;[373] and that, not only in regard of the matter contained in it, but also in respect of the authority of God the Creator who gave it.[374] Neither doth Christ in the Gospel any way dissolve, but much strengthen this obligation.[375]

06. Although true believers be not under the law, as a covenant of works, to be thereby justified or condemned,[376] yet it is of great use to them as well as to others in that as a rule of life informing them of the will of God and their duty, it directs and binds them to walk accordingly,[377] discovering also the sinful pollutions of their nature, hearts and lives;[378] so as, examining themselves thereby, they may come to further conviction of, humiliation for and hatred against sin,[379] together with a clearer sight of the need they have of Christ and the perfection of His obedience.[380] It is likewise of use to the regenerate, to restrain their corruptions, in that it forbids sin,[381] and the threatenings of it serve to show what even their sins deserve and what afflictions in this life they may expect for them, although freed from the curse thereof threatened in the law.[382] The promises of it, in like manner, show them God's approbation of obedience and what blessings they may expect upon the performance thereof,[383] although not as due to them by the law as a covenant of works.[384] So as a man's doing good and refraining from evil because the law encourageth to the one and deterreth from the other is no evidence of his being under the law and not under grace.[385]

07. Neither are the forementioned uses of the law contrary to the grace of the Gospel, but do sweetly comply with it,[386] the Spirit of Christ subduing and enabling the will of man to do that freely and cheerfully, which the will of God, revealed in the law, requireth to be done.[387]

20. Of Christian Liberty and Liberty of Conscience

01. The liberty which Christ has purchased for believers under the Gospel consists in their freedom from the guilt of sin, the condemning wrath of God, the curse of the moral law,[388] and in their being delivered from this present evil world, bondage to Satan and dominion of sin,[389] from the evil of afflictions, the sting of death, the victory of the grave and everlasting damnation,[390] as also in their free access to God[391] and their yielding obedience unto Him not out of slavish fear, but a child-like love and willing mind.[392] All which were common also to believers under the law.[393] But under the new testament the liberty of Christians is further enlarged in their freedom from the yoke of the ceremonial law to which the Jewish Church was subjected,[394] and in greater boldness of access to the throne of grace,[395] and in fuller communications of the free Spirit of God, than believers under the law did ordinarily partake of.[396]

02. God alone is Lord of the conscience[397] and hath left it free from the doctrines and commandments of men which are, in any thing, contrary to His Word, or beside it, in matters of faith or worship.[398] So that to believe such doctrines, or to obey such commands, out of conscience, is to betray true liberty of conscience,[399] and the requiring of an implicit faith and an absolute and blind obedience is to destroy liberty of conscience and reason also.[400]

03. They who upon pretence of Christian liberty do practice any sin or cherish any lust, do thereby destroy the end of Christian liberty, which is that being delivered out of the hands of our enemies we might serve the Lord without fear, in holiness and righteousness before Him, all the days of our life.[401]

04. And because the powers which God hath ordained and the liberty which Christ hath purchased are not intended by God to destroy, but mutually to uphold and preserve one another, they who upon pretence of Christian liberty shall oppose any lawful power of the lawful exercise of it, whether it be civil or ecclesiastical, resist the ordinance of God.[402] And for their publishing of such practices as are contrary to the light of nature, or to the known principles of Christianity (whether concerning faith, worship or conversation), or to the power of godliness, or such erroneous opinions and practices as either in their own nature or in the manner of publishing or maintaining them, are destructive to the external peace and order which Christ hath established in the Church, they may lawfully be called to account and proceeded against, by the censures of the Church,[403] and by the power of the civil magistrate.[404]

21. Of Religious Worship and the Sabbath Day

01. The light of nature showeth that there is a God who hath lordship and sovereignty over all, is good and doth good unto all, and is therefore to be feared, loved, praised, called upon, trusted in and served with all the heart and with all the soul and with all the might.[405] But the acceptable way of worshipping the true God is instituted by Himself and so limited by His own revealed will that He may not be worshipped according to the imaginations and devices of men or the suggestions of Satan, under any visible representation, or any other way not prescribed in the Holy Scripture.[406]

02. Religious worship is to be given to God the Father, Son and Holy Ghost, and to Him alone,[407] not to angels, saints or any other creature,[408] and since the fall, not without a Mediator, nor in the mediation of any other but Christ alone.[409]

03. Prayer with thanksgiving, being one special part of religious worship,[410] is by God required of all men,[411] and that it may be accepted, it is to be made in the name of the Son[412] by the help of His Spirit,[413] according to His will,[414] with understanding, reverence, humility, fervency, faith, love and perseverance,[415] and if vocal, in a known tongue.[416]

04. Prayer is to be made for all things lawful[417] and for all sorts of men living or that shall live hereafter,[418] but not for the dead[419] nor for those of whom it may be known that they have sinned the sin unto death.[420]

05. The reading of the Scriptures with godly fear,[421] the sound preaching[422] and conscionable hearing of the Word in obedience unto God, with understanding, faith and reverence,[423] singing of psalms with grace in the heart,[424] as also the due administration and worthy receiving of the sacraments instituted by Christ, are all parts of the ordinary religious worship of God;[425] beside religious oaths,[426] and vows,[427] solemn fastings[428] and thanksgivings upon special occasions[429] which are, in their several times and seasons, to be used in an holy and religious manner.[430]

06. Neither prayer nor any other part of religious worship is now, under the Gospel, either tied unto or made more acceptable by any place in which it performed, or towards which it is directed;[431] but God is to be worshipped everywhere[432] in spirit and truth,[433] as in private families[434] daily[435] and in secret, each one by himself,[436] so more solemnly in the public assemblies, which are not carelessly or wilfully to be neglected or forsaken when God, by His Word or providence, calleth thereunto.[437]

07. As it is the law of nature that in general a due proportion of time be set apart for the worship of God, so in His Word by a positive, moral and perpetual commandment binding all men in all ages, He hath particularly appointed one day in seven for a Sabbath to be kept holy unto Him;[438] which from the beginning of the world to the resurrection of Christ was changed into the first day of the week,[439] which in Scripture is called the Lord's Day,[440] and is to be continued to the end of the world as the Christian Sabbath[441]

08. This Sabbath is then kept holy unto the Lord when men, after a due

preparing of their hearts and ordering of their common affairs beforehand, do not only observe an holy rest all the day, from their own works, words and thoughts about their worldly employments and recreations,[442] but also are taken up the whole time in the public and private exercises of His worship, and in the duties of necessity and mercy.[443]

22. Of Lawful Oaths and Vows

01. A lawful oath is part of religious worship[444] wherein, upon just occasion, the person swearing solemnly calleth God to witness what he asserteth or promiseth, and to judge him according to the truth or falsehood of what he sweareth.[445]

02. The name of God only is that by which men ought to swear and therein it is to be used with all fear and reverence.[446] Therefore, to swear vainly or rashly by that glorious and dreadful name or to swear at all by any other thing, is sinful and to be abhorred.[447] Yet as in matters of weight and moment an oath is warranted by the Word of God under the new testament as well as under the old,[448] so a lawful oath, being imposed by lawful authority in such matters, ought to be taken.[449]

03. Whosoever taketh an oath ought duly to consider the weightiness of so solemn ac act, and therein to avouch nothing but what he is fully persuaded is the truth;[450] neither may any man bind himself by oath to anything but what is good and just and what he believeth so to be, and what he is able and resolved to perform.[451] Yet is a sin to refuse an oath touching anything that is good and just being imposed by lawful authority.[452]

04. An oath is to be taken in the plain and common sense of the words, without equivocation or mental reservation.[453] It cannot oblige to sin, but in anything not sinful, being taken, it binds to performance, although to a man's own hurt[454]. Nor is it to be violated, although made to heretics or infidels.[455]

05. A vow is of the like nature with a promissory oath and ought to be made with the like religious care and to be performed with the like faithfulness.[456]

06. It is not to be made to any creature but to God alone,[457] and that it may be accepted, it is to be made voluntarily, out of faith and conscience of duty, in way of thankfulness for mercy received or for the obtaining of what we want, whereby we more strictly bind ourselves to necessary duties, or to other things, so far and so long as they may fitly conduce thereto.[458]

07. No man may vow to do anything forbidden in the Word of God or what would hinder any duty therein commanded, or which is not in his own power, and for the performance whereof he hath no promise of ability from God.[459] In which respects popish monastical vows of perpetual single life, professed poverty and regular obedience are so far from being degrees of higher perfection that they are superstitious and sinful snares in which no Christian may entangle himself.[460]

23. Of the Civil Magistrate

01. God, the supreme Lord and King of all the world, hath ordained civil magistrates to be, under Him, over the people for His own glory and the public good, and to this end hath armed them with the power of the sword for the defense and encouragement of them that are good, and for the punishment of evil doers.[461]

02. It is lawful for Christians to accept and execute the office of a magistrate when called thereunto;[462] in the managing whereof, as they ought especially to maintain piety, justice and peace, according to the wholesome laws of each commonwealth,[463] so for that end they may lawfully, now under the new testament, wage war upon just and necessary occasion.[464]

03. The civil magistrate may not assume to himself the administration of the Word and Sacraments or the power of the keys of the kingdom of heaven,[465] yet he hath authority and it is his duty to take order that unity and peace be preserved in the Church, that the truth of God be kept pure and entire, that all blasphemies and heresies be suppressed, all corruptions and abuses in worship and discipline prevented or reformed, and all the ordinances of God duly settled, administered and observed.[466] For the better effecting whereof he hath power to call synods, to be present at them and to provide that whatsoever is transacted in them be according to the mind of God.[467]

04. It is the duty of people to pray for magistrates,[468] to honor their persons,[469] to pay them tribute or other dues,[470] to obey their lawful commands and to be subject to their authority for conscience sake.[471] Infidelity or difference in religion doth not make void the magistrate's just and legal authority nor free the people from their due obedience to them;[472] from which ecclesiastical persons are not exempted,[473] much less hath the Pope any power and jurisdiction over them in their dominions, or lives, if he shall judge them to be heretics, or upon any other pretense whatsoever.[474]

24. Of Marriage and Divorce

01. Marriage is between one man and one woman, neither is it lawful for any man to have more than one wife nor for any woman to have more than one husband at the same time.[475]

02. Marriage was ordained for the mutual help of husband and wife,[476] for the increase of mankind with a legitimate issue and of the Church with an holy seed[477], and for preventing of uncleanness.[478]

03. It is lawful for all sorts of people to marry, who are able with judgement to give their consent.[479] Yet it is the duty of Christians to marry only in the Lord.[480] And therefore such as profess the true Reformed religion should not marry with infidels, papists or other idolaters, neither should such as are godly be unequally yoked, by marrying with such as are notoriously wicked in their life, or maintain damnable heresies.[481]

04. Marriage ought not to be within the degrees of consanguinity or affinity forbidden by the Word.[482] Nor can such incestuous marriages ever be made lawful by any law of man or consent of parties, so as those persons may live together as man and wife.[483] The man may not marry any of his wife's kindred nearer in blood than he may of his own,[484] nor the woman of her husband's kindred nearer in blood than of her own.

05. Adultery or fornication committed after a contract, being detected before marriage, giveth just occasion to the innocent party to dissolve that contract.[485] In the case of adultery after marriage, it is lawful for the innocent party to sue out a divorce[486] and after the divorce, to marry another, as if the offending party were dead.[487]

06. Although the corruption of man be such as is apt to study arguments unduly to put asunder those whom God hath joined together in marriage, yet nothing but adultery or such wilful desertion as can no way be remedied by the Church or civil magistrate, is cause sufficient of dissolving the bond of marriage,[488] wherein a public and orderly course of proceeding is to be observed, and the persons concerned in it not left to their own wills and discretion, in their own case.[489]

25. Of the Church

01. The catholic or universal Church which is invisible, consists of the whole number of the elect that have been, are, or shall be gathered into one, under Christ the head thereof; and is the spouse, the body, the fullness of Him that filleth all in all.[490]

02. The visible Church which is also catholic or universal under the Gospel (not confined to one nation, as before under the law), consists of all those throughout the world that profess the true religion,[491] and of their children;[492] and is the kingdom of the Lord Jesus Christ,[493] the house and family of God,[494] out of which there is no ordinary possibility of salvation.[495]

03. Unto this catholic, visible Church Christ hath given the ministry, oracles and ordinances of God, for the gathering and perfecting of the saints in this life, to the end of the world; and doth by His own presence and Spirit, according to His promise, make them effectual thereunto.[496]

04. This catholic Church has been sometimes more, sometimes less visible.[497] And particular churches which are members thereof, are more or less pure, according as the doctrine of the Gospel is taught and embraced, ordinances administered and public worship performed or less purely in them.[498]

05. The purest churches under heaven are subject both to mixture and error,[499] and some have so degenerated as to become no churches of Christ but synagogues of Satan.[500] Nevertheless there shall always be a Church on earth to worship God according to His will.[501]

06. There is no other head of the Church but the Lord Jesus Christ.[502] Nor can the Pope of Rome in any sense be head thereof, but is that Antichrist, that man of sin and son of perdition that exalteth himself in the Church, against Christ and all that is called God.[503]

26. Of the Communion of Saints

01. All saints that are united to Jesus Christ their head, by His Spirit and by faith, have fellowship with Him in His grace, sufferings, death, resurrection and glory,[504] and being united to one another in love, they have communion in each other's gifts and graces[505] and are obliged to the performance of such duties, public and private, as do conduce to their mutual good, both in the inward and outward man.[506]

02. Saints by profession are bound to maintain an holy fellowship and communion in the worship of God and in performing such other spiritual services as tend to their mutual edification,[507] as also in relieving each other in outward things according to their several abilities and necessities. Which communion, as God offereth opportunity, is to be extended unto all those who, in every place, call upon the name of the Lord Jesus.[508]

03. This communion which the saints have with Christ doth not make them in any wise partakers of the substance of His Godhead or to be equal with Christ in any respect, either of which to affirm is impious and blasphemous.[509] Nor doth their communion with one another as saints take away or infringe the title or propriety which each man hath in his goods and possessions.[510]

27. Of the Sacraments

01. Sacraments are holy signs and seals of the covenant of grace,[511] immediately instituted by God[512] to represent Christ and His benefits and to confirm our interest in Him,[513] as also to put a visible difference between those that belong unto the Church and the rest of the world,[514] and solemnly engage them to the service of God in Christ, according to His Word.[515]

02. There is in every sacrament a spiritual relation or sacramental union between the sign and the thing signified, whence it comes to pass that the names and effects of the one are attributed to the other.[516]

03. The grace which is exhibited in or by the sacraments rightly used is not conferred by any power in them, neither doth the efficacy of a sacrament depend upon the piety or intention of him that doth administer it,[517] but upon the work of the Spirit[518] and the word of institution, which contains, together with a precept authorizing the use thereof, a promise of benefit to worthy receivers.[519]

04. There be only two sacraments ordained by Christ our Lord in the Gospel, that is to say, baptism and the supper of the Lord, neither of which may be dispensed by any but by a minister of the Word lawfully ordained.[520]

05. The sacraments of the old testament, in regard of the spiritual things thereby signified and exhibited, were for substance the same with those of the new.[521]

28. Of Baptism

01. Baptism is a sacrament of the new testament ordained by Jesus Christ[522] not only for the solemn admission of the party baptized into the visible Church[523] but also to be unto him a sign and seal of the covenant of grace,[524] of his ingrafting into Christ,[525] of regeneration,[526] of remission of sins[527] and of his giving up unto God, through Jesus Christ, to walk in newness of life[528]. Which sacrament is by God's own appointment to be continued in His Church until the end of the world.[529]

02. The outward element to be used in this sacrament is water, wherewith the party is to be baptized in the name of the Father and of the Son and of the Holy Ghost, by a minister of the Gospel lawfully called thereunto.[530]

03. Dipping of the person into the water is not necessary, but baptism is rightly administered by pouring or sprinkling water upon the person.[531]

04. Not only those that do actually profess faith in and obedience unto Christ,[532] but also the infants of one or both believing parents are to be baptized.[533]

05. Although it be a great sin to condemn or neglect this ordinance,[534] yet grace and salvation are not so inseparably annexed unto it as that no person can be regenerated or saved without it,[535] or that all that are baptized are undoubtedly regenerated.[536]

06. The efficacy of baptism is not tied to that moment of time wherein it is administered,[537] yet notwithstanding, by the right use of this ordinance the grace promised is not only offered but really exhibited and conferred by the Holy Ghost to such (whether of age or infants) as that grace belongeth unto, according to the counsel of God's own will, in His appointed time.[538]

07. The sacrament of baptism is but once to be administered unto any person.[539]

29. Of the Lord's Supper

01. Our Lord Jesus in the night wherein He was betrayed instituted the sacrament of His body and blood, called the Lord's Supper, to be observed in His Church unto the end of the world for the perpetual remembrance of the sacrifice of Himself in His death, the sealing all benefits thereof unto true believers, their spiritual nourishment and grown in Him, and to be a bond and pledge of their communion with Him and with each other, as members of His mystical body.[540]

02. In this sacrament Christ is not offered up to His Father nor any real sacrifice made at all for remission of sins of the quick or dead,[541] but only a commemoration of that one offering up of Himself, by Himself, upon the cross, once for all; and a spiritual oblation of all possible praise unto God for the same,[542] so that the popish sacrifice of the mass (as they call it) is most abominably injurious to Christs, one, only sacrifice, the alone propitiation for all the sins of His elect.[543]

03. The Lord Jesus hath in this ordinance appointed His ministers to declare His word of institution to the people, to pray and bless the elements of bread and wine, and thereby to set them apart from a common to an holy use, and to take and break the bread, to take the cup and (they communicating also themselves) to give both to the communicants,[544] but to none who are not then present in the congregation.[545]

04. Private masses or receiving the sacrament by a priest or any other, alone;[546] as likewise the denial of the cup to the people,[547] worshipping the elements, the lifting them up or carrying them about for adoration, and the reserving them for any pretended religious use, are all contrary to the nature of this sacrament and to the institution of Christ.[548]

05. The outward elements in this sacrament, duly set apart to the uses ordained by Christ, have such relation to Him crucified as that truly, yet sacramentally only, they are sometimes called by the name of the things they represent, to wit, the body and blood of Christ;[549] albeit in substance and nature they still remain truly and only bread and wine as they were before.[550]

06. That doctrine which maintains a change of the substance of bread and wine into the substance of Christ's body and blood (commonly called transubstantiation) by consecration of a priest or by any other way, is repugnant not to Scripture alone, but even to common sense and reason, overthroweth the nature of a sacrament and hath been, and is, the cause of manifold superstitions, yea, of gross idolatries.[551]

07. Worthy receivers, outwardly partaking of the visible elements in this sacrament[552] do then also inwardly by faith, really and indeed, yet not carnally and corporally but spiritually, receive and feed upon Christ crucified, and all benefits of His death; the body and blood of Christ being then not corporally or carnally in, with or under the bread and wine, yet as really, but spiritually present to the faith of believers in that ordinance, as the elements themselves are to their outward senses.[553]

08. Although ignorant and wicked men receive the outward elements in this sacrament, yet they receive not the thing signified thereby, but by their unworthy coming thereunto, are guilty of the body and blood of the Lord, to their own damnation. Wherefore all ignorant and ungodly persons, as they are unfit to enjoy communion with Him, so are they unworthy of the Lord's table, and cannot, without great sin against Christ, while they remain such, partake of these holy mysteries[554] or be admitted thereunto.[555]

30. Of Church Censures

01. The Lord Jesus as King and Head of His Church hath therein appointed a government in the hand of Church officers, distinct from the civil magistrate.[556]

02. To these officers the keys of the kingdom of heaven are committed, by virtue whereof they have power respectively to retain and remit sins, to shut that kingdom against the impenitent both by the Word and censures, and to open it unto penitent sinners by the ministry of the Gospel, and by absolution from censures as occasion shall require.[557]

03. Church censures are necessary for the reclaiming and gaining of offending brethren, for deterring of others from the like offenses, for purging out of that leaven which might infect the whole lump, for vindicating the honour of Christ and the holy profession of the Gospel, and for preventing the wrath of God which might justly fall upon the Church if they should suffer His covenant and the seals thereof, to be profaned by notorious and obstinate offenders.[558]

04. For the better attaining of these ends the officers of the Church are to proceed by admonition, suspension from the sacrament of the Lord's Supper for a season and by excommunication from the Church, according to the nature of the crime and demerit of the person.[559]

31. Of Synods and Councils

01. For the better government and further edification of the Church there ought to be such assemblies as are commonly called synods or councils.[560]

02. As magistrates may lawfully call a synod of ministers and other fit persons to consult and advise with about matters of religion,[561] so if magistrates be open enemies to the Church, the ministers of Christ of themselves, by virtue of their office, or they with other fit persons upon delegation from their churches, may meet together in such assemblies.[562]

03. It belongeth to synods and councils ministerially to determine controversies of faith and cases of conscience, to set down rules and directions for the better ordering of the public worship of God and government of His Church, to receive complaints in cases of maladministration and authoritatively to determine the same, which decrees and determinations, if consonant with the Word of God, are to be received with reverence and submission, not only for their agreement with the Word, but also for the power whereby they are made, as being an ordinance of God appointed thereunto in His Word.[563]

04. All synods or councils since the Apostles' times, whether general or particular, may err and many have erred. Therefore they are not to be made the rule of faith or practice, but to be used as a help in both.[564]

05. Synods and councils are to handle or conclude nothing but that which is ecclesiastical, and are not to intermeddle with civil affairs which concern the commonwealth unless by way of humble petition in cases extraordinary, or by way of advice for satisfaction of conscience, if they be thereunto required by the civil magistrate.[565]

32. Of the State of Men after Death and of the Resurrection of the Dead

01. The bodies of men after death return to dust and see corruption.[566] but their souls, which neither die nor sleep, having an immortal subsistence, immediately return to God who gave them;[567] the souls of the righteous being then made perfect in holiness are received into the highest heavens where they behold the face of God in light and glory, waiting for the full redemption of their bodies.[568] And the souls of the wicked are cast into hell where they remain in torments and utter darkness, reserved to the judgement of the great day.[569] Beside these two places, for souls separated from their bodies, the Scripture acknowledgeth none.

02. At the last day such as are found alive shall not die but be changed[570] and all the dead shall be raised up, with the selfsame bodies, and none other (although with different qualities), which shall be united again to their souls forever.[571]

03. The bodies of the unjust shall, by the power of Christ, be raised to dishonour; the bodies of the just, by His Spirit, unto honour, and be made conformable to His own glorious body.[572]

33. Of the Last Judgement

01. God hath appointed a day wherein He will judge the world in righteousness by Jesus Christ,[573] to whom all power and judgement is given of the Father.[574] In which day not only the apostate angels shall be judged[575] but likewise all persons that have lived upon earth shall appear before the tribunal of Christ, to give an account of their thoughts, words and deeds, and to receive according to what they have done in the body, whether good or evil.[576]

02. The end of God's appointing this day is for the manifestation of the glory of His mercy in the eternal salvation of the elect,[577] and of His justice in the damnation of the reprobate who are wicked and disobedient.[578] For then shall the righteous go into everlasting life and receive that fullness of joy and refreshing which shall come from the presence of the Lord,[579] but the wicked who know not God and obey not the Gospel of Jesus Christ, shall be cast into eternal torments, and be punished with everlasting destruction from the presence of the Lord and from the glory of His power.[580]

03. As Christ would have us to be certainly persuaded that there shall be a day of judgement, both to deter all men from sin and for the greater consolation of the godly in their adversity,[581] so will He have that day unknown to men, that they may shake off all carnal security and be always watchful, because they know not at what hour the Lord will come, and may be ever prepared to say, Come Lord Jesus, come quickly. Amen.[582]

[1] Ro 2:14-15; 1:19-20; Ps 19:1-3; Ro 1:32; 2:1.

[2] I Co 1:21; 2:13-14.

[3] He 1:1.

[4] Pr 22:19-21; Lk 1:3-4; Ro 15:4; Mt 4:4, 7, 10; Is 8:19-20.

[5] II Ti 3:15; II Pe 1:19.

[6] He 1:1-2.

[7] Lk 16:29, 31; Ep 2:20; Re 22:18-19; II Ti 3:16.

[8] Lk 24:27-44; Ro 3:2; II Pe 1:21.

[9] II Pe 1:19, 21; II Ti 3:16; I Jn 5:9; I Th 2:13.

[10] I Ti 3:15.

[11] I Jn 2:20, 27; Jn 16:13-14; I Co 2:10-12; Is 59:21.

[12] II Ti 3:15-17; Ga 1:8-9; II Th 2:2.

[13] Jn 6:45; I Co 2:9-12.

[14] I Co 11:13-14; 14:26, 40.

[15] II Pe 3:16.

[16] Ps 119:105, 130.

[17] Mt 5:18.

[18] Is 8:20; Ac 15:15; Jn 5:39, 46.

[19] Jn 5:39.

[20] I Co 14:6, 9, 11, 12, 24, 27, 28.

[21] Cl 3:16.

[22] Ro 15:4.

[23] II Pe 1:20-21; Ac 15:15.

[24] Mt 22:29-31; Ep 2:20; Ac 28:25.

[25] De 6:4; I Co 8:4, 6.

[26] I Th 1:9; Je 10:10.

[27] Jb 11:7-9; 26:14.

[28] Jn 4:24.

[29] I Ti 1:17.

[30] De 4:15-16; Jn 4:24; Lk 24:39.

[31] Ac 14:11, 15.

[32] Ja 1:17; Ma 3:6.

[33] I Ki 8:27; Je 23:23-24.

[34] Ps 90:2; I Ti 1:17.

[35] Ps 145:3.

[36] Gn 17:1; Re 4:8.

[37] Ro 16:27.

[38] Is 6:3; Re 4:8.

[39] Ps 115:3.

[40] Ex 3:14.

[41] Ep 1:11.

[42] Pr 16:4; Ro 11:36.

[43] I Jn 4:8, 16.

[44] Ex 34:6, 7.

[45] He 11:6.

[46] Ne 9:32, 33.

[47] Ps 5:5, 6.

[48] Na 1:2,3; Ex 34:7.

[49] Jn 5:26.

[50] Ac 7:2.

[51] Ps 119:68.

[52] I Ti 6:15; Ro 9:5.

[53] Ac 17:24, 25.

[54] Jb 22:2, 3.

[55] Ro 11:36.

[56] Re 4:11; I Ti 6:15; Da 4:25, 35.

[57] He 4:13.

[58] Ro 11:33, 34; Ps 147:5.

[59] Ac 15:18; Ek 11:5.

[60] Ps 145:17; Ro 7:12.

[61] Re 5:12-14.

[62] I Jn 5:7; Mt 3:16, 17; 28:19; II Co 13:14.

[63] Jn 1:14, 18.

[64] Jn 15:26; Ga 4:6.

[65] Ep 1:11; Ro 11:33; He 6:17; Ro 9:15, 18.

[66] Ja 1:13, 17; I Jn 1:5.

[67] Ac 2:23; Mt 17:12; Ac 4:27, 28; Jn 19:11; Pr 16:33.

[68] Ac 15:18; I Sa 23:11, 12; Mt 11:21, 23.

[69] Ro 9:11, 13, 16, 18.

[70] I Ti 5:21; Mt 25:41.

[71] Ro 9:22, 23; Ep 1:5, 6; Pr 16:4.

[72] II Ti 2:19; Jn 13:18.

[73] Ep 1:4, 9, 11; Ro 8:30; II Ti 1:9; I Th 5:9.

[74] Ro 9:11, 13, 16; Ep 1:4, 9.

[75] Ep 1:6, 12.

[76] I Pe 1:2; Ep 1:4, 5; 2:10; II Th 2:13.

[77] I Th 5:9, 10; Tt 2:14.

[78] Ro 8:30; Ep 1:5; II Th 2:13.

[79] I Pe 1:5.

[80] Jn 17:9; Ro 8:28-33; Jn 6:64, 65; 10:26; 8:47; I Jn 2:19.

[81] Mt 11:25, 26; Ro 9:17, 18, 21, 22; II Ti 2:19, 20; Ju 4; I Pe 2:8.

[82] Ro 9:20; 11:33; De 29:29.

[83] II Pe 1:10.

[84] Ep 1:6; Ro 11:33.

[85] Ro 11:5, 6, 20; II Pe 1:10; Ro 8:33; Lk 10:20.

[86] He 1:2; Jn 1:2, 3; Gn 1:2; Jb 26:13; 33:4.

[87] Ro 1:20; Je 10:12; Ps 104:24; 33:5, 6.

[88] Gn 1; He 11:3; Cl 1:16; Ac 17:24.

[89] Gn 1:27.

[90] Gn 2:7; Ec 12:7; Lk 23:43; Mt 10:28.

[91] Gn 1:26; Cl 3:10; Ep 4:24.

[92] Ro 2:14, 15.

[93] Ec 7:29.

[94] Gn 3:6; Ec 7:29.

[95] Gn 2:17; 3:8-11, 23.

[96] Gn 1:26, 28.

[97] He 1:3.

[98] Da 4:34, 35; Ps 135:6; Ac 17:25, 26, 28; Jb 38-41.

[99] Mt 10:29-31.

[100] Pr 15:3; Ps 104:24; 145:17.

[101] Ac 15:18; Ps 94:8-11.

[102] Ep 1:11; Ps 33:10, 11.

[103] Is 63:14; Ep 3:10; Ro 9:17; Gn 45:7, Ps 145:7.

[104] Ac 2:23.

[105] Gn. 8:22; Je 31:35; Ex 21:13; De 19:5; I Ki 22:28, 34; Is 10:6-7.

[106] Ac 27:31, 44; Is 55:10, 11; Ho 2:21-22.

[107] Ho 1:7; Mt 4:4; Jb 34:10.

[108] Ro 4:19-21.

[109] II Ki 6:6; Da 3:27.

[110] Ro 11:32-34; II Sa 24:1; I Ch 21:1; I Ki 22:22, 23; I Ch 10:4, 13, 14; II Sa 16:10; Ac 2:23; 4:27-28.

[111] Ac 14:16.

[112] Ps 76:10; II Ki 19:28.

[113] Gn 50:20; Is 10:6, 7, 12.

[114] Ja 1:13, 14, 17; I Jn 2:16; Ps 50:21.

[115] II Ch 32:25, 26, 31; II Sa 24:1.

[116] II Co 12:7-9; Ps 73; 77:1, 10, 12; Mk 14:66-72; Jn 21:15, 17.

[117] Ro 1:24, 26, 28; 11:7, 8.

[118] De 29:4.

[119] Mt 13:12; 25:29.

[120] De 2:30; II Ki 8:12, 13.

[121] Ps 81:11-12; II Th 2:10-12.

[122] Ex 7:3; 8:15, 32; II Co 2:15, 16; Is 8:14; I Pe 2:7-8; Is 6:9-10; Ac 28:26-27.

[123] I Ti 4:10; Am 9:8, 9; Ro 8:28; Is 43:3-5, 14.

[124] Gn 3:13; II Co 11:3.

[125] Ro 11:32.

[126] Gn 3:6-8; Ec 7:29; Ro 3:23.

[127] Gn 2:17; Ep 2:1.

[128] Tt 1:15; Gn 6:5; Je 17:9; Ro 3:10-19.

[129] Gn 1:27-28; 2:16-17; Ac 17:26; Ro 5:12, 15-19; I Co 15:21, 22, 45, 49.

[130] Ps 51:5; Gn 5:3; Jb 14:4; 15:14.

[131] Ro 5:6; 8:7; 7:18; Cl 1:21.

[132] Gn 6:5; 8:21; Ro 3:10-12.

[133] Ja 1:14-15; Ep 2:2, 3; Mt 15:19.

[134] I Jn 1:8-10; Ro 7:14, 17, 18, 23; Ja 3:2; Pr 20:9; Ec 7:20.

[135] Ro 7:5, 7, 8, 25; Ga 5:17.

[136] I Jn 3:4.

[137] Ro 2:15; 3:9, 19.

[138] Ep 2:3.

[139] Ga 3:10.

[140] Ro 6:23.

[141] Ep 4:18.

[142] Ro 8:20; La 3:39.

[143] Mt 25:41; II Th 1:9.

[144] Is 40:13-17; Jb 9:32, 33; I Sa 2:25; Ps 113:5, 6; 100:2, 3; Jb 22:2, 3; 35:7, 8; Lk 17:10; Ac 17:24, 25.

[145] Ga 3:12.

[146] Ro 10:5; 5:12-20.

[147] Gn 2:17; Ga 3:10.

[148] Ga 3:21; Ro 8:3; 3:20, 21; Gn

3:15; Is 42:6.

[149] Mk 16:15, 16; Jn 3:16; Ro 10:6, 9; Ga 3:11.

[150] Ek 36:26, 27; Jn 6:44, 45.

[151] He 9:15-17; 7:22; Lk 22:20; I Co 11:25.

[152] II Co 3:6-9.

[153] He 8-10; Ro 4:11; Cl 2:11-12; I Co 5:7.

[154] I Co 10:1-4; He 11:13; Jn 8:56.

[155] Ga 3:7-9; 14.

[156] Ga 2:17.

[157] Mt 28:19, 20; I Co 11:23-25.

[158] He 12:22-28; Je 31:33, 34.

[159] Mt 28:19; Ep 2:15-19.

[160] Lk 22:20.

[161] Ga 3:14, 16; Ac 15:11; Ro 3:21-23, 30; Ps 32:1; Ro 4:3, 6, 16, 17, 23, 24; He 13:8.

[162] Is 42:1; I Pe 1:19, 20; Jn 3:16; II Ti 2:5.

[163] Ac 3:22.

[164] He 5:5,6.

[165] Ps 2:6; Lk 1:33.

[166] Ep 5:23.

[167] He 1:2.

[168] Ac 17:31.

[169] Jn 17:6; Ps 22:30; Is 53:10.

[170] I Ti 2:6; Is 55:4, 5; I Co 1:30.

[171] Jn 1:1, 14; I Jn 5:20; Ph 2:6; Ga 4:4.

[172] He 2:14, 16, 17; 4:15.

[173] Lk 1:27, 31, 35; Ga 4:4.

[174] Lk 1:35; Cl 2:9; Ro 9:5; I Pe 3:18; I Ti 3:16.

[175] Ro 1:3, 4; I Ti 2:5.

[176] Ps 45:7; Jn 3:34.

[177] Cl 2:3.

[178] Cl 1:19.

[179] He 7:26; Jn 1:14.

[180] Ac 10:38; He 12:24; 7:22.

[181] He 5:4, 5.

[182] Jn 5:22, 27; Mt 28:18; Ac 2:36.

[183] Ps 40:7, 8; He 10:5-10; Jn 10:18; Ph 2:8.

[184] Ga 4:4.

[185] Mt 3:15; 5:17.

[186] Mt 26:37-38; Lk 22:44, Mt 27:46.

[187] Mt 26-27.

[188] Ph 2:8.

[189] Ac 2:23, 24, 27; 13:37; Ro 6:9.

[190] I Co 15:3-4.

[191] Jn 20: 25, 27.

[192] Mk 16:19.

[193] Ro 8:34; He 9:24; 7:25.

[194] Ro 14:9, 10; Ac 1:11; 10:42; Mt 13:40-42; Ju 6; II Pe 2:4.

[195] Ro 5:19; He 9:14, 16; 10:14; Ep 5:2; Ro 3:25, 26.

[196] Da 9:24, 26; Cl 1:19, 20; Ep 1:11, 14; Jn 17:2; He 9:12, 15.

[197] Ga 4:4, 5; Gn 3:15; Re 13:8; He 13:8.

[198] He 9:14; I Pe 3:18.

[199] Ac 20:28; Jn 3:13; I Jn 3:16.

[200] Jn 6:37, 39; 10:15, 16.

[201] I Jn 2:1, 2; Ro 8:34.

[202] Jn 15:13, 15; Ep 1:7-9; Jn 17:6.

[203] Jn 14:16; He 12:2; II Co 4:13; Ro 8:9, 14; 15:18, 19; Jn 17:17.

[204] Ps 110:1; I Co 15:25, 26; Ml 4:2, 3; Cl 2:15.

[205] Mt 17:12; Ja 1:14; De 30:19.

[206] Ec 7:29; Gn 1:26.

[207] Gn 2:16, 17; 3:6.

[208] Ro 5:6; 8:7; Jn 15:5.

[209] Ro 3:10-12.

[210] Ep 2:1, 5; Cl 2:13.

[211] Jn 6:44, 65; Ep 2:2-5; I Co 2:14; Tt 3:3-5.

[212] Cl 1:13; Jn 8:34, 36.

[213] Ph 2:13; Ro 6:18, 22.

[214] Ga 5:17; Ro 7:15, 18, 19, 21, 23.

[215] Ep 4:13; He 12:23; I Jn 3:2; Ju 24.

[216] Ro 8:30; 11:7; Ep 1:10, 11.

[217] II Th 2:13, 14; II Co 3:3, 6.

[218] Ro 8:2; Ep 2:1-5; II Ti 1:9, 10.

[219] Ac 26:18; I Co 2:10, 12; Ep 1:17, 18.

[220] Ek 36:26.

[221] Ek 11:19; Ph 2:13; De 30:6; Ek 36:27.

[222] Ep 1:19; Jn 6:44, 45.

[223] So 1:4; Ps 110:3; Jn 6:37; Ro 6:16-18.

[224] II Ti 1:9; Tt 3:4, 5; Ep 2:4, 5, 8, 9;

Ro 9:11.
[225] I Co 2:14; Ro 8:7; Ep 2:5.
[226] Jn 6:37; Ek 36:27; Jn 5:25.
[227] Lk 18:15, 16; Ac 2:38, 39; Jn 3:3, 5; I Jn 5:12; Ro 8:9.
[228] Jn 3:8.
[229] I Jn 5:12; Ac 4:12.
[230] Mt 22:14.
[231] Mt 7:22; 13:20, 21; He 6:4, 5.
[232] Jn 6:64-66; 8:24.
[233] Ac 4:12; Jn 14:6; Ep 2:12; Jn 4:22; 17:3.
[234] II Jn 9-11; I Co 16:22; Ga 1:6-8.
[235] Ro 8:30; 3:24.
[236] Ro 4:5-8; II Co 5:19, 21; Ro 3:22, 24, 25, 27, 28; Tt 3:5, 7; Ep 1:7, Je 23:6; I Co 1:30, 31; Ro 5:17-19.
[237] Ac 10:44; Ga 2:16; Ph 3:9; Ac 13:38, 39; Ep 2:7, 8.
[238] Jn 1:12; Ro 3:28; 5:1.
[239] Ja 2:17, 22, 26; Ga 5:6.
[240] Ro 5:8-10, 19; I Ti 2:5, 6; He 10:10, 14; Da 9:24, 26; Is 53:4-6, 10-12.
[241] Ro 8:32.
[242] II Co 5:21; Mt 3:17; Ep 5:2.
[243] Ro 3:24; Ep 1:7.
[244] Ro 3:26; Ep 2:7.
[245] Ga 3:8; I Pe 1:2, 19, 20; Ro 8:30.
[246] Ga 4:4; I Ti 2:6; Ro 4:25.
[247] Cl 1:21, 22; Ga 2:16; Tt 3:4-7.
[248] Mt 6:12; I Jn 1:7, 9; 2:1, 2.
[249] Lk 22:32; Jn 10:28; He 10:14.
[250] Ps 89:31-33; 51:7-12; 32:5; Mt 26:75; I Co 11:30, 32; Lk 1:20.
[251] Ga 3:9, 13, 14; Ro 4:22-24; He 13:8.
[252] Ep 1:5; Ga 4:4, 5.
[253] Ro 8:17; Jn 1:12.
[254] Je 14:9; II Co 6:18; Re 3:12.
[255] Ro 8:15.
[256] Ep 3:12; Ro 5:2.
[257] Ga 4:6.
[258] Ps 103:13.
[259] Pr 14:26.
[260] Mt 6:30, 32; I Pe 5:7.
[261] He 12:6.
[262] La 3:31.
[263] Ep 4:30.
[264] He 6:12.
[265] I Pe 1:3, 4; He 1:14.
[266] I Co 6:11; Ac 20:32; Ph 3:10; Ro 6:5, 6.
[267] Jn 17:17; Ep 5:26; II Th 2:13.
[268] Ro 6:6, 14.
[269] Ga 5:24; Ro 8:13.
[270] Cl 1:11; Ep 3:16-19.
[271] II Co 7:1; He 12:14.
[272] I Th 5:23.
[273] I Jn 1:10; Ro 7:18, 23; Ph 3:12.
[274] Ga 5:17; I Pe 2:11.
[275] Ro 7:23.
[276] Ro 6:14; I Jn 5:4; Ep 4:15, 16.
[277] II Pe 3:18; II Co 3:18.
[278] II Co 7:1.
[279] He 10:39.
[280] II Co 4:13; Ep 1:17-19; 2:8.
[281] Ro 10:14, 17.
[282] I Pe 2:2; Ac 20:32; Ro 4:11; Lk 17:5; Ro 1:16, 17.
[283] Jn 4:42; I Th 2:13; I Jn 5:10; Ac 24:14.
[284] Ro 16:26.
[285] Is 66:2.
[286] He 11:13; I Ti 4:8.
[287] Jn 1:12; Ac 16:31; Ga 2:20; Ac 15:11.
[288] He 5:13, 14; Ro 4:19, 20; Mt 6:30; 8:10.
[289] Lk 22:31, 32; Ep 6:16; I Jn 5:4, 5.
[290] He 6:11, 12; 10:22; Cl 2:2.
[291] He 12:2.
[292] Ze 12:10; Ac 11:18.
[293] Lk 24:47; Mk 1:15; Ac 20:21.
[294] Ek 18:30, 31; Is 30:22; Ps 51:4; Je 31:18, 19; Jo 2:12, 13; Am 5:15; Ps 119:128; II Co 7:11.
[295] Ps 119:6, 59, 106; Lk 1:6; II Ki 23:25.
[296] Ek 36:31, 32; 16:61-63.
[297] Ho 14:2, 4; Ro 3:24; Ep 1:7.
[298] Lk 13:3, 5; Ac 17:30, 31.
[299] Ro 6:23; 5:12; Mt 12:36.
[300] Is 55:7; Ro 8:1; Is 1:16, 18.
[301] Ps 19:13; Lk 19:8; I Ti 1:13, 15.

302 Ps 51:4, 5, 7, 9, 14; 32:5, 6.

303 Pr 28:13; I Jn 1:9.

304 Ja 5:16; Lk 17:3, 4; Js 7:19; Ps 51.

305 II Co 2:8.

306 Mi 6:8; Ro 12:2; He 13:21.

307 Mt 15:9; Is 29:13; I Pe 1:18; Ro 10:2; Jn 16:2; I Sa 15:21-23.

308 Ja 2:18, 22.

309 Ps 116:12, 13; I Pe 2:9.

310 I Jn 2:3, 5; II Pe 1:5-10.

311 II Co 9:2; Mt 5:16.

312 Tt 2:5, 9-12; I Ti 6:1.

313 I Pe 2:15.

314 I Pe 2:12; Ph 1:11; Jn 15:8.

315 Ep 2:10.

316 Ro 6:22.

317 Jn 15:4-6; Ek 36:26, 27.

318 Ph 2:13; 4:13; II Co 3:5.

319 Ph 2:12; He 6:11, 12; II Pe 1:3, 5, 10, 11; Is 64:7; II Ti 1:6; Ac 26:6-7; Ju 20, 21.

320 Lk 17:10; Ne 13:22; Jb 9:2, 3; Ga 5:17.

321 Ro 3:20; 4:2, 4, 6; Ep 2:8, 9; Tt 3:5-7; Ro 8:18; Ps 16:2; Jb 22:2, 3; 35:7, 8.

322 Lk 17:10.

323 Ga 5:22, 23.

324 Is 64:6; Ga 5:17; Ro 7:15, 18; Ps 143:2; 130:3.

325 Ep 1:6; I Pe 2:5; Ex 28:38; Gn 4:4; He 11:4.

326 Jb 9:20; Ps 143:2.

327 He 13:20, 21; II Co 8:12; He 6:10; Mt 25:21, 23.

328 II Ki 10:30, 31; I Ki 21:27, 29; Ph 1:15, 16, 18.

329 Gn 4:3-5; He 11:4, 6.

330 I Co 13:3; Is 1:12.

331 Mt 6:2, 5, 16.

332 Hg 2:14; Tt 1:15; Am 5:21, 22; Ho 1:4; Ro 9:16; Tt 3:5.

333 Ps 14:4; 36:3; Jb 21:14, 15; Mt 25:41-45; 23:23.

334 Ph 1:6; II Pe 1:10; Jn 10:28, 29; I Jn 3:9; I Pe 1:5, 9.

335 II Ti 2:18, 19; Je 31:3.

336 He 10:10, 14; 13:20, 21; 9:12-15; Ro 8:33-39; Jn 17:11, 24; Lk 22:32.

337 Jn 14:16, 17; I Jn 2:27; 3:9.

338 Je 32:40.

339 Jn 10:28; II Th 3:3; I Jn 2:19.

340 Mt 26:70, 72, 74.

341 Ps 51:14.

342 Is 64:5, 7, 9; II Sa 11:27.

343 Ep 4:30.

344 Ps 51:8, 10, 12; Re 2:4; So 5:2-4, 6.

345 Is 36:17; Mk 6:52; 16:14.

346 Ps 32:3, 4; 51:8.

347 II Sa 12:14.

348 Ps 89:31, 32; I Co 11:32.

349 Jb 8:13, 14; Mi 3:11; De 29:19; Jn 8:41.

350 Mt 7:22, 23.

351 I Jn 2:3; 3:14, 18, 19, 21, 24; 5:13.

352 Ro 5:2, 5.

353 He 6:11, 19.

354 He 6:17, 18.

355 II Pe 1:4, 5, 10, 11; I Jn 2:3; 3:14; II Co 1:12.

356 Ro 8:15, 16.

357 Ep 1:13, 14; 4:30; II Co 1:21, 22.

358 I Jn 5:13; Is 50:10; Mk 9:24; Ps 88; 77:1-12.

359 I Co 2:12; I Jn 4:13; He 6:11, 12; Ep 3:17-19.

360 II Pe 1:10.

361 Ro 5:1, 2, 5; 14:17; 15:13; Ep 1:3, 4; Ps 4:6, 7; 119:32.

362 I Jn 2:1, 2; Ro 6:1, 2; Tt 2:11, 12, 14; II Co 7:1; Ro 8:1, 12; I Jn 3:2, 3; Ps 130:4; I Jn 1:6, 7.

363 So 5:2, 3, 6; Ps 51:8, 12, 14; Ep 4:30, 31; Ps 77:1-10; Mt 26:69-72; Ps 31:22; 88; Is 50:10.

364 I Jn 3:9; Lk 22:32; Jb 13:15; Ps 73:15; 51:8; 12; Is 50:10.

365 Mi 7:7-9; Je 52:40; Is 54:7-10; Ps 22:1; 88.

366 Gn 1:26, 27; 2:17; Ro 2:14, 15; 10:5; 5:12, 19; Ga 3:10, 12; Ec 7:29; Jb 28:28.

367 Ja 1:25; 2:8, 10-12; Ro 13:8, 9; De 5:32; 10:4; Ex 34:1.

[368] Mt 22:37-40.

[369] He 9; 10:1; Ga 4:1-3; Cl 2:17.

[370] I Co 5:7; II Co 6:17; Ju 23.

[371] Cl 2:14, 16, 17; Da 9:27; Ep 2:15, 16.

[372] Ex 21; 22:1-29; Gn 49:10; I Pe 2:13, 14; Mt 5:17, 38, 39; I Co 9:8-10.

[373] Ro 13:8-10; Ep 6:2; I Jn 2:3, 4, 7, 8.

[374] Ja 2:10, 11.

[375] Mt 5:17-19; Ja 2:8; Ro 3:31.

[376] Ro 6:14; Ga 2:16; 3:13; 4:4, 5; Ac 13:39; Ro 8:1.

[377] Ro 7:12, 22, 25; Ps 119:4-6; I Co 7:19; Ga 5:14, 16, 18-23.

[378] Ro 7:7; 3:20.

[379] Ja 1:23-25; Ro 7:9, 14, 24.

[380] Ga 3:24; Ro 7:24, 25; 8:3, 4.

[381] Ja 2:11; Ps 119:101, 104, 128.

[382] Ez 9:13, 14; Ps 89:30-34.

[383] Le 26:1, 10, 14; II Co 6:16; Ep 6:2, 3; Ps 37:11; Mt 5:5; Ps 19:11.

[384] Ga 2:16; Lk 17:10.

[385] Ro 6:12, 14; I Pe 3:8-12; Ps 34:12-16; He 12:28, 29.

[386] Ga 3:21.

[387] Ek 36:27; He 8:10; Je 31:33.

[388] Tt 2:14; I Th 1:10; Ga 3:13.

[389] Ga 1:4; Cl 1:13; Ac 26:18; Ro 6:14.

[390] Ro 8:28; Ps 119:71; I Co 15:54-57; Ro 8:1.

[391] Ro 5:1, 2.

[392] Ro 8:14, 15; I Jn 4:18.

[393] Ga 3:9, 14.

[394] Ga 4:1-3, 6, 7; 5:1; Ac 15:10, 11.

[395] He 4:14, 16; 10:19-22.

[396] Jn 7:38, 39; II Co 3:13, 17, 18.

[397] Ja 4:12; Ro 14:4.

[398] Ac 4:19; 5:29; I Co 7:23; Mt 23:8-10; II Co 1:24; Mt 15:9.

[399] Cl 2:20, 22, 23; Ga 1:10; 2:4, 5; Ps 5:1.

[400] Ro 10:17; 14:23; Is 8:20; Ac 17:11; Jn 4:22; Ho 5:11; Re 13:12, 16, 17; Je 8:9.

[401] Ga 5:13; I Pe 2:16; II Pe 2:19; Jn

8:34; Lk 1:74, 75.

[402] Mt 12:25; I Pe 2:13, 14, 16; Ro 13:1-8; He 13:17.

[403] Ro 1:32, I Co 5:1, 5, 11, 13; II Jn 10, 11; II Th 3:14; I Ti 6:3-5; Tt 1:10, 11, 13; 3:10; Mt 18:15-17; I Ti 1:19, 20; Re 2:2, 14, 15, 20; 3:9.

[404] De 13:6-12; Ro 13:3, 4; II Jn 10, 11; Ez 7:23-28; Re 17:12, 16, 17; Ne 13:15, 17, 21, 22, 25, 30; II Ki 23:5, 6, 9, 20, 21; II Ch 34:33; 15:12, 13, 16; Da 3:29; I Ti 2:2; Is 49:23; Ze 13:2, 3.

[405] Ro 1:20; Ac 17:24; Ps 119:68; Je 10:7; Ps 31:23; 18:3; Ro 10:12; Ps 62:8; Js 24:14; Mk 12:33.

[406] De 12:32; Mt 15:9; Ac 17:25; Mt 4:9-10; De 4:15-20; Ex 20:4-6; Cl 2:23.

[407] Mt 4:10; Jn 5:23; II Co 13:14.

[408] Cl 2:18; Re 19:10; Ro 1:25.

[409] Jn 14:6; I Ti 2:5; Ep 2:18; Cl 3:17.

[410] Ph 4:6.

[411] Ps 65:2.

[412] Jn 14:13, 14; I Pe 2:5.

[413] Ro 8:26.

[414] I Jn 5:14.

[415] Ps 47:7; Ec 5:1, 2; He 12:28; Gn 18:27; Ja 5:16; 1:6, 7; Mk 11:24; Mt 6:12, 14, 15; Cl 4:2; Ep 6:18.

[416] I Co 14:14.

[417] I Jn 5:14.

[418] I Ti 2:1, 2; Jn 17:20; II Sa 7:29; Ru 4:12.

[419] II Sa 12:21-23; Lk 16:25, 26; Re 14:13.

[420] I Jn 5:16.

[421] Ac 15:21; Re 1:3.

[422] II Ti 4:2.

[423] Ja 1:22; Ac 10:33; Mt 13:19; He 4:2; Is 66:2.

[424] Cl 3:16; Ep 5:19; Ja 5:13.

[425] Mt 28:19; I Co 11:23-29; Ac 2:42.

[426] De 6:13; Ne 10:29.

[427] Is 19:21; Ec 5:4, 5.

[428] Jo 2:12; Es 4:16; Mt 9:15; I Co 7:5.

[429] Ps 107; Es 9:22.
[430] He 12:28.
[431] Jn 4:21.
[432] Ma 1:11; I Ti 2:8.
[433] Jn 4:23, 24.
[434] Je 10:25; De 6:6, 7; Jb 1:5; II Sa 6:18, 20; I Pe 3:7; Ac 10:2.
[435] Mt 6:11.
[436] Mt 6:6; Ep 6:18.
[437] Is 56:7; He 10:25; Pr 1:20, 21, 24; 8:34; Ac 13:42; Lk 4:16; Ac 2:42.
[438] Ex 20:8, 10, 11; Is 56:2, 4, 6, 7.
[439] Gn 2:2, 3; I Co 16:1, 2; Ac 20:7.
[440] Re 1:10.
[441] Ex 20:8, 10; Mt 5:17, 18.
[442] Ex 20:8; 16:23, 25, 26, 29, 30; 31:15-17; Is 58:13; Ne 13:15-22.
[443] Is 58:13; Mt 12:1-13.
[444] De 10:20.
[445] Ex 20:7; Le 19:12; II Co 1:23; II Ch 6:22, 23.
[446] De 6:13.
[447] Ex 20:7; Je 5:7; Mt 5:34, 37; Ja 5:12.
[448] He 6:16; II Co 1:23; Is 65:16.
[449] I Ki 8:31; Ne 13:25; Ez 10:25.
[450] Ex 20:7; Je 4:2.
[451] Gn 24:2, 3, 5, 6, 8, 9.
[452] Nu 5:19, 21; Ne 5:12; Ex 22:7-11.
[453] Je 4:2; Ps 24:4.
[454] I Sa 25:22, 32-34; Ps 15:4.
[455] Ek 17:16, 18, 19; Js 9:18, 19; II Sa 21:1.
[456] Is 19:21; Ec 5:4-6; Ps 61:8; 66:13, 14.
[457] Ps 76:11; Je 44:25, 26.
[458] De 23:21-23; Ps 50:14; Gn 28:20-22; I Sa 1:11; Ps 66:13, 14; 132:2-5.
[459] Ac 23:12, 14; Mk 6:26; Nu 30:5, 8, 12, 13.
[460] Mt 19:11, 12; I Co 7:2, 9; Ep 4:28; I Pe 4:2; I Co 7:23.
[461] Ro 13:1-4; I Pe 2:13, 14.
[462] Pr 8:15, 16; Ro 13:1, 2, 4.
[463] Ps 2:10-12; I Ti 2:2; Ps 82:3, 4; II Sa 23:3; I Pe 2:13.
[464] Lk 3:14; Ro 13:4; Mt 8:9, 10; Ac

10:1, 2; Re 17:14, 16.
[465] II Ch 26:18; Mt. 18:17; 16:19; I Co 12:28, 29; Ep 4:11, 12; I Co 4:1, 2; Ro 10:15; He 5:4.
[466] Is 49:23; Ps 122:9; Ez 7:23, 25-28; Le 24:16; De 13:5, 6, 12; II Ki 18:4; I Ch 13:1-9; II Ki 24:1-26; II Ch 34:33; 15:12, 13.
[467] II Ch 19:8-11; 29-30; Mt 2:4, 5.
[468] I Ti 2:1, 2.
[469] I Pe 2:17.
[470] Ro 13:6, 7.
[471] Ro 13:5; Tt 1:3.
[472] I Pe 2:13, 14, 16.
[473] Ro 13:1; I Ki 2:35; Ac 25:9-11; II Pe 2:1, 10, 11; Ju 8-11.
[474] II Th 2:4; Re 13:15-17.
[475] Gn 2:24; Mt 19:5, 6; Pr 2:17.
[476] Gn 2:18.
[477] Ma 2:15.
[478] I Co 7:2, 9.
[479] He 13:4; I Ti 4:3; I Co 7:36-38; Gn 24:57, 58.
[480] I Co 7:39.
[481] Gn 34:14; Ex 34:16; De 7:3, 4; I Ki 11:4; Ne 13:25-27; Ma 2:11, 12; II Co 6:14.
[482] Le 18; I Co 5:1; Am 2:7.
[483] Mk 6:18; Le 18:24-28.
[484] Le 20:19-21.
[485] Mt 1:18-20.
[486] Mt 5:31, 32.
[487] Mt 19:9; Ro 7:2,3.
[488] Mt 19:8, 9; I Co 7:15; Mt 19:6.
[489] De 24:1-4.
[490] Ep 1:10, 22, 23; 5:23; 27, 32; Cl 1:18.
[491] I Co 1:2; 12:12, 13; Ps 2:8; Re 7:9; Ro 15:9-12.
[492] I Co 7:14; Ac 2:39; Ek 16:20, 21; Ro 11:16; Gn 3:15; 17:7.
[493] Mt 13:47; Is 9:7.
[494] Ep 2:19; 3:15.
[495] Ac 2:47.
[496] I Co 12:23; Ep 4:11-13; Mt 28:19, 20; Is 59:21.
[497] Ro 11:3, 4; Re 12:6, 14.
[498] Re 2-3; I Co 5:6, 7.

[499] I Co 13:12; Re 2-3; Mt 13:24-30, 47.

[500] Re 18:2; Ro 11:18-22.

[501] Mt 16:18; Ps 72:17; 102:28; Mt 28:19, 20.

[502] Cl 1:18; Ep 1:22.

[503] Mt 23:8-10; II Th 2:3, 4, 8, 9; Re 13:6.

[504] I Jn 1:3; Ep 3:16-19; Jn 1:16; Ep 2:5, 6; Ph 3:10; Ro 6:5,6; II Ti 2:12.

[505] Ep 4:15-16; I Co 12:7; 3:21-23; Cl 2:13.

[506] I Th 5:11, 14; Ro 1:11, 12, 14; I Jn 3:16-18; Ga 6:10.

[507] He 10:24, 25; Ac 2:42, 46; Is 2:3; I Co 11:20.

[508] Ac 2:44, 45; I Jn 3:17; II Co 8:8-9; Ac 11:29, 30.

[509] Cl 1:18, 19; I Co 8:6; Is 42:8; I Ti 6:15, 16; Ps 45:7; He 1:8, 9.

[510] Ex 20:15; Ep 4:28; Ac 5:4.

[511] Ro 4:11; Gn 17:7, 10.

[512] Mt 28:19; I Co 11:23.

[513] I Co 10:16; 11:25, 26; Ga 3:27.

[514] Ro 15:8; Ex 12:48; Gn 34:14.

[515] Ro 6:3, 4; I Co 10:16, 21.

[516] Gn 17:10; Mt 26:27, 28; Tt 3:5.

[517] Ro 2:28, 29; I Pe 3:21.

[518] Mt 3:11; I Co 12:13.

[519] Mt 26:27, 28; 28:19, 20.

[520] Mt 28:19; I Co 11:20, 23; 4:1; He 5:4.

[521] I Co 10:1-4.

[522] Mt 28:19.

[523] I Co 12:13.

[524] Ro 4:11; Cl 2:11, 12.

[525] Ga 3:27; Ro 6:5.

[526] Tt 3:5.

[527] Mk 1:4.

[528] Ro 6:3, 4.

[529] Mt 28:19, 20.

[530] Mt 3:11; Jn 1:33; Mt 28:19, 20.

[531] He 9:10, 19-22; Ac 2:41; 16:33; Mk 7:4.

[532] Mk 16:15, 16; Ac 8:37, 38.

[533] Gn 17:7, 9; Ga 3:9, 14; Cl 2:11, 12; Ac 2:38, 39; Ro 4:11, 12; I Co

7:14; Mt 28:19; Mk 10:13-16; Lk 18:15.

[534] Lk 7:30; Ex 4:24-26.

[535] Ro 4:11; Ac 10:2, 4, 22, 31, 45, 47.

[536] Ac 8:13, 23.

[537] Jn 3:5, 8.

[538] Ga 3:27; Tt 3:5; Ep 5:25, 26; Ac 2:38, 41.

[539] Tt 3:5.

[540] I Co 11:23-26; 10:16, 17, 21; 12:13.

[541] He 9:22, 25, 26, 28.

[542] I Co 11:24-26; Mt 26:26, 27.

[543] He 7:23, 24, 27; 10:11, 12, 14, 18.

[544] Mt 26:26-28; Mk 14:22-24; Lk 22:19, 20; I Co 11:23-27.

[545] Ac 20:7; I Co 11:20.

[546] I Co 10:6.

[547] Mk 14:23; I Co 11:25-29.

[548] Mt 15:9.

[549] Mt 26:26-28.

[550] I Co 11:26-28; Mt 26:29.

[551] Ac 3:21; I Co 11:24-26; Lk 24:6, 39.

[552] I Co 11:28.

[553] I Co 10:16.

[554] I Co 11:27-29; II Co 6:14-16.

[555] I Co 5:6, 7, 13; II Th 3:6, 14, 15; Mt 7:6.

[556] Is 9:6, 7; I Ti 5:17; I Th 5:12; Ac 20:17, 28; He 13:7, 17, 24; I Co 12:28; Mt 28:18-20.

[557] Mt 16:19; 18:17, 18; Jn 20:21-23; II Co 2:6-8.

[558] I Co 5; I Ti 5:20; Mt 7:6; I Ti 1:20; I Co 11:27; Ju 23.

[559] I Th 5:12; II Th 3:6, 14, 15; I Co 5:4, 5, 13; Mt 18:17; Tt 3:10.

[560] Ac 15:2, 4, 6.

[561] Is 49:23; I Ti 2:1, 2; II Ch 19:8-11; 29-30; Mt 2:4, 5; Pr 11:14.

[562] Ac 15:2, 4, 22, 23, 25.

[563] Ac 15:15, 19, 24, 27-31; 16:4; Mt 18:17-20.

[564] Ep 2:20; Ac 17:11; I Co 2:5; II Co 1:24.

[565] Lk 12:13-14; Jn 18:36.

[566] Gn 3:19; Ac 13:36.

[567] Lk 23:43; Ec 12:7.

[568] He 12:23; II Co 5:1, 6, 8; Ph 1:23; Ac 3:21; Ep 4:10.

[569] Lk 16:23, 24; Ac 1:15; Ju 6, 7; I Pe 3:19.

[570] I Th 4:17; I Co 15:51, 52.

[571] Jb 19:26, 27; I Co 15:42-44.

[572] Ac 24:15; Jn 5:28, 29; I Co 15:42; Ph 3:21.

[573] Ac 17:31.

[574] Jn 5:22, 27.

[575] I Co 6:3; Ju 6; II Pe 2:4.

[576] II Co 5:10; Ec 12:14; Ro 2:16; 14:10, 12; Mt 12:36, 37.

[577] Ro 9:23; Mt 25:21.

[578] Ro 2:5-6; II Th 1:7,8; Ro 9:22.

[579] Mt 25:31-34; Ac 3:19; II Th 1:7.

[580] Mt 25:41, 46; II Th 1:9.

[581] II Pe 3:11, 14; II Co 5:10, 11; II Th 1:5-7; Lk 21:27, 28; Ro 8:23-25.

[582] Mt 24:36, 42-44; Mk 13:35-37; Lk 12:35, 36; Re 22:20.

47. THE SAVOY DECLARATION, 1658

History

By the time Oliver Cromwell died (03 October 1658) it was clear that the precarious unity of the commonwealth Church of England would not long endure. The basic quarrel was between the Presbyterians, who wanted a centralized Church, and the Independents, who wanted the local congregation to have full autonomy. The former were prepared, if necessary, to make their peace with Charles II, and in return they hoped for a more clearly Protestant (i.e. Calvinist) national Church. They were to be disappointed in this, but at the time it did not seem to be an unreasonable expectation.

The Independents, or Congregationalists (as we now call them) had no desire to see the Church controlled by a centralizing state, and many of them were gradually moving towards a position of outright separatism. In the Savoy Declaration, they put their case before the public in a document which after 1662 became the doctrinal basis of the Congregationalist churches. It was later accepted by the established Church of Massachusetts (Boston, 1680) and by the established Church of Connecticut (Saybrook, 1708).

The Savoy Declaration consists of a lengthy Preface, a revised Westminster Confession, and a series of Articles dealing with ecclesiastical order. For this edition, the first and last of these are printed in full. As for the Confession, only the revisions are included, with appropriate references to the Westminster Confession. For a complete table of correspondences between this declaration, the Westminster Confession, and later Baptist confessions, see Appendix 08.

Theology

The theology of the Savoy Declaration is Calvinist, in the Westminster mould, but it is also separatistic. Those who framed it wanted to see a Church largely independent of the state, and free to develop its own theology. They also wanted local control to predominate over central organization – the point at which their views came into sharpest conflict with the Presbyterians.

N.B. The paragraph numbering of the Preface has been supplied for this edition. The other parts of the Declaration are numbered according to the original document.

A Preface

01. Confession of the faith that is in us, when justly called for, is so indispensable a due all owe to the glory of the sovereign God that it is ranked among the duties of the First Commandment, such as prayer is; and therefore by Paul yoked with faith itself, as necessary to salvation: with the heart man believeth unto righteousness, and with the mouth confession is made unto salvation. Our Lord Christ himself, when he was accused of his doctrine, considered simply as a matter of fact by preaching, refused to answer; because as such, it lay upon evidence and matter of testimony of others, unto whom therefore he refers himself. But when both the high priest and Pilate expostulate his faith, and what he held himself to be, he without any demur at all cheerfully makes declaration that he was the Son of God (so to the high priest) and that he was a King, and born to be a King (thus to Pilate). Though upon the uttering of it his life lay at the stake, which holy profession of his is celebrated for our example (I Ti 6:13).

02. Confessions, when made by a company of professors of Christianity jointly meeting to that end, the most genuine and natural use of such confessions is that under the same form of words, they express the substance of the same common salvation or unity of their faith, whereby *speaking the same things, they show themselves perfectly joined in the same mind and in the same judgement* (I Co 1:10).

03. And accordingly such a transaction is to be looked upon but as a meet or fit medium or means whereby to express that their common faith and salvation, and no way to be made use of as an imposition upon any. Whatever is of force or constraint in matters of this nature causeth them to degenerate from the name and nature of confessions, and turns them from being confessions of faith into exactions and impositions of faith.

04. And such common confessions of the orthodox faith, made in simplicity of heart by any such body of Christians, with concord among themselves, ought to be entertained by all others that love the truth as it is in Jesus, with an answerable rejoicing. For if the unanimous opinions and assertions but in some few points of religion, and that when by two churches, namely that of Jerusalem and the messengers of Antioch met, assisted by some of the Apostles, were by the believers of those times received with so much joy (as it is said: *They rejoiced for the consolation*[1]) much more this is to be done when the whole substance of faith and form of wholesome words, shall be declared by the messengers of a multitude of churches, though wanting those advantages of counsel and authority of the Apostles, which that assembly had.

05. Which acceptation is then more specially due when these shall (to choose) utter and declare their faith, in the same substance for matter, yea, words, for the most part, that other churches and assemblies, reputed the most orthodox, have done before them. For upon such a correspondency all may see that actually accomplished, which the Apostle did but exhort unto, and pray for, in those two more eminent churches of the Corinthians and the Romans, (and so in them for all the Christians of his time), that both Jew and Gentile, that is, men of different persuasions (as they were) might glorify God with one mind and with one mouth. And truly, the very turning of the Gentiles to the owning of the same faith, in the substance of it, with the Christian Jew (though differing in greater points than we do from our brethren) is presently after dignified by the Apostle with this style, that it is the confession of Jesus Christ himself, not as the object only, but as the author and maker thereof: *I will confess to thee* (saith Christ to God) *among the Gentiles*[2]) So that in all such accords Christ is the great and first confessor, and we and all our faith uttered by us are but the epistles (as Paul) and confessions (as Isaiah there) of their Lord and ours, he but expressing what is written in his heart, through their hearts and mouths, to the glory of God the Father. And shall not we all rejoice herein, when as Christ himself is said to do it upon this occasion, as it there also follows: *I will sing unto thy name*?[3]

06. Further, as the soundness and wholesomeness of the matter gives the vigour and life to such confessions, so the inward freeness, willingness and readiness of the spirits of the confessors do contribute the beauty and loveliness thereunto; as it is in prayer to God, so in confessions made to men. If two or three met, do agree, it renders both to either the more acceptable. The Spirit of Christ is in himself too free, great and generous a Spirit to suffer himself to be used by any human arm, to whip men into belief. He drives not, but gently leads into all truth and persuades men to dwell in the tents of like precious faith, which would lose of its preciousness and value if that sparkle of freeness shone not in it. The character of his people is to be a willing people in the day of his power (not man's) in the beauties of holiness, which are the assemblings of the saints, one glory of which assemblings in that first church is said to have been: *They met with one accord*;[4] which is there in that psalm prophesied of in the instance of that first Church, for all other that should succeed.

07. And as this great Spirit is in himself free, when and how far and in whom to work, so where and when he doth work he carrieth it with the same freedom, and is said to be a free Spirit, as he both is and works in us. And where the Spirit of the Lord is, there is liberty.

08. Now as to this confession of ours, besides that a conspicuous conjunction of the particulars mentioned hath appeared therein, there are also four remarkable attendants thereon, which added, might perhaps, in the eyes of sober and indifferent spirits, give the whole of this transaction a room and rank amongst other many good and memorable things of this age. At least all set together do cast s clear a gleam and manifestation of God's power and presence as hath appeared in any such kind of confessions, made by so numerous a company these later years.

09. The first is the temper (or distemper rather) of the times during which these churches have been gathering, and which they have run through. All do (out of a general sense) complain that the times have been perilous or difficult times (as the Apostle foretold), and that in respect to danger from

seducing spirits, more perilous than the hottest seasons of Persecution.

10. We have failed through an estuation, fluxes and refluxes of great varieties of spirits, doctrines, opinions and occurrences, and especially in the matter of opinions, which have been accompanied in their several seasons with powerful persuasions and temptations, to seduce those of our way. It is known, men have taken the freedom (notwithstanding what authority hath interposed to the contrary) to vent and vend their own vain and accursed imaginations, contrary to the great and fixed truths of the Gospel, insomuch as take the whole round and circle of delusions the Devil hath in this small time run. It will be found that every truth, of greater or lesser weight, hath by one or other hand, at one time or another, been questioned and called to the bar amongst us, yea and impleaded under the pretext (which hath some degree of justice in it) that all should not be bound up to the traditions of former times, nor take religion upon trust.

11. Whence it hath come to pass that many of the soundest professors were put upon a new search and disquisition of such truths as they had taken for granted, and yet had lived upon the comfort of, to the end that they might be able to convince others and establish their own hearts against that darkness and unbelief that is ready to close with error, or at least to doubt of the truth when error is speciously presented. And hereupon we do professedly account it one of the greatest advantages gained out of the temptations of these times, yea the honour of the saints and ministers of these nations, that after they had sweetly been exercised in, and had improved practical and experimental truths, this should be their further lot, to examine and discuss, and indeed, anew to learn over every doctrinal truth, both out of the Scriptures and also with a fresh taste thereof in their own hearts; which is no other than what the Apostle exhorts to: *Try all things, hold fast to that which is good.*[5] Conversion unto God at first, what is it else than a savoury and affectionate application, and the bringing home to the heart with spiritual light and life, all truths that are necessary to salvation, together with other lesser truths? All which we had afore conversion taken in but notionally from common education and tradition.

12. Now that after this first gust those who have been thus converted should be put upon a new probation and search out of the Scriptures, not only of all principles explicitly ingredients to conversion, (unto which the Apostle referreth the Galatians when they had diverted from them), but of all other superstructures as well as fundamentals, and together therewith, anew to experiment the power and sweetness of all these in their own souls. What is this, but tried faith indeed, and equivalent to a new conversion unto the truth? An anchor that is proved to be sure and steadfast, that will certainly hold in all contrary storms. This was the eminent seal and commendation which those holy Apostles that lived and wrote last (Peter, John and Jude in their Epistles) did set and give to the Christians of the latter part of those primitive times. And besides, it is clear and evident by all the other Epistles, from first to last, that it cost the Apostles as much and far more care and pains, to preserve them they had converted, in the truth, than they had taken to turn them thereunto at first; and it is in itself as great a work and instance of the power of God that keeps, yea, guards us through faith unto salvation.

13. Secondly, let this be added (or superadded rather) to give full weight and measure, even to running over, that we have all along this season held forth (though quarrelled with for it by our brethren) this great principle of these times, that amongst Christian states and churches, there ought to be vouchsafed a forebearance and mutual indulgence unto saints of all persuasions that keep unto and hold fast the necessary foundations of faith and holiness, in all other matters extra fundamental, whether of faith or order.

14. This to have been our constant principle, we are not ashamed to confess to the whole Christian world. Wherein yet we desire we may be understood, not as if in the abstract we stood indifferent to falsehood or truth or were careless whether faith or error, in any truths but fundamental, did obtain or not, so we had our liberty in our petty and smaller differences; or as if to make sure of that, we had cut out this wide cloak for it. No, we profess that the whole, and every particle of that faith delivered to the saints (the substance of which we have according to our light here professed) is, as to the propagation and furtherance of it by all Gospel means, as precious to us as our lives, or what can be supposed to be dear to us, and in our sphere we have endeavoured to promote them accordingly. But yet withal, we have and do contend (and if we had all the power which any or all of our brethren of differing opinions have desired to have over us, or others, we should freely grant it unto them all), we have and do contend for this, that in the concrete, the persons of all such gracious saints, they and their errors, as they are in them, when they are but such errors as do and may stand with communion with Christ, though they should not repent of them, as not being convinced of them to the end of their days; that those, with their errors (that are purely spiritual and entrench and overthrow not civil societies), as concrete with their persons, should for Christ's sake be borne withal by all Christians in the world, and they notwithstanding be permitted to enjoy all ordinances and spiritual privileges according to their light, as freely as any other of their brethren that pretend to the greatest orthodoxy; as having an equal and as fair a right in and unto Christ, and all the holy things of Christ, than any other can challenge to themselves.

15. And this doth afford a full and invincible testimony on our behalf, in that whiles we have so earnestly contended for this just liberty of saints in all the churches of Christ, we ourselves have no need of it; that is, as to the matter of the profession of faith which we have maintained together with others, and of this, this subsequent confession of faith gives sufficient evidence. So as we have the confidence in Christ to utter in the words of those two great Apostles: That *we have stood fast in the liberty wherewith Christ hath made us free*[6] (in the behalf of others, rather than ourselves),

and having been free, have not made use of our liberty for a cloak of error or maliciousness in ourselves. And yet lo, whereas from the beginning of the rearing of these churches that of the Apostle hath been (by some) prophesied of us, and applied to us: *That while we promised* (unto others) *liberty, we ourselves would become servants of corruption, and be brought in bondage*[7] to all sorts of fancies and imaginations, yet the whole world may now see after the experience of many years run through (and it is manifest by this confession), that the great and gracious God hath not only kept us in that common unity of the faith and knowledge of the Son of God, which they whole community of saints have and shall in their generations come unto, but also in the same truths, both small and great, that are built thereupon, that any other of the best and more pure reformed churches in the best times (which were their first times) have arrived unto; this confession withal holding forth a professed opposition unto the common errors and heresies of these times.

16. These two considerations have been taken from the seasons we have gone through.

17. Thirdly, let the space of time itself, or days, wherein from first to last the whole of this confession was framed and consented to by the whole of us, be duly considered by sober and ingenuous spirits; the whole of days in which we had meetings about it (set aside the two Lord's Days, and the first day's meeting, in which we considered and debated what to pitch upon) were but eleven days, part of which also was spent by some of us in prayer, others in consulting, and in the end all agreeing. We mention this small circumstance but to this end (which still adds unto the former) that it gives demonstration, not of our freeness and willingness only, but of our readiness and preparedness unto so great a work; which otherwise and in other assemblies hath ordinarily taken up long and great debates, and in such a variety of matters of such concernment, may well be supposed to fall out. And this is no other than what the Apostle Peter exhorts unto: *Be ready always to give an answer to every man that asketh you a reason, or account of the hope that is in you.*[8] The Apostle Paul saith of the spiritual truths of the Gospel: *That God hath prepared them for those that love him.*[9] The inward and innate constitution of the new creature being in itself such as is suited to all those truths, as congenial thereunto, but although there be this mutual adeptness between these two, yet such is the mixture of ignorance, darkness and unbelief, carnal reason, preoccupation of judgement, interest of parties, wantonness in opinion, proud adhering to our own persuasions and perverse oppositions and averseness to agree with others, and a multitude of such like distempers common to believing man; all which are not only mixed with, but at times (especially in such times as have passed over our heads) are ready to overcloud our judgements, and to cause our eyes to be double, and sometimes prevail as well as lusts, and do bias our wills and affections. And such is their mixture that although there may be existent an habitual preparedness in men's spirits, yet not always a present readiness to be found, specially not in such a various multitude of men, to make a solemn and deliberate profession of all truths, it being as great a work to find the spirits of the just (perhaps the best of saints) ready for every truth, as to be prepared to every good work.

18. It is therefore to be looked at, as a great and special work of the Holy Ghost, that so numerous a company of ministers and other principal brethren, should so readily, speedily and jointly give up themselves unto such a whole body of truths that are after godliness.

19. This argues they had not their faith to seek; but as is said of Ezra, that they were ready scribes, and (as Christ) instructed unto the kingdom of heaven, being as the good householders of so many families of Christ, bringing forth of their store and treasury New and Old. It shows these truths had been familiar to them, and they acquainted with them, as with their daily food and provision (as Christ's allusion there insinuates). In a word, that so they had preached, and that so their people had believed, as the Apostle speaks upon one like particular occasion. And the Apostle Paul considers (in cases of this nature) the suddenness or length of the time, either one way or the other; whereas it were in men's forsaking or learning of the truth. Thus the suddenness in the Galatians' case in leaving the truth, he makes a wonder of it: *I marvel that you are so soon* (that is, in so short a time) *removed from the true Gospel unto another*.[10] Again on the contrary, in the Hebrews he aggravates their backwardness: *That when for the time you ought to be teachers, you had need that one teach you the very first principles of the oracles of God*.[11] The parallel contrary to both these having fallen out in this transaction, may have some ingredient and weight with ingenuous spirits in its kind, according to the proportion is put upon either of these forementioned in their adverse kind, and obtain the like special observation.

20. This accord of ours hath fallen out without having held any correspondency together, or prepared consultation, by which we might come to be advised of one another's minds. We allege not this as a matter of commendation in us; no, we acknowledge it to have been a great neglect. And accordingly, one of the first proposals for union amongst us was that there might be a constant correspondence held among the churches for counsel and mutual edification, so for time to come to prevent the like omission.

21. We confess that from the first, everyone, or at least the generality of our churches, have been in a manner like so many ships (though holding forth the same general colours) launched singly, and sailing apart and alone in the vast ocean of these tumultuating times, and they exposed to every wind of doctrine, under no other conduct than the Word and Spirit, and their particular elders and principal brethren, without associations among ourselves, or so much as holding out common lights to others, whereby to know where we were.

22. But yet whilst we thus confess to our own shame this neglect, let all acknowledge that God hath ordered it for his high and greater glory, in that his singular care and power should have so watched over each of these, as that all should be found to have steered their course by the same chart, and to have been bound for one and the same port, and that upon this general search now made, that the same holy and blessed truths of all sorts, which are current and warrantable amongst all the other churches of Christ in the world, should be found to be our landing.

23. The whole, and every one of these things when put together, do cause us (whatever men of prejudiced and opposite spirits may find out to slight them) with a holy admiration, to say that this is no other than the Lord's doing, and which we with thanksgiving do take from his hand as a special token upon us for good, and doth show that God is faithful and upright towards those that are planted in his house. And that as the faith was but once for all, and intentionally first delivered unto the saints, so the saints, when not abiding scattered, but gathered under their respective pastors according to God's heart into an house, and churches unto the living God, such together are, as Paul forespake it, the most steady and firm pillar and seat of truth that God hath anywhere appointed to himself on earth, where his truth is best conserved and publicly held forth, there being in such assemblies weekly a rich dwelling of the Word amongst them, that is, a daily open house kept by the means of those good householders, their teachers and other instructors respectively appropriated to them, whom Christ, in the virtue of his ascension, continues to give as gifts to his people, himself dwelling amongst them, to the end that by this, as the most sure standing permanent means, the saints might be perfected, till we all (even as the saints in present and future ages) do come by this constant and daily ordinance of his unto the unity of the faith and knowledge of the Son of God unto a perfect man, unto the measure of the stature of the fullness of Christ (which though growing on by parts and piecemeal, will yet appear complete when that great and general assembly shall be gathered; then when this world is ended and these dispensations have had their fullness and period) and so that from henceforth (such a provision being made for us) we be no more children tossed to and fro, and carried about with every wind of doctrine.

24. And finally, this doth give a fresh and recent demonstration that the great Apostle and high priest of our profession is indeed ascended into heaven and continues there with power and care, faithful as a son over his own house, whose house are we if we hold fast the confidence and the rejoicing of the hope firm unto the end; and shows that he will, as he hath promised, be with his own institutions to the end of the world.

25. It is true that many sad miscarriages, divisions, breaches, fallings off from holy ordinances of God, have along this time of temptation (especially in the beginning of it) been found in some of our churches; and no wonder, if what hath been said be fully considered. Many reasons might further be given hereof that would be a sufficient apology, without the help of a retortion upon other churches (that promised themselves peace) how that more destroying ruptures have befallen them, and that in a wider sphere and compass; which though it should not justify us, yet may serve to stop others' mouths.

26. Let Rome glory of the peace in, and obedience of, her children, against the reformed churches for their divisions that occurred (especially in the first rearing of them) whilst we all know the causes of their dull and stupid peace to have been carnal interests, worldly correspondencies and coalitions, strengthened by gratifications of all sorts of men by that religion, the principles of blind devotion, traditional faith, ecclesiastical tyranny, by which she keeps her children in bondage to this day. We are also certain that the very same prejudices that from hence they would cast upon the reformed (if they were just) do lie as fully against those pure churches raised up by the Apostles themselves in those first times; for as we have heard of their patience, sufferings, consolations and the transcending gifts poured out, and graces shining in them, so we have heard complaints of their divisions too, of the forsakings of their assemblies, as the custom or manner of some was (which later were in that respect *felo de se*, and needed no other delivering up to Satan as their punishment, than what they executed upon themselves.) We read of the shipwreck also of faith and a good conscience, and overthrowings of the faith of some; and still but of some, not all, nor the most; which is one piece of an apology the Apostle again and again inserts to future ages, and through mercy we have the same to make.

27. And truly we take the confidence professedly to say that these temptations common to the purest churches of saints separated from the mixture of the world, though they grieve us (for who is offended, and we burn not?), yet they do not at all stumble us, as to the truth of our way, had they been many more. We say it again, these stumble us no more (as to that point) than it doth offend us against the power of religion itself to have seen, and to see daily in particular persons called out and separated from the world by an effectual work of conversion, that they for a while do suffer under disquietments, vexations, turmoils, unsettlements of spirit, that they are tossed with tempests and horrid temptations such as they had not in their former estate, whilst they walked according to the course of this world. For Peter hath sufficiently instructed us whose business it is to raise such storms - even the devil's; and also whose design it is that after they have suffered a while, thereby they shall be settled, perfected, stablished, that have so suffered, even the God of all grace. And look what course of dispensation God holds to saints personally, he doth the like to bodies of saints in churches, and the Devil the same for his part too; and that consolatory maxim of the Apostle: *God shall tread down Satan under your feet shortly*,[12] which Paul uttereth concerning the Church of Rome, shows how both God and Satan have this very hand therein; for he speaks that very thing in reference unto their divisions, as the coherence clearly manifests, and so you have both designs expressed at once.

28. Yea, we are not a little induced to think that the divisions, breaches, etc., of those primitive churches would not have been so frequent among the people themselves, and not the elders only, had not the freedom, liberties and rights of the members (the brethren, we mean) been stated and exercised in those churches, the same which we maintain and contend for to be in ours.

29. Yea (which perhaps may seem more strange to many) had not those churches been constituted of members enlightened further than with notional and traditional knowledge, by a new and more powerful light of the Holy Ghost, wherein they had been made partakers of the Holy Ghost and the heavenly gift, and their hearts had tasted the good Word of God, and the powers of the world to come, and of such members at lowest, there had not fallen out those kinds of divisions among them.

30. For experience hath shown that the common sort of mere doctrinal professors (such as the most are nowadays), whose highest elevation is but freedom from moral scandal, joined with devotion to Christ through mere education, such as in many Turks is found towards Mohammed, that these finding and feeling themselves not much concerned in the active part of religion, so they may have the honour (especially upon a reformation of a new refinement) that themselves are approved members, admitted to the Lord's Supper, and their children to the ordinance of baptism; they regard not other matters (as Gallio did not), but do easily and readily give themselves up unto their guides, being like dead fishes carried with the common stream, whereas those that have a further renewed light by a work of the Holy Ghost, whether saving or temporary, are upon the quite contrary grounds apt to be busy about, and inquisitive into what they are to receive and practise, or wherein their consciences are professedly concerned and involved. And thereupon they take the freedom to examine and try the spirits, whether of God or no; and from hence are more apt to dissatisfaction, and from thence to run into division, and many of such, proving to be enlightened but with a temporary, not saving faith (who have such a work of the Spirit upon them, and profession in them, as will and doth approve itself to the judgement of saints, and ought to be so judged until they be otherwise discovered), who at long run prove hypocrites, through indulgence unto lusts, and then out of their lusts persist to hold up these divisions unto breach of, or departings from churches, and the ordinances of God, and God is even with them for it, they waxing worse and worse, deceiving and being deceived. And even many of those that are sincere, through a mixture of darkness and erroneousness in their judgements, are for a season apt, out of conscience, to be led away with the error of others which lie in wait to deceive.

31. Insomuch as the Apostle, upon the example of those first times, foreseeing also the like events in following generations upon the like causes,

hath been bold to set this down as a ruled case, that likewise in other churches so constituted and *de facto* emprivileged as that of the church of Corinth was (which single church, in the sacred records about it, is the completest mirror of Church constitution, order and government, and events thereupon ensuing, of any one church whatever that we have story of), his maxim is: *There must be also divisions among you;*[13] he setly inserts an *also* in the case, as that which had been in his own observation, and that which would be *epi to poly* the fate of other churches like thereunto, so prophesieth he. And he speaks this as peremptorily as he doth elsewhere in that other: *We must through many tribulations enter into the kingdom of heaven;*[14] yea and that *all that will live godly in Christ Jesus shall suffer persecution.*[15] There is a *must* upon both alike, and we bless God that we have run through both, and do say, and we say no more, that as it was then, so it is now in both respects.

32. However, such hath been the powerful hand of God's providence in these, which have been the worst of our trials, that out of an approved experience and observation of the issue, we are able to add that other part of the Apostle's prediction, that therefore *such rents must be, that they which are approved may be made manifest among you.*[16] Which holy issue God (as having aimed at it therein) doth frequently and certainly bring about in churches, as he doth bring upon them that other fate of division. Let them therefore look unto it, that are the authors of such disturbances, as the Apostle warneth (Ga 5:10). The experiment is this, that we have seen and do daily see, that multitudes of holy and precious souls and, in the Holy Ghost's word, approved saints, have been and are the more rooted and grounded by means of these shakings, and do continue to cleave the faster to Christ and the purity of his ordinances, and value them the more by this cost God hath put them to for the enjoying of them; who having been planted in the house of the Lord have flourished in the courts of our God, in these evil times, to show that the Lord is upright. And this experimented event from out of such divisions hath more confirmed us, and is a louder apology for us, than all that our opposites are able from our breaches to allege and to prejudice us.

33. We will add a few words for conclusion, and give a more particular account of this our declaration. In drawing up this confession of faith we have had before us the Articles of Religion (i.e. the Westminster Confession, *ed.*), approved and passed by both Houses of Parliament after advice had with an assembly of divines, called together by them for that purpose. To which confession, for the substance of it, we fully assent, as do our brethren of New England, and the churches also of Scotland, as each in their general synods have testified.

34. A few things we have added for obviating some erroneous opinions that have been more broadly and boldly here of late maintained by the asserters than in former times, and made other additions and alterations in method, here and there, and some clearer explanations, as we found occasion.

35. We have endeavoured throughout to hold to such truths in this our confession, as are more properly termed matters of faith, and what is of Church order we dispose in certain propositions by itself. To this course we are led by the example of the honourable Houses of Parliament, observing what was established and what omitted by them in that confession the assembly presented to them. Who thought it not convenient to have matters of discipline and Church government put into a confession of faith, especially such particulars thereof as then were, and still are, controverted and under dispute by men orthodox and found in faith. The thirtieth chapter therefore of that confession, as it was presented to them by the assembly, which is of Church censures, their use, kinds and in whom placed. As also Chapter 31, of synods and councils, by whom to be called, of what force in their decrees and determinations. And the fourth paragraph of the twentieth chapter, which determines what opinions and practices disturbs the peace of the Church, and how such disturbers ought to be proceeded against by the censures of the Church, and punished by the civil magistrate. Also a great part of the twenty-fourth chapter of marriage and divorce. These were such doubtful assertions and so unsuitable to a confession of faith, as the honourable Houses in their great wisdom thought fit to lay them aside, there being nothing that tends more to heighten dissensions among brethren than to determine and adopt the matter of their difference under so high a title as to be an Article of our faith. So that there are two whole chapters, and some paragraphs in other chapters in their confession, that we have upon this account omitted, and the rather do we give this notice because that copy of the Parliament followed by us is in few men's hands. The other, as it came from the assembly, being approved of in Scotland, was printed and hastened into the world before the Parliament had declared their resolutions about it, which was not till 20 June 1648, and yet hath been, and continueth to be the copy (ordinarily) only sold, printed and reprinted for these eleven years.

36. After the nineteenth chapter, *Of the Law*, we have added a chapter *Of the Gospel*, it being a title that may not well be omitted in a confession of faith, in which chapter what is dispersed, and by intimation in the assemblies' confession, with some little addition, is here brought together, and more fully, under one head.

37. That there are not Scriptures annexed, as in some confessions (though in divers others it is otherwise), we give the same account as did the reverend assembly in the same case, which was this: "The confession being large, and so framed as to meet with the common errors, if the Scriptures should have been alleged with any clearness, and by showing where the strength of the proof lieth, it would have required a volume."

38. We say further, it being our utmost end in this (as it is indeed of a confession) humbly to give an account what we hold and assert in these matters, that others, especially the churches of Christ, may judge of us accordingly. This we aimed at, and not so much to instruct others or convince gainsayers. These are the proper works of other institutions of Christ and are to be done in the strength of express Scripture. A confession is an ordinance of another nature.

39. What we have laid down and asserted about churches and their government we humbly conceive to be the order which Christ himself hath appointed to be observed, we have endeavoured to follow Scripture's light; and those also that went before us according to that rule, desirous of nearest uniformity with reforming churches, as with our brethren in New England, so with others that differ from them and us.

40. The models and platforms of this subject, laid down by learned men and practised by churches, are various. We do not judge it brotherly or grateful to insist upon comparisons, as some have done, but this experience teacheth that the variety, and possibly the disputes and emulations arising thence, have much strengthened, if not fixed, this unhappy persuasion in the minds of some learned and good men, namely, that there is no settled order laid down in Scripture but it is left to the prudence of the Christian magistrate to compose or make choice of such a form as is most suitable and consistent with their civil government. Where this opinion is entertained in the persuasion of governors, there, churches asserting their power and order to be *iure divino*, and the appointment of Jesus Christ, can have no better nor more honourable entertainment than a toleration or permission.

41. Yet herein there is this remarkable advantage to all parties that differ about what in government is of Christ's appointment, in that such magistrates have afar greater latitude in conscience to tolerate and permit the several forms of each so bound up in their persuasion, that they have to submit unto what the magistrate shall impose. And thereupon the magistrate exercising an indulgency and forbearance, with protection and encouragement to the people of God, so differing from him and amongst themselves, doth therein discharge as great a faithfulness to Christ and love to his people as can any way be supposed and expected from any Christian magistrate, of what persuasion soever he is. And where this clemency from governors is shown to any sort of persons, or churches of Christ, upon such a principle, it will in equity produce this just effect, that all that so differ from him, and amongst themselves, standing in equal and alike difference from the principle of such a magistrate, he is equally free to give alike liberty to them, one as well as the other.

42. This faithfulness in our governors we do with thankfulness to God acknowledge, and to their everlasting honour, which appeared much in the late reformation. The hierarchy, common prayer book, and all other things grievous to God's people, being removed, they made choice of an assembly of learned men to advise what government and order is meet to be established in the room of these things. And because it was known there were different opinions (as always hath been among godly men) about forms of Church government, there was by the ordinance first sent forth to call an assembly, not only a choice made of persons of several persuasions to sit as members there, but liberty given to a lesser number, if dissenting, to report their judgements and reasons, as well and as freely as the major part.

43. Hereupon the honourable House of Commons (an indulgence we hope will never be forgotten) finding any papers received from them, that the members of the assembly were not like to compose differences amongst themselves, so as to join in the same rule for Church government, did order further as followeth: That a committee of Lords and Commons, etc., do take into consideration the differences of the opinions in the assembly of divines in point of Church government, and to endeavour a union if it be possible; and in case that cannot be done, to endeavour the finding out some way, how far tender consciences, who cannot in all things submit to the same rule which that be established, may be born with according to the Word, and as may stand with the public peace.

44. By all which it is evident, the Parliament purposed not to establish the rule of Church government with such rigour as might not permit and bear with a practice different from what they had established, in persons and churches of different principles, if occasion were. And this Christian clemency and indulgence in our governors hath been the foundation of that freedom and liberty in the managing of Church affairs which our brethren, as well as we that differ from them, do now and have many years enjoyed.

45. The honourable Houses, by several ordinances of Parliament, after much consultation, having settled rules for Church government, and such an ecclesiastical order as they judged would best joint with the laws and government of the kingdom, did publish them, requiring the practice hereof throughout the nation, and in particular, by the ministers of the Parliament of London. But (upon the former reason, or the like charitable consideration) these rules were not imposed by them under any penalty, or rigorous enforcement, though frequently urged thereunto by some.

46. Our reverend brethren of the province of London, having considered of these ordinances and the Church government laid down in them, declared their opinions to be that there is not a complete rule in those ordinances; also, that there are many necessary things not yet established, and some things wherein their consciences are not so fully satisfied. These brethren, in the same paper, have published also their joint resolution to practise in all things according to the rule of the Word, and according to these ordinances so far as they conceive them to correspond to it, and in so doing, they trust they shall not grieve the spirit of the truly godly, nor give any just occasion to them that are contrary minded, to blame their proceedings.

47. We humbly conceive that (we being dissatisfied in these things as our brethren) the like liberty was intended by the honourable Houses, and may be taken by us of the Congregational way (without blame or grief to the spirits of those brethren at least), to resolve or rather, to continue in the same resolution and practice in these matters, which indeed were our practices in times of greatest opposition, and before this reformation was begun.

48. And as our brethren the ministers of London drew up and published their opinions and apprehensions about Church government into an entire system, so we now give the like public account of our consciences and the rules by which we have constantly practised hitherto, which we have here drawn up and do present. Whereby it will appear how much or how little we differ in these things from our Presbyterian brethren.

49. And we trust there is no just cause why any man, either for our differing from the present settlement, it being out of conscience and not out of contempt, or our differences one from another, being not wilful, should charge either of us with that odious reproach of schism. And indeed, if not for our differing from the state settlement, much less because we differ from our brethren, our differences being in some lesser things and circumstances only, as themselves acknowledge. And let it be further considered that we have not broken from them or their order by these differences (but rather they from us) and in that respect we less deserve their censure, our practice being no other than what it was in our breaking from episcopacy, and long before presbytery or any such form as now they are in was taken up by them, and we will not say how probable it is that the yoke of episcopacy had been upon our neck to this day if some such way (as formerly, and now is, and hath been termed schism) had not with much suffering been then practised and since continued in.

50. For novelty wherewith we are likewise both charged by the enemies of both, it is true, in respect of the public and open profession, either of presbytery or independency, this nation had been a stranger to each way, it is possible, ever since it hath been Christian; though for ourselves, we are able to trace the footsteps of an Independent Congregational way in the ancientest customs of the Churches, as also in the writings of our soundest Protestant divines, and (that which we are much satisfied in) a full concurrence throughout in all the substantial parts of Church government, with our reverend brethren the old Puritan Non-Conformists, who being instant in prayer and much sufferings, prevailed with the Lord, and we reap with joy what they sowed in tears. Our brethren also that are for presbyterial subordinations profess what is of weight against novelty for their way.

51. And now therefore, seeing the Lord, in whose hand is the heart of princes, hath put into the hearts of our governors to tolerate and permit (as they have done many years) persons of each persuasion, to enjoy their consciences, though neither come up to the rule established by authority; and that which is more, to give us both protection and the same encouragement that the most devoted Conformists in those former superstitious times enjoyed, yea and by a public law to establish this liberty for time to come; and yet further, in the midst of our fears, to set over us a prince that owns this establishment and cordially resolves to secure our churches in the enjoyment of these liberties if we abuse them not, to the disturbance of the civil peace.

52. This should be a very great engagement upon the hearts of all, though of different persuasions, to endeavour our utmost, jointly to promote the honour and prosperity of such a government and governors by whatsoever means which in our callings as ministers of the Gospel, and as churches of Jesus Christ the Prince of Peace, we are any way able to do; as also to be peaceably disposed one towards another, and with mutual toleration to love as brethren, notwithstanding such differences, remembering, as it is very equal we should, the differences that are between Presbyterians and Independents being differences between fellow-servants, and neither of them having authority given from God or man to impose their opinions one more than the other. That our governors, after so solemn an establishment, should thus bear with us both in our greater differences from their rule, and after this, for any of us to take a fellow-servant by the throat, upon the account of a lesser reckoning, and nothing due to him upon it, is to forget, at least not to exercise, the compassion and tenderness we have found where we had less ground to challenge or expect it.

53. Our prayer unto God is: That whereto we have already attained, we all may walk by the same rule, and that wherein we are otherwise minded, God would reveal it to us in his due time.

A Declaration of Faith

The following modifications have been made to the Westminster Confession:

A new Chapter 20 has been added, causing all subsequent chapters to alter their number accordingly, e.g. WC 20 = SD 21, etc. The additional chapter reads as follows:

20. Of the Gospel, and of the extent of the grace thereof.

01. The covenant of works being broken by sin and made unprofitable unto life, God was pleased to give unto the elect the promise of Christ, the seed of the woman, as the means of calling them, and begetting in them faith and repentance. In this promise the Gospel, as to the substance of it, was revealed and was therein effectual for the conversion and salvation of sinners.

02. The promise of Christ and salvation by him is revealed only in and by the Word of God; neither do the works of creation or providence, with the light of nature, make discovery of Christ or of grace by him, so much as in a general or obscure way; much less that men, destitute of the revelation of him by the promise of the Gospel, should be enabled thereby to attain saving faith or repentance.

03. The revelation of the Gospel unto sinners, made in divers times and by sundry parts, with the addition of promises and precepts for the obedience required therein, as to the nations and persons to whom it is granted, is merely of the sovereign will and good pleasure of God, not being annexed by virtue of any promise to the due improvement of men's natural abilities, by virtue of common light received without it, which none ever did make, or can so do; and therefore in all ages the preaching the Gospel hath been granted unto persons and nations, as to the extent or straitening of it, in great variety, according to the counsel of the will of God.

04. Although the Gospel be the only outward means of revealing Christ and saving grace, and is as such abundantly sufficient thereunto; yet that men who are dead in trespasses may be born again, quickened or regenerated, there is moreover necessary an effectual, irresistible work of the Holy Ghost upon the whole soul, for the producing in them of a new spiritual life, without which no other means are sufficient for their conversion unto God.

In Chapter 21 (WC 20), there are slight revisions to two sections as follows. (Additions are in **bold type**; subtractions are in (parentheses).

02. God alone is Lord of the conscience and hath left it free from the doctrines and commandments of men which are in anything contrary to his Word, **or not contained in it** (or beside it, in matters of faith or worship); so that to believe such doctrines, or to obey such commands out of conscience, is to betray true liberty of conscience; and the requiring of an implicit faith and an absolute and blind obedience is to destroy liberty of conscience and reason also.

03. They who, upon pretense of Christian liberty, do practise any sin or cherish any lust, **as they** do thereby **pervert the main design of the grace of the Gospel to their own destruction; so they wholly** destroy the end of Christian liberty, which is that being delivered out of the hands of our enemies, we might serve the Lord without fear, in holiness and righteousness before him all the days of our life.

Section 04 of WC 20 is omitted entirely.
In Chapter 24 (WC 23) Section 03 is replaced as follows:

03. Although the magistrate is bound to encourage, promote and protect the professors and profession of the Gospel, and to manage and order civil administrations in a due subserviency to the interest of Christ in the world, and to that end to take care that men of corrupt minds and conversations do not licentiously publish and divulge blasphemy and errors, in their own nature subverting the faith and inevitably destroying the souls of them that receive them; yet in such differences about the doctrines of the Gospel, or ways of the worship of God, as may befall men exercising a good conscience, manifesting it in their conversation, and holding the foundation, not disturbing others in their ways of worship that differ from them, there is no warrant for the magistrate under the Gospel to abridge them of their liberty.

In Chapter 25 the last clause of Section 04 and the whole of Sections 05 and 06 of WC 24 are omitted.

In Chapter 26, Sections 02, 03 and 04 of WC 25 are omitted. Instead, there is a new Section 02 and a section 05 which have no counterparts in the WC. In addition, Section 03 corresponds, with modifications, to Section 03 of the WC, and Section 05 with Section 06 of the WC. These correspondences may be tabulated as follows:

SD 26		WC 25
01		01
–		02
02		–
–		03
–		04
03	is a modified form of	05
04	is a modified form of	06
05		–

The added/modified text of the Savoy Declaration reads as follows:

02. The whole body of men throughout the world, professing the faith of the Gospel, and obedience unto God by Christ according unto it, not destroying their own profession by any errors everting the foundation, or unholiness of conversation, are and may be called the visible Catholic Church of Christ, although as such it is not entrusted with the administration of any ordinances, or hath any officers to rule or govern in or over the whole body.

03. (WC 25.05) The purest churches under heaven are subject both to mixture and error, and some have so degenerated as to become no churches of Christ, but synagogues of Satan. Nevertheless, **Christ always hath had and ever shall have a visible kingdom in this world, to the end thereof, of such as believe in him and make profession of his name** (there shall be always a Church on earth to worship God according to his will).

04. (WC 25.06) There is no other head of the Church but the Lord Jesus Christ, nor can the Pope of Rome in any sense be head thereof; but he is that Antichrist, that man of sin and son of perdition that exalteth himself in the Church against Christ and all that is called God, **whom the Lord shall destroy with the brightness of his coming**.

05. As the Lord is in care and love towards his Church, hath in his infinite wise providence exercised it with great variety in all ages, for the good of them that love him, and to his own glory; so, according to his promise, we expect that in the latter days, Antichrist being destroyed, the Jews called, and the adversaries of the kingdom of his dear Son broken, the churches of Christ being enlarged and edified through a free and plentiful communication of light and grace, shall enjoy in this world a more quiet, peaceable and glorious condition than they have enjoyed.

WC 30 and WC 31 are omitted altogether.

Of the institution of churches and the order appointed in them by Jesus Christ

01. By the appointment of the Father, all power for the calling, institution, order or government of the Church is invested in a supreme and sovereign manner in the Lord Jesus Christ, as King and Head thereof.

02. In the execution of this power wherewith he is so entrusted, the Lord Jesus calleth out of the world unto communion with himself those that are given unto him by his Father, that they may walk before him in all the ways of obedience which he prescribed to them in his Word.

03. Those thus called (through the ministry of the Word by his Spirit) he commandeth to walk together in particular societies or churches, for their mutual edification and the due performance of that public worship which he requireth of them in this world.

04. To each of these churches thus gathered, according unto his mind declared in his Word, he hath given all that power and authority which is any way needful for their carrying on that order in worship and discipline which he hath instituted for them to observe with commands and rules for the due and right exerting and executing of that power.

05. These particular churches thus appointed by the authority of Christ and entrusted with power from him for the ends before expressed, are each of them as unto those ends the seat of that power which he is pleased to communicate to his saints or subjects in this world, so that as such they receive it immediately from himself.

06. Besides these particular churches there is not instituted by Christ any Church more extensive or catholic, entrusted with power for the administration of his ordinances or the execution of any authority in his name.

07. A particular church gathered and completed according to the mind of Christ, consists of officers and members; the Lord Christ having given to his called ones (untied according to his appointment in Church order) liberty and power to choose persons fitted by the Holy Ghost for that purpose, to be over them and to minister to them in the Lord.

08. The members of these churches are saints by calling, visibly manifesting and evidencing (in and by their profession and walking) their obedience unto that call of Christ, who being further known to each other by their confession of the faith wrought in them by the power of God, declared by themselves or otherwise manifested, do willingly consent to walk together according to the appointment of Christ, giving up themselves to the Lord and to one another by the will of God, in professed subjection to the ordinances of the Gospel.

09. The officers appointed by Christ to be chosen and set apart by the Church so called, and gathered for the peculiar administration of ordinances and execution of power or duty which he intrusts them with, or calls them to, to be continued to the end of the world, are pastors, teachers, elders and deacons.

10. Churches thus gathered and assembling for the worship of God are thereby visible and public and their assemblies (in what place soever they are, according as they have liberty or opportunity) are therefore Church or public assemblies.

11. The way appointed by Christ for the calling of any person, fitted and gifted by the Holy Ghost, unto the office of pastor, teacher or elder in a church, is that he be chosen thereunto by the common suffrage of the church itself, and solemnly set apart by fasting and prayer, with imposition of hands of the eldership of that church if there be any before constituted therein. And of a deacon, that he be chosen by like suffrage and set apart by prayer and the like imposition of hands.

12. The essence of this call of a pastor, teacher or elder unto office consists in the election of the church, together with his acceptation of it, and separation by fasting and prayer, and those who are so chosen, though not set apart by imposition of hands, are rightly constituted ministers of Jesus Christ, in whose name and authority they exercise the ministry to them so committed. The calling of deacons consisteth in the like election and acceptation, with separation by prayer.

13. Although it be incumbent on the pastors and teachers of the churches to be instant in preaching the Word by way of office, yet the work of preaching the Word is not so peculiarly confined to them but that others also gifted and fitted by the Holy Ghost for it, and approved (being by lawful ways and means in the providence of God called thereunto), may publicly, ordinarily and constantly perform it so that they give themselves up thereunto.

14. However, they who are engaged in the work of public preaching and enjoy the public maintenance upon that account, are not thereby obliged to dispense the seals to any other than such as (being saints by calling and gathered according to the order of the Gospel) they stand related to as pastors and teachers, yet ought they not to neglect others living within their parochial bounds, but besides their constant public preaching to them, they ought to enquire after their profiting by the Word, instructing them in and pressing upon them (whether young or old) the great doctrines of the Gospel, even personally and particularly, so far as their strength and time will admit.

15. Ordination alone, without the election or precedent consent of the church by those who formerly have been ordained by virtue of that power they have received by their ordination, doth not constitute any person a church officer, or communicate office power unto him.

16. A church furnished with officers (according to the mind of Christ) hath full power to administer all his ordinances, and where there is want of any one or more officers required, that officer, or those which are in the church, may administer all the ordinances proper to their particular duty and offices, but where there are no teaching officers none may administer the seals, nor can the church authorize any so to do.

17. In the carrying on of church administrations, no person ought to be added to the church but by the consent of the church itself, that so love (without dissimulation) may be preserved between all the members thereof.

18. Whereas the Lord Jesus Christ hath appointed and instituted as a means of edification that those who walk not according to the rules and laws appointed by him (in respect of faith and life, so that just offence doth arise to the church thereby) be censured in his name and authority, every church hath power in itself to exercise and execute all those censures appointed by him, in the way and order prescribed in the Gospel.

19. The censures so appointed by Christ are admonition and excommunication, and whereas some offences are or may be known only to some, it is appointed by Christ that those to whom they are so known do first admonish the offender in private (in public offences where any sin, before all), and in case of non-amendment upon private admonition, the offence being related to the Church, and the offender not manifesting his repentance, he is to be duly admonished in the name of Christ by the whole church, by the ministry of the elders of the church; and if this censure prevail not for his repentance then he is to be cast out by excommunication, with the consent of the church.

20. As all believers are bound to join themselves to particular churches, when and where they have opportunity so to do, so none are to be admitted unto the privileges of the churches who do not submit themselves to the rule of Christ in the censures for the government of them.

21. This being the way prescribed by Christ in case of offence, no Church members, upon any offences taken by them, having performed their duty required of them in this matter, ought to disturb any church order or absent themselves from the public assemblies or the administration of any ordinances upon that pretence, but to wait upon Christ in the further proceeding of the church.

22. The power of censures being seated by Christ in a particular church is to be exercised only towards particular members of each church respectively as such, and there is no power given by him unto any synods or ecclesiastical assemblies to excommunicate, or by their public edicts to

threaten excommunication or other church censures against churches, magistrates or their people, upon any account, no man being obnoxious to that censure but upon his personal miscarriage as a member of a particular church.

23. Although the Church is a society of men assembling for the celebration of the ordinances according to the appointment of Christ, yet every society assembling for that end or purpose, upon the account of cohabitation within any civil precincts or bounds, is not thereby constituted a church, seeing there may be wanting among them what is essentially required thereunto; and therefore a believer living with others in such a precinct may join himself with any church for his edification.

24. For the avoiding of differences that may otherwise arise, for the greater solemnity in the celebration of the ordinances of Christ, and the opening a way for the larger usefulness of the gifts and graces of the Holy Ghost, saints living in one city or town, or within such distances as that they might conveniently assemble for divine worship, ought rather to join in one church for their mutual strengthening and edification than to set up many distinct societies.

25. As all churches and all the members of them are bound to pray continually for the good or prosperity of all the churches of Christ in all places, and upon all occasions to further it (every one within the bounds of their places and callings, in the exercise of their gifts and graces), so the churches themselves (when planted by the providence of God so as they may have opportunity and advantage for it) ought to hold communion amongst themselves for their peace, increase of love and mutual edification.

26. In cases of difficulties or differences, either in point of doctrine or in administrations, wherein either the churches in general are concerned, or any one church, in their peace, union and edification, or any member or members of any church are injured in or by any proceeding in censures not agreeable to truth and order, it is according to the mind of Christ that many churches, holding communion together, do by their messengers meet in a synod or council to consider and give their advice in or about that matter in difference, to be reported to all the churches concerned. Howbeit, these synods so assembled are not entrusted with any church power properly so called or with any jurisdiction over the churches themselves, to exercise any censures either over any churches or persons, or to impose their determinations on the churches or officers.

27. Besides these occasioned synods or councils, there are not instituted by Christ any stated synods in a fixed combination of churches or their officers in lesser or greater assemblies, nor are there any synods appointed by Christ in a way of subordination to one another.

28. Persons that are joined in church fellowship ought not lightly or without just cause to withdraw themselves from the communion of the church whereunto they are so joined. Nevertheless, where any person cannot

continue in any church without his sin, either for war
of any ordinances instituted by Christ or by his be
privileges, or compelled to anything in practice no
or in case of persecution, or upon the account of c
he, consulting with the church, or the office
peaceably depart from the communion of the churc
walked to join himself with some other church where he
ordinances in the purity of the same, for his edification and conso

29. Such reforming churches as consist of persons sound in the faith, an
of conversation becoming the Gospel, ought not to refuse the communion
of each other, so far as may consist with their own principles respectively,
though they walk not in all things according to the same rules of church
order.

30. Churches gathered and walking according to the mind of Christ,
judging other churches (though less pure) to be true churches, may receive
unto occasional communion with them such members of those churches as
are credibly testified to be godly and to live without offence.

[1] Ac 15:31	[5] I Th 5:21	[9] I Co 2:9	[13] I Co 11:19
[2] Ro 15:9	[6] Ga 5:1	[10] Ga 1:16	[14] Ac 14:22
[3] Ro 15:9	[7] II Pe 2:19	[11] He 5:12	[15] II Ti 3:12
[4] Ac 2:46	[8] I Pe 3:15	[12] Ro 16:20	[16] I Co 11:19

8. THE DECLARATION OF BREDA, 1660

History

As a restoration of the monarchy became increasingly likely, Charles II bent over backwards to placate those numerous of his future subjects who were not at all sympathetic to a restoration of the civil or ecclesiastical order which had prevailed before 1640. The following declaration was intended as a guarantee that the past would not be held against anyone, and that in future, liberty of conscience would be preserved. It was drafted on 04 April (Old Style) or 14 April (New Style) 1660, and read in both Houses of Parliament on 01 May (Old Style). The king arrived at Dover later in May and made his triumphal entry into London on 29 May 1660 (Old Style).

It seems that the king himself was sincere enough in his statements, but he was surrounded by men who were thirsting for revenge. Once he was safely back on his throne, Charles found that he had to make concessions to these extremists, and the good intentions of Breda were seriously compromised as a result. Nevertheless, they remained as a sign that toleration was a realizable goal, and in spite of many setbacks, something very like it was finally achieved in 1689.

Charles, by the grace of God, king of England, Scotland, France and Ireland, Defender of the Faith etc., to all our loving subjects, of what degree or quality soever, greeting.

If the general distraction and confusion which is spread over the whole kingdom doth not awaken all men to a desire and longing that those wounds which have so many years together been kept bleeding, may be bound up, all we can say will be to no purpose; however, after this long silence, we have thought it our duty to declare how much we desire to contribute thereunto; and that as we can never give over the hope, in good time, to obtain the possession of that right which God and nature hath made our due, so do we make it our daily suit to the Divine Providence, that he will, in compassion to us and our subjects after so long misery and sufferings, remit and put us into a quiet and peaceable possession of that our right, with as little blood and damage to our people as is possible; nor do we desire more to enjoy what by law is theirs, by a full and entire administration of justice throughout the land, and by extending our mercy where it is wanted and deserved.

And to the end that the fear of punishment may not engage any, conscious to themselves of what is past, to a perseverance in guilt for the future, by opposing the quiet and happiness of their country, in the restoration both of king, peers and people to their just, ancient and fundamental rights, we do by these presents declare that we do grant a free and general pardon, which we are ready upon demand to pass under our great seal of England, to all our subjects, of what degree or quality soever, who within forty days after the publishing hereof shall lay hold upon this our grace and favour, and shall, by any public act, declare their doing so, and that they return to the loyalty and obedience of good subjects; excepting only such persons as shall hereafter be excepted by Parliament.

Those only excepted, let all our subjects, how faulty soever, rely upon the word of a king, solemnly given by this present declaration, that no crime whatsoever, committed against us or our royal father before the publication of this, shall ever rise in judgement or be brought in question against any of them, to the least endamagement of them, either in their lives, liberties or estates, or (as far forth as lies in our power) so much as to the prejudice of their reputations, by any reproach or term of distinction from the rest of our best subjects; we desiring and ordaining that henceforward all notes of discord, separation and difference of parties be utterly abolished among all our subjects, whom we invite and conjure to a perfect union among themselves, under our protection, for the resettlement of our just rights and theirs in a free Parliament, by which, upon the word of a king, we will be advised.

And because the passion and uncharitableness of the times have produced several opinions in religion, by which men are engaged in parties and animosities against each other (which, when they shall hereafter unite in a freedom of conversation, will be composed or better understood), we do declare a liberty to tender consciences, and that no man shall be disquieted or called in question for differences of opinion in matter of religion, which do not disturb the peace of the kingdom; and that we shall be ready to consent to such an Act of Parliament as, upon mature deliberation, shall be offered to us, for the full granting that indulgence.

And because, in the continued distractions of so many years, and so many and great revolutions, many grants and purchases of estates have been made to and by many officers, soldiers and others, who are now possessed of the same, and who may be liable to actions at law upon several titles, we are likewise willing that all such differences, and all things relating to such grants, sales and purchases, shall be determined in Parliament, which can best provide for the just satisfaction of all men who are concerned.

And we do further declare that we will be ready to consent to any Act or Acts of Parliament to the purposes aforesaid, and for the full satisfaction of all arrears due to the officers and soldiers of the army under the command of General Monk; and that they shall be received into our service upon as good pay and conditions as they now enjoy.

Given under our sign manual and privy signet, at our court at Breda, this 04/14 day of April 1660, in the twelfth year of our reign.

49. THE ACT OF UNIFORMITY, 1662
(14 Charles II, c. 4)

History

The Restoration of 1660 ended the period in which Puritan Calvinism was in the ascendant in the Church of England, although a large number of ministers continued to uphold broadly Puritan views. At first there was some hope that these could be reconciled in a new settlement of the Church along Elizabethan lines, but negotiations to this end broke down, owing to the intransigence of the returning Episcopalians and the reluctance of the Puritans to compromise the principles for which they had fought the Civil War. The king continued to look for a solution which would comprehend all but the die-hard extremists, and this was the hope of the Act of Uniformity, which received royal assent on 19 May 1662. It was decided to make St Bartholomew's Day (24 August) 1662 the deadline for subscription, but when it became apparent that a large number of ministers had not conformed by that date, the deadline was extended to 25 December 1663, to give the Bishops time to persuade more waverers. Penalties for non-compliance were far less severe than in previous Acts of Uniformity, which perhaps indicates that popular support for the measure was not great.

This Act continues to be a fundamental constitutional document of the Church of England, though most parts of it have since been repealed or modified, especially since the middle years of the nineteenth century. In 1706 the Act was reaffirmed as a prelude to the Act of Union with Scotland in the following year, and its provisions were extended to Ireland by the Act of Union (1800), which came into force on 01 January 1801.

Penalties and disabilities prescribed in the Act were repealed by statute in 1844 and 1846, since when most of the rest has been removed as well. The history of repeal can be briefly summarized as follows:

1863	Statute Law Revision Act: Sections 09, 27
1865	Clerical Subscription Act: Sections 04, 06 (part), 07, 15 (part)
1871	Universities Tests Act: Section 06 (part), 08
1871	Promissory Oaths Act: Section 06 (rest)
1888	Statute Law Revision Act: Section 10 (part)
1945	Statute Law Revision Act: Section 10 (part)
1948	Statute Law Revision Act: Section 25
1967	Statute Law Revision Act: Sections 02, 03
1969	Statute Law Revision Act: Section 17

1973   Statute Law Revision Act: Sections 11, 22, 23
1974   Worship and Doctrine Measure: Sections 01, 05, 10 (part), 12,
        13, 14, 16, 18, 19, 20, 21, 24, 26

In addition, all application of the Act to Ireland ceased when the Church of Ireland was disestablished on 01 January 1871, and likewise to Wales, since the disestablishment of the Church in Wales on 31 March 1920. Since 01 November 1988 the Church of England has had the power, by virtue of the Ecumenical Relations Measure (1988), to suspend the operation of the Act in certain circumstances, largely to do with ecumenical services and the use of Church buildings by other denominations.

At the present time, only parts of sections 10 and 15 are still in force; these are printed in **bold type** in the present edition. For a complete history of the process of repeal, see *Halsbury's Statutes of England and Wales*, Fourth Edition, London, 1986, Vol. 14, pp. 735-737.

Theology

When the Act of Uniformity was passed, over 1700 ministers (about 20% of the total) resigned their livings and left the Church of England. Almost all of these were Puritans, and so the Act may be said to represent the expulsion of Puritanism from the national Church. The Dissenters, as these ministers were called, formed churches of their own, most of which still exist as "Free Churches". Within the Church of England, the main doctrinal impact of the Act was to reinforce the position of the Thirty-nine Articles as the only statement of faith, and of the Book of Common Prayer as its expression in worship. The Prayer Book was essentially Protestant in doctrine, though it contained certain elements of ceremonial which had been introduced by Archbishop William Laud (1633-1645) in the controversies leading up to the Civil War.

An Act for the Uniformity of Public Prayers and Administration of Sacraments and other Rites and Ceremonies and for establishing the Form of Making, Ordaining and Consecrating Bishops, Priests and Deacons in the Church of England.

01. Whereas in the first year of the late Queen Elizabeth (1559) there was one uniform order of common service and prayer and of the administration of sacraments, rites and ceremonies in the Church of England (agreeable to the Word of God and usage of the primitive Church), compiled by the reverend bishops and clergy, set forth in one book entitled *The Book of Common Prayer and Administration of Sacraments and other Rites and Ceremonies in the Church of England*, and enjoined to be used by act of Parliament holden in the said first year of the said late Queen, entitled *An*

Act for the Uniformity of Common Prayer and Service in the Church and Administration of the Sacraments, very comfortable to all good people desirous to live in Christian conversation and most profitable to the estate of this realm, upon the which the mercy, favour and blessing of Almighty God is in no wise so readily and plentifully poured as by common prayers, due using of the sacraments and often preaching of the Gospel with devotion of the hearers; and yet this notwithstanding, a great number of people in divers parts of this realm, following their own sensuality, and living without knowledge and due fear of God, do wilfully and schismatically abstain and refuse to come to their parish churches and other public places where common prayer, administration of the sacraments, and preaching of the Word of God is used upon the Sundays and other days ordained and appointed to be kept and observed as holy days, and whereas by the great and scandalous neglect of ministers in using the said order or liturgy so set forth and enjoined as aforesaid, great mischiefs and inconveniences during the times of the late unhappy troubles have arisen and grown, and many people have been led into factions and schisms, to the great decay and scandal of the reformed religion of the Church of England, and to the hazard of many souls (for prevention whereof in time to come, for settling the peace of the Church, and for allaying the present distempers which the indisposition of the time hath contracted, the King's Majesty, according to his declaration of the five and twentieth of October, One thousand six hundred and sixty (25 October 1660), granted his commission under the great seal of England to several bishops and other divines to review the Book of Common Prayer and to prepare such alterations and additions as they thought fit to offer, and afterwards the Convocations of both the provinces of Canterbury and York, being by his Majesty called and assembled and now sitting, his Majesty hath been pleased to authorize and require the said presidents of the said Convocations and other the bishops and clergy of the same, to review the said Book of Common Prayer and the Book of the Form and Manner of the Making and Consecrating of Bishops, Priests and deacons, and that after mature consideration, they should make such additions and alterations in the said Books respectively, as to them should seem meet and convenient, and should exhibit and present the same to his Majesty in writing for his further allowance and confirmation, since which time upon full and mature deliberation, they the said presidents, bishops and clergy of both provinces have accordingly reviewed the said Books and have made some alterations which they think fit to be inserted to the same, and some additional prayers to the said Book of Common Prayer, to be used upon proper and emergent occasions, and have exhibited and presented the same unto his Majesty in writing, in one Book entitled *The Book of Common Prayer and Administration of the Sacraments and other Rites and Ceremonies of the Church according to the Use of the Church of England*, together with the Psalter or Psalms of David pointed as they are to be said or sung in churches, and the form and manner of making, ordaining and consecrating of bishops, priests and deacons, all which his Majesty, having duly considered, hath fully approved and allowed the same and recommended to this present Parliament that the said Books of Common Prayer and of the Form of Ordination and Consecration of Bishops, Priests and Deacons, with the alterations and additions which have been so made and presented to his Majesty by the said Convocations, be the Book which shall be appointed to be used by all that officiate in all cathedral and collegiate churches and chapels, and in all chapels of colleges and halls in both the Universities and the Colleges of Eton and Winchester, and in all parish churches and chapels within the Kingdom of England, Dominion of Wales and Town of Berwick upon Tweed, and by all that make or consecrate bishops, priests or deacons in any of the said places, under such sanctions and penalties as the Houses of Parliament shall think fit. Now in regard that nothing conduceth more to the settling of the peace of this nation (which is desired of all good men), nor to the honour of our religion and the propagation thereof, than an universal agreement in the public worship of Almighty God, and to the intent that every person within this realm may certainly know the rule to which he is to conform in public worship and administration of sacraments, and other rites and ceremonies of the Church of England, and the manner how and by whom bishops, priests and deacons are and ought to be made, ordained and consecrated:

Be it enacted by the King's most excellent Majesty, by the advice and with the consent of the Lords spiritual and temporal and of the Commons in this present Parliament assembled, and by the authority of the same, that all and singular ministers in any cathedral, collegiate or parish church or chapel, or other place of public worship within this Realm of England, Dominion of Wales and Town of Berwick upon Tweed, shall be bound to say and use the morning prayer, evening prayer, celebration and administration of both the sacraments, and all other the public and common prayer in such order and form as is mentioned in the said book annexed and joined to this present Act, and entitled, *The Book of Common Prayer and Administration of the Sacraments and other Rites and Ceremonies of the Church according to the Use of the Church of England*, together with the Psalter or Psalms of David, pointed as they are to be said or sung in churches, and the form or manner of making, ordaining and consecrating of bishops, priests and deacons. And that the morning and evening prayers therein contained shall upon every Lord's Day, and upon all other days and occasions, and at the times therein appointed, be openly and solemnly read by all and every minister or curate in every church, chapel or other place of public worship within this Realm of England and places aforesaid.

02. And to the end that uniformity in the public worship of God (which is so much desired) may be speedily effected, be it further enacted by the authority aforesaid, that every parson, vicar or other minister whatsoever,

who now hath and enjoyeth any ecclesiastical benefice or promotion within this realm of England and places aforesaid, shall in the church, chapel or place of public worship belonging to his said benefice or promotion, upon some Lord's Day before the feast of St Bartholomew, which shall be in the year of our Lord God One thousand six hundred sixty and two (24 August 1662), openly, publicly and solemnly read the morning and evening prayer appointed to be read by and according to the said Book of Common Prayer at the times thereby appointed, and after such reading thereof shall openly and publicly, before the congregation there assembled, declare his unfeigned assent and consent to the use of all things in the said Book contained and prescribed, in these words and no other:

I, A. B., do declare my unfeigned assent and consent to all and everything contained and prescribed in and by the Book entitled *The Book of Common Prayer and Administration of the Sacraments and other Rites and Ceremonies of the Church according to the Use of the Church of England*, together with the Psalter or Psalms of David pointed as they are to be sung or said in churches, and the form or manner of making, ordaining and consecrating of bishops, priests and deacons.

03. And that all and every such person who shall (without some lawful impediment to be allowed and approved of by the ordinary of the place) neglect or refuse to do the same within the time aforesaid (or in case of such impediment), within one month after such impediment removed shall (*ipso facto*) be deprived of all his spiritual promotions, and that from thenceforth it shall be lawful to and for all patrons and donors of all and singular the said spiritual promotions or of any of them according to their respective rights and titles, to present or collate to the same as though the person or persons so offending or neglecting were dead.

04. And be it further enacted by the authority aforesaid, that every person who shall hereafter be presented or collated or put into any ecclesiastical benefice or promotion within this Realm of England and places aforesaid, shall in the church, chapel or place of public worship belonging to his said benefice or promotion, within two months next after that he shall be in the actual possession of the said ecclesiastical benefice or promotion, upon some Lord's Day, openly, publicly and solemnly read the morning and evening prayers appointed to be read by and according to the said Book of Common Prayer at the times thereby appointed, and after such reading thereof shall openly and publicly before the congregation there assembled, declare his unfeigned assent and consent to the use of all things therein contained and prescribed according to the form before appointed, and that all and every such person who shall (without some lawful impediment to be allowed and approved by the ordinary of the place), neglect or refuse to do the same within the time aforesaid (or in case of such impediment within one month after such impediment removed), shall (*ipso facto*) be deprived of all his said ecclesiastical benefices and promotions, and that from thenceforth it shall and may be lawful to and for all patrons and donors of all and singular the said ecclesiastical benefices and promotions or any of them (according to their respective rights and titles), to present or collate to the same as though the person or persons so offending or neglecting were dead.

05. And be it further enacted by the authority aforesaid that in all places where the proper incumbent of any parsonage or vicarage, or benefice with cure, doth reside on his living, and keep a curate, the incumbent himself in person (not having some lawful impediment to be allowed by the ordinary of the place) shall once (at the least) in every month openly and publicly read the common prayers and service in and by the said Book prescribed and (if there be occasion) administer each of the sacraments and other rites of the Church in the parish council or chapel of, or belonging to, the same parsonage, vicarage or benefice in such order, manner and form as in and by the said Book is appointed, upon pain to forfeit the sum of five pounds to the use of the poor of the parish for every offence upon conviction, by confession or proof of two credible witnesses upon oath before two justices of the peace of the county, city or town corporate where the offence shall be committed, which oath the said justices are hereby empowered to administer, and in default of payment within ten days, to be levied by distress and sale of the goods and chattels of the offender by the warrant of the said justices, by the churchwardens or overseers of the poor of the said parish, rendering the surplusage to the party.

06. And be it further enacted by the authority aforesaid that every dean, canon and prebendary of every cathedral or collegiate church, and all masters and other heads, fellows, chaplains and tutors of or in any college, hall, house of learning or hospital, and every public professor and reader in either of the universities and in every college elsewhere, and every parson, vicar, curate, lecturer and every other person in Holy Orders, and every schoolmaster keeping any public or private school, and every person instructing or teaching any youth in any house or private family as a tutor or schoolmaster, who upon the first day of May which shall be in the year of our Lord God One thousand six hundred sixty-two (01 May 1662), or at any time thereafter shall be incumbent, or have possession of any deanery, canonry, prebend, mastership, headship, fellowship, professor's place or reader's place, parsonage, vicarage or any other ecclesiastical dignity or promotion, or of any curate's place, lecture or school, or shall instruct or teach any youth as tutor or schoolmaster, shall before the feast day of St Bartholomew, which shall be in the year of our Lord One thousand six hundred sixty-two (24 August 1662), or at or before his or their respective admission to be incumbent or have possession aforesaid, subscribe the declaration or acknowledgement following, scilicet:

I, A. B., do declare that it is not lawful upon any pretence whatsoever to take arms against the King, and that I do abhor that traitorous position of taking arms by his authority against his person, or against those that are commissionated by him, and that I will conform to the liturgy of the Church of England as it is now by law established, and I do declare that I do hold there lies no obligation upon me or on any other person from the oath commonly called the Solemn League and Covenant, to endeavour any change or alteration of government either in Church or state, and that the same was in itself an unlawful oath, and imposed upon the subjects of this realm against the known laws and liberties of this Kingdom.

Which said declaration and acknowledgement shall be subscribed by every the said masters and other heads, fellows, chaplains and tutors of or in any college, hall or house of learning, and by every public professor and reader in either of the universities before the Vice-Chancellor of the respective universities for the time being of his deputy, and the said declaration or acknowledgement shall be subscribed before the respective archbishop, bishop or ordinary of the diocese by every other person hereby enjoined to subscribe the same, upon pain that all and every of the persons aforesaid falling in such subscription shall lose and forfeit such respective deanery, canonry, prebend, mastership, headship, fellowship, professor's place, reader's place, parsonage, vicarage, ecclesiastical dignity or promotion, curate's place, lecture and school, and shall be utterly disabled and (*ipso facto*) deprived of the same, and that every such respective deanery, canonry, prebend, mastership, headship, fellowship, professor's place, reader's place, parsonage, vicarage, ecclesiastical dignity or promotion, curate's place, lecture and school shall be void, as if such person so failing were naturally dead.

07. And if any schoolmaster or other person instructing or teaching youth in any private house or family as a tutor or schoolmaster, shall instruct or teach any youth as a tutor or schoolmaster before licence obtained from his respective archbishop, bishop or ordinary of the diocese, according to the laws and statutes of this realm (for which he shall pay twelve pence only), and before such subscription and acknowledgement made as aforesaid, then every such schoolmaster and other instructing and teaching as aforesaid shall for the first offence suffer three months imprisonment without bail or mainprize, and for every second and other such offence shall suffer three months imprisonment without bail or mainprize, and also forfeit to his Majesty the sum of five pounds. And after such subscription made, every such parson, vicar, curate and lecturer shall procure a certificate under the hand and seal of the respective archbishop, bishop or ordinary of the diocese (who are hereby enjoined and required upon demand to make and deliver the same), and shall publicly and openly read the same, together with the declaration or acknowledgement aforesaid upon some Lord's Day within three months then the next following, in his parish church where he is to officiate in the presence of the congregation there assembled in the time of divine service, upon pain that every person failing therein shall lose such parsonage, vicarage or benefice, curate's place or lecturer's place respectively, and shall be utterly disabled and (*ipso facto*) deprived of the same,

and that the said parsonage, vicarage or benefice, curate's place or lecturer's place shall be void, as if he were naturally dead.

08. Provided always that from and after the twenty-fifth day of March which shall be in the year of our Lord God One thousand six hundred eighty-two (25 March 1682) there shall be omitted in the said declaration or acknowledgement so to be subscribed and read, these words following, scilicet:

And I do declare that I do hold there lies no obligation upon me or on any other person from the oath commonly called the Solemn League and Covenant, to endeavour any change or alteration of government either in Church or state, and that the same was in itself an unlawful oath, and imposed upon the subjects of this realm against the known laws and liberties of this Kingdom.

So as none of the persons aforesaid shall from thenceforth be at all obliged to subscribe or read part of the said declaration or acknowledgement.

09. Provided always and be it enacted that from and after the feast of St Bartholomew which shall be in the year of our Lord One thousand six hundred sixty and two (24 August 1662), no person who now is incumbent and in possession of any parsonage, vicarage or benefice, and who is not already in Holy Orders by episcopal ordination, or shall not before the said feast day of St Bartholomew be ordained priest or deacon according to the form of episcopal ordination, shall have, hold or enjoy the said parsonage, vicarage, benefice with cure, or other ecclesiastical promotion within this Kingdom of England or the Dominion of Wales or Town of Berwick upon Tweed, but shall be utterly disabled and (*ipso facto*) deprived of the same, and all his ecclesiastical promotions shall be void as if he was naturally dead.

10. And be it further enacted by the authority aforesaid, that **no person whatsoever shall thenceforth be capable to be admitted to any parsonage, vicarage, benefice or other ecclesiastical promotion or dignity whatsoever,** nor shall presume to consecrate and administer the holy sacrament of the Lord's Supper, **before such time as he be ordained priest according to the form and manner in and by the said Book prescribed, unless he have formerly been made priest by episcopal ordination,** upon pain to forfeit for every offence the sum of one hundred pounds, one moiety [i.e. half, *ed.*] thereof to the King's Majesty, the other moiety thereof to be equally divided between the poor of the parish where the offence shall be committed, and such person or persons as shall sue for the same by action of debt, bill, plaint or information in any of his Majesty's courts of record, wherein no essoin, protection or wager of law shall be allowed, and to be disabled from taking or being admitted into the order of priest by the space of one whole year then next following.

11. Provided that the penalties in this Act shall not extend to the foreigners or aliens of the foreign reformed Churches allowed or to be allowed by the King's Majesty, his heirs and successors in England.

12. Provided always that no title to confer or present by lapse shall accrue by any avoidance or deprivation (*ipso facto*) by virtue of this statute, but after six months after notice of such voidance or deprivation given by the ordinary to the patron, or such sentence of deprivation openly and publicly read in the parish church of the benefice, parsonage or vicarage becoming void, or whereof the incumbent shall be deprived by virtue of this Act.

13. And be it further enacted by the authority aforesaid that no form or order of common prayers, administration of sacraments, rites or ceremonies shall be openly used in any church, chapel or other public place of or in any college or hall in either of the universities, the colleges of Westminster, Winchester or Eton, or any of them other than what is prescribed and appointed to be used in and by the said Book, and that the present governor or head of every college and hall in the said universities and of the said colleges or halls hereafter to be elected or appointed within one month next after his election or collation and admission into the same government or headship, shall openly and publicly in the church, chapel or other public place of the same college or hall, and in the presence of the fellows and scholars of the same, or the greater part of them then resident, subscribe unto the Nine and Thirty Articles of Religion mentioned in the statute made in the thirteenth year of the reign of the late Queen Elizabeth, and unto the said Book and declare his unfeigned assent and consent unto and approbation of the said Articles and of the same Book, and to the use of all the prayers, rites and ceremonies, forms and orders in the said Book prescribed, and contained according to the form aforesaid, and that all such governors or heads of the said colleges and halls or any of them as are or shall be in Holy Orders shall once (at least) in every quarter of the year (not having a lawful impediment) openly and publicly read the morning prayer and service in and by the said Book appointed to be read in the church, chapel and other public place of the same college or hall, and if any governor or head of any college or hall suspended for not subscribing unto the said Articles and Book, or for not reading of the morning prayer and service as aforesaid, shall not at or before the end of six months next after such suspension, subscribe unto the said Articles and Book, and declare his consent thereunto as aforesaid, or read the morning prayer and service as aforesaid, then such government or headship shall be (*ipso facto*) void.

14. Provided always that it shall and may be lawful to use the morning and evening prayer and all other prayers and service prescribed in and by the said Book in the chapels or other public places of the respective colleges and halls in both the universities, in the colleges of Westminster, Winchester and Eton, and in the Convocations of the clergies of either province in Latin, anything in this Act contained to the contrary notwithstanding.

15. And be it further enacted by the authority aforesaid that **no person shall be or be received as a lecturer, or permitted, suffered or allowed to preach as a lecturer, or to preach or read any sermon or lecture in**

any church, chapel or other place of public worship within this realm of England or the Dominion of Wales and Town of Berwick upon Tweed, unless he be first approved and thereunto licensed by the archbishop of the province or bishop of the diocese, or (in case the see be void), by the guardian of the spiritualities under his seal and shall in presence of the same archbishop or bishop, read the Nine and Thirty Articles of Religion mentioned in the statute of the thirteenth year of the late Queen Elizabeth, with declaration of his unfeigned assent to the same, and that every person and persons who now is or hereafter shall be licensed, assigned or appointed or received as a lecturer, to preach upon any day of the week in any church, chapel or place of public worship within this Realm of England or places aforesaid, the first time he preacheth (before his sermon) shall openly, publicly and solemnly read the common prayers and service in and by the said book appointed to be read for that time of the day, and then and there publicly and openly declare his assent unto and approbation of the said Book, and to the use of all the prayers, rites and ceremonies, forms and orders therein contained and prescribed according to the form before appointed in this Act, and also shall upon the first lecture day of every month afterwards, so long as he continues lecturer or preacher there at the place appointed for his said lecture or sermon, before his said lecture or sermon openly, publicly and solemnly read the common prayers and service in and by the said Book appointed to be read for that time of the day at which the said lecture or sermon is to be preached, and after such reading thereof shall openly and publicly before the congregation there assembled, declare his unfeigned assent and consent unto and approbation of the said Book, and to the use of all the prayers, rites and ceremonies, forms and orders therein contained and prescribed according to the form aforesaid. And that all and every such person and persons who shall neglect or refuse to do the same shall from henceforth be disabled to preach the said or any other lecture or sermon in the said or any other church, chapel or place of public worship, until such time as he and they shall openly, publicly and solemnly read the common prayers and service appointed by the said Book, and conform in all points to the things therein appointed and prescribed according to the purport, true intent and meaning of this Act.

16. Provided always that if the said sermon or lecture to be preached or read in any cathedral or collegiate church or chapel, it shall be sufficient for the said lecturer openly at the time aforesaid to declare his assent and consent to all things contained in the said Book according to the form aforesaid.

17. And be it further enacted by the authority aforesaid, that if any person who is by this Act disabled to preach any lecture or sermon, shall during the time that he shall continue and remain so disabled, preach any sermon or lecture, that then for every such offence the person and persons so offending shall suffer three months imprisonment in the common gaol

without bail or mainprize, and that any two justices of the peace of any county of this kingdom and places aforesaid, and the mayor or other chief magistrate of any city or town corporate within the same, upon certificate from the ordinary of the place made to him or them, of the offence committed, shall and are hereby required to commit the person or persons so offending to the gaol of the same county, city or town corporate accordingly.

18. Provided always and be it further enacted by the authority aforesaid, that at all and every time and times when any sermon or lecture is to be preached, the common prayers and service in and by the said Book appointed to be read for that time of day, shall be openly, publicly and solemnly read by some priest or deacon in the church, chapel or place of public worship where the said sermon or lecture is to be preached, before such sermon or lecture be preached, and that the lecturer then to preach shall be present at the reading thereof.

19. Provided nevertheless that this Act shall not extend to the university churches in the universities of this realm, or either of them, when or at such times as any sermon or lecture is preached or read in the said churches or any of them, for or as the public university sermon or lecture, but that the same sermons and lectures may be preached or read in such sort and manner as the same have been heretofore preached or read, this Act or anything herein contained to the contrary thereof in any wise notwithstanding.

20. And be it further enacted by the authority aforesaid, that the several good laws and statutes of this realm which have been formerly made and are now in force for the uniformity of prayer and the administration of the sacraments within this Realm of England and the places aforesaid, shall stand in full force and strength to all intents and purposes whatsoever for the establishing and confirming of the said Book, entitled *The Book of Common Prayer and Administration of the Sacraments and other Rites and Ceremonies of the Church according to the Use of the Church of England,* together with the Psalter or Psalms of David, pointed as they are to be sung or said in churches, and the form or manner of making, ordaining and consecrating of bishops, priests and deacons, herein before mentioned to be joined and annexed to this Act, and shall be applied, practised and put in ure for the punishing of all offences contrary to the said laws, with relation to the Book aforesaid and none other.

21. Provided always and be it further enacted by the authority aforesaid that in all those prayers, litanies and collects which do in any way relate to the King, Queen or royal progeny, the names be altered and changed from time to time and fitted to the present occasion according to the direction of lawful authority.

22. Provided also and be it enacted by the authority aforesaid, that a true and printed copy of the said Book entitled *The Book of Common Prayer and Administration of the Sacraments and other Rites and Ceremonies of* *the Church according to the Use of the Church of England*, together with the Psalter or Psalms of David, pointed as they are to be sung or said in churches, and the form or manner of making, ordaining and consecrating of bishops, priests and deacons, shall at all costs and charges of the parishioners of every parish church and chapelry, cathedral church, college and hall, be attained and gotten before the feast day of St Bartholomew in the year of our Lord One thousand six hundred sixty and two (24 August 1662), upon pain of forfeiture of three pounds by the month, for so long time as they shall then after be unprovided thereof, by every parish or chapelry, cathedral church, college and hall making default therein.

23. Provided always and be it enacted by the authority aforesaid, that the bishops of Hereford, St David's, St Asaph, Bangor and Llandaff, and their successors, shall take such order among themselves for the souls' health of the flock committed to their charge within Wales, that the Book hereto annexed be truly and exactly translated into the British or Welsh tongue, and that the same so translated and being by them or any three of them at the least viewed, perused and allowed, be imprinted to such number at least, so that one of the said Books so translated and imprinted may be had for every cathedral, collegiate and parish church and chapel of ease in the said respective dioceses and places in Wales where the Welsh is commonly spoken or used, before the first day of May One thousand six hundred sixty-five (01 May 1665). And that from and after the imprinting and publishing of the said Book so translated, the whole divine service shall be used and said by the ministers and curates throughout all Wales within the said dioceses where the Welsh tongue is commonly used, in the British or Welsh tongue in such manner and form as is prescribed according to the Book hereunto annexed to be used in the English tongue, differing nothing in any order or form from the said English Book, for which Book so translated and imprinted, the churchwardens of every the said parishes shall pay out of the parish monies in their hands for the use of the respective churches, and be allowed the same on their account, an that the said bishops and their successors, or any three of them at the least, shall set and appoint the price for which the said Book shall be sold, and one other Book of Common prayer in the English tongue shall be bought and had in every church throughout Wales, in which the Book of Common prayer in Welsh is to be had by force of this Act, before the first day of May One thousand six hundred sixty and four (01 May 1664), and the same book to remain in such convenient places within the said churches, that such as understand them may resort at all convenient times to read and peruse the same, and also such as do not understand the said language may, by conferring both tongues together, the sooner attain to the knowledge of the English tongue, anything in this Act to the contrary notwithstanding, and until printed copies of the said Book so to be translated may be had and provided, the form of common prayer established by Parliament before the making of this Act shall be used as formerly in such parts of Wales where the English tongue is not commonly understood.

24. And to the end that the true and perfect copies of this Act, and the said Book hereunto annexed, may be safely kept and perpetually preserved, and for the avoiding of all disputes for the time to come, be it therefore enacted by the authority aforesaid, that the respective deans and chapters of every cathedral or collegiate church within England and Wales shall at their proper costs and charges, before the twenty-fifth day of December One thousand six hundred sixty and two (25 December 1662), obtain under the great seal of England, a true and perfect printed copy of this Act and the said Book annexed hereunto, to be by the said deans and chapters and their successors kept and preserved in safety for ever, and to be also produced and showed forth in any court of record as often as they shall be thereunto lawfully required, and also there shall be delivered true and perfect copies of this Act and of the same Book, into the respective courts at Westminster, and into the Tower of London, to be kept and preserved for ever among the records of the said courts and the records of the Tower, to be also produced and showed forth in any court as need shall require, which said Books so to be exemplified under the great seal of England shall be examined by such persons as the King's Majesty shall appoint under the great seal of England for that purpose, and shall be compared with the original Book hereunto annexed, and shall have power to correct and amend in writing any error committed by the printer in the printing of the same Book, or of anything therein contained, and shall certify in writing under their hands and seals, or the hands and seals of any three of them at the end of the same Book, that they have examined and compared the same Book and find it to be a true and perfect copy, which said Books and every one of them so exemplified under the great seal of England as aforesaid, shall be deemed, taken, adjudged and expounded to be good and available in the law to all intents and purposes whatsoever, and shall be accounted as good records as this Book itself hereunto annexed, any law or custom to the contrary in any wise notwithstanding.

25. Provided also that this Act or anything therein contained shall not be prejudicial or hurtful unto the King's professor of the law within the University of Oxford for or concerning the prebend of Shipton within the cathedral church of Sarum, united and annexed unto the place of the same King's professor for the time being, by the late King James of blessed memory.

26. Provided always that whereas the six and thirtieth Article of the Nine and Thirty Articles agreed upon by the archbishops and bishops of both provinces and the whole clergy in the Convocation holden at London in the year of our Lord One thousand five hundred sixty-two (i.e. 1652), for the avoiding of diversities of opinions and for the establishing of consent touching true religion, is in these words following, viz.:

That the Book of Consecration of Archbishops and Bishops and Ordaining of Priests and Deacons lately set forth in the time of King Edward the Sixth, and confirmed at the same time by authority of Parliament, doth contain all things necessary to such consecrating and ordaining, neither hath it anything that of itself is superstitious and ungodly, and therefore whosoever are consecrated or ordered according to the rites of that Book since the second year of the aforenamed King Edward unto this time, or hereafter shall be consecrated or ordered according to the same rites, we decree all such to be rightly, orderly and lawfully consecrated and ordered.

It be enacted, and be it therefore enacted by the authority aforesaid, that all subscriptions hereafter to be had or made unto the said Articles by any deacon, priest or ecclesiastical person or other person whatsoever, who by this Act or any other law now in force is required to subscribe unto the said Articles, shall be construed and be taken to extend and shall be applied (for and touching the said Six and Thirtieth Article) unto the Book containing the form and manner of making, ordaining and consecrating bishops, priests and deacons, in this Act mentioned, in such sort in the time of King Edward the Sixth mentioned in the said Six and Thirtieth Article, anything in the said Article or in any statute, act or canon heretofore had or made to the contrary thereof, in any wise notwithstanding.

27. Provided also that *The Book of Common Prayer and Administration of the Sacraments and other Rites and Ceremonies of this Church of England, together with the Form or Manner of Ordaining and Consecrating Bishops, Priests and Deacons* heretofore in use, and respectively established by Act of Parliament in the first (1559) and eighth (1566) years of Queen Elizabeth, shall be still used and observed in the Church of England until the feast day of St Bartholomew, which shall be in the year of our Lord God One thousand six hundred sixty and two (24 August 1662).

50. THE PREFACE TO THE BOOK OF COMMON PRAYER, 1662

History

The reintroduction of the 1559 Book of Common Prayer was one of the major demands of the episcopalian party which surrounded Charles II. A few minor changes were considered and introduced, but in all essentials it was the old book which was reinstated. Puritan ministers, who objected to set forms of prayer and prescribed worship, now left the Church of England in droves.

Theology

The Book of Common Prayer of 1662 reflects the same kind of moderate Protestantism which Elizabeth I approved of in 1559. The belief in a uniform, common prayer, shared by priest and people alike, was fundamental to established Anglicanism, and continued to be the major difference between it and the other Protestant churches. This however, is not the same thing as liturgical worship, a concern which is much more recent within the Church of England. From a purely liturgical point of view, the Book of Common Prayer has often been considered defective, and the Liturgical Renewal of the mid-twentieth century has not hesitated to criticize and even to rewrite it. But it must be remembered that in 1662, it was uniformity which appealed to the Church more than liturgy – the latter was merely an aid to the former. In this respect, it is not without interest to note that the revival of interest in liturgy has signalled the death of uniformity, and the virtual loss of a truly **common** prayer in the Church of England.

It hath been the wisdom of the Church of England, ever since the first compiling of her public liturgy, to keep the mean between the two extremes, of too much stiffness in refusing, and of too much easiness in admitting any variation from it. For, as on the one side common experience showeth that where a change hath been made of things advisedly established (no evident necessity so requiring) sundry inconveniences have thereupon ensued; and those many times more and greater than the evils that were intended to be remedied by such change; so, on the other side, the particular forms of divine worship and the rites and ceremonies appointed to be used therein, being things in their own nature indifferent and alterable, and so acknowledged; it is but reasonable that upon weighty and important considerations, according to the various exigency of times and occasions, such changes and alterations should be made therein, as to those that are in place of authority should from time to time seem either necessary or expedient. Accordingly we find that in the reigns of several princes of blessed memory since the Reformation, the Church, upon just and weighty considerations her thereunto moving, hath yielded to make such alterations in some particulars, as in their respective times were thought convenient; yet so as the main body and essentials of it (as well in the chiefest materials as in the frame and order thereof) have still continued the same unto this day, and do yet stand firm and unshaken, notwithstanding all the vain attempts and impetuous assaults made against it, by such men as are given to change, and have always discovered a greater regard to their own private fancies and interests than to that duty they owe to the public.

By what undue means, and for what mischievous purposes the use of the liturgy (though enjoined by the laws of the land, and those laws never yet repealed) came, during the late unhappy confusions, to be discontinued, is too well known to the world, and we are not willing here to remember. But when, upon his Majesty's happy restoration, it seemed probable that, amongst other things, the use of the liturgy also would return of course (the same having never been legally abolished) unless some timely means were used to prevent it; those men who under the late usurped powers had made it a great part of their business to render the people disaffected thereunto, saw themselves in point of reputation and interest concerned (unless they would freely acknowledge themselves to have erred, which such men are very hardly brought to do) with their utmost endeavours to hinder the restitution thereof. In order whereunto divers pamphlets were published against the Book of Common Prayer, the old objections mustered up, with the addition of some new ones, more than formerly had been made, to make the number swell. In fine, great importunities were used to his sacred Majesty that the said book might be revised, and such alterations therein and additions thereunto made, as should be thought requisite for the ease of tender consciences; whereunto his Majesty, out of his pious inclination to give satisfaction (so far as could be reasonably expected) to all his subjects of what persuasion soever, did graciously condescend.

In which review we have endeavoured to observe the like moderation as we find to have been used in the like case in former times. And therefore, of the sundry alterations proposed unto us, we have rejected all such as were of dangerous consequence (as secretly striking at some established doctrine or laudable practice of the Church of England, or indeed of the whole catholic Church of Christ) or else of no consequence at all, but utterly frivolous and vain. But such alterations as were tendered to us (by what persons, under what pretences, or to what purpose soever so tendered) as seemed to us in any degree requisite or expedient, we have willingly and of our own accord assented unto, not enforced so to do by any strength of argument, convincing us of the necessity of making the said alterations; for we are fully persuaded in our judgements (as we here profess it to the world) that the Book, as it stood before established by law, doth not contain in it anything contrary to the Word of God or to sound doctrine, or which a godly man may not with a good conscience use and submit unto, or which is not fairly defensible against any that shall oppose the same; if it shall be allowed such just and favourable construction as in common equity ought to be allowed to all human writings, especially such as are set forth by authority, and even to the very best translations of the Holy Scripture itself.

Our general aim therefore in this undertaking was, not to gratify this or that party in any their unreasonable demands, but to do that which to our best understandings we conceived might most tend to the preservation of peace and unity in the Church, the procuring of reverence, and exciting of piety and devotion in the public worship of God; and the cutting off occasion from them that seek occasion of cavil or quarrel against the liturgy of the Church. And as to the several variations from the former Book, whether by alteration, addition or otherwise, it shall suffice to give this general account, that most of the alterations were made, either first, for the better direction of them that are to officiate in any part of divine service, which is chiefly done in the calendars and rubrics; or secondly, for the more proper expressing of some words or phrases of ancient usage in terms more suitable to the language of the present times and the clearer explanation of some other words and phrases that were either of doubtful signification, or otherwise liable to misconstruction; or thirdly, for a more perfect rendering of such portions of Holy Scripture as are inserted into the liturgy, which in the Epistles and Gospels especially, and in sundry other places, are now ordered to be read according to the last translation; and that it was thought convenient that some prayers and thanksgivings, fitted to special occasions, should be added in their due places; particularly for those at sea, together with an office for the baptism of such as are of riper years; which, although not so necessary when the former book was compiled, yet by the growth of anabaptism, through the licentiousness of the late times crept in amongst us, is now becoming necessary, and may always be useful for the baptizing of natives in our plantations and others converted to the Faith. If any man who shall desire a more particular account of the several alterations in any part of the liturgy shall take the pains to compare the present Book with the former, we doubt not but the reason of the change may easily appear.

And having thus endeavoured to discharge our duties in this weighty affair, as in the sight of God, and to approve our sincerity therein (so far as lay in us) to the consciences of all men; although we know it impossible (in such variety of apprehensions, humours and interests as are in the world) to please all; nor can expect that men of factious, peevish and perverse spirits should be satisfied with anything that can be done in this kind by any other than themselves; yet we have good hope that what is here presented, and hath been by the Convocations of both Provinces with great diligence examined and approved, will be also well accepted and approved by all sober, peaceable and truly conscientious sons of the Church of England.

51. THE TEST ACT, 1673 (25 Charles II c. 2)

History

After the Restoration of 1660, it became imperative to establish the religious loyalty of everyone who was engaged in public service. As early as May 1661, the so-called Corporation Act decreed that: "no person or persons shall for ever hereafter be placed, elected or chosen, in or to any the offices or places aforesaid (i.e. any local government position), that shall not have, within one year next before such election or choice, taken the sacrament of the Lord's Supper according to the rites of the Church of England...". Following the Act of Uniformity and the exclusion of nearly 20% of the Church's ministers, dissent from this requirement became a real and growing danger. To make matters worse, Roman Catholicism seemed to be on the increase, at least to the extent that there were many in the royal household who were sympathetic to it. Charles II was to become a Catholic on his deathbed, and his brother and heir, the Duke of York, converted in 1673. That event sparked off renewed concern about "popery", which in turn inspired the Test Act.

This Act, like the Corporation Act before it, remained on the statute books until 1828, when first Protestant Dissenters and then, a year later, Roman Catholics, were emancipated.

Theology

The Test Act reflects the theology of High Church Anglicanism, according to which the state was the political manifestation of the Christian people of England, and therefore subject to Church control. No-one who was not a member in good standing of the national Church could claim the full privileges of citizenship. From the Church's point of view, this restriction was necessary, because Parliament was its only legislative body. Because the Church's doctrine and worship could be, and were, regulated by Acts of Parliament, it was essential that all Members be communicants, and therefore subject to Church discipline. This view was increasingly challenged as time went on, but it remained characteristic of die-hard High Churchmen until the end. George IV hesitated before allowing repeal of the Act, because he felt that it went against his coronation oath, in which he had sworn to uphold the Protestant religion, and many churchpeople were equally disturbed. The prospect of a Parliament composed of non-Anglicans having jurisdiction over Church affairs was sufficiently alarming to induce John Keble to preach a university sermon in Oxford on the theme of "national apostasy" (14 July 1833) – the famous occasion which is generally held to mark the beginning of the so-called Oxford, or Tractarian Movement.

An Act for preventing dangers which may happen from Popish Recusants.

01. For preventing dangers which may happen from popish recusants, and quieting the minds of his Majesty's good subjects, be it enacted by the King's most excellent Majesty, by and with the advice and consent of the Lords spiritual and temporal, and the Commons, in this present Parliament assembled, and by authority of the same, that all and every person or persons, as well peers as commoners, that shall bear any office or offices, civil or military, or shall receive any pay, salary, fee, or wages, by reason of any patent or grant from his Majesty, or shall have command or place of trust from or under his Majesty, or from any of his Majesty's predecessors, or by his or their authority, or by authority derived from him or them, within the realm of England, dominion of Wales, or town of Berwick-upon-Tweed, or in his Majesty's navy, or in the several islands of Jersey and Guernsey, or shall be of the household or in the service or employment of his Majesty, or of his royal highness the Duke of York, who shall inhabit, reside, or be within the city of London or Westminster, or within thirty miles distant from the same, on the first day of Easter term that shall be in the year of our Lord 1673 (02 February 1673), or at any time during the said term, all and every the said person or persons shall personally appear before the end of the said term, or of Trinity term next following, in his Majesty's High Court of Chancery, or in his Majesty's Court of King's Bench, and there in public and open court, between the hours of nine of the clock and twelve in the forenoon, take the several oaths of supremacy and allegiance – which oath of allegiance is contained in a statute made in the third year of King James (1605) – by law established; and during the time of the taking thereof by the said person and persons, all pleas and proceedings in the said respective courts shall cease: and that all and every of the said respective persons and officers, not having taken the said oaths in the said respective courts aforesaid, shall on or before the first day of August, 1673 (01 August 1673), at the quarter sessions for that county or place where he or they shall be, inhabit or reside on the twentieth day of May (20 May 1673), take the said oaths in open court between the said hours of nine and twelve of the clock in the forenoon; and the said respective officers aforesaid shall also receive the sacrament of the Lord's Supper, according to the usage of the Church of England, at or before the first day of August in the year of our Lord 1673 (01 August 1673), in some parish church, upon some Lord's Day, commonly called Sunday, immediately after divine service and sermon.

02. And be it further enacted by the authority aforesaid, that all and every person or persons that shall be admitted, entered, placed or taken into any office or offices, civil or military, or shall receive any pay, salary, fee or wages by reason of any patent or grant of his Majesty, or shall have command or place of trust from or under his Majesty, his heirs or successors, or by his or their authority or by authority derived from him or them, within this realm of England, dominion of Wales, or town of Berwick-upon-Tweed, or in his Majesty's navy, or in the several islands of Jersey and Guernsey, or that shall be admitted into any service or employment in his Majesty's or royal highness's household or family, after the first day of Easter term aforesaid (02 February 1673), and shall inhabit, be, or reside, when he or they is or are so admitted or placed, within the cities of London or Westminster, or within thirty miles of the same, shall take the said oaths aforesaid in the said respective court or courts aforesaid, in the next term after such his or their admittance or admittances into the office or offices, employment or employments aforesaid, between the hours aforesaid and no other, and the proceedings to cease as aforesaid; and that all and every such person or persons to be admitted after the said first day of Easter term (02 February 1673) as aforesaid, not having taken the said oaths in the said courts aforesaid, shall at the quarter sessions for that county or place where he or they shall reside, next after such his admittance or admittances into any of the said respective offices or employments aforesaid, take the several and respective oaths as aforesaid; and all and every such person and persons so to be admitted as aforesaid shall also receive the sacrament of the Lord's Supper according to the usage of the Church of England, within three months after his or their admittances in or receiving their said authority and employment, in some public church, upon some Lord's Day, commonly called Sunday, immediately after divine service and sermon.

And every of the said persons in the respective court where he takes the said oaths shall first deliver a certificate of such his receiving the said sacrament as aforesaid, under the hands of the respective minister and churchwardens, and shall then make proof of the truth thereof by two credible witnesses at the least, upon oath; all which shall be inquired of, and put upon record in the respective courts.

03. And be it further enacted by the authority aforesaid, that all and every the person or persons aforesaid, that do or shall neglect or refuse to take the said oaths and sacrament in the said courts and places, and at the respective times aforesaid, shall be *ipso facto* adjudged incapable and disabled in law, to all intents and purposes whatsoever, to have, occupy, or enjoy the said office or offices, employment or employments, or any part of them, or any matter or thing aforesaid, or any profit or advantage appertaining to them or any of them; and every such office and place, employment and employments shall be void, and is hereby adjudged void.

04. And be it further enacted, that all and every such person or persons that shall neglect or refuse to take the said oaths or the sacrament as aforesaid, within the times and in the places aforesaid, and in the manner aforesaid, and yet after such neglect and refusal shall execute any of the said offices or employments after the said times expired, wherein he or they ought to have taken the same, and being thereupon lawfully convicted, in

or upon any information, presentment or indictment, in any of the King's courts at Westminster, or at the assizes, every such person and persons shall be disabled from thenceforth to sue or use any action, bill, plaint or information in course of law, or to prosecute any suit in any court of equity, or to be guardian of any child, or executor or administrator of any person, or capable of any legacy or deed of gift, or to bear any office within this realm of England, dominion of Wales or town of Berwick-upon-Tweed; or shall forfeit the sum of five hundred pounds, to be recovered by him or them that shall sue for the same, to be prosecuted by any action of debt, suit, bill, plaint or information, in any of his Majesty's courts at Westminster, wherein no essoin, protection or wager of law shall lie.

05. And be it further enacted by the authority aforesaid, that the names of all and singular such persons and officers aforesaid, that do or shall take the oaths aforesaid, shall be, in the respective courts of Chancery and King's Bench and the quarter sessions enrolled, with the day and time of their taking the same, in rolls made and kept only for that intent and purpose, and for no other; the which rolls, as for the Court of Chancery, shall be publicly hung up in the office of the petty-bag, and the roll for the King's Bench in the Crown Office of the said court, and in some public place in every quarter sessions, and there remain during the whole term, every term, and during the whole time of the said sessions, in every quarter sessions, for everyone to resort to and look upon without fee or reward; and likewise none of the person or persons aforesaid shall give or pay as any fee or reward to any officer or officers belonging to any of the courts as aforesaid, above the sum of twelve pence for his or their entry of his or their taking of the said oaths aforesaid.

06. And further, that it shall and may be lawful to and for the respective courts aforesaid, to give and administer the said oaths aforesaid to the person or persons aforesaid, in manner as aforesaid; and upon the due tender of any such person or persons to take the said oaths, the said courts are hereby required and enjoined to administer the same.

07. And be it further enacted, that if any person or persons, not bred up by his or their parent or parents from their infancy in the popish religion, and professing themselves to be popish recusants, shall breed up, instruct, or educate his or their child or children, or suffer them to be instructed or educated in the popish religion, every such person, being thereof convicted, shall be from thenceforth disabled of bearing any office or place of trust or profit in Church or state; and all such children as shall be so brought up, instructed, or educated, are and shall be hereby disabled of bearing any such office or place of trust or profit, until he and they shall be perfectly reconciled and converted to the Church of England, and shall take the oaths of supremacy and allegiance aforesaid before the justices of the peace in the open quarter sessions of the county or place where they shall inhabit, and thereupon receive the sacrament of the Lord's Supper after the usage of the

Church of England, and obtain a certificate thereof under the hands of two or more of the said justices of the peace.

08. And be it further enacted by the authority aforesaid, that at the same time when the persons concerned in this Act shall take the aforesaid oaths of supremacy and allegiance, they shall likewise make and subscribe this declaration following, under the same penalties and forfeitures as by this Act is appointed:

"I, A. B., do declare that I do believe that there is not any transubstantiation in the sacrament of the Lord's Supper, or in the elements of bread and wine, at or after the consecration thereof by any person whatsoever."

Of which subscription there shall be the like register kept, as of the taking of the oaths aforesaid.

09. Provided always that neither this Act nor anything therein contained, shall extend, be judged or interpreted any ways to hurt or prejudice the peerage of any peer of this realm, or to take away any right, power, privilege or profit which any person (being a peer of this realm) has or ought to enjoy by reason of his peerage, either in time of Parliament or otherwise, or to take away creation money or bills of impost, nor to take away or make void any pension or salary granted by his Majesty to any person for valuable and sufficient consideration for life, lives or years, other than such as relate to any office, or to any place of trust under his Majesty, and other than pensions of bounty or voluntary pensions; not to take away or make void any estate of inheritance granted by his Majesty, or any his predecessors, to any person or persons of or in any lands, rents, tithes or hereditaments, not being offices; nor to take away or make void any pension or salary already granted by his Majesty to any persons who was instrumental in the happy preservation of his sacred Majesty after the battle of Worcester in the year 1651, until his Majesty's arrival beyond the seas; nor to take away or make void the grant of any office or offices of inheritance, or any fee, salary or reward for executing such office or offices, or thereto any way belonging, granted by his Majesty, or any his predecessors, to, or enjoyed, or which hereafter shall be enjoyed, by any person or persons who shall refuse or neglect to take the said oaths, or either of them, or to receive the sacrament, or to subscribe the declaration mentioned in this Act, in manner therein expressed. Nevertheless so as such person or persons having or enjoying any such office or offices of inheritance, do or shall substitute and appoint his or their sufficient deputy or deputies (which such officer or officers respectively are hereby empowered from time to time to make or change, any former law or usage to the contrary notwithstanding) to exercise the said office or offices shall voluntarily in the Court of Chancery, before the lord chancellor or lord keeper for the time being, or in the Court of King's Bench, take the said oaths, and receive the sacrament according to law, and subscribe the said declaration, and so as all and every the deputy and deputies, so as aforesaid to be appointed, take the said oaths, receive the sacrament, and subscribe the said declaration from time to time, as they shall happen to be so appointed, in manner as by this Act such officers, whose deputies they be, are appointed to do; and so as such deputies be from time to time approved of by the King's Majesty under his privy signet; but that all and every the peers of this realm shall have, hold, and enjoy what is provided for as aforesaid, and all and every other person or persons before mentioned, denoted or intended within this proviso, shall have, hold and enjoy what is provided for as aforesaid, notwithstanding any incapacity or disability mentioned in this Act.

10. Provided also that the said peers and every of them may take the said oaths, and make the said subscription, and deliver the said certificates, before the peers sitting in Parliament, if the Parliament be sitting, within the time limited for doing thereof, and in the intervals of Parliament, in the High Court of Chancery, in which respective courts all the said proceedings are to be recorded in manner aforesaid.

11. Provided always that no married woman or person under the age of eighteen years, or being beyond or upon the seas, or found by the lawful oaths of twelve men to be *non compos mentis*, and so being and remaining at the end of Trinity term in the year of our Lord 1673 (31 July 1673), having any office, shall by virtue of this Act lose or forfeit any such his or her office (other than such married woman during the life of her husband only) for any neglect or refusal of taking the oaths, and doing the other things required by this Act to be done by persons having offices, so as such respective persons within four months after the death of the husband, coming to the age of eighteen years, returning into this kingdom, and becoming of sound mind, shall respectively take the said oaths, and perform all other things in manner as by this Act is appointed for persons to do, who shall happen to have any office or offices to them given or fallen after the end of the said Trinity term.

12. Provided also that any person who by his or her neglect or refusal, according to this Act, shall lose or forfeit any office, may be capable, by a new grant, of the said office, or of any other, and to have and hold the same again, such person taking the said oaths, and doing all other things required by this Act, so as such office be not granted to, and actually enjoyed by, some other person at the time of the regranting thereof.

13. Provided also that nothing in this Act contained shall extend to make any forfeiture, disability or incapacity in, by or upon any non-commissioned officer or officers in his Majesty's navy, if such officer or officers shall only subscribe the declaration therein required, in manner as the same is directed.

14. Provided also that nothing in this Act contained shall extend to prejudice George, Earl of Bristol, or Anne, Countess of Bristol, his wife, in the pension or pensions granted to them by patent, under the great seal of England, bearing date the sixteenth day of July in the year of our Lord 1669 (16 July 1669), being in lieu of a just debt due to the said Earl from his Majesty, particularly expressed in the said patent.

15. Provided also that this Act, or anything therein contained, shall not extend to the office of any high constable, petty constable, tithingman, headborough, overseer of the poor, churchwardens, surveyor of the highways, or any like inferior civil office, or to any office of forester, or keeper of any park, chase, warren or game, or of bailiff of any manor or lands, or to any like private offices, or to any person or persons having only the before-mentioned or any the like offices.

52. THE TOLERATION ACT, 1689
(1 William III and Mary II, c.18)

History

The ecclesiastical settlement of 1662 was intended to be comprehensive and permanent, but it soon became apparent that a substantial minority of the population was not prepared to conform to its requirements. The departure of about a fifth of the Church's ministers was a heavy blow, felt all the more because there was still considerable sympathy for Puritan theology within the Establishment. There were also a number of Dissenters, like Richard Baxter, who were not separatists, and who continued to hope that the Church of England might be reunited on a more Reformed basis.

Before long the king was trying to effect a compromise, which would allow Dissenters to practise their form of Protestantism within the bounds of the law. Unfortunately, it was well known that the libertine Charles II (1660-1685) was not motivated by the religious fervour which had driven the Dissenters out of the Establishment, and it was widely suspected that his desire for toleration was really an attempt to legalize Roman Catholicism. His brother James II (1685-1688), who was a practising Catholic, tried to advocate toleration for all, but met with the same objection. Most Englishmen were prepared to accept Protestant Dissent, but not legalized Roman Catholicism, which was obviously James' main concern.

Political and religious events soon combined to force the issue to a head. In France, the Huguenots (Protestants) were finally expelled in 1685, and many took refuge in England, where they were welcomed with open arms. Protestant solidarity suddenly seemed more important than the issues which divided the Establishment from Dissent. James' Catholicism was a legal anomaly which stirred memories of persecution under the last Catholic sovereign, Mary I. A situation in which the king practised a proscribed religion, whilst he was at the same time the Supreme Governor of a Church which he was supposed to regard as heretical, was clearly untenable. It was resolved by the flight of James in 1688 and Parliament's invitation to his daughter, Mary II (1689-1694), and her husband, William III of Orange (1689-1702), to come to England as joint sovereigns. This "Glorious Revolution" created a state in which Protestantism was the accepted religion, although the new king, a Dutch Calvinist, was not a member of the Church of England. Seven bishops, including the Archbishop of Canterbury, refused to recognize this revolution, and remained loyal to James II, even though they were unsympathetic to his Roman Catholicism. These legitimists, who were known as "non-jurors" because of their refusal to swear the oath of allegiance to William and Mary, left the Church of England and continued an independent episcopal succession which lasted until 1805.

William and Mary consolidated their triumph by confirming the establishment of the Church of England, by allowing the Church of Scotland to return to a Presbyterian form of government, and by granting toleration to the English Dissenters. The Toleration Act which was passed during their first Parliament remained in force until 1828, when it was superseded by an Act of Emancipation, giving Dissenters full civil and ecclesiastical rights. (Roman Catholics were similarly emancipated in 1829).

Theology

The Toleration Act established the principle that England was henceforth to be a Protestant state with an established Anglican Church, but with toleration for those Protestants who could not accept the worship and discipline of the Establishment. It did not introduce freedom of religion in the modern sense, but was an important contribution to it, because it recognized that one could be loyal to the state without belonging to the king's Church. A certain degree of pluralism within the overall umbrella of Protestantism was also recognized, and the exclusivist claims of High Church Anglicans were rejected.

An Act for exempting their Majesties' Protestant Subjects dissenting from the Church of England from the Penalties of certain Laws

01. Forasmuch as some ease to scrupulous consciences in the exercise of religion may be an effectual means to unite their Majesties' Protestant subjects in interest and affection, be it enacted by the King and Queen's most excellent Majesties, by and with the advice and consent of the Lords spiritual and temporal, and the Commons in this present Parliament assembled, and by the authority of the same, that neither the statute made in the three and twentieth year of the reign of the late Queen Elizabeth (1581), intitled *An Act to retain the Queen's Majesty's Subjects in their due Obedience*, nor the statute made in the twenty-ninth year of the said Queen (1587), intitled *An Act for the more speedy and due Execution of certain Branches of the Statute made in the three and twentieth year of the Queen's Majesty's reign*, viz. the aforesaid Act, nor that branch or clause of a statute made in the first year of the reign of the said Queen (1559), intitled *An Act for the Uniformity of Common Prayer and Service in the Church and Administration of the Sacraments*, whereby all persons having no lawful or reasonable excuse to be absent are required to resort to their parish church or chapel, or some usual place where the Common Prayer shall be used, upon pain of punishment by the censures of the Church; and also upon pain that every person so offending shall forfeit for every such offence twelve pence; not the statute made in the third year of the late King James the First (1605), entitled *An Act for the better Discovering and Repressing Popish Recusants*; nor that other statute made in the same year, intitled *An Act to* *prevent and avoid Dangers which may grow by Popish Recusants*; nor any other law or statute of this realm made against Papists or Popish Recusants, except the statute made in the five and twentieth year of King Charles the Second (1673), intitled *An Act for preventing Dangers which may happen from Popish Recusants*, and except also the statute made in the thirtieth year of the said King Charles the Second (1678), intitled *An Act for the more effectual preserving the King's Person and Government by disabling Papists from sitting in either House of Parliament*, shall be construed to extend to any person or persons dissenting from the Church of England that shall take the oaths mentioned in a statute made in this present Parliament, intitled *An Act for removing and preventing all Questions and Disputes concerning the Assembling and Sitting of this present Parliament*; and shall make and subscribe the declaration mentioned in a statute made in the thirtieth year of the reign of King Charles the Second (1678), intitled *An Act to prevent Papists from sitting in either House of Parliament*, which oaths and declaration the justices of peace at the general sessions of the peace to be held for the county or place where such persons shall live, are hereby required to tender and administer to such persons as shall offer themselves to take, make and subscribe the same, and thereof to keep a register; and likewise none of the persons aforesaid shall give or pay as any fee or reward to any officer or officers belonging to the Court aforesaid, above the sum of sixpence, nor that more than once for his or her entry of his taking the said oaths and making and subscribing the said declaration, nor above the further sum of sixpence for any certificate of the same to be made out and signed by the officer or officers of the said court.

02. And be it further enacted by the authority aforesaid, that all and every person or persons already convicted or prosecuted in order to conviction of recusancy by indictment, information, action of debt or otherwise grounded upon the aforesaid statutes or any of them that shall take the said oaths mentioned in the said statute made in this present Parliament, and make and subscribe the declaration aforesaid in the Court of Exchequer or assizes or General or Quarter Sessions to be held for the county where such person lives, and to be thence respectively certified into the Exchequer, shall be thenceforth exempted and discharged from all the penalties, seizures, forfeitures, judgements and executions incurred by force of any of the aforesaid statutes, without any composition fee or further charge whatsoever.

03. And be it further enacted by the authority aforesaid that all and every person and persons that shall, as aforesaid, take the said oaths and make and subscribe the declaration aforesaid, shall not be liable to any pains, penalties or forfeitures mentioned in an Act made in the five and thirtieth year of the reign of the late Queen Elizabeth (1593), intitled *An Act to retain the Queen's Majesty's Subjects in their due Obedience*, nor in an Act made in the two and twentieth year of the reign of the late King Charles the Second (1670), intitled *An Act to prevent and suppress seditious Conventicles*, nor

shall any of the said persons be prosecuted in any ecclesiastical court for or by reason of their non-conforming to the Church of England.

04. Provided always and be it enacted by the authority aforesaid, that if any assembly of persons dissenting from the Church of England shall be had in any place for religious worship with the doors locked, barred or bolted during the time of such meeting, together all and every person or persons that shall come to and be at such meeting shall not receive any benefit from this law, but be liable to all the pains and penalties of all the aforesaid laws recited in this Act for such their meeting, notwithstanding his taking the oaths and his making and subscribing the declaration aforesaid, provided always that nothing herein contained shall be construed to exempt any of the persons aforesaid from paying of tithes or other parochial duties, or any other duties to the Church or minister, nor for any prosecution in any ecclesiastical court or elsewhere for the same.

05. And be it further enacted by the authority aforesaid, that if any person dissenting from the Church of England as aforesaid, shall hereafter be chosen or otherwise appointed to bear the office of High Constable or Petty Constable, churchwarden, overseer of the poor, or any other parochial or ward office, and such person shall scruple to take upon him any of the said offices, in regard of the oaths or any other matter or thing required by the law to be taken or done in respect of such office, every such person shall and may execute such office or employment by a sufficient deputy by him to be provided, that shall comply with the laws on this behalf, provided always the said deputy be allowed and approved by such person and/or persons in such manner as such officer or officers respectively should by law have been allowed and approved.

06. And be it further enacted by the authority aforesaid, that no person dissenting from the Church of England in Holy Orders, or pretending to Holy Orders, nor any preacher or teacher of any congregation of dissenting Protestants that shall make and subscribe the declaration aforesaid, and take the said oaths at the General or Quarter Sessions of the peace to be held for the county town, parts or division where such person lives, which court is hereby empowered to administer the same and shall also declare his approbation of and subscribe the Articles of religion mentioned in the statute made in the thirteenth year of the reign of the late Queen Elizabeth (1571), except the thirty-fourth, thirty-fifth and thirty-sixth, and these words of the twentieth Article, viz.: "the Church hath power to decree rites or ceremonies, and authority in controversies of faith and yet" shall be liable to any of the pains and penalties mentioned in an Act made in the seventeenth year of the reign of King Charles the Second (1665), intitled, *An Act for restraining Non-Conformists from inhabiting in Corporations*, nor the penalties mentioned in the aforesaid Act made in the two and twentieth year of his said late Majesty's reign (1670), for or by reason of such persons preaching at any meeting for the exercise of religion, nor to the penalty of one hundred

pounds mentioned in an Act made in the thirteenth and fourteenth of King Charles the Second (1662), intitled *An Act for the Uniformity of Public Prayers and Administration of Sacraments and other Rites and Ceremonies, and for establishing the Form of Making, Ordaining and Consecrating of Bishops, Priests and Deacons in the Church of England* for officiating in any congregation for the exercise of religion permitted and allowed by this Act (provided always that the making and subscribing the said declaration and the taking the said oaths and making the declaration of approbation and subscription to the said Articles in manner as aforesaid by every respective person or persons herein before mentioned at such General or Quarter Sessions of the peace as aforesaid, shall be then and there entered of record in the said court, for which sixpence shall be paid to the clerk of the peace and no more), provided that such person shall not at any time preach in any place but with the doors not locked, barred or bolted as aforesaid.

07. And whereas some dissenting Protestants scruple the baptizing of infants, be it enacted by the authority aforesaid, that every person in pretended Holy Orders, or pretending to Holy Orders, or preacher or teacher that shall subscribe the aforesaid Articles of Religion, except before excepted, and also except part of the seven and twentieth Article touching infant baptism, and shall take the said oaths and make and subscribe the declaration aforesaid in manner aforesaid, every such person shall enjoy all the privileges, benefits and advantages which any other dissenting minister as aforesaid might have or enjoy by virtue of this Act.

08. And be it further enacted by the authority aforesaid, that every teacher or preacher in Holy Orders or pretended Holy Orders, that is a minister, preacher or teacher of a congregation that shall take the oaths herein required, and make and subscribe the declaration aforesaid, and also subscribe such of the aforesaid Articles of the Church of England as are required by this Act in manner aforesaid, shall be thenceforth exempted from serving upon any jury or from being chosen or appointed to bear the office of churchwarden, overseer of the poor, or any other parochial or ward office, or other office in any hundred of any shire, city, town, parish, division or wapentake.

09. And be it further enacted by the authority aforesaid, that every justice of the peace may at any time hereafter require any person that goes to any meeting for exercise of religion, to make and subscribe the declaration aforesaid, and also to take the said oaths or declaration of fidelity after mentioned, in case such person scruples the taking of an oath, and upon refusal thereof, such justice of the peace is hereby required to commit such person to prison without bail or mainprize, and to certify the name of such person to the next General or Quarter Sessions of the peace to be held for that county, town, part or division where such person then resides, and if such person so committed shall upon a second tender at the General or Quarter Sessions refuse to make and subscribe the declaration aforesaid,

such person refusing shall be then and there recorded, and he shall be taken thenceforth to all intents and purposes for a Popish Recusant convict, and suffer accordingly, and incur all the penalties and forfeitures of all the aforesaid laws.

10. And whereas there are certain other persons, dissenters from the Church of England, who scruple the taking of any oath, be it enacted by the authority aforesaid that every such person shall make and subscribe the aforesaid declaration and also this declaration of fidelity following, viz.:

I, A. B., do sincerely promise and solemnly declare before God and the world that I will be true and faithful to King William and Queen Mary, and I do solemnly profess and declare that I do from my heart abhor, detest and renounce as impious and heretical, that damnable doctrine and position, that princes excommunicated or deprived by the Pope or any authority of the See of Rome, may be deposed or murdered by their subjects or any other whatsoever, and I do declare that no foreign (prince, person), prelate, state or potentate hath or ought to have any power, jurisdiction, superiority, pre-eminence or authority ecclesiastical or spiritual within this realm.

(And shall subscribe a profession of their Christian belief in these words:

I, A. B., profess faith in God the Father and in Jesus Christ his eternal Son, the true God, and in the Holy Spirit, one God blessed for evermore, and do acknowledge the Holy Scriptures of the Old and New Testament to be given by divine inspiration.

Which declarations and subscription shall be made and entered of record at the general Quarter Sessions of the peace of the county, city or place where every such person shall then reside),[1] and every such person that shall make and subscribe the two declarations and profession aforesaid being thereunto required, shall be exempted from all the pains and penalties of all and every the aforementioned statutes made against Popish Recusants or Protestant Non-conformists, and also from the penalties of an Act made in the fifth year of the reign of the late Queen Elizabeth (1563), intitled *An Act for the Assurance of the Queen's Royal Power over all Estates and Subjects within her Dominions*, for or by reason of such persons not taking, or refusing to take the oath mentioned in the said Act, and also from the penalties of an Act made in the thirteenth and fourteenth years of the reign of King Charles the Second (1662), intitled *An Act for preventing Mischiefs that may arise by certain Persons called Quakers refusing to take the lawful Oaths*, and enjoy all other the benefits, privileges and advantages under the like limitations, provisos and conditions which any other dissenters shall or ought to enjoy by virtue of this Act.

11. Provided always, and be it enacted by the authority aforesaid, that in case any person shall refuse to take the said oaths when tendered to them, which every justice of the peace is hereby empowered to do, such person shall not be admitted to make and subscribe the two declarations aforesaid, though required thereunto either before any justice of the peace, or at the

General and Quarter Sessions, before or after any conviction of Popish Recusancy as aforesaid, unless such person can within thirty-one days after such tender of the declarations to him, produce two sufficient Protestant witnesses to testify upon oath that they believe him to be a Protestant Dissenter, or a certificate under the hands of four Protestants who are conformable to the Church of England, or have taken the oaths and subscribed the declaration above mentioned, and shall also produce a certificate under the hands and seals of six or more sufficient men of the congregation to which he belongs, owning him for one of them.

12. Provided also, and be it enacted by the authority aforesaid, that until such certificate under the hands of six of his congregation as aforesaid be produced, and two Protestant witnesses come to attest his being a Protestant Dissenter or a certificate under the hands of four Protestants as aforesaid be produced, the justice of the peace shall, and hereby is required to take a recognizance with two sureties in the penal sum of fifty pounds (to be levied of his goods and chattels, lands and tenements, to the use of the King and Queen's Majesties, their heirs and successors) for his producing the same, and if he cannot give such security, to commit him to prison, there to remain until he has produced such certificates, or two witnesses as aforesaid.

13. Provided always, and it is the true intent and meaning of this Act, that all the laws made and provided for the frequenting of divine service on the Lord's Day, commonly called Sunday, shall be still in force and executed against all persons that offend against the said laws, except such persons come to some congregation or assembly of religious worship allowed or permitted by this Act.

14. Provided always and be it further enacted by the authority aforesaid, that neither this Act nor any clause, article or thing herein contained, shall extend or be construed to extend to give any ease, benefit or advantage to any Papist or Popish Recusant whatsoever, or any person that shall deny in his preaching or writing the doctrine of the Blessed Trinity, as it is declared in the aforesaid Articles of Religion.

15. Provided always, and be it enacted by the authority aforesaid, that if any person or persons at any time or times after the tenth day of June (10 June 1689) do, and shall willingly and of purpose maliciously or contemptuously come into any cathedral or parish church, chapel or other congregation permitted by this Act, and disquiet or disturb the same, or misuse any preacher or teacher; such person or persons upon proof thereof before any justice of peace, by two or more sufficient witnesses, shall find two sureties to be bound by recognizance in the penal sum of fifty pounds, and in default of such sureties shall be committed to prison, there to remain till the next General or Quarter Sessions, and upon conviction of the said offence at the said General or Quarter Sessions shall suffer the pain and penalty of twenty pounds (to the use of the King and Queen's Majesties, their heirs and successors).

16. Provided always that no congregation or assembly for religious worship shall be permitted or allowed by this Act, until the place of such meeting shall be certified to the Bishop of the Diocese or to the archdeacon of the archdeaconry (or to the justices of the peace at the General or Quarter Sessions of the peace for the county, city or place) in which such meeting shall be held, and registered in the said bishop's or archdeacon's court respectively, or recorded at the said General or Quarter Sessions. The Register or Clerk of the peace whereof respectively is hereby required to register the same, and to give certificate thereof to such person as shall demand the same, for which there shall be none greater fee nor reward taken than the sum of sixpence.

[1] In the original Act, this section was annexed in a separate schedule.

53. THE SECOND LONDON (BAPTIST) CONFESSION OF FAITH, 1689

History

Almost from the beginning of the Reformation there were some who rejected what they saw as the half-measures being taken by the leading proponents of Reform. These radicals, as we now think of them, wanted root-and-branch change; in effect, a new start on the basis of the New Testament. Symbolic of this was their insistence on rebaptism, because to their minds only an adult, consciously professing faith, could really be said to belong to Christ and to inherit the promise of new birth which baptism implied.

These so-called Anabaptists were strongly opposed by all the mainline Reformers because their Augustinian stance led them to insist that baptism was the cleansing of original sin, and children inherited this from their parents. To deny infant baptism was therefore to deny infant sinfulness, and to fall into the Pelagian heresy. Whether most Anabaptists were truly guilty of this heresy is hard to determine, but they were certainly opposed to the standard Augustinian (and later Calvinist) teaching on grace, placing much more emphasis on personal decision for Christ.

By the end of the sixteenth century, Anabaptists had coalesced into a number of small groups, of which the most prominent were those associated with the Dutchman, Menno Simons (1496-1561). In England they were never a real presence, but early in the seventeenth century there were a few extreme separatists who began to preach rebaptism. They could not meet freely in England, and so the first active "Baptist" congregations were formed in Holland. These groups were influenced by the Mennonites, but were accepted by the latter only after lengthy investigation and discussion, and Mennonite-Baptist links were never close.

In 1609 an English Baptist pastor, John Smyth, wrote a short confession of faith to explain Baptist views. It was generally supportive of the Arminian position in the controversies then raging within the Dutch Reformed Church, and it caused division even among the Baptists themselves. Two years later another pastor, Thomas Helwys, published an anti-Arminian confession, which was smuggled back to England.

It is therefore possible to say that from the beginning, English Baptists were divided between Arminian and Calvinist tendencies, and this is reflected in the numerous Baptist confessions which appeared during the seventeenth century. The most significant and influential of these was the First London Confession (1644), which was strongly Calvinistic in tone, even though it probably represented only a minority of Baptists.

One difficulty was that "Baptists" at this time were not really a denomination in the modern sense. Rather they were a loose association of people who shared the same views about baptism, but might not have much else in common. As far as the theological articulation of their position was concerned, the Calvinists soon gained the upper hand. In 1677 they produced what was to become the nucleus of the Second London Confession, and when the Act of Toleration became law (24 May 1689) these Baptists met to produce a public statement of their beliefs.

In the event they did little more than modify the Savoy Declaration of 1658, to take peculiarly Baptist views into account. However, the resulting Confession of Faith became very influential, and formed the principal basis of Baptist belief (though without attracting the assent of all Baptists) until the nineteenth century. The Confession was particularly influential in the American Colonies, where Baptists had long been a force to contend with. In 1742 it was adopted by their assembly at Philadelphia, which added two articles of its own. Because of this, the Confession is sometimes (erroneously) referred to as the Philadelphia Confession of 1688/1689.

A complete history of Baptist Confessions lies outside the scope of this volume, but may be found, together with the relevant texts, in William L. Lumpkin, *Baptist Confessions of Faith*, Judson Press, Valley Forge, 1959 (Revised Edition, 1969).

Theology

The theology of the Confession is basically the same as that of the Westminster Confession of 1647, though with Baptist distinctives added. The most important of these concern the mode and subjects of baptism, as well as the separation of Church and state, which was a Baptist principle from the beginning.

N.B. For this edition, it was not thought necessary to repeat the many Articles of the Confession which are identical to those of the Westminster Confession and/or the Savoy Declaration. Only those Articles which represent a distinctively Baptist position are reprinted here. For the precise relationship of this Confession to its reformed relatives, see Appendix 08.

Chapter 20 is taken from the Savoy Declaration, and has no equivalent in the Westminster Confession. The numbering of the chapters thus follows the Savoy Declaration, and not the Westminster Confession, from this point onwards.

Chapter 21 Article 04 of Chapter 20 of the Westminster Confession is omitted.

Chapter 24 Article 03 and 04 of Chapter 23 of the Westminster Confession are omitted. In their place, the following is inserted:

Civil Magistrates being set up by God for the ends aforesaid, subjection in all lawful things commanded by them ought to be yielded by us in the Lord, not only for wrath, but for conscience' sake; and we ought to make supplications and prayers for kings and all that are in authority, that under them we may live a quiet and peaceable life, in all godliness and honesty.

Chapter 26: This chapter, corresponding to Chapter 25 of the Westminster Confession, was completely rewritten as follows. Articles which are taken from the Savoy Declaration are italicized.

01. The Catholic or universal Church which (with respect to the internal work of the Spirit of truth and grace) may be called invisible, consists of the whole number of the elect, that have been, are, or shall be gathered into one, under Christ, the head thereof: and is the spouse, the body, the fullness of him that filleth all in all.

02. *All persons throughout the world, professing the faith of the Gospel and obedience unto God by Christ according unto it, not destroying their own profession by any errors, everting the foundation, or unholiness of conversation, are and may be called visible saints; and of such ought all particular congregations to be constituted.*

03. *The purest churches under heaven are subject to mixture and error; and some have so degenerated as to become no churches of Christ, but synagogues of Satan; nevertheless, Christ always hath had and ever shall have a kingdom in this world to the end thereof, of such as believe in him, and make profession of his name.*

04. The Lord Jesus Christ is the Head of the Church, in whom, by the appointment of the Father, all power for the calling, institution, order, or government of the Church is invested in a supreme and sovereign manner; neither can the Pope of Rome, in any sense, be head thereof, but is no other than Antichrist, that man of sin and son of perdition, that exalteth himself in the Church against Christ, and all that is called God: whom the Lord shall destroy with the brightness of his coming.

05. In the execution of this power wherewith he is so intrusted, the Lord Jesus calleth out of the world unto himself, through the ministry of his Word, by his Spirit, those that are given unto him by his Father, that they may walk before him in all the ways of obedience which he prescribeth to them in his Word. Those thus called he commandeth to walk together in particular societies or churches, for their mutual edification, and the due performance of that public worship which he requireth of them in the world.

06. The members of these churches are saints by calling, visibly manifesting and evidencing (in and by their profession and walking) their obedience unto that call of Christ; and do willingly consent to walk together according to the appointment of Christ, giving up themselves to the Lord and one to another, by the will of God, in the professed subjection to the ordinances of the Gospel.

07. To each of these churches thus gathered, according to his mind declared in his Word, he hath given all that power and authority which is in any way needful for their carrying on that order in worship and discipline which he hath instituted for them to observe, with commands and rules for the due and right exerting and executing of that power.

08. A particular church gathered and completely organized, according to the mind of Christ, consists of officers and members; and the officers appointed by Christ to be chosen and set apart by the Church (so-called and gathered) for the peculiar administration of ordinances, and execution of power and duty, which he intrusts them with or calls them to, to be continued to the end of the world, are bishops or elders and deacons.

09. The way appointed by Christ for the calling of any person, fitted and gifted by the Holy Spirit, unto the office of bishop or elder in the church is that he be chosen thereunto by the common suffrage of the church itself, and solemnly set apart by fasting and prayer, with imposition of hands of the eldership of the church, if there be any before constituted therein; and of a deacon, that he be chosen by the like suffrage, and set apart by prayer, and the like imposition of hands.

10. The work of pastors being constantly to attend the service of Christ in his churches, in the ministry of the Word and prayer, with watching for their souls, as they that must give an account to him, it is incumbent on the churches to whom they minister, not only to give them all due respect, but also to communicate to them all their good things, according to their ability, so as they may have a comfortable supply, without being themselves entangled with secular affairs; and may also be capable of exercising hospitality towards others; and this is required by the law of nature, and by the express order of our Lord Jesus, who hath ordained that they that preach the Gospel should live of the Gospel.

11. Although it be incumbent on the bishops or pastors of the churches to be instant in preaching the Word by way of office, yet the work of preaching the Word is not so peculiarly confined to them but that others also, gifted and fitted by the Holy Spirit for it, and approved and called by the Church, may and ought to perform it.

12. As all believers are bound to join themselves to particular churches, when and where they have opportunity so to do, so that all that are admitted unto the privileges of a church are also under the censures and government thereof, according to the rule of Christ.

13. No church members, upon any offence taken by them, having performed their duty required of them towards the person they are offended at, ought to disturb any church order, or absent themselves from the assemblies of the church or administration of any ordinances upon the account of such offence at any of their fellow-members, but to wait upon Christ in the further proceeding of the church.

14. As each church, and all the members of it, are bound to pray continually for the good and prosperity of all the churches of Christ, in all places, and upon all occasions to further it (every one within the bounds of their places and callings, in the exercise of their gifts and graces), so the churches (when planted by the providence of God so as they may enjoy opportunity and advantage of it) ought to hold communion among themselves for their peace, increase of love, and mutual edification.

15. In cases of difficulties or differences, either in point of doctrine or administration, wherein either the churches in general are concerned or any one church, in their peace, union and edification; or any member or members of any church are injured, in or by any proceedings in censures not agreeable to truth and order: it is according to the mind of Christ that many churches, holding communion together, do by their messengers meet to consider and give their advice in or about that matter in difference, to be reported to all the churches concerned; howbeit these messengers assembled are not intrusted with any church power properly so called, or with any jurisdiction over the churches themselves, to exercise any censures either over any churches or persons, to impose their determination on the churches or officers.

Chapter 28 This replaces Chapter 27 of the Westminster Confession with the following:

01. Baptism and the Lord's Supper are ordinances of positive and sovereign institution, appointed by the Lord Jesus, the only Lawgiver, to be continued in his Church to the end of the world.

02. These holy appointments are to be administered by those only who are qualified, and thereunto called, according to the commission of Christ.

Chapter 29 This replaces Chapter 28 of the Westminster Confession. Articles 02-04 are rearranged, as indicated below:

01. Baptism is an ordinance of the New Testament ordained by Jesus Christ to be unto the party baptized a sign of his fellowship with him in his death and resurrection; of his being engrafted into him; of remission of sins; and of his giving up unto God, through Jesus Christ, to live and walk in newness of life.

02. (WC 04) Those who do actually profess repentance towards God, faith in and obedience to our Lord Jesus, are the only proper subjects of this ordinance.

03. (WC 02) The outward element to be used in this ordinance is water, wherein the party is to be baptized in the name of the Father, and of the Son and of the Holy Spirit.

04. (WC 03) Immersion, or dipping of the person in water, is necessary to the due administration of this ordinance.

Chapters 30 and 31 of the Westminster Confession are entirely omitted.

In 1742 the Philadelphia Assembly of Baptists adopted the 1689 Confession, adding two further Articles. These were the following (numbers are those of the Philadelphia Confession):

23. Of Singing of Psalms

01. We believe that singing the praises of God is a holy ordinance of Christ, and not a part of natural religion or a moral duty only; but that it is brought under divine institution, it being enjoined on the churches of Christ to sing psalms, hymns and spiritual songs; and that the whole Church, in their public assemblies (as well as private Christians), ought to sing God's praises according to the best light they have received. Moreover, it was practised in the great representative Church by our Lord Jesus Christ with his disciples after he had instituted and celebrated the sacred ordinance of his holy supper as a commemorative token of his redeeming love.

31. Of Laying on of Hands

01. We believe that laying on of hands, with prayer, upon baptized believers, as such, is an ordinance of Christ, and ought to be submitted unto by all such persons that are admitted to partake of the Lord's Supper, and that the end of this ordinance is not for the extraordinary gifts of the Spirit, but for a farther reception of the Holy Spirit of promise, or for the addition of the graces of the Spirit, and the influences thereof to confirm, strengthen and comfort them in Christ Jesus; it being ratified and established by the extraordinary gifts of the Spirit in the primitive times, to abide in the Church, as meeting together on the first day of the week was (Ac 2:1), that being the day of worship, or Christian Sabbath, under the Gospel, and as preaching the Word was (Ac 10:44) and as baptism was (Mt 3:16) and prayer was (Ac 4:31) and singing psalms etc. was (Ac 16:25-26), so this laying on of hands was (Ac 8 and 19); for as the whole Gospel was confirmed by signs and wonders, and divers miracles and gifts of the Holy Ghost in general, so was every ordinance in like manner confirmed in particular.

54. THE ACT OF SETTLEMENT, 1700 (12-13 William III, c. 2)

History

The rôle of the Crown in Church and state was always central to the success or failure of the Reformation. Quite possibly, Protestantism would never have taken root had Henry VIII not felt compelled, for dynastic reasons, to seek a divorce from Katherine of Aragon. Henry clearly expected the country to follow his lead in religious matters, and the same policy was continued by his successors. When Mary I wished to return to Catholicism she took the country with her, and had little difficulty getting legislation to that effect through Parliament. Similarly, Elizabeth I was able to impose a Protestant settlement on the nation without serious opposition. Even as late as 1603, the Puritans hoped that the arrival of James VI of Scotland, with his Calvinist upbringing, would favour their cause.

The notion that the people would follow their monarch in religious matters was put to its greatest test under Charles I, when it became apparent that the King's wishes, and his policies, differed from that of an influential body of his subjects. Rather than compromise with Parliament, the King dissolved it and ruled alone, with the result that when pressure for change became too strong to resist, civil war erupted and both King and Church were swept away. The Restoration theoretically brought back the *status quo ante*, but it was clear that there could be no going back on matters of substance. Charles II was not able to deliver the toleration which he had promised to his dissenting subjects, nor could he openly proclaim his own sympathy with, and eventual conversion to, Roman Catholicism. However, his brother and heir became a Catholic in 1673, and there was no means to prevent his succession to the throne in 1685. Great Britain thus found itself with a Catholic monarch who was supreme governor of the Church of England. Such an anomaly proved to be intolerable, and when James unexpectedly produced a male heir, he was chased into exile.

Parliament then extended an invitation to James's elder daughter, Mary II and her husband, William III of Orange, to come to Britain to claim the crown. In the Bill of Rights passed in 1689, it was decreed that no Roman Catholic could thenceforth inherit the throne, thus barring James II and his son, also called James, from reclaiming their inheritance. All was well until 1700, when the young Duke of Gloucester, heir and only surviving son of princess Anne, the second daughter of James II, died. This left no heir to the throne once Anne herself was dead, and it became necessary to establish a Protestant succession which would be universally accepted. The nearest Protestant heir to the throne was Princess Sophia of Hanover, granddaughter of James VI and I, and she was duly designated as the successor to Anne. As it turned out, Sophia died shortly before Anne did, in 1714, and the throne passed to her son, who became King George I. This succession was contested, not least by James, the Old Pretender (and later by his son, Charles, the Young Pretender), but on the whole it was accepted by the country. This event marked the final end of the English Reformation, and the establishment of a political settlement which, at least with respect to the Crown, has lasted until the present time.

Theology

The notion that the sovereign should accept the religion professed by the people, and not the other way round, was the great innovation of this Act. In effect, it made a reversal of the Reformation impossible, and paved the way for the development of the monarchy into the representative symbol of the Church. That this is not a fiction was demonstrated as recently as 1936, when King Edward VIII was forced to abdicate because his proposed marriage violated Church law – a far cry indeed from the situation under Henry VIII! More recently, a case could even be made for saying that the preservation of the monarchy today rests, at least to some degree, on its ability to incarnate the moral and spiritual values of the nation, which (in theory at least) are supposed to be articulated in and through the national Church. Neither Charles II nor James II could ever have subscribed to such a view – a clear indication, if any were needed, of how far the relationship between Crown and nation has changed since their time.

N.B. Most of the Act is still in force, but sections which have been repealed are indicated in bold type. Dates of repeal are given in footnotes.

An Act for the further Limitation of the Crown and better securing the Rights and Liberties of the Subject.

01. Whereas in the first year of the reign of your Majesty, and of our late most gracious sovereign lady Queen Mary (of blessed memory), an Act of Parliament was made, entitled: *An Act for declaring the rights and liberties of the subject, and for settling the succession of the Crown* (1689), wherein it was, amongst other things, enacted, established and declared that the Crown and regal government of the kingdoms of England, France and Ireland, and the dominions thereunto belonging, should be and continue to your Majesty and the said late Queen, during the joint lives of your Majesty and the said Queen, and to the survivor; and that after the decease of your Majesty and of the said Queen, the said Crown and regal government should be and remain to the heirs of the body of the said late Queen; and for default of such issue, to her royal highness the Princess Anne of Denmark, and the heirs of her body; and for default of such issue, to the heirs of the body of your Majesty. And it was thereby further enacted that all and every person and persons that then were, or afterwards should be reconciled to, or shall hold communion with the See or Church of Rome, or should profess the popish religion, or marry a papist, should be excluded, and are by that Act made for ever incapable to inherit, possess or enjoy the Crown and government of this realm, and Ireland, and the dominions thereunto belonging, or any part of the same, or to have, use or exercise any real power, authority or jurisdiction within the same; and in all and every such case and cases the people of these realms shall be and are thereby absolved of their allegiance; and that the said Crown and government shall from time to time descend to, and be enjoyed by, such person or persons, being Protestants, as should have inherited and enjoyed the same, in case the said person or persons, so reconciled, holding communion, professing or marrying, as aforesaid, were naturally dead:

After the making of which statute, and the settlement therein contained, your Majesty's good subjects, who were restored to the full and free possession and enjoyment of their religion, rights and liberties, by the providence of God giving success to your Majesty's just undertakings and unwearied endeavours for that purpose, had no greater temporal felicity to hope or wish for, than to see a royal progeny descending from your Majesty, to whom (under God) they owe their tranquillity, and whose ancestors have for many years been the principal assertors of the reformed religion and the liberties of Europe, and from our said most gracious sovereign lady, whose memory will always be precious to the subjects of these realms; and it having since pleased Almighty God to take away our said sovereign lady, and also the most hopeful Prince William, Duke of Gloucester (the only surviving issue of her royal highness the Princess Anne of Denmark), to the unspeakable grief and sorrow of your Majesty and your said good subjects, who under such losses being sensibly put in mind, that it standeth wholly in the pleasure of Almighty God to prolong the lives of your Majesty and of her royal highness, and to grant to your Majesty, or to her royal highness, such issue as may be heritable to the Crown and regal government aforesaid, by the respective limitations in the said recited Act contained, do constantly implore the divine mercy for those blessings; and your Majesty's said subjects having daily experience of your royal care and concern for the present and future welfare of these kingdoms, and particularly recommending from your throne a further provision to be made for the succession of the Crown in the Protestant line, for the happiness of the nation, and the security of our religion; and it being absolutely necessary for the safety, peace and quiet of this realm, to obviate all doubts and contentions in the same, by reason of any pretended titles to the Crown, and to maintain a certainty in the succession thereof, to which your subjects may safely have recourse for their protection, in case the limitations in the said recited Act should determine:

Therefore for a further provision of the succession of the Crown in the

Protestant line, we your Majesty's most dutiful and loyal subjects, the Lords spiritual and temporal, and Commons, in this present Parliament assembled, do beseech your Majesty that it may be enacted and declared, and be it enacted and declared by the King's most excellent Majesty, by and with the advice and consent of the Lords spiritual and temporal, and Commons, in this present Parliament assembled, and by the authority of the same, that the most excellent Princess Sophia, electress and duchess dowager of Hanover, daughter of the most excellent Princess Elizabeth, late Queen of Bohemia, daughter of our late sovereign lord King James I, of happy memory, be and is hereby declared to be the next in succession, in the Protestant line, to the imperial Crown and dignity of the said realms of England, France and Ireland, with the dominions and territories thereto belonging, after his Majesty and the Princess Anne of Denmark, and in default of issue of the said Princess Anne and of his Majesty respectively; and that from and after the deceases of his said Majesty, our now sovereign lord, and of her royal highness the Princess Anne of Denmark, and for default of issue of the said Princess Anne and of his Majesty respectively, the crown and regal government of the said kingdoms of England, France and Ireland, and of the dominions thereunto belonging, with the royal state and dignity of the said realms, and all honours, styles, titles, regalities, prerogatives, powers, jurisdictions and authorities to the same belonging and appertaining, shall be, remain and continue to the said most excellent Princess Sophia and the heirs of her body, being Protestants; and thereto the said Lords spiritual and temporal, and Commons, shall and will, in the name of all the people of this realm, most humbly and faithfully submit themselves, their heirs and posterities; and do faithfully promise that after the deceases of his Majesty and her royal highness, and the failure of the heirs of their respective bodies, to stand to, maintain and defend the said Princess Sophia, and the heirs of her body, being Protestants, according to the limitation and succession of the crown in this Act specified and contained, to the utmost of their powers, with their lives and estates, against all persons whatsoever that shall attempt anything to the contrary.

02. Provided always and it is hereby enacted that all and every person and persons, who shall or may take or inherit the said Crown, by virtue of the limitation of this present Act, and is, are, or shall be reconciled to, or shall hold communion with, the See or Church of Rome, or shall profess the popish religion, or shall marry a papist, shall be subject to such incapacities and in such case or cases are by the said recited Act provided, enacted and established; and that every King or Queen of this realm, who shall come to and succeed in the imperial Crown of this kingdom, by virtue of this Act, shall have the coronation oath administered to him, her or them, at their respective coronations, according to the Act of Parliament made in the first year of the reign of his Majesty and the said late Queen Mary, entitled: *An Act for establishing the coronation oath* (1689), and shall make, subscribe and repeat the declaration in the Act first above recited mentioned or referred to, **in the manner and form thereby prescribed.**[1]

03. And whereas it is requisite and necessary that some further provision be made for securing our religion, laws and liberties, from and after the death of his Majesty and Princess Anne of Denmark, and in default of such issue of the body of the said princess and of his Majesty respectively; be it enacted by the King's most excellent Majesty, by and with the advice and consent of the Lords spiritual and temporal, and Commons, in Parliament assembled, and by the authority of the same:

That whosoever shall hereafter come to the possession of this Crown shall join in communion with the Church of England, as by law established.

That in case the Crown and imperial dignity of this realm shall hereafter come to any person, not being a native of this kingdom of England, this nation be not obliged to engage in any war for the defence of any dominions or territories which do not belong to the Crown of England, without the consent of Parliament.

That no person who shall hereafter come to the possession of this Crown shall go out of the dominions of England, Scotland or Ireland, without consent of Parliament.

That from and after the time that the further limitation by this Act shall take effect, all matters and things relating to the well governing of this kingdom, which are properly cognizable in the Privy Council by the laws and customs of this realm, shall be transacted there, and all resolutions taken thereupon shall be signed by such of the Privy Council as shall advise and consent to the same.[2]

That after the said limitation shall take effect as aforesaid, no person born out of the kingdoms of England, Scotland or Ireland, or the dominions thereunto belonging (although he be **naturalized or**[3] made a denizen, except such as are born of English parents), shall be capable to be of the Privy Council, or a Member of either House of Parliament, or to enjoy any office or place of trust, either civil or military, or to have any grant of lands, tenements, or hereditaments from the Crown, to himself or to any other or others in trust for him.

That no person who has an office or place of profit under the King, or receives a pension from the Crown, shall be capable of serving as a member of the House of Commons.

That after the said limitation shall take effect as aforesaid, judges commissions be made *quamdiu se bene gesserint***, and their salaries ascertained and established; but upon the address of both Houses of Parliament it may be lawful to remove them.**[4]

04. That no pardon under the great seal of England be pleadable to an impeachment by the Commons in Parliament.

And whereas the laws of England are the birthright of the people thereof, and all the kings and queens, who shall ascend the throne of this realm, ought to administer the government of the same according to the said laws, and all their officers and ministers ought to serve them respectively according to the same; the said Lords spiritual and temporal, and Commons, do therefore further humbly pray, that all the laws and statutes of this realm for securing the established religion and the rights and liberties of the people thereof, and all other laws and statutes of the same now in force, may be ratified and confirmed, and the same are by his Majesty, by and with the advice and consent of the said Lords spiritual and temporal, and Commons, and by authority of the same, ratified and confirmed accordingly.

[1] The form of the oath was altered in 1910.

[2] Repealed in 1705, and again in 1714.

[3] Repealed in 1914.

[4] Repealed in 1705.

Supplementary Texts

01. THE FIRST AND SECOND STATUTES OF PROVISORS, 1351 AND 1390 (25 Edward III, s. 5 and 13 Richard II, s. 2)

History

During the Middle Ages it had become the practice of certain Popes to grant English ecclesiastical appointments to foreigners, who remained at Rome or Avignon, receiving the revenues of the appointment without exercising the corresponding responsibilities. The injustice of this was long recognized, but nothing was done to stop it until 1351, when Edward III caused a statute forbidding the practice to be enacted by Parliament. This statute was renewed and extended by Richard II in 1390. It became one of the principal legal weapons invoked by Henry VIII in his campaign against the Papacy, and it is for that reason that the second statute (which embraces the first) is printed here. The first statute is highlighted in bold type.

Item, whereas the noble King Edward, grandfather of our lord the King that now is, at his Parliament holden at Westminster on the Octave of the Purification of our Lady, the five and twentieth year of his reign (09 February 1351), caused to be rehearsed the statute made at Carlisle in the time of King Edward (I), son of King Henry (III), touching the estate of the Holy Church of England; the said grandfather of the king that now is, by the assent of the great men of his realm, being in the same Parliament, holden the said five and twentieth year (1351), to the honour of God and of Holy Church, and of all his realm, did ordain and establish, that the free elections to archbishoprics, bishoprics and all other dignities and benefices elective in England, should hold from thenceforth in the manner as they were granted by his progenitors, and by the ancestors of other lords, founders; and that all prelates and other people of Holy Church, which had advowsons of any benefices of the gift of the King, or of his progenitors, or of other lords and donors, should freely have their collations and presentments; and thereupon a certain punishment was ordained in the same statute for those who accept any benefice or dignity contrary to the said statute made at Westminster the said twenty-fifth year, as is aforesaid; which statute our lord the King has caused to be recited in this present Parliament at the request of his Commons in the same Parliament, the tenor whereof is such as hereafter follows:
Whereas of late in the Parliament of Edward of good memory, King of England, grandfather of our lord the King that now is, in the twenty-fifth year of his reign, holden at Carlisle, the petition heard, put before

the said grandfather and his council in the said Parliament by the commonalty of the said realm, containing: That whereas the Holy Church of England was founded in the estate of prelacy, within the realm of England, by the said grandfather and his progenitors, and the earls, barons and other nobles of his said realm, and their ancestors, to inform them and the people of the law of God, and to make hospitalities, alms and other works of charity in the places where the churches were founded, for the souls of the founders, their heirs and all Christians; and certain possessions, as well in fees, lands, rents and in advowsons, which extend to a great value, were assigned by the said founders to the prelates and other people of the Holy Church of the said realm, to sustain the same charge, and especially of the possessions which were assigned to archbishops, bishops, abbots, priors, religious and all other people of Holy Church, by the kings of the said realm, earls, barons, and other great men of his realm; the same kings, earls, barons and other nobles, as lords and advowees, have had and ought to have the custody of such voidances, and the presentments and the collations of the benefices being of such prelacies.

And the said kings in times past were wont to have the greatest part of their council for the safeguard of the realm, when they had need of such prelates and clerks so advanced; the Pope of Rome, accroaching to him the seignories of such possessions and benefices, does give and grant the same benefices to aliens who never dwelt in England, and to cardinals who could not dwell here, and to others, as well aliens as denizens, as if he had been patron or advowee of the said dignities and benefices, as he was not of right by the law of England; whereby if these should be suffered, there would scarcely be any benefice within a short time in the said realm, but that it should be in the hands of aliens and denizens by virtue of such provisions, against the good will and disposition of the founders of the same benefices; and so the elections of archbishops, bishops and other religious should fail, and the alms, hospitalities and other works of charity, which should be done in the said places, should be withdrawn, the said grandfather and other lay patrons, in the time of such voidances, should lose their presentments, the said council should perish and goods without number should be carried out of the realm, to the annulling of the estate of the Holy Church of England, and disherison of the said grandfather, and the earls, barons and other nobles of the said realm, and in offence and destruction of the laws and rights of his realm, and to the great damage of his people, and in subversion of all the estate of all his said realm, and against the good disposition and will of the first founders, by the assent of the earls, barons and other nobles, and of all the said commonalty, at their instant request, the damage and grievances aforesaid being considered in the said full Parliament, it was provided, ordained and established, that the said oppressions, grievances and damages in the same realm from henceforth should not be suffered in any manner.

And now it is shown to our lord the King in this present Parliament holden at Westminster, on the Octave of the Purification of our Lady, the five and twentieth year of his reign in England and the twelfth of France (09 February 1351), by the grievous complaint of all the Commons of his realm, that the grievances and mischiefs aforesaid do daily abound, to the greater damage and destruction of all the realm of England, more than ever were before, viz. that now anew our holy father the Pope, by procurement of clerks and otherwise, has reserved, and doth daily reserve to his collation generally and especially, as well archbishoprics, bishoprics, abbeys and priories, as all other dignities and other benefices of England, which are of the advowsons of people of Holy Church, and gives the same as well to aliens as to denizens, and takes of all such benefices the first-fruits, and many other profits, and a great part of the treasure of the said realm is carried away and dispended out of the realm, by the purchasers of such graces aforesaid; and also by such privy reservations, many clerks, advanced in this realm by their true patrons, which have peaceably holden their advancements by long time, are suddenly put out; whereupon the said Commons have prayed our said lord the King, that since the right of the Crown of England, and the law of the said realm is such, that upon the mischiefs and damages which happen to his realm, he ought, and is bound by his oath, with the accord of his people in his Parliament thereof, to make remedy and law, for the removing of the mischiefs and damages which thereof ensue, that it may please him to ordain remedy therefor.

Our lord the King, seeing the mischiefs and damages before mentioned, and having regard to the said statute made in the time of his said grandfather, and to the causes contained in the same; which statute holds always its force, and was never defeated, repealed, nor annulled in any point, and insomuch as he is bound by his oath to cause the same to be kept as the law of his realm, though that by suffrance and negligence it has been since attempted to the contrary; also having regard to the grievous complaints made to him by his people in divers his Parliaments holden heretofore, willing to ordain remedy for the great damages and mischiefs which have happened, and daily do happen to the Church of England by the said cause; by the assent of all the great men and the commonalty of the said realm, to the honour of God and profit of the said Church of England, and of all his realm, has ordered and established; that the free election of archbishops, bishops and all other dignities and benefices elective in England shall hold from henceforth in the manner as they were granted by the King's progenitors, and the ancestors of other lords, founders.

And that all prelates and other people of Holy Church, which have advowsons of any benefices of the King's gift, or of any of his progenitors, or of other lords and donors, to do divine service, and other charges thereof ordained, shall have their collations and presentments freely to do the same, in the manner as they were enfeoffed by their donors. And in case that reservation, collation, or provision be made by the court of Rome, to any archbishopric, bishopric, dignity or other benefice, in disturbance of the free elections, collations or presentations aforenamed, that, at the same time of the voidance, as such reservations, collations, and provisions ought to take effect, our lord the King and his heirs shall have and enjoy, for the same time, the collations to the archbishoprics, bishoprics and other dignities elective, which be of his advowson, such as his progenitors had before that free election was granted; seeing that the election was first granted by the King's progenitors upon a certain form and condition, as to demand licence of the King to choose, and after the election to have his royal assent, and not in other manner. Which conditions not being kept, the thing ought by reason to resort to its first nature.

And if any such reservation, provision, or collation be made of any house of religion of the King's advowson, in disturbance of free election, our sovereign lord the King, and his heirs, shall have, for that time, the collation to give this dignity to a convenient person. And in case that collation, reservation or provision be made by the court of Rome to any church, prebend, or other benefice, which is of the advowson of people of Holy Church, whereof the King is advowee paramount immediate, that at the same time of the voidance, at which time the collation, reservation or provision ought to take effect as is aforesaid, the King and his heirs shall thereof have the presentation or collation for that time – and so from time to time, whensoever such people of Holy Church shall be disturbed of their presentments or collations by such reservations, collations or provisions, as is aforesaid. Saving to them the right of their advowsons and their presentments, when no collation or provision by the court of Rome is made thereof, or where that the said people of Holy Church shall or will, to the same benefices, present or make collation; and that their presentees may enjoy the effect of their collations or presentments. And in the same manner every other lord, of what condition he be, shall have the collations or presentments to the houses of religion which are of his advowson, and other benefices of Holy Church which pertain to the same houses. And if such advowees do not present to such benefices within the half-year after such voidances, nor the bishop of the place give the same by lapse of time within a month after half a year, that then the King shall have thereof the presentments and collations, as he has of others of his own advowson demesne.

And in case that the presentees of the King – or the presentees of other patrons of Holy Church, or of their advowees, or they to whom the King, or such patrons or advowees aforesaid, have given benefices pertaining to their presentments or collations to them made, or that they which are in possession of such benefices be impeached upon their said possessions by such provisors, then the said provisors, their procurators, executors and notaries, shall be attached by their bodies and brought in to answer; and if they be convicted, they shall abide in prison without being let to mainprize or bail, or otherwise delivered, till they have made fine and ransom to the King at his will, and satisfaction to the party that shall feel himself grieved. And nevertheless before that they be delivered, they shall make full renunciation, and find sufficient surety that they will not attempt such things in time to come, nor sue any process by themselves, nor by others, against any man in the said court of Rome, nor in any part elsewhere, for any such imprisonments or renunciations, nor any other thing depending of them. And in case that such provisors, procurators, executors or notaries be not found, that the exigent shall run against them by due process, and that writs shall go forth to take their bodies wherever they be found, as well at the King's suit, as at the suit of the party.

And that in the meantime the King shall have the profits of such benefices so occupied by such provisors, except abbeys, priories and other houses, which have colleges or convents, and in such houses the colleges or convents shall have the profits; saving always to our lord the King, and to all other lords, their old right.

And this statute shall hold good as well as to reservations, collations, and provisions made and granted in times past against all them which have not yet obtained corporal possession of the benefices granted to them by the same reservations, collations and provisions, as against all others in time to come. And this statute ought to hold place and to begin at the said Octave (09 February 1351).

Our lord the King that now is, with the assent of the great men of his realm, being in this present Parliament, has ordained and established that for all archbishoprics, bishoprics and other dignities and benefices elective, and all other benefices of Holy Church, which began to be void in deed the twenty-ninth day of January, the thirteenth year of the reign of our lord King Richard (II) that now is (29 January 1390), or after, or which shall be void in time to come within the realm of England, the said statute, made in the said twenty-fifth year, shall be firmly held for ever, and put in due execution from time to time in all manner of points. And if any do accept a benefice of Holy Church contrary to this statute, and that duly proved, and be beyond the sea, he shall abide exiled and banished out of the realm for ever, and his lands and tenements, goods and chattels shall be forfeited to the King; and if he be within the realm, he shall also be exiled and banished, as is aforesaid, and shall incur the same forfeiture, and take his way, so that he be out of the realm within six weeks next after such acceptation. And if any receive any such person banished coming from beyond the sea, or being within the realm after the said six weeks, having knowledge thereof, he shall be also exiled and banished, and incur such forfeiture as is aforesaid. And that their procurators, notaries, executors and summoners have the pain and forfeiture aforesaid.

Provided nevertheless that all they for whom the Pope or his predecessors have provided any archbishopric, bishopric or other dignity, or other benefices of Holy Church, of the patronage of people of Holy Church, in respect of any voidance before the said twenty-ninth day of January, and thereof were in actual possession before the same twenty-ninth day, shall have and enjoy the said archbishoprics, bishoprics, dignities and other benefices peaceably for their lives, notwithstanding the statutes and ordinances aforesaid. And if the King send by letter, or in other manner, to the court of Rome, at the entreaty of any person, or if any other send or sue to the same court, whereby anything is done contrary to this statute, touching any archbishopric, bishopric, dignity or other benefice of Holy Church within the said realm, if he that makes such motion or suit be a prelate of Holy Church, he shall pay to the King the value of his temporalities for one year; and if he be a temporal lord, he shall pay to the King the value of his lands and possessions not moveable for one year; and if he be another person of a more mean estate, he shall pay to the King the value of the benefice for which suit is made, and shall be imprisoned for one year.

And it is the intent of this statute, that of all dignities and benefices of Holy Church, which were void in deed the said twenty-ninth day of January (29 January 1390), which are given, or to which it is provided by the Apostolic See before the same twenty-ninth day, that they to whom such gifts or provisions be made may freely, of such gifts and provisions, sue execution without offence of this statute. Provided always, that of no dignity or benefice which was full the said twenty-ninth day of January shall any man, because of any collation, gift, reservation and provision, or other grace of the Apostolic See, not executed before the said twenty-ninth day, sue thereof execution, upon the pains and forfeitures contained in this present statute.

Also it is ordained and established that if any man bring or send within the realm, or the King's power, any summons, sentences or excommunications, against any person, of what condition soever he be, for the cause of making motion, assent, or execution of the said Statute of Provisors, he shall be taken, arrested and put in prison, and forfeit all his lands and tenements, goods and chattels for ever, and incur the pain of life and of member. And if any prelate make execution of such summons, sentences or excommunications, that his temporalties be taken and abide in the King's hands, till due redress and correction be thereof made. And if any person of less estate than a prelate, of what condition soever he be, make such execution, he shall be taken, arrested and put in prison, and have imprisonment, and make fine and ransom at the discretion of the council of our said lord the King.

The King's Writ directing proclamation of the Statute

The King to the sheriff of Kent, greeting. We command you, firmly enjoining that without delay you cause to be read and on our behalf publicly proclaimed and to be firmly kept and observed according to the form of the statutes and ordinances aforesaid, certain statutes and ordinances by us, with the assent of the nobles and commonalty of our realm of England, made in our last Parliament holden at Westminster, which we send you under our great seal in open form, within your county, in places where it may be most expedient. And this under instant peril you shall in no wise omit. Witness the King at Westminster the fifteenth day of May (15 May 1390).

(Similar writs were directed to all the sheriffs of England).

02. THE FIRST STATUTE OF *PRAEMUNIRE*, 1353
(27 Edward III, s. 1)

History

This statute was made necessary by the Statute of Provisors (1351), and made it treason to appeal to the Pope against the King. A second statute, to the same effect, was passed in 1393, following the second Statute of Provisors. Henry VIII resurrected both of them in his battle of wits against the Pope in 1529-1534.

Our lord the King, by the assent and prayer of the great men, and the Commons of his realm of England, at his great council holden at Westminster, on Monday next after the feast of St Matthew the Apostle, the twenty-seventh year of his reign of England, and of France the fourteenth (23 September 1353), in amendment of his said realm, and maintenance of the laws and usages, has ordained and established these things under written:

First, because it is shown to our lord the King, by the grievous and clamorous complaints of the great men and Commons aforesaid, how that divers of the people be, and have been drawn out of the realm to answer for things, whereof the cognizance pertains to the King's court; and also that the judgements given in the same court be impeached in another court, in prejudice and disherison of our lord the King, and of his Crown, and of all the people of his said realm, and to the undoing and destruction of the common law of the same realm at all times used.

Whereupon, good deliberation being had with the great men and others of his said council, it is assented and accorded by our lord the King, and the great men and Commons aforesaid, that all the people of the King's allegiance, of whatsoever condition they be, which shall draw any out of the realm in plea, whereof the cognizance pertains to the King's court, or of things whereof judgements be given in the King's court, or which do sue in any other court, to defeat or impeach the judgements given in the King's court, shall have a day, within the space of two months, by warning to be made to them in the place where the possessions be, which are in debate, or otherwise where they have lands or other possessions, by the sheriffs or other the King's ministers, to appear before the King and his council, or in his chancery, or before the King's justices in his places of the one bench or the other, or before other the King's justices which to the same shall be deputed, to answer in their proper persons to the King, of the contempt done in this behalf.

And if they come not at the said day in their proper persons to be at the law, they, their procurators, attorneys, executors, notaries and maintainers, shall from that day forth be put out of the King's protection, and their lands, goods and chattels forfeited to the King, and their bodies, wheresoever they may be found, shall be taken and imprisoned, and ransomed at the King's will; and upon the same a writ shall be made to take them, by their bodies, and to seize their lands, goods, and possessions, into the King's hands; and if it be returned that they be not found, they shall be put in exigent, and outlawed.

Provided always, that at what time they come before they be outlawed, and will yield themselves to the King's prison to be justified by the law, and to receive that which the court shall award in this behalf, that they shall be thereto received; the forfeiture of lands, goods and chattels abiding in force, if they do not yield themselves within the said two months, as is aforesaid.

03. THE SECOND STATUTE OF *PRAEMUNIRE*, 1393
(16 Richard II, c. 5)

History

As with the first Act of *Praemunire*, so the second forbade appeals from the King's courts to those of the Pope. Like its predecessor, it was resurrected by Henry VIII and used against the clergy in his struggle against Rome.

Item, whereas the Commons of the realm in this present Parliament have showed to our redoubtable lord the King, grievously complaining, that whereas the said our lord the King, and all his liege people, ought of right, and of old time were wont, to sue in the King's court to recover their presentments to churches, prebends, and other benefices of Holy Church, to the which they had the right to present, the cognizance of plea, of which presentment belongs only to the King's court of the old right of his Crown, used and approved in the time of all his progenitors Kings of England; and when judgement shall be given in the same court upon such a plea and presentment, the archbishops, bishops and other spiritual persons which have institution to such benefice within their jurisdiction, are bound, and have made execution of such judgements by the King's commandment by all the time aforesaid without interruption (for another layperson cannot make such execution), and also are bound of right to make execution of many other of the King's commandments, of which right the crown of England has been peaceably seized, as well in the time of our said lord the King that now is, as in the time of all his progenitors till this day:

But now of late divers processes are made by the holy father the Pope, and censures of excommunication upon certain bishops of England, because they have made execution of such commandments, to the open disherison of the said Crown and destruction of our said lord the King, his law, and all his realm, if remedy be not provided.

And also it is said, and a common clamour is made, that the said holy father the Pope has ordained and purposed to translate some prelates of the same realm, some out of the realm, and some from one bishopric to another within the same realm, without the King's assent and knowledge, and without the assent of the prelates, which so shall be translated, which prelates be much profitable and necessary to our said lord the King, and to all his realm; by which translations, if they should be suffered, the statutes of the realm would be defeated and made void; and his said liege sages of his council, without his assent, and against his will, carried away and gotten out of his realm, and the substance and treasure of the realm shall be carried away, and so the realm be destitute as well of council as of substance, to the final destruction of the same realm; and so the Crown of England, which has been so free at all times, that it has been in no earthly subjection, but immediately subject to God in all things touching the royalty of the same Crown, and to none other, should be submitted to the Pope, and the laws and statutes of the realm by him defeated and avoided at his will, to the perpetual destruction of the sovereignty of our lord the King, his Crown and his royalty, and of all his realm, which God defend.

And moreover, the Commons aforesaid say, that the said things so attempted are clearly against the King's Crown and his royalty, used and approved from the time of all his progenitors; wherefore they and all the liege Commons of the same realm will stand with our said lord the King, and his said Crown and his royalty, in the cases aforesaid, and in all other cases attempted against him, his Crown and his royalty in all points, to live and to die.

And moreover they pray the King, and require him by way of justice, that he would examine all the lords in the Parliament, as well spiritual as temporal, severally, and all the estates of the Parliament, how they think of the cases aforesaid, which be so openly against the King's Crown, and in derogation of his royalty, and how they will stand in the same cases with our lord the King, in upholding the rights of the said Crown and royalty.

Whereupon the Lords temporal so demanded, have answered every one by himself, that the cases aforesaid are clearly in derogation of the King's Crown, and of his royalty, as it is well known, and has been for a long time known, and that they will be with the same Crown and royalty in these cases specially, and in all other cases which shall be attempted against the same crown and royalty in all points with all their power.

And moreover it was demanded of the Lords spiritual there being, and the procurators of others being absent, there advice and will in all these cases; which lords, that is to say, the archbishops, bishops and other prelates – being in the said Parliament severally examined, making protestations that it is not their mind to deny nor affirm that our holy father the Pope may not excommunicate bishops, not that he may make translation of prelates after the law of Holy Church – answered and said that if any executions of processes made in the King's court, as before were made, by any, and censures of excommunications be made against any bishops of England, or any other of the King's liege people, for that they have made execution of such commandments; and that if any executions of such translations be made of any prelates of the same realm, which prelates be very profitable and necessary to our said lord the King, and to his said realm, or that the sage people of his council, without his assent, and against his will, be removed and carried out of the realm, so that the substance and treasure of the realm maybe consumed – that the same is against the King and his Crown, as it is contained in the petition before named.

And likewise the same procurators, every one by himself examined upon the said matters, have answered and said in the name of and for their lords, as the said bishops have said and answered, and that the said Lords spiritual will and ought to be with the King in these cases in lawfully maintaining his Crown, and in all other cases touching his Crown and his royalty, as they are bound by their allegiance;

Whereupon our said lord the King, by the assent aforesaid, and at the request of his said Commons, has ordained and established, that if any purchase or pursue, or cause to be purchased or pursued, in the court of Rome, or elsewhere, any such translations, processes and sentences of excommunication, bulls, instruments, or any other things whatsoever, which touch our lord the King, against him, his Crown and his royalty, or his realm, as is aforesaid, and they which bring the same within the realm, or receive them, or make thereof notification, or any other execution whatsoever within the same realm or without, that they, their notaries, procurators, maintainers, abettors, favourers and counsellors, shall be put out of the King's protection, and their lands and tenements, goods and chattels, forfeited to our lord the King; and that they be attached by their bodies, if they may be found, and brought before the King and his council, there to answer to the cases aforesaid, or that process be made against them by *Praemunire facias*, in manner as it is ordained in other statutes concerning provisors, and others who sue, in any other court, in derogation of the royalty of our lord the King.

04. THE AUGSBURG CONFESSION, 1530

History

The Augsburg Confession, which is also often known by its Latin name, *Confessio Augustana*, was the first confessional document drawn up by the Lutherans as an expression of their beliefs. It was presented to the Emperor Charles V, and designed to be a statement of points on which the Lutherans dissented from Rome. It has remained one of the defining documents of Lutheranism, but its importance for the English Reformation lies in the fact that it was the starting-point of negotiations between Luther and the Church of England once Henry VIII had declared himself Supreme Head (under Christ) of the Church. Its influence can easily be seen in the Wittenberg Articles (1536) and later in the Thirteen Articles (1538). Lutheranism was a less powerful force in English affairs after that, but signs of the *Augustana*'s impact persist in the Articles of Religion which Cranmer drew up in 1553.

N.B. It should be noted that the Latin version was the official text used by Cranmer and his associates, though it differs slightly from the German. The English translation provided here is unofficial. In the Second Part of the Confession, the articles are numbered twice; first according to the original text, and second (in parentheses) in sequence, following the First Part, e.g. 01 (23), etc.

01. De Deo

Ecclesiae magno consensu apud nos docent, decretum Nicaenae synodi verum, et sine ulla dubitatione credendum esse. Videlicet, quod sit una essentia divina, quae et appellatur et est Deus, aeternus, incorporeus, impartibilis, immensa potentia, sapientia, bonitate, creator et conservator omnium rerum visibilium et invisibilium, et tamen tres sint personae eiusdem essentiae et potentiae, et coaeternae, Pater, Filius et Spiritus Sanctus. Et nomine personae utuntur ea significatione qua usi sunt in hac causa scriptores

01. Of God

The churches, with common consent among us, do teach the decree of the Council of Nicaea to be true and without any doubt to be believed, viz. that there is one divine essence which is both called and is God, eternal, incorporeal, indivisible, of immense power, wisdom and goodness, creator and preserver of all things visible and invisible, and yet there are three persons of the same essence and power, coeternal, Father, Son and Holy Spirit; and they use the name Person in the same sense as it was used by writers of the Church,

ecclesiastici, ut significet non partem aut qualitatem in alio, sed quod proprie subsistit. Damnant omnes haereses contra hunc articulum exortas, ut Manichaeos, qui duo principia ponebant, bonum et malum: item Valentinianos, Arianos, Eunomianos, Mahometistas et omnes horum similes. Damnant et Samosatenos, veteres et neotericos, qui cum tantum unam personam esse contendent, de Verbo et Spiritu Sancto astute et impie rhetoricantur, quod non sint personae distinctae, sed quod Verbum significet verbum vocale, et Spiritus motum in rebus creatum.

i.e. as signifying not a part or a quality in another being, but what subsists in itself. They condemn all the heresies which have arisen against this article, e.g. the Manichees, who posited two principles, one good and one evil; likewise the Valentinians, Arians, Eunomians, Muslims and all like them. They also condemn the Adoptionists, ancient and modern, who argue that there is only one person, and cleverly and impiously prate that the Word and the Holy Spirit are not distinct persons, but that the Word is just a verbal utterance and the Spirit just a movement created in things.

02. De peccato originis

Item docent, quod post lapsum Adae omnes homines, secundum naturam propagati, nascantur cum peccato originali; hoc est, sine metu Dei, sine fiducia erga Deum, et cum concupiscentia; quodque hic morbus seu vitium originis vere sit peccatum, damnans et afferens nunc quoque aeternam mortem his qui non renascuntur per baptismum et Spiritum Sanctum. Damnamus Pelagianos, et alios, qui vitium originis negant esse peccatum, et ut extenuent gloriam meriti et beneficiorum Christi, disputant hominem propriis viribus rationis coram Deo iustificari posse.

02. Of Original Sin

Also they teach that after the fall of Adam all men, engendered according to nature, are born with original sin; that is, without fear of God or trust towards God, and with concupiscence. And this illness or original flaw is truly sin, condemning, and now also bringing eternal death to those who are not born again by baptism and the Holy Spirit. We condemn the Pelagians and others who deny that the original flaw is sin, and in order to dissipate the glory of the merit and of the benefits of Christ, argue that man can be declared righteous before God by the strength of his own reason.

03. De Filio Dei

Item docent, quod Verbum, hoc est, Filius Dei, assumpserit humanam naturam in utero Beatae Mariae Virginis, ut sint duae naturae, divina

03. Of the Son of God

They also teach that the Word, that is, the Son of God, took unto him human nature in the womb of the blessed Virgin Mary, so that there are

et humana in unitate personae inseparabiliter coniunctae unus Christus vere Deus, et vere homo, natus ex Virgine Maria, vere passus, crucifixus, mortuus et sepultus, ut reconciliaret nobis Patrem, et hostia esset non tantum pro culpa originis, sed etiam pro omnibus actualibus hominum peccatis. Item descendit ad inferos, vere resurrexit tertia die, deinde ascendit ad caelos, ut sedeat ad dexteram Patris et perpetuo regnet et dominetur omnibus creaturis, sanctificet credentes in ipsum, misso in corde eorum Spiritu Sancto, qui regat, consoletur, ac vivificet eos, ac defendat adversus Diabolum et vim peccati. Idem Christus palam est rediturus ut iudicet vivos et mortuos etc., iuxta Symbolum Apostolorum.

two natures, the divine and the human, inseparably joined together in unity of person; one Christ, true God and true man, born of the Virgin Mary; (who) truly suffered, was crucified, dead and buried, that he might reconcile the Father unto us, and might be a sacrifice, not only for original guilt, but also for all actual sins of men. The same also descended into hell, and truly rose again the third day. Afterward he ascended into heaven to sit at the right hand of the Father, and reign for ever, and have dominion over all creatures; and to sanctify those who believe in him by sending the Holy Spirit into their hearts, to rule, comfort and quicken them, and defend them against the Devil and the power of sin. The same Christ shall openly return to judge the living and the dead etc., as the Apostles' Creed states.

04. De iustificatione

Item docent, quod homines non possint iustificari coram Deo propriis viribus, meritis aut operibus, sed gratis iustificentur propter Christum per fidem, cum credunt se in gratiam recipi, et peccata remitti propter Christum, qui sua morte pro nostris peccatis satisfecit. Hanc fidem imputat Deus pro iustitia coram ipso (Ro 3, 4).

04. Of Justification

Likewise they teach that men cannot be justified before God by their own strength, merits or works, but are justified freely by faith on account of Christ, when they believe that they have been received into grace and that their sins have been forgiven on account of Christ, who by his death has made satisfaction for our sins. God reckons this faith as righteousness in his sight (Ro 3, 4).

05. De ministerio ecclesiastico

Ut hanc fidem consequamur, institutum est ministerium docendi evangelii et porrigendi sacramenta. Nam per verbum et sacramenta tam-

05. Of the Ministry of the Church

For us to obtain this faith, the ministry of teaching the Gospel and administering the sacraments was instituted. For by the Word and sacra-

quam per instrumenta donatur Spiritus Sanctus, qui fidem efficit, ubi et quando visum est Deo, in his qui audiunt evangelium, scilicet quod Deus non propter nostra merita sed propter Christum iustificet paenitentes, qui credunt se propter Christum in gratiam recipi. Damnamus Anabaptistas et alios, qui sentiunt Spiritum Sanctum contingere sine verbo externo hominibus per ipsorum praeparationes et opera.

ments, as by instruments, the Holy Spirit is given; who produces faith where and when it pleases God, in those that hear the Gospel, i.e. that God, not for our merits' sake, but for Christ's sake, justifies the Penitent who believe that for Christ's sake they are received into grace. We condemn the Anabaptists and others, who believe that the Holy Spirit comes to men without any external word, through their own preparation and works.

06. De nova oboedientia

Item docent quod fides illa debeat bonos fructus parere, et quod oporteat bona opera, mandata a Deo, facere propter voluntatem Dei, non ut confidamus per ea opera iustificationem coram Deo mereri. Nam remissio peccatorum et iustificatio fide appraehenditur, sicut testatur et vox Christi (Lc 17:10): *Cum feceritis haec omnia, dicite, servi inutiles sumus.* Item docent et veteres scriptores ecclesiastici. Ambrosius enim inquit: *Hoc constitutum est a Deo, ut qui credit in Christum salvus sit, sine opere, sola fide, gratis accipiens remissionem peccatorum.*

06. Of New Obedience

Also they teach that this faith should bring forth good fruits, and that men ought to do the good works commanded of God because it is God's will, and not on any confidence of meriting justification before God by their works. For remission of sins and justification is apprehended by faith, as also the voice of Christ witnesseth (Lk 17:10): *When ye have done all these things say, we are unprofitable servants.* The same also do the ancient writers of the Church teach, for Ambrose saith: *This is ordained of God, that he that believeth in Christ shall be saved without works, by faith alone, freely receiving remission of sins.*

07. De Ecclesia

Item docent quod una sancta Ecclesia perpetuo mansura sit. Est autem Ecclesia congregatio sanctorum, in qua Evangelium recte docetur et recte administrantur sacramenta. Et ad veram unitatem Ecclesiae satis est consentire de doctrina Evangelii et administratione sacra-

07. Of the Church

Also they teach that one holy Church is to continue for ever. But the Church is the congregation of saints in which the Gospel is rightly taught and the sacraments rightly administered. And unto the true unity of the Church, it is sufficient to agree concerning the doctrine of the

mentorum. Nec necesse est ubique esse similes traditiones humanas, seu ritus aut ceremonias ab hominibus institutas. Sicut inquit Paulus (Ep 4:5-6): *Una fides, unum baptisma, unus Deus et Pater omnium, etc.*

Gospel and the administration of the sacraments. Nor is it necessary that human traditions, rites or ceremonies instituted by men should be everywhere alike, as St Paul saith (Ep. 4:5-6): *There is one faith, one baptism, one God and Father of all etc.*

08. *Quid sit Ecclesia*

Quamquam Ecclesia proprie sit congregatio sanctorum et vere credentium, tamen cum in hac vita multi hypocritae et mali admixti sint, licet uti sacramentis quae per malos administrantur, iuxta vocem Christi (Mt 23:2): *Sedent scribae et Pharisaei in cathedra Moysi, etc.* Et sacramenta et verbum propter ordinationem et mandatum Christi sunt efficacia, etiamsi per malos exhibeantur.

Damnant Donatistas et similes qui negabant licere uti ministerio malorum in Ecclesia, et sentiebant ministerium malorum inutile et inefficax esse.

08. *What the Church is*

Though the Church be properly the congregation of saints and true believers, yet seeing that in this life many hypocrites and evil persons are mingled with it, it is lawful to use the sacraments administered by evil men according to the voice of Christ (Mt 23:2): *The scribes and Pharisees sit in Moses's seat, etc.* And the sacraments and the Word are effectual by reason of the institution and commandment of Christ, though they be delivered by evil men.

They condemn the Donatists and such like, who denied that it was lawful to use the ministry of evil men in the Church, and thought that the ministry of evil men is useless and ineffective.

09. *De baptismo*

De baptismo docent quod sit necessarius ad salutem, quodque per baptismum offeratur gratia Dei, et quod pueri sint baptizandi, qui per baptismum oblati Deo recipiantur in gratiam Dei. Damnant Anabaptistas qui improbant baptismum puerorum et affirmant pueros sine baptismo salvos fieri.

09. *Of Baptism*

Of baptism they teach that it is necessary to salvation and that by baptism the grace of God is offered, and that children are to be baptized, who by baptism, being offered to God, are received into God's favour. They condemn the Anabaptists who allow not the baptism of children, and affirm that children are saved without baptism.

10. De coena Domini

De coena Domini docent quod corpus et sanguis Christi vere adsint et distribuantur vescentibus in Coena Domini, et improbant secus docentes.

11. De confessione

De confessione docent quod absolutio privata in ecclesiis retinenda sit, quamquam in confessione non sit necessaria omnium delictorum enumeratio. Est enim impossibilis iuxta Ps 19:12: *Delicta quis intelligit?*

12. De paenitentia

De paenitentia docent, quod lapsis post baptismum contingere possint remissio peccatorum, quocunque tempore cum convertuntur, et quod Ecclesia talibus redeuntibus ad paenitentiam absolutionem impartiri debeat. Constat autem paenitentia proprie his duabus partibus: altera est contritio seu terrores incussi conscientiae agnito peccato. Altera est fides quae concipitur ex Evangelio seu absolutione, et credit propter Christum remitti peccata, et consolatur conscientiam, et ex terroribus liberat. Deinde sequi debent bona opera, quae sunt fructus paenitentiae. Damnant Anabaptistas qui negant semel iustificatos posse amittere Spiritum Sanctum. Item, qui contendunt quibusdam tantam perfectionem in hac vita contingere, ut peccare non possint. Damnantur et Novatiani qui nolebant absolvere

10. Of the Lord's Supper

Of the Supper of the Lord they teach that the body and blood of Christ are truly present, and are communicated to those that eat in the Lord's Supper. And they disapprove of those that teach otherwise.

11. Of Confession

Concerning confession, they teach that private confession be retained in the churches, though enumeration of all offences be not necessary in confession. For it is impossible, according to Ps 19:12: *Who can understand his errors?*

12. Of Penitence

Touching penitence, they teach that such as have fallen after baptism may find remission of sins at what time they are converted, and that the Church should give absolution unto such as return to penitence. Now penitence consisteth properly of these two parts: one is contrition, or terrors stricken into the conscience through the acknowledgement of sin. The other is faith, which is conceived by the Gospel, or absolution, and doth believe that for Christ's sake sins be forgiven, and comforteth the conscience, and freeth it from terrors. Then should follow good works, which are fruits of penitence. They condemn the Anabaptists who deny that men once justified can lose the Spirit of God, and do contend that some men may attain to such a perfection in this life that they cannot sin. The Novatians are also con-

lapsos post baptismum redeuntes ad paenitentiam. Reiiciuntur et isti qui non docent remissionem peccatorum per fidem contingere, sed iubent nos mereri gratiam per satisfactiones nostras.

demned, who would not absolve such as had fallen after baptism, though they returned to penitence. They also that do not teach that remission of sins is obtained by faith, and who command us to merit grace by satisfactions, are rejected.

13. De usu sacramentorum

De usu sacramentorum docent quod sacramenta instituta sint, non modo ut sint notae professionis inter homines, sed magis ut sint signa et testimonia voluntatis Dei erga nos, ad excitandam et confirmandam fidem in his, qui utuntur, proposita. Itaque utendum est sacramentis ita, ut fides accedat, quae credat promissionibus, quae per sacramenta exhibentur et ostenduntur. Damnant igitur illos qui docent, quod sacramenta ex opere operato iustificent, nec docent fidem requiri in usu sacramentorum, quae credat remitti peccata.

13. Of the Use of Sacraments

Concerning the use of the sacraments, they teach that they were ordained not only to be marks of profession among men, but rather that they should be signs and testimonies of the will of God towards us, set forth unto us to stir up and confirm faith in such as use them. Therefore men must use sacraments so as to join faith with them, which believes the promises that are offered and declared unto us by the sacraments. Wherefore they condemn those that teach that the sacraments do justify *ex opere operato*, and do not teach that faith which believes the remission of sins is requisite in the use of the sacraments.

14. De ordine ecclesiastico

De ordine ecclesiastico docent quod nemo debeat in Ecclesia publice docere aut sacramenta administrare nisi rite vocatus.

14. Of Ecclesiastical Orders

Concerning ecclesiastical orders they teach that no man should publicly in the Church teach or administer the sacraments unless he be rightly called.

15. De ritibus ecclesiasticis

De ritibus ecclesiasticis docent quod ritus illi servandi sint qui sine peccato servari possunt, et prosunt ad tranquillitatem et bonum ordinem in Ecclesia, sicut certae feriae, festa

15. Of Ecclesiastical Rites

Concerning ecclesiastical rites they teach that those rites are to be observed which may be observed without sin, and are profitable for tranquillity and good order in the

et similia. De talibus rebus tamen admonentur homines, ne conscientiae onerentur, tamquam talis cultus ad salutem necessarius sit. Admonentur etiam quod traditiones humanae institutae ad placandum Deum, ad promerendam gratiam et satisfaciendum pro peccatis, adversentur Evangelio et doctrinae fidei. Quare vota et traditiones de cibis et diebus etc., institutae ad promerendam gratiam et satisfaciendum pro peccatis inutiles sint et contra Evangelium.

16. De rebus civilibus

De rebus civilibus docent quod legitimae ordinationes civiles sint bona opera Dei, quod Christianis liceat gerere magistratus, exercere iudicia, iudicare res ex imperatoriis et aliis praesentibus legibus, supplicia iure constituere, iure bellare, militare, lege contrahere, tenere proprium, iusiurandum postulantibus magistratibus dare, ducere uxorem, nubere. Damnant Anabaptistas qui interdicunt haec civilia officia Christianis. Damnant et illos qui evangelicam perfectionem non collocant in timore Dei et fide, sed in deserendis civilibus officiis, quia Evangelium tradit iustitiam aeternam cordis. Interim non dissipat politiam aut oeconomiam, sed maxime postulat conservare tamquam ordinationes Dei, et in talibus ordinationibus exercere caritatem. Itaque necessario debent Christiani oboedire magistratibus suis et legibus, nisi cum iubent

Church, such as are set holidays, feasts and the like. Yet concerning such things, men are to be admonished that consciences are not to be burdened as if such worship were necessary unto salvation. They are also to be admonished that human traditions, instituted to placate God, to merit grace and make satisfaction for sins, are opposed to the Gospel and the doctrine of faith. Wherefore vows and traditions concerning foods and days etc., instituted to merit grace and make satisfaction for sins, are useless and contrary to the Gospel.

16. Of Civil Affairs

Concerning civil affairs, they teach that such civil ordinances as are lawful are good works of God; that Christians may lawfully bear civil office, sit in judgements, determine matters by the imperial laws, and other laws in present force, appoint just punishments, engage in just war, act as soldiers, make legal bargains and contracts, hold property, take an oath when the magistrates require it, marry a wife, or be given in marriage. They condemn the Anabaptists who forbid Christians these civil offices. They condemn also those that place the perfection of the Gospel, not in the fear of God and in faith, but in forsaking civil offices, inasmuch as the Gospel teacheth an everlasting righteousness of the heart. In the meantime, it doth not disallow order and government of commonwealths or families, but requireth especially the preservation and maintenance thereof, as of God's

peccare, tunc etiam magis debent oboedire Deo quam hominibus (Ac 5:29).

own ordinances, and that in such ordinances we should exercise love. Christians therefore must necessarily obey their magistrates and laws, save only when they command any sin, for then they must rather obey God than men (Ac 5:29).

17. De Christi reditu ad iudicium

Item docent quod Christus apparebit in consummatione mundi ad iudicandum et mortuos omnes resuscitabit, piis et electis dabit vitam aeternam et perpetua gaudia, impios autem homines ac diabolos condemnabit, ut sine fine crucientur. Damnant Anabaptistas qui sentiunt hominibus damnatis ac diabolis finem poenarum futurum esse. Damnant et alios qui nunc spargunt Iudaicas opiniones, quod ante resurrectionem mortuorum pii regnum mundi occupaturi sint, ubique oppressis impiis.

17. Of Christ's Return to Judgement

Also they teach that in the consummation of the world Christ shall appear to judge, and shall raise up all the dead, and shall give unto the godly and elect eternal life and everlasting joys; but ungodly men and the devils shall he condemn unto endless torments. They condemn the Anabaptists who think that to condemned men and the devils shall be an end of torments. They condemn others also, who now scatter Jewish opinions that, before the resurrection of the dead, the godly shall occupy the kingdom of the world, the wicked being everywhere suppressed.

18. De libero arbitrio

De libero arbitrio docent quod humana voluntas habeat aliquam libertatem ad efficiendam civilem iustitiam et deligendas res rationi subiectas. Sed non habet vim sine Spiritu Sancto efficiendae iustitiae spiritualis, quia animalis homo non percipit ea, quae sunt Spiritus Dei (I Co 2:14); sed haec fit in cordibus, cum per Verbum Spiritus Sanctus concipitur. Haec totidem verbis dicit Augustinus (*Hypognosticon 3*): *Esse fatemur liberum arbitrium omnibus hominibus, habens quidem iudicium rationis, non per quod sit idoneum*

18. Of Free Will

Concerning free will they teach that man's will hath some liberty to work a civil righteousness, and to choose such things as reason can reach unto, but that it hath no power to work the righteousness of God, or a spiritual righteousness, without the Holy Spirit; because that the soulish man receiveth not the things of the Spirit of God (I Co 2:14). But this is wrought in the heart when men do receive the Holy Spirit through the Word. These things are in as many words affirmed by St Augustine (*Hypognosticon 3*): *We confess that*

in eis, quae ad Deum pertinent, sine Deo aut inchoare aut certe peragere, sed tantum in operibus vitae praesentis tam bonis, quam etiam malis. Bonis dico, quae de bono naturae oriuntur, i.e. velle laborare in agro, velle manducare et bibere, velle habere amicum, velle habere indumenta, velle fabricare domum, uxorem velle ducere, pecora nutrire, artem discere diversarum rerum bonarum, vel quicquid bonum ad praesentem pertinet vitam. Quae omnia non sine divino gubernaculo subsistunt, imo ex ipso et per ipsum sunt et esse coeperunt. Malis vero dico, ut est, velle idolum colere, velle homicidium, etc. Damnant Pelagianos et alios qui docent quod sine Spiritu Sancto, solis naturae viribus possimus Deum super omnia diligere; item praecepta Dei facere, quoad substantiam actuum. Quamquam enim externa opera aliquo modo efficere natura possit, potest enim continere manus a furto, a cede; tamen interiores motus non potest efficere, ut timorem Dei, fiduciam erga Deum, castitatem, patientiam, etc.

there is in all men a free will which hath indeed the judgement of reason, not that it is thereby fitted, without God, either to begin or to perform anything in matters pertaining to God, but only in works belonging to this present life, whether they be good or evil. By good works I mean those which are of the goodness of nature, as to will to labour in the field, to desire to eat and drink, to desire to have a friend, to desire apparel, to desire to build a house, to marry a wife, to nourish cattle, to learn the art of divers good things, to desire any good thing pertaining to this present life; all which are not without God's government, yea, they are and had their beginning from God and by God. Among evil things I account such as these: to desire to worship an image, to will manslaughter, etc. They condemn the Pelagians and others who teach that by the powers of nature alone, without the Holy Spirit, we are able to love God above all things; also to perform the commandments of God, as touching the substance of our actions. For although nature be able in some sort to do the external works (for it is able to withhold the hands from theft and murder), yet it cannot work the inward notions, such as the fear of God, trust in God, chastity, patience and such like, etc.

19. De causa peccati

De causa peccati docent quod tametsi Deus creat et conservat naturam, tamen causa peccati est voluntas malorum, videlicet Diaboli et impiorum, quae non adiuvante Deo

19. Of the Cause of Sin

Touching the cause of sin they teach that although God doth create and preserve nature, yet the cause of sin is the will of the wicked; to wit, of the Devil and ungodly men, which

avertit se a Deo, sicut Christus ait (Io 8:44): *Cum loquitur mendacium, ex se ipso loquitur.*

will, God not aiding, turneth itself from God, as Christ saith (Jn 8:44): *When he speaketh a lie, he speaketh of his own.*

20. De bonis operibus

Falso accusantur nostri, quod bona opera prohibeant. Nam scriptaeorum, quae extant de decem praeceptis et alis simili argumento testantur, quod utiliter docuerint de omnibus vitae generibus et officiis, quae genera vitae, quae opera in qualibet vocatione Deo placeant. De quibus rebus olim parum docebant concionatores, tantum puerilia et non necessaria opera urgebant, ut certas ferias, certa ieiunia, fraternitates, peregrinationes, cultus sanctorum, rosaria, monachatum et similia. Haec adversarii nostri admoniti nunc dediscunt, nec perinde praedicant haec inutilia opera, ut olim. Praeterea incipiunt fidei mentionem facere, de qua olim mirum erat silentium. Docent nos non tantum operibus iustificari, sed coniungunt fidem et opera, et dicunt nos fide et operibus iustificari. Quae doctrina tolerabilior est priore, et plus afferre potest consolationis quam vetus ipsorum doctrina.

20. Of Good Works

Ours are falsely accused of forbidding good works. For their writings extant upon the Ten Commandments, and others of the like argument, do bear witness that they have to good purpose taught concerning every kind of life and its duties; what kinds of life and what works in every calling do please God. Of which things preachers in former times taught little or nothing, only they urged certain childish and needless works, as keeping of certain holidays, set fasts, fraternities, pilgrimages, worshipping of saints, the use of rosaries, monasticism, and such like. Whereof our adversaries having had warning, they do now unlearn them and do not preach concerning these unprofitable works, as they used to. Besides, they begin now to make mention of faith, concerning which there was formerly a deep silence. They teach that we are not justified by works alone, but they conjoin faith and works, and say we are justified by faith and works. Which doctrine is more tolerable than the former one, and can afford more consolation than their old doctrine.

Cum igitur doctrina de fide, quam oportet in Ecclesia praecipuam esse, tam diu iacuerit ignota, quemadmodum fateri omnes necesse est, de fidei iustitia altissimum silentium fuisse in concionibus, tantum doc-

Whereas therefore the doctrine of faith, which should be the chief one in the Church, hath been so long unknown, as all men must needs grant, that there was the deepest silence about the righteousness of

trinam operum versatam esse in ecclesiis, nostri de fide sic admonuerunt ecclesias. Principio, quod opera nostra non possint reconciliare Deum aut mereri remissionem peccatorum et gratiam et iustificationem, sed hanc tantum fide consequimur, credentes quod propter Christum recipiamur in gratiam, qui solus positus est Mediator et propitiatorium (I Ti 2:5), per quem reconcilietur Pater. Itaque qui confidit operibus se mereri gratiam, is aspernatur Christi meritum et gratiam, et quaerit sine Christo humanis viribus viam ad Deum, cum Christus de se dixerit (Io 14:6): *Ego sum via, veritas et vita.*

Haec doctrina de fide ubique in Paulo tractatur (Ep 2:8-9): *Gratia salvi facti estis per fidem, et hoc non ex vobis, Dei donum est, non ex operibus, etc.* Et ne quis cavilletur, a nobis novam Pauli interpretationem excogitari, tota haec causa habet testimonia Patrum. Nam Augustinus multis voluminibus defendit gratiam et iustitiam fidei contra merita operum. Et similia docet Ambrosius *De vocatione gentium*, et alibi. Sic enim inquit de vocatione gentium: *Vilesceret redemptio sanguinis Christi, nec misericordiae Dei humanorum operum praerogativa succumberet, si iustificatio, quae fit per gratiam, meritis praecedentibus deberetur, ut non munus largientis, sed merces esset operantis.*

faith in their sermons, and that the doctrine of works was usual in the churches; for this cause our divines did thus admonish the churches. First, that our works cannot reconcile God or deserve remission of sins, grace and justification at his hands, but that these we obtain by faith only, when we believe that we are received into favour for Christ's sake, who alone is appointed the Mediator and propitiatory (I Ti 2:5), by whom the Father is reconciled. He therefore that trusteth by his works to merit grace, doth despise the merit and grace of Christ, and seeketh by his own power, without Christ, to come unto the Father; whereas Christ hath said expressly of himself (Jn 14:6): *I am the way, the truth and the life.*

This doctrine of faith is handled by Paul almost everywhere (Ep 2:8-9): *By grace are ye saved through faith, and that not of yourselves; it is the gift of God, not of works, etc.* And lest any here should cavil that we bring in a new interpretation of Paul, this whole cause is sustained by testimonies of the Fathers. Augustine doth in many volumes defend grace and the righteousness of faith, against the merit of works. So doth Ambrose in his book *De vocatione gentium* and elsewhere, for thus he saith of the calling of the Gentiles: *The redemption made by the blood of Christ would be of small account, and the prerogative of man's works would not give place to the mercy of God, if the justification which is by grace were due to merits going before; so as it should not be the generosity of the giver but the wages of hire of the labourer.*

Quamquam autem haec doctrina contemnitur ab imperitis, tamen experiuntur piae ac pavidae conscientiae, plurimum eam consolationis afferre, quia conscientiae non possunt reddi tranquillae per ulla opera, sed tantum fide cum certo statuunt, quod propter Christum habeant placatum Deum; quemadmodum Paulus docet (Ro 5:1): *Iustificati per fidem, pacem habenus apud Deum.* Tota haec doctrina ad illud certamen perterrefactae conscientiae referenda est, nec sine ullo certamine intelligi potest. Quare male iudicant de ea re homines imperiti et profani, qui Christianam iustitiam nihil esse somniant, nisi civilem et philosophicam iustitiam.

Olim vexabantur conscientiae doctrina operum, non audiebant ex Evangelio consolationem. Quosdam conscientia expulit in desertum, in monasteria, sperantes ibi se gratiam merituros esse per vitam monasticam. Alii alia excogitaverunt opera ad promerendam gratiam et satisfaciendum pro peccatis. Ideo magnopere fuit opus, hanc doctrinam de fide in Christum tradere et renovare, ne deesset consolatio pavidis conscientiis, sed scirent fide in Christum appraehendi gratiam et remissionem peccatorum et iustificationem. Admonentur etiam homines, quod hic nomen fidei non significet tantum historiae notitiam, qualis est in impiis et Diabolo, sed significet fidem, quae credit non tantum historiam, sed etiam effectum historiae, videlicet hunc articulum,

This doctrine, though it be contemned of the unskillful, yet godly and fearful consciences find by experience that it bringeth very great comfort, because that consciences cannot be quieted by any works, but by faith alone, when they believe assuredly that they have a God who is placated for Christ's sake, as St Paul teacheth (Ro 5:1): *Being justified by faith, we have peace with God.* This doctrine doth wholly belong to the conflict of a troubled conscience, and cannot be understood, but where the conscience hath felt that conflict. Wherefore all such as have had no experience thereof, and all that are profane men, who dream that Christian righteousness is naught else but a civil and philosophical righteousness, are poor judges of this matter.

Formerly men's consciences were vexed with the doctrine of works; they did not hear any comfort out of the Gospel. Whereupon conscience drove some into the desert, into monasteries, hoping there to merit grace by a monastical life. Others devised other works whereby to merit grace and to satisfy for sin. There was very great need therefore to teach and renew this doctrine of faith in Christ, to the end that fearful consciences might not want comfort, but might know that grace and forgiveness of sins and justification are received by faith in Christ. Another thing which we teach men is that in this place the name of faith doth not only signify a knowledge of the history which may be in the wicked, and in the Devil, but that it signifieth a faith which believeth not

remissionem peccatorum, quod videlicet per Christum habeamus gratiam, iustitiam et remissionem peccatorum. Iam qui scit se per Christum habere propitium Patrem, is vere novit Deum, scit, se ei curae esse, invocat eum; denique non est sine Deo, sicut gentes. Nam diaboli et impii non possunt hunc articulum credere, remissionem peccatorum. Ideo Deum tamquam hostem oderunt, non invocant eum, nihil boni ab eo expectant. Augustinus etiam de fidei nomine hoc modo admonet lectorem et docet, in Scripturis nomen fidei accipi, non pro notitia, qualis est in impiis, sed pro fiducia, quae consolatur et erigit perterrefactas mentes.

only the history, but also the effect of the history, to wit, the article of remission of sins; namely that by Christ we have grace, righteousness and remission of sins. Now he that knoweth that he hath the Father merciful to him through Christ, this man knoweth God truly. He knoweth that God hath a care of him, he loveth God and calleth upon him, in a word, he is not without God as the Gentiles are. For the devils and the wicked can never believe this article of the remission of sins, and therefore they hate God as their enemy; they call not upon him, they look for no good thing at his hands. After this manner doth Augustine admonish the reader touching the name of faith, and teacheth that this word faith is taken in Scriptures, not for such a knowledge as is in the wicked, but for a trust which doth comfort and lift up disquieted minds.

Praeterea docent nostri quod necesse sit bona opera facere, non ut confidamus per ea gratiam mereri, sed propter voluntatem Dei. Tantum fide appraehenditur remissio peccatorum ac gratia. Et quia per fidem accipitur Spiritus Sanctus, iam corda renovantur et induunt novos affectus, ut parere bona opera possint. Sic enim ait Ambrosius: *Fides bonae volutatis et iustae actionis genitrix est*. Nam humanae vires sine Spiritu Sancto plenae sunt impiis affectibus, et sunt imbecilliores quam ut bona opera possint efficere coram Deo. Ad haec, sunt in potestate Diaboli, qui impellit homines ad varia peccata, ad impias opiniones, ad manifesta scelera. Quemadmodum est videre in philosophis, qui et ipsi

Moreover, ours teach that it is necessary to do good works, not that we may trust that we deserve grace by them, but because it is the will of God that we should do them. By faith alone is apprehended remission of sins and grace. And because the Holy Spirit is received by faith, our hearts are now renewed, and so put on new affections, so that they are able to bring forth good works. For thus saith Ambrose: *Faith is the begetter of a good will and righteous behaviour*. For man's powers, without the Holy Spirit, are full of wicked affections and are too weak to perform any good deed before God. Besides, they are in the Devil's power, who driveth men forward into divers sins, into profane opinions

conati honeste vivere, tamen id non potuerunt efficere, sed contaminati sunt multis manifestis sceleribus. Talis est imbecillitas hominis, cum est sine fide et sine Spiritu Sancto, et tantum humainis viribus se gubernat. Hinc facile apparet, hanc doctrinam non esse accusandam, quod bona opera prohibeat, sed multo magis laudandam, quod ostendit, quomodo bona opera facere possimus. Nam sine fide nullo modo potest humana natura primi aut secundi praecepti opera facere. Sine fide non invocat Deum, a Deo nihil expectat, non tollerat crucem, sed quaerit humana praesidia, confidit humanis praesidiis. Ita regnant in corde omnes cupiditates et humana consilia, cum abest fides et fiducia erga Deum. Quare et Christus dixit (Io. 15:5): *Sine me nihil potestis facere*. Et Ecclesia canit: *Sine tuo numine nihil est in homine, nihil est innoxium.*

and into heinous crimes; as was to be seen in the philosophers who, trying to live an honest life, could not attain unto it, but were defiled with many heinous crimes. Such is the weakness of man when he is without faith and the Holy Spirit, and hath no other guide but the natural powers of man. Hereby every man may see that this doctrine is not to be accused, as forbidding good works; but rather is much to be commended, because it showeth after what sort we must do good works. For without faith the nature of man can by no means perform the works of the First or Second Table. Without faith it cannot call upon God, hope in God, bear the cross; but seeketh help from man, and trusteth in man's help. So it cometh to pass that all lusts and human counsels reign in the heart so long as faith and trust in God are absent. Wherefore also Christ saith (Jn 15:5): *Without me ye can do nothing* and the Church singeth: *Without thy power is naught in man, naught that is innocent.*

21. De cultu sanctorum

De cultu sanctorum docent quod memoria sanctorum proponi potest, ut imitemur fidem eorum et bona opera iuxta vocationem; ut Caesar imitari potest exemplum Davidis in bello gerendo ad depellendos Turcas a patria. Nam uterque rex est. Sed Scriptura non docet invocare sanctos seu petere auxilium a sanctis, quia unum Christum nobis proponit mediatorem, propitiatorium, pontificem et intercessorem. Hic invocandus est et promisit, se exauditurum

21. Of the Worship of Saints

Touching the worship of saints, they teach that the memory of saints may be set before us that we may follow their faith and good works according to our calling, as the Emperor may follow David's example in making war to drive away the Turks from his country, for either of them is a king. But the Scripture teacheth not to invoke saints, or to ask help of saints, because it propoundeth unto us one Christ the Mediator, propitiatory, high priest and intercessor. This

esse preces nostras, et hunc cultum maxime prodat, videlicet, ut invocetur in omnibus afflictionibus (I Io 2:1): *Si quis peccat, habemus advocatum apud Deum, etc.*

Christ is to be invoked, and he hath promised that he will hear our prayers, and liketh this worship especially, to wit, that he be invoked in all afflictions (I Jn 2:1): *If any man sin, we have an advocate with God, etc.*

22.

Haec fere summa est doctrinae apud nos, in qua cerni potest, nihil inesse, quod discrepet a Scripturis, vel ab Ecclesia Catholica, vel ab Ecclesia Romana quatenus ex scriptoribus nota est. Quod cum its sint, inclementer iudicant isti qui nostros pro haereticis haberi postulant. Sed dissensio est de quibusdam abusibus, qui sine certa auctoritate in ecclesias irrepserunt, in quibus etiam, si qua esset dissimilitudo, tamen decebat haec lenitas episcopos, ut propter confessionem, quam modo recensuimus, tolerarent nostros, quia ne canones quidem tam duri sunt, ut eosdem ritus ubique esse postulent, neque similes unquam omnium ecclesiarum ritus fuerunt. Quamquam apud nos magna ex parte veteres ritus diligenter servantur. Falsa enim calumnia est, quod omnes ceremoniae, omnia vetera instituta in ecclesiis nostris aboleantur. Verum publica querela fuit, abusus quosdam in vulgaribus ritibus haerere. Hi quia non poterant bona conscientia probari, aliqua ex parte correcti sunt.

22.

This is about the sum of doctrine among us, in which can be seen that there is nothing which is discrepant with the Scriptures, or with the Church Catholic, or even with the Roman Church, so far as that Church is known from writers. This being the case, they judge us harshly who insist that we shall be regarded as heretics. But the dissension is concerning certain abuses which, without any certain authority, have crept into the churches; in which things, even if there were some difference, yet would it be a becoming lenity on the part of the bishops that, on account of the confession which we have now presented, they should bear with us, since not even the canons are so severe as to demand the same rites everywhere, nor were the rites of all churches at any time the same. Although among us in large part the ancient rites are diligently observed. For it is a calumnious falsehood that all the ceremonies, all the things instituted of old, are abolished in our churches. But the public complaint was that certain abuses were connected with the rites in common use. These, because they could not with good conscience be approved, have to some extent been corrected.

Pars II: Articuli in quibus recensentur abusus mutati

Cum ecclesiae apud nos de nullo articulo fidei dissentiant ab Ecclesia Catholica, tantum paucos quosdam abusus omittant, qui novi sunt, et contra voluntatem canonum vitio temporum recepti, rogamus, ut Caesarea Maiestas clementer audiat, et quid sit mutatum, et quae fuerint causae, quo minus coactus sit populus illos abusus contra conscientiam observare. Nec habest fidem Caesarea Maiestas istis, qui, ut inflamment odia hominum adversus nostros, miras calumnias spargunt in populum. Hoc modo irritatis animis bonorum virorum initio praebuerunt occasionem huic dissidio, et eadem arte conantur nunc augere discordias. Nam Caesarea Maiestas haud dubie comperiet tolerabiliorem esse formam et doctrinae et ceremoniarum apud nos, quam qualem homines iniqui et malevoli describunt. Porro veritas ex vulgi rumoribus aut maledictis inimicorum colligi non potest. Facile autem hoc iudicari potest, nihil magis prodesse ad dignitatem ceremoniarum conservandam et alendam reverentiam ac pietatem in populo, quam si ceremoniae rite fiant in ecclesiis.

Part II: Articles in which are recounted the abuses which have been corrected

Inasmuch as the churches among us dissent in no article of faith from the Church Catholic, and only omit a few certain abuses which are novel and, contrary to the purport of the canons, have been received by the fault of the times, we beg that your imperial Majesty would clemently hear both what ought to be changed and what are the reasons that the people ought not to be forced against their consciences to observe those abuses. Nor should your imperial Majesty have faith in those who, that they may inflame the hatred of men against us, scatter amazing slanders among the people. In this way the minds of good men being angered at the beginning, they gave occasion to this dissension, and by the same art they now endeavour to increase the discords. For beyond doubt your imperial Majesty will find that the form, both of doctrines and of ceremonies, among us is far more tolerable than that which these wicked and malicious men describe. The truth, moreover, cannot be gathered from common rumours and the reproaches of enemies. But it is easy to judge this, that nothing is more profitable to preserve the dignity of ceremonies and to nurture reverence and godliness among the people than that the ceremonies should be rightly performed in the churches.

01 (23). De utraque specie

Laicis datur utraque species sacra-

01 (23). Of Both Kinds

Both kinds of the sacrament of the

menti in Coena Domini, quia hic mos habet mandatum Domini (Mt 26:27): *Bibite ex hoc omnes*. Ubi manifeste praecepit Christus de poculo, ut omnes bibant, et ne quis possit cavillari, quod hoc ad sacerdotes tantum pertineat, Paulus ad Corinthios exemplum recitat (I Co 11:26) in quo apparet, totam ecclesiam utraque specie usam esse. Et diu mansit hic mos in Ecclesia, nec constat quando aut quo auctore mutatus sit, tametsi Cardinalis Cusanus recitet, quando sit approbatus. Cyprianus aliquot locis testatur, populo sanguinem datum esse. Idem testatur Hieronymus, qui ait, *sacerdotes Eucharistiae ministrant, et sanguinem Christi populis dividunt*. Imo Gelasius Papa mandat, ne dividatur sacramentum (*Diss. de consec. 2; cap. Comperimus*). Tantum consuetudo non ita vetus aliud habet. Constat autem, quod consuetudo, contra mandata Dei introducta, non sit probanda, ut testantur canones (*Diss. 8 cap. Veritate*) cum sequentibus. Haec vero consuetudo non solum contra Scripturam sed etiam contra veteres canones et exemplum Ecclesiae recepta est. Quare si qui maluerunt utraque specie sacramenti uti, non fuerunt cogendi, ut aliter facerent cum offensione conscientiae. Et quia divisio sacramenti non convenit cum institutione Christi, solet apud nos omitti processio, quae hactenus fieri solita est.

Lord's Supper are given to the laity, because this custom hath the commandment of the Lord (Mt 26:27): *Drink ye all of this*, where Christ doth manifestly command concerning the cup that all should drink. And that no man might cavil that this doth only pertain to the priests, the example of Paul to the Corinthians witnesseth that the whole church did use both kinds in common (I Co 11:26). And this custom remained a long time in the Church, neither is it certain when or by what authority it was changed, although Cardinal (Nicholas of) Cusa relates when it was approved. Cyprian in certain places doth witness that the blood was given to the people, the same thing doth Jerome testify, saying: *The priests do minister the Eucharist, and communicate the blood of Christ to the people*. Nay, Pope Gelasius commandeth that the sacrament be not divided (*Diss. de consec. 2; cap. Comperimus*). Only a custom, not that ancient, doth otherwise. But it is manifest that a custom, brought in contrary to the commandments of God, is not to be approved, as the canons do witness (*Diss. 8; cap. Veritate*) with the words which follow. Now this custom has been received, not only against the Scripture, but also against the ancient canons and the example of the Church. Therefore if any would rather use both kinds in the sacrament, they are not to be compelled to do otherwise, with the offence of their conscience. And because that the division of the sacrament doth not agree with the institution of

Christ, among us it is the custom to omit that procession which hitherto hath been in use.

02 (24). De coniugio sacerdotum

Publica querela fuit de exemplis sacerdotum, qui non continebant. Quam ob causam et Pius Papa dixisse fertur, fuisse aliquas causas, cur ademptum sit sacerdotibus coniugium, sed multo maiores esse causas, cur reddi debeat; sic enim scribit Platina. Cum igitur sacerdotes apud nos publica illa scandala vitare vellent, duxerunt uxores ac docuerunt, quod liceat ipsis contrahere matrimonium. Primum, quia Paulus dicit (I Co 7:2): *Unusquisque habeat uxorem suam propter fornicationem.* Item (v. 9): *Melius est nubere quam uri.* Secundo, Christus inquit (Mt 19:12): *Non omnes capiunt verbum hoc,* ubi docet, non omnes homines ad coelibatum idoneos esse, quia Deus creavit hominem ad procreationem (Gn 1:28). Nec est humanae potestatis, sine singulari dono et opere Dei creationem mutare. Igitur qui non sunt idonei ad coelibatum, debent contrahere matrimonium. Nam mandatum Dei et ordinationem Dei nulla lex humana, nullum votum tollere potest. Et his causis docent sacerdotes, sibi licere uxores ducere. Constat etiam, in Ecclesia veteri sacerdotes fuisse maritos. Nam et Paulus ait (I Ti 3:2): *Episcopum eligendum esse, qui sit maritus.* Et in Germania, primum ante annos quadrigentos sacerdotes vi coacti sunt ad coelibatum, qui quidem adeo adversati sunt, ut archiepiscopus

02 (24). Of the Marriage of Priests

There was a common complaint of the examples of such priests as were not celibate. For which cause Pope Pius (II) is reported to have said that there were certain causes for which marriage was forbidden to priests, but there were many weightier causes why it should be permitted again, for so Platina writeth. Whereas therefore, the priests among us seek to avoid these public offences, they have married wives and have taught that it is lawful for them to enter into marriage. First, because that Paul saith (I Co 7:2): *To avoid fornication, let every man have his wife*; again (v. 9): *It is better to marry than to burn.* Secondly Christ saith (Mt 19:11): *All men cannot receive this word,* where he showeth that all men are not fit for a single life, because that God created mankind male and female (Gn 1:28). Nor is it in man's power, without a special gift and work of God, to alter his creation. Therefore such as are not meet for a single life ought to contract marriage. For no law of man, no vow, can take away the commandment of God and his ordinance. By these reasons the priests do prove that they may lawfully take wives. And it is well known that in the ancient churches priests were married. For Paul saith (I Ti 3:2): *That a bishop must be chosen which is a husband.* And in Germany, not until about four hundred years ago

Moguntinus, publicaturus edictum Romani Pontificis de ea re, paene ab iratis sacerdotibus per tumultum oppressus sit. Et res gesta est tam inciviliter, ut non solum in posterum coniugia prohiberentur, sed etiam praesentia, contra omnia iura divina et humana, contra ipsos etiam canones, factos non solum a Pontificibus, sed a laudatissimis synodis, distraherentur. Et cum senescente mundo paulatim natura humana fiat imbecillior, convenit prospicere, ne plura vitia serpant in Germaniam. Porro Deus instituit coniugium ut esset remedium humanae infirmitatis. Ipsi canones veterem rigorem interdum posterioribus temporibus propter imbecillitatem hominum laxandum esse dicunt, quod optandum est, ut fiat et in hoc negotio. Ac videntur ecclesiis aliquando defuturi pastores, si diutius prohibeatur coniugium.

Cum autem extet mandatum Dei, cum mos Ecclesiae notus sit, cum impurus coelibatus plurima pariat scandala, adulteria et alia scelera, digna animadversione boni magistratus; tamen mirum est, nulla in re maiorem exerceri saevitatem, quam adversus coniugium sacerdotum. Deus praecepit honore afficere coniugium. Leges in omnibus rebus publicis bene constitutis, etiam apud ethnicos, maximis honoribus ornaverunt. At nunc capitalibus poenis

were the priests by violence compelled to live a single life; who then were so wholly bent against the matter that the Archbishop of Mainz, being about to publish the Pope of Rome's decree to that effect, was almost murdered in a tumult by the priests in their anger. And the matter was handled so rudely that not only were marriages forbidden for the time to come, but also such as were then contracted were broken asunder, contrary to all laws divine and human, contrary to the canons themselves, that were before made, not only by Popes, but also by most famous councils. And seeing that as the world decayeth, man's nature by little and little waxeth weaker, it is well to look to it, that no more vices do overspread Germany. Furthermore, God ordained marriage to be a remedy for man's infirmity. The canons themselves do say that the old rigour is now and then in latter times to be released because of the weakness of men. Which it were to be wished might be done in this matter also. And if marriage be forbidden any longer, the churches may at length want pastors.

Seeing then that there is a plain commandment of God, seeing the custom of the Church is well known, seeing that impure single life bringeth forth very many offences, adulteries and other enormities worthy to be punished by the good magistrate, it is a marvel that greater cruelty should be showed in no other thing than against the marriage of priests. God hath commanded to honour marriage; the laws in all well-ordered commonwealths, even

excruciantur, et quidem sacerdotes, contra canonum voluntatem, nullam aliam ob causam, nisi propter coniugium. Paulus vocat doctrinam daemoniorum, quae prohibet coniugium (I Ti 4:1,3). Id facile nunc intelligi potest, cum talibus suppliciis prohibitio coniugii defenditur.

Sicut autem nulla lex humana potest mandatum Dei tollere, ita nec votum potest tollere mandatum Dei. Proinde etiam Cyprianus suadet, ut mulieres nubant, quae non servant promissam castitatem. Verba eius sunt haec (*1, Ep. 11*): *Si autem perseverare nolunt, aut non possunt, melius est ut nubant, quam ut in ignem deliciis suis cadant; certe nullum fratribus aut sororibus scandalum faciant.* Et aequitate quadam utuntur ipsi canones erga hos, qui ante iustam aetatem voverunt, quomodo fere hactenus fieri consuevit.

03 (25). De missa

Falso accusantur ecclesiae nostrae, quod missam aboleant; retinetur enim missa apud nos, et summa reverentia celebratur. Servantur et usitatae ceremoniae fere omnes, praeterquam quod Latinis cantionibus admiscentur alicubi Germanicae, quae additae sunt ad docendum populum. Nam ad hoc unum opus est ceremoniis, ut doceant imperitos. Et non modo Paulus praecipit (I Co 14:9) uti lingua intellecta populo in ecclesia, sed

among the heathen, have adorned marriage with very great honours. But now men are cruelly put to death, yea, and priests also, contrary to the mind of the canons, for no other cause but marriage. Paul calleth that a doctrine of devils, which forbiddeth marriage (I Ti 4:1, 3); which may now very well be seen, since the forbidding of marriage is maintained by such punishments.

But as no law of man can take away the law of God, no more can any vow take away the law of God. Therefore Cyprian also giveth counsel, that those women should marry who do not keep their vowed chastity. His words are these (*1, Ep. 11*): *If they will not or are not able to endure, it is far better they should marry than that they should fall into the fire by their importunate desires. In any wise let them give no offence to their brethren or sisters.* Yea even the canons show some kind of justice towards such as before their ripe years did vow chastity, as hitherto the use hath for the most part been.

03 (25). Of the Mass

Our churches are wrongfully accused to have abolished the mass. For the mass is retained still among us and celebrated with great reverence; yea, and almost all the ceremonies which are in use, except that with the things sung in Latin we mix certain things sung in German at various parts of the service, which are added for the people's instruction. For therefore alone we have need of ceremonies, that they may teach the unlearned.

etiam ita constitutum est humano iure. Assuevit populus, ut una utantur sacramento, si qui sunt idonei, id quoque auget reverentiam ac religionem publicarum ceremoniarum. Nulli enim admittuntur, nisi antea explorati. Admonentur etiam homines de dignitate et usu sacramenti, quantam consolationem afferat pavidis conscientiis, ut discant Deo credere, et omnia bona a Deo expectare et petere.

Hic cultus delectat Deum, talis usus sacramenti alit pietatem erga Deum. Itaque non videntur apud adversarios missae maiore religione fieri, quam apud nos. Constat autem hanc quoque publicam et longe maximam querelam omnium bonorum virorum diu fuisse, quod missae turpiter profanarentur, collatae ad quaestum. Neque enim obscurum est, quam late pateat hic abusus in omnibus templis, a qualibus celebrentur missae, tantum propter mercedem aut stipendium, quam multi contra interdictum canonum celebrent. Paulus autem graviter minatur his, qui indigne tractant Eucharistiam, cum ait (I Co 11:27): *Qui ederit panem hunc, aut biberit calicem Domini indigne, reus erit corporis et sanguinis Domini.* Itaque cum apud nos admonerentur sacerdotes de hoc peccato, desierunt apud nos privatae missae, cum fere nullae privatae missae nisi quaestus causa fierent. Neque ignoraverunt hos abusus episcopi, qui si

This is not only commanded by St Paul, to use in church a tongue that the people understand (I Co 14:9), but man's law hath also appointed it. We accustom the people to receive the sacrament together, if so be any be found fit thereunto; and that is a thing that doth increase the reverence and due estimation of the public ceremonies. For none are admitted, except they be first proved. Besides, we put men in mind of the worthiness and use of the sacrament, how great comfort it bringeth to timid consciences, that they may learn to believe God, and to look for and crave all good things from God.

This worship doth please God; such a use of the sacrament doth nourish piety towards God. Therefore it seemeth not that masses be more religiously celebrated among our adversaries than with us. But it is evident that of long time this hath been the public and most grievous complaint of all good men, that masses are basely profaned, being used for gain. And it is not unknown how far this abuse hath spread itself in all churches; of what manner of men masses are used, only for a reward, or for wages; and how many do use them against the prohibition of the canons. But Paul doth grievously threaten those who treat the Lord's Supper unworthily, saying (I Co 11:27): *He that eateth this bread or drinketh this cup of the Lord unworthily, shall be guilty of the body and blood of the Lord.* Therefore, when the priests among us were admonished of this sin, private masses were laid aside among us, seeing that for the most

correxissent eos in tempore, minus nunc esset dissensionum. Antea sua dissimulatione multa vitia passi sunt in Ecclesiam serpere. Nunc sero incipiunt quaeri de calumnitatibus Ecclesiae, cum hic tumultus non aliunde sumpserit occasionem, quam ex illis abusibus, qui tam manifesti erant, ut tolerari amplius non possent. Magnae dissensiones de missa, de sacramento extiterunt. Fortasse dat poenas orbis tam diuturnae profanationis missarum, quam in ecclesiis tot saeculis toleraverunt isti, qui emendare et poterant et debebant. Nam in Decalogo scriptum est (Ex 20:7): *Qui Dei nomine abutitur, non erit impunitus.* At ab initio mundi nulla res divina its videtur unquam ad quaestum collata fuisse, ut missa.

Accessit opinio, quae auxit privatas missas in infinitum, videlicet quod Christus sua passione satisfecerit pro peccato originis, et instituerit missam, in qua fieret oblatio pro quotidianis delictis, mortalibus et venialibus. Hinc manavit publica opinio, quod missa sit opus delens peccata vivorum et mortuorum ex opere operato. Hic coeptum est disputari, utrum una missa, dicta pro pluribus, tantundem valeat, quantum singulae pro singulis. Haec disputatio peperit istam infinitam multitudinem mis-

part there were no private masses but only for lucre's sake. Neither were the bishops ignorant of these abuses, and if they had amended them in time, there would now be fewer dissensions. Heretofore, by their dissembling, they suffered much corruption to creep into the Church; now they begin, though it be late, to complain of the calamities of the Church, seeing that this tumult was raised up by no other mean than by those abuses, which were so evident that they could no longer be tolerated. There were many dissensions concerning the mass, concerning the sacrament. And perhaps the world is punished for so long a profaning of masses, which they, who both could and ought to have amended it, have so many years tolerated in the churches. For in the ten Commandments it is written (Ex 20:7): *He that taketh in vain the name of the Lord shall not be held guiltless.* And from the beginning of the world there neither was nor is any divine thing which seems so to have been employed for gain as the mass.

There was added an opinion, which increased private masses infinitely; to wit, that Christ by his passion did satisfy for original sin, and appointed the mass, wherein an oblation should be made for daily sins, both mortal and venial. Hereupon a common opinion was received, that the mass is a work that taketh way the sins of the quick and the dead, and that *ex opere operato*. Here men began to dispute whether one mass said for many was of as great force as particular masses said for particular men. This disputation

sarum. De his opinionibus nostri admonuerunt, quod dissentiant a Scripturis Sanctis, et laedant gloriam passionis Christi. Nam passio Christi fuit oblatio et satisfactio, non solum pro culpa originis sed etiam pro omnibus reliquis peccatis, ut ad Hebraeos scriptum est (He 10:10): *Sanctificati sumus per oblationem Iesu Christi semel*. Item (He 10:14): *Una oblatione consumavit in perpetuum sanctificatos*. Item, Scriptura docet, nos coram Deo iustificari per fidem in Christum, cum credimus, nobis remitti peccata propter Christum. Iam si missa delet peccata vivorum et mortuorum ex opere operato, contingit iustificatio ex opere missarum, non ex fide, quod Scriptura non patitur. Sed Christus iubet (Lc 22:19): *facere in sui memoriam*, quare missa instituta est, ut fides in eis, qui utuntur sacramento, recordetur, quae beneficia accipiat per Christum, et erigat et consoletur pavidam conscientiam. Nam id est meminisse Christi, beneficia meminisse, ac sentire, quod vere exhibeantur nobis. Nec satis est historiam recordari, quia hanc etiam Iudaei et impii recordari possunt. Est igitur ad hoc facienda missa, ut ibi porrigatur sacramentum his, quibus opus est consolatione, sicut Ambrosius ait: *Quia semper pecco, semper debeo accipere medicinam.*

hath brought forth that infinite multitude of masses. Our preachers have admonished concerning these opinions that they do depart from the Holy Scriptures, and diminish the glory of the passion of Christ. For the passion of Christ was an oblation and satisfaction, not only for original sin, but also for all other sins, as it is written to the Hebrews (He 10:10): *We are sanctified by the oblation of Jesus Christ once made*; also (He 10:14): *By one oblation he hath perfected for ever them that are sanctified*. The Scripture also teacheth that we are justified before God through faith in Christ, when we believe that our sins are forgiven for Christ's sake. Now if the mass do take away the sins of the quick and the dead, even *ex opere operato*, then justification cometh by the work of masses, and not by faith; which the Scripture cannot endure. But Christ commandeth us: *Do this in remembrance of me* (Lk 22:19), therefore the mass has been instituted that faith in them which use the sacrament may remember what benefits it receiveth by Christ, and that it may raise and comfort the fearful conscience. For this is to remember Christ, to wit, to remember his benefits and to feel and perceive that they be indeed imparted unto us. Nor is it sufficient to call to mind the history, because that the Jews also, and the wicked, can do. Therefore the mass must be used to this end, that there the sacrament may be reached unto them that have need of comfort, as Ambrose saith: *Because I do always sin, therefore I ought always to receive the medicine.*

Cum autem missa sit talis communicatio sacramenti, servatur apud nos una communis missa singulis feriis atque aliis etiam diebus, si qui sacramento velint uti, ubi porrigitur sacramentum his, qui petunt. Neque hic mos in Ecclesia novus est, nam veteres ante Gregorium non faciunt mentionem privatae missae; de communi missa plurimum loquuntur. Chrysostomus ait: *Sacerdotem quotidie stare ad altare, et alios ad communionem accersere, alios arcere.* Et ex canonibus veteribus apparet, unum aliquem celebrasse missam, a quo reliqui presbyteri et diaconi sumpserunt corpus Domini. Sic enim sonant verba canonis Nicaeni: *Accipiant diaconi secundum ordinem post presbyteros ab episcopo vel a presbytero sacram communionem.* Et Paulus (I Co 11:33) de communion iubet, ut alii alios expectent, ut fiat communis participatio.

Postquam igitur missa apud nos habet exemplum Ecclesiae, ex Scriptura et patribus, confidimus improbari eam non posse, maxime cum publicae ceremoniae magna ex parte similes usitatis serventur; tantum numerus missarum est dissimilis, quem propter maximos et manifestos abusus certe moderari podesset. Nam olim etiam in ecclesiis frequentissimis non fiebat quotidie missa, ut testatur *Historia Tripartita 9,38*: *Rursus autem in Alexandria quarta et sexta feria Scripturae leguntur, easque doctores interpretantur, et omnia fiunt praeter solemnem oblationis morem.*

And seeing that the mass is such a communion of the sacrament, we do observe one common mass every holy day, and on other days, if any will use the sacrament, at which times it is offered to them that desire it. Neither is this custom new to the Church. For the ancients, before Gregory's time, make no mention of any private mass; of the common mass they speak much. Chrysostom saith that *the priest doth daily stand at the altar, and call some unto the Communion, and put back others.* And by the ancient canons it is evident that someone did celebrate the mass, of whom the other elders and deacons did receive the body of the Lord. For so the words of the Nicene canon do sound: *Let the deacons in their order, after the elders, receive the Holy Communion of a bishop, or of an elder.* And Paul (I Co 11:33), concerning the Communion, commandeth that one tarry for another, that so there may be a common participation.

Seeing therefore that the mass amongst us hath the example of the Church, out of the Scripture and the Fathers, we trust that it cannot be disapproved, especially since our public ceremonies are kept, the most part, like unto the usual ceremonies; only the number of masses is not alike, the which, by reason of very great and manifest abuses, it were certainly far better to be moderated. For in times past also, in the churches whereunto was greatest resort, it was not the use to have mass said every day, as the *Tripartite History 9,38* doth witness: *Again,* saith it, *in Alexandria, every fourth and sixth*

day of the week, the Scriptures are read and the doctors do interpret them; and all other things are done also, except only the celebration of the Eucharist.

04 (26). De confessione

Confessio in ecclesiis apud nos non est abolita, non enim solet porrigi corpus Domini, nisi antea exploratis et absolutis. Et docetur populus diligentissime de fide absolutionis, de qua ante haec tempora magnum erat silentium. Docentur homines, ut absolutionem plurimi faciant, quia sit vox Dei et mandato Dei pronuncietur.

Ornatur potestas clavium et commemoratur quantam consolationem afferat perterrefactis conscientiis, et quod requirat Deus fidem, ut illi absolutioni tamquam voci de caelo sonanti credamus, et quod illa fides in Christum vere consequatur et accipiat remissionem peccatorum. Antea immodice extollebantur satisfactiones; fidei et meriti Christi ac iustitiae fidei nulla fiebat mentio; quare in hac parte minime sunt culpandae ecclesiae nostrae. Nam hoc etiam adversarii tribuere nobis coguntur, quod doctrina de paenitentia diligentissime a nostris tractata ac patefacta sit.

Sed de confessione docent quod enumeratio delictorum non sit necessaria, nec sint onerandae conscientiae cura enumerandi omnia

04 (26). Of Confession

Confession is not abolished in our churches. For it is not usual to communicate the body of our Lord except to those who have been previously examined and absolved. And the people are taught most carefully concerning the faith required to absolution, about which before these times there has been a great silence. Men are taught that they should highly regard absolution, inasmuch as it is God's voice, and pronounced by God's command.

The power of the keys is honoured, and mention is made how great consolation it brings to terrified consciences, and that God requires faith that we believe that absolution as a voice sounding from heaven, and that this faith in Christ truly obtains and receives remission of sins. Aforetime satisfactions were immoderately extolled; of faith and the merit of Christ, and justification by faith, no mention was made. Wherefore on this point our churches are by no means to be blamed. For this even our adversaries are compelled to concede in regard to us, that the doctrine of repentance is most diligently treated and laid open by us.

But of confession our churches teach that the enumeration of sins is not necessary, nor are consciences to be burdened with the care of enumer-

delicta, quia impossibile est omnia delicta recitare, ut testatur Ps 19:12: *Delicta quis intelligit?* Item Ieremias (17:9): *Pravum est cor hominis et inscrutabile.* Quod si nulla peccata nisi recitata remitterentur, numquam adquiescere conscientiae possent, quia plurima peccata neque vident, neque meminisse possunt. Testantur et veteres scriptores enumerationem non esse necessariam. Nam in Decretis citatur Chrysostomus, qui sic ait: *Non tibi dico, ut te prodas in publicum, neque apud alios te accuses, sed oboedire te volo prophetae dicenti: "Revela ante Deum viam tuam". Ergo tua confitere peccata apud Deum, verum iudicem, cum oratione. Delicta tua pronuntia non lingua, sed conscientiae tuae memoria, etc.* Et Glossa (*De paen. Diss. 5, cap. Consideret*), fatetur humani iuris esse confessionem. Verum confessio, cum propter maximum absolutionis beneficium, tum propter alias conscientiarum utilitates apud nos retinetur.

ating all sins, inasmuch as it is impossible to recount all sins, as Ps 19:12 testifies: *Who can understand his errors?* So also Jeremiah (Je 17:9): *The heart is deceitful above all things and desperately wicked. Who can know it?* But if no sins were remitted except what were recounted, consciences could never find peace because very many sins they neither see nor can remember. The ancient writers also testify that the enumeration is not necessary. For in the Decrees Chrysostom is cited, who speaks thus: *I do not say to thee that thou shouldst discover thyself in public, or accuse thyself before others, but I would have thee obey the prophet when he says: "Reveal thy way unto the Lord". Therefore with prayer confess thy sins before God the true judge. Pronounce thine errors, not with the tongue but with the memory of the conscience.* And the Gloss (*Of Repentance, Diss. 5, ch. Consideret*), admits that confession is of human right only. Nevertheless, on account of the very great benefit of absolution, as well as for other uses to the conscience, confession is retained among us.

05 (27). *De discrimine ciborum*

Publica persuasio fuit non tantum vulgi, sed etiam docentium in ecclesiis, quod discrimina ciborum et similes traditiones humanae sint opera utilia ad promerendam gratiam et satisfactoria pro peccatis. Et quod sic senserit mundus, apparet ex eo, quia quotidie instituebantur novae ceremoniae, novi ordines, novae feriae, nova ieiunia, et doctores in

05 (27). *Of the Distinction of Meats*

It hath been a general opinion, not of the people alone, but also of such as are teachers in the churches, that the differences of meats and such like human traditions are works available to merit grace, and are satisfactions for sins. And that the world thus thought is apparent by this – that daily new ceremonies, new orders, new holidays, new fasts were

templis exigebant haec opera tamquam necessarium cultum ad promerendam gratiam, et vehementer terrebant conscientias si quid omitterent. Ex hac persuasione de traditionibus multa incommoda in Ecclesia secuta sunt. Primo, obscurata est doctrina de gratia et iustitia fidei, quae est praecipua pars Evangelii, et quam maxime oportet, extare et eminere in Ecclesia, ut meritum Christi bene cognoscatur, et fides, quae credit remitti peccata propter Christum, longe supra opera collocetur. Quare et Paulus in hunc locum maxime incumbit, legem et traditiones humanas removet, ut ostendat iustitiam Christianam aliud quiddam esse, quam huiusmodi opera, videlicet fidem, quae credit peccata gratis remitti propter Christum. At haec doctrina Pauli paene tota oppressa est per traditiones, quae pepererunt opinionem, quod per discrimina ciborum et similes cultus oporteat mereri gratiam et iustitiam. In paenitentia nulla mentio fiebat de fide, tantum haec opera satisfactoria proponebantur, in his videbatur paenitentia tota consistere.

Secundo, hae traditiones obscuraverunt praecepta Dei, quia traditiones longe praeferebantur praeceptis Dei. Christianismus totus putabatur esse observatio certarum feriarum, rituum, ieiuniorum, vestitus. Hae observationes erant in possessione honestissimi tituli, quod

appointed; and the teachers in the churches did exact these works as worship necessary to deserve grace; and they did greatly terrify men's consciences, if aught were omitted. Of this persuasion concerning traditions many disadvantages have followed in the Church. For first, the doctrine of grace is obscured by it, and also the righteousness of faith, which is the principal part of the Gospel, and which it behoveth most of all to stand forth and to have the pre-eminence in the Church, that the merit of Christ may be well known, and faith, which believeth that sins are remitted for Christ's sake, may be exalted far above works. For which cause also Paul lays much stress on this point; he removeth the law and and human traditions, that he may show that Christian righteousness is a far other thing than such works as these be, namely, a faith which believeth that sins are freely remitted for Christ's sake. But this doctrine of Paul is almost wholly smothered by traditions, which have bred an opinion that, by making difference in meats, and such services, a man should merit grace and justification. In their doctrine of penitence there was no mention of faith; only these works of satisfaction were spoken of; penitence seemed to consist wholly in these.

Secondly, these traditions obscured the commandments of God because traditions were preferred far above the commandments of God. All Christianity was thought to be an observation of certain holidays, rites, fasts and attire. These observations were in possession of a most goodly

essent vita spiritualis et vita perfecta. Interim mandata Dei iuxta vocationem nullam laudem habebant, quod paterfamilias educabat sobolem, quod mater pariebat, quod princeps regebat rem publicam, haec putabantur esse opera mundana et imperfecta et longe deteriora illis splendidis observationibus. Et hic error valde cruciavit pias conscientias, quae dolebant se teneri imperfecto vitae genere, in coniugio, in magistratibus, aut aliis functionibus civilibus, mirabantur monachos et similes, et falso putabant illorum observationes Deo gratiores esse.

Tertio, traditiones attulerunt magna pericula conscientiis, quia impossibile erat omnes traditiones servare, et tamen homines arbitrabantur has observationes necessarios esse cultus. Gerson scribit: *multos incidisse in desperationem, quosdam etiam sibi mortem coscivisse, quia senserant, se non posse satisfacere traditionibus*, et interim consolationem nullam de iustitia fidei et de gratia audierant. Videmus Summistas et theologos colligere traditiones, et quaerere *epieikeias*, ut levent conscientias, non satis tamen expediunt, sed interdum magis iniiciunt laqueos conscientiis. Et in colligendis traditionibus ita fuerunt occupatae scholae et conciones, ut non vacaverit attingere Scripturam, et quaerere utiliorem doctrinam de fide, de cruce, de spe, de dignitate civilium rerum, de consolatione conscientiarum in arduis tentation-

title, that they were the spiritual life and the perfect life. In the meantime God's commandments, touching every man's calling, were of small estimation; that the father brought up his children, that the mother nurtured them, that the prince governed the commonwealth. These were reputed worldly affairs and imperfect, and far inferior to those glittering observances. And this error did greatly torment godly consciences, which were grieved that they were held by an imperfect kind of life, in marriage, in magistracy, or in other civil functions. They had the monks, and such like, in admiration, and falsely imagined that the observances of these men were more pleasing to God than their own.

Thirdly, traditions brought great danger to men's consciences, because it was impossible to keep all traditions, and yet men thought the observation of them to be necessary [services of] worship. Gerson writeth that: *many fell into despair and some murdered themselves because they perceived that they could not keep the traditions*, and all this while they never heard the comfort of the righteousness of faith, or of grace. We see the Summists and divines gather together the traditions, and seek qualifications of them, to unburden men's consciences; and yet all will not serve, but meantime they bring more snares upon the conscience. The schools and pulpits have been so busied in gathering together the traditions that they had not leisure to touch the Scripture and to seek out a more profitable doctrine – of faith, of the cross, of

ibus. Itaque Gerson et alii quidam theologi graviter quaesti sunt, se his rixis traditionum impediri, quo minus versari possent in meliore genere doctrinae. Et Augustinus vetat onerare conscientias huiusmodi observationibus, et prudenter admonet Ianuarium, ut sciat eas indifferentur observandas esse; sic enim loquitur.

Quare nostri non debent videri hanc causam temere attigisse, aut odio episcoporum, ut quidam falso suspicantur. Magna necessitas fuit, de illis erroribus, qui nati erant ex traditionibus male intellectis, admonere ecclesias. Nam Evangelium cogit urgere doctrinam in ecclesiis de gratia et iustitia fidei, quae tamen intelligi non potest, si putent homines se mereri gratiam per observationes ab ipsis electas. Sic igitur docuerunt, quod per observationem traditionum humanarum non possimus gratiam mereri aut iustificari, quare non est sentiendum, quod huiusmodi observationes sint necessarius cultus. Addunt testimonia ex Scriptura. Christus (Mt 15:3) excusat Apostolos qui non servaverant usitatam traditionem, quae tamen videbatur de re non illicita, sed media esse, et habere cognationem cum baptismatibus legis; et dicit (v.9): *Frustra colunt me mandatis hominum.* Igitur non exigit cultum inutilem. Et paulo post addit (v. 11): *Omne quod intrat in os, non inquinat hominem.* Item (Ro

hope, of the dignity of civil affairs, of the comfort of conscience in arduous trials. Wherefore Gerson and some other divines have made grievous complaints, that they were hindered by these strifes about traditions, so that they could not be occupied in some better kind of doctrine. And Augustine forbiddeth than men's consciences should be burdened with observations of this kind, and doth very prudently warn Januarius to know that they are to be observed as things indifferent; for so he speaketh.

Wherefore our ministers must not be thought to have touched this matter rashly, or from hatred of the bishops, as some do falsely surmise. There was great need to admonish the churches of those errors which did arise from mistaking of traditions, for the Gospel compelleth men to urge the doctrine of grace and of the righteousness of faith in the Church; which yet can never be understood if men suppose that they can merit remission of sins and justification by observances of their own choice. Thus therefore, they teach us that we cannot merit grace or justification by the observation of man's traditions, and therefore we must not think that such observations are necessary worship. Hereunto they add testimonies out of Scripture. Christ (Mt 15:3) excuseth his Apostles who kept not the received tradition (which yet seemed to be about a matter not unlawful, but indifferent, and to have some affinity with the baptisms of the law), and saith (v. 9): *They worship me in vain with the commandments of men.*

14:17): *Regnum Dei non est esca aut potus. Cl 2:16: Nemo iudicet vos in cibo, potu, sabbato aut die festo.* Item (v. 20 seq.): *Si mortui estis cum Christo ab elementis mundi, quare tamquam viventes in mundo decreta facitis: Ne attingas, ne gustes, ne contrectes?* Ait Petrus (Ac 15:10-11): *Quare tentatis Deum, imponentes iugum super cervices discipulorum, quod neque nos neque patres nostri portare potuimus, sed per gratiam Domini nostri Iesu Christi credimus salvari, quemadmodum et illi.* Hic vetat Petrus onerare conscientias pluribus ritibus sive Moysi, sive aliis. Et (I Ti 4:1-3) vocat prohibitionem ciborum doctrinam daemoniorum, quia pugnat cum Evangelio, talia opera instituere aut facere, ut per ea mereamur gratiam, aut quod non possit existere Christianismus sine tali cultu.

Hic obiiciunt adversarii quod nostri prohibeant disciplinam et mortificationem carnis, sicut Iovinianus, Verum aliud deprehendetur ex scriptis nostrorum. Semper enim docuerunt de cruce, quod Christianos oporteat tollerare afflictiones. Haec est vera, seria et non simulata mortificatio, variis afflictionibus exerceri et crucifigi cum Christo. Insuper docent, quod quilibet Christianus debeat se corporali disciplina aut corporalibus exercitiis et laboribus sic exercere et

Christ therefore exacteth no unprofitable worship. And a little after, he addeth (v. 11): *Whatsoever entereth in at the mouth defileth not the man.* So also Ro 14:17: *The kingdom of God is not meat and drink.* Cl 2:16: *Let no man judge you in meat or drink, or in respect of the Sabbath-days, or of a holiday.* Again (vv. 20-21): *If ye be dead with Christ to the rudiments of the world, are ye subject to traditions: Touch not, taste not, handle not?* Peter saith (Ac 15:10-11): *Why tempt ye God, laying a yoke upon the necks of the disciples which neither we nor our fathers were able to bear? But we believe that through the grace of the Lord Jesus Christ we shall be saved even as they.* Here Peter forbiddeth to burden the consciences with many rites, whether they be of Moses's or of any others' appointing. And I Ti 4:1-3 calleth the forbidding of meats a doctrine of devils, because that it is against the Gospel to appoint or do such works to the end that by them we may merit grace or justification, or as though Christianity could not exist without such worship.

Here our adversaries object against us, that our ministers hinder all good discipline and mortification of the flesh, as Jovinian did. But the contrary may be seen by our [men's] writings. For they have always taught, touching the cross, that Christians ought to bear afflictions. This is the true, earnest and unfeigned mortification, to be exercised with divers afflictions, and to be crucified with Christ. Moreover they teach that every Christian must so by bodily discipline, or bodily

coercere, ne saturitas aut desidia extimulet ad peccandum, non ut per illa exercitia mereamur gratiam, aut satis faciamus pro peccatis. Et hanc corporalem disciplinam oportet semper urgere, non solum paucis et constitutis diebus. Sicut Christus praecipit (Lc 21:34): *Cavete ne corpora vestra graventur crapula.* Item (Mt 17:21): *Hoc genus daemoniorum non eiicitur nisi ieiunio et oratione.* Et Paulus ait (I Co 9:27): *Castigo corpus meum et redigo in servitutem.* Ubi clare ostendit, se idea castigare corpus, non ut per eam disciplinam mereatur remissionem peccatorum, sed ut corpus habeat obnoxium et idoneum ad res spirituales et ad faciendum officium iuxta vocationem suam. Itaque non damnantur ipsa ieiunia, sed traditiones quae certos dies, certos cibos praescribunt, cum periculo conscientiae, tamquam istiusmodi opera sint necessarius cultus.

Servantur tamen apud nos pleraeque traditiones, quae conducunt ad hoc, ut res ordine geratur in Ecclesia; ut ordo lectionum in missa et praecipuae feriae. Sed interim homines admonentur, quod talis cultus non iustificet coram Deo, et quod non sit ponendum peccatum in talibus rebus, si omittantur sine scandalo. Haec libertas in ritibus humanis non fuit ignota Patribus. Nam in Oriente alio tempore servaverunt Pascha quam Romae, et cum Romani propter hanc dissimilitudinem accusarent Orientem schismatis, admoniti sunt ab aliis, tales mores non oportere ubique

exercises and labour, exercise and keep himself under, that plenty and sloth do not stimulate him to sin; not that he may by such exercises merit grace or satisfy for sins. And this corporal discipline should be used always, not only on a few and set days, according to the commandment of Christ (Lk 21:34): *Take heed lest your bodies be weighed down with drunkeness.* Again (Mt 17:21): *This kind goeth not out but by prayer and fasting.* And Paul saith (I Co 9:27): *I keep under my body and bring it into subjection*, where he plainly showeth that he did therefore chastise his body; not that by that discipline he might merit remission of sins, but that his body might be apt and fit for spiritual things, and to do his duty according to his calling. Therefore we do not condemn fasts themselves, but the traditions which prescribe certain days and certain meats, with danger to the conscience, as though such works as these were a necessary worship.

Yet most of the traditions are observed among us which tend unto this end, that things may be done orderly in the Church, as namely, the order of lessons in the mass and the chiefest holidays. But in the meantime, men are admonished that such a worship doth not justify before God, and that it is not to be supposed there is sin in such things, if they be left undone without scandal. This liberty in human rites and ceremonies was not unknown to the Fathers. For in the East they kept Easter at another time than they did in Rome, and when they of Rome accused the East of schism for this

similes esse. Et Irenaeus inquit: *Dissonantia ieiunii fidei consonantiam non solvit*; sicut et Gregorius Papa (*Dist. 12*) significat, talem dissimilitudinem non laedere unitatem Ecclesiae. Et in *Historia Tripartita 9*, multa colliguntur exempla dissimilium rituum, et recitantur haec verba: *Mens Apostolorum fuit, non de diebus festis sancire, sed praedicare bonam conversationem et pietatem.*

diversity, they were admonished by others that such customs need not be alike everywhere. And Irenaeus saith: *The disagreement about fasting doth not break off the agreement of faith.* Besides, Pope Gregory, in the twelfth Distinction, intimates that such diversity doth not hurt the unity of the Church; and in the *Tripartite History 9*, many examples of dissimilar rites are gathered together, and these words are there rehearsed: *The mind of the Apostles was not to give precepts concerning holidays, but to preach godliness and a holy life.*

06 (28). De votis monachorum

Quid de votis monachorum apud nos doceatur, melius intelliget si quis meminerit qualis status fuerit monasteriorum, quam multa contra canones in ipsis monasteriis quotidie fiebant. Augustini tempore erant libera collegia, postea, corrupta disciplina, ubique addita sunt vota ut tamquam excogitatio carcere disciplina restitueretur. Additae sunt paulatim supra vota aliae multae observationes. Et haec vincula multis ante iustam aetatem contra canones iniecta sunt. Multi inciderunt errore in hoc vitae genus, quibus etiam si non deessent anni, tamen iudicium de suis viribus defuit. Qui sic irretiti erant, cogebantur manere, etiam si quidam beneficio canonum liberari possent. Et hoc accidit magis etiam in monasteriis virginum, quam monachorum, cum sexui imbecilliori magis parcendum esset. Hic rigor displicuit multis bonis viris ante haec tempora, qui videbant puellas et

06 (28). Of Monastic Vows

What is taught among us touching the vows of monks will be better understood if one calls to mind what was the state of the monasteries, and how many things were every day committed in the monasteries contrary to the canons. In Augustine's time cloister fraternities were free, but afterwards, when discipline was corrupted, vows were everywhere laid upon them, that, as it were in a newly devised prison, the discipline might be restored again. Over and besides vows, many other observances little by little were added. And these bands and snares were cast upon many, before they came to ripe years, contrary to the canons. Many through error fell into this kind of life unawares, who, though they wanted not years, yet they wanted discretion to judge of their strength and ability. They who were once got within these nets were constrained to abide in them, though

adolescentes in monasteria detrusi propter victum, videbant, quam infeliciter succederet hoc consilium quae scandala pareret, quos laqueos conscientiis iniiceret. Dolebant auctoritatem canonum in re periculosissima omnino negligi et contemni. Ad haec mala accedebat talis persuasio de votis, quam constat etiam olim displicuisse ipsis monachis, si qui paulo cordatiores fuerunt. Docebant vota paria esse baptismo, docebant se hoc vitae genere mereri remissionem peccatorum et iustificationem coram Deo. Imo addebant, vitam monasticam non tantum iustitiam mereri coram Deo, sed amplius etiam, quia servaret non modo praecepta, sed etiam consilia evangelica. Ita persuadebant monasticam professionem longe meliorem esse baptismo, vitam monasticam plus mereri, quam vitam magistratuum, vitam pastorum et similium, qui in mandatis Dei sine facticiis religionibus suae vocationi serviunt. Nihil horum negari potest, extant enim in libris eorum.

Quid fiebat postea in monasteriis? Olim erant scholae sacrarum litterarum et aliarum disciplinarum quae

by the benefit of the canons, some might be set at liberty. And that fell out rather in the monasteries of nuns than of monks, although the weaker sex ought more to have been spared. This rigour and severity displeased many good men heretofore, when they saw young maids and young men thrust into monasteries, there to get their living. They saw what an unhappy issue this counsel had, what offences it bred, and what snares it laid upon consciences. They were grieved that the authority of the canons was wholly neglected and contemned in a thing most dangerous. To all these evils there was added such a persuasion concerning vows as, it is well known, did in former times displease the monks themselves, if any of them were somewhat wiser than the rest. They taught that vows were equal to baptism, they taught that by this kind of life they merited remission of sins and justification before God; yea, they added that the monk's life did not only merit righteousness before God, but more than that, because it observed not only the commandments, but also the counsels of the Gospel. And thus they taught that the monk's profession was better than baptism, that the monk's life did merit more than the life of magistrates, of pastors, and such like, who, in obedience to God's commandment, followed their calling without any such religions of man's making. None of these things can be denied; they are to be seen in their writings.

What occurred afterwards in the monasteries? In old time they were schools for the study of sacred letters

sunt utiles Ecclesiae, et sumebantur inde pastores et episcopi. Nunc alia res est; nihil opus est recitare nota. Olim ad discendum conveniebant; nunc fingunt institutum esse vitae genus ad promerendam gratiam et iustitiam; imo praedicant esse statum perfectionis, et longe praeferunt omnibus aliis vitae generibus a Deo ordinatis. Haec ideo recitavimus nihil odiose exaggerantes, ut melius intelligi posset de hac re doctrina nostrorum. Primum de his qui matrimonia contrahunt, sic docent apud nos quod liceat omnibus, qui non sunt idonei ad coelibatum, contrahere matrimonium, quia vota non possunt ordinationem ac mandatum Dei tollere. Est autem hoc mandatum Dei (I Co 7:2): *Propter fornicationem habeat unusquisque uxorem suam.* Neque mandatum solum sed etiam creatio et ordinatio Dei cogit hos ad coniugium, qui sine singulari Dei opere non sunt excepti, iuxta aliud (Gn 2:18): *Non est bonum homini esse solum.* Igitur non peccant isti, qui obtemperant huic mandato et ordinationi Dei. Quid potest contra haec opponi? Exaggeret aliquis obligationem voti, quantum volet, tamen non poterit efficere, ut votum tollat mandatum Dei. Canones docent: *in omni voto ius superioris excipi*, quare multo minus haec vota contra mandata Dei valent. Quodsi obligatio votorum nullas haberet causas, cur mutari possit; nec Romani Pontifices dispensassent, neque enim licet homini obligationem, quae simpliciter est iuris divini, rescindere. Sed prudenter iudicaverunt Romani Pontifices aequitatem in hac

and other branches of knowledge which were profitable to the Church, and thence were pastors and bishops taken, but now the case is altered. It is needless to rehearse what is notorious. In old time they came together into such places to learn, but now they feign that it is a kind of life taken up to merit remission of sins and justification; yea, they say it is a state of perfection and prefer it to all other kinds of life, the kinds that God ordained. We have therefore mentioned these things, not to excite hatred, exaggerating nothing, to the end that the doctrine of our churches touching this matter might be understood. First, concerning such as contract marriage, thus they teach among us: that it is lawful for any to marry that are not adapted for a single life, forasmuch as vows cannot take away God's ordinance and commandment. The commandment of God is (I Co 7:2): *To avoid fornication, let every man have his own wife.* And not only the commandment, but also the creation and ordinance of God, compelleth such unto marriage as without the special work of God are not exempted, according to that saying (Gn 2:18): *It is not good for man to be alone.* They therefore, that are obedient to this commandment and ordinance of God do not sin. What can be said against these things? Let a man exaggerate the bond of a vow as much as he will, yet he can never bring to pass that the vow shall take away God's commandment. The canons teach that *in every vow the right of the superior is excepted.* Much less therefore, can these vows

obligatione adhibendam esse. Ideo saepe de votis dispensasse leguntur. Nota est historia de rege Aragonum, revocato ex monasterio, et extant exempla nostri temporis.

Deinde, cur obligationem exaggerant adversarii seu effectum voti, cum interim de ipsa voti natura sileat, quod debet esse in re possibili, quod debet esse voluntarium, sponte et consulto conceptum. At quomodo sit in potestate hominis perpetua castitas, non est ignotum. Et quotusquisque sponte et consulto vovit? Puellae et adolescentes, priusquam iudicare possunt, persuadentur ad vovendum, interdum etiam coguntur. Quare non est aequum tam rigide de obligatione disputare, cum omnes fateantur contra voti naturam esse, quod non sponte quod inconsulto admittitur. Plerique canones rescindunt vota ante annum XV. contracta, quia ante illam aetatem non videtur tantum esse iudicii, ut de perpetua vita constitui possit. Alius canon, plus concedens hominum imbecillitati, addit annos aliquot, vetat enim ante annum XVIII. votum fieri. Sed utrum sequemur? Maxima pars habet excusationem, cur monasteria deserant, quia plurimi

which are contrary to God's commandment be of force. If so be that the obligation of vows has no causes why it might be changed, then could not the Roman Pontiffs have dispensed therewith. For neither is it lawful for man to disannul that bond which doth simply belong to the law of God. But the Roman Pontiffs have judged very prudently that in this obligation, equity must be used. Therefore they often, as we read, have dispensed with vows. The history of the King of Aragón being called back out of a monastery is well known, and there are examples in our own time.

Secondly, why do our adversaries exaggerate the obligation or the effect of the vow, when in the meantime they speak not a word of the very nature of a vow, that it ought to be in a thing possible, ought to be voluntary and taken up of a man's own accord, and with deliberation? But it is not unknown how far perpetual chastity is in the power of a man. And how many a one amongst them is there that doth vow of his own accord and well advised? Maidens and youths, before they know how to judge, are persuaded, yea, sometimes also compelled to vow. Wherefore it is not meet to dispute so rigorously of the obligation, seeing that all men confess that it is against the nature of a vow that it is not done of a man's own accord, not advisedly. The canons for the most part disannul vows which are made before fifteen years of age because before one come to that age there seemeth not to be so much judgement that deter-

ante hanc aetatem voverunt. Postremo, etiam si voti violatio repraehendi posset, tamen non videtur statim sequi, quod coniugia talium personarum dissolvenda sint. Nam Augustinus negat debere dissolvi (*Q. 27,1 cap. Nuptiarum*); cuius non est levis auctoritas, etiamsi alii postea aliter senserunt.

Quamquam autem mandatum Dei de coniugio videatur plerosque liberare a votis, tamen afferunt nostri et aliam rationem de votis, quod sint irrita, quia omnis cultus Dei, ab hominibus sine mandato Dei institutus et electus ad promerendam iustificationem et gratiam, impius est, sicut Christus ait (Mt 15:9): *Frustra colunt me mandatis hominum.* Et Paulus ubique docet, iustitiam non esse quaerendam ex nostris observationibus et cultibus, qui sint excogitati ab hominibus, sed contingere eam per fidem credentibus, se recipi in gratiam a Deo propter Christum. Constat autem monachos docuisse, quod factitiae religiones satisfaciant pro peccatis, mereantur gratiam et iustificationem. Quid hoc est aliud, quam de gloria Christi detrahere, et obscurare ac negare iustitiam fidei? Sequitur

mination may be made concerning a perpetual life. Another canon, permitting more to the weakness of men, doth add some years more; for it forbiddeth a vow to be made before one be eighteen years of age. But which of these shall we follow? The greatest part have this excuse for forsaking monasteries, because most of them vowed before they came to this age. Last of all, even though the breaking of a vow were to be reprehended, yet it seems not to follow directly that the marriages of such persons are to be dissolved. For Augustine (*Q.27,1 ch. Of Marriages*), doth deny that they ought to be dissolved, and his authority is not lightly to be esteemed, although others afterwards have thought otherwise.

And although the commandment of God touching wedlock doth free most men from vows, yet our teachers do also bring another reason concerning vows, to show that they are void; because that all the worship of God, instituted of men without the commandment of God and chosen to merit justification and grace, is wicked, as Christ saith (Mt 15:9): *In vain they do worship me, teaching for doctrines the commandments of men.* And Paul doth everywhere teach that righteousness is not to be sought of our own observances, and services which are devised by men, but that it cometh by faith to those that believe that they are received into favour by God for Christ's sake. But it is evident that the monks did teach that these counterfeited religions satisfy for sins, and merit grace and justification. What else is

igitur, ista vota usitata impios cultus fuisse, quare sunt irrita. Nam votum impium et factum contra mandata Dei non valet, neque enim debet votum vinculum esse iniquitatis, ut canon dicit. Paulus dicit (Ga 5:4): *Evacuati estis a Christo, qui in lege iustificamini, a gratia excidistis.* Ergo etiam, qui votis iustificari volunt, evacuantur a Christo, et a gratia excidunt. Nam et hi, qui votis tribuunt iustificationem, tribuunt propriis operibus hoc, quod proprie ad gloriam Christi pertinet. Neque vero negari potest, quin monachi docuerint, se per vota et observationes suas iustificari et mereri remissionem peccatorum, imo affinxerunt absurdiora, dixerunt se aliis mutuari sua opera. Haec si quis velit odiose exaggerare, quam multa possit colligere, quorum iam ipsos monachos pudet.

Ad haec persuaserunt hominibus, factitias religiones esse statum Christianae perfectionis. Annon est hoc iustificationem tribuere operibus? Non est leve scandalum in Ecclesia, populo proponere certum cultum ab hominibus excogitatum sine mandato Dei, et docere, quod talis cultus iustificet homines; quia iustitia fidei, quam maxime oportet tradi in Ecclesia, obscuratur, cum illae mirifice religiones angelorum, simulatio paupertatis et humilitatis,

this than to detract from the glory of Christ, and to obscure and deny the righteousness of faith? Wherefore it followeth that these common vows were wicked services and are therefore void. For a wicked vow, and that which is made against the commandment of God, is one of no force; neither as the canon saith, ought a vow to be a bond of iniquity. Paul saith (Ga 5:4): *Christ is become of no effect unto you, whosoever of you are justified by the law; ye are fallen from grace.* They therefore, who wish to be justified by vows, are made void of Christ and fall from grace. For they also who attribute justification to their vows, attribute to their own works what properly belongs to the glory of Christ. Nor truly can it be denied that the monks taught that they are justified by their vows and observances, and merit the remission of sins; nay, they invented yet greater absurdities and said they could transfer their good works to others. If any man wished to expand these things so as to excite hatred, how many things might he rehearse whereof the monks themselves are now ashamed!

Moreover, they would persuade men that these invented religious orders are a state of Christian perfection. Is this not attributing justification to works? It is no light offence in the Church to propound unto the people a certain service devised by men, without the commandment of God, and to teach that such a service doth justify men, because the righteousness of faith, which ought especially to be taught in the Church, is obscured when

et coelibatus offunduntur oculis hominum. Praeterea obscurantur praecepta Dei et verus cultus Dei, cum audiunt homines, solos monachos esse in statu perfectionis, quia perfectio Christiana est serio timere Deum, et rursus concipere magnam fidem et confidere propter Christum, quod habeamus Deum placatum, petere a Deo, et certo expectare auxilium in omnibus rebus gerendis, iuxta vocationem; interim foris diligenter facere bona opera, et servire vocationi. In his rebus est vera perfectio et verus cultus Dei, non est in coelibatu aut mendicitate, aut veste sordida.

Verum populus concipit multas perniciosas opiniones ex illis falsis praeconiis vitae monasticae. Audit sine modo laudari coelibatum; ideo cum offensione conscientiae versatur in coniugio. Audit solos mendicos esse perfectos; ideo cum offensione conscientiae retinet possessiones, negotiatur. Audit consilium evangelicum esse de non vindicando; ideo alii in privata vita non verentur ulcisci, audiunt enim consilium esse, non praeceptum. Alii omnes magistratus et civilia officia iudicant indigna esse Christianis. Leguntur exempla hominum, qui desero coniugio, deserta reipublicae administratione, abdiderunt se in monasteria. Id vocabant fingere ex mundo, et quaerere vitae genus, quod Deo magis placeret, nec videbant, Deo serviendum esse in illis mandatis,

those marvellous religions of angels, the pretence of poverty and humility, and of celibacy, are cast before men's eyes. Moreover, the commandments of God and the true worship of God are obscured when men hear that monks alone are in that state of perfection, because that Christian perfection is this, to fear God sincerely, and again, to conceive great faith and to trust assuredly that God is pacified towards us, for Christ's sake; to ask, and certainly to look for help from God in all our affairs, according to our calling; and outwardly to do good works diligently, and to attend to our vocation. In these things doth true perfection and the true worship of God consist; it doth not consist in singleness of life, in beggary, or in vile apparel.

Truely the people doth also conceive many pernicious opinions from these false commendations of the monastic life. They hear celibacy praised above measure; therefore with offence of conscience they live in marriage. They hear that mendicants only are perfect; therefore with offence of conscience they keep their possessions, and buy and sell. They hear that the Gospel only giveth counsel not to take revenge; therefore some in private life are not afraid to avenge themselves, for they hear that it is a counsel, not a commandment. Others do think that all magistracy and civil offices are unworthy Christian men. We read examples of men who, forsaking wedlock, and leaving the government of the commonwealth, have hid themselves in monasteries. This they

quae ipse tradidit, non in mandatis, que sunt excogitata ab hominibus. Bonum et perfectum vitae genus est, quod habet mandatum Dei. De his rebus necesse est admonere homines. Et ante haec tempora repraehendit Gerson errorem monachorum de perfectione et testatur, suis temporibus novam vocem fuisse, quod vita monastica sit status perfectionis. Tam multae impiae opiniones haerent in votis, quod iustificent, quod sint perfectio Christiana, quod servent consilia et praecepta, quod habeant opera supererogationis. Haec omnia cum sint falsa et inania, faciunt vota irrita.

called flying out of the world and seeking a kind of life which is more acceptable to God; neither did they see that God is to be served in those commandments which he himself hath delivered, not in the commandments which are devised by men. That is a good and perfect kind of life which hath the commandment of God for it. It is necessary to admonish men of these things. And before these times Gerson did reprehend this error of the monks concerning perfection, and witnesseth that in his time this was a new saying, that the monastical life is a state of perfection. Thus many wicked opinions do cleave fast unto vows, as that they merit remission of sins and justification, that they are Christian perfection, that they do keep the counsels and commandments, that they have works of supererogation. All these things (seeing they be false and vain) do make vows to be of none effect.

07 (29). De potestate ecclesiastica

Magnae disputationes fuerunt de potestate episcoporum, in quibus nonnulli incommode commiscuerunt potestatem ecclesiasticam et potestatem gladii. Et ex hac confusione maxima bella, maximi motus extiterunt, dum Pontifices, freti potestate clavium, non solum novos cultus instituerunt reservatione casuum, violentis excommunicationibus conscientias oneraverunt, sed etiam regna mundi transferre et imperatoribus adimere imperium conati sunt. Haec vitia multo ante repraehenderunt in Ecclesia homines

07 (29). Of Ecclesiastical Power

There have been great controversies touching the power of bishops, in which many have incommodiously mingled together the ecclesiastical power and the power of the sword. And out of this confusion there have sprung very great wars and tumults, while the Pontiffs, trusting in the power of the keys, have not only appointed new kinds of service and burdened men's consciences by reserving of cases and by violent excommunications; but have also endeavoured to transfer worldly kingdoms from one to another, and

pii et eruditi. Itaque nostri ad consolandas conscientias coacti sunt ostendere discrimen ecclesiasticae potestatis et potestatis gladii, et docuerunt utramque propter mandatum Dei religiose venerandam et honore afficiendam esse, tamquam summa Dei beneficia in terris.

Sic autem sentiunt, potestatem clavium seu potestatem episcoporum, iuxta Evangelium, potestatem esse seu mandatum Dei, praedicandi Evangelii, remittendi et retinendi peccata, et administrandi sacramenta. Nam cum hoc mandato Christus mittit Apostolos (Jn 20:21-23): *Sicut misit me Pater, ita et ego mitto vos. Accipite Spiritum Sanctum, quorum remiseritis peccata, remittuntur eis, et quorum retinueritis peccata, retenta sunt.* (Mc 16:15): *Ite, praedicate Evangelium omni creaturae, etc.* Haec potestas tantum exercetur docendo seu praedicando Verbum, et porrigendo sacramenta, vel multis vel singulis iuxta vocationem, quia conceduntur non res corporales, sed res aeternae, iustitia aeterna, Spiritus Sanctus, vita aeterna. Haec non possunt contingere nisi per ministerium Verbi et sacramentorum, sicut Paulus dicit (Ro 1:16): *Evangelium est potentia Dei ad salutem omni credenti.*

to despoil emperors of their power and authority. These faults did godly and learned men long since reprehend in the Church; and for that cause our teachers were compelled, for the comfort of men's consciences, to show the difference between the ecclesiastical power and the power of the sword. And they have taught that both of them, because of God's commandment, are dutifully to be reverenced and honoured, as the chiefest blessings of God upon earth.

Now their judgement is this, that the power of the keys, or the power of the bishops, by the rule of the Gospel, is a power or commandment from God, of preaching the Gospel, of remitting or retaining sins, and of administering the sacraments. For Christ doth send his Apostles with this charge (Jn 20:21-23): *As the Father hath sent me, even so send I you. Receive ye the Holy Ghost; whosoever sins ye remit, they are remitted unto them, and whosesoever sins ye retain, they are retained.* Mk 16:15: *Go and preach the Gospel to every creature, etc.* This power is put in execution only by teaching or preaching the Word and administering the sacraments, either to many or to single individuals, in accordance with their call. For thereby not corporal things, but eternal are granted; as an eternal righteousness, the Holy Ghost, life everlasting. These things cannot be got but by the ministry of the Word and of the sacraments, as Paul saith (Ro 1:16): *The Gospel is the power of God to salvation to every one that believeth.*

Itaque cum potestas ecclesiastica concedat res aeternas, et tantum exerceatur per ministerium Verbi, non impedit politicam adminis- trationem, sicut ars canendi nihil impedit politicam administrationem. Nam politica administratio versatur circa alias res quam Evangelium; magistratus defendit non mentes sed corpora et res corporales adversus manifestas iniurias, et coercet homines gladio et corporalibus poenis, ut iustitiam civilem et pacem retineat. Non igitur commiscendae sunt potestates ecclesiastica et civilis; ecclesiastica suum mandatum habet Evangelii docendi et adminis- trandi sacramenta. Non irrumpat in alienum officium, non transferat regna mundi, non abroget leges magistratuum, non tollat legitimam oboedientiam, non impediat iudicia de ullis civilibus ordinationibus aut contractibus, non praescribat leges magistratibus de forma rei publicae, sicut dicit Christus (Io 18:36): *Regnum meum non est de hoc mundo.* Item (Lc 12:14): *Quis constituit me iudicem aut divisorem super vos?* Et Paulus ait (Ph 3:20): *Nostra politia in caelis est.* II Co 10:4: *Arma militiae nostrae non sunt carnalia, sed potentia Dei, ad destruendas cogitationes, etc.* Ad hunc modum discernunt nostri utriusque potestatis officia, et iubent utramque honore afficere et agnoscere, utramque Dei donum et beneficium esse.

Si quam habent episcopi

Seeing then that the ecclesiastical power concerneth things eternal and is exercised only by the ministry of the Word, it hindereth not the political government any more than the art of singing hinders political government. For the political ad- ministration is occupied about other matters than is the Gospel. The magistracy defends not the minds but the bodies, and bodily things, against manifest injuries, and coerces men by the sword and corporal punish- ments, that it may uphold civil justice and peace. Wherefore the ecclesias- tical and civil powers are not to be confounded. The ecclesiastical power hath its own commandment to preach the Gospel and administer the sacraments. Let it not by force enter into the office of another, let it not a transfer worldly kingdoms, let it not abrogate the magistrate's laws, let it not withdraw from them lawful obedience, let it not hinder judge- ments touching any civil ordinances or contracts, let it not prescribe laws to the magistrate touching the form of the commonwealth, as Christ saith (Jn 18:36): *My kingdom is not of this world.* Again (Lk 12:14): *Who made me a judge or a divider over you?* And Paul saith (Ph 3:20): *Our citizenship is in heaven.* II Co 10:4: *The weapons of our warfare are not carnal, but mighty through God, casting down imaginations, etc.* In this way do our teachers distinguish between the duties of each power one from the other, and do warn all men to honour both powers, and to acknowledge both to be the gift and blessing of God.

If it so be that the bishops have

potestatem gladii, hanc non habent episcopi ex mandato Evangelii, sed iure humano donatam a regibus et imperatoribus, ad administrationem civilem suorum bonorum. Haec interim alia functio est, quam ministerium Evangelii. Cum igitur de iurisdictione episcoporum quaeritur, discerni debet imperium ab ecclesiastica iurisdictione. Porro secundum Evangelium, seu ut loquuntur, de iure divino, nulla iurisdictio competit episcopis, ut episcopis, hoc est, his, quibus est commissum ministerium Verbi et sacramentorum, nisi remittere peccata, item, cognoscere doctrinam, et doctrinam ab Evangelio dissentientem reiicere, et impios, quorum nota est impietas, excludere communione Ecclesiae, sine vi humana, sed Verbo. Hic necessario et de iure divino debent eis Ecclesiae praestare oboedientiam, iuxta illud (Lc 10:16): *Qui vos audit, me audit.*

Verum cum aliquid contra Evangelium docent aut statuunt, tunc habent ecclesiae mandatum Dei, quod oboedientiam prohibet (Mt 7:15): *Cavete a pseudoprophetis.* Ga 1:8: *Si angelus de caelo aliud Evangelium evangelizaverit, anathema sit.* II Co 13:8: *Non possumus aliquid contra veritatem, sed pro veritate.* Item (v. 10): *Data est nobis potestas ad aedificationem, non ad destructionem.* Sic et canones praecipiunt (*Q. 2, 7 cap. Sacerdotes* et *cap. Oves*). Et Augustinus contra Petiliani epistolam inquit: *Ne*

any power of the sword, they have it not as bishops by the commandment of the Gospel, but by man's law given unto them of kings and emperors, for the civil government of their goods. This however is a kind of function diverse from the ministry of the Gospel. Therefore, when the question touches the jurisdiction of bishops, government must be distinguished from ecclesiastical jurisdiction. Again, by the Gospel, or as they term it, by divine right, bishops as bishops – that is, those who have the administration of the Word and sacraments committed to them – have no other jurisdiction at all, but only to remit sin, also to take cognizance of doctrine, and to reject doctrine inconsistent with the Gospel, and to exclude from the communion of the Church, without human force, but by the Word, those whose wickedness is known. And herein of necessity the churches ought by divine right to render obedience unto them, according to the saying of Christ (Lk 10:16): *He that heareth you heareth me.*

But when they teach or determine anything contrary to the Gospel, then have the churches a commandment of God which forbiddeth obedience to them (Mt 7:15): *Beware of false prophets.* Ga 1:8: *If an angel from heaven preach any other Gospel, let him be accursed.* II Co 13:8: *We cannot do anything against the truth, but for the truth.* Also (v. 10): *This power is given us to edify, and not to destroy.* So do the canons command (*Q.2,7 ch. Sacerdotes* and *ch. Oves*). And Augustine, in his treatise against Petilian's epistle,

Catholicis episcopis consentiendum est, sicubi forte falluntur, aut contra canonicas Dei Scripturas aliquid sentiunt. Si quam habent aliam vel potestatem, vel iurisdictionem in cognoscendis certis causis, videlicet matrimonii, aut decimarum, etc., hanc habent humano iure; ubi cessantibus ordinariis coguntur principes, vel inviti, suis subditis ius dicere, ut pax retineatur.

Praeter haec disputatur, utrum episcopi seu pastores habeant ius instituendi ceremonias in Ecclesia, et leges de cibis, feriis, gradibus ministrorum, seu ordinibus, etc., condendi. Hoc ius qui tribuunt episcopis allegant testimonium (Io 16:12): *Adhuc multa habeo vobis dicere, sed non potestis portare modo. Cum autem venerit ille Spiritus veritatis, docebit vos omnem veritatem.* Allegant etiam exemplum Apostolorum, qui prohibuerunt abstinere a sanguine et suffocato (Ac 15:29). Allegant sabbatum mutatum in diem dominicum, contra Decalogum ut videtur. Nec ullum exemplum magis iactatur, quam mutatio sabbati. Magnam contendunt Ecclesiae potestatem esse, quod dispensaverit de praecepto Decalogi.

Sed de hac quaestione nostri sic docent, quod episcopi non habent potestatem statuendi aliquid contra Evangelium, ut supra ostensum sit, docent idem canones (*Distinct. 9*).

saith: *Neither must we subscribe to catholic bishops if they chance to err, or determine anything contrary to the canonical divine Scriptures.* If it so be that they have any other power or jurisdiction, in hearing and understanding certain cases, as namely, of matrimony and tithes, etc., they hold it by human right. But when the ordinaries fail, princes are constrained, whether they wish to do so or not, to declare the law to their subjects, for maintaining of peace.

Besides these things, there is a controversy whether bishops or pastors have power to institute ceremonies in the Church, and to make laws concerning meats and holidays, degrees or orders of ministers, etc. They that ascribe this power to the bishops allege this testimony for it (Jn 16:12): *I have yet many things to say unto you, but ye cannot bear them now. But when that Spirit of truth shall come, he shall teach you all truth.* They allege also the examples of the Apostles, who commanded to abstain from blood and that which was strangled (Ac 15:29). They allege the change of the Sabbath into the Lord's Day, contrary, as it seemeth, to the Ten Commandments; and they have no example more in their mouths than the change of the Sabbath. They will needs have the Church's power to be very great, because it hath dispensed with a precept of the Ten Commandments.

But of this question ours do thus teach, that the bishops have no power to ordain anything contrary to the Gospel, as was shown before. The same also do the canons teach (*Dis-*

Porro contra Scripturam est, traditiones condere aut exigere, ut per eam observationem satis faciamus pro peccatis, aut mereamur gratiam et iustitiam. Laeditur enim gloria meriti Christi, cum talibus observationibus conamur mereri iustificationem. Constat autem propter hanc persuasionem, in Ecclesia paene in infinitum crevisse traditiones, oppressa interim doctrina de fide et iustitia fidei, quia subinde plures feriae factae sunt, ieiunia indicta, ceremoniae novae, novi honores sanctorum instituti sunt, quia arbitrabantur se auctores talium rerum his operibus mereri gratiam. Sic olim creverunt canones paenitentiales, quorum adhuc in satisfactionibus vestigia quaedam videmus.

Item, auctores traditionum faciunt contra mandatum Dei, cum collocant peccatum in cibis, in diebus et similibus rebus, et onerant Ecclesiam servitute legis, quasi oporteat apud Christianos ad promerendam iustificationem cultum esse similem levitico, cuius ordinationem commiserit Deus Apostolis et episcopis. Sic enim scribunt quidam et videntur Pontifices aliqua ex parte exemplo legis Mosaicae decepti esse. Hinc sunt illa onera, quod peccatum mortale sit, etiam sine offensione aliorum, in feriis laborare manibus, quod sit peccatum mortale omittere horas canonicas, quod certi cibi polluant conscientiam, quod ieiunia sint opera placantia Deum, quod peccatum in casu reservato non possit remitti, nisi accesserit auc-

tinct. 9). Moreover, it is against the Scripture to ordain or require the observation of any traditions to the end that we may make satisfaction for sins, or merit grace and justification. For the glory of Christ's merit suffers when we seek by such observances to merit justification. And it is very apparent that through this persuasion traditions grew into an infinite number in the Church. In the meanwhile the doctrine concerning faith, righteousness of faith, was quite suppressed, for thereupon there were new holidays made, new fasts appointed, new ceremonies, new honours for saints, instituted; because that the authors of such things supposed by these works to merit grace. After the same manner heretofore did the penitential canons increase, whereof we still see some traces in satisfactions.

Moreover, the authors of traditions do contrary to the command of God when they find matters of sin in foods, in days, and like things, and burden the Church with the servitude of the law, as if there ought to be among Christians, in order to merit justification, a service like the levitical, the ordination of which God hath committed to the Apostles and bishops. For this some of them write, and the Pontiffs in some measure seem to be misled by the example of the law of Moses. From hence are those burdens, that it is mortal sin, even without offence to others, to do manual labour on the festivals, that it is a mortal sin to omit the canonical hours, that certain foods defile the conscience, that fastings are works which appease God, that sin (in a

toritas reservantis, cum quidem ipsi canones non de reservatione culpae, sed de reservatione poenae ecclesiasticae loquantur. Unde habent ius episcopi has traditiones imponendi ecclesiis ad illaqueandas conscientias, cum Petrus (Ac 15:10) vetet imponere iugum discipulis, cum Paulus (II Co 13:10) dicat, potestatem ipsis datam esse ad aedificationem, non ad destructionem. Cur igitur augent peccata per has traditiones?

Verum extant clara testimonia quae prohibent condere tales traditiones ad promerendam gratiam, aut tamquam necessarias ad salutem. Paulus (Cl 2:16): *Nemo vos iudicet in cibo, potu, parte diei festi, novilunio aut sabbatis.* Item (v. 20-23): *Si mortui estis cum Christo ab elementis mundi, quare tamquam viventes in mundo, decreta factis? Non attingas, non gustes, non contrectes; quae omnia pereunt usu, et sunt mandata et doctrinae hominum, quae habent speciem sapientiae.* Item, Tt 1:14 aperte prohibet traditiones: *Non attendentes Iudaicis fabulis et mandatis hominum aversantium veritatem.* Et Christus (Mt 15:14) inquit de his, qui exigunt traditiones: *Sinite illos, caeci sunt et duces caecorum.* Et improbat cultus (v. 13): *Omnis plantatio quam non plantavit Pater meus caelestis, eradicabitur.*

reserved case) cannot be pardoned but by the authority of him that reserved it, whereas the canons speak only of reserving of ecclesiastical penalty, and not of the reserving of the fault. Whence then have the bishops power and authority of imposing these traditions upon the churches for the ensnaring of men's consciences, when Peter forbids (Ac 15:10) to put a yoke upon the neck of the disciples, and St Paul says (II Co 13:10) that the power given him was to edification, not to destruction? Why therefore do they increase sins by these traditions?

For there are divers clear testimonies which prohibit the making of such traditions, either to merit grace, or as things necessary to salvation. Paul saith (Cl 2:16): *Let no man judge you in meat or in drink or in respect of a holiday, or of the new moon, or of the Sabbath days.* Again (vv. 20-23): *If ye be dead with Christ from the rudiments of the world, why, as though living in the world, are ye subject to ordinances – touch not, taste not, handle not, which are all to perish with the using – after the commandments and doctrines of men? Which things indeed have a show of wisdom.* And to Titus (Tt 1:14) he doth plainly forbid traditions, for he saith: *Not giving heed to Jewish fables and to commandments of men, that turn from the truth.* And Christ saith of them which urge traditions (Mt 15:14): *Let them alone; they be blind leaders of the blind.* And he condemneth such services (v. 13): *Every plant which my heavenly*

Father hath not planted shall be rooted up.

Si ius habent episcopi onerandi ecclesias infinitis traditionibus, et illaqueandi conscientias, cur toties prohibet Scriptura condere et audire traditiones? Cur vocat eas doctrinas daemoniorum (I Ti 4:1)? Num frustra haec praemonuit Spiritus Sanctus? Relinquitur igitur cum ordinationes institutae tamquam necessariae, aut cum opinione promerendae gratiae, pugnent cum Evangelio quod non liceat ullis episcopis tales cultus instituere aut exigere. Necesse est enim in ecclesiis retineri doctrinam de libertate Christiana, quod non sit necessaria servitus legis ad iustificationem; sicut in Galatis scriptum est (Ga 5:1): *Nolite iterum iugo servitutis subiici.* Necesse est retineri praecipuum Evangelii locum, quod gratiam per fidem in Christum, gratis consequamur, non propter certas observationes, aut propter cultus ab hominibus institutos. Quid igitur sentiendum est de die dominico et similibus ritibus templorum? Ad haec respondent quod liceat episcopis seu pastoribus facere ordinationes, ut res ordine gerantur in Ecclesia, non ut per illas mereamur gratiam, aut satis faciamus pro peccatis, aut obligentur conscientiae, ut iudicent esse necessarios cultus, ac sentiant se peccare, cum sine offensione aliorum violant. Sic Paulus ordinat (I Co 11:6, 15) ut in congregatione mulieres velent capita; (I Co 14:27) ut ordine audiantur in ecclesia interpretes, etc. Tales ordinationes convenit ecclesias propter caritatem et tranquillitatem

If bishops have the authority to burden the churches with innumerable traditions and to snare men's consciences, why doth the Scripture so oft forbid to make and to listen to traditions? Why doth it call them the doctrine of devils (I Ti 4:1)? Hath the Holy Spirit warned us of them to no purpose? It remaineth then, that (seeing ordinances, instituted as necessary, or with the opinion of meriting grace, are repugnant to the Gospel) it is not lawful for any bishops to institute or exact such worship. For it is necessary that the doctrine of Christian liberty should be maintained in the churches, that the bondage of the law is not necessary unto justification, as it is written to the Galatians (Ga 5:1): *Be not entangled again with the yoke of bondage.* It is necessary that the chiefest point of all the gospel should be holden fast, that we do freely obtain grace by faith in Christ, not because of certain observances or of worship devised by men. What is then, to be thought of the Lord's Day and of like rites of temples? Hereunto they answer that it is lawful for bishops or pastors to make ordinances whereby things may be done in order in the Church, not that by them we may merit grace or satisfy for sins, or that men's consciences should be bound to esteem them as necessary worship, and think that they sin when they violate them, without the offence of others. So Paul ordained (I Co 11:6, 15) that women should cover their heads in the congregation; (I Co 14:27) that

servare eatenus, ne alius alium offendat, ut ordine et sine tumultu omnia fiant in ecclesiis (I Co 14:40; cf. Ph 2:14); verum ita ne conscientiae onerentur, ut ducant res esse necessarias ad salutem, ac iudicent se peccare, cum violant eas sine aliorum offensione, sicut nemo dixerit peccare mulierem, quae in publicum non velato capite procedit, sine offensione hominum.

Talis est observatio diei dominici, Paschatis, Pentecostes et similium feriarum et rituum. Nam qui iudicant Ecclesiae auctoritate pro sabbato institutam esse diei dominici observationem, tamquam necessariam, longe errant. Scriptura abrogavit sabbatum, quae docet omnes ceremonias Mosaicas, post revelatum Evangelium omitti posse. Et tamen quia opus erat constituere certum diem, ut sciret populus, quando convenire deberet, apparet Ecclesiam ei rei destinasse diem dominicum, qui ob hanc quoque causam videtur magis placuisse, ut haberent homines exemplum Christianae libertatis, et scirent, nec sabbati nec alterius diei observationem necessariam esse. Extant prodigiosae disputationes de mutatione legis, de ceremoniis novae legis, de mutatione sabbati, quae omnes ortae sunt ex falsa persuasione, quod oporteat in Ecclesia cultum esse similem levitico, et quod Christus commiserit Apostolis et

the interpreters of Scripture should be heard in order in the church, etc. Such ordinances it behoveth the churches to keep for charity and quietness' sake, so that one offend not another, that all things may be done in order, and without tumult in the churches (I Co 14:40; cf. Ph 2:14), but so that consciences be not burdened, so as to account them as things necessary to salvation and think they sin when they violate them, without offence of others; as no-one would say that a woman sins if she went into public with her head uncovered, provided it were without the offence of men.

Such is the observation of the Lord's Day, of Easter, of Pentecost, and like holidays and rites. For they that think that the observation of the Lord's day was appointed by the authority of the Church, instead of the Sabbath, as necessary, are greatly deceived. The Scripture, which teacheth that all the Mosaical ceremonies can be omitted after the Gospel is revealed, has abrogated the Sabbath. And yet, because it was requisite to appoint a certain day that the people might know when they ought to come together, it appears that the Church did for that purpose appoint the Lord's Day; which for this cause also seemed to have been pleasing, that men might have an example of Christian liberty and might know that the observation, neither of the Sabbath, nor of another day, was of necessity. There are certain marvellous disputations touching the changing of the law, and the ceremonies of the new law, and the change of the Sabbath, which all

episcopis excogitare novas ceremonias, quae sint ad salutem
necessariae. Hi errores serpserunt in
Ecclesiam, cum iustitia fidei non
satis clare doceretur. Aliqui disputant, diei dominici observationem
non quidem iuris divini esse, sed
quasi iuris divini; praescribunt de
feriis, quatenus liceat operari.
Huiusmodi disputationes quid sunt
aliud, nisi laquei conscientiarum?
Quamquam enim conentur epii-
keizare traditiones, tamen numquam
potest aequitas depraehendi, donec
manet opinio necessitatis, quam
manere necesse est, ubi ignorantur
iustitia fidei et libertas Christiana.
Apostoli iusserunt (Ac 15:20)
abstinere a sanguine. Quis nunc
observat? Neque tamen peccant qui
non observant, quia ne ipsi quidem
Apostoli voluerunt onerare conscientias tali servitute, sed ad tempus
prohibuerunt propter scandalum. Est
enim perpetuo voluntas Evangelii
consideranda in decreto. Vix ulli
canones servantur accurate, et multi
quotidie exolescunt apud illos etiam,
qui diligentissime defendunt
traditiones. Nec potest conscientiis
consuli, nisi haec aequitas servetur,
ut sciamus eos sine opinione necessitatis servari, nec laedi conscientias,
etiamsi traditiones exolescant.

arose from the false persuasion that
there should be a service in the
Church like to the levitical, and that
Christ committed to the apostles and
bishops the devising of new ceremonies which should be necessary to
salvation. These errors crept into the
Church when the righteousness of
faith was not plainly enough taught.
Some dispute that the observation of
the Lord's Day is not indeed of the
law of god, but as it were of the law
of God; and touching holidays they
prescribe how far it is lawful to work
on them. What else are such
disputations but snares for men's
consciences? For though they seek to
moderate traditions, yet the equity of
them can never be perceived so long
as the opinion of necessity remaineth; which must needs remain where
the righteousness of faith and Christian liberty are not known. The Apostles commanded (Ac 15:20) to abstain from blood. Who observeth that
nowadays? And yet they do not sin
that observe it not. For the Apostles
themselves would not burden men's
consciences with such a servitude,
but they forbade it for a time because
of scandal. For in the decree, the will
of the Gospel is always to be considered. Scarcely any canons are
precisely kept, and many grow out of
use daily, yea, even among them that
do most busily defend traditions.
Neither can there be sufficient care
had of men's consciences, except
this equity be kept, that we should
know that such rites are not to be
observed with any opinion of
necessity, and that men's consciences
are not hurt, though traditions grow
out of use.

Facile autem possent episcopi legitimam oboedientiam retinere, si non urgerent servare traditiones, quae bona conscientia servari non possunt. Nunc imperant coelibatum, nullos recipiunt, nisi iurent se puram Evangelii doctrinam nolle docere. Non petunt ecclesiae ut episcopi honoris sui iactura sarciant concordiam, quod tamen decebat bonos pastores facere. Tantum petunt ut iniusta onera remittant, quae nova sunt, et praeter consuetudinem Ecclesiae Catholicae recepta. Fortassis initio quaedam constitutiones habuerunt probabiles causas, quae tamen posterioribus temporibus non congruunt.

Apparet etiam quasdam errore receptas esse, quare Pontificiae clementiae esset, illas nunc mitigare, quia talis mutatio non labefacit Ecclesiae unitatem. Multae enim traditiones humanae tempore mutatae sunt, ut ostendunt ipsi canones. Quod si non potest impetrari, ut relaxentur observationes, quae sine peccato non possunt praestari, oportet nos regulam Apostolicam sequi (Ac 5:29), quae praecipit Deo magis oboedire quam hominibus. Petrus (I Pe 5:3) vetat episcopos dominari, et ecclesiis imperare. Nunc non id agitur, ut dominatio eripiatur episcopis, sed hoc unum petitur, ut patiantur Evangelium pure doceri, et relaxent paucas quasdam observationes, quae sint peccato servari non possunt. Quod si nihil remiserint, ipsi viderint, quomodo Deo rationem reddituri sint, quod pertinacia sua causam schismati praebent.

The bishops might easily retain lawful obedience if they would not urge men to observe such traditions as cannot be kept with a good conscience. Now they command single life, and they admit none, except they will swear not to teach the pure doctrine of the Gospel. The churches do not desire of the bishops that they would repair peace and concord with the loss of their honour (which yet good pastors ought to do); they only desire that they would remit unjust burdens which are both new and are received contrary to the custom of the Catholic Church. It may well be that some constitutions had some probable reasons when they began, which yet will not agree to latter times.

It is evident that some were received through error. Wherefore it would be a matter for the pontifical gentleness to mitigate them now; for such a change would not overthrow the unity of the Church. For many human traditions have been changed in time, as the canons themselves declare. But if it cannot be obtained that those observances may be relaxed which cannot be kept without sin, then we must follow the Apostles' rule, which willeth to obey God rather than men (Ac 5:29). Peter forbiddeth bishops to be lords and to be imperious over the churches (I Pe 5:3). Now our meaning is not to have rule taken from the bishops, but this one thing only is requested, that they would suffer the Gospel to be purely taught and that they would relax a few observances which cannot be held without sin. But if they will remit none, let them look how they will give account to God for this, that by their obstinacy they provide a cause for schism.

APPENDIXES

01. SOVEREIGNS OF ENGLAND (1485–1714) AND ARCHBISHOPS OF CANTERBURY (1486–1715)

Sovereigns		Archbishops	
1485–1509	Henry VII	1486–1500	John Morton
		1501-1503	Henry Deane
1509-1547	Henry VIII	1504–1532	William Warham
1547-1553	Edward VI	1533–1556	Thomas Cranmer
1553–1558	Mary I		
		1556–1558	Reginald Pole
1558–1603	Elizabeth I		
		1559–1575	Matthew Parker
		1576–1583	Edmund Grindal
		1583–1604	John Whitgift
1603–1625	James I (VI of Scotland)		
		1604–1610	Richard Bancroft
		1611–1633	George Abbot
1625–1649	Charles I		
		1633–1645	William Laud
	INTERREGNUM		
1649–1658	Oliver Cromwell	VACANT	
1658–1659	Richard Cromwell		
	RESTORATION		
1660–1685	Charles II	1660–1663	William Juxon
		1663–1677	Gilbert Sheldon
		1677–1690	William Sancroft
1685–1688	James II (VII of Scotland)		
1689–1702	William III		
1689–1694	Mary II		
		1691–1694	John Tillotson
		1694–1715	Thomas Tenison
1702-1714	Anne		

02. SOVEREIGNS BY REGNAL YEARS (Old Style)

Henry VII	22 August 1485–21 April 1509
Henry VIII	22 April 1509–28 January 1547
Edward VI	28 January 1547–06 July 1553
Mary I	19 July 1553–17 November 1558
Philip (II of Spain)	25 July 1554–17 November 1558*
Elizabeth I	17 November 1558–24 March 1603
James I	24 March 1603–27 March 1625
Charles I	27 March 1625–30 January 1649
Charles II	30 January 1649–06 February 1685
James II	06 February 1685–23 December 1688**
William III	13 February 1689–08 March 1702
Mary II	13 February 1689–28 December 1694
Anne	08 March 1702–01 August 1714

* King of England by marriage to Mary I only
** This was the date of James's flight. Parliament officially recognised 11 December 1688 as the end of his reign, but it appears that documents signed by James between then and his final departure were accepted as valid.

03. POPES 1484–1721

Dates given are those of election and death.
From 15 October 1582 the Gregorian Calendar (New Style) is used.

Innocent VIII	29 August 1484–25 July 1492
Alexander VI	11 August 1492–18 August 1503
Pius III	22 September 1503–18 October 1503
Julius II	01 November 1503–21 February 1513
Leo X	11 March 1513–01 December 1521
Hadrian VI	09 January 1522–14 September 1523
Clement VII	18 November 1523–26 September 1534
Paul III	13 October 1534–10 November 1549
Julius III	07 February 1550–23 March 1555
Marcellus II	09 April 1555–30 April 1555
Paul IV	23 May 1555–18 August 1559
Pius IV	25 December 1559–09 December 1565
Pius V	07 January 1566–01 May 1572
Gregory XIII	13 May 1572–10 April 1585
Sixtus V	24 April 1585–27 August 1590

Urban VII	15 September 1590–27 September 1590
Gregory XIV	05 December 1590–15 October 1591
Innocent IX	29 October 1591–30 December 1591
Clement VIII	30 January 1592–05 March 1605
Leo XI	01 April 1605–27 April 1605
Paul V	16 May 1605–28 January 1621
Gregory XV	09 February 1621–08 July 1623
Urban VIII	06 August 1623–29 July 1644
Innocent X	15 September 1644–07 January 1655
Alexander VII	07 April 1655–22 May 1667
Clement IX	20 June 1667–09 December 1669
Clement X	29 April1670–22 July 1676
Innocent XI	21 September 1676–12 August 1689
Alexander VIII	06 October 1689–01 February 1691
Innocent XII	12 July 1691–27 September 1700
Clement XI	23 November 1700–19 March 1721

04. DATES OF EASTER AND MOVEABLE FEASTS 1485–1715

EASTER

1485	03 April		1505	23 March
1486	26 March		1506	12 April
1487	15 April		1507	04 April
1488	06 April		1508	23 April
1489	19 April		1509	08 April
1490	11 April		1510	31 March
1491	03 April		1511	20 April
1492	22 April		1512	11 April
1493	07 April		1513	27 March
1494	30 March		1514	16 April
1495	19 April		1515	08 April
1496	03 April		1516	23 March
1497	26 May		1517	12 April
1498	15 April		1518	04 April
1499	31 March		1519	24 April
1500	19 April		1520	08 April
1501	11 April		1521	31 March
1502	27 March		1522	20 April
1503	16 April		1523	05 April
1504	07 April		1524	27 March

1525	16 April		1554	25 March
1526	01 April		1555	14 April
1527	21 April		1556	05 April
1528	12 April		1557	18 April
1529	28 March		1558	10 April
1530	17 April		1559	26 March
1531	09 April		1560	14 April
1532	31 March		1561	06 April
1533	13 April		1562	29 March
1534	05 April		1563	11 April
1535	28 March		1564	02 April
1536	16 April		1565	22 April
1537	01 April		1566	14 April
1538	21 April		1567	30 March
1539	06 April		1568	18 April
1540	28 March		1569	10 April
1541	17 April		1570	26 March
1542	09 April		1571	15 April
1543	25 April		1572	06 April
1544	13 April		1573	22 March
1545	05 April		1574	11 April
1546	25 April		1575	03 April
1547	10 April		1576	22 April
1548	01 April		1577	07 April
1549	21 April		1578	30 March
1550	06 April		1579	19 April
1551	29 March		1580	03 April
1552	17 April		1581	26 March
1553	02 April		1582	15 April

	Julian Calendar (Old Style)	Gregorian Calendar (New Style)		Julian Calendar (Old Style)	Gregorian Calendar (New Style)
1583	31 March	10 April*	1593	15 April	18 April
1584	19 April	01 April	1594	31 March	10 April*
1585	11 April	21 April*	1595	20 April	26 March
1586	03 April	06 April	1596	11 April	14 April
1587	16 April	29 March	1597	27 March	06 April*
1588	07 April	17 April*	1598	16 April	22 March
1589	30 March	02 April	1599	08 April	11 April
1590	19 April	22 April	1600	23 March	02 April*
1591	04 April	14 April*	1601	12 April	22 April*
1592	26 March	29 March	1602	04 April	07 April

1603	24 April	30 March	1647	18 April	21 April
1604	08 April	18 April*	1648	02 April	12 April*
1605	31 March	10 April*	1649	25 March	04 April*
1606	20 April	26 March	1650	14 April	17 April
1607	05 April	15 April*	1651	30 March	09 April*
1608	27 March	06 April*	1652	18 April	31 March
1609	16 April	19 April	1653	10 April	13 April
1610	08 April	11 April	1654	26 March	05 April*
1611	24 March	03 April*	1655	15 April	28 March
1612	12 April	22 April*	1656	06 April	16 April*
1613	04 April	07 April	1657	29 March	01 April
1614	24 April	30 March	1658	11 April	21 April*
1615	09 April	19 April*	1659	03 April	13 April*
1616	31 March	03 April*	1660	22 April	28 March
1617	20 April	26 March	1661	14 April	17 April
1618	05 April	15 April*	1662	30 March	09 April*
1619	28 March	31 March	1663	19 April	25 March
1620	16 April	19 April	1664	10 April	13 April
1621	01 April	11 April*	1665	26 March	05 April*
1622	21 April	27 March	1666	15 April	25 April*
1623	13 April	16 April	1667	07 April	10 April
1624	28 March	07 April*	1668	22 March	01 April*
1625	17 April	30 March	1669	11 April	21 April*
1626	09 April	12 April	1670	03 April	06 April
1627	25 March	04 April*	1671	23 April	29 March
1628	13 April	23 April*	1672	07 April	17 April*
1629	05 April	15 April*	1673	30 March	02 April
1630	28 March	31 March	1674	19 April	25 March
1631	10 April	20 April*	1675	04 April	14 April*
1632	01 April	11 April*	1676	26 March	05 April*
1633	21 April	27 March	1677	15 April	18 April
1634	06 April	16 April*	1678	31 March	10 April*
1635	29 March	08 April*	1679	20 April	02 April
1636	17 April	23 March	1680	11 April	21 April*
1637	09 April	12 April	1681	03 April	06 April
1638	25 March	04 April*	1682	16 April	29 March
1639	14 April	24 April*	1683	08 April	18 April*
1640	05 April	08 April	1684	30 March	02 April
1641	25 April	31 March	1685	19 April	22 April
1642	10 April	20 April*	1686	04 April	14 April*
1643	02 April	05 April	1687	27 March	30 March
1644	21 April	27 March	1688	15 April	18 April
1645	06 April	16 April*	1689	31 March	10 April*
1646	29 March	01 April	1690	20 April	26 March

1691	12 April	15 April	1703	28 March	08 April*
1692	27 March	06 April*	1704	16 April	23 March
1693	16 April	22 March	1705	08 April	12 April
1694	08 April	11 April	1706	24 March	04 April*
1695	24 March	03 April*	1707	13 April	24 April*
1696	12 April	22 April*	1708	04 April	08 April
1697	04 April	07 April	1709	24 April	31 March
1698	24 April	30 March	1710	09 April	20 April*
1699	09 April	19 April*	1711	01 April	05 April
1700	31 March	11 April*	1712	20 April	27 March
1701	20 April	17 April	1713	05 April	16 April*
1702	05 April	16 April*	1714	28 March	01 April
			1715	17 April	21 April

*Same actual day in both calendars

THE MOVEABLE FEASTS

These can be calculated from the date of Easter, according to the following table. The second date in February applies to leap years. Note that 1700 was a leap year in the Julian, but not in the Gregorian Calendar.

Easter	Ash Wednesday	Whitsun (Pentecost)	Easter	Ash Wednesday	Whitsun (Pentecost)
22 March	04/05 Feb	10 May	09 April	22/23 Feb	28 May
23	05/06	11	10	23/24	29
24	06/07	12	11	24/25	30
25	07/08	13	12	25/26	31
26	08/09	14	13	26/27	01 June
27	09/10	15	14	27/28	02
28	10/11	16	15	28/29	03
29	11/12	17	16	01 March	04
30	12/13	18	17	02	05
31	13/14	19	18	03	06
01 April	14/15	20	19	04	07
02	15/16	21	20	05	08
03	16/17	22	21	06	09
04	17/18	23	22	07	10
05	18/19	24	23	08	11
06	19/20	25	24	09	12
07	20/21	26	25	10	13
08	21/22	27			

05. FROM THE AUGSBURG CONFESSION TO THE 39 ARTICLES: A COMPARATIVE TABLE

This table gives the various articles of faith treated in the Augsburg Confession (1530), the Wittenberg Articles (1536), the Ten Articles (1536), the Thirteen Articles (1538), the Forty–two Articles (1553), the Eleven Articles (1559) and the Thirty–nine Articles (1571). It should be noted that the Thirty–eight Articles (1563) follow the 1571 list exactly, apart from Article 29, which was inserted at the later date. The order of subjects broadly follows that of the 42/39 Articles. It should be pointed out that the comparison is one of subjects treated, and does not guarantee that the text of the articles in question is identical, or even similar. Readers are requested to consult the documents in question for a detailed comparison of this kind.

Subject	AC	WA	10	13	42	11	39
01. God/Trinity	1			1	1	1	1
02. Incarnation	3			3	2		2
03. Descent into Hell					3		3
04. Resurrection	3				4		4
05. Holy Spirit							5
06. Holy Scripture		1	1		5	2	6
07. Old Testament					6		7
08. Three Creeds		1	1		7	2	8
09. Original Sin	2	2		2	8		9
10. Free Will	18				9		10
11. Grace					10		
12. Justification	4	4	5	4	11		11
13. Good Works	20	5					12
14. Works before Justif.	5				12		13
15. Works/Supererogation	6				13		14
16. Sinlessness of Christ					14		15
17. Sins after Baptism					15		16
18. Blasphemy/Holy Spirit					16		
19. Predestination					17		17
20. Salvation					18		18
21. Moral Law					19		
22. Church	7/8	9		5	20	3	19
23. Church Authority		10			21	3	20
24. Conciliar Authority					22		21
25. Purgatory			10		23		22

Subject	AC	WA	10	13	42	11	39
26. Ministry	14	9		10	24	4	23
27. Language of Worship					25		24
28. Sacraments	13	8		9	26		25
29. Unworthy Ministers	5	9			27		26
30. Baptism	9	3	2	6	28	8	27
31. Lord's Supper	10/23	6/12	4	7	29		28
32. Unworthy Reception							29
33. Both Kinds	22	13				10	30
34. Perfect Oblation					30	9	31
35. Clerical Celibacy	22/26	14			31		32
36. Excommunicates					32		33
37. Traditions	15/25	10	9	11	33	11	34
38. Homilies					34		35
39. Prayer Book/Ordinal					35	7	36
40. Civil Magistrate	16/27	11		12	36	5/6	37
41. Private Property		11			37		38
42. Oaths		11			38		39
43. Resurrection of Dead	17			13	39		
44. Last Things					40–42		

06. FROM THE 39 ARTICLES TO THE WESTMINSTER CONFESSION: A COMPARATIVE TABLE

This table compares the 39 Articles (1571) with the Lambeth Articles (1595), the Irish Articles (1615) and the Westminster Confession (1647) following the same procedure used above. However, for this table, the order of the Irish Articles has been taken as normative.

Subject	39	LA	IA	WC
01. Holy Scripture	6		1–6	1
02. Three Creeds	8		7	
03. God/Trinity	1		8–9	2
04. Holy Spirit	5		10	
05. Predestination	17	1–8	11–17	3/10
06. Man/Creation			18–21	4
07. Original Sin	9		22–24	6
08. Free Will	10	9	25	9

Subject	39	LA	IA	WC
09. Works before Justification	13		26	
10. Actual Sin			27–28	
11. Incarnation	2–4		29	8
12. Sinlessness of Christ	15		30	8
13. Salvation	18		31	
14. Grace			32–33	
15. Justification	11	5–6	34–38	11
16. Good Works	12		39–45	16
17. Works/Super-erogation	14		41	10
18. Sins after Baptism	16		44	6
19. Worship			46–56	21
20. Civil Magistrate	37		57–62	23
21. Private Property	38		63–67	26
22. Church	19		68–69/78	25
23. Unworthy Ministers	26		70	27
24. Ministry	23		71	
25. Language	24		72	
26. Excommunicates	33		73	30
27. Absolution			74	
28. Church Authority	20		75/77	30
29. Conciliar Authority	21		76	31
30. Papacy			79–80	
31. Old Testament	7		81–84	7/19
32. Sacraments	25		85–88	27
33. Baptism	27		89–91	28
34. Lord's Supper	28		92–95/98	29
35. Unworthy Reception	29		96	
36. Both Kinds	30		97	
37. Perfect Oblation	31		99	
38. Private Masses			100	
39. Last Things			101–104	32–33
40. Purgatory	22		24	
41. Clerical Celibacy	32			24
42. Traditions	34			
43. Homilies	35			
44. Prayer Book/Ordinal	36			
45. Oaths	39			22

07. THE WESTMINSTER CONFESSION AND THE 39 ARTICLES DIRECTLY COMPARED

This table outlines how the Westminster Confession compares with the 39 Articles, using the former as the model. Articles not covered by the Confession are listed separately at the end.

Subject Westminster Conf.	39 Articles	Subject Westminster Conf.	39 Articles
01. Holy Scripture	6	18. Assurance	
02. God/Trinity	1	19. Law of God	7
03. Eternal Decree	17–18	20. Christian Liberty	
04. Creation		21. Worship	24
05. Providence		22. Oaths	39
06. Fall/Sin	9/16	23. Civil Magistrate	37
07. Covenant	7	24. Marriage/Divorce	32
08. Christ as Mediator	2–4/15	25. Church	19/34
09. Free Will	10	26. Communion of Saints	38
10. Effectual Calling	17	27. Sacraments	25/26
11. Justification		28. Baptism	27
12. Adoption		29. Lord's Supper	28–31
13. Sanctification		30. Church Censures	20/33
14. Saving Faith		31. Synods/Councils	21
15. Repentance unto Life		32. Resurrection of the Dead	22
16. Good Works	12–14	33. Last Judgement	
17. Perseverance of the Saints			

ARTICLES NOT COVERED BY THE WESTMINSTER CONFESSION

05. Holy Spirit
08. Three Creeds
23. Ministry (assumed in WC 25, 27 but not explicitly stated)
35. Homilies
36. Prayer Book/Ordinal

08. THE WESTMINSTER CONFESSION AND ITS OFFSPRING COMPARED

This table compares the Westminster Confession of 1647 with three of its more important revisions. The first is the Savoy Declaration (1658), the next is the Second London (Baptist) Confession (1689) and the last is the Philadelphia Confession (1742), which is only a minor revision of the Second London Confession. The subjects are not listed; readers are referred to the relevant documents, all of which are published in this collection.

WC	SD	2LC	PhC		WC	SD	2LC	PhC
1–19	1–19	1–19	1–19		25	26	26**	27
	20	20	20		27	28	28**	29
20	21*	21	21		28	29	29**	30
21	22	22	22					31
		23			29	30	30	32
22	23	23	24		30	31		
23	24*	24**	25		31	32		
24	25*	25	26		32	33	31	33
25	26	26**	27		33	34	32	34

*These chapters from the Westminster Confession were modified in the Savoy Declaration. Unless otherwise indicated, they were taken over without further modification in the Second London and Philadelphia Confessions.

**These chapters from the Savoy Declaration were modified in the Second London Confession. They were then taken over without further modification in the Philadelphia Confession.

INDEX OF PROPER NAMES

This index contains the names of people (except Biblical characters), certain documents, and Church councils mentioned in the texts. Reigning sovereigns of England are not indexed in documents authorised by them. Similarly, ecclesiastical and civil offices (e.g. Archbishop of Canterbury, Lord Chancellor) are not indexed, except when they refer to specific individuals.

INDEX TO THE SCRIPTURE REFERENCES

Entries in bold refer to Scripture quotations in all the documents. References to quotations contained in the Westminster Confession appear in normal type; the numbers correspond to the corresponding notes (pp. 512-520).